ADVANCED TEXTS IN ECONOMETRICS

General Editors

CO-INTEGRATION, ERROR CORRECTION, AND THE ECONOMETRIC ANALYSIS OF NON-STATIONARY DATA

Anindya Banerjee, Juan J. Dolado,
John W. Galbraith, and David F. Hendry

OXFORD UNIVERSITY PRESS
1993

Oxford University Press, Walton Street, Oxford OX2 6DP
Oxford New York Toronto
Delhi Bombay Calcutta Madras Karachi
Kuala Lumpur Singapore Hong Kong Tokyo
Nairobi Dar es Salaam Cape Town
Melbourne Auckland Madrid
and associated companies in
Berlin Ibadan

Oxford is a trade mark of Oxford University Press

Published in the United States
by Oxford University Press Inc., New York

British Library Cataloguing in Publication Data
Data available

Library of Congress Cataloging in Publication Data
Co-integration, error correction, and the econometric analysis of non-stationary data / Anindya Banerjee . . . [et al.].
(Advanced texts in econometrics)
Includes index.
1. Econometric models. I. Banerjee, Anindya. II. Series.
HB141.C62 1993 330'.01'5195–dc20 92–27344

ISBN 0–19–828700–3
ISBN 0-19-828810-7 (Pbk)

Typeset by Keytec Typesetting Ltd, Bridport, Dorset

Printed in Great Britain by
Bookcraft Ltd.
Midsomer Norton, Avon

Preface

This book is intended as a guide to the literature on co-integration and modelling of integrated processes. Time-series econometrics has developed rapidly during the past decade, but especially so in the analysis of non-stationarity. In particular, the study of integrated processes has grown in importance from the status of an exotic topic, discussed only in technical journals, to being an essential part of the econometrician's collection of techniques. It has thereby developed into an area of interest for econometric theorists and applied econometricians alike. This book is aimed at graduate students in economics, applied econometricians, econometric theorists, and the general audience of economists who use empirical methods to analyse time series.

Despite the growing importance of the literature on integration and co-integration, most accounts of this literature remain confined to journals, edited collections of papers, or survey papers. While some of the surveys are quite detailed, space restrictions usually do not allow a full exposition of many of the theoretical points. This book attempts to bridge the gap between accounts such as surveys, which are mainly descriptive, and accounts that are mainly theoretical. It explains the important concepts informally and also presents them formally. The asymptotic theory of integrated processes is described and the tools provided by this theory are used to derive, in some detail, the distributions of estimators. By taking readers step by step through some of the main derivations, our hope is to make the theory readily accessible to a wide audience.

We have tried to make the book as self-contained as possible. A knowledge of econometrics, statistics, and matrix algebra at the level of a final-year undergraduate or first-year graduate course in econometrics is assumed, but otherwise all of the important statistical concepts and techniques are described.

A book such as this one, which discusses an area that is developing rapidly, is inevitably incomplete and runs the risk of not being quite up-to-date. To limit the time taken in writing and revising, we did not seek to chase a frontier that was expanding in many directions. Rather, the topics covered reflect our views of issues, models, and methods that are likely to remain important for some time to come, many of which will continue to provide the platform for future research.

Acknowledgements

Our book was written in two continents, three years, and four universities, so the list of people, across time, space, and departments, to whom we owe extensive debts of gratitude has grown formidably large. A major part of this debt is owed to the Departments of Economics at the Universities of California at San Diego, Florida in Gainesville, McGill, and Oxford, and the Bank of Spain, where the authors either worked or visited for substantial periods. Their generous support of our work is much appreciated.

The book has also benefited greatly from the patient scrutiny of several of our colleagues, who read the entire typescript and made detailed comments. We have pleasure in thanking Michael Clements, Rob Engle, Neil Ericsson, Tony Hall (and several of his students), Colin Hargreaves, Søren Johansen, Katarina Juselius, Teun Kloek, James MacKinnon, G. S. Maddala, Grayham Mizon, Jean-François Richard, Mark Rush, Neil Shephard, Timo Teräsvirta, and four anonymous referees for their help. They have made a great contribution to this book, and found many infelicities in earlier versions, but of course are not responsible for any that remain.

Early versions of the book were inflicted by us upon our graduate students. Among those who suffered from the confusion caused by obscure notation and prose, but continued unflinchingly, Hughes Dauphin, Carol Dole, Jesus Gonzalo, Catherine Liston, Claudio Lupi, Neil Rickman, and Geeta Singh deserve special thanks.

We are also indebted to Julia Campos, Michael Clements, Steven Cook, Neil Ericsson and Claudio Lupi for proof reading.

The financial support of the Economic and Social Research Council (UK) under grants B01250024 and R231184 and the Fonds pour la Formation des Chercheurs et l'Aide à la Recherche (Quebec) is gratefully acknowledged. Finally, we thank Andrew Schuller and the editors of this series, who remained encouraging about the project despite its many difficulties.

Oxford	A. B.
Madrid	J. J. D.
Montreal	J. W. G.
Oxford	D. F. H.

Contents

Notational Conventions, Symbols, and Abbreviations

The following notational conventions will be used throughout the text:

Y, y	endogenous variables
X, Z, x, z	exogenous variables, or vectors containing both y and z
Greek letters	population values (parameters)
Greek letters with $\hat{}$ or $\tilde{}$	sample values (estimates)
Bold lower case (Roman or Greek)	vectors
Bold upper case (Roman or Greek)	matrices

Equation numbers

Equations are numbered consecutively in each chapter and referred to within that chapter by this number alone. Equations from other chapters are referred to by the chapter number and equation number within chapter; e.g. the fifth equation in Chapter 2 is (5) within Chapter 2, and (2.5) elsewhere.

Symbols

L	lag operator: $Lx_t = x_{t-1}$.
Δ	first-difference operator: $\Delta x_t = (1 - L)x_t = x_t - x_{t-1}$.
$\otimes$	Kronecker product
$\forall$	for all
$\|x\|$	modulus or absolute value of x, where x is a scalar
$\|\mathbf{A}\|$	determinant of $\mathbf{A}$, where $\mathbf{A}$ is a matrix
$(x\|y)$	x conditional on y
$\Rightarrow$	weak convergence
$\xrightarrow{d}$	convergence in distribution
$\xrightarrow{p}$	convergence in probability

Abbreviations

ADF	augmented Dickey–Fuller
ADL	autoregressive-distributed lag

AR	autoregression
ARIMA	autoregressive integrated moving average
ARMA	autoregressive-moving average
ARMAX	ARMA + additional exogenous processes
ASE	Asymptotic standard error
BM	Brownian motion
CI(d, b)	co-integrated of order d, b
CLT	central limit theorem
COMFAC	common factor error representation
CRDW	co-integrating regression DW statistic
diag	diagonal matrix
d.f.	degrees of freedom
DF	Dickey–Fuller
DGP	data-generation process
DW	Durbin–Watson statistic
ECM	error-correction model/mechanism
ESE	(average) estimated standard error
FCLT	functional central limit theorem/s
FIML	full-information maximum likelihood
GLS	generalized least squares
GNP	gross national product
I(d)	integrated of order d
ID	independently distributed
IID	independently and identically distributed
IMA	integrated moving average
IN(μ, σ^2)	independently and normally distributed with mean μ and variance σ^2
IV	instrumental variables
LIML	limited-information maximum likelihood
MA	moving average
MDS	martingale difference sequence
MLE	maximum likelihood estimator
N(μ, σ^2)	normally distributed with mean μ and variance σ^2
NI	near-integrated
OLS	ordinary least squares
SC	Schwarz information criterion
SD	standard deviation
SE	standard error
SI	seasonally integrated
SSD	sample standard deviation
T	sample size or last observation in a time-series
TFE	total final expenditure
VAR	vector autoregression
var	variance

vec	vectorizing operator
$W(r)$	Wiener (Brownian motion) process with increments of variance r

1

Introduction and Overview

This book considers the econometric analysis of both stationary and non-stationary processes which may be linked by equilibrium relationships. It exposits the main tools, techniques, models, concepts, and distributions involved in econometric modelling of possibly non-stationary time-series data. Since the focus is on equilibrium concepts, including co-integration and error correction, the analysis begins with a discussion of the application of these concepts to stationary empirical models. Later we will show that integrated processes can be reduced to this case by suitable transformations that take advantage of co-integrating (equilibrium) relationships. In this chapter we will introduce some important concepts from time-series analysis and the theory of stochastic processes, and in particular the theory of Brownian motion processes. We also offer several empirical examples which use these concepts.

A significant re-evaluation of the statistical basis of econometric modelling took place during the 1980s. Its analytical basis expanded from the assumption of stationarity to include integrated processes. The effect of this shift is far from complete, but is already radical, influencing the choice of model forms, modelling practices, statistical inference, distribution theory, and the interpretation of many traditional concepts such as simultaneity, measurement errors, collinearity, forecasting, and exogeneity. This book attempts to analyse these issues, describe the tools necessary to investigate integrated processes, and relate the new methods to those more familiar to econometricians. Research is continuing at a rapid pace, and since this book cannot cover all of the techniques that have been explored, we will concentrate on those that we believe will remain useful.

Time-series econometrics is concerned with the estimation of relationships among groups of variables, each of which is observed at a number of consecutive points in time. The relationships among these variables may be complicated; in particular, the value of each variable may depend on the values taken by many others in several previous time periods. In consequence, the effect that a change in one variable has on another depends upon the time horizon that we consider. It is easy to imagine examples in which a change in one quantity has little or no effect on another at first and a substantial effect later. Alternatively, a variable may have a substantial effect on another for a time, but that effect may eventually die out.

It is useful, therefore, to distinguish what are often called 'short-run' relationships (those holding over a relatively short period) from 'long-run' relationships. The former relate to links that do not persist. For example, a sudden storm may temporarily reduce the supply of fresh fish and increase its price, but later fair weather will lead to the re-establishing of the earlier price if demand is unaltered. The long-run relationships determine the generally prevailing price–quantity combinations transacted in the market, and so are closely linked to the concepts of equilibrium relationships in economic theory and of persistent co-movements of economic time series in econometrics. Our first task is to clarify these concepts.

1.1. Equilibrium Relationships and the Long Run

An *equilibrium state* is defined as one in which there is no inherent tendency to change. A disequilibrium is any situation that is not an equilibrium and hence characterizes a state that contains the seeds of its own destruction. An equilibrium state may or may not have the property of either local or global stability; thus, it may or may not be true that the system tends to return to the equilibrium state when it is perturbed. However, we generally consider only stable equilibria, since unstable equilibria will not persist given that there are stochastic shocks to the economy. That is, equilibria are states to which the system is attracted, other things being equal. It may also be possible in some circumstances to view the forces tending to push the system back into equilibrium as depending upon the magnitude of the deviation from equilibrium at a given point in time.

Equilibrium may be either general or partial. In the latter case, a given market is viewed as having attained equilibrium in spite of the fact that we have not taken account of the feedback from other markets. In both cases, an equilibrium relationship is expressed through a function $\mathbf{f}(x_1, x_2, \ldots, x_n) = \mathbf{0}$, which describes the relationships that hold among the n variables x_1 to x_n when the system is in equilibrium. The phrase 'long-run equilibrium' is also used to denote the equilibrium relationship to which a system converges over time. Over finite periods of time, the long-run or equilibrium relationships may fail to hold, but they will eventually hold to any degree of accuracy if the equilibrium is stable, and if the system does not experience further shocks from outside. Expressed differently, a long-run equilibrium relationship entails a systematic co-movement among economic variables which an economic system exemplifies precisely in the long run; we will write equations representing such co-movements without time subscripts as, e.g. $x_1 = \beta x_2$ to denote a linear long-run relation between x_1 and x_2.

Our definition of equilibrium is therefore *not* that in which 'equilibrium' refers to clearing in a particular market and where 'disequilibrium' means that supply is not equal to demand, as in Quandt (1978, 1982): we use the term 'market-clearing' for the former and a 'non-clearing market' for the latter. A non-clearing market involves quantity rationing of some agents and, depending on the institutional structure, may or may not involve a deviation from an equilibrium functional relationship.

There is of course a connection between the meaning of 'equilibrium' used in econometrics by Quandt and others, and that used here, which is more common in time-series analysis. When a market clears, an equilibrium relationship of the type we have defined may also occur because clearing of that market may return the system to a state in which some functional relationship among observable variables holds. Our definition is intended to be general and therefore to incorporate market-clearing equilibria, as well as others which may arise through the behaviour of a variety of different types of systems. For example, we would say that an equilibrium relationship exists between aggregate consumption and income if consumption tends toward a fraction γ of income in the absence of shocks which may temporarily perturb the relationship. This need not be an equilibrium in the Quandt (1978) sense, however, because it may not correspond to the clearing of markets. (All consumers may remain credit-rationed, for example.)

Even if shocks to a system are constantly occurring so that the economic system is never in equilibrium, the concept of long-run equilibrium may nonetheless be useful. The present is the long-run outcome of the distant past and, as will be made precise below, a long-run relationship will often hold 'on average' over time. Moreover, a stable equilibrium has the property that a given deviation from the equilibrium becomes more and more unlikely as the magnitude of the deviation is greater, so that one may be reasonably confident that the discrepancy between the actual relationship connecting variables and this long-run relationship is within certain bounds. Precise definitions are provided in Chapter 5.

Methods for investigating such long-run relationships are our concern here. An examination of these methods will lead us to discuss aspects of time-series analysis, of dynamic modelling in general, and of the rapidly growing literature treating co-integration, error correction, and inference from non-stationary data. The first step is to clarify the statistical notion of stationarity and its links to the concept of equilibrium.

1.2. Stationarity and Equilibrium Relationships

In economic theory, the concept of equilibrium is well established and well defined. The statistical concept of equilibrium centres on that of a *stationary process*, which will be defined formally below. A substantial body of methods is developing around the statistical features of equilibrium relationships among time-series processes, and the concepts of stationarity and particular forms of non-stationarity are crucial to these methods.

If a particular relationship such as $x_1 = \beta x_2$ emerges as the economic system is allowed to settle down, this will describe an equilibrium to an econometrician just as to a theorist. In actual time series, however, the relation $x_{1t} = \beta x_{2t}$ may never be observed to hold. Consequently, we look for ways of characterizing the relationships that can be observed to hold between x_{1t} and x_{2t}.

Roughly speaking—again, terms will be defined precisely in Chapter 5—we say that an equilibrium relationship $f(x_1, x_2) = 0$ holds between two variables x_1 and x_2 if the amount $\varepsilon_t \equiv f(x_{1t}, x_{2t})$ by which actual observations deviate from this equilibrium is a median-zero stationary process.[1] That is, the 'error' or discrepancy between outcome and postulated equilibrium has a fixed distribution, centred on zero, that does not change over time. This error cannot therefore grow indefinitely; if it did, the relationship could not have been an equilibrium one since the system is free to move ever further away from it. Of course, it may be difficult to distinguish in finite samples between an ever-growing discrepancy in an hypothesized equilibrium relationship and a random fluctuation; formal statistical tests for problems such as this are discussed in later chapters.

Given the characterization above, the short-run discrepancy ε_t in an equilibrium relationship must have no tendency to grow systematically over time. However, since this error represents shocks that are constantly occurring and affecting economic variables, in a real economic system there is no systematic tendency for this error to diminish over time either. It would fall away to zero only if shocks were to cease.

This definition of an equilibrium relationship holds automatically when applied to series that are themselves stationary. For *any* two stationary series $\{x_{1t}\}$ and $\{x_{2t}\}$, irrespective of any substantive economic relationship between these two alone, a difference of the form

[1] Later we will consider more precisely the properties that the deviation must have. The requirement is usually stated as being that the deviation from the equilibrium relationship be integrated of order zero (see below); alternatively, we might impose only the weaker requirement that the unconditional expectation of the deviation from the equilibrium relationship be zero, implying that only the first moment need exist and be constant. For simplicity, we omit intercepts from the present discussion.

$\{x_{1t} - bx_{2t}\}$ must be a stationary series for any b. Thus, whether or not there exists a non-zero β which describes a true equilibrium relationship, corresponding to a non-zero derivative between x_1 and x_2, any arbitrarily chosen b will meet the statistical equilibrium condition. This does not imply that we cannot use statistical methods to determine the parameters of a long-run relationship, but simply that one stage of the process, in which we look for a stationary discrepancy, is unnecessary.

However, this concept of statistical equilibrium is necessary and useful in examining equilibrium relationships between variables tending to grow over time. In such cases, if the actual relationship is $x_1 = \beta x_2$, the discrepancy $x_{1t} - bx_{2t}$ will be non-stationary for any $b \neq \beta$, since the discrepancy deviates from the true relationship by the constant proportion $(b - \beta)$ of the growing variable x_{2t}; only the true relationship can yield a stationary discrepancy. With more than two variables, however, there may be more than one equilibrium relation, and this leads to another of the statistical problems that is currently being pursued: the empirical determination of the number of equilibrium relationships between three or more non-stationary time series.

1.3. Equilibrium and the Specification of Dynamic Models

Equilibrium relationships have played an explicit role in econometric modelling since its foundations (see Morgan 1990). If there exists a stable equilibrium $x_1 = \beta x_2$, the discrepancy $\{x_{1t} - \beta x_{2t}\}$ evidently contains useful information since on average the system will move towards that equilibrium if it is not already there. In particular, $(x_{1t-1} - \beta x_{2t-1})$ represents the previous disequilibrium. Suppose the equilibrium relationship is between a variable $\{y_t\}$ to be modelled and some series $\{z_t\}$ which is exogenous in an appropriate sense. If we let $x_{1t} = y_t$ and $x_{2t} = z_t$ to distinguish their status, and denote the equilibrium by $y = \beta z$, then the discrepancy, or error, $\{y_t - \beta z_t\}$ should be a useful explanatory variable for the next direction of movement of y_t. In particular, when $y_t - \beta z_t$ is positive, y_t is too high relative to z_t, and on average we might expect a fall in y in future periods relative to its trend growth. The term $(y_{t-1} - \beta z_{t-1})$, called an *error-correction mechanism*, is therefore sometimes included in dynamic regressions (see Sargan 1964, Hendry and Anderson 1977, and Davidson, Hendry, Srba, and Yeo 1978).

The true parameter β characterizing the relationship is not known in general. This need not prevent the error-correction mechanism from being useful, however, since the unknown parameter can either be estimated separately in a prior analysis or estimated in the course of modelling the variable of interest. Moreover, the general error-correction mechanism can be shown to be equivalent to various other transformations of a general linear model incorporating past values of both the variable of interest and the explanatory variables (see Chapter 2). A particular advantage of the error-correction mechanism is that the extent of adjustment in a given period to deviations from long-run equilibrium is given by the estimated equation without any further calculation. Other forms of the estimated model are also convenient in that they allow the implied long-run relation itself to be seen directly. Considerations such as these are discussed in the following chapter.

The practice of exploiting information contained in the current deviation from an equilibrium relationship, in explaining the path of a variable, has benefited from the formalization of the concept of co-integration by Granger (1981) and Engle and Granger (1987). The informal definition of statistical equilibrium discussed above is based upon a special case of the definition of co-integration. Further, the practice of modelling co-integrated series is closely related to error-correction mechanisms: error-correcting behaviour on the part of economic agents will induce co-integrating relationships among the corresponding time series and vice versa.

A series that is tending to grow over time cannot be stationary (although it may possibly be stationary around some deterministic trend), but the *changes* in that series might be. To take a mechanical example, if an object has a fixed average position around which it moves, always returning after some interval to this position like a randomly perturbed weight at the end of a spring, then its displacement may be a stationary series. An object that has no such fixed position may nevertheless have a velocity (the change in position per unit time), or acceleration (the change in the velocity per unit time), that is stationary. For example, if the object is moving ever further from its point of origin, but with velocity fluctuating around some fixed positive mean according to a fixed distribution function, then the velocity of the object is a stationary series.

A series is said to be integrated of order 1 (I(1)) if, although it is itself non-stationary, the changes in this series form a stationary series. It is said to be integrated of order 2 (I(2)) if, although the changes are non-stationary, the *changes in the changes* form a stationary series. In other words, if the series must be differenced exactly k times to achieve stationarity, then the series is I(k), so that a stationary series is I(0). We will use the term 'integrated process' to refer to a series with order of integration strictly greater than zero: precise definitions are given in Chapter 3.

We can now consider the concept of co-integration, its relation to the definition of long-run equilibrium between series given above, and its use as part of a statistical description of the behaviour of time series that satisfy some equilibrium relationship. A simple example concerns two series, each of which is integrated of order 1. Assume that a long-run equilibrium relationship holds between them, and that it is linear: $x_1 = \beta x_2$. Then $(x_1 - \beta x_2)$ must be equal to zero in equilibrium and the series $\{x_{1t} - \beta x_{2t}\}$ has a constant unconditional mean of zero. This need not imply that $\{x_{1t} - \beta x_{2t}\}$ is stationary: the variance of $\{x_{1t} - \beta x_{2t}\}$ might be non-constant, for example. The definition of co-integration given by Engle and Granger (1987), and discussed in Chapter 5, does however require stationarity of the deviation $\{x_{1t} - \beta x_{2t}\}$. When stationarity does hold, we say that x_1 and x_2 are co-integrated (1, 1), denoted CI(1, 1); that is, they are each integrated of order 1, and there exists some linear combination $\{x_{1t} - \beta x_{2t}\}$ which is integrated of an order one lower than the components (i.e. is I(0) here). If $\{x_{1t} - \beta x_{2t}\}$ has a constant unconditional mean but is not stationary, then we may still want to say that an equilibrium relationship holds; the series will not, however, fit the strict Engle–Granger definition of co-integration, which requires that some linear combination be stationary.

A substantive long-run equilibrium relationship is something from which the variables involved can deviate, but not by an ever-growing amount. That is, the discrepancy or error in the relationship cannot be integrated of any order greater than zero. Series integrated of strictly positive orders which are linked by such an equilibrium relationship must, therefore, be co-integrated with each other. In the example just given, the fact that the integrated series x_1 and x_2 move together in the long run is reflected in the fact that they are co-integrated; a linear relation yields a stationary deviation.

More generally, we can speak of variables that are co-integrated (a, b) when $a > b$ and $b > 0$, where a is the order of integration of the variables and b is the reduction in order of integration produced by the linear combination, which then has order of integration $a - b$. When $b > 0$, a linear relation exists between the variables which is integrated of lower order than either of the variables themselves, but which may none the less not be I(0). In the latter case $(a - b > 0)$, the variables may deviate from the linear relationship by an ever-growing amount, and so it is not the kind of relationship that we have been calling a long-run equilibrium. Nevertheless, variables that are CI(a, b) for $b > 0$ do contain some information about the long-run behaviour of the series involved.

Since a relationship between co-integrated variables can be shown to be representable using an error-correction mechanism (see Chapter 5), and since such representations have been found to be valuable in empirical modelling, there is a formal counterpart to the informal argument above suggesting the usefulness of equilibrium information in specifying dynamic regression models.

1.4. Estimation of Long-Run Relationships and Testing for Orders of Integration and Co-integration

The existence of long-run relationships between variables, the potential orders of integration of particular time series, and the implications of these for the specification of dynamic econometric models can be understood as mathematical properties without implying that we know whether or not such relationships exist, let alone what their forms for a particular empirical problem would be.

When an estimated regression equation implies an equilibrium relationship between two processes, it is a straightforward operation to extract the estimated long-run equilibrium relation regardless of the form in which the equation is estimated. The calculation can be made by expressing the equation in an equilibrium form and taking its expectation. This is analogous to assuming a state in which the values of the variables do not change, so that the dating of variables becomes irrelevant and the equation is treated as deterministic. Computing the derivative between the two series is then straightforward. Approximations to the variances of estimated long-run multipliers can also be computed. Chapter 2 explores various transformations of the linear model that are convenient for these and related calculations.

Testing for the existence of such an equilibrium relationship is not nearly so simple. First, it is difficult empirically to establish the orders of integration of individual time series. Second, the order of integration of a linear relationship among variables is even harder to discover than the order of integration of a single series: drawing inferences is complicated by the fact that the parameters of the relationship are in general unknown.

Testing whether an individual series is I(1) as opposed to I(0) is the problem that has been widely discussed as that of testing for a 'unit root' in a time series. Strategies for performing such testing have had to contend with the problem that I(0) alternatives in which the series is 'close' to being I(1) (so that the power of the test is low) are very plausible in many economic circumstances. Further, the form of the data generation process (e.g. the orders of dynamics; the question of which exogenous variables enter; etc.) is not known, and critical values of test statistics are typically sensitive to the structure of the process.

Fuller (1976) and Dickey and Fuller (1979) emphasized that testing for non-stationarity (again, I(1) as opposed to I(0) series) is more difficult than conventional t-tests of the hypothesis that the autoregressive parameter is equal to one in an AR(1) model. In fact, where there are roots greater than or equal to one, conventionally used tests do not have standard asymptotic distributions. The original tests were variants of conventional tests, with critical values retabulated using Monte Carlo experiments to reflect the changes in distribution when, under the null, the series are non-stationary.

These original tests were based on simple forms of autoregressive model: an AR(1) model, with or without drift and time trend terms (i.e. $y_t = \alpha y_{t-1}$ $[+\beta]$ $[+\gamma t] + \varepsilon_t$). Such simple forms may often be poor approximations to the data generation process. This will manifest itself in the failure of the estimated model to pass various mis-specification tests. In particular, tests for residual autocorrelation will often reflect autocorrelated processes that have been omitted from the model specification. One way of dealing with the problem of finding an adequate model within which to test for non-stationarity has therefore been to retain a simple autoregressive model form, but with a non-parametric correction to the values of the test statistic to allow for a general form of autocorrelation in the residuals. Another approach attempts to capture the autocorrelation through the addition of extra lagged terms in the dependent variable. These issues are addressed in Chapter 4.

When series may contain more than one 'unit root'—i.e. where they may be I(2) or of higher orders—testing becomes yet more difficult because the sequence in which different hypotheses are tested can affect inference. Such issues are also considered in Chapter 4.

A related method can be applied to the problem of testing for an equilibrium relation between integrated variables. A prior step must be added to the method above, in which a linear relationship between or among the variables in question is estimated. Testing for co-integration then entails testing the order of integration of the error in this relationship. For example, a stationary error in a model relating integrated series entails an equilibrium relationship. Conversely, if there were no equilibrium relationship, there would be nothing to tie these series to any estimated linear relation, and this would imply non-stationarity of the residuals.

It might appear at first sight, for example, that testing for co-integration between I(1) series $\{x_{1t}\}$ and $\{x_{2t}\}$ would be precisely the same as a test of the hypothesis that $\{\varepsilon_t\} = \{x_{1t} - \beta x_{2t}\}$ is I(1) against the alternative that $\{\varepsilon_t\}$ is I(0). However, this is true only under very strong assumptions. Necessary conditions include that there is only one co-integrating relation and the values of its parameters are known. In the bivariate case, when β is estimated, the series that one tests for stationarity is $\{\hat{\varepsilon}_t\} = \{x_{1t} - \hat{\beta} x_{2t}\}$. Since linear regression minimizes the variance of $\hat{\varepsilon}_t$, the estimated series of deviations from equilibrium has a smaller variance than the true deviations $\{x_{1t} - \beta x_{2t}\}$, assuming that β

exists. That is, the method by which β is usually estimated amounts to choosing $\hat{\beta}$ in such a way that the two variables are given the best chance to appear to move together. Regression makes co-integration appear to be present more often than it should, so that the critical values of test statistics must be adjusted to reflect the fact that β is estimated. Co-integration tests are therefore similar, but not identical, to standard stationarity tests.

Chapter 7 explores these tests for co-integration, and Chapter 8 extends the discussion to estimation and testing in systems of equations.

1.5. Preliminary Concepts and Definitions

We assume that readers are acquainted with the fundamental principles and methods of econometrics and statistical inference. It is nonetheless worth reviewing some important concepts and definitions that will be used in later chapters, establishing terminology as we do so.

1.5.1. Stochastic Processes and Time-series Models

A number of concepts from standard time-series analysis will be necessary. Box and Jenkins (1970) give a thorough treatment of these models.

A *stochastic process* is an ordered sequence of random variables $\{x(s, t),\ s \in \mathbb{S},\ t \in \mathbb{T}\}$, such that, for each $t \in \mathbb{T}$, $x(\cdot, t)$ is a random variable on the sample space $\mathbb{S}$ and, for each $s \in \mathbb{S}$, $x(s, \cdot)$ is a realization of the stochastic process on the index set $\mathbb{T}$ (that is, an ordered set of values, each corresponding to one value of the index set). A given realization of the process may be represented as $\{x(t),\ t \in \mathbb{T}\}$, and this notation is also often used for the stochastic process itself. In later chapters we will typically refer to realizations of stochastic processes by the notation x_t for a value at t, and $\{x_t\}_1^T$ (or $\{x_t\}$ or $\{x_t\}_{t=1}^T$) for a full set of values corresponding to an index set $\mathbb{T} = \{1, 2, \ldots, T\}$. We will also restrict our attention to discrete stochastic processes, for which the index set is a discrete set, in which case we generally use the notation x_t rather than $x(t)$, which may apply also to continuous processes.

Next, let $\{x(t),\ t \in \mathbb{T}\}$ be a stochastic process such that $E(|x(t)|) < \infty$ for all $t \in \mathbb{T}$, and $E(x(t)|\mathcal{I}_{t-1}) = x(t-1)$ for all $t \in \mathbb{T}$, where $E(\cdot)$ is the expectations operator and $\mathcal{I}_{t-1}$ represents a particular information set of data realized by time $t-1$. Then $\{x(t),\ t \in \mathbb{T}\}$ is called a *martingale* with respect to $\{\mathcal{I}_t,\ t \in \mathbb{T}\}$. A *martingale difference sequence* can then be defined by $\{y(t) = x(t) - x(t-1), t \in \mathbb{T}\}$. It follows that $E(|y(t)|) < \infty\ \ \forall\ t \in \mathbb{T}$ and that $E(y(t)|\mathcal{I}_{t-1}) = 0\ \ \forall\ t \in \mathbb{T}$.

A stochastic process is called *strictly stationary* if, for any subset $(t_1, t_2, \ldots, t_n)$ of $\mathbb{T}$ and any real number h such that $t_i + h \in \mathbb{T}$, $i = 1, 2, \ldots, n$, we have

$$F(x(t_1), x(t_2), \ldots, x(t_n)) = F(x(t_1 + h), x(t_2 + h), \ldots, x(t_n + h)),$$

where $F(\cdot)$ is the joint distribution function of the n values. Strict stationarity therefore implies that all existing moments of the process are constant through time. The process is *weakly stationary* (or *second-order stationary* or *covariance stationary*) if

$$E[x(t_i)] = E[x(t_i + h)] = \mu < \infty,$$
$$E[(x(t_i))^2] = E[(x(t_i + h))^2] = \mu_2 < \infty, \qquad \text{and}$$
$$E[x(t_i)x(t_j)] = E[x(t_i + h)x(t_j + h)] = \mu_{ij} < \infty,$$

where μ, μ_2, and the μ_{ij} are constant over t, for all $t \in \mathbb{T}$ and h such that $t_r + h \in \mathbb{T}$ $(r = i, j)$. Thus, the contemporaneous second moments do not depend on time, and the lag dependencies are functions only of lag length. That the first two raw moments are constant also implies that the variance of the process is constant. If we consider a vector process $\{\mathbf{x}(t)\} = \{x_1(t), x_2(t), \ldots, x_m(t)\}'$, then we require in addition that covariances of the form $E[x_k(t_i)x_l(t_j)]$ are finite constants and are functions of i, j, k, l only, for any admissible i, j, k, and l.

We will not offer a rigorous definition of an integrated process at this stage but we can highlight a number of the issues involved. An *integrated process* is one that can be made stationary by differencing. A discrete process integrated of order d must be differenced d times to reach stationarity; that is, $\Delta^d x_t$ is stationary where the differencing operator Δ^d is defined by $(1 - L)^d$ (using the lag operator L, itself defined by $L^n x_t = x_{t-n}$). For example, the first difference is $\Delta x_t = x_t - x_{t-1}$, and the second difference is $\Delta^2 x_t = \Delta x_t - \Delta x_{t-1} = x_t - 2x_{t-1} + x_{t-2} = (1 - L)^2 x_t$. The process $(1 - L)x_t = \varepsilon_t$, where $\{\varepsilon_t\}$ is a white-noise series (see below), is called a *random walk* and is a simple example of a process integrated of order 1.

Two issues merit comment. First, if x_t is stationary then so is Δx_t or even $\Delta^d x_t$ for $d > 0$. Thus, the stationarity of $\Delta^d x_t$ is not sufficient for x_t to be I(d). (Recall that an I(d) process is one that *must* be differenced d times to achieve stationarity.) Secondly, consider the stable autoregressive process, $x_t = \alpha_0 + \alpha_1 x_{t-1} + \varepsilon_t$, where $|\alpha_1| < 1$, $x_0 = 0$, and $\varepsilon_t \sim \text{IN}(0, \sigma^2)$, $t = 1, \ldots, T$. Then $\{x_t\}$ is non-stationary since $E(x_t) = \alpha_0(1 - \alpha_1^t)(1 - \alpha_1)^{-1}$ which is not constant over t, although

$\{x_t\}$ is asymptotically stationary (see e.g. Spanos 1986). Hence we have a non-stationary series that is not an integrated process in the sense we wish to use. Chapter 3 offers precise definitions.

A *white-noise process* is a stationary process which has a zero mean and is uncorrelated over time; that is, $\{x(t),\ t \in \mathbb{T}\}$ is white noise if $\forall\, t \in \mathbb{T}$, $E[x(t)] = 0$, $E[(x(t))^2] = \sigma^2 < \infty$ and $E[x(t)x(t+h)] = 0$ where $h \neq 0$ and $t + h \in \mathbb{T}$. A white-noise process is therefore necessarily second-order stationary, and if $x(t)$ is normally distributed it is strictly stationary as well since in this case higher-order moments are functions of the first two.

An innovation $\{v(t)\}$ against an information set $\mathcal{I}_{t-1}$ is a process whose distribution $D[v(t)|\mathcal{I}_{t-1}]$ does not depend on $\mathcal{I}_{t-1}$; also, $v(t)$ is a mean innovation if $E[v(t)|\mathcal{I}_{t-1}] = 0$. Thus, an innovation must be white noise if $\mathcal{I}_{t-1}$ contains a history of $\{v(t-1), \ldots, v(0)\}$, but not conversely. Consequently, an innovation must be a martingale difference sequence. (See Spanos (1986) for further discussion.)

For a stationary process, the covariance between two realizations at different points in time (indices) will depend only upon the difference between those indices, and not on the indices themselves. We can therefore define, for a process $\{x_t\}$ that is at least second-order stationary with $E(x_t) = \mu < \infty$, the *autocovariance function*

$$\gamma(h) = E[(x(t) - \mu)(x(t + h) - \mu)].$$

Stationarity implies that $\gamma(h) = \gamma(-h)$, since the autocovariance between two values depends only on the distance between them. The *autocorrelation function* is defined similarly, as

$$\rho(h) = \gamma(h)/\gamma(0),$$

$\gamma(0)$ being the variance of the process.

Our understanding of and ability to forecast stochastic processes is often enhanced by fitting models. The autoregressive-moving average (ARMA) class of models is widely used for univariate time-series modelling, and we will make frequent reference to such models. An ARMA(p, q) model (with p autoregressive (AR) and q moving-average (MA) parameters) for a process $\{x_t\}_1^T$ is of the form

$$x_t = \sum_{i=1}^{p} \alpha_i x_{t-i} + \sum_{j=0}^{q} \theta_j \varepsilon_{t-j},$$

with $\theta_0 = 1$ and $\{\varepsilon_t\}_1^T$ a white-noise process.

Using polynomials in the lag operator, we can express the ARMA model as

$$\alpha(L)x_t = \theta(L)\varepsilon_t, \tag{1}$$

with

$$\alpha(L) = 1 - \sum_{i=1}^{p} \alpha_i L^i \qquad \text{and} \qquad \theta(L) = 1 + \sum_{j=1}^{q} \theta_j L^j.$$

The polynomials $\alpha(L)$ and $\theta(L)$ can be expressed in terms of their factors as

$$\alpha(L) = \prod_{i=1}^{p} (1 - \lambda_i L) \qquad \text{and} \qquad \theta(L) = \prod_{j=1}^{q} (1 - \delta_j L).$$

If any factor $(1 - \lambda_m L)$ from $\alpha(L)$ matches any $(1 - \delta_k L)$ from $\theta(L)$, then these are said to be common factors, and can be cancelled from both sides of (1). This is important because, if $\gamma(L)$ is any arbitrary polynomial of order n, from (1) it is also true that

$$\gamma(L)\alpha(L)x_t = \gamma(L)\theta(L)\varepsilon_t \qquad \text{or} \qquad \alpha^*(L)x_t = \theta^*(L)\varepsilon_t.$$

Such redundant common factors must be cancelled to ensure a unique representation. If the AR polynomial $\alpha(L)$ contains the factor $(1 - L)$, (that is, if there is some λ_i equal to one), then the process is said to contain a *unit root*.[2]

When the parameters $\{\alpha_i\}$ and $\{\theta_j\}$ are chosen to fit the autocorrelations of the observed process as well as possible, the resulting ARMA process may be a useful predictive device. An autoregressive integrated moving-average (ARIMA) process allows for an integrated component in the underlying time series; thus, an ARIMA(p, d, q) process is an I(d) process for which the dth difference follows an ARMA(p, q).

An ARMA model with given parameters implies particular autocovariance and autocorrelation functions; see Box and Jenkins (1970: 74 ff.) for a description of an algorithm by which these can be calculated for a general ARMA(p, q) process.

If the parameters of the ARMA process are known, checking stationarity is not difficult. Provided that $\alpha(L)$ and $\theta(L)$ contain no common factors, stationarity of an ARMA(p, q) process depends only on the p parameters of the autoregressive part. An AR or ARMA model is stationary if and only if the roots of the AR polynomial $(1 - \alpha_1 L - \ldots - \alpha_p L^p)$ lie *outside* the unit circle (or, equivalently, if and only if the latent roots of the polynomial, being the roots of $(z^p - \alpha_1 z^{p-1} - \ldots - \alpha_p)$, lie *inside* the unit circle). An analogous condition must hold in the MA polynomial to guarantee *invertibility* of the process; see Box and Jenkins (1970) or Fuller (1976).

[2] Factors such as $(1 + L)$ or $(1 + L^2)$ yield roots with moduli of unity.

Examples of processes having these forms will be given later in this chapter.

1.5.2. Orders of Magnitude, Convergence in Probability, and Convergence in Distribution

During the course of the analysis, we will examine the limiting behaviour of many random variables. In particular, we will often be interested in determining whether or not a given sequence of random variables converges or tends to a limiting value (or to a limit random variable), and the rate at which any such convergence occurs. The definitions given below, taken from Fuller (1976) and based on Mann and Wald (1943), make these concepts of convergence rigorous.

It is useful to start with a sequence of variables—say, real numbers—that are non-stochastic.

Let $\{a_T\}_{T=1}^{\infty}$ be a sequence of real numbers and $\{g_T\}_{T=1}^{\infty}$ be a sequence of positive real numbers. Then

1. a_T is of smaller order (in magnitude) than g_T, denoted $a_T = o(g_T)$, if $\lim_{T\to\infty} a_T/g_T = 0$.
2. a_T is at most of order (in magnitude) g_T, denoted $a_T = O(g_T)$, if there exists a real number M such that $g_T^{-1}|a_T| \leqslant M$ for all T.

For a sequence of random or stochastic variables, 'order in probability' is the relevant concept. Let $\{X_T\}$ be a sequence of random variables with $\{g_T\}$ as above. Then

3. The sequence $\{X_T\}$ *converges in probability* to the random variable X, denoted either $X_T \xrightarrow{\text{p}} X$ or $\text{plim}\, X_T = X$, if, for every $\varepsilon > 0$, $\lim_{T\to\infty} \Pr\{|X_T - X| > \varepsilon\} = 0$. The *probability limit* of X_T is X.
4. X_T is of smaller order in probability than g_T, denoted $X_T = o_p(g_T)$, if $\text{plim}\, X_T/g_T = 0$.
5. X_T is at most of order in probability g_T, denoted $X_T = O_p(g_T)$, if, for every $\varepsilon > 0$, there exists a positive real number M_ε such that $\Pr\{|X_T| \geqslant M_\varepsilon g_T\} \leqslant \varepsilon$.

Two important points should be noted. First, the distinction between the little-o and big-O concepts of convergence may be understood intuitively by thinking of the former as scaling a random variable such that the scaled variable tends to zero in the limit; for the latter, all that is required is that the scaled variable remains bounded by a finite interval of the real line. In a trivial case, say X_T is $o_p(1)$. (Here the sequence $\{g_T\}$ is a degenerate sequence of 1s.) That is, unscaled, $X_T \xrightarrow{\text{p}} 0$. Then it is certainly true that X_T is $O_p(1)$. The converse is not true in general.

The second point concerns the specific use made of these convergence concepts in this book. The sequence $\{X_T\}$ will in general be a sequence of estimators. The sequence of ordinary least squares (OLS) estimators in a regression model is a good example. The estimator $\hat{\beta}_T$ is derived from a sample of size T, where in time-series analysis T denotes time. A sample of size T is therefore composed of observations on a set of variables for T time periods, usually denoted $t = 1, 2, \ldots, T$. Thus, $\hat{\beta}_T \xrightarrow{p} \beta$ if and only if $\lim_{T\to\infty} \Pr\{|\hat{\beta}_T - \beta| > \varepsilon\} = 0$.

The corresponding sequence $\{g_T\}$ is usually a power function of time. Thus, for OLS estimators when the variables are stationary, $g_T = T^{-1/2}$ and $\{\hat{\beta}_T - \beta\} = O_P(T^{-1/2})$. In an alternative terminology, we often say that $\hat{\beta}$ tends to β at rate $T^{1/2}$. If the variables are integrated, $g_T = T^{-1}$ or larger, which is the case of super- (or faster than $T^{1/2}$) convergence.

The lemmata given below are often useful in determining orders in magnitude and in probability of functions (sums, differences, products, and quotients) of random variables (see Fuller 1976, and White 1984).

LEMMA 1. Let $\{a_T\}$, $\{b_T\}$ be sequences of real numbers. Let $\{f_T\}$ and $\{g_T\}$ be sequences of positive real numbers.

(i) If $a_T = o(f_T)$ and $b_T = o(g_T)$, then

$$a_T b_T = o(f_T\, g_T)$$
$$|a_T|^s = o(f_T^s) \qquad \text{for } s > 0$$
$$a_T + b_T = \max\{o(f_T), o(g_T)\}.$$

(ii) If $a_T = O(f_T)$ and $b_T = O(g_T)$, then

$$a_T b_T = O(f_T\, g_T)$$
$$|a_T|^s = O(f_T^s) \qquad \text{for } s \geqslant 0$$
$$a_T + b_T = \max\{O(f_T), O(g_T)\}.$$

(iii) If $a_T = o(f_T)$ and $b_T = O(g_T)$, then

$$a_T b_T = o(f_T\, g_T)$$
$$a_T + b_T = O(g_T).$$

LEMMA 2. Let $\{f_T\}$, $\{g_T\}$ be sequences of positive real numbers and let $\{X_T\}$ and $\{Y_T\}$ be sequences of random variables.

(i) If $X_T = o_p(f_T)$ and $Y_T = o_p(g_T)$, then

$$X_T Y_T = o_p(f_T\, g_T)$$
$$|X_T|^s = o_p(f_T^s) \qquad \text{for } s > 0$$
$$X_T + Y_T = \max\{o_p(f_T), o_p(g_T)\}.$$

(ii) If $X_T = O_p(f_T)$ and $Y_T = O_p(g_T)$, then

$$X_T Y_T = O_p(f_T\, g_T)$$
$$|X_T|^s = O_p(f_T^s) \qquad \text{for } s \geqslant 0$$
$$X_T + Y_T = \max\{O_p(f_T),\, O_p(g_T)\}.$$

(iii) If $X_T = o_p(f_T)$ and $Y_T = O_p(g_T)$, then

$$X_T Y_T = o_p(f_T\, g_T)$$
$$X_T + Y_T = O_p(g_T).$$

A second type of convergence is the convergence of a sequence of distribution functions to a limit function. Important examples of such convergence are central limit theorems, where a sequence of distribution functions converges point-wise to the normal distribution function. The appendix to this chapter uses the Liapunov central limit theorem to derive the asymptotic distribution of a scaled function of the sample mean.

6. If $\{X_T\}$ is a sequence of random variables with distribution functions $\{F_{X_T}(x)\}$, then $\{X_T\}$ is said to converge in distribution to the random variable X with distribution function $F_X(x)$, denoted $X_T \xrightarrow{\text{d}} X$, if $\lim_{T\to\infty} F_{X_T}(x) = F_X(x)$, at all points of continuity x.

Finally, convergence in probability implies convergence in distribution. Thus,

7. Let $\{X_T\}$ be a sequence of random variables. If there exists a random variable X such that $\text{plim}\, X_T = X$, then $X_T \xrightarrow{\text{d}} X$.

1.5.3. Ergodicity and Mixing Processes

The following definitions are based on Davidson and MacKinnon (1992), Spanos (1986), and White (1984), which readers can consult for further details.

Ergodicity, uniform mixing, and strong mixing are three types of asymptotic independence, implying that two realizations of a time series become ever closer to independence as the distance between them increases. Generically, a stochastic process $\{y_t\}$ is defined as *asymptotically independent* if

$$\left|F(y_1, \ldots, y_n, y_{h+1}, \ldots, y_{h+n}) - F(y_1, \ldots, y_n)F(y_{h+1}, \ldots, y_{h+n})\right| \to 0$$

as $h \to \infty$; that is, the joint distribution function of the two subsequences of $\{y_t\}$ approaches the product of the distributions of each of the sub-sequences as the distance between the sub-sequences increases without bound.

A process $\{y_t\}$ is defined as *ergodic* if it is stationary and if, for any t,

$$\lim_{T\to\infty}\left(T^{-1}\sum_{\tau=1}^{T}\operatorname{cov}(y_t, y_{t+\tau})\right) = 0.$$

A sufficient but not necessary condition for this to hold is that $\operatorname{cov}(y_t, y_{t+\tau}) \to 0$ as $\tau \to \infty$. Thus ergodicity is a weak form of average asymptotic independence, and usually we will assume that stronger conditions hold which imply ergodicity.

If two events A and B are independent, then the quantities $P(A|B) - P(A)$ and $P(A\cap B) - P(A)P(B)$ are both equal to zero, where $P(A|B)$ is the conditional probability of A given B and $P(A\cap B)$ is the joint probability of A and B. The concepts of *uniform mixing* and *strong mixing* are based on these two quantities respectively, and require that expressions having these forms be equal to zero asymptotically. Uniform mixing and strong mixing are also called ϕ-mixing and α-mixing, after the sequences of numbers $\{\phi_n\}$ and $\{\alpha_n\}$ used in defining them. Uniform mixing implies strong mixing, and for a stationary process either of these implies ergodicity.

Begin by defining the bounded mappings $G_1(y_i, \ldots, y_{i+h})$ and $G_2(y_i, \ldots, y_{i+k})$ onto the real line. Then the sequence $\{y_t\}$ is defined as ϕ-mixing if there exists a sequence $\{\phi_n\}$, with $\phi_n > 0\ \forall\ n$, where $\phi_n \to 0$ as $n \to \infty$, such that for $n \gg h$

$$\left|E[G_1(y_t, \ldots, y_{t+h})|G_2(y_{t+n}, \ldots, y_{t+n+k})] - E[G_1(y_t, \ldots, y_{t+h})]\right| < \phi_n.$$

The sequence $\{y_t\}$ is defined as α-mixing if there exists a sequence $\{\alpha_n\}$ with $\alpha_n > 0\ \forall\ n$ and where $\alpha_n \to 0$ as $n \to \infty$, such that

$$\left|E[G_1(y_t, \ldots, y_{t+h})G_2(y_{t+n}, \ldots, y_{t+n+k})] - E[G_1(y_t, \ldots, y_{t+h})]E[G_2(y_{t+n}, \ldots, y_{t+n+k})]\right| < \alpha_n.$$

1.5.4. Exogeneity

While our primary focus is on integrated series and the problems they imply for standard econometric analyses, rather than on the problems created by a failure of exogeneity (in the appropriate sense), it will be important to consider exogeneity at several points.

Econometric analysis often proceeds on the basis of a single-equation model of a process of interest. Implicitly, we assume that knowledge of the processes generating the explanatory variables would carry no information relevant to the parameters of interest. As Engle, Hendry, and Richard (1983) indicate, concepts of exogeneity relate to the circumstances in which this assumption is valid. Rather than refer to particular variables as exogenous in general, Engle *et al.* refer to a variable as exogenous *with respect to a particular parameter* if knowledge of the process generating the exogenous variable contains no information about that parameter.

The three different concepts introduced by Engle *et al.* are called weak, strong, and super exogeneity and correspond to three different ways in which a parameter estimate may be used: inference, forecasting conditional on forecasts of the exogenous variables, and policy analysis. These different uses require that different conditions must be met for exogeneity to hold. These conditions can be examined with the following definitions.

Let $\mathbf{x}_t = (y_t, z_t)'$ be generated by the process with conditional density function $D(\mathbf{x}_t|\mathbf{X}_{t-1}, \boldsymbol{\lambda})$, where $\mathbf{X}_{t-1}$ denotes the history of the variable $\mathbf{x}$: $\mathbf{X}_{t-1} = (\mathbf{x}_{t-1}, \mathbf{x}_{t-2}, \ldots, \mathbf{X}_0)$. Let the parameters $\boldsymbol{\lambda} \in \boldsymbol{\Lambda}$ be partitioned into $(\boldsymbol{\lambda}_1, \boldsymbol{\lambda}_2)$ to support the factorization

$$D(\mathbf{x}_t|\mathbf{X}_{t-1}, \boldsymbol{\lambda}) = D(y_t|z_t, \mathbf{X}_{t-1}, \boldsymbol{\lambda}_1)D(z_t|\mathbf{X}_{t-1}, \boldsymbol{\lambda}_2).$$

Then $[(y_t|z_t; \boldsymbol{\lambda}_1), (z_t; \boldsymbol{\lambda}_2)]$ operates a *sequential cut* on $D(\mathbf{x}_t|\mathbf{X}_{t-1}, \boldsymbol{\lambda})$ if and only if $\boldsymbol{\lambda}_1$ and $\boldsymbol{\lambda}_2$ are *variation free*; that is, if and only if

$$(\boldsymbol{\lambda}_1, \boldsymbol{\lambda}_2) \in \boldsymbol{\Lambda}_1 \times \boldsymbol{\Lambda}_2, \qquad \text{where } \boldsymbol{\lambda}_1 \in \boldsymbol{\Lambda}_1 \text{ and } \boldsymbol{\lambda}_2 \in \boldsymbol{\Lambda}_2,$$

so that the parameter space $\boldsymbol{\Lambda}$ is the direct product of $\boldsymbol{\Lambda}_1$ and $\boldsymbol{\Lambda}_2$. In other words, for any values of $\boldsymbol{\lambda}_1$ and $\boldsymbol{\lambda}_2$, admissible values of the parameters $\boldsymbol{\lambda}$ of the joint distribution can be recovered. The essential element of weak exogeneity is that the marginal distribution contains no information relevant to $\boldsymbol{\lambda}_1$ (for an exposition, see Ericsson 1992).

Weak exogeneity: z_t is weakly exogenous for a set of parameters of interest $\boldsymbol{\psi}$ if and only if there exists a partition $(\boldsymbol{\lambda}_1, \boldsymbol{\lambda}_2)$ of $\boldsymbol{\lambda}$ such that (i) $\boldsymbol{\psi}$ is a function of $\boldsymbol{\lambda}_1$ alone, and (ii) $[(y_t|z_t; \boldsymbol{\lambda}_1), (z_t; \boldsymbol{\lambda}_2)]$ operates a sequential cut.

Strong exogeneity: z_t is strongly exogenous for $\boldsymbol{\psi}$ if and only if z_t is weakly exogenous for $\boldsymbol{\psi}$ and

$$D(z_t|\mathbf{X}_{t-1}, \boldsymbol{\lambda}_2) = D(z_t|\mathbf{Z}_{t-1}, \mathbf{Y}_0, \boldsymbol{\lambda}_2),$$

so that y does not Granger-cause z.

Super exogeneity: z_t is super exogenous for $\boldsymbol{\psi}$ if and only if z_t is weakly exogenous for $\boldsymbol{\psi}$ and $\boldsymbol{\lambda}_1$ is invariant to interventions affecting $\boldsymbol{\lambda}_2$.

Weak exogeneity ensures that there is no loss of information about parameters of interest from analysing only the conditional distribution; a variable z_t is weakly exogenous for a set of parameters $\boldsymbol{\psi}$ if inference concerning $\boldsymbol{\psi}$ can be made conditional on z_t with no loss of information relative to that which could be obtained using the joint density of y_t and

z_t. Strong exogeneity is necessary for multi-step forecasting which proceeds by forecasting future zs and then forecasting ys conditional on those zs. Super exogeneity sustains policy analysis on $\boldsymbol{\lambda}_1$ when the marginal distribution of z_t is altered.

Engle *et al.* contrast these three types of exogeneity with the traditional concepts of *strict exogeneity* and *pre-determinedness*. If u_t is the error term in a model, then z_t is said to be strictly exogenous if $E[z_t u_{t+i}] = 0 \;\forall\, i$, whereas z_t is said to be predetermined if $E[z_t u_{t+i}] = 0$ $\forall\, i \geqslant 0$. Engle *et al.* show that the latter concepts are neither necessary nor sufficient for valid inference since neither relates to parameters of interest.

The following example (from Engle *et al.* 1983) seeks to clarify these concepts. Consider the DGP:

$$y_t = \beta z_t + \xi_{1t}$$
$$z_t = \delta_1 z_{t-1} + \delta_2 y_{t-1} + \xi_{2t},$$

with

$$\begin{bmatrix} \xi_{1t} \\ \xi_{2t} \end{bmatrix} \sim \mathrm{IN}\left[\begin{pmatrix} 0 \\ 0 \end{pmatrix}, \begin{pmatrix} \sigma_{11} & \sigma_{12} \\ \sigma_{21} & \sigma_{22} \end{pmatrix}\right].$$

The parameters $(\beta, \delta_1, \delta_2, \sigma_{11}, \sigma_{12}, \sigma_{22})$ are assumed to be variation free beyond the requirements that ensure the error covariance matrix is positive definite. β is the parameter of interest. The reduced-form equation for y_t is

$$y_t = \beta\delta_1 z_{t-1} + \beta\delta_2 y_{t-1} + v_t,$$

with

$$\begin{bmatrix} v_t \\ \xi_{2t} \end{bmatrix} \sim \mathrm{IN}\left[\begin{pmatrix} 0 \\ 0 \end{pmatrix}, \begin{pmatrix} \sigma_{11} + 2\beta\sigma_{12} + \beta^2\sigma_{22} & \sigma_{12} + \beta\sigma_{22} \\ \sigma_{12} + \beta\sigma_{22} & \sigma_{22} \end{pmatrix}\right]$$

and $E[y_t | z_t, \mathbf{Y}_{t-1}, \mathbf{Z}_{t-1}] = bz_t + c_1 z_{t-1} + c_2 y_{t-1}$, where

$$b = \beta + \sigma_{12}\sigma_{22}^{-1} \quad \text{and} \quad c_i = -\delta_i\sigma_{12}\sigma_{22}^{-1}, \quad i = 1, 2.$$

The corresponding conditional variance $\mathrm{var}\,(y_t | z_t, \mathbf{Y}_{t-1}, \mathbf{Z}_{t-1})$ is given by

$$\sigma^2 = \sigma_{11} - \sigma_{12}^2\sigma_{22}^{-1}.$$

Consider now the regression model

$$y_t = bz_t + c_1 z_{t-1} + c_2 y_{t-1} + u_t, \qquad u_t \sim \mathrm{IN}\,(0, \sigma^2).$$

If $\sigma_{12} = 0$, by substituting this value into the expressions for b, c_i, and σ^2, we see that $E[y_t | z_t, \mathbf{Y}_{t-1}, \mathbf{Z}_{t-1}] = \beta z_t$ and that the conditional variance is σ_{11}. Also, $E[z_t | \mathbf{Z}_{t-1}, \mathbf{Y}_{t-1}] = \delta_1 z_{t-1} + \delta_2 y_{t-1}$ with variance σ_{22}. Hence the conditional density of (y_t, z_t) factorizes as in our earlier definition of a sequential cut, so that (β, σ_{11}) and $(\delta_1, \delta_2, \sigma_{22})$

correspond to $\boldsymbol{\lambda}_1$ and $\boldsymbol{\lambda}_2$ respectively. Since the parameter β is (trivially) a function of $\boldsymbol{\lambda}_1$ only, z_t is weakly exogenous for β. In the context of the regression model, this shows up in the fact that β can be derived from the parameters of this regression, without knowledge of the parameters of the process generating z_t. Here, in fact, $\sigma_{12} = 0$ implies $b = \beta$. If $\sigma_{12} \neq 0$, then β cannot be obtained from the parameters b_1, c_1, c_2, and σ^2 of the regression model (or of the conditional distribution).

As long as $\delta_2 \neq 0$, lagged ys affect z and so z is neither strongly nor strictly exogenous for β irrespective of its weak exogeneity status. When $\sigma_{12} \neq 0$, and β is an invariant parameter, changes in the parameters (δ_1, δ_2, σ_{22}) determining the marginal process affect the parameters of the conditional process, b and c_i. Thus, the failure of z_t to be weakly exogenous can lead to a failure of constancy in the conditional model when the marginal process changes. Conversely, when $\sigma_{12} = 0$ and (β, σ_{11}) are invariant to changes in $(\delta_1, \delta_2, \sigma_{22})$, z_t is super exogenous for β. This holds even when $\delta_2 \neq 0$ and z_t is not strongly exogenous for β.

1.5.5. Functions of Deterministic Trends

Various sums of powers of trends appear regularly in the derivations in this book and so it is convenient to record the most common of these here:

$$\sum_{t=1}^{T} t = (1/2)T(T + 1) = O(T^2);$$

$$\sum_{t=1}^{T} t^2 = (1/6)T(T + 1)(2T + 1) = O(T^3);$$

$$\sum_{t=1}^{T} t^3 = [(1/2)T(T + 1)]^2 = O(T^4);$$

$$\sum_{t=1}^{T} t^4 = (1/6)T(T + 1)(2T + 1)\{(1/5)[3T(T + 1) - 1]\} = O(T^5).$$

In each case, we also have that $T^{-m}\sum_{t=1}^{T} t^{m-1} \to 1/m$.

These formulae are well known and easy, if tedious, to establish, and can be checked by induction. Let

$$\sum_{t=1}^{T} t^j = a_1 T + a_2 T^2 + a_3 T^3 + a_4 T^4 + \ldots + a_{j+1} T^{j+1}.$$

Then for $T = 1, 2, 3, \ldots, j + 1$, solve the resulting simultaneous system. For example, when $j = 1$, $\sum_{t=1}^{T} t = a_1 T + a_2 T^2$. At $T = 1$, $1 = a_1 + a_2$, while at $T = 2$, $3 = 2a_1 + 4a_2$. Solving for a_1 and a_2 gives $a_1 = 1/2$ and $a_2 = 1/2$, so that

$$\sum_{t=1}^{T} t = \tfrac{1}{2}T + \tfrac{1}{2}T^2 = \tfrac{1}{2}T(T+1).$$

Also, $T^{-2}[(1/2)T + (1/2)T^2] \to 1/2$. The polynomial that is fitted to $\sum_{t=1}^{T} t^j$ is assumed to be of order $j+1$. To show that this is the correct order to use, consider what would happen if $\sum_{t=1}^{T} t$ had been set equal to a third-order polynomial $a_1T + a_2T^2 + a_3T^3$. Solving as above for a_1, a_2, and a_3 would yield $a_1 = a_2 = 1/2$ (as before) with $a_3 = 0$.

We can summarize some of the relations above as follows. Let $A_1 = (1/2)T(T+1)$, $A_2 = (1/3)(2T+1)$, and $A_3 = (1/5)[3T(T+1) - 1]$. Then

$$\sum_{t=1}^{T} t = A_1, \quad \sum_{t=1}^{T} t^2 = A_1A_2, \quad \sum_{t=1}^{T} t^3 = A_1^2 \quad \text{and}$$

$$\sum_{t=1}^{T} t^4 = A_1A_2A_3.$$

These sums are of orders $O(T^2)$, $O(T^3)$, $O(T^4)$, and $O(T^5)$ respectively, because $T^{-2}A_1 \to 1/2$, $T^{-3}A_1A_2 \to 1/3$, $T^{-4}A_1^2 \to 1/4$, and $T^{-5}A_1A_2A_3 \to 1/5$.

1.5.6. Wiener Processes

Wiener, or Brownian motion, processes are used in exploring the properties of statistics involving integrated data. We begin our discussion by constructing an integrated process, and then map a transformation of it into a Wiener process.

Let $\{x_t\}$ be a normally distributed, zero-mean, unit variance, stationary, and ergodic martingale difference sequence, so that $x_t \sim \text{IN}(0,1)$, and let

$$S_T = \sum_{t=1}^{T} x_t, \tag{2}$$

with $S_0 = 0$. The sample mean is $\bar{x} = T^{-1}S_T$. For $0 \leq \kappa < \tau < T$, $E[S_T - S_\kappa] = 0$ so that

$$E[(S_T - S_\kappa)^2] = E\left[\left(\sum_{t=\kappa+1}^{T} x_t\right)^2\right] = T - \kappa$$

and

$$E[(S_T - S_\tau)(S_{\tau-1} - S_\kappa)] = 0.$$

Thus, $S_T \sim \text{N}(0, T)$ and is an I(1) process with independent increments. Specifically, S_T is a random walk: $S_T = S_{T-1} + x_T$. More generally, when the distribution of $\{x_t\}$ is well behaved, the limiting distribution of a suitably standardized S_T will also be well behaved.

The analysis of regressions with integrated series uses the concept of limit theorems in function spaces known as *functional limit theorems*. These are also called *invariance principles* because the same form of limiting distribution results for a wide range of processes $\{x_t\}$, having different degrees of heterogeneity and memory (see Phillips 1987*a*). Figure 1.1 illustrates a sample realization of a random walk S_T for $T = 10$. We will describe the various stages of analysis in terms of this example. We first consider convergence of the transformation $S_T/\sqrt{T}$ from (2) to a continuous *Wiener process* denoted by $\mathrm{W}(r)$ for $r \in [0, 1]$.

A Wiener process is like a continuous random walk defined on the interval [0, 1] (regard this as the horizontal axis), but has unbounded variation despite being continuous, and so can be imagined as moving extremely erratically in the vertical direction. In any sub-interval $[a, b]$ of [0, 1], $\mathrm{W}(r)$ for $r \in [a, b]$ remains equally erratic. In general, a continuous process $V(t)$, $t \geqslant 0$, is a Wiener process if (i) for all $t \geqslant 0$, $E[V(t)] = 0$; (ii) for all fixed $t \geqslant 0$, $V(t)$ is normally distributed and non-degenerate; (iii) $V(t)$ has independent increments; and (iv) $\Pr\{V(0) = 0\} = 1$. A Wiener process may be thought of as the limit of a discrete-time random walk as the interval between realizations goes to zero. Its derivative is a continuous-time normally distributed white-noise process, which is an abstraction, not a physically realizable process. Nonetheless, the limiting distributions described by the Wiener process may be useful approximations in many circumstances.

There are few convenient analytical expressions for functions of the distribution of $\mathrm{W}(r)$, $r \in [0, 1]$, although as we have noted

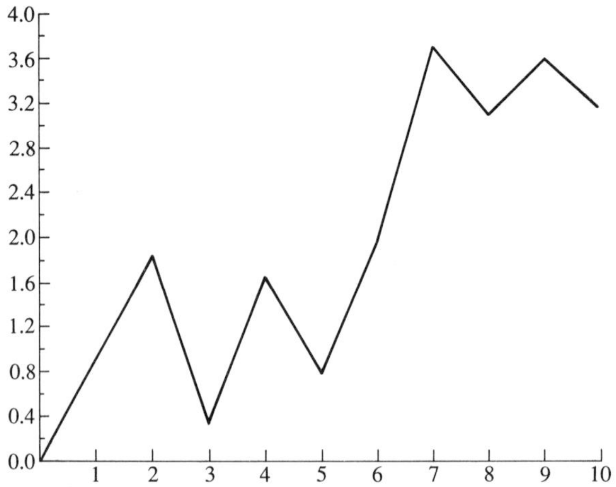

FIG 1.1. Realization of a random walk over 10 points

$W(r) \sim N(0, r)$ for fixed r, and $W(r)$ has independent increments. Various functions of $W(r)$ have been tabulated, usually by simulation.

The following formulation maps the increasing interval from 0 to T into the fixed interval [0, 1] so that results will be invariant to the actual value of T. To do so, we construct from S_T a new random step function $R_T(r)$ as follows. Let $[rT]$ denote the integer part of rT, where $r \in [0, 1]$. For example, if $T = 100$ and $r = 0.101$, then $[rT] = [10.1] = 10$. Divide the interval [0, 1] into $T + 1$ parts at 0, $1/T$, $2/T$, . . ., 1, and let

$$R_T(r) = S_{[rT]}/\sqrt{T} \qquad \text{for } r \in [0, 1]. \tag{3}$$

For example, $R_{100}(0.101) = S_{10}/10$ whereas $R_{100}(0.11) = S_{11}/10$. Thus, $R_T(r)$ is constant for values of r within jumps at successive integers, and is a right-continuous random variable defined over [0, 1]. Figure 1.2 shows this second-stage mapping, leading to the step function graph of $R_T(r)$ in Fig. 1.3. As $T \to \infty$, $R_T(r)$ becomes increasingly dense on [0, 1]. Figures 1.4 and 1.5 show this happening for $T = 100$ and $T = 1000$. The horizontal axis length is fixed, so the vertical axis variability increases as T grows.

Let $\Rightarrow$ denote weak convergence in the sense that the probability measures converge: this is the analogue for function spaces, of convergence in distribution for random variables (see Hall and Heyde 1980). Then, under weak assumptions about $\{x_t\}$,

$$R_T(r) \Rightarrow W(r) \qquad \text{for } r \in [0, 1] \text{ as } T \to \infty. \tag{4}$$

Furthermore, if $f(\cdot)$ is a continuous functional on [0, 1], then

$$f(R_T(r)) \Rightarrow f(W(r)). \tag{5}$$

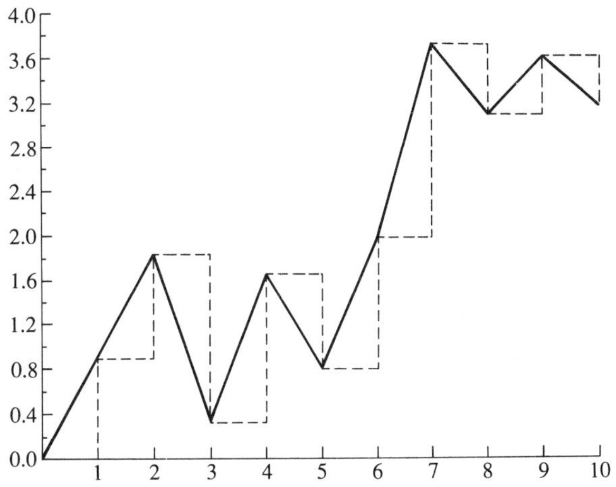

FIG 1.2. Mapping the 10-point graph on to a step function

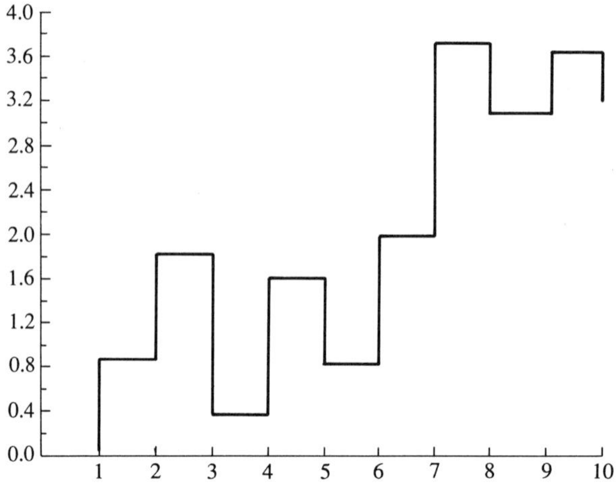

FIG 1.3. Step representation of a random walk over 10 points

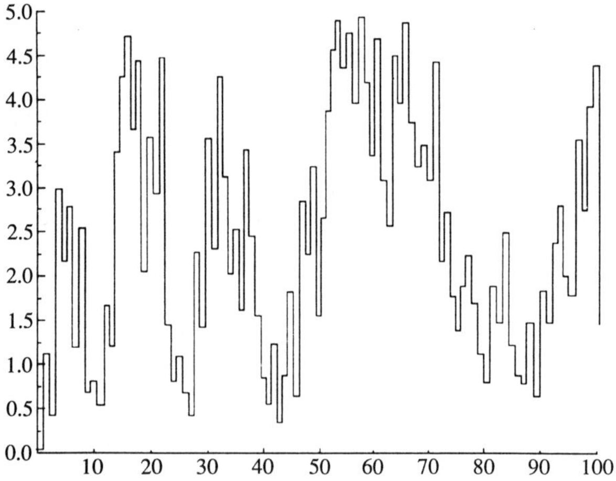

FIG 1.4. Step representation of a random walk over 100 points

For further details, see Billingsley (1968), Dickey and Fuller (1979, 1981), Hall and Heyde (1980), and Phillips (1986, 1987*a*).

In distributions involving I(1) variables, functionals of Wiener processes arise quite generally, whereas conventional methods of obtaining limiting distributions tend to be specific to the assumptions made about the data or error process.[3] Also, many of the statistics regularly used in

[3] By this we mean that only weak restrictions need to be satisfied by the $\{x_t\}$ sequence for convergence results such as (4) and (5) to hold. Phillips (1987*a*) provides a good account of this issue, and a discussion is also contained in Ch. 3.

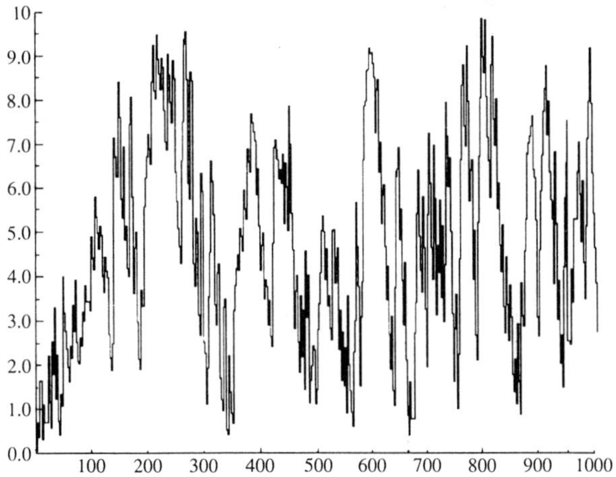

FIG 1.5. Step representation of a random walk over 1000 points

empirical research involving I(1) time series have different distributions from those that arise with I(0) data. In particular, many statistics in I(1) processes do not converge to constants, as in the I(0) case, but instead converge to random variables. Thus, different critical values may be required for tests, depending on the degree of integration of the time series.

Consider the random walk, $y_t = y_{t-1} + e_t$, with $e_t \sim \text{IN}(0, 1)$ and $y_0 = 0$. Then

$$E[y_t] = E\left[\sum_{i=1}^{t} e_i\right] = 0, \tag{6}$$

and

$$\text{var}(y_t) = E[y_t^2] = E\left[\left(\sum_{i=1}^{t} e_i\right)^2\right] = \sum_{i=1}^{t}\sum_{j=1}^{t} E[e_i e_j] = t, \tag{7}$$

since $E[e_i e_j] = 1$ if $i = j$, and 0 if $i \neq j$.

From (6) and (7), $y_t \sim \text{N}(0, t)$. Furthermore,

$$\text{cov}(y_t, y_{t-1}) = E[y_t y_{t-1}] = E\left[\left(\sum_{i=1}^{t} e_i\right)\left(\sum_{j=1}^{t-1} e_j\right)\right] = \sum_{i=1}^{t}\sum_{j=1}^{t-1} E[e_i e_j] = t - 1.$$

Alternatively, from (7),

$$E(y_t y_{t-1}) = E(y_{t-1}^2 + y_{t-1}e_t) = E(y_{t-1}^2) = t - 1.$$

Next, $$\operatorname{corr}^2(y_t, y_{t-1}) = [E(y_t y_{t-1})]^2/[E(y_t^2)E(y_{t-1}^2)]$$
$$= (t-1)^2/t(t-1) = 1 - t^{-1}. \qquad (8)$$

Similarly, $\operatorname{corr}^2(y_t, y_{t-k})$ has a numerator of $(t-k)^2$ and a denominator of $t(t-k)$ for $k > 0$, and so equals $1 - k/t$. When $k < 0$, let $s = t - k$ so that $t = s + k$, and let $r = -k > 0$, in which case

$$\operatorname{corr}^2(y_t, y_{t-k}) = \operatorname{corr}^2(y_{s+k}, y_s) = \operatorname{corr}^2(y_s, y_{s-r}) = 1 - r/s$$
$$= 1 + k/(t-k).$$

Since $y_0 = 0$, we have that

$$E\left(T^{-1}\sum_{t=1}^{T} y_{t-1}e_t\right) = 0$$

and (see Fuller 1976: 367) since $E(y_t^4) = 3t^2$

$$E\left(T^{-1}\sum_{t=1}^{T} y_t^2\right) = T^{-1}\sum_{t=1}^{T} t = T^{-1}T(T+1)/2 = (T+1)/2 \qquad (9a)$$

$$E\left(T^{-1}\sum_{t=1}^{T} y_t y_{t-1}\right) = T^{-1}\sum_{t=2}^{T}(t-1) = T^{-1}T(T-1)/2 = (T-1)/2 \qquad (9b)$$

$$\operatorname{var}\left(T^{-1}\sum_{t=1}^{T} y_t^2\right) = E\left[T^{-1}\sum_{t=1}^{T} y_t^2 - (T+1)/2\right]^2$$
$$= T^{-2}\sum_{t=1}^{T}\sum_{s=1}^{T} E(y_t^2 y_s^2) - (T+1)^2/4$$
$$= T^{-2}\left[3\sum_{t=1}^{T} t^2 + 2\sum_{t=2}^{T}\sum_{s=1}^{t-1}(ts + 2s^2)\right] - \frac{(T+1)^2}{4}$$
$$\cong (T+1)^2/3 + O(T). \qquad (9c)$$

The last approximation uses $\sum_{t=1}^{T} t^2 = T(T+1)(2T+1)/6$ and $\sum_{t=1}^{T} t^3 = [T(T+1)/2]^2$.

To illustrate the use of Wiener processes in deriving distributions involving I(1) variables, we will derive the limiting distribution of the sample mean, $\bar{y} = T^{-1}\sum_{t=1}^{T} y_t$. Because $\{y_t\}$ is a random walk, its mean converges to a functional of a Wiener process. Let $R_T(r) = y_{[rT]}/\sqrt{T} = y_{i-1}/\sqrt{T}$ for $(i-1)/T \leq r < i/T$ $(i = 1, \ldots, T)$, and $R_T(1) = y_T/\sqrt{T}$. $R_T(r)$ is a step function with steps at i/T, for $i = 1, \ldots, T$, and is constant between steps. Thus,

$$\int_0^1 R_T(s)\,\mathrm{d}s = \sum_{i=1}^{T}\int_{(i-1)/T}^{i/T} R_T(s)\,\mathrm{d}s = \sum_{i=1}^{T} T^{-1}R_T\left(\frac{i-1}{T}\right) = T^{-1}\sum_{i=1}^{T} y_{i-1}/\sqrt{T}$$
$$= T^{-3/2}\sum_{t=1}^{T} y_{t-1}.$$

The last expression is $\bar{y}_1/\sqrt{T}$, where $\bar{y}_1$ is the lagged mean. This result uses the fact that, for any constant c,

$$\int_{(i-1)/T}^{i/T} c\,\mathrm{d}r = cr\Big]_{r=(i-1)/T}^{r=i/T} = ic/T - (i-1)c/T = cT^{-1}.$$

From (3) and (4),

$$\bar{y}_1/\sqrt{T} = \int_0^1 R_T(s)\,\mathrm{d}s \Rightarrow \int_0^1 W(r)\,\mathrm{d}r$$

and hence

$$\bar{y}_1/\sqrt{T} \Rightarrow \int_0^1 W(r)\,\mathrm{d}r. \tag{10}$$

The unlagged sample mean has the same limiting distribution.

An interesting aspect of (10) is that the Lindeberg–Feller central limit theorem[4] (which applies to independent but heterogeneously distributed observations; see White 1984) can be applied to obtain the distribution of $\bar{y}$ and hence show that

$$\int_0^1 \mathrm{W}(r)\mathrm{d}r \sim \mathrm{N}(0, 1/3). \tag{11}$$

Thus, some functionals of Wiener processes are familiar random variables in disguise and we will develop this aspect as we proceed. A proof of (11) is given in the Appendix.

1.5.7. Monte Carlo Simulation

The purpose of Monte Carlo simulation is to evaluate by experiment quantities that would be very difficult or impossible to evaluate analytically. Such experiments typically begin by creating a set of data with known statistical properties. This is achieved by specifying every aspect of a data-generating process, or class of such processes, and replacing the random errors of the DGP by pseudo-random numbers. Pseudo-random numbers are numbers generated deterministically to mimic a random process with a particular distribution. An investigator typically generates a large number of such artificial data sets (called replications) to investigate statistical techniques which analyse these data *as if the process generating them were not known*. The performance of the statistical technique in revealing some characteristic of the data set may

[4] Strictly speaking, the version we use here is a special case of this theorem, sometimes called the Liapunov central limit theorem.

then be evaluated by generating its distribution from independent replications of the experiment and comparing the results with the known characteristics of the process generating the data.

For example, an econometrician may wish to examine the performance of the standard t-test in data generated by a random walk. Artificial data-sets following a random walk may easily be constructed using pseudo-random disturbances, and the empirical distribution of the t-statistic in samples of size T can be generated by replicating N sets of T observations. The mean, variance, or various critical values of the t-statistic can be calculated from the empirical distribution and, for sufficiently large N, will be close to their population (i.e. analytic) counterparts. The investigator can also vary the parameters of the DGP in order to observe their effects on the outcome. In each experiment, the investigator knows the true parameters of the process, and so can evaluate the estimators and tests used.

Unlike analytical studies, Monte Carlo simulations cannot produce exact results; any result from a Monte Carlo experiment comes from a (pseudo-)random sample, and therefore has some variability attached to it. Moreover, Monte Carlo experiments are inevitably specific to the particular data generation processes examined (although it may be possible to prove analytically that results will be invariant to certain parameters in the process). Nonetheless, Monte Carlo results are useful when analytical results are difficult to obtain. In particular, Monte Carlo experiments are often used to investigate the finite-sample performance of statistical techniques, the analytical properties of which are known only asymptotically.

There are a number of subtleties to the design and interpretation of Monte Carlo experiments which demand careful attention, including the methods used to generate pseudo-random numbers, variance-reduction methods such as common random numbers, antithetic random numbers and control variates intended to improve precision, the calculation of standard errors of the experimental estimates of unknown quantities, the use of response surfaces to summarize and interpolate results, and recursive updating of quantities of interest. Expositions of Monte Carlo methods may be found in, for example, Hammersley and Handscomb (1964), Hendry (1984), Ripley (1987), Hendry, Neale, and Ericsson (1990), and Davidson and MacKinnon (1992).

1.6. Data Representation and Transformations

Since data transformations play an important role in econometrics generally, we briefly consider their impact on I(1) data. Consider the hypothesis that a set of integrated data can be described by a linear model with a constant error variance. In particular, a normally distributed random walk with drift is often postulated so that $\Delta x_t \sim \mathrm{IN}(\mu, \sigma^2)$. Many economic time series (such as consumption, national income and expenditure, or the price level) do grow over time, but the amount by which they grow in each period also tends to rise. However, $\Delta x_t = x_t - x_{t-1}$ will be stationary only if the absolute amount of growth is stationary, in which case for $\mu > 0$, σ/x_t will tend to zero. Percentage growth, by contrast, often displays no obvious tendency to rise or fall, making it a more likely candidate for stationarity. Since the levels of many economic variables are initially positive, and recalling that

$$\Delta \log(x_t) = \log(x_t) - \log(x_{t-1}) = \log(x_t/x_{t-1}),$$

we see that stationarity of the rate of growth implies stationarity of $\Delta \log(x_t)$. Changes in the logarithms of economic data series such as those just mentioned, therefore, seem more likely to be stationary than changes in the levels. We will return to this point in Chapter 6 below, where we consider how co-integration is affected by the logarithmic transformation. We illustrate some of these points with actual data series.

The time series that we analyse is real net national product (Y, in 1929 £million) for the United Kingdom over 1872–1975. The data are taken from Friedman and Schwartz (1982) and are also investigated in Hendry and Ericsson (1991*a*). Figures 1.6–1.9 plot this data series and

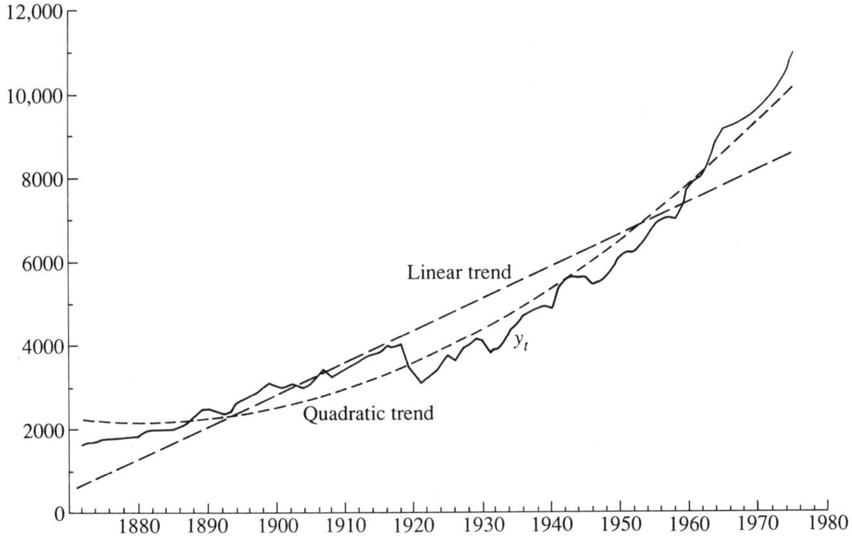

FIG 1.6. UK real net national product (Y in 1929 £million), 1872–1975

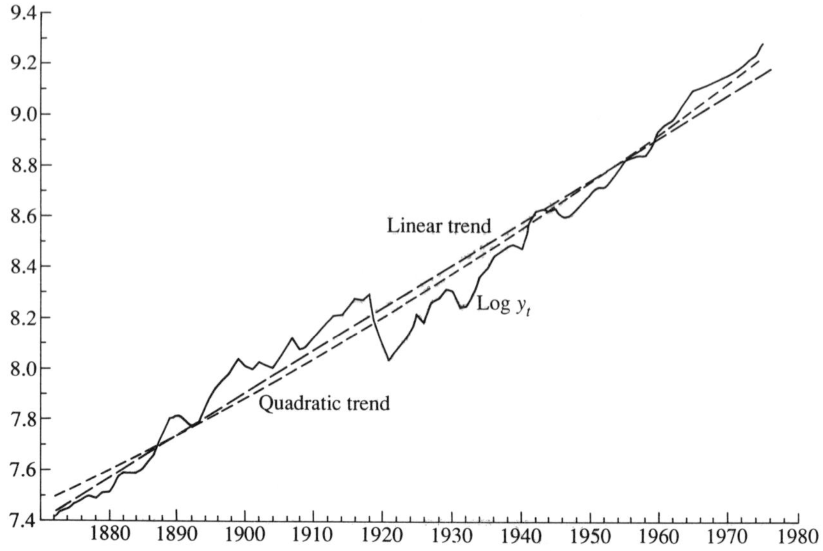

FIG 1.7. Logarithm (log Y) of UK real net national product

various transformations of it. Figure 1.6 plots the untransformed series Y_t; the series is tending to grow by increasing amounts, and so would be better approximated by a convex function than by a straight line. This is visible from the upward curvature and the much closer fit of the quadratic trend line compared with the linear trend. In Fig. 1.7, we plot the logarithm of the series: the curvature is no longer apparent, and the quadratic and linear trends are very similar and fit about equally well. Thus, the logarithm of the series is relatively well approximated by a straight line and, while growing, there is no evident tendency for the growth rate to change over time.

Figure 1.8 plots the changes, ΔY_t. There is a tendency for both the mean and the variance to grow over time, and the linear trend shown highlights the former. (It requires more careful inspection to see the latter owing to the very large shock in 1919–20.) Differencing the initial series has therefore not produced a stationary series. In Fig. 1.9, however, where $\Delta \log Y_t$ is plotted, there is no longer any major change in the mean or variability of the series over the sample, with perhaps a slight tendency for the variance to be smaller in the period since 1945. Certainly, any trend in the mean of $\Delta \log Y_t$ is negligible. This series, then, may well be stationary, although neither the logarithmic transformation nor the first-difference transformation produced a stationary series on its own. Since the differences in the logarithms appear stationary, we might expect to find that the logarithms of the original

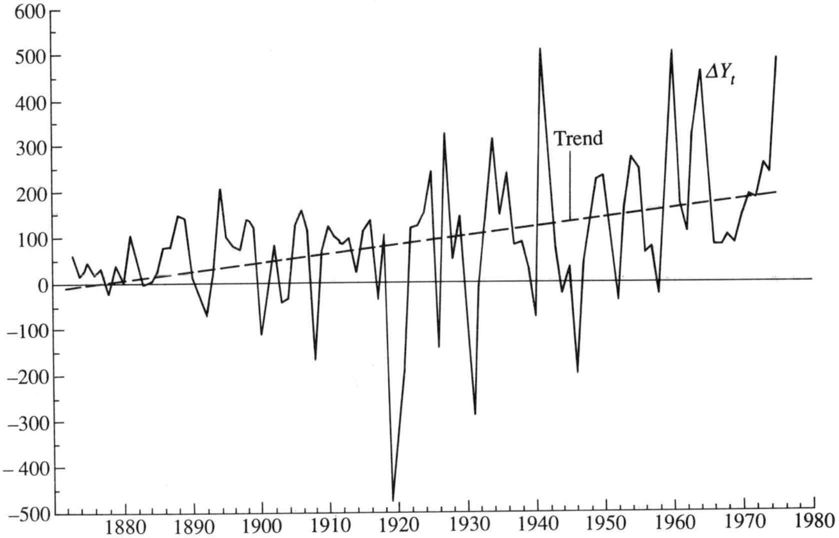

FIG 1.8. Changes (ΔY) in UK real net national product

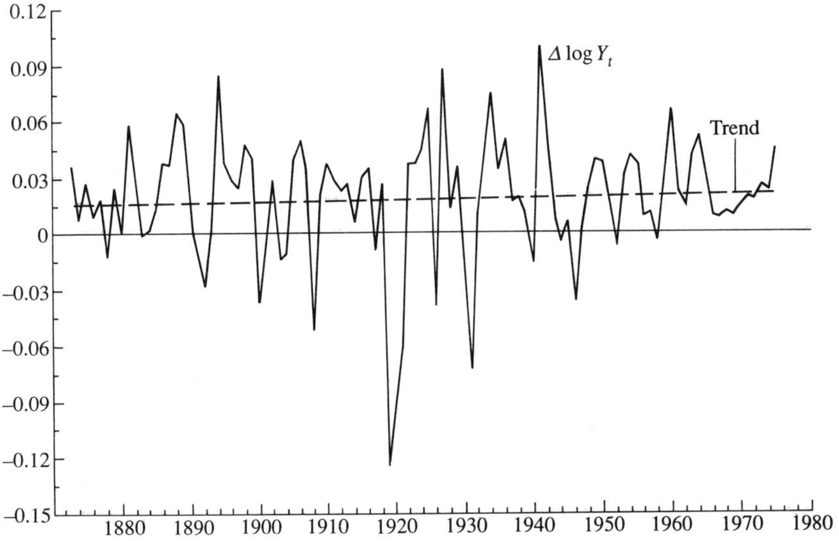

FIG 1.9. Changes in the logarithm ($\Delta \log Y$) of UK real net national product

series are I(1), while the untransformed initial series apparently is not and differencing it is not sufficient to produce stationarity.

Alternatively, any linear model of ΔY_t will have an error term, which we denote by u_t, with a standard deviation σ_u that must be in the same units as Y_t. Since these are 1929 £million, the linear model assumes a constant absolute error standard deviation. However, net national product has grown about six-fold over the sample so that σ_u/Y_t (the relative error) will be much smaller in 1975 than in 1875. It would be difficult to imagine reasons for such a decline.

The log-linear model, by way of contrast, assumes a constant relative error standard deviation (e.g. $2\frac{1}{2}$ percent of Y_t at all points in time), which seems much more plausible. Failing to transform the data adequately violates the statistical model of an I(1) or I(0) series, and can induce trending means and variances, making testing less reliable. Certainly, a relatively long time series is needed to make such factors obvious, but they operate even within post-war quarterly data (see e.g. Ermini and Hendry 1991). Moreover, changes in means and variances over time are very apparent in nominal time series, and can confuse attempts to determine co-integration. Granger and Hallman (1991) analyse general transformations in I(1) time series, and Chapter 4 below explores formal statistical tests of hypotheses about the degree of integration of individual time series.

1.7. Examples: Typical ARMA Processes

Figures 1.10–1.20 present graphs of typical examples of series generated by special cases of ARMA(1, 1) processes. For ease of comparison, each series is computer-generated using the same set of 200 observations on normally distributed white-noise errors $\varepsilon_t \sim \text{IN}(0, 1)$ with $u_0 = 0$. The data generation processes are:

Fig. 1.10	$u_t = \varepsilon_t$	[white noise]
Fig. 1.11	$u_t = \varepsilon_t + 0.8\varepsilon_{t-1}$	[MA(1), stationary]
Fig. 1.12	$u_t = \varepsilon_t - 0.8\varepsilon_{t-1}$	[MA(1), stationary]
Fig. 1.13	$u_t = 0.5\, u_{t-1} + \varepsilon_t$	[AR(1), stationary]
Fig. 1.14	$u_t = 0.5\, u_{t-1} + \varepsilon_t + 0.8\varepsilon_{t-1}$	[ARMA(1, 1), stationary]
Fig. 1.15	$u_t = 0.5\, u_{t-1} + \varepsilon_t - 0.8\varepsilon_{t-1}$	[ARMA(1, 1), stationary]
Fig. 1.16	$u_t = 0.9\, u_{t-1} + \varepsilon_t$	[AR(1), stationary]
Fig. 1.17	$u_t = 0.9\, u_{t-1} + \varepsilon_t + 0.8\varepsilon_{t-1}$	[ARMA(1, 1), stationary]
Fig. 1.18	$u_t = 0.99\, u_{t-1} + \varepsilon_t$	[AR(1), stationary]
Fig. 1.19	$u_t = 1.00\, u_{t-1} + \varepsilon_t$	[AR(1), non-stationary]
Fig. 1.20	$u_t = 1.01\, u_{t-1} + \varepsilon_t$	[AR(1), non-stationary]

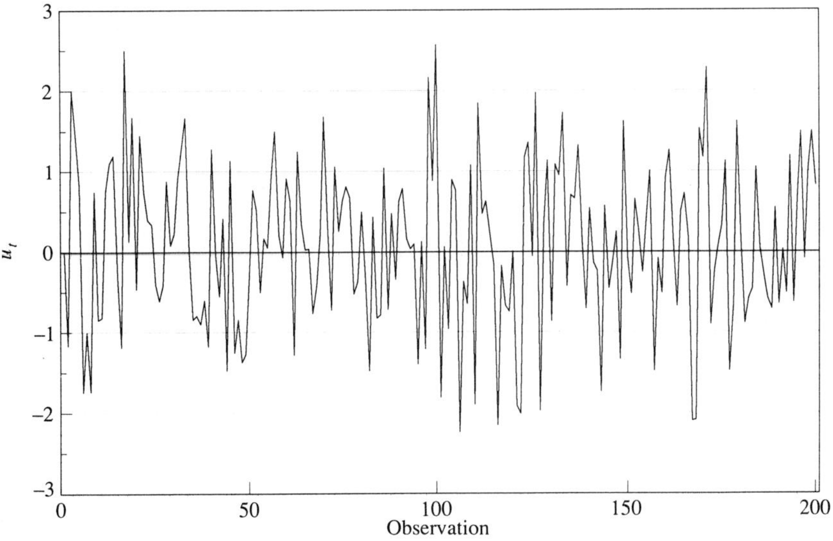

FIG 1.10. AR = 0.0; MA = 0.0

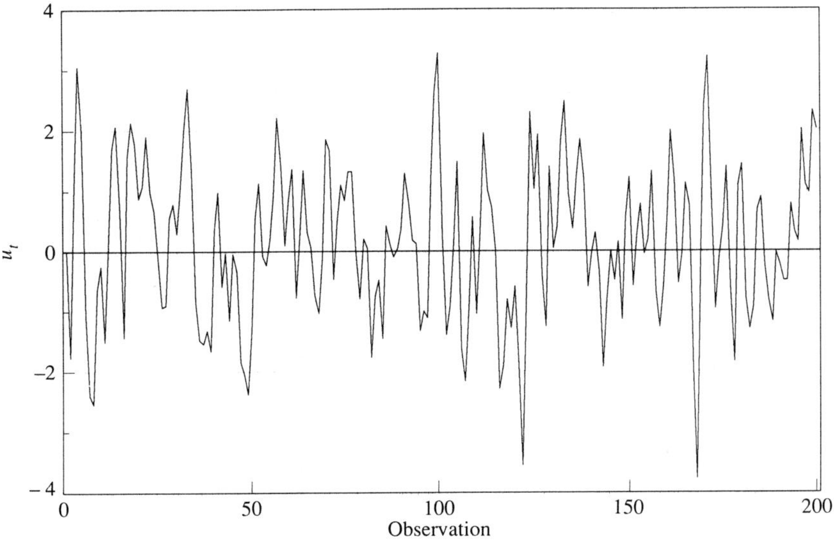

FIG 1.11. AR = 0.0; MA = 0.8

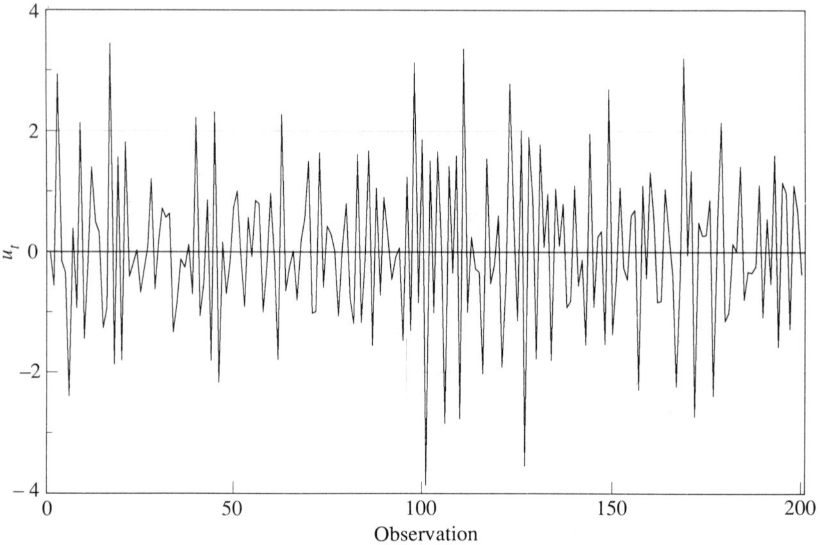

FIG 1.12. AR = 0.0; MA = −0.8

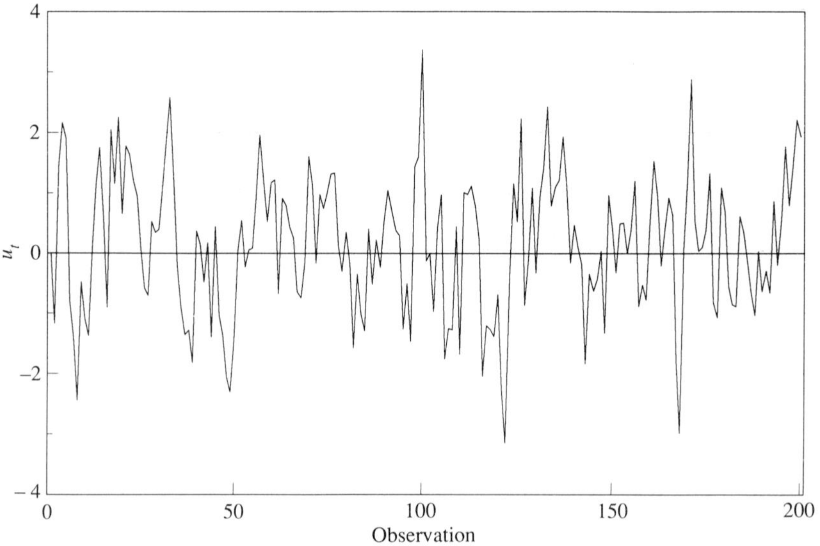

FIG 1.13. AR = 0.5; MA = 0.0

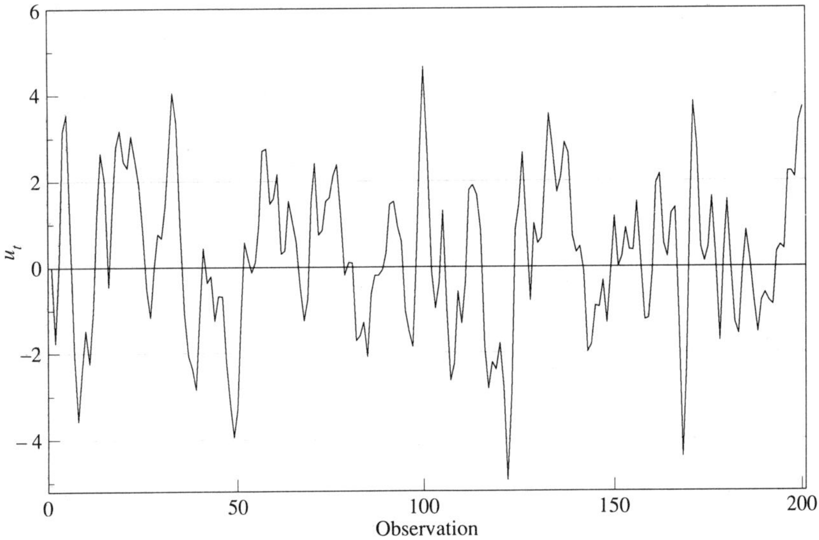

FIG 1.14. AR = 0.5; MA = 0.8

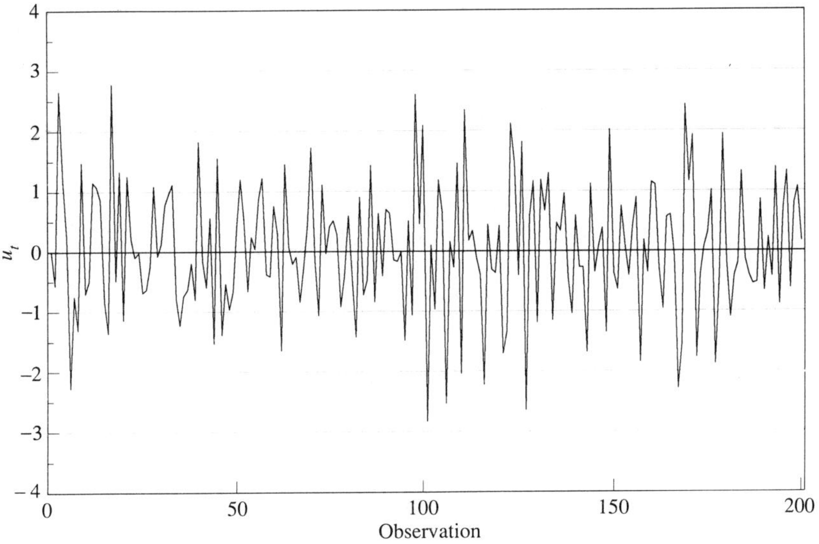

FIG 1.15. AR = 0.5; MA = −0.8

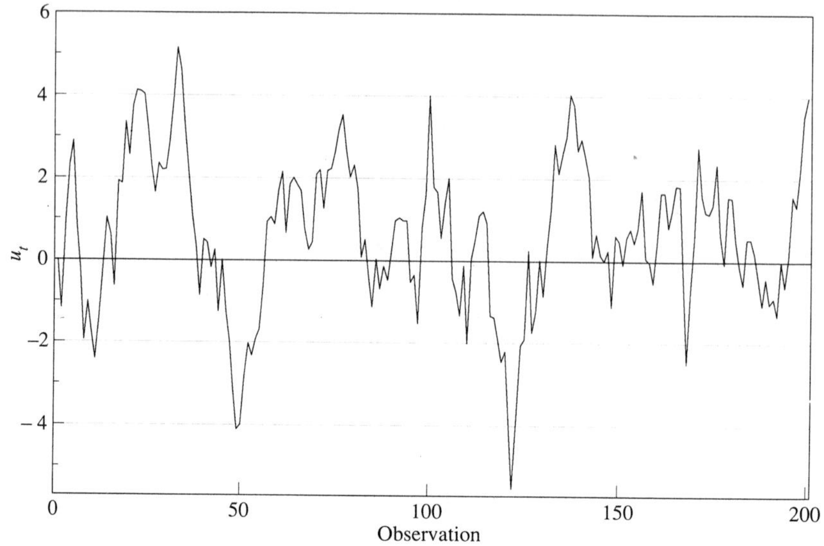

FIG 1.16. AR = 0.9; MA = 0.0

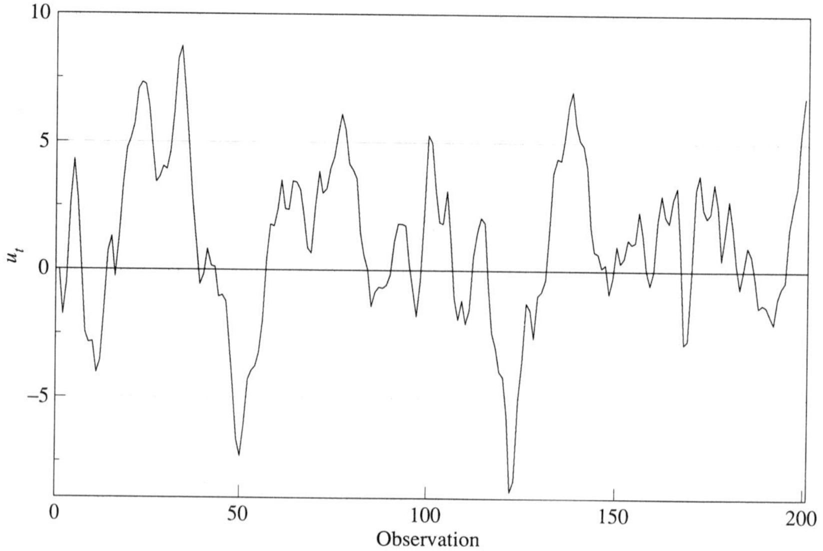

FIG 1.17. AR = 0.9; MA = 0.8

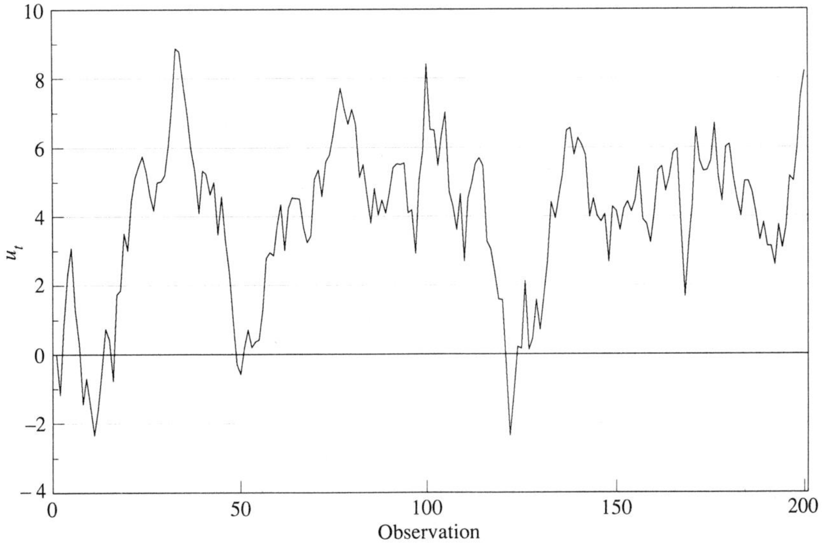

FIG 1.18. AR = 0.99; MA = 0.0

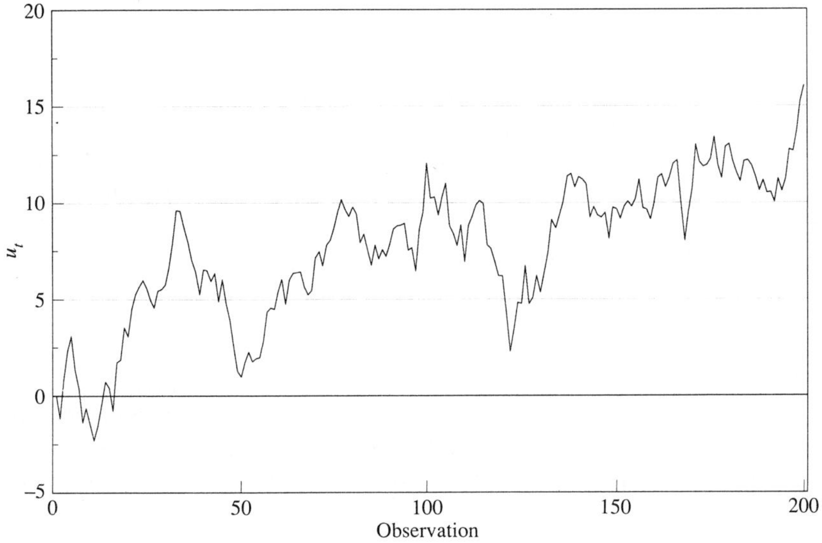

FIG 1.19. AR = 1.00; MA = 0.00

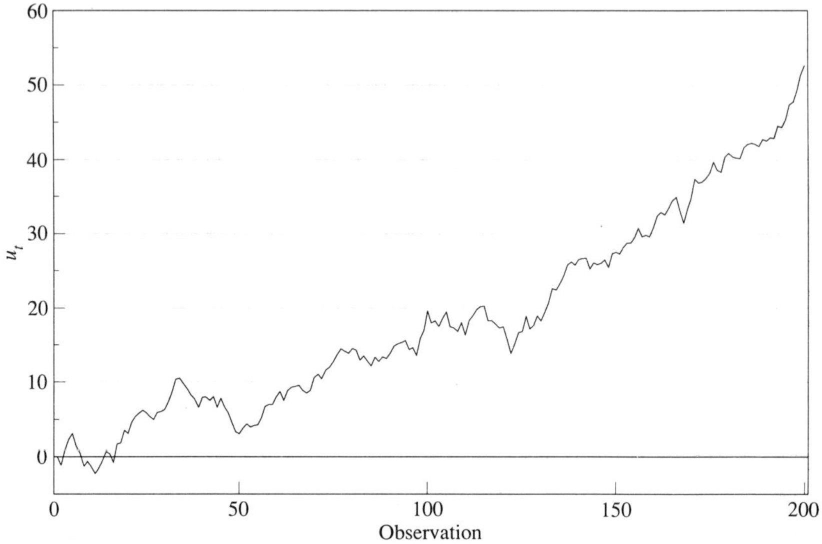

FIG 1.20. AR = 1.01; MA = 0.00

A process such as that in Fig. 1.19, an AR(1) with a unit root, is a random walk and may also be expressed as ARIMA(0, 1, 0).

The scales on the graphs in Figs. 1.10–1.20 are not identical; for the non-stationary processes, in particular, the graphs show very wide movements relative to those of the stationary series. Non-stationary processes with roots strictly greater than unity grow very quickly even where those roots are quite close to 1, as can be seen from Fig. 1.20, an AR(1) with a root in the autoregressive part of 1.01. The stationary processes in Figs. 1.10–1.18 have unconditional means of zero and finite unconditional variances. They are 'tied' to this zero mean in the sense that deviations from it cannot accumulate indefinitely. By contrast, the process with a single root of exactly unity (Fig. 1.19) has an unconditional variance which increases over time and will tend to wander widely (see equation (7)) with an unbounded expected crossing time of the origin. The process with a root greater than unity (Fig. 1.20) is explosive and will tend to either $+\infty$ or $-\infty$.

Figures 1.11, 1.14, and 1.17 add a positive MA component to the series in Figs. 1.10, 1.13, and 1.16 respectively, to highlight the 'smoothing' effect of a positive MA term. By contrast, the series in Figs. 1.12 and 1.15 add a negative MA term of the same absolute magnitude; these negative MA terms have the opposite effect, making the series appear less smooth than the pure AR series in Figs. 1.10 and 1.13. Figure 1.15 resembles Fig. 1.10, however, reflecting the fact that the

AR and MA lag polynomials are close to cancelling. (If the AR coefficient were 0.8, then the AR and MA polynomials would each be $(1 - 0.8L)$, and these redundant common factors could be cancelled, leaving white noise as in Fig. 1.10). In each of the sets Figs. 1.10–1.12, 1.13–1.15, 1.16 and 1.17, respectively, the data series plotted have the same AR root, and differ only in their MA parts.

Knowing the generating mechanism, the differences among the ARMA processes given in the figures are fairly clear. In practice, however, it is not easy to solve the converse problem of determining the generating mechanisms from observations on the variables; it may even be difficult to determine from a moderately sized sample whether or not a process is stationary. Although the distinctions among the examples of stationary and non-stationary processes above are substantial, those among 'borderline' stationary and non-stationary processes may not be. For example, $u_t = 0.99u_{t-1} + \varepsilon_t$ is a (borderline) stationary process, but will closely resemble the random walk $u_t = u_{t-1} + \varepsilon_t$ for samples of the size reproduced in Figs. 1.18 and 1.19.

It is interesting to compare the latter two processes by rewriting the AR(1) in MA form. For the process $u_t = \alpha u_{t-1} + \varepsilon_t$, it follows that $u_{t-1} = \alpha u_{t-2} + \varepsilon_{t-1}$ also. Substituting this into the first equation, we have $u_t = \alpha(\alpha u_{t-2} + \varepsilon_{t-1}) + \varepsilon_t$. If we continue to eliminate each subsequent lag of u, we find

$$u_t = \alpha^n u_{t-n} + \sum_{l=0}^{n-1} \alpha^l \varepsilon_{t-l}.$$

For the stationary process, $|\alpha| < 1$, so the first term and the contributions of more distant errors disappear as $n \to \infty$, and u_t may be approximated by an MA(n) process with increasing accuracy as $n \to \infty$. If $\alpha = 1$, however, the first term does not disappear, and the approximation fails; this follows from the failure of the stationarity condition stated above. When $\alpha = 1$,

$$u_t = u_{t-n} + \sum_{l=0}^{n-1} \varepsilon_{t-l},$$

so that u_t is the sum of a starting value, u_{t-n}, and all the errors accruing between $t - n + 1$ and t. This representation of the process $\{u_t\}$ as a sum of past contributions is the source of the relationship of *integration* in this time-series sense and integration in the integral calculus, where the integral of a function may be thought of as the limit of a sum of discrete areas under a curve. Figure 1.19 is the cumulative sum, or discrete integral, of the errors recorded in Fig. 1.10.

Many economic time series have been modelled using ARMA or ARIMA processes, and models of these types will be used frequently in the following chapters in describing the methods and tests. Priestley (1989) provides examples of other types of models that may be used to characterize non-stationary processes.

1.8. Empirical Time Series: Money, Prices, Output, and Interest Rates

Figure 1.21 graphs the logarithms of quarterly, seasonally adjusted, nominal M1 and prices (the implict deflator of total final expenditure, TFE) in the UK over the period 1963–89. The series (denoted $\log M_t$ and $\log P_t$) have strong trends and are relatively smooth, although their growth rates alter perceptibly around 1974 and again around 1980. Such data are not unlike realizations from highly autoregressive (I(1)) processes. Figure 1.22 shows their first differences $\Delta \log (M_t)$ and $\Delta \log (P_t)$. These are more erratic but are still highly autocorrelated. The growth

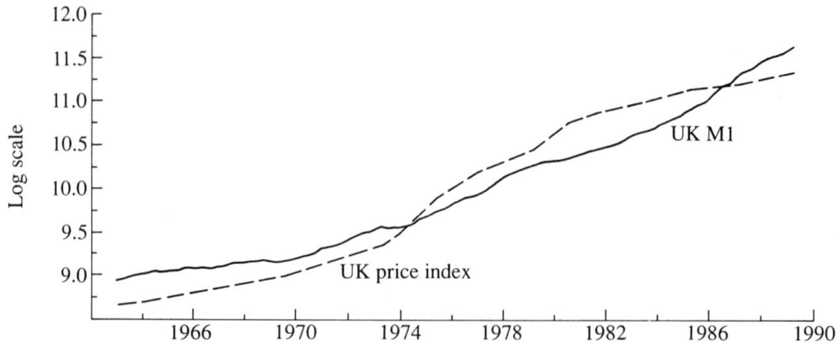

FIG 1.21. Time series of money (M1) and prices (implicit deflator of total final expenditure) in the UK, seasonally adjusted, in logs

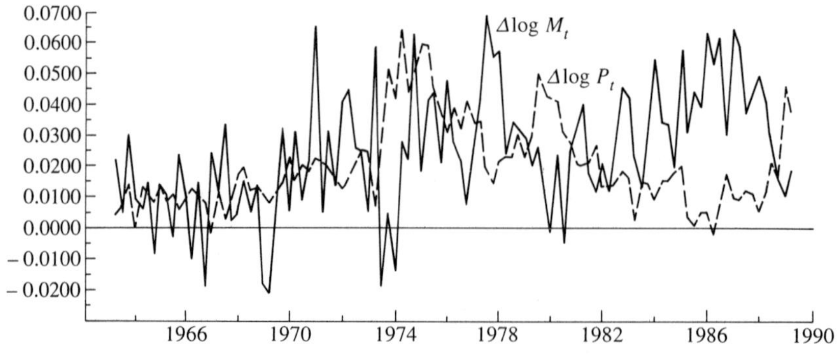

FIG 1.22. Time series of $\Delta \log M_t$ and $\Delta \log P_t$

rate of M appears to have increased over time, whereas that of P has fallen, especially after 1980. These data do not seem to be stationary although the graphs by themselves do not reveal the source of the non-stationarity.

Next, Fig. 1.23 shows the behaviour of logs of the real money supply ($\log(M_t/P_t)$) and real TFE ($\log(Y_t)$). It might have been anticipated from Fig. 1.21 that $\log(M_t)$ and $\log(P_t)$ moved sufficiently closely over the whole sample for this differential to be stationary, but Fig. 1.23 shows that the real money supply is non-stationary. The formal apparatus of testing for co-integration developed in Chapter 7 is designed to detect such relationships statistically. By way of contrast, $\log(Y_t)$ looks more like a series with a constant linear trend, subject to perturbations in 1973/4 and 1979/80.

In economic terms, surprising features of Figs. 1.22–1.23 are the low pairwise correlations between $\Delta\log(M_t)$ and $\Delta\log(P_t)$, and between $\log(M_t/P_t)$ and $\log(Y_t)$, respectively. However, such results have no implications for the existence or otherwise of well defined relationships between these variables. Monetary theory suggests that the opportunity cost of holding money is an important determinant of the demand for money, so Fig. 1.24 shows the time series of the interest rate (R_t, a three-month local authority bill rate adjusted for financial innovation) and the rate of inflation, plotted in units that maximize their apparent correlation. The series $\{R_t\}$ also seems to be non-stationary, but with a different time profile from the other series. In particular, it is much less smooth than the other level series, but less erratic than their changes. Finally, Fig. 1.25 shows $\Delta\log(Y_t)$ and ΔR_t. These are possibly weakly stationary, although both appear to have higher variances in the middle of the sample than at the ends. However, neither is highly autocorrelated, nor do they drift noticeably in any direction. We will analyse the four series $\log(M_t)$, $\log(P_t)$, $\log(Y_t)$, and R_t as a system in later chapters. (See Hendry and Ericsson (1991b), who provided the data.)

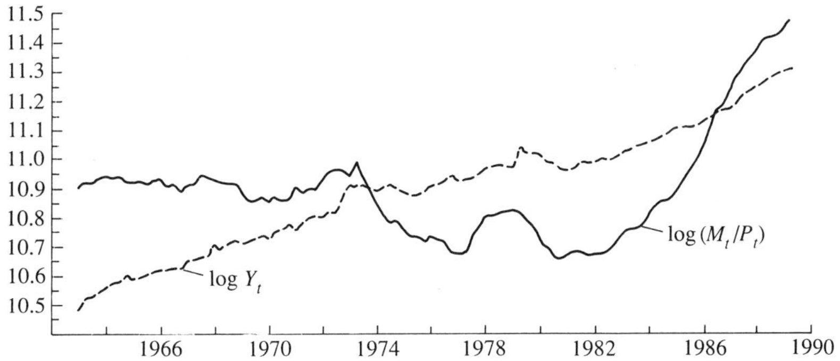

Fig 1.23. Time series of real money ($\log M_t/P_t$) and real TFE ($\log Y_t$)

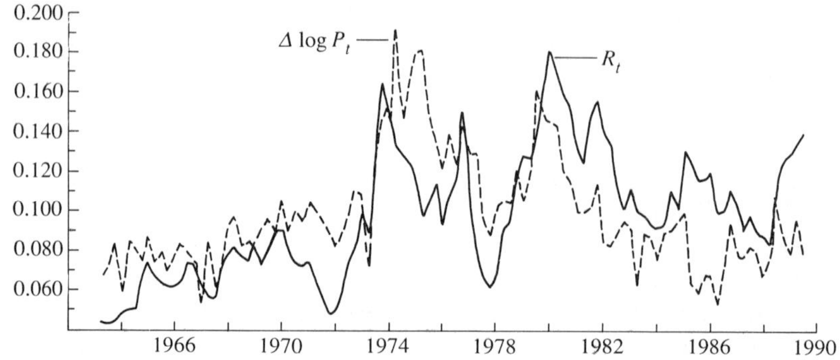

FIG 1.24. Time series of a three-month interest rate (R_t) and the rate of inflation ($\Delta \log P_t$) in the UK

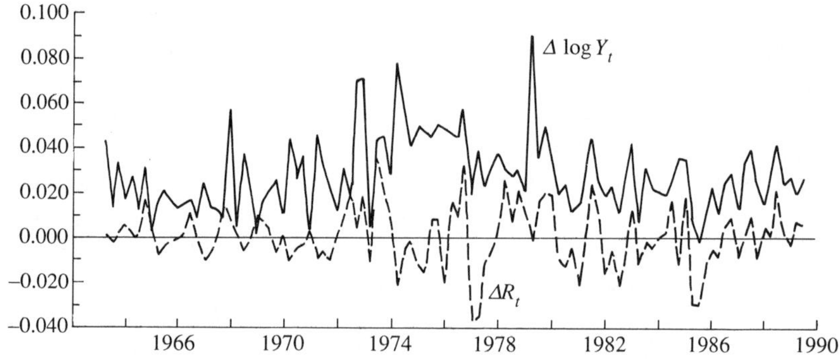

FIG 1.25. Time series of $\Delta \log Y_t$ and ΔR_t

1.9. Outline of Later Chapters

Chapter 2 discusses dynamic models for stationary processes. This allows us to introduce, in a familiar context, a number of considerations which will prove important later. Various equivalent transformations of linear autoregressive-distributed lag models are considered, especially error-correction, Bewley, and Bårdsen forms. The role of expectations in stationary processes is also investigated and is related to the absence of weak exogeneity for the parameters of the economic agents' decision functions.

Chapter 3 then considers the analysis of I(1) variables, and explores the concepts of unit roots, non-stationarity, orders of integration, and near integration. The behaviour of least-squares estimators applied to spurious relationships is investigated and a number of results established for Wiener processes (see Phillips 1987*a*). Univariate tests for unit roots are discussed in Chapter 4, and the formal definitions in Chapter 3 are related to the properties of integrated series. Monte Carlo results illustrate the various distributions. Extensions to multiple unit roots and seasonal data are considered, and several examples are described in detail.

Chapter 5 moves on to the topic of co-integration. Following a bivariate example and formal definitions, the Granger Representation Theorem is described, linking co-integration to error correction, and clarifying the status of other representations such as common trends. The original Engle–Granger two-step estimator of the co-integrating relationship is analysed. Chapter 6 first considers inconsistent regressions sometimes used in orthogonality tests; the analysis then turns to distributions of estimators in dynamic regressions with I(1) data, based on the results in Sims, Stock, and Watson (1990), and is illustrated by a number of examples.

Chapter 7 discusses testing for co-integration. A range of tests is considered, based on testing for a unit root in the residuals from the static regression. While widely used, such tests have drawbacks, and Monte Carlo experiments are used to illustrate some of these. Tests based on single-equation dynamic models are also considered.

Finally, in Chapter 8, co-integration in systems of equations is analysed. Linear co-integrated systems are expressed in error-correction form and maximum likelihood estimation and inference for co-integrating vectors is discussed, focusing on the approach proposed by Johansen (1988). A range of extensions is considered, as are various other estimators. The analysis is again illustrated by a number of examples and simulation experiments.

Appendix

Equation (11)

To prove (11), we need to construct a random variable X_t, where

$$X_t \sim ID(\mu_t, \sigma_t^2) \qquad \text{with } |\mu_t| < \infty,\ 0 < \sigma_t^2 < \infty,$$
$$E[|X_t - \mu_t|^3] = m_{3t}, \qquad \text{with } |m_{3t}| < \infty. \tag{A1}$$

Define

$$\bar{X}_T = T^{-1}\sum_{t=1}^{T} X_t, \qquad \bar{\mu}_T = T^{-1}\sum_{t=1}^{T}\mu_t, \qquad \text{and} \qquad C_T^2 = \sum_{t=1}^{T}\sigma_t^2.$$

If

$$\lim_{T\to\infty} (C_T)^{-1}\left(\sum_{t=1}^{T} m_{3t}\right) = 0,$$

then, by the Liapunov central limit theorem,

$$(\bar{X}_T - \bar{\mu}_T)/(C_T/T) \xrightarrow{\text{d}} \text{N}(0, 1).$$

The proof of (11) is in three steps. First, consider (from (6)) the sample mean:

$$\begin{aligned}
\bar{y} &= T^{-1} \sum_{t=1}^{T} \sum_{j=1}^{t} e_j \\
&= e_1 + [(T-1)/T]e_2 + \ldots + (2/T)e_{T-1} + (1/T)e_T \\
&= \sum_{t=1}^{T} X_t
\end{aligned}$$

where $X_t = [(T-t+1)/T]e_t$. Then

$$E[X_t] = [(T-t+1)/T]E(e_t) \equiv \mu_t = 0,$$
$$\text{var}[X_t] = [(T-t+1)/T]^2 E(e_t^2) = [(T-t+1)/T]^2 \equiv \sigma_t^2 < \infty,$$

and

$$E(X_t X_s) = [(T-t+1)/T][(T-s+1)/T]E(e_t e_s) = 0, \ \forall\, t \neq s.$$

Thus $X_t \sim \text{ID}(0, \sigma_t^2)$, as required. Further, noting that

$$X_t^3 = [(T-t+1)/T]^3 e_t^3,$$

and using normality of e_t, $E(X_t^3) = 0$. Next, $\bar{\mu}_T = 0$ and for $T > 6$

$$\begin{aligned}
C_T^2 &= \sum_{t=1}^{T} [(T-t+1)/T]^2 = T^{-2} \sum_{t=1}^{T} (T^2 - 2Tt + t^2 + 2(T-t) + 1) \\
&\cong T - 2T^{-1}T(T-1)/2 + T^{-2}T(T+1)(2T+1)/6 \cong T/3,
\end{aligned}$$

as $T \to \infty$. Since $m_{3t} = 0$,

$$\lim_{T\to\infty} (C_T)^{-1}\left(\sum_{t=1}^{T} m_{3t}\right) = 0$$

and all the conditions of the Liapunov theorem are satisfied. Therefore,

$$(\bar{X}_T - \bar{\mu}_T)/(C_T/T) \xrightarrow{\text{d}} \text{N}(0, 1).$$

Finally, using the results above, and noting that $\bar{y} = T\bar{X}_T$,

$$(\bar{X}_T - \bar{\mu}_T)/(C_T/T) = \bar{y}/C_T \approx \bar{y}/(T/3)^{1/2}. \tag{A2}$$

Hence, $\bar{y}/(T/3)^{1/2} \xrightarrow{\text{d}} \text{N}(0, 1)$.

Since $\bar{y}/\sqrt{T} \Rightarrow \int_0^1 W(r)\,\mathrm{d}r$ from results above, we have that $\bar{y}/\sqrt{T}$ converges to both $\int_0^1 W(r)\,\mathrm{d}r$ and to N(0, 1/3). Therefore

$$\int_0^1 W(r)\,\mathrm{d}r \sim \mathrm{N}(0, 1/3).$$

The derivations of later results follow similar lines.

2

Linear Transformations, Error Correction, and the Long Run in Dynamic Regression

We begin by considering the properties of linear autoregressive-distributed lag (ADL) models for stationary data processes. Transformations of the ADL model to error correction and to various other forms are described. We discuss the estimation of long-run multipliers from dynamic models, and the equivalence of the estimates of these multipliers (and their variances) from any of several different forms. Finally, we consider inference about long-run multipliers where expectational variables are present, and the potential problems are shown to be special cases of the general invalidity of inference when the regressors are not weakly exogenous for parameters of interest.

In later chapters, we will concentrate on the importance of integrated processes for econometric modelling, and in particular on the detection of the stochastic trends embodied in integrated processes, on identifying series that share stochastic trends and therefore satisfy long-run equilibrium relations, and on the implications of such properties for the estimation of economic relationships. Before beginning to explore these concepts, however, there are a number of aspects of the use and specification of dynamic econometric models which can be reviewed without a thorough knowledge of integrated processes, and which will be useful in later discussion. The calculation of the parameters of long-run relationships from estimated models, the interpretation of linear transformations, and the forms of particular models such as the error-correction model are among these topics. The variables used in this chapter may all be treated as being stationary, but readers who are familiar with the concepts examined in later chapters will recognize that the same results apply if the variables are co-integrated.

One simple but fundamental problem that we address is the following: given a variable which in general depends upon its own past and on the values of various exogenous variables, how can we determine the long-run equilibrium relationship between the endogenous variable and the exogenous variables? If an endogenous variable y_t is expressed as a function only of the value of a set of exogenous variables z_t at the same point in time, the effect of z_t on y_t is immediate and complete; however, if a lag distribution applies to every variable in the model, the long-run effect must be derived as a function of all the lag distributions. Moreover, there are other types of information that can be revealed by a dynamic equation; any of a number of equivalent forms will provide the same information about, say, short-run and long-run adjustment, but different forms of the equation will reveal different types of information conveniently.

We will consider a number of ways in which to estimate long-run multipliers from dynamic regression models, and in doing so will examine several different types of model. After describing the general autoregressive-distributed lag (ADL) model from which the other models are derived, we first concentrate upon the error-correction model, in which the terms representing the extent of deviation from equilibrium are explicitly present in the estimated equation, and which therefore immediately displays information about the adjustment that a process makes to a deviation from some long-run equilibrium.

This chapter will emphasize two important points about linear transformations. First, each of the transformations contains precisely the same information: the estimated values of long-run multipliers, hypothesis test statistics, and explanatory powers of the differently transformed models are all identical. The choice of transformation can be made purely on the basis of convenience, and we will consider which ones are convenient for different purposes. The second point is a corollary of the first, but is worth emphasizing: the estimates of short-run adjustment parameters from the error-correction model do not depend upon the parameter θ, used in defining the error-correction term $y_{t-1} - \theta z_{t-1}$, as long as other levels terms are present to allow for adjustment to the chosen parameter. In particular, a value of unity for θ may be chosen, leading to what is called 'homogeneity' (an error-correction term of $y_{t-1} - z_{t-1}$), as long as the necessary extra terms are present.

Next, we consider several other transformations of the autoregressive-distributed lag model, due to Bewley (1979) (and discussed by Wickens and Breusch 1988) and Bårdsen (1989). Each of these transformations can be related to the error-correction transformation, and we indicate some of the implications of this fact for estimation using one or other of the transformations. Finally, we will discuss some potential difficulties in the estimation of long-run equilibrium relations and their interpretation, following McCallum (1984), Kelly (1985), and Hendry and Neale (1988).

While this chapter deals explicitly with stationary (I(0)) processes, many of the models considered can be used with co-integrated processes as well, as explored in Chapters 5 and 6. In particular, the equivalence of these transformations (in the sense that each form can be derived from any other by operating linearly on the variables) is relevant when dealing with the Granger Representation Theorem, also discussed in Chapter 5. This equivalence has implications for derivations of the distributions of coefficient estimates in co-integrated systems. In a particular transformation, for example, the variables may all be integrated of order zero, so that the asymptotic theory of stationary processes applies to the distributions of the estimates. Such a parameterization might be convenient for inference, because its information content is identical to that of the original parameterization, if for example that form contained both I(1) and I(0) variables. These issues are considered at length in Chapter 6, and the analysis in this chapter provides useful background for that discussion.

2.1. Transformations of a Simple Model

Before beginning a general treatment, we consider the first-order linear autoregressive-distributed lag model, denoted ADL(1, 1), as an example and derive several linear transformations of it. Each transformation is equivalent in the sense that each implies the same relationship between exogenous and endogenous variables. The ADL(1, 1) is

$$y_t = \alpha_0 + \alpha_1 y_{t-1} + \beta_0 x_t + \beta_1 x_{t-1} + \varepsilon_t, \tag{1a}$$

where $\varepsilon_t \sim \text{IID}(0, \sigma^2)$ and $|\alpha_1| < 1$ (see Hendry, Pagan, and Sargan 1984).

First consider a static equilibrium defined, as above, as an environment in which all change has ceased, recalling that we are treating (y_t, x_t) as jointly stationary. The long-run values are given by the unconditional expectations of the form $E(y_t)$ in (1a). Defining $y^* = E(y_t)$ and $x^* = E(x_t)\ \forall\, t$, we have, since $E(\varepsilon_t) = 0$,

$$y^* = \alpha_0 + \alpha_1 y^* + \beta_0 x^* + \beta_1 x^*,$$

and hence

$$y^* = \frac{\alpha_0 + (\beta_0 + \beta_1)x^*}{(1 - \alpha_1)} \equiv k_0 + k_1 x^*,$$

or

$$E(y_t) = k_0 + k_1 E(x_t).$$

Then k_1 is the *long-run multiplier* of y with respect to x.

Now subtract y_{t-1} from both sides of (1a) and then add and subtract $\beta_0 x_{t-1}$ on the right-hand side to get[1]

[1] Equation (1a) is invariant to such linear transformations which preserve the error process $\{\varepsilon_t\}$.

$$\Delta y_t = \alpha_0 + (\alpha_1 - 1)y_{t-1} + \beta_0 \Delta x_t + (\beta_0 + \beta_1)x_{t-1} + \varepsilon_t, \quad (1b)$$

and finally add and subtract $(\alpha_1 - 1)x_{t-1}$ on the right side, yielding

$$\Delta y_t = \alpha_0 + (\alpha_1 - 1)(y_{t-1} - x_{t-1}) + \beta_0 \Delta x_t + (\beta_0 + \beta_1 + \alpha_1 - 1)x_{t-1} + \varepsilon_t. \quad (1c)$$

Alternatively, we could have added and subtracted $(\beta_0 + \beta_1)x_{t-1}$ on the right side, to get

$$\Delta y_t = \alpha_0 + (\alpha_1 - 1)(y_{t-1} - k_1 x_{t-1}) + \beta_0 \Delta x_t + \varepsilon_t. \quad (1d)$$

All of these equations imply the same relationship, because any one can be derived from another without violating the equality. In equations (1c) and (1d), however, terms representing the discrepancy between y_{t-1} and x_{t-1} or between y_{t-1} and $k_1 x_{t-1}$ appear explicitly; the coefficient (the same for each form) on these terms can be taken as a measure of the speed of adjustment of y to a discrepancy between y and x in the previous period. We examine such *error-correction* models in detail in the next section.

Equation (1b) is similar to (1c) and (1d) in that the same information appears explicitly as a coefficient; that is, $(\alpha_1 - 1)$ represents the short-run adjustment to a 'discrepancy', and this coefficient can be read directly from any of the three. Equation (1b) will be seen to be a special case of (5) below, just as (1c) is a special case of (3) below.

Finally, let us return to (1a) and take a different route. Subtracting $\alpha_1 y_t$ from both sides, we have

$$y_t(1 - \alpha_1) = \alpha_0 - \alpha_1 \Delta y_t + \beta_0 x_t + \beta_1 x_{t-1} + \varepsilon_t.$$

Defining $\lambda_1 = (1 - \alpha_1)^{-1}$ and adding and subtracting $\beta_1 x_t$, we have

$$y_t = \lambda_1 \alpha_0 - \lambda_1 \alpha_1 \Delta y_t + \lambda_1(\beta_0 + \beta_1)x_t - \lambda_1 \beta_1 \Delta x_t + \lambda_1 \varepsilon_t. \quad (1e)$$

This is again a special case of one of the general forms of transformed ADL models given below (equation (4)). This form, following Bewley (1979), conveniently reveals the long-run equilibrium multiplier as the coefficient of x_t in (1e) since $\lambda_1(\beta_0 + \beta_1) = k_1$. However, because a contemporaneous value of the dependent variable appears on the right side of the equation, ordinary least-squares estimates are not consistent; consistent estimation can be carried out using instrumental variables.

Next, consider a data-generation process having the form of a general autoregressive-distributed lag model (Hendry *et al.* 1984). An ADL(m, n) model with a constant and p exogenous variables, which we will also write as ADL(m, n; p), is given by[2]

[2] We use the same n for each of the p exogenous variables without loss of generality, because any β_{ji} may be set equal to zero, so that n is simply the maximum, rather than uniform, lag length of the x_j.

$$y_t = \alpha_0 + \sum_{i=1}^{m} \alpha_i y_{t-i} + \sum_{j=1}^{p} \sum_{i=0}^{n} \beta_{ji} x_{jt-i} + \varepsilon_t, \tag{2}$$

where $\varepsilon_t \sim \text{IID}(0, \sigma^2)$. We might also write this, using the lag operator $L^n z_t \equiv z_{t-n}$, as

$$\alpha(L) y_t = \alpha_0 + \sum_{j=1}^{p} \beta_j(L) x_{jt} + \varepsilon_t,$$

where $\alpha(L) = 1 - \sum_{i=1}^{m} \alpha_i L^i$ and $\beta_j(L) = \sum_{i=0}^{n} \beta_{ji} L^i$. As before, there are a number of possible transformations of this equation which, because they do not add or remove any linearly independent columns from the data matrix, are equivalent projections of the dependent variable on to the data. Given joint stationarity, the long-run solution of (2) is

$$\begin{aligned} E(y_t) &= \left(1 - \sum_{i=1}^{m} \alpha_i\right)^{-1} \left[\alpha_0 + \sum_{j=1}^{p} \sum_{i=0}^{n} \beta_{ji} E(x_{jt})\right] \\ &= (\alpha(1))^{-1} \left[\alpha_0 + \sum_{j=1}^{p} \beta_j(1) E(x_{jt})\right] \\ &\equiv \theta_0 + \sum_{j=1}^{p} \theta_j E(x_{jt}), \end{aligned}$$

where $\alpha(1)$ and $\beta_j(1)$ represent the substitution of unity for the lag operator L in the lag polynomials.

2.2. The Error-correction Model

The first of the general forms that we examine is the error-correction model. Error-correction terms were used by Sargan (1964), Hendry and Anderson (1977), and Davidson *et al.* (1978) as a way of capturing adjustments in a dependent variable which depended not on the level of some explanatory variable, but on the extent to which an explanatory variable deviated from an equilibrium relationship with the dependent variable. When the equilibrium relationship is of the form $y^* = \theta x^*$, then an error-correction term is one such as $(y_t - \theta x_t)$, if the parameter in the equilibrium relationship is presumed known, or $(y_t - \hat{\theta} x_t)$ if it is estimated. However, even $(y_t - x_t)$ could be used, since the possibility of a coefficient other than unity on x_t can be captured through other terms in the regression, as we will see below.

We can derive a generalized error-correction model (ECM), corresponding to the ADL($m, n; p$) model with p exogenous variables $x_1, \ldots, x_p$, by steps similar to those used in the specific cases above. The result, which allows us to specify directly a general dynamic regression model in the form of an ECM, is (for $r \leqslant m$)

$$\Delta y_t = \alpha_0 + \sum_{i=1}^{r} \eta_i \left(y_{t-i} - \sum_{j=1}^{p} x_{jt-i} \right) + \sum_{j=1}^{p} \beta_{j0} \Delta x_{jt} + \sum_{j=1}^{p} \sum_{i=1}^{r} \zeta_{ji} x_{jt-i}$$

$$+ \sum_{j=1}^{p} \sum_{i=r+1}^{n} \beta_{ji} x_{jt-i} + \sum_{i=r+1}^{m} \alpha_i y_{t-i} + \varepsilon_t, \qquad (3)$$

with

$$\eta_1 = \alpha_1 - 1, \qquad \eta_i = \alpha_i, \qquad i = 2, \ldots, r; \qquad r \equiv \min(m, n);$$

$$\zeta_{j1} = \alpha_1 - 1 + \beta_{j0} + \beta_{j1}, \qquad \zeta_{ji} = \alpha_i + \beta_{ji}, \qquad i = 2, \ldots, r,$$

and

$$\Delta x_{jt-i} \equiv (x_{jt-i} - x_{jt-i-1}).$$

By convention, in the case of any term for which summations begin from $r + 1$, the term does not enter at all if the lower limit of the summation exceeds the upper limit. For each of the 'error-correction' terms $(y_{t-i} - \sum_{j=1}^{p} x_{jt-i})$, one lagged term in x_{jt} is present to break 'homogeneity': that is, to allow the error-correction term to take the form $(y_{t-i} - \sum_{j=1}^{p} \theta_j x_{jt-i})$, where θ_j is not equal to one. The θ_j are the equilibrium multipliers given above: $\theta_j = \beta_j(1)/\alpha(1)$; and if the θ_j were known, they could be inserted directly into the ECM terms in (3) and the terms in lagged x could be eliminated.[3] In terms of the parameters of (3),

$$\theta_j = -\left(\sum_{i=1}^{r} \eta_i + \sum_{i=r+1}^{m} \alpha_i \right)^{-1} \left[\sum_{i=1}^{r} (\zeta_{ji} - \eta_i) + \sum_{i=r+1}^{n} \beta_{ji} \right].$$

Since the ECM is simply a linear transformation of the ADL model, we might ask what its distinguishing feature is. The answer is that in the ECM formulation, parameters describing the extent of short-run adjustment to disequilibrium are immediately provided by the regression. Although the form in (3) is analytically convenient, it is not a useful empirical specification. In practice, a single error-correction term at lag r is preferable, as it induces a more interpretable and more nearly orthogonal parameterization.

The error-correction mechanism will be of particular value where the extent of an adjustment to a deviation from equilibrium is especially interesting. It is clear that the ECM provides this information when the error-correction terms are of the form $(y_{t-i} - \sum_{j=1}^{p} \theta_j x_{jt-i})$, with θ_j a known parameter. If θ_j is not known it can be estimated; moreover, an unknown θ_j can implicitly be allowed for in the error-correction term

[3] Note that this requires $\sum_{i=1}^{m} \alpha_i < 1$.

through the inclusion of extra lags in the x_j, without affecting the magnitude of the estimated coefficients η_i in (3). Hence these parameters do not need to be estimated at an earlier stage in order to allow us to use the ECM. In fact, an important point in favour of the generalized ECM (3) is that the estimated coefficients on the error-correction terms are unaffected by the incorporation of any constant θ into the term; this will be proved after we have established some other results which will simplify the proof. The implication is that we can interpret the coefficients η_i in (3) directly as adjustments to disequilibrium even though the true disequilibrium term is given by $(y_{t-i} - \sum_{j=1}^{p} \theta_j x_{jt-i})$ and not by $(y_{t-i} - \sum_{j=1}^{p} x_{jt-i})$. Hence the use of a generalized ECM *does not imply homogeneity* $(\theta = 1)$ as long as extra lags in the x_j are incorporated, even though the error-correction terms that enter (3) do not explicitly allow for $\theta \neq 1$.

2.3. An Example

An example of the use of the error-correction mechanism can be found in Davidson *et al.* (1978), who use a homogeneous $(\theta = 1)$ error-correction mechanism in the modelling of consumers' expenditure. The 'error' to which adjustment is made in the model is the difference between the logarithms of consumption and income, each lagged four quarters. The error-correction term is significant in a wide variety of specifications. In particular, using quarterly seasonally unadjusted data from the United Kingdom, expressed at constant prices over the sample period of 1958(I)–1970(IV), the authors favour the model[4] (standard errors in parentheses):

$$\begin{aligned}\widehat{\Delta_4 \log C_t} = {} & \underset{(0.04)}{0.47}\,\Delta_4 \log Y_t - \underset{(0.05)}{0.21}\,\Delta_1\Delta_4 \log Y_t - \underset{(0.02)}{0.10}\,\log(C/Y)_{t-4} \\ & + \underset{(0.003)}{0.01}\,\Delta_4 D_t^o - \underset{(0.07)}{0.13}\,\Delta_4 \log P_t - \underset{(0.15)}{0.28}\,\Delta_1\Delta_4 \log P_t,\end{aligned}$$

$$R^2 = 0.77, \quad \hat{\sigma} = 0.0061, \quad DW = 1.8, \quad z_1(20) = 21.8, \quad z_2(12) = 19,$$

where the statistics z_1 and z_2 are asymptotic χ^2 tests for parameter constancy and serially independent residuals, respectively with degrees of freedom in parentheses; $\hat{C}_t$ is the fitted value of real consumers' expenditure on non-durable goods and services C_t; Y_t is real personal disposable income; P_t is the price deflator for consumption; and D_t^o is a dummy variable for changes in taxation. The error-correction term has a

[4] The symbol $\Delta_1\Delta_4$ represents the first difference of the fourth difference; e.g. $\Delta_4 \log Y_t - \Delta_4 \log Y_{t-1} \equiv \Delta_1\Delta_4 \log Y_t$.

coefficient that is reasonably substantial as well as statistically significant at conventional levels. The model can readily be derived from an ADL model, noting that $\log(C/Y)_{t-4} \equiv \log C_{t-4} - \log Y_{t-4} = c_{t-4} - y_{t-4}$, using lower-case letters to denote logarithms.

On the additional assumption that $\Delta_4 c_t$, $\Delta_4 y_t$, and $\Delta_4 p_t$ are stationary, with $E(\Delta_4 c_t) = g_c$, $E(\Delta_4 y_t) = g_y$, and $E(\Delta_4 p_t) = \dot{p}_a$ (the annual rate of inflation), then, taking expectations of the equation above for fixed values of the estimated parameters,

$$g_c = 0.47 g_y - 0.13 \dot{p}_a - 0.10(c^* - y^*).$$

Hence $C^* = kY^*$ where $k = \exp(-5.3 g_y - 1.3 \dot{p}_a)$, noting that $g_c = g_y$ given the proportional long-run solution. This form of solution is consistent with the life-cycle hypothesis (see Deaton and Muellbauer 1980), in which case the coefficients of g_y and $\dot{p}_a$ should correspond to the negatives of the annual wealth–income and liquid asset–income ratios. The resulting values seem sensible.

For positive real growth or inflation, $k < 1$, and k falls as g_y or $\dot{p}_a$ rises. Representative values of g_y and $\dot{p}_a$ are 0.025 and 0.05 respectively. These imply a value of k of $e^{-0.2} = 0.82$, and therefore a (savings + durable expenditure) to income ratio of $(1 - 0.82)$ or 18%.

This model has an additional interpretation which can often be given to an error-correction term. The coefficient of -0.10 on $\log(C/Y)_{t-4}$ suggests, first of all, that the greater is the excess of income over consumption (in logarithms) for the corresponding quarter one year ago, the higher is consumption now. That is, as income exceeds consumption by more, it becomes optimal to raise consumption in the future. The 'error' which is partially corrected is this discrepancy; consumers may consume unusually much (or little) at some point in time, but will then tend to consume relatively less (or more) at some point in the future. This is implied simply by the negative sign of the effect; in addition, we have an estimate of its magnitude, and it is apparent that the effect is substantial. Moreover, by adjusting expenditure in this way, consumption and income are tied together in the long run, despite the growth over time in the level of each. Consequently the model formulation actually entails the co-integration of consumption and income, given that these series are individually integrated: see Chapter 5. For a recent update, see Hendry, Muellbauer, and Murphy (1990).

2.4. Bårdsen and Bewley Transformations

Two other transformations of the ADL$(m, n; p)$ are those of Bewley (1979) and Bårdsen (1989). The Bewley transformation has the form

$$y_t = \lambda\alpha_0 - \lambda \sum_{i=1}^{m} \alpha_i(y_t - y_{t-i})$$
$$+ \sum_{j=1}^{p} \left(\lambda \sum_{i=0}^{n} \beta_{ji}\right) x_{jt} - \sum_{j=1}^{p} \lambda \left[\sum_{i=1}^{n} \beta_{ji}(x_{jt} - x_{jt-i})\right] + \lambda\varepsilon_t, \tag{4}$$

where λ is defined in (6) below. Note that in (4), as in (2) and in (5) below, there are $k \equiv 1 + m + [p(n+1)]$ coefficients to be estimated.

The transformation treated by Bårdsen can be seen as a variant of an error-correction mechanism, and may be written as

$$\Delta y_t = \alpha_0 + \sum_{i=1}^{m-1} \alpha_i^* \Delta y_{t-i} + \sum_{j=1}^{p} \sum_{i=0}^{n-1} \beta_{ji}^* \Delta x_{jt-i}$$
$$+ \alpha_m^* y_{t-m} + \sum_{j=1}^{p} \beta_{jn}^* x_{jt-n} + \varepsilon_t, \tag{5}$$

where the coefficients are related to those in (2) and (4) by

$$\alpha_i^* = \sum_{l=1}^{i} \alpha_l - 1 = \sum_{l=1}^{i} \eta_l, \quad \text{and} \quad \beta_{ji}^* = \sum_{l=0}^{i} \beta_{jl}.$$

Finding the long-run multiplier implied by any one of these forms (ADL, ECM, Bewley, Bårdsen) is quite straightforward. Define θ_j as the long-run effect of a change in x_j on y. Recall that in an equilibrium state there are no stochastic shocks and values of all variables are therefore constant, so that, writing $y^* = E(y_t)$ and $x_j^* = E(x_{jt})$,

$$y^* = \alpha_0 + \sum_{i=1}^{m} \alpha_i y^* + \sum_{j=1}^{p} \sum_{i=0}^{n} \beta_{ji} x_j^*.$$

Then, corresponding to the ADL model (2), we have

$$\theta_j \equiv \frac{\partial y^*}{\partial x_j^*} = \lambda \sum_{i=0}^{n} \beta_{ji} \tag{6}$$

where $\lambda \equiv (1 - \sum_{i=1}^{m} \alpha_i)^{-1} = [\alpha(1)]^{-1}$. It is important to note that this formula is applicable only where $|\sum_{i=1}^{m} \alpha_i|$ is strictly less than 1. Otherwise, no long-run equilibrium can be said to exist between y and x, as these quantities may diverge increasingly as $t \to \infty$. In particular, the unconditional expectations are not well defined.

Corresponding to the Bewley transform (4), we also have

$$\theta_j = \lambda \sum_{i=0}^{n} \beta_{ji},$$

and this can be read directly from the estimated regression (4) as the coefficient on x_{jt}. Finally, using the Bårdsen transformation (5), we have

$$\theta_j = \frac{\beta^*_{jn}}{-\alpha^*_m}. \tag{7}$$

This expression can be computed from Bårdsen's regression (5) simply by dividing the coefficient on x_{jt-n} by the negative of that on y_{t-m}.

Each of these transformations leads to numerically identical estimates of the long-run multiplier (the same estimated equilibrium relationship) if (2) and (5) are estimated by ordinary least squares (OLS) and (4) by instrumental variables (IV), using the regressors from the ADL model (2) as instruments. The necessity of IV for consistent estimation of (4) stems from the presence of *contemporaneous* terms in the dependent variable y_t on the right-hand side of (4), rendering the error term correlated with those explanatory variables.

Finally, it is worth pointing out the sense in which the Bårdsen transform is an error-correction form. The coefficients α^*_i are *sums* of the terms η_i in the ECM representing adjustment to disequilibrium (as shown following (5) above) and the α^*_i may therefore be thought of as cumulative adjustments: α^*_i represents the sum of the effects of error-correction terms 1, . . ., i. For some purposes these cumulative adjustments are of particular interest, in which case the Bårdsen form will be especially convenient.

2.5. Equivalence of Estimates from Different Transformations

Wickens and Breusch (1988) show that the Bewley transformation (estimated by IV with ADL regressors as instruments) yields precisely the same estimates of the long-run multipliers θ_j as does the untransformed ADL (2) estimated by OLS. The same is true of the Bårdsen transform (5) estimated by OLS, and of the general error-correction mechanism (again estimated by OLS), as Banerjee, Galbraith, and Dolado (1990*b*) show. In demonstrating these points we will make use of the general structure that Wickens and Breusch use to compare linear transformations of regression models.

Take as a basic structure the regression model

$$\mathbf{y} = \mathbf{X}\gamma + \varepsilon, \tag{8}$$

where the $\mathbf{X}$ matrix contains lagged (but not contemporaneous) y as well as contemporaneous and lagged x terms, and γ is a $k \times 1$ vector. Define this as corresponding to the ADL model (2). The representations (4) and (5) involve transforming the matrices $\mathbf{y}$ and $\mathbf{X}$ by a transformation matrix $\mathbf{A}$, such that, following Wickens and Breusch,

$$[\tilde{\mathbf{y}} : \tilde{\mathbf{X}}] \equiv [\mathbf{y} : \mathbf{X}]\mathbf{A} \tag{9a}$$

so that

$$\tilde{\mathbf{y}} = \tilde{\mathbf{X}}\boldsymbol{\delta} + \mathbf{u}. \tag{9b}$$

For example, take $m = n = 2$ and $p = 1$ in (2) so that the matrix of the transformation to the Bårdsen form (5) is

$$\mathbf{A}_a = \begin{bmatrix} 1 & 0 & 0 & 0 & 0 & 0 & 0 \\ 0 & 1 & 0 & 0 & 0 & 0 & 0 \\ -1 & 0 & 1 & 0 & 0 & 0 & 0 \\ 0 & 0 & -1 & 0 & 0 & 1 & 0 \\ 0 & 0 & 0 & 1 & 0 & 0 & 0 \\ 0 & 0 & 0 & -1 & 1 & 0 & 0 \\ 0 & 0 & 0 & 0 & -1 & 0 & 1 \end{bmatrix}, \tag{10a}$$

since $\mathbf{x}_t' = [y_t, 1, y_{t-1}, y_{t-2}, x_t, x_{t-1}, x_{t-2}]$ maps onto $\tilde{\mathbf{x}}_t' = [\Delta y_t, 1, \Delta y_{t-1}, \Delta x_t, \Delta x_{t-1}, y_{t-2}, x_{t-2}]$ in (5). For the Bewley transformation (4) and the same case ($m = n = 2$, $p = 1$), the transformation matrix is

$$\mathbf{A}_b = \begin{bmatrix} 1 & 0 & 1 & 1 & 0 & 0 & 0 \\ 0 & 1 & 0 & 0 & 0 & 0 & 0 \\ 0 & 0 & -1 & 0 & 0 & 0 & 0 \\ 0 & 0 & 0 & -1 & 0 & 0 & 0 \\ 0 & 0 & 0 & 0 & 1 & 1 & 1 \\ 0 & 0 & 0 & 0 & 0 & -1 & 0 \\ 0 & 0 & 0 & 0 & 0 & 0 & -1 \end{bmatrix}, \tag{10b}$$

since $[y_t, 1, y_{t-1}, y_{t-2}, x_t, x_{t-1}, x_{t-2}]$ in (2) maps onto

$$[y_t, 1, (y_t - y_{t-1}), (y_t - y_{t-2}), x_t, (x_t - x_{t-1}), (x_t - x_{t-2})].$$

First, let us summarize the relation between the error processes $\mathbf{u}$ and $\boldsymbol{\varepsilon}$. Begin by partitioning the general matrix $\mathbf{A}$ (which may be $\mathbf{A}_a$, $\mathbf{A}_b$, or another transformation) to be conformable with $[\mathbf{y} : \mathbf{X}]$:

$$\mathbf{A} = \begin{bmatrix} a_{11} & \mathbf{a}_{12} \\ \mathbf{a}_{21} & \mathbf{A}_{22} \end{bmatrix}.$$

When there are k regressors, the elements of the partition have the following dimensions: a_{11}, 1×1; $\mathbf{a}_{12}$, $1 \times k$; $\mathbf{a}_{21}$, $k \times 1$; $\mathbf{A}_{22}$, $k \times k$.

When there are no contemporaneous y variables on the right-hand side of the transformed model $\mathbf{a}_{12} = \mathbf{0}$, and presuming that $\mathbf{A}$ is of full rank, then the two sets of errors are identical: $\mathbf{u} \equiv \boldsymbol{\varepsilon}$. If $\mathbf{a}_{12} \neq \mathbf{0}$, as in the Bewley transformation, then a contemporaneous y_t (multiplied by a scalar) has been added to the right-hand side of the equation, and therefore to the left to preserve the equality. For estimation, the equation must then be renormalized so that we have only y_t (unscaled) on the left, and all elements must be multiplied by the normalization factor. This normalization will have to be accounted for later to convert back to the original parameters.

Transformation by $\mathbf{A}$ requires renormalizing by dividing the entire equation by the factor $(a_{11} - \mathbf{a}_{12}\boldsymbol{\delta}) \neq 0$ to deliver (8) from (9*a*) and (9*b*), so the errors of the new process are given by

$$\mathbf{u} = (a_{11} - \mathbf{a}_{12}\boldsymbol{\delta})\boldsymbol{\varepsilon} \equiv a^{-1}\boldsymbol{\varepsilon}, \tag{11}$$

where a is the normalization constant. For example, if we begin with

$$y_t = \beta_1 y_{t-1} + \beta_2[\cdot] + \varepsilon_t$$

(where $[\cdot]$ does not depend on $y_{t-i}\ \forall\, i$) and transform to

$$y_t = \delta_1(y_t - y_{t-1}) + \delta_2[\cdot] + u_t,$$

we do so by subtracting $\beta_1 y_t$ from each side and dividing the entire equation by $(1 - \beta_1)$, so that $\delta_1 = -\beta_1/(1 - \beta_1)$, $\delta_2 = \beta_2/(1 - \beta_1)$, and $u_t = \varepsilon_t/(1 - \beta_1)$. The parameters satisfy the general formula

$$a\mathbf{A}\begin{bmatrix} 1 \\ -\boldsymbol{\delta} \end{bmatrix} = \begin{bmatrix} 1 \\ -\boldsymbol{\gamma} \end{bmatrix}, \tag{12}$$

with $a = (1 - \beta_1)$, $\boldsymbol{\delta} = [-\beta_1/(1 - \beta_1){:}\ \beta_2/(1 - \beta_1)]'$, $\boldsymbol{\gamma} = [\beta_1{:}\ \beta_2]'$, and

$$\mathbf{A} = \begin{bmatrix} 1 & 1 & 0 \\ 0 & -1 & 0 \\ 0 & 0 & 1 \end{bmatrix}.$$

Now consider the relationship between estimates of long-run multipliers in transformed and untransformed models, starting with the Bårdsen transformation which can be estimated consistently by OLS. Different calculations must be performed on the two sets of regression estimates to get long-run multipliers; if we estimate (2) we must perform the calculation (6), and if we use (5) we must perform the division (7). We want to show that the actual estimates that we get will be numerically identical whichever method we use. We know from the definition of the OLS estimator of the transformed model ((9*b*) or, explicitly (5)) that

$$\widetilde{\mathbf{X}}'\,(\tilde{\mathbf{y}} : \widetilde{\mathbf{X}})\begin{bmatrix} 1 \\ -\hat{\boldsymbol{\delta}} \end{bmatrix} = \mathbf{0}, \tag{13}$$

as is easily verified by substituting the formula for the OLS estimator of $\boldsymbol{\delta}$, $\hat{\boldsymbol{\delta}} = (\widetilde{\mathbf{X}}'\widetilde{\mathbf{X}})^{-1}\widetilde{\mathbf{X}}'\tilde{\mathbf{y}}$. By definition of the OLS estimator in (8) (corresponding to (2)),

$$\mathbf{X}'(\mathbf{y}:\mathbf{X})\begin{bmatrix} 1 \\ -\hat{\gamma} \end{bmatrix} = \mathbf{0}, \tag{14}$$

again, easily checked using the formula $\hat{\gamma} = (\mathbf{X}'\mathbf{X})^{-1}\mathbf{X}'\mathbf{y}$.

Now in the case of the Bårdsen transform, $\mathbf{a}_{12} = \mathbf{0}$ and $\mathbf{A}$ has the form

$$\mathbf{A}_a = \left[\begin{array}{c|ccccccc} 1 & 0 & 0 & 0 & \ldots & 0 & 0 & 0 \\ \hline 0 & & & & & & & \\ -1 & & & & & & & \\ 0 & & & & & & & \\ \vdots & & & \mathbf{A}_{22} & & & & \\ 0 & & & & & & & \\ 0 & & & & & & & \end{array}\right],$$

so that (13) and $(\tilde{\mathbf{y}}:\tilde{\mathbf{X}}) = (\Delta\mathbf{y}:\mathbf{X}\mathbf{A}_{22})$ together imply

$$(\mathbf{A}_{22}'\mathbf{X}')(\mathbf{y}:\mathbf{X})\mathbf{A}_a\begin{bmatrix} 1 \\ -\hat{\boldsymbol{\delta}} \end{bmatrix} = \mathbf{0},$$

so

$$\mathbf{X}'(\mathbf{y}:\mathbf{X})\mathbf{A}_a\begin{bmatrix} 1 \\ -\hat{\boldsymbol{\delta}} \end{bmatrix} = \mathbf{0}, \tag{15}$$

since $\mathbf{A}_{22}$ is of full rank. From (14) and (15), we can deduce that[5]

$$\mathbf{A}_a\begin{bmatrix} 1 \\ -\hat{\boldsymbol{\delta}} \end{bmatrix} = \begin{bmatrix} 1 \\ -\hat{\gamma} \end{bmatrix}, \tag{16}$$

where the equality follows from the facts that the matrix $\mathbf{X}'(\mathbf{y}:\mathbf{X}) \equiv \boldsymbol{\Gamma}$ has dimension $k \times (k+1)$ and rank k, where again $k \equiv 1 + m + [p(n+1)]$, and that $\boldsymbol{\Gamma}$ can be partitioned as $[\boldsymbol{\Gamma}_1 : \boldsymbol{\Gamma}_2]$ with $\boldsymbol{\Gamma}_1$ having dimension $k \times 1$ and $\boldsymbol{\Gamma}_2$ having dimension $k \times k$ and rank k.

So the same relationship holds between estimated parameters $\hat{\gamma}$ and $\hat{\boldsymbol{\delta}}$ as between the true parameters γ and $\boldsymbol{\delta}$ (i.e. (16) has the same form as (12)). What this means is that the estimates of, say, multipliers will be the same whichever transformation is used. To make this last step in the argument, let Ψ_A be a quantity calculated from the true parameters of model A, and Ψ_B be the same quantity calculated from the true parameters of the transformed model B. Clearly, $\Psi_A \equiv \Psi_B$ since the calculation is adapted to produce the same underlying quantity in each case. Let the functions describing the calculations be $\mathbf{f}[{}^{\;1}_{-\gamma}]$ and $\mathbf{g}[{}^{\;1}_{-\boldsymbol{\delta}}]$ respectively. Then, by (12),

$$\mathbf{f}\begin{bmatrix} 1 \\ -\gamma \end{bmatrix} \equiv \mathbf{g}\begin{bmatrix} 1 \\ -\boldsymbol{\delta} \end{bmatrix} \text{ implies } \mathbf{f}\left(\mathbf{A}_a\begin{bmatrix} 1 \\ -\boldsymbol{\delta} \end{bmatrix}\right) = \mathbf{g}\begin{bmatrix} 1 \\ -\boldsymbol{\delta} \end{bmatrix}.$$

[5] The normalizing constant a does not appear here because it happens that $\mathbf{u} = \boldsymbol{\varepsilon}$ in (8) ($\mathbf{a}_{12} = \mathbf{0}$) for the case of the Bårdsen transform, so that $a = 1$. For the Bewley transform, there is a non-zero normalizing constant.

But since this holds for any γ, it must hold for $\hat{\gamma}$, and so

$$\mathbf{f}\begin{bmatrix} 1 \\ -\hat{\gamma} \end{bmatrix} = \mathbf{f}\left(\mathbf{A}_a\begin{bmatrix} 1 \\ -\hat{\delta} \end{bmatrix}\right) = \mathbf{g}\begin{bmatrix} 1 \\ -\hat{\delta} \end{bmatrix},$$

the second equality following from (16). This implies that $\hat{\Psi}_A \equiv \hat{\Psi}_B$: we get the same *estimated* quantity from either model, using the appropriate transformation matrix.

One can therefore obtain the coefficients of either the transformed or untransformed model from the other, using the original transformation matrix $\mathbf{A}$. For example, in calculating $\hat{\theta}_j$ from the ADL, we use (6); (6) is one part of the transformation $\mathbf{A}$ applied to the original parameters γ. If the parameters of the Bårdsen transform are δ, then the θ_j are ratios of elements of δ as in (7). Calculating θ_j from the ADL amounts to using ratios of sums of selected elements of the vector $\mathbf{A}^{-1}\left[\begin{smallmatrix} 1 \\ -\hat{\gamma} \end{smallmatrix}\right]$ in the calculation; by (16), this formula yields the corresponding elements of $\left[\begin{smallmatrix} 1 \\ -\hat{\delta} \end{smallmatrix}\right]$, and so these results are precisely the same as those obtained from the Bårdsen transformation and (7). The same holds true for any linear transformation where $\mathbf{A}$ is of full rank ($\mathbf{A}^{-1}$ is non-singular).

In the case of transformations for which $\mathbf{a}_{12} \neq \mathbf{0}$, such as Bewley's, OLS estimation is inconsistent because of the correlation between the error term and the contemporaneous dependent variables on the right-hand side. This brings us to IV estimation.

Where the instrumental variables used in estimation are those of the untransformed ADL model, IV estimation of the Bewley transformation also yields estimates of the long-run multipliers identical to those from the ADL. In this case, analogously with (13), if we let δ_b represent the parameters of the model (4) and $\mathbf{A}_b$ the matrix of that transformation, we have

$$\mathbf{X}'(\tilde{\mathbf{y}} : \tilde{\mathbf{X}})\begin{bmatrix} 1 \\ -\hat{\delta}_{b,\text{IV}} \end{bmatrix} = \mathbf{0}, \qquad (17)$$

where $\hat{\delta}_{b,\text{IV}}$ is the IV estimator of δ_b; again, this formula is immediately verifiable by substituting[6] $\hat{\delta}_{b,\text{IV}} = (\mathbf{X}'\tilde{\mathbf{X}})^{-1}\mathbf{X}'\tilde{\mathbf{y}}$. From (17),

$$\mathbf{X}'(\mathbf{y} : \mathbf{X})\mathbf{A}_b\begin{bmatrix} 1 \\ -\hat{\delta}_{b,\text{IV}} \end{bmatrix} = \mathbf{0}. \qquad (18)$$

We must then normalize by $\hat{a}_b$ (defined to be the constant that normalizes the dependent variable's coefficient to unity, analogous to a in (11)) before we compare this estimator with another which has been normalized to have the dependent variable enter with a coefficient of one, and we then obtain (Wickens and Breusch 1988), following steps similar to those above,

[6] The IV estimator takes this form because the original $\mathbf{X}$s are being used as instruments in the transformed regression model involving $\tilde{\mathbf{y}}$ and $\tilde{\mathbf{X}}$.

$$\mathbf{A}_b \hat{a}_b \begin{bmatrix} 1 \\ -\hat{\boldsymbol{\delta}}_{b,\text{IV}} \end{bmatrix} = \begin{bmatrix} 1 \\ -\hat{\boldsymbol{\gamma}} \end{bmatrix}. \tag{19}$$

Comparing (19) with (16), it is clear that once again the estimates from the transformed model can be related back to those from OLS on the ADL model, or to those from the other transformation $\mathbf{A}_a$, through the known transformation matrices. Moreover, comparing (19) with (12), the same relation holds in estimated parameters as in the true parameters, so that estimates of functions of these parameters (such as the long-run multipliers) will be the same regardless of the model from which they are calculated. Here, using the Bewley transformation, the long-run multipliers θ_j appear directly in $\boldsymbol{\delta}_b$; to calculate them from the ADL parameters, we would use

$$\hat{a}_b^{-1}\mathbf{A}_b^{-1} \begin{bmatrix} 1 \\ -\hat{\boldsymbol{\gamma}} \end{bmatrix}.$$

2.6. Homogeneity and the ECM as a Linear Transformation of the ADL

The results just established allow a straightforward proof of the earlier statement that, by incorporating lags of the levels of explanatory variables, the generalized ECM makes no implicit homogeneity assumptions. Consider the two regressions

$$\Delta y_t = \alpha_0 + \sum_{i=1}^{r} \gamma_i \left(y_{t-i} - \sum_{j=1}^{p} x_{jt-i} \right) + \sum_{j=1}^{p} \beta_{j0} \Delta x_{jt} + \sum_{j=1}^{p} \sum_{i=1}^{r} \zeta_{ji} x_{jt-i}$$
$$+ \sum_{j=1}^{p} \sum_{i=r+1}^{n} \beta_{ji} x_{jt-i} + \sum_{i=r+1}^{m} \alpha_i y_{t-i} + \varepsilon_t \tag{20a}$$

and

$$\Delta y_t = \alpha_0 + \sum_{i=1}^{r} \delta_i \left(y_{t-i} - \sum_{j=1}^{p} \theta_j x_{jt-i} \right) + \sum_{j=1}^{p} \beta_{j0} \Delta x_{jt} + \sum_{j=1}^{p} \sum_{i=1}^{r} \zeta_{ji}^{*} x_{jt-i}$$
$$+ \sum_{j=1}^{p} \sum_{i=r+1}^{n} \beta_{ji} x_{jt-i} + \sum_{i=r+1}^{m} \alpha_i y_{t-i} + \varepsilon_t, \tag{20b}$$

where $r = \min(m, n)$. The difference between (20a) and (20b) lies in the fact that the θ_j in (20b) are set to unity in (20a). We will prove that the coefficients on the error-correction terms are none the less equal, i.e. that $\hat{\gamma}_i = \hat{\delta}_i$ for all i and arbitrary θ_j. The ADL model is

$$y_t = \alpha_0 + \sum_{i=1}^{m} \lambda_i y_{t-i} + \sum_{j=1}^{p} \sum_{i=0}^{n} \phi_{ji} x_{jt-i} + \varepsilon_t. \tag{20c}$$

We will call the full parameter vectors from (20a), (20b), and (20c) $\hat{\mathbf{a}}$, $\hat{\mathbf{b}}$, and $\hat{\mathbf{c}}$ respectively. Then, from our examination of general linear transformations above, redefining the particular transformation matrix $\mathbf{A}_b$:

$$\mathbf{A}_a\begin{bmatrix} 1 \\ -\hat{\mathbf{a}} \end{bmatrix} = \begin{bmatrix} 1 \\ -\hat{\mathbf{c}} \end{bmatrix} = \mathbf{A}_b\begin{bmatrix} 1 \\ -\hat{\mathbf{b}} \end{bmatrix}. \tag{21}$$

In the $m = n = 2$, $p = 1$ case, for example, $\mathbf{A}_a$ and $\mathbf{A}_b$ are equal to

$$\mathbf{A}_a = \begin{bmatrix} 1 & 0 & 0 & 0 & 0 & 0 & 0 \\ 0 & 1 & 0 & 0 & 0 & 0 & 0 \\ -1 & 0 & 1 & 0 & 0 & 0 & 0 \\ 0 & 0 & 0 & 1 & 0 & 0 & 0 \\ 0 & 0 & 0 & 0 & 1 & 0 & 0 \\ 0 & 0 & -1 & 0 & -1 & 1 & 0 \\ 0 & 0 & 0 & -1 & 0 & 0 & 1 \end{bmatrix};$$

$$\mathbf{A}_b = \begin{bmatrix} 1 & 0 & 0 & 0 & 0 & 0 & 0 \\ 0 & 1 & 0 & 0 & 0 & 0 & 0 \\ -1 & 0 & 1 & 0 & 0 & 0 & 0 \\ 0 & 0 & 0 & 1 & 0 & 0 & 0 \\ 0 & 0 & 0 & 0 & 1 & 0 & 0 \\ 0 & 0 & -\theta & 0 & -1 & 1 & 0 \\ 0 & 0 & 0 & -\theta & 0 & 0 & 1 \end{bmatrix}.$$

Since the first $(\min(m, n) + 3)$ rows remain unaffected by the new terms θ_j, the first $(\min(m, n) + 3)$ entries in

$$\mathbf{A}_a\begin{bmatrix} 1 \\ -\hat{\mathbf{a}} \end{bmatrix} = \mathbf{A}_b\begin{bmatrix} 1 \\ -\hat{\mathbf{b}} \end{bmatrix} \tag{22}$$

are unaffected by the arbitrary constants θ_j. Hence the first $(\min(m, n) + 2)$ elements of the parameter vectors $\hat{\mathbf{a}}$ and $\hat{\mathbf{b}}$, which correspond to the error-correction terms, must be identical.

Thus the generalized ECM, using lagged terms in the exogenous variables to break homogeneity, produces precisely the same estimates of the responses to 'disequilibrium' whether or not the error-correction terms involve postulated values of long-run multipliers explicitly.

2.7. Variances of Estimates of Long-Run Multipliers

We want to be able to compute not only the estimates of long-run multipliers, but also the variances or standard errors of these estimates. Since the long-run multipliers are calculated as ratios of coefficients or sums of coefficients, and since there is no general formula for the exact variance of a quotient of items with known variances, we must use an approximation to the variance of the quotient. In the case of the Bewley transformation, since the long-run multipliers appear as coefficients on the x_{jt}, we can read the variances on these estimated coefficients from the usual estimator of the variance–covariance matrix of IV coefficient estimates; this estimate implicitly embodies an approximation to the variance of the quotient, although it might appear to be an exact estimate.[7] In fact, the different transformations yield equivalent results, in that the natural approximate estimator of the variances is the same for each.

For the Bewley transformation (4), since the $\hat{\theta}_j$ are coefficients in the regression, we apply the formula for the covariance matrix of coefficients estimated in an instrumental variables regression. Using $\hat{\mathbf{V}}_{\hat{\gamma}}$ to represent the estimated variance of $\hat{\gamma}$, the estimated parameter vector,

$$\hat{\mathbf{V}}_{\boldsymbol{\delta}_{b,\text{IV}}} = \frac{\hat{\mathbf{u}}'\hat{\mathbf{u}}}{T}[\tilde{\mathbf{X}}'\mathbf{X}(\mathbf{X}'\mathbf{X})^{-1}\mathbf{X}'\tilde{\mathbf{X}}]^{-1} \quad \text{where} \quad \hat{\mathbf{u}} = (\tilde{\mathbf{y}} : \tilde{\mathbf{X}})\begin{bmatrix} 1 \\ -\hat{\boldsymbol{\delta}}_{b,\text{IV}} \end{bmatrix}. \tag{23}$$

Wickens and Breusch (1988: 198) show that this is equal to the covariance matrix of the same parameter vector $\hat{\boldsymbol{\delta}}_{b,\text{IV}}$, calculated (indirectly) by applying the transformation $\mathbf{A}_b$ to the original parameters γ and using the Jacobian of this transformation to approximate the estimated covariance matrix $\hat{\mathbf{V}}_{\boldsymbol{\delta}_{b,\text{IV}}}$. That is,

$$\hat{\mathbf{V}}_{\boldsymbol{\delta}_b} \cong \left[\frac{\partial \boldsymbol{\delta}_b(\hat{\gamma})}{\partial \gamma}\right] \hat{\mathbf{V}}_{\gamma} \left[\frac{\partial \boldsymbol{\delta}_b(\hat{\gamma})}{\partial \gamma}\right]' \tag{24}$$

and $\hat{\mathbf{V}}_{\boldsymbol{\delta}_b}$ can be reduced from this to the same expression as that given for $\hat{\mathbf{V}}_{\boldsymbol{\delta}_{b,\text{IV}}}$ in (23).

Both the original ADL model and Bårdsen's transformation involve a calculation of the θ_j as nonlinear functions of coefficients in the original regression. Following Bårdsen, a standard formula for an approximation to the variance of a nonlinear function of elements with known variances can be used to compute $\widehat{\text{var}(\hat{\theta}_j)}$. Let $f = f(a_1, a_2, \ldots, a_H)$; then $\hat{f} = f(\hat{a}_1, \hat{a}_2, \ldots, \hat{a}_H)$ and

$$\widehat{\text{var}(\hat{f})} \cong \sum_{h=1}^{H} \left(\frac{\partial \hat{f}}{\partial a_h}\right)^2 \widehat{\text{var}(\hat{a}_h)} + 2 \sum_{g<h} \left(\frac{\partial \hat{f}}{\partial a_g}\right)\left(\frac{\partial \hat{f}}{\partial a_h}\right) \widehat{\text{cov}(\hat{a}_g, \hat{a}_h)}. \tag{25a}$$

In the case of the ADL, we have $\hat{f} = \hat{\theta}_j = \hat{\lambda}\sum_{i=0}^{n}\hat{\beta}_{ji}$ where

[7] It might seem impossible that the Bewley transformation could involve a ratio, being a case of a linear transformation matrix $\mathbf{A}_b$ applied to the original linear regression. Recall, however, that there is also a normalization factor applied, through which division by another linear function of the original coefficients is accomplished.

$\hat{\lambda} \equiv (1 - \sum_{i=1}^{m} \hat{\alpha}_i)^{-1}$, as implied by (6) above. The estimated variances and covariances of the parameter estimates $\hat{\gamma}$ are based on $\hat{\sigma}^2(\mathbf{X}'\mathbf{X})^{-1}$ from (8).

For the Bårdsen transformation, (25*a*) takes a particularly simple form, since $\hat{\theta}_j$ is calculated from the ratio of only two parameters. Hence if estimation is via (5), we have, after taking derivatives, that

$$\widehat{\operatorname{var}(\hat{\theta}_j)} \cong \left(\frac{1}{-\hat{\alpha}_m^*}\right)^2 \widehat{\operatorname{var}(\hat{\beta}_{jn}^*)} + \left[\frac{\hat{\beta}_{jn}^*}{(\hat{\alpha}_m^*)^2}\right]^2 \widehat{\operatorname{var}(\hat{\alpha}_m^*)}$$

$$+ 2\left(\frac{1}{-\hat{\alpha}_m^*}\right)\left[\frac{\hat{\beta}_{jn}^*}{(\hat{\alpha}_m^*)^2}\right] \widehat{\operatorname{cov}(\hat{\beta}_{jn}^*, \hat{\alpha}_m^*)},$$

recalling that $\widehat{\operatorname{var}(\hat{\beta}_{jn}^*)}$, $\widehat{\operatorname{var}(\hat{\alpha}_m^*)}$, and $\widehat{\operatorname{cov}(\hat{\beta}_{jn}^*, \hat{\alpha}_m^*)}$ are easily calculated from $\hat{\sigma}^2(\tilde{\mathbf{X}}'\tilde{\mathbf{X}})^{-1}$.

An equivalent way of writing (25*a*) is to express it in the form of (24). For $f = f(a_1, a_2, \ldots, a_H)$, as above, let $\hat{\mathbf{V}}_a$ be the $H \times H$ covariance matrix of which the $(g, h)th$ element is $\widehat{\operatorname{cov}(\hat{a}_g, \hat{a}_h)}$. Then, using the Jacobian of the transformation $f(\cdot)$, defined as

$$\mathbf{J}_f' = \left(\frac{\partial f}{\partial a_1}, \frac{\partial f}{\partial a_2}, \ldots, \frac{\partial f}{\partial a_H}\right),$$

we have

$$\widehat{\operatorname{var}(\hat{f})} = \hat{\mathbf{J}}_f{}'\hat{\mathbf{V}}_a\hat{\mathbf{J}}_f. \tag{25b}$$

Wickens and Breusch show that, substituting $\hat{\theta}_j$ for $\hat{f}$ and comparing the results of (23) and (24) with those of (25*a*) and (25*b*), the estimated variances of long-run multipliers calculated from the ADL model are the same as those provided in the IV estimator of the Bewley transform. We show now that the same is also true of the error-correction transformation, or any other linear transformation, using the form (25*b*). That is, the method of proof does not use the features of the ECM or of any other particular transformation, but instead applies to the estimates from any non-singular linear transformation. The important point, as above, is the equivalence of results yielded by different linear transformations of the model.

Consider the long-run multiplier vector as calculated from the ADL,

$$\hat{\boldsymbol{\theta}} = \mathbf{f}(\hat{\boldsymbol{\alpha}}, \hat{\boldsymbol{\beta}}). \tag{26}$$

The ADL approximation to the variance of the multiplier is

$$\operatorname{var}_A(\hat{\boldsymbol{\theta}}) \cong \mathbf{J}_\mathbf{f}' \operatorname{var}(\hat{\boldsymbol{\alpha}}, \hat{\boldsymbol{\beta}})\mathbf{J}_\mathbf{f}, \tag{27}$$

where $\mathbf{J}_\mathbf{f}$ is the Jacobian of the transformation represented by the function $\mathbf{f}(\cdot, \cdot)$. The long-run multiplier vector calculated from the ECM is

$$\hat{\boldsymbol{\theta}} = \mathbf{g}(\hat{\boldsymbol{\eta}}, \hat{\boldsymbol{\zeta}}), \tag{28}$$

and the ECM approximation to the variance is

$$\text{var}_E(\hat{\boldsymbol{\theta}}) \cong \mathbf{J}_g' \,\text{var}(\hat{\boldsymbol{\eta}}, \hat{\boldsymbol{\zeta}})\mathbf{J}_g, \tag{29}$$

where $\mathbf{J}_g$ corresponds to the function $\mathbf{g}(\cdot, \cdot)$. We can prove that

$$\mathbf{J}_g' = \mathbf{J}_f'\mathbf{A}_{22} \tag{30}$$

for $\mathbf{J}_f$ and $\mathbf{J}_g$ representing general linear transformations, so that we now have for the variances, as well as the point estimates, the result that the estimates obtained do not depend on which transformation is used. That is, $\text{var}_A(\hat{\boldsymbol{\theta}}) = \text{var}_E(\hat{\boldsymbol{\theta}})$ if and only if $\mathbf{J}_f'\mathbf{A}_{22} = \mathbf{J}_g'$, because, by (27) and the relation

$$\begin{bmatrix} \hat{\boldsymbol{\alpha}} \\ \hat{\boldsymbol{\beta}} \end{bmatrix} = \mathbf{A}_{22}\begin{bmatrix} \hat{\boldsymbol{\eta}} \\ \hat{\boldsymbol{\zeta}} \end{bmatrix}, \tag{31}$$

it follows that

$$\text{var}_A(\hat{\boldsymbol{\theta}}) \cong \mathbf{J}_f'\mathbf{A}_{22}\,\text{var}(\hat{\boldsymbol{\eta}}, \hat{\boldsymbol{\zeta}})\mathbf{A}_{22}'\,\mathbf{J}_f, \quad \text{and} \quad \text{var}_E(\hat{\boldsymbol{\theta}}) \cong \mathbf{J}_g'\,\text{var}(\hat{\boldsymbol{\eta}}, \hat{\boldsymbol{\zeta}})\mathbf{J}_g.$$

To prove (30), define

$$\hat{\mathbf{a}} = \begin{bmatrix} \hat{\boldsymbol{\alpha}} \\ \hat{\boldsymbol{\beta}} \end{bmatrix} \quad \text{and} \quad \hat{\mathbf{h}} = \begin{bmatrix} \hat{\boldsymbol{\eta}} \\ \hat{\boldsymbol{\zeta}} \end{bmatrix}.$$

We know that $\mathbf{f}(\mathbf{a}) = \boldsymbol{\theta} = \mathbf{g}(\mathbf{h})$. Now $\mathbf{J}_f' = \partial\mathbf{f}(\mathbf{a})/\partial\mathbf{a}'$ and $\mathbf{J}_g' = \partial\mathbf{g}(\mathbf{h})/\partial\mathbf{h}'$, while (31) states that $\mathbf{a} = \mathbf{A}_{22}\mathbf{h}$. Hence

$$\mathbf{J}_f' = \frac{\partial\mathbf{g}(\mathbf{h})}{\partial\mathbf{a}'} = \frac{\partial\mathbf{g}(\mathbf{h})}{\partial\mathbf{h}'}\frac{\partial\mathbf{h}}{\partial\mathbf{a}'} = \mathbf{J}_g'\mathbf{A}_{22}^{-1}.$$

Rearranging yields (30) immediately.

So, estimating the ECM or another linear transformation and transforming to get the variance of the long-run multiplier leads to the same result as obtained by transforming the ADL model. Wickens and Breusch (1988) showed the corresponding results for the Bewley estimator; the information revealed by all three transformations is the same. As with the Bårdsen transformation, $\mathbf{a}_{12} = \mathbf{0}$ for the ECM, and its parameters are therefore consistently estimated by OLS.

2.8. Expectational Variables and the Interpretation of Long-Run Solutions

So far, long-run solutions have been derived for models with valid conditioning on regressors or instruments. McCallum (1984) and Kelly (1985) have suggested potential problems in the interpretation of long-run solutions in the presence of expectational variables in the processes generating the data. The problems are, however, readily interpreted as resulting from invalid (weak) exogeneity assumptions, and do not uniquely concern long-run solutions; short-run effects may be badly estimated also. Moreover, if the variables concerned are non-stationary and have particular integration and co-integration properties (see Chapters 3–5), then the long-run solution, but not the short-run multipliers, can be estimated consistently despite the expectational variables. We follow McCallum and Kelly in describing the circumstances in question, and Hendry and Neale (1988) in relating these to weak exogeneity and non-stationarity.

McCallum (1984) offers the following example. Consider the relationship between interest rates and inflation, and in particular the Fisher effect. Let Π_t denote the inflation rate and i_t the nominal interest rate. Then, in the relationship

$$i_t = \beta_0 + \beta_1 \Pi_t + v_t, \tag{32}$$

the Fisher hypothesis is interpreted as stating that $\beta_1 = 1$; i.e. in long-run equilibrium, the nominal interest rate reflects inflation one for one. Now imagine that the actual generation of these series is according to the processes

$$i_t = \rho + \hat{\Pi}_{t+1|t} + \upsilon_t \tag{33}$$

and

$$\Pi_t = \mu_0 + \mu_1 \Pi_{t-1} + e_t, \tag{34}$$

with $|\mu_1| < 1$; υ_t and e_t white-noise processes; $E(e_t \upsilon_s) = 0 \ \forall \, t, s$, where ρ is a constant real interest rate and $\hat{\Pi}_{t+1|t}$ represents agents' forecasts of Π_{t+1} made at time t. Equation (33) implies that the Fisher hypothesis is valid in each period, rather than as a long-run equilibrium only. Imagine further that information is costless and that agents understand the $\{\Pi_t\}$ process so that $\hat{\Pi}_{t+1|t} = \mu_0 + \mu_1 \Pi_t$. Then

$$i_t = \rho + \mu_0 + \mu_1 \Pi_t + \upsilon_t. \tag{35}$$

Hence estimation of (32) by a consistent method such as OLS will produce a coefficient estimate $\hat{\beta}_1$ which converges to $\mu_1 < 1$. McCallum emphasizes the hazards of frequency-domain time-series techniques for estimating long-run (zero-frequency) effects, but the conclusion is equally well applicable to time-domain methods. In spite of the validity of the Fisher hypothesis, the investigator examining the long-run solution through a model such as (32) would falsely conclude that it fails to hold.

Kelly (1985) and Hendry and Neale (1988) use the following more general structure in order to examine the issue. The data are generated by

$$\phi(L)y_t = \alpha + \beta(L)\hat{x}_{t|t-1} + \gamma(L)z_t + \varepsilon_t, \tag{36}$$

where $\phi(L)$, $\beta(L)$, and $\gamma(L)$ are finite-order polynomials in the lag operator of the form

$$\phi(L) = \phi_0 - \sum_{i=1}^{K} \phi_i L^i, \qquad \beta(L) = \sum_{j=0}^{I} \beta_j L^j, \qquad \text{and} \qquad \gamma(L) = \sum_{j=0}^{M} \gamma_j L^j.$$

Furthermore, $\phi_0 = 1$, and for simplicity in this example we take

$$\hat{x}_{t|t-1} \equiv E(x_t|\mathbf{\Omega}_{t-1}), \qquad \mathbf{\Omega}_{t-1} \equiv (\mathbf{Y}_{t-1}, \mathbf{X}_{t-1}, \mathbf{Z}_t). \tag{37}$$

The lag operator in the polynomial $\beta(L)$ is interpreted as applying to the first subscript of $\hat{x}_{t|t-1}$ only, so that

$$L^k(\hat{x}_{t|t-1}) \equiv \hat{x}_{t-k|t-1} = x_{t-k},\ k \geqslant 1.$$

The underlying series $\{x_t\}$ is generated according to

$$x_t = \delta_0 + \delta(L)x_{t-1} + \eta_t, \qquad \delta(L) = \sum_{j=1}^{J} \delta_j L^{j-1}. \tag{38}$$

The error terms ε_t and η_t are mutually and serially uncorrelated white noise. Combining (37) and (38), we have

$$\hat{x}_{t|t-1} = \delta_0 + \delta(L)x_{t-1}$$

and

$$y_t = \alpha + \beta_0\hat{x}_{t|t-1} + \beta^*(L)x_{t-1} + \gamma(L)z_t + \phi^*(L)y_{t-1} + \varepsilon_t, \tag{39}$$

where $\beta^*(L) = \sum_{i=1}^{I}\beta_i L^i$ and $\phi^*(L) = \sum_{k=1}^{K}\phi_k L^k$. Finally, using (38):

$$\begin{aligned} y_t &= (\alpha + \beta_0\delta_0) + [\beta_0\delta(L) + \beta^*(L)]x_{t-1} + \gamma(L)z_t + \phi^*(L)y_{t-1} + \varepsilon_t \\ &= E(y_t|\mathbf{\Omega}_{t-1}) + \varepsilon_t. \end{aligned} \tag{40}$$

The parameters β_i cannot be determined from (40) without knowledge of the marginal process (38); hence, recalling the definition of weak exogeneity in Chapter 1, x_t is not weakly exogenous for the β_i in (40). If, however, we somehow observed $\hat{x}_{t|t-1}$ directly, then we would be able to estimate the β_i from (39).

The problem identified by McCallum and Kelly is therefore simply one aspect of a broader, and well-known, one: we cannot in general count on unbiased estimates from models in which the explanatory variables are not (weakly) exogenous for the parameters of interest. The solution, in this circumstance, is therefore joint estimation of (40) and (38). If (40) alone is estimated, not only is the long-run solution not consistently estimated, but the short-run adjustment coefficients are incorrectly estimated as well; where $\hat{x}_{t|t-1}$ is omitted from the model, coefficients on x_{t-1} are not $\beta^*(L)$ but $\beta_0\delta(L) + \beta^*(L)$. If we do not have weak exogeneity, we cannot conduct valid conditional inference.

This point is independent of whether our primary interest is in long-run equilibrium solutions or in short-run effects.

It is also interesting to note that non-stationarity in the series y_t and x_t, and co-integration between them, can lead to consistent estimation of the long-run solution in spite of the lack of weak exogeneity. To make this clear, as well as to clarify the position of 'strict' exogeneity, express (39) as

$$y_t = \alpha + \beta_0 x_t + \beta^*(L)x_{t-1} + \gamma(L)z_t + \phi^*(L)y_{t-1} + \varepsilon_{2t}, \quad (41)$$

where $\varepsilon_{2t} \equiv (\varepsilon_t - \beta_0\eta_t)$ and where $x_t = \hat{x}_{t|t-1} + \eta_t$ from (38); x_t is in effect an error-laden measurement of $\hat{x}_{t|t-1}$. Now group the latter regressors to get

$$y_t = \beta_0 x_t + \xi'\mathbf{w}_t + \varepsilon_{2t}, \quad (42)$$

and define

$$\mathbf{C} = \begin{bmatrix} E(x_t^2) & E(x_t\mathbf{w}_t') \\ E(\mathbf{w}_t x_t) & E(\mathbf{w}_t\mathbf{w}_t') \end{bmatrix}^{-1} = \begin{bmatrix} c_{11} & \mathbf{c}_{12} \\ \mathbf{c}_{21} & \mathbf{C}_{22} \end{bmatrix}. \quad (43)$$

From (38), x_t is correlated with ε_{2t} in (41) and (42) since ε_{2t} depends upon η_t. However we can redefine the parameters in (42) (i.e. re-parameterize) to eliminate this correlation, using (43). Write

$$y_t = \beta_0(1 - c_{11}\sigma_\eta^2)x_t + (\xi - \beta_0\sigma_\eta^2\mathbf{c}_{21})'\mathbf{w}_t + \mu_t, \quad (44)$$

yielding $\mu_t = \varepsilon_t - \beta_0\eta_t + \beta_0 c_{11}\sigma_\eta^2 x_t + \beta_0\sigma_\eta^2\mathbf{c}_{21}'\mathbf{w}_t$, from which, again using $x_t = \hat{x}_{t|t-1} + \eta_t$, and assuming that $\hat{x}_{t|t-1}$ is uncorrelated with ε_t and η_t, we can calculate that

$$E(\mu_t x_t) = E(\varepsilon_t\eta_t) + \beta_0\sigma_\eta^2[-1 + c_{11}E(x_t^2) + \mathbf{c}_{21}'E(\mathbf{w}_t x_t)],$$
$$= 0,$$

since the first right-hand-side term is equal to zero by assumption, and from the definition of $\mathbf{C}$ and the fact that $\mathbf{CC}^{-1} = \mathbf{I}$, the square-bracketed term is zero as well.

So the re-parameterized equation (44) has an error term that is uncorrelated with the regressors; $E(\mu_t x_t) = 0$. Note that, since this re-parameterization has rendered x_t 'strictly exogenous' (Engle *et al.* 1983) in this example, the inferential problems do not stem from a lack of exogeneity in that sense: strict exogeneity, unlike weak exogeneity, is neither necessary nor sufficient for valid inference.

Equation (44) allows us to see the large-sample results of estimating (42) by regression, because (44) is expressed such that the error is uncorrelated with the regressors so that the coefficients represent the impacts of conditional expectations. There are two points to note. First, the existence of biases in (44) (e.g. $\beta_0(1 - c_{11}\sigma_\eta^2) \neq \beta_0$) depends upon a non-zero value for σ_η^2, and therefore on the discrepancy between x_t and the expectation $\hat{x}_{t|t-1}$; that is, the biases are attributable to the lack of weak exogeneity implied by the fact that we use x_t in place of $\hat{x}_{t|t-1}$. If this problem were not present, both short run and long run would be estimable with no bias; since the problem *is* present, neither short nor long run is estimated without bias (for I(0) processes).

Second, if x_t is not stationary but integrated of order 1, and if y_t has the same order of integration and is co-integrated with x_t (that is, if there is a long-run equilibrium relationship between them) while η_t remains a stationary process, then $c_{11}\sigma_\eta^2 \rightarrow 0$ as $t \rightarrow \infty$ (see Chapter 3). In the limit as t increases without bound, therefore, the estimated coefficient on x_t will tend to β_0, and we have the possibility of consistent estimation of the long-run solution. Nevertheless, the short-run coefficients remain mis-estimated.

Clearly, a lack of weak exogeneity creates serious inferential problems, but these are not restricted to the estimation of long-run solutions. Further, there is a marked difference in the long-run outcomes between the I(0) and I(1) situations, leading us to study the properties of integrated and co-integrated processes.

3

Properties of Integrated Processes

A knowledge of the fundamental properties of integrated processes is essential for an understanding of tests for both non-stationarity and the existence of long-run equilibrium relationships. Here we define and present the important properties of integrated processes. We deal with the issue of spurious regressions and show how a consideration of the theory of integrated processes helps us to understand the behaviour of standard estimators in models involving non-stationary data. Several examples illustrate the use of Wiener distribution theory in deriving asymptotic results for such models.

Much conventional asymptotic theory for least-squares estimation (e.g. the standard proofs of consistency and asymptotic normality of OLS estimators) assumes stationarity of the explanatory variables, possibly around a deterministic trend. Not all economic time series are stationary, as we saw in Chapter 1, and for many important ones, including aggregate consumption and national income, stationarity is not even a sensible approximation.

Nonetheless, regression methods have often appeared to be effective when analysing such series, and it was not clear that methods developed for stationary series would not be valid elsewhere. To some extent, therefore, many analyses of unadjusted non-stationary series have been carried out on the assumption that the non-stationarity would not matter. As some potential problems in doing so became clear, however, econometricians naturally looked for methods of transforming their data in such a way that the resulting series *would* be stationary, and therefore amenable to analysis using 'traditional' econometric or time-series methods.

One illustration of the difficulties that can arise when performing regression with clearly non-stationary series is the problem of *nonsense regression*, so named by Yule (1926), or *spurious regression*, in the terminology of Granger and Newbold (1974): given two completely unrelated but integrated series, regression of one on the other will tend to produce an apparently significant relationship.[1] The realization that such things could occur led to the interest in transformations to induce stationarity. Differencing data was one of these; 'removing' a deterministic trend from a series was another.[2]

Although these transformations enjoyed some popularity, it eventually became clear for a wide class of processes that standard significance tests for the hypothesis that there is no trend are biased in favour of rejecting the hypothesis even though it is true (see Granger and Newbold 1974, *inter alia*). Moreover, spurious correlations between unrelated integrated processes appear even in regressions containing deterministic trends. The simple method of de-trending before drawing inferences from non-stationary data was therefore found to be flawed.

3.1. Spurious Regression

The standard proof of the consistency of ordinary least squares regression uses an assumption such as that $\text{plim}\,(1/T)(\mathbf{X}'\mathbf{X}) = \mathbf{Q}$, where $\mathbf{X}$ is the matrix containing the data on the explanatory variables and $\mathbf{Q}$ is a fixed matrix. That is, with increasing sample information, the sample moments of the data settle down to their population values. In order to have fixed population moments to which these sample moments converge, the data must be stationary—otherwise, as for example in the case of integrated series, the data might be tending to increase over time, in which case there are no fixed values in the matrix of expectations of sums of squares and cross-products of these data.[3]

Some examples of what can emerge when standard regression techniques are used with non-stationary data were re-emphasized by Granger and Newbold, who considered the following data generation process:

$$y_t = y_{t-1} + u_t, \qquad u_t \sim \text{IID}\,(0, \sigma_u^2) \tag{1}$$

$$x_t = x_{t-1} + v_t, \qquad v_t \sim \text{IID}\,(0, \sigma_v^2) \tag{2}$$

$$E(u_t v_s) = 0 \;\forall\, t, s; \qquad E(u_t\, u_{t-k}) = E(v_t\, v_{t-k}) = 0 \quad \forall\, k \neq 0.$$

[1] The change in terminology may be misleading, since Yule also used the term 'spurious relationships', referring to a correlation induced between two variables that are causally unrelated but are both dependent on other common variables.

[2] This is accomplished either by including a function of time as a regressor, or by subtracting a function of time from all series used. By the Frisch–Waugh theorem, regressing all series on time and using their residuals in a further regression is numerically equivalent to including time as a regressor when using the unadjusted series.

[3] Anderson (1958) extends the standard asymptotic distribution theory to deal with the de-trending of deterministic variables that can be suitably standardized. However, here we are concerned with integrated stochastic processes.

That is, x_t and y_t are uncorrelated random walks. Since x_t neither affects nor is affected by y_t, one would hope that the coefficient β_1 in the regression model

$$y_t = \beta_0 + \beta_1 x_t + \varepsilon_t \qquad (3)$$

would converge in probability to zero, reflecting the lack of a relation between the series, and that the coefficient of determination (R^2) from this regression would also tend to zero. However, this is not the case. Regression methods detect correlations, and in non-stationary series (as Yule 1926 showed) spurious correlations may persist in large samples despite the absence of any connection between the underlying series. If two time series are each growing, for example, they may be correlated even though they are increasing for entirely different reasons and by increments that are uncorrelated. Hence a correlation between integrated series cannot be interpreted in the way that it could be if it arose among stationary series.

In (3), both the null hypothesis $\beta_1 = 0$ (implying $y_t = \beta_0 + \varepsilon_t$), and the alternative $\beta_1 \neq 0$ lead to false models, since the true DGP is not nested within (3). From this perspective it is not surprising that the null hypothesis, implying that $\{y_t\}$ is a white-noise process, is rejected; the autocorrelation in the random walk $\{y_t\}$ tends to project onto $\{x_t\}$, also a random walk and therefore also strongly autocorrelated. Tests based on badly specified models can often be misleading. Nonetheless, the spurious regression problem that appears among integrated processes is distinct from the inferential problems that may appear among stationary processes. If $\{y_t\}$ and $\{x_t\}$ were made stationary by introducing a coefficient between zero and one on each of the lagged terms in (1) and (2), the OLS-estimated regression coefficient $\widehat{\beta}_1$ and the non-centrality of its t-statistic *would* both converge to zero, even though (3) does not nest the true process (although the t-test would over-reject). That is, in the stationary case, regression on a set of variables independent of the regressand produces coefficients that converge to zero; in the non-stationary case, this need not be so.

To characterize precisely some of the analytical results for integrated processes, we refer to Phillips (1986). A simple case uses (1) and (2) above as the data generation process, with the assumptions concerning the error processes u_t and v_t capable of being weakened substantially. Then, estimation of the model (3) by ordinary least squares can be shown to lead to results that cannot be interpreted within the conventional testing procedure. To begin with, conventionally calculated 't-statistics' on $\widehat{\beta}_0$ and $\widehat{\beta}_1$ do not have t-distributions, do not have any limiting distributions, and in fact diverge in distribution as the sample size T increases; hence, for any fixed critical value, rejection rates will tend to increase with sample size. The null hypothesis that is being rejected here is $H_0{:}\beta_1 = 0$; hence a rejection rate increasing with sample size implies that a null of *no* relationship between the series will tend to be rejected more and more frequently in larger samples. The t-statistics are of order $T^{1/2}$. Thus, the invalid inference that there is in fact a relationship is traceable directly to the non-stationarity in the data-generation process (1) and (2). When (1) and (2) are replaced with stable autoregressive processes, the non-centrality of the t-statistic to test $H_0{:}\beta_1 = 0$ converges to zero, reflecting the lack of relationship between the series. We will examine these asymptotic results in more detail in Section 3.5.2, after reviewing some of the necessary concepts from Wiener distribution theory.

Further analytical results concerning the distribution of the F-statistic for the hypothesis that $\beta_0 = \beta_1 = 0$, and those of standard autocorrelation test statistics, are also given in Phillips (1986). The F-statistic also diverges, leading to rejections growing with the sample size T, despite the lack of relation between $\{y_t\}$ and $\{x_t\}$; residual autocorrelation tests, however, provide an indication to the investigator that the model is mis-specified, by converging in probability to the values implied by a serial correlation coefficient of unity. That is, although the t- and F-statistics for the null hypothesis of interest are grossly misleading, some information which would suggest that the regression (3) is mis-specified *is* provided by a test for residual autocorrelation. This underlines again the importance of thoroughly testing any regression model for mis-specification, and basing inference only upon those in which no evidence of serious mis-specification is found; see e.g. Spanos (1986).

Consider now the following bivariate DGP, which extends (1) and (2) by allowing the inclusion of intercepts corresponding to potential drifts in the unit-root processes:

$$\Delta y_t = \alpha + \varepsilon_t, \qquad \text{where } \varepsilon_t \sim \text{IID}(0, \sigma_\varepsilon^2); \tag{4}$$

$$\Delta z_t = \gamma + v_t, \qquad \text{where } v_t \sim \text{IID}(0, \sigma_v^2). \tag{5}$$

To simplify the analysis, we assume that the two shocks ε_t and v_t are independent at all points in time, which implies that

$$E(\varepsilon_t v_s) = 0 \quad \forall\, t, s. \tag{6}$$

Assume also that the initial values y_0 and z_0 are zero. We will mainly consider the case where $\alpha = \gamma = 0$, so that both variables are simple random walks and y_t and z_t are the sums of all of their respective past shocks. When α and γ are not zero, y_t and z_t depend on linear trends which reflect the accumulation of the successive intercepts. This completes the formulation of the statistical generating mechanism in (4) and (5), other than stating a specific form for the error distributions.

Turn now to the specification of an economic hypothesis. An economist may wish to describe the relationship between $\{y_t\}$ and $\{z_t\}$ with the model

$$y_t = \beta_0 + \beta_1 z_t + u_t, \tag{7}$$

where β_1 is interpreted as the derivative of y_t with respect to z_t. Conventionally, equations such as (7) are estimated by ordinary least squares, treating $\{u_t\}$ as an IID process independent of z_t. Since y_t and z_t are causally unrelated here by construction, the derivative β_1 is zero in the sense that no relation exists; it is not true to say that setting β_1 to zero in (7) gives the true DGP. We want to examine the properties of the conventional estimation and hypothesis testing procedure applied to (7) when the unknown DGP is in fact (4)–(6).

Standard regression theory for models involving stationary regressors would suggest that $\text{plim}\,(\hat{\beta}_1) = \beta_1 = 0$, and that the probability of the absolute value of the t-statistic for $H_0\!:\!\beta_1 = 0$ exceeding 1.96 is 5 per cent. Because these regressors are integrated, however, this is not so. Reconsider (7). Since $\{y_t\}$ and $\{z_t\}$ are both integrated processes, (7) could be a well-defined regression with a non-zero β_1, if a relationship between these two variables existed. If however $\beta_1 = 0$, as is true here by (4)–(6), we have $y_t = \beta_0 + u_t$. Now since $\{y_t\}$ is I(1), $\{u_t\}$ must be I(1), which violates the assumption made about $\{u_t\}$ above. There is an internal inconsistency in conducting hypothesis testing in the standard way here, because it is not possible for the error term to be I(0) when β_1 is zero.

We can use Monte Carlo methods to examine typical results, in finite samples, of regressions such as (7) where $\{y_t\}$ and $\{z_t\}$ are independent non-stationary processes. In the exercise that follows, we generate $\{y_t\}$ using the DGP (4), with $T = 100$, $\alpha = 0$, $y_0 = 0$, and $\sigma_\varepsilon = 1$. Similarly, $\{z_t\}$ is generated with $\gamma = 0$, $z_0 = 0$, and $\sigma_v = 1$ in (5). The random errors are normally distributed and generated independently, consistent with (6). At each replication, we record (i) the estimated coefficients, (ii) the estimated standard errors, (iii) whether the null hypothesis $\beta_1 = 0$ is rejected when conventional 5 per cent critical values of the t-distribution are used, (iv) the value of the sample correlation between y and z, and (v) the value of the Durbin–Watson statistic for residual serial correlation. There are $N = 10{,}000$ replications using PC-NAIVE.

In this experiment, the Monte Carlo estimate of the mean value of $\hat{\beta}_1$ for the experiment is $\tilde{E}[\hat{\beta}_1] = -0.012$, with Monte Carlo standard error (that is, the standard error of the Monte Carlo estimate of the mean of $\hat{\beta}_1$) of 0.006. Because we are estimating a mean using independent replications, a central limit theorem applies to the Monte Carlo results, so that the sample mean is asymptotically normally distributed (i.e. as $N \to \infty$). Hence we can reject the hypothesis that $E[\hat{\beta}_1] = 0$ at $T = 100$, despite the fact that the estimated mean value of $\widehat{\beta}_1$ is relatively small. The frequency distribution of $\widehat{\beta}_1$ is shown in Fig. 3.1, standardized to zero mean and unit variance. The sample standard deviation (SSD) of the values of $\{\widehat{\beta}_{1i}, i = 1, 2, \ldots, 10{,}000\}$ is 0.63 where SSD is defined as

$$\mathrm{SSD}(\widehat{\beta}_1) = \left\{(N-1)^{-1} \sum_{i=1}^{N} [\widehat{\beta}_{1i} - \widetilde{E}(\widehat{\beta}_1)]^2\right\}^{1/2}.$$

The distribution plotted in Fig. 3.1 is that of $\bar{\beta}_i = (\widehat{\beta}_{1i} - \widetilde{E}[\widehat{\beta}_1])/\mathrm{SSD}(\widehat{\beta}_{1i})$, so that $\{\bar{\beta}_i\}$ has a standard deviation of unity. The Monte Carlo standard error is $\sigma = \mathrm{SSD}(\widehat{\beta}_1)/N^{1/2}$.

The probability of rejecting H_0 at the conventional significance level of 0.05 is 0.753; that is, even when the null hypothesis is true, we will reject it 75.3 per cent of the time, and therefore make the wrong decision most of the time. Figure 3.2 reveals that it is not the shape of the standardized t-distribution that is at fault. Rather, the actual statistic

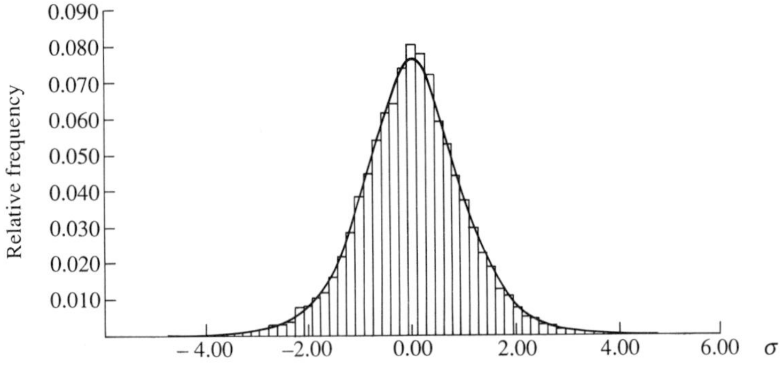

FIG 3.1. Frequency distribution of the spurious regression coefficient, standardized to zero mean, unit variance

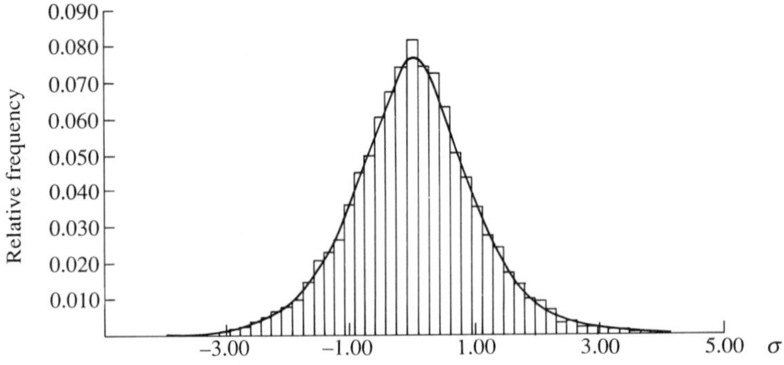

FIG 3.2. Frequency distribution of the 't-test' of $\beta = 0$, standardized to zero mean, unit variance

calculated does not have a zero mean, unit variance distribution. In fact, where $\bar{t}$ is the mean t-statistic, $\bar{t} = -0.12$ (0.07) and SSD(t) = 7.3. Values of $|t| > 1.96$ are very likely with such a large standard deviation, and the empirical critical values in the experiment that ensure a test with a size of 5 per cent are approximately $\pm$ 14.5. However, these critical values are not appropriate at other sample sizes.

This is the *spurious regression* problem: regression of an integrated series on another unrelated integrated series produces t-ratios on the slope parameter which indicate a relationship much more often than they should at the nominal test level. The phenomenon is of course not specific to this sample size, and in particular the problem will not disappear as the sample size is increased. The distribution of the t-ratio will, however, depend on the sample size; Fig. 3.3 shows the graph of $\widetilde{E}[\widehat{\beta}_1|T]$ for $T = 20, 21, \ldots, 100$, together with $\pm 2\sigma$ at each T, where σ denotes the Monte Carlo standard error in the graph. The bias is significantly different from zero only at the larger sample sizes, but does not change noticeably with T. Moreover, the value of σ does not fall greatly with T, which differs from what one would expect if conventional asymptotic theory were applicable.

Figure 3.4 records the mean value of the regression coefficient together with the SSD and the mean estimated standard error (ESE) of the coefficient. There is a great difference between the two measures of uncertainty: ESE is the estimated standard error of the coefficient $\widehat{\beta}_1$ that the investigator would obtain on average, in a regression of the form of (7) given the DGP in (4)–(6); the SSD is the Monte Carlo estimate of the true standard deviation of this parameter estimate. As Fig. 3.4 shows, the economist would report a severe underestimate of the uncertainty in the estimate of β_1.

The mean value of the t-statistic shown in Fig. 3.5 changes little as T increases from 20 to 100, but the standard deviation of t increases

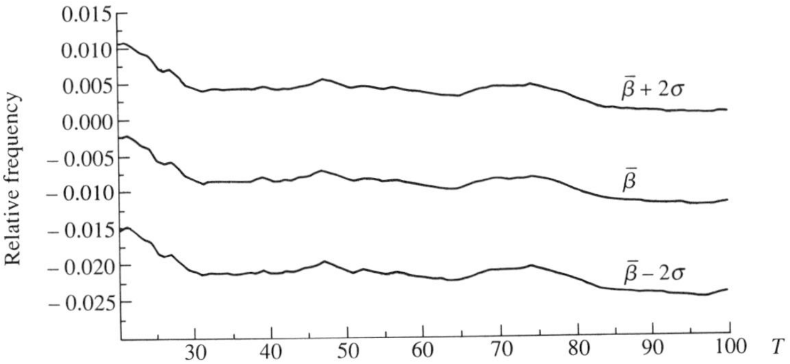

FIG 3.3. Mean value of the spurious regression coefficient with $\pm 2\sigma$ (the Monte Carlo standard error)

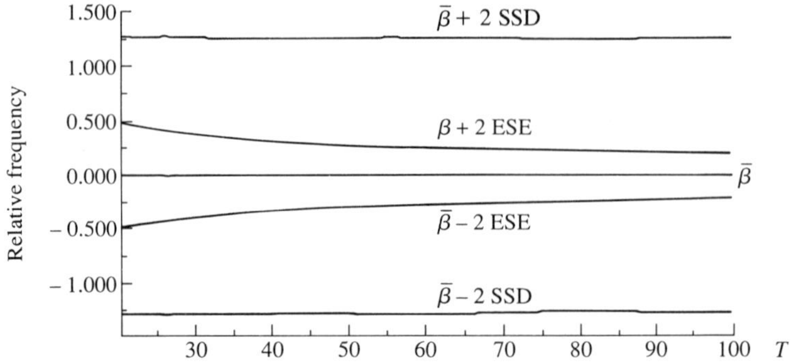

FIG 3.4. Mean value of the spurious regression coefficient with the estimated standard error (ESE) and sampling standard deviation (SSD) across sample sizes

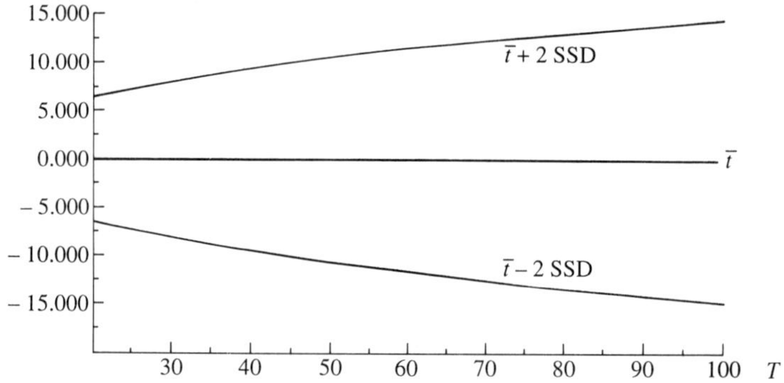

FIG 3.5. Mean value of the 't-test' of $H_0{:}\beta_1 = 0$, with $\pm$2SSD (the Monte Carlo based sampling standard deviation)

rapidly. Thus the problem becomes *worse* as T increases; rejection of the null hypothesis of *no* relation between the y_t and z_t series becomes more likely, despite one's initial intuition that, if the series really are unrelated, this feature should eventually dominate as $T \to \infty$. Figure 3.6 records the rejection frequencies for every sample size considered in the simulation exercise; $\Pr(|t(\beta_1 = 0)| \geqslant 2)$ is 0.30 at $T = 20$, already greater than the nominal size of the test, and the problem worsens as T is increased because the rejection frequencies also increase steadily with T. The outcomes of the simulations reveal the dangers of using critical values justified in one context (e.g. IID processes) to conduct inferences with statistics computed from data generated by a very different probability mechanism.

With the DGP in (4) and (5), the problem of discriminating between genuine interdependence and spurious regressions is difficult to solve

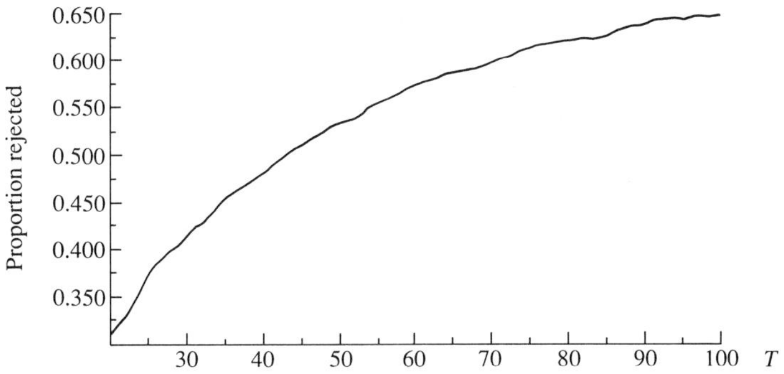

FIG 3.6. Rejection frequency of the 't-test' of $H_0{:}\beta_1 = 0$ when the hypothesis is true

because, under both the null and the alternative hypotheses, y_t and z_t have a high sample correlation (denoted R). In both cases we reject $H_0{:}\beta_1 = 0$ most of the time in large samples.

An early analysis of the spurious regressions problem is due, as we have said, to Yule (1926), who also used Monte Carlo simulations. Yule's observations on the distribution of R remain noteworthy and may be considered in three parts, representing three different situations: (i) where the $\{y_t\}$ and $\{z_t\}$ series are both mean–zero IID processes; (ii) where they are IID processes integrated once; and (iii) where they are IID processes integrated twice.[4] In each case, the figures given below represent the frequency distribution of R obtained from estimating equation (7) 10,000 times with a sample size of 100; $\beta_0 = \beta_1 = 0$ in all the simulations (except for an irrelevant location change in case (i), owing to a program restriction, when $\beta_0 = 1$). The following features of the different cases may be observed.

Case (i). When both variables are I(0) and IID, as Fig. 3.7 shows, R is well behaved and has a symmetric, nearly Gaussian, distribution centred on zero although bounded by $\pm$ 1.

Case (ii). When both variables are I(1) and the first differences are IID, the density of R, $f_R(r)$, is closer to a semi-ellipse with excess frequency at both ends of the distribution (see Fig. 3.8). Consequently, values of R well away from zero are far more likely here than in case (i).

Case (iii). When both variables are I(2), the second differences are IID. In this situation (see Fig. 3.9) $f_R(r)$ becomes U-shaped, and the

[4] Order of integration was defined informally in Chapter 1; it is explored formally in Section 3.3 below.

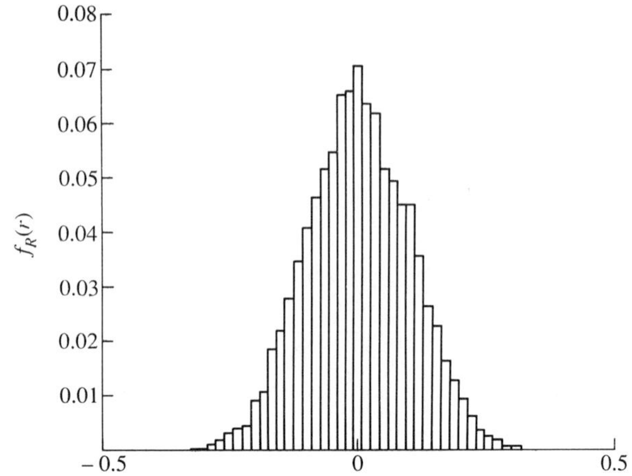

FIG 3.7. Frequency distribution for the correlation R between two IID independent processes

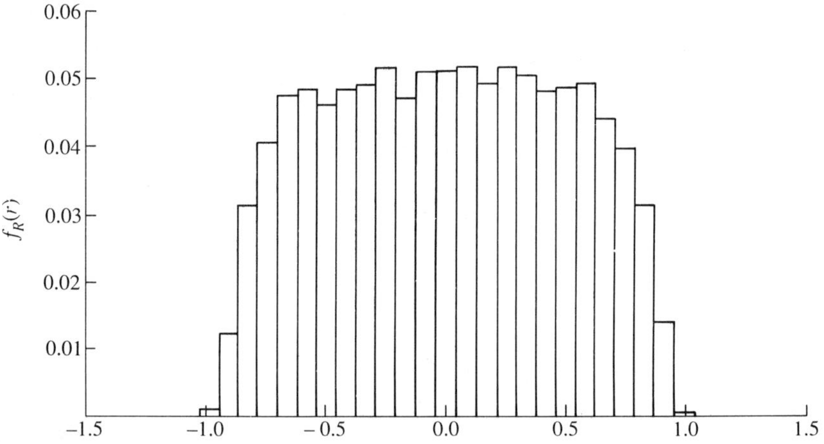

FIG 3.8. Frequency distribution for R between two I(1) processes with independent IID first differences

most likely correlations between two such I(2) unrelated series are ± 1, which is precisely what would occur if the series were truly related.

If a test statistic, based on R, assumes the distribution to be the one applying to case (i) when in fact the correct distribution is the one that applies to case (ii), the rejection frequency will greatly exceed the nominal size of the test (given by the expected number of rejections if (i) were true). Case (iii) is even worse: the least likely outcome here would seem to be the discovery of the truth. There is almost no

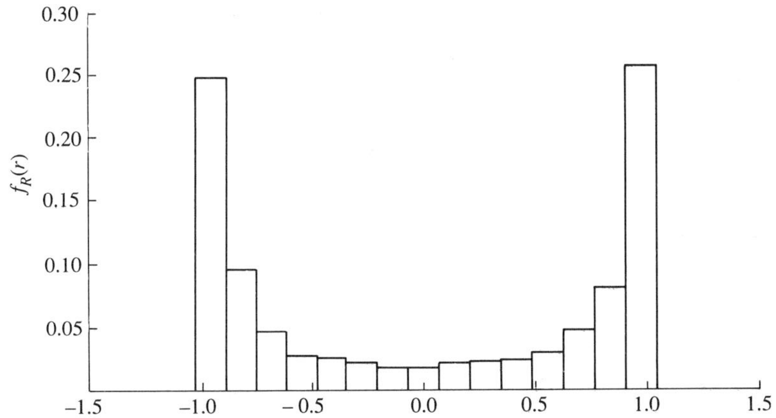

FIG 3.9. Frequency distribution of R for two I(2) processes with independent IID second differences

probability of finding $R \simeq 0$ in this last case, although the population value anticipated under the null is zero. The most likely sample value is $R \simeq \pm 1$.

If the degrees of integration of the data series are unknown, mixtures of cases (i)–(iii) are possible. For $T = 100$, Table 3.1 summarizes the outcomes.

Denote the order of integration of y_t and x_t by d_1 and d_2 respectively, and let $d = \max\{d_1, d_2\}$. The mean of R is close to zero in every case, but its standard deviation increases with $d_1 + d_2$. The estimate of the mean of β_1 is relatively small compared with the SSD, especially when

TABLE 3.1. Features of regressions among series with various orders of integration

Type[a]	$[d_1 + d_2]$	$\bar{R}$	SSD(R)	$\hat{\beta}_1$	ESE	SSD	$\Pr(\lvert t(\beta_1 = 0)\rvert \geqslant 2)$
I(0), I(0)	0	0.0004	0.101	0.0004	0.101	0.102	0.0493
I(1), I(1)	2	−0.006	0.490	−0.009	0.102	0.631	0.7570
I(2), I(2)	4	0.004	0.818	0.015	0.103	1.974	0.9406
I(0), I(1)	1	0.0004	0.099	−0.0001	0.031	0.033	0.0458
I(1), I(0)	1	0.0008	0.101	0.003	0.384	0.417	0.0486
I(2), I(1)	3	−0.023	0.613	−1.84	3.84	33.52	0.8530
I(1), I(2)	3	−0.013	0.610	−0.0005	0.0054	0.036	0.8444

[a] The notation I(j), I(k) describes a regression of an I(j) variable on an I(k) variable, j, $k = 0, 1, 2$. Thus, I(0), I(0) is a case (i) regression, I(1), I(1) a case (ii) regression, and I(2), I(2) a case (iii) regression. The remaining cases are mixtures of the primitive (i)-, (ii)-, and (iii)-type regressions.

$d_1 = d_2$. The mean ESE reported by OLS is virtually unaffected by d when $d_1 = d_2$, but varies greatly when $d_1 \neq d_2$. The SSD also increases as $d_1 + d_2$ increases unless the regressor is of higher order of integration than the regressand, namely when $d_1 < d_2$. The ESE underestimates the SSD by a factor in the neighbourhood of 10 to 20 for $d = 2$. The probability of falsely rejecting the null that $\beta_1 = 0$ rises to about 94 per cent as d increases.

Thus, the difficulties are not restricted to spurious regressions generated by regressing independent series *of the same order* on each other. Severe problems are revealed in regressions of an I(2) on an I(1) series (or vice versa). Less serious problems occur in regressions of I(1) on I(0) series (or vice versa). Figure 3.10 reports the distribution of R for an I(1) on an I(2) series and reveals a U-shaped distribution, as with two I(2) series. (This also occurs for an I(2) on I(1) series.) Figure 3.11 shows the distribution of the least-squares coefficient estimate for an I(2) on I(1) series; the distribution here is long-tailed but peaked and is distinctly non-normal. The t-rejection frequencies are similar in these two cases and lie between the rejection frequencies given by the case (ii)- and case (iii)-type regressions. The distribution of R, when one of the series is I(0), is similar to the distribution of this statistic when both series are I(0).[5] Overall, we see a pattern of potential nonsense once both time series become integrated.

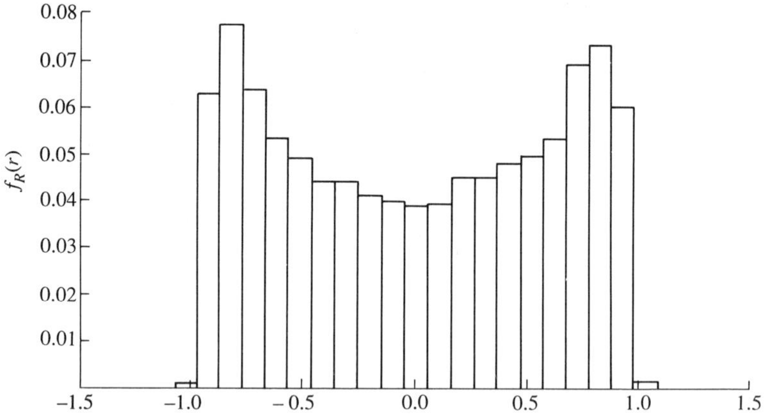

FIG 3.10. Frequency distribution of R between an I(1) and an I(2) process with independent IID first and second differences respectively

[5] There is good reason, as we shall see in Ch. 6, for this similarity in behaviour. In a regression of one I(0) series on another I(0) series, independent of the first series, the estimate of the regression coefficient β_1 tends in probability to zero. However, when an I(0) series is regressed on an I(1) series, the only way in which OLS can make the regression consistent and minimize the sum of squares is to drive the coefficient on the I(1) variable to zero. Thus equivalent results arise. These possibilities do not occur when both series are integrated.

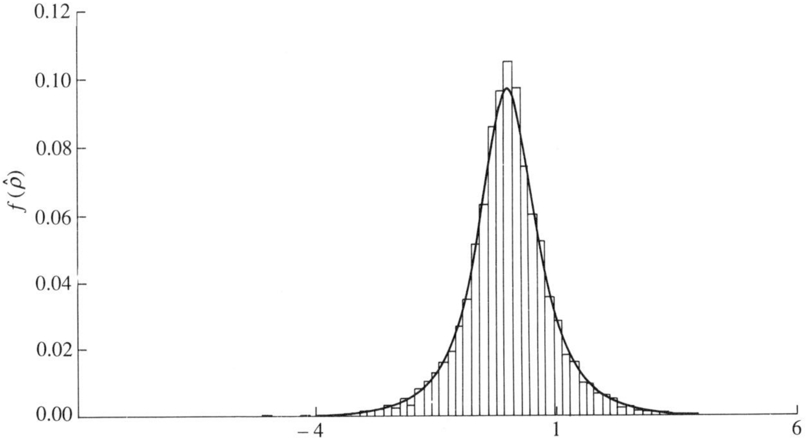

FIG 3.11. Histogram and estimated density for the regression coefficient of an I(2) series regressed on an I(1) series

Phillips (1986) also demonstrates that the Durbin–Watson statistic calculated from the residuals of (7) converges to zero as the sample size tends to infinity. When the two series are genuinely related, the DW statistic converges to a non-zero value. The behaviour of the DW statistic therefore provides one way of discriminating between spurious and genuine regressions, but a test based on this statistic may have poor power properties in small samples. Phillips's analytical results are useful in understanding the simulation evidence that Granger and Newbold (1974) advanced, bearing on the regression R^2 as well as the DW statistic. These authors suggested treating any regression for which $R^2 > \text{DW}$ as one that is likely to be spurious. This could be interpreted as a sign of a lack of any equilibrium relationship among the variables in the regression, which in turn implies a non-stationary error term and so very strong autocorrelation in the regression residuals.

Overall, simulation and analytical results show that the problem of drawing inference from non-stationary data is a serious one; OLS regression interpreted in the standard fashion can be very misleading. Resolution of this problem will lead us into a more detailed consideration of the integration properties of time series, but first we will examine the practice of de-trending time series.

3.2. Trends and Random Walks

One potential solution suggested for dealing with integrated series was to assume that the source of non-stationarity could be captured by, or approximated by, a deterministic function of time. If this were so, it would be possible to break up an integrated series into a deterministic (and therefore completely predictable) component, and a stationary series of deviations from this 'trend'. Methods for analysing stationary series could be applied to the deviations, and the whole series thereby modelled.

Unfortunately, subsequent evidence from Monte Carlo and analytical studies (e.g. Phillips 1986) showed that inference in models that contained time trends could not be carried out in the straightforward way that practitioners had hoped. First of all, time trends would appear to be statistically significant in models where they should not be, much more often than conventional test sizes would suggest. That is, the standard statistics (especially t-statistics) for the hypothesis that the time trend should not appear do not have standard t-distributions.

Second, deterministic trends did not solve the spurious regression problem, even leaving aside the difficulty involved in deciding whether or not they should be present in the regression model. The reason is that spurious correlation will tend to emerge even with deterministically 'de-trended' random walks.

We will now look at some more precise questions and their answers. The analytical results that we summarize are found in Durlauf and Phillips (1988); Monte Carlo studies of models with time trends present can be found in Said and Dickey (1984) and Schwert (1989). Section 3.5.1 describes the asymptotic theory applicable.

The two questions that we will address are: (i) What problems of inference appear in using time trends? and (ii) Can de-trending yield stationary series and therefore a solution to the problem of spurious regression?

Consider a series $\{y_t\}$ which is generated according to the random walk

$$y_t = y_{t-1} + \varepsilon_t, \qquad \varepsilon_t \sim \text{IID}(0, \sigma^2). \tag{8}$$

An investigator faced with such a series (without, of course, knowing this data-generation process precisely) might decide to attempt to deal with the apparent non-stationarity by de-trending: that is, by including a time trend in a regression equation or by removing the fitted values from a regression on time from the series. The investigator might therefore use the regression model

$$y_t = c + \gamma t + u_t. \tag{9}$$

As Durlauf and Phillips (1988) show, there are once again problems in conducting inference in this environment. When $c = \gamma = 0$, by (8), $\hat{\gamma}$ has a degenerate limiting distribution at 0 (as in a stationary model with a trend), whereas $\hat{c}$ has a divergent distribution; that is, the unscaled parameter estimate $\hat{c}$ has a variance that grows with the sample size. We will deal more rigorously with these limiting distributions later in the chapter.

Moreover, inference concerning γ will be unreliable even though the estimate of that parameter is converging to its true value of zero. While the parameter estimate converges to zero, the t- and F-statistics for the hypothesis H_0: $\gamma = 0$ do not converge to zero, and are in fact asymptotically unbounded with probability 1. (That is, there exists some $\delta > 0$ such that, for ζ representing either of the test statistics, $T^{-\delta}\zeta \rightarrow \infty$ with probability 1.) As in the spurious regression case above, the investigator must look to mis-specification tests—in particular, tests for autocorrelated errors—for a suggestion that there is something wrong with the regression model.

Since the spurious regression problem between integrated series remains with deterministically de-trended series, inclusion of a time trend is not a solution. Consider again the DGP (1)–(2), and an investigator who chooses this time to attempt to 'take account of' the potential non-stationarity in these series by including a time trend in the regression. The model is therefore

$$y_t = c + \beta x_t + \gamma t + u_t. \tag{10}$$

The results from (10) are much as one would expect given those implied by (3) and (9) above (see, again, Durlauf and Phillips 1988). As before, the distribution of $\hat{c}$ diverges and $\hat{\gamma}$ tends in probability to zero, but $\hat{\beta}$ has a non-degenerate distribution asymptotically (i.e. does not converge to zero). Tests for H_0: $\beta = 0$ diverge in distribution, tending to lead the investigator falsely to reject this null hypothesis. Estimation of the regressions in (9) and (10) will produce substantial residual autocorrelation. It might be thought that modelling the autoregressive error using, say, the Cochrane–Orcutt algorithm should remove the unit root and thereby allow valid tests of $\beta = 0$ in (10). Granger and Newbold (1977) present Monte Carlo evidence suggesting that such a strategy is ineffective in practice when based on conventional critical values.

In summary, the problem of falsely concluding that a relationship exists between two unrelated non-stationary series, a problem that persists even as the sample size grows without bound, is not alleviated by an attempt to remove a trend from the underlying series.

In working with non-stationary data, the investigator must be particularly careful. While one solution is to transform the series to achieve stationarity (at the cost of losing some information about long-run behaviour, as we shall see below), it is essential that the investigator be aware of the non-stationarity in the data if procedures for modelling data of this type are to be applied appropriately. As it happens, testing for non-stationarity is also potentially misleading, in that non-standard distributions appear where the data are non-stationary, so that inferential procedures must differ from those applicable when the series are stationary.

Our discussion has therefore led us to two major areas which must be understood when working with potentially non-stationary data. The first is composed of techniques for determining whether or not series are stationary (more generally, the order of integration of a series). Chapter 4 will concentrate on these techniques, which we use to decide whether methods of inference for non-stationary data are necessary to overcome the problems that have been illustrated to this point. Methods that can be used with non-stationary data comprise the second area that we should examine, and form the subject matter of Chapter 6. Moreover, it must be noted that, in spite of the inadequacy of deterministic trends as models for series that are in fact random walks, it remains conceivable that economic time series do actually contain such deterministic components; some of the tests that we consider later will allow for this possibility.

3.3. Some Statistical Features of Integrated Processes

Before we consider testing for integration in time series, we must first define orders of integration and consider some of the properties that integrated series usually display.

> DEFINITION 1.[6] A series with no deterministic component and which has a stationary and invertible autoregressive moving average (ARMA) representation after differencing d times, but which is not stationary after differencing only $d-1$ times, is said to be integrated of order d, denoted $x_t \sim \mathrm{I}(d)$.

The definition can be extended to allow for polynomials in time of the form $\sum_{i=0}^{p} \mu_i t^i$. When $\Delta^d x_t$ contains a polynomial of order p in time, x_t depends on a polynomial of order $p+d$.

The properties of series integrated of strictly positive orders differ substantially from those of I(0) series. Consider a series containing a single unit root:

$$y_t = \rho y_{t-1} + u_t; \qquad y_0 = 0, \qquad u_t \sim \mathrm{I}(0), \tag{11a}$$

[6] This definition is similar to that of Engle and Granger (1987), but rules out some anomalies. Consider the stationary, I(−1), series $z_t = \varepsilon_t - \varepsilon_{t-1}$, where ε_t is I(0). Integrating $\{z_t\}$ gives a series that is I(0); but if we call $\{z_t\}$ itself an I(0) series, then we would expect its integral $\{\varepsilon_t\}$ to be I(1).

or, after integrating,

$$y_t = S_t, \tag{11b}$$

where $S_t \equiv \sum_{i=0}^{t-1}\rho^i u_{t-i}$. If $|\rho| \geq 1$, y_t is non-stationary, and if $\rho = 1$, it is integrated of order 1 (i.e. I(1)) since y_t is then the sum of all previous errors $\{u_j\}$, $j = 1, \ldots, t$. The sequence $\{u_t\}$ need not be an innovation sequence; u_t may itself follow a stationary ARMA(p, q) process, for example. Below we will assume a fairly general set of properties for the $\{u_t\}$ process. First, however, we consider two special cases of (11*a*):

$$y_t = \rho y_{t-1} + u_{1t}; \qquad |\rho| < 1; \qquad u_{1t} \sim \text{IID}(0, \sigma_1^2) \tag{12}$$

and

$$y_t = y_{t-1} + u_{2t}; \qquad y_0 = 0; \qquad u_{2t} \sim \text{IID}(0, \sigma_2^2). \tag{13}$$

In (12), to ensure stationarity, let us assume that y_0 is drawn from the unconditional distribution of y; that is, $y_0 \sim \text{IID}[0, \sigma_1^2/(1 - \rho^2)]$.

It is interesting to compare several properties of these series, viewed as possible DGPs. Table 3.2 summarizes some of the differences between autoregressive series that are stationary, and those containing one (or more) unit roots (which require differencing to be made stationary). The properties in the right-hand column of the table hold for integrated series generally. Nonetheless, the specification (13) is a special one, and in a general treatment we want a less restrictive

TABLE 3.2. Some properties of stationary and integrated processes

	DGP (12) (I(0))	DGP (13) (I(1))
Variance	Finite ($\sigma_1^2(1-\rho^2)^{-1}$)	Unbounded (grows as $t\sigma_2^2$)
Conditional variance	σ_1^2	σ_2^2
Autocorrelation function at lag i	$\rho_i = \rho^i$	$\rho_i = \sqrt{1-(i/t)} \rightarrow 1\ \forall\ i$ as $t \rightarrow \infty$
Expected time between crossings of $y = 0$	Finite	Infinite
Memory[a]	Temporary	Permanent[b]

[a]We say that a series has a permanent memory if the effect of a shock does not disappear as $t \rightarrow \infty$.

[b]In a multivariate context, an integrated process may have some components that do not remain in the series indefinitely. If a series is integrated, there must be at least one component that will have permanent effects, but there may be others with temporary memory. For example, a random walk process plus an unrelated stationary process would yield an integrated process, but memory would be permanent only for the random walk component.

specification which will cover a greater variety of series. We can find one by adopting (11*a*), for example, but the properties of the error term remain to be specified since (11*a*) requires only that it be I(0). We do not, however, wish to adopt the very restrictive specification in (12) and (13), whereby the error is required to be orthogonal to its own past. However some restrictions must be placed on the errors to guarantee non-degenerate limiting distributions for the statistics described below. A weak set of restrictions which suffices for many purposes is given below and is discussed in detail by Phillips (1987*a*); the model (11), supplemented with error terms $\{u_t\}$ required to meet only these conditions, is capable of representing a wide variety of univariate data-generation processes, including those with exogenous variables, as long as the exogenous variables are I(0) and so are capable of being subsumed in $\{u_t\}$ in (11). These conditions are given in (16*a*)–(16*d*) below.

Series that are I(0) have the important property that certain functions of the sample values converge to constants as the number of sample values increases without bound. For example, laws of large numbers (see e.g. White 1984) guarantee the convergence in probability of the sample mean to the true mean of the process for a class of processes that includes stationary time series. Other functions of the sample can have constant probability limits as well; for example, a variance estimator may converge in probability to the true variance of the series. One of the primary facts about integrated processes, however, is that convergence theorems of this type, where convergence is to constants, generally fail to hold, and such convergence theorems as can be derived will involve convergence of sample moments to *random variables*. Analytical results concerning limiting distributions must therefore be based on an extended asymptotic theory.

For a vector time series $\mathbf{x}_t$ with n components, we define $\mathbf{x}_t \sim \mathrm{I}(d)$ if d is the highest order of integration of the individual series: $x_{it} \sim \mathrm{I}(d_i)$ and $d = \max(d_1, d_2, \ldots, d_n)$.

3.4. Asymptotic Theory for Integrated Processes

We will now review and develop some of the asymptotic theory appropriate to integrated random variables. We use the Wiener processes introduced in Chapter 1, so that the properties of estimators and test statistics for I(1) series will be more readily interpretable. Most of our attention will be devoted to the statistical properties of series containing a single unit root (i.e. I(1) processes), extending to the more general I(*d*) class only where necessary.

Begin by considering the following data generation process:

$$y_t = \mu + \rho y_{t-1} + u_t; \qquad \rho = 1,\ y_0 = 0, \qquad t = 1, 2, \ldots, \tag{14}$$

where $\{u_t\}_1^\infty$ is a weakly stationary, mean–zero *innovation* sequence.

After integrating the process in (14),

$$y_t = \mu t + S_t; \qquad S_t = \sum_{i=1}^{t} u_i, \qquad t = 1, 2, \ldots. \tag{15}$$

In general, I(1) series such as y_t are linear functions of time, with a slope of zero where $\mu = 0$. The deviations from this function of time are I(1), being the accumulation of past random shocks: the effects of these shocks do not die out. For example, let $u_t \sim \mathrm{IN}(0, 1)$. Then, for $0 \leqslant \tau \leqslant T$, we have that $E(S_T - S_\tau) = 0$, and

$$E[(S_T - S_\tau)^2] = E\left(\sum_{t=\tau+1}^{T} u_t^2\right) = T - \tau,$$

because $\sum_{t=\tau+1}^{T} u_t^2$ is distributed as χ^2 with $T - \tau$ degrees of freedom. Hence $S_T \sim N(0, T)$, a random walk with independent normally distributed increments.

In general, the formulation in (14) need not assume that the $\{u_t\}$ are white-noise disturbances, but only that they satisfy conditions given in (16) below. To complete the specification of the DGP, we impose these restrictions on $\{u_t\}_1^\infty$. The conditions are strong enough to sustain the derivation of non-degenerate limiting distributions for the statistics to be discussed below and weak enough to be relevant for many economic time series. This set of conditions is defined in detail in Phillips (1987*a*), and can be summarized as follows.

Let $\{u_t\}_1^\infty$ be a stochastic process such that, for $S_T = \sum_{i=1}^{T} u_i$,

- $E(u_t) = 0$ for all t; (16*a*)
- $\sup_t E(|u_t|^\beta) < \infty$ for some $\beta > 2$; (16*b*)
- $\sigma^2 = \lim_{T\to\infty} E(T^{-1} S_T^2)$ exists, and $\sigma^2 > 0$;
- u_t is strongly mixing, with mixing coefficients $\{\alpha_m\}$ such that $\sum_{m=1}^{\infty} \alpha_m^{(1-2/\beta)} < \infty$. (16*c*)
- for stationary $\{u_t\}$, σ^2 can be written as

$$\sigma^2 = \sigma_u^2 + 2\lambda \qquad \text{with } \sigma_u^2 = E(u_1^2) \text{ and } \lambda = \sum_{j=2}^{\infty} E(u_1 u_j). \tag{16d}$$

Each of these conditions relates to an important aspect of the behaviour of the $\{u_t\}$ process. The first, in (16*a*), is the conventional one of having a zero unconditional mean such that all drawings of $\{u_t\}$ have the same mean. Next, (16*b*) is sufficient to ensure the existence of the variance and a higher non-integer moment of $\{u_t\}$ $\forall\, t$. However, it is a weak condition in that $E(|u_t|^\beta)$ is not assumed to be constant, so that heterogeneity is allowed in the error process. Often, third or even fourth moments will be assumed to exist, thereby ensuring that (16*b*) holds: normality, for example, entails that all moments of finite order exist. The third condition is needed to ensure non-degenerate limiting distributions, and either (16*c*) or a closely related condition is required in most central limit theorems to guarantee that information continues to accrue. Finally, we discussed mixing conditions in Chapter 1, and these serve as a useful intermediate assumption which ensures ergodicity yet allows a considerable degree of temporal dependence in the $\{u_t\}$ process. The β in (16*b*) is the same as that in (16*c*): the more heterogeneity that is allowed, the less the possible temporal dependence, and vice versa.

These conditions imply that the process generating the error term in (14) may take any one of a large number of forms. Possible examples include most stationary ARMA models, and ARMAX models where the exogenous variables are I(0). Note that $\sigma^2 = \sigma_u^2$ only if the error term in (14) is IID$(0, \sigma_u^2)$. This restrictive case is of interest in that it is the case for which most limiting distributions have been tabulated; nevertheless, it will not hold in many empirical applications.[7] For example, if u_t is the MA(1) process $u_t = \varepsilon_t - \theta\varepsilon_{t-1}$, then $\sigma_u^2 = \sigma_\varepsilon^2(1 + \theta^2)$, whereas $\sigma^2 = \sigma_\varepsilon^2(1 - 2\theta + \theta^2) = \sigma_\varepsilon^2(1 - \theta)^2$.

As noted above, ordinary probability limits and central limit theorems do not apply in the case of integrated processes I(d), $d \geqslant 1$. In order to derive limiting distributions, it is necessary as in the stationary case to use sequences of random variables, the convergence of which is ensured by appropriate transformations. The evolution of a time-series process dominated by a growing secular component can be suitably smoothed by a choice of horizontal and vertical axes which control for explosivity and curvature, respectively. More precisely, in the I(1) framework, we need to focus on the sequence $\{S_t\}$ which can be transformed such that each element of the sequence lies in the space of real-valued functions on the interval [0, 1] which are right-continuous, and have finite left limits; this space is denoted D(0, 1). The transformation is achieved by substituting a concentrated series for the stochastic component S_t of the original series. In particular, we will map a transformation of S_t onto the Wiener process. The first step, as we saw in Chapter 1, is to map the interval $[0, T]$ onto the fixed interval [0, 1] by dividing the latter into $T + 1$ parts at $0, 1/T, 2/T, \ldots, 1$; next, we construct a new random function on [0, 1] (see Phillips 1987*a*).

A suitable concentrated series is then

$$R_T(r) = \frac{S_{[Tr]}}{\sigma T^{1/2}} = \frac{S_{t-1}}{\sigma T^{1/2}}, \tag{17}$$

[7] The parameter σ^2 has a clear interpretation in the frequency domain: it is equal to $2\pi f_u(0)$, where $f_u(0)$ is the spectral density at frequency zero.

with $(t-1)/T \leqslant r < t/T$ and $t = 1, 2, \ldots, T$, so that $r \in [0, 1]$. Here $[z]$ represents the integer part of any rational number z. In this way we are able to concentrate the original horizontal axis of 1 to T to the closed interval $[0, 1]$, indexing the observations by r. If, for example, $T = 100$, the original observation y_{50} will be indexed by $r \in [0.50, 0.51)$, and so on. The choice of the power of T in the denominator of (17) is such that the series R_T is neither explosive nor converges to zero. Since, for example, when u_t is IID$(0, \sigma_u^2)$, then $\mathrm{var}(S_T) = \sigma_u^2 T$, the standard deviation of S_T will be $O(T^{1/2})$, and this is precisely the power chosen to modify the ordinate axis.

We then have that, as T grows without bound,

$$R_T(r) \Rightarrow \mathrm{W}(r). \tag{18}$$

The symbol $\Rightarrow$ is used here to signify weak convergence of the associated probability measure,[8] while $\mathrm{W}(r)$ is a scalar Wiener process with variance r, also known as a Brownian motion process, which lies in the space $C[0, 1]$ of all real-valued continuous functions on the interval $[0, 1]$. Result (18) is known as *Donsker's theorem*; interested readers are referred to Billingsley (1968) for details and proof.

An extension of the Slutsky theorem in conventional asymptotic theory (see e.g. White 1984) also applies in this framework, in the sense that, if $g(\cdot)$ is any continuous functional on $C[0, 1]$, then $R_T(r) \Rightarrow W(r)$ implies that

$$g[R_T(r)] \Rightarrow g[W(r)]. \tag{19}$$

This result is called the *continuous mapping theorem* (see Billingsley 1968).

The most striking difference between conventional asymptotic theory and this theory appropriate to integrated processes is that, whereas in the former the sample moments converge to constants, in the latter suitably normalized sample functions converge to random variables. Similarly, as a result of the absence of stationarity and ergodicity in the series $\{y_t\}$, traditional central limit theorems are replaced by functional central limit theorems (FCLT).

A useful contrast between this asymptotic theory and that applicable to stationary processes is provided by the distribution of the sample mean considered in Chapter 1. Rewrite (14) as

$$y_t = \rho^t y_0 + \left(\sum_{i=0}^{t-1} \rho^i\right) \mu + \sum_{i=0}^{t-1} \rho^i u_{t-i},$$

and consider the behaviour of the last term for $\rho < 1$ and $\rho = 1$

[8] This concept, used in function spaces, is analogous to convergence in distribution for ordinary random variables. See Hall and Heyde (1980).

respectively. In the former case, this term is I(0) and a straightforward application of a Law of Large Numbers (again see, e.g., White 1984) will show that

$$\operatorname{plim} T^{-1} \sum_{i=0}^{T-1} \rho^i u_{T-i} = 0, \tag{20}$$

since $E(u_{t-i}) = 0$. In the I(1) case, when $\rho = 1$ this last term is given by $S_t = \sum_{i=1}^{t} u_i$, and can be written in terms of the corresponding Wiener process using the standardized sum (see Phillips 1986 and Sect. 1.5.6):[9]

$$T^{-3/2} \sum_{t=1}^{T} S_t = \sigma T^{-1} \sum_{t=1}^{T} [(\sigma T^{1/2})^{-1} S_{t-1}] + T^{-3/2} \sum_{t=1}^{T} u_t$$
$$\Rightarrow \sigma \int_0^1 W(r)\,\mathrm{d}r. \tag{21}$$

Similarly:

$$T^{-2} \sum_{t=1}^{T} S_t^2 \Rightarrow \sigma^2 \int_0^1 [W(r)]^2 \mathrm{d}r. \tag{22}$$

Since

$$\sum_{t=1}^{T} S_t^2 = \sum_{t=1}^{T} (S_{t-1} + u_t)^2 = \sum_{t=1}^{T} S_{t-1}^2 + \sum_{t=1}^{T} u_t^2 + 2\sum_{t=1}^{T} S_{t-1} u_t,$$
$$\sum_{t=1}^{T} S_{t-1} u_t = \tfrac{1}{2}\left[\sum_{t=1}^{T} S_t^2 - \sum_{t=1}^{T} S_{t-1}^2 - \sum_{t=1}^{T} u_t^2\right] = \tfrac{1}{2}\left[S_T^2 - \sum_{t=1}^{T} u_t^2\right].$$

Thus:

$$T^{-1} \sum_{t=1}^{T} S_{t-1} u_t \Rightarrow (\sigma^2/2)[W(1)^2 - \sigma_u^2/\sigma^2] \equiv (\sigma^2/2)[W(1)^2 - 1] + \lambda, \tag{23}$$

where $\lambda = (\sigma^2 - \sigma_u^2)/2$, because $T^{-1} S_T^2 \Rightarrow \sigma^2 W(1)^2$. Finally:

$$T^{-5/2} \sum_{t=1}^{T} t S_t \Rightarrow \sigma \int_0^1 r W(r)\,\mathrm{d}r. \tag{24}$$

Note the difference between the orders of magnitude of these limiting distributions and the conventional stationary distributions: i.e. $O_p(T^{3/2})$ in (21) instead of $O_p(T)$, $O_p(T^2)$ in (22) instead of $O_p(T)$, $O_p(T)$ in (23) instead of $O_p(T^{1/2})$, and $O_p(T^{5/2})$ in (24) instead of $O_p(T^{3/2})$. These differences are behind a number of unconventional features of the distributions of test statistics for hypotheses involving integrated series.

[9] $T^{-3/2} \sum_{t=1}^{T} u_t$ is $o_p(1)$ since $T^{-1} \sum_{t=1}^{T} u_t \xrightarrow{\mathrm{p}} E(u_t)$, given the restrictions embodied in (16).

Many of the functionals to which these sample moments converge can be expressed in terms of normal densities. Table 3.3 provides a set of distributional results for a number of these functionals for IID errors with unit variance. Section 1.5.6 and the appendix to Chapter 1 provide examples of the method of proof of these results by showing that the sample moment in example 1 of Table 3.3 converges to both the functional $\int_0^1 W(r)\mathrm{d}r$ and the density N(0, 1/3), implying that the functional must have this density (also see Phillips 1987*a*, *b*, and Chan and Wei 1988).

3.5. Using Wiener Distribution Theory

We now present two examples of the application of the asymptotic distribution theory for integrated processes to help understand regression with non-stationary data. Recall that results on sums of powers of trend terms are summarized in Section 1.5.5 above, and that the relationships among sample moments, functionals of Wiener processes, and densities from the normal family are summarized in Table 3.3.

TABLE 3.3. Convergence results for normalized sample moments[a]

Functional	Density	Sample moment[b]
1: $\int_0^1 W(r)\,\mathrm{d}r$	N(0, 1/3)	$T^{-1/2}\bar{y}$
2: $\int_0^1 r\,\mathrm{d}W(r)$	N(0, 1/3)	$T^{-3/2}\sum_{t=1}^{T} tu_t$
3: $W(1)$	N(0, 1)	$y_T/\sqrt{T}$
4: $\int_0^1 W(r)\,\mathrm{d}W(r)$	$(1/2)(\chi^2(1) - 1)$	$T^{-1}\sum_{t=1}^{T} y_{t-1}u_t$
5: $\left[\int_0^1 W(r)^2\,\mathrm{d}r\right]^{-1/2}\int_0^1 W(r)\,\mathrm{d}V(r)$	N(0, 1)	—
6: $\int_0^1 (r-a)W(r)\,\mathrm{d}r$	N(0, $\mathcal{V}$), where $\mathcal{V} = (1/60)\cdot(8 - 25a + 20a^2)$	$T^{-5/2}\sum_{t=1}^{T} ty_t\ (a = 0)$

[a] In example 5, $V(r)$ is another Wiener process independent of $W(r)$. Note that a special case of example 6, which we will use later, is $a = 0$, which yields a density of N(0, 2/15).

[b] These are examples of sample moments which converge to the corresponding functionals in the first column for $y_0 = \mu = 0$ and $\sigma_u^2 = 1$.

3.5.1. Example: Spurious De-trending (Durlauf and Phillips 1988)

Let $\{y_t\}_1^\infty$ be generated as in (14) above; then

$$y_t = \mu t + S_t. \tag{25}$$

Consider the model

$$y_t = c + \gamma t + e_t. \tag{26}$$

This is a model which fails to take account of the presence of the stochastic trend in the data series and thereby attempts to de-trend spuriously.

The OLS estimator of c in (26) is

$$\hat{c} = d^{-1}\left[\left(\sum_{t=1}^{T} t^2\right)\left(\sum_{t=1}^{T} y_t\right) - \left(\sum_{t=1}^{T} ty_t\right)\left(\sum_{t=1}^{T} t\right)\right], \tag{27}$$

where $d = T\sum_{t=1}^{T} t^2 - (\sum_{t=1}^{T} t)^2$.

Substituting (25) into (27) and rearranging, we obtain

$$T^{-1/2}\hat{c} =$$

$$(T^{-4}d)^{-1}\left[T^{-3}\left(\sum_{t=1}^{T} t^2\right)\left(T^{-3/2}\sum_{t=1}^{T} S_t\right) - T^{-2}\left(\sum_{t=1}^{T} t\right)\left(T^{-5/2}\sum_{t=1}^{T} tS_t\right)\right]. \tag{28}$$

However, by (21);

$$T^{-3/2}\sum_1^T S_t \Rightarrow \sigma_u \int_0^1 W(r)\,\mathrm{d}r$$

by (24);

$$T^{-5/2}\sum_1^T tS_t \Rightarrow \sigma_u \int_0^1 rW(r)\,\mathrm{d}r$$

also;

$$T^{-3}\sum_1^T t^2 \rightarrow 1/3;\ T^{-2}\sum_1^T t \rightarrow 1/2;$$

and $T^{-4}d \rightarrow 1/12$ (see Section 1.5.5). Thus,

$$\begin{aligned} T^{-1/2}\hat{c} &\Rightarrow 12\left[(1/3)\sigma_u \int_0^1 W(r)\,\mathrm{d}r - (1/2)\sigma_u \int_0^1 rW(r)\,\mathrm{d}r\right] \\ &= 4\sigma_u \int_0^1 W(r)\,\mathrm{d}r - 6\sigma_u \int_0^1 rW(r)\,\mathrm{d}r \\ &= -6\sigma_u \int_0^1 (r - 2/3)W(r)\,\mathrm{d}r. \end{aligned}$$

The density of this functional can be found from example 6 in Table 3.3, by substituting $a = 2/3$; it reduces to $\mathrm{N}(0, 2\sigma_u^2/15)$. Note in particular that $\hat{c}$ has a divergent limiting distribution.

Similarly, the OLS estimate of γ in (26) is

$$\hat{\gamma} = d^{-1}\left[T\sum_{t=1}^{T} ty_t - \left(\sum_{t=1}^{T} t\right)\left(\sum_{t=1}^{T} y_t\right)\right].$$

Using (25) and rearranging yields

$$(\hat{\gamma} - \mu) = d^{-1}\left[T\sum_{t=1}^{T} tS_t - \left(\sum_{t=1}^{T} t\right)\left(\sum_{t=1}^{T} S_t\right)\right].$$

Further,

$$T^{1/2}(\hat{\gamma} - \mu) = (T^{-4}d)^{-1}\left[T^{-5/2}\sum_{t=1}^{T} tS_t - T^{-2}\left(\sum_{t=1}^{T} t\right)\left(T^{-3/2}\sum_{t=1}^{T} S_t\right)\right].$$

It then follows, from the limiting results given above, that

$$T^{1/2}(\hat{\gamma} - \mu) \Rightarrow 12\sigma_u\left[\int_0^1 rW(r)\mathrm{d}r - (1/2)\int_0^1 W(r)\,\mathrm{d}r\right] \tag{29}$$

$$= 12\sigma_u \int_0^1 (r - 1/2)W(r)\,\mathrm{d}r = \mathrm{N}(0, 6\sigma_u^2/5),$$

where the last equality follows from setting $a = 1/2$ in example 6 of Table 3.3. Using similar techniques, Durlauf and Phillips (1988) show that $T^{-1/2}t_{\hat{\gamma}}$, $T^{-1/2}t_{\hat{c}}$, $T^{-1}\hat{\sigma}_u^2$, R^2, and $T\cdot\mathrm{DW}$ have functionals of Wiener processes as their asymptotic distributions.[10] Since the estimated coefficient on the trend converges to μ, as suggested by (29), and as the distribution of its t-statistic is divergent, interpreting the results at face value will lead the investigator to suppose that the trend is an important determinant of the series $\{y_t\}$. In fact, the series would be better modelled with a stochastic trend as in (25), which would lead to a stationary residual series.

3.5.2. Example: Spurious Regression (see Phillips 1986)

Let $\{y_t\}_1^\infty$ and $\{x_t\}_1^\infty$ be generated as pure random walks:

$$y_t = y_{t-1} + u_t$$

$$x_t = x_{t-1} + \varepsilon_t$$

$$u_t \sim \mathrm{IID}(0, \sigma_u^2), \qquad \varepsilon_t \sim \mathrm{IID}(0, \sigma_\varepsilon^2), \qquad \text{and } E(u_t\varepsilon_s) = 0 \ \ \forall\ t, s.$$

The spurious regression model is

$$y_t = c + \beta x_t + e_t. \tag{30}$$

In order to derive the asymptotic distributions of the estimators and test statistics for (30), it is convenient to define $W_u(r)$ and $W_\varepsilon(r)$ as the independent Wiener processes on $C[0, 1]$ obtained from cumulating the $\{u_t\}_1^\infty$ and $\{\varepsilon_t\}_1^\infty$ series, respectively. Let $\bar{x}$ and $\bar{y}$ be the sample means of the $\{x_t\}$ and $\{y_t\}$ series. Then

[10] R is the multiple correlation coefficient of the estimated model, and DW is the Durbin–Watson statistic computed from the $\hat{u}_t$.

$$\hat{\beta} = \left[\sum_{t=1}^{T} y_t(x_t - \bar{x})\right]\left[\sum_{t=1}^{T} (x_t - \bar{x})^2\right]^{-1}$$
$$= \left[T^{-2}\sum_{t=1}^{T} y_t x_t - T^{-1}\bar{y}\bar{x}\right]\left[T^{-2}\sum_{t=1}^{T} (x_t - \bar{x})^2\right]^{-1}$$
$$= \left[T^{-2}\sum_{t=1}^{T} y_t x_t - T^{-1/2}\bar{y}(T^{-1/2}\bar{x})\right]\left[T^{-2}\sum_{t=1}^{T} x_t^2 - T^{-1}\bar{x}^2\right]^{-1}. \quad (31)$$

From (21),

$$T^{-1/2}\bar{y} \Rightarrow \sigma_u \int_0^1 W_u(r)\,dr, \quad (32)$$

$$T^{-1/2}\bar{x} \Rightarrow \sigma_\varepsilon \int_0^1 W_\varepsilon(r)\,dr. \quad (33)$$

From (22),

$$T^{-2}\sum_{t=1}^{T} x_t^2 \Rightarrow \sigma_\varepsilon^2 \int_0^1 W_\varepsilon(r)^2\,dr. \quad (34)$$

It may also be shown, using the same method of proof, that

$$T^{-2}\sum_{t=1}^{T} y_t x_t \Rightarrow \sigma_u\sigma_\varepsilon \int_0^1 W_u(r)W_\varepsilon(r)\,dr. \quad (35)$$

Substituting (32)–(35) into (31), it follows that

$$\hat{\beta} \Rightarrow \frac{\sigma_u\sigma_\varepsilon^{-1}\left[\int_0^1 W_u(r)W_\varepsilon(r)\,dr - \int_0^1 W_u(r)\,dr\int_0^1 W_\varepsilon(r)\,dr\right]}{\left\{\int_0^1 W_\varepsilon(r)^2\,dr - \left[\int_0^1 W_\varepsilon(r)\,dr\right]^2\right\}}$$
$$\equiv \sigma_u\sigma_\varepsilon^{-1}\zeta. \quad (36)$$

Also,

$$T^{-1/2}\hat{c} = T^{-3/2}\sum_{1}^{T} y_t - \hat{\beta}T^{-3/2}\sum_{1}^{T} x_t. \quad (37)$$

From (21) and (36),

$$T^{-1/2}\hat{c} \Rightarrow \sigma_u\left[\int_0^1 W_u(r)\,dr - \zeta\int_0^1 W_\varepsilon(r)\,dr\right]. \quad (38)$$

The spurious regression problem becomes clear upon inspection of (36). The true value of the derivative of y_t with respect to x_t is zero because the errors generating the $\{x_t\}$ and $\{y_t\}$ series in the regression (30) are independent. Yet $\hat{\beta}$ fails to converge in probability to zero and instead has a non-degenerate distribution.

Using similar techniques, Phillips (1986) shows that $T^{-1/2}t_\beta$ has a non-degenerate distribution, or in other words that the t-statistic for $\hat{\beta}$ has a divergent distribution. Hence as $T \to \infty$, the probability of a significant t-value arising in a regression such as (30) approaches 1, leading to spurious inferences about the existence of a relationship between y_t and x_t (see Banerjee and Hendry 1992, for an exposition).

3.6. Near-integrated Processes

In later chapters we will deal with variables that are 'borderline-' or 'near-'integrated. By this we mean that the process generating the variables has a root close to but not on the unit circle. Phillips (1987*b*) presents asymptotic results for 'unit-root' and 'near-unit-root' processes within a unified framework to explain the special properties of regressions estimated using borderline-stationary variables and we follow his approach.

Consider the AR(1) model

$$y_t = \rho y_{t-1} + u_t, \tag{39}$$

where $u_t \sim \mathrm{IN}(0, \sigma^2)$. When $|\rho| < 1$ and $y_0 \sim \mathrm{N}[0, \sigma^2(1-\rho^2)^{-1}]$, $\{y_t\}$ is a stationary process. When $\rho = 1$ and $y_0 = 0$, it is I(1) and non-stationary. Apparently, therefore, there is a discontinuity at $\rho = 1$ where stationarity disappears, and the constant unconditional variance $(\sigma^2(1-\rho^2)^{-1})$ becomes a trend $(t\sigma^2)$.

In fact, if $y_0 = 0$ in (39) and $|\rho| < 1$ but is close to unity, say $\rho = 1 + \varepsilon$ with $\varepsilon < 0$ for small ε, then

$$E(y_t) = 0$$

and

$$\begin{aligned} \operatorname{var}(y_t) &= \sigma^2[1 + (1+\varepsilon)^2 + \ldots + (1+\varepsilon)^{2(t-1)}] \\ &= \sigma^2 t[1 + \varepsilon(t-1)] \qquad \text{to } O(\varepsilon). \end{aligned}$$

Thus, the variance acts like a trend for finite t when terms of $O(\varepsilon^2)$ or smaller are negligible, and there is really no discontinuity in practical terms: for sufficiently small ε and finite t, the process behaves like an I(1) process even though it is asymptotically stationary. Paraphrasing, in finite samples, for ε close to zero, a better approximation is to treat the process as I(1) than as I(0), even though asymptotically, the expansion for the variance above approaches a finite limit not dependent upon t.

A more convenient parameterization of nearly integrated processes is given by writing $\rho = \exp(\varepsilon/T)$, for $\varepsilon < 0$. This parameterization defines a sequence of local alternatives to $\rho = 1$ for the process. When $\varepsilon = 0$,

$\rho = 1$, while ρ is less than but close to unity for small $\varepsilon < 0$ and as $T \rightarrow \infty$, $\rho \rightarrow 1$. A process with such a value of ρ is called 'near-integrated' because for small negative ε it behaves rather like an I(1) process.[11]

There are three advantages to considering near-integrated time series. The first is the link they provide between conventional asymptotic distribution theory and the Wiener theory described above, stressing the continuity of the breakdown in stationarity as a root approaches unity. The sketch of the relevant theory provided below reinforces this consideration. The second advantage is that the resulting theory may be empirically more relevant than that deriving from the assumption of an exact unit root. It is too early to reach a final judgement on that issue, but the algebra below suggests that very similar finite-sample behaviour would be observed in unit-root and near-integrated processes.

The final advantage, and the real reason for our interest, is that near-integration is needed when examining the power functions of unit-root tests against stationary local alternatives. Phillips (1988) emphasizes this role, and Johansen (1991*a*) and Haldrup and Hylleberg (1991) present applications to deriving power functions. We describe and draw upon some of their results in the next chapter when discussing testing for a unit root.

Reconsider (39) with $\rho = \exp(\varepsilon/T)$, $y_0 = 0$, and with the $\{u_t\}_1^\infty$ sequence satisfying the set of conditions given by (16*a*)–(16*d*). In order to derive the limiting distribution of $\hat{\rho}$, the OLS estimator of ρ, under H_0, it is convenient to define the functional $K_\varepsilon(r)$:

$$K_\varepsilon(r) = W(r) + \varepsilon \int_0^r \exp[\varepsilon(r - s)]W(s)\,\mathrm{d}s.$$

$K_\varepsilon(r)$ is also known as an *Ornstein–Uhlenbeck* process and, for fixed r, is distributed normally with mean zero and variance $(1/2)\varepsilon^{-1}[\exp(2r\varepsilon) - 1]$.[12] $K_\varepsilon(r)$ is a first-order diffusion process and is closely related to $W(r)$. (See e.g. Grimmet and Stirzaker (1982) for details.) It is like an error-correction process, having been generated by the stochastic differential equation

$$\mathrm{d}K_\varepsilon(s) = \varepsilon K_\varepsilon(s) + \mathrm{d}W(s).$$

Using arguments analogous to those employed earlier in this chapter to derive distributions for unit root processes, Phillips (1987*b*) proves the following asymptotic results for (39) when $\rho = \exp(\varepsilon/T)$:[13]

[11] See Chan and Wei (1988) and Phillips (1987*b*).

[12] Note that $\lim_{\varepsilon \rightarrow 0}(\varepsilon^{-1}/2)[\exp(2r\varepsilon) - 1] = r$ (using L'Hôpital's rule). This is as expected because, as $\varepsilon \rightarrow 0$, $K_\varepsilon(r) \rightarrow \mathrm{W}(r)$, and for fixed r, $\mathrm{W}(r) \sim \mathrm{N}(0, r)$. Alternatively, use a Taylor series expansion to give $\exp(2r\varepsilon) = 1 + 2r\varepsilon + O(\varepsilon^2)$ and the result follows.

[13] The definitions of $S_{[Tr]}$, S_t, λ, and σ^2 are given in equations (14)–(23).

$$\frac{S_{[Tr]}}{\sigma T^{1/2}} \Rightarrow K_{\varepsilon}(r); \tag{40}$$

$$T^{-2} \sum_{t=1}^{T} S_t^2 \Rightarrow \sigma^2 \int_0^1 [K_{\varepsilon}(r)]^2 \, dr; \tag{41}$$

$$T^{-1} \sum_{t=1}^{T} S_{t-1}u_t \Rightarrow (\sigma^2/2)[K_{\varepsilon}(1)^2 - 1] - \varepsilon \int_0^1 [K_{\varepsilon}(r)]^2 \, dr + \lambda. \tag{42}$$

For example, to demonstrate (40), construct step-processes given by

$$T^{-1/2} y_{[Tr]} = \sum_{j=1}^{[Tr]} \exp[\varepsilon T^{-1}([Tr] - j)] \, u_j \qquad \text{for } r \in [0, 1]$$

and then show that

$$T^{-1/2} y_{[Tr]} = T^{-1/2} S_{[Tr]} \Rightarrow \sigma K_{\varepsilon}(r).$$

Using the power-series expansion for $\exp(\varepsilon/T)$,

$$\rho = 1 + \varepsilon/T + O(T^{-2}). \tag{43}$$

Now, from (39),

$$T(\hat{\rho} - \rho) = \left(T^{-2} \sum_{t=1}^{T} y_{t-1}^2\right)\left(T^{-1} \sum_{t=1}^{T} y_{t-1}u_t\right).$$

Thus, from (43),

$$T(\hat{\rho} - 1) = \varepsilon + O(T^{-1}) + \left(T^{-2} \sum_{t=1}^{T} y_{t-1}^2\right)\left(T^{-1} \sum_{t=1}^{T} y_{t-1}u_t\right). \tag{44}$$

Finally, using (41) and (42) in (44),

$$T(\hat{\rho} - 1) \Rightarrow \varepsilon + [(1/2)\{K_{\varepsilon}(1)^2 - 1\} - \varepsilon\sigma^{-2} \int_0^1 (K_{\varepsilon}(r))^2 \, dr + \lambda/\sigma^2] \left[\int_0^1 (K_{\varepsilon}(r))^2 \, dr\right]^{-1}. \tag{45}$$

When the non-centrality parameter ε is set to zero, $K_{\varepsilon}(r) \equiv W(r)$ and the Dickey–Fuller distribution is recovered as a special case of (45). Using the Dickey–Fuller distribution as a benchmark, it can also be seen from (45) that the effects of near-integration are revealed in a shift in location (given by ε) and a change in shape of the limiting distribution of $\hat{\rho}$: $\hat{\rho}$ converges to 1 (which is the null value of ρ as $T \to \infty$) at rate T^{-1}. This is the usual Dickey–Fuller rate of convergence: see Chapter 4.

Results in Banerjee and Dolado (1987) and Banerjee, Dolado, and

Galbraith (1990*a*) show that some of the important distributional features for the near-integrated case (for example, the lower-tail critical values) can be recovered from the Dickey–Fuller tables simply by shifting the Dickey–Fuller distribution by fixed numbers. These results suggest that, even in fairly large samples, the non-centrality parameter in (45) is the most important determinant of the shape of the distribution of $\hat{\rho}$. The more subtle distributional features, which involve changes in shape and are given by the second part of (45), become relevant only asymptotically.

4

Testing for a Unit Root

This chapter describes methods of testing for a unit root in an observed series. Both parametric regression tests and non-parametric adjustments to these test statistics are considered, and we give the tables of critical values necessary for the application of commonly used tests. We also use functionals of Wiener processes to describe the asymptotic distributions of important test statistics.

Since an I(1) series becomes stationary upon being differenced once, it must contain one unit root. For example, if we take a random walk as the DGP, then we can immediately derive that its first difference is stationary. If by contrast the underlying data-generating process is

$$y_t = \rho_1 y_{t-1} + u_{1t},$$

where $|\rho_1| > 1$, then we have

$$y_t - y_{t-1} \equiv \Delta y_t = (\rho_1 - 1)y_{t-1} + u_{1t}. \tag{1}$$

From (1) it is clear that Δy_t is no longer stationary: it depends not only upon the stationary process u_{1t}, but also upon the non-stationary process y_{t-1} (since $\rho_1 - 1 > 0$). Hence an AR(1) process with a coefficient of 1 is I(1), but the same process with a coefficient of 1.01 is not, since differencing will not reduce this process to stationarity.

Many economic time series may contain an exact unit root if we consider logarithmic transformations of the form routinely applied to economic time series. Otherwise, roots very close to, but slightly greater than, unity imply non-stationary series that are not I(d) for any d. Roots slightly less than unity generate near-integrated series. Such processes will tend to be difficult to distinguish from those with roots of exactly unity on moderately sized samples; such processes are discussed in Chapter 3. Roots substantially greater than unity, by contrast, will be easily detected as the explosive character of the series will be clear with even fairly small samples.

Consider the simplest data-generation process within which we can discuss tests for unit roots:

$$y_t = \rho y_{t-1} + u_t; \qquad u_t \sim \text{IID}(0, \sigma_u^2); \tag{2}$$

$$y_0 = 0.$$

If one were testing the true hypothesis $H_0: \rho = \rho_0$ for $|\rho_0| < 1$, the test would be easily performed. Running the regression (2), the t-statistic $(\hat{\rho} - \rho_0)/\mathrm{SE}(\hat{\rho})$ has, asymptotically, a standard normal distribution and can be compared with tables of significance points for $N(0, 1)$. In small samples the statistic is approximately t-distributed, although the coefficient estimate $\hat{\rho}$ is biased downward slightly.

For $\rho_0 = 1$, however, this result no longer holds. The distribution of the test statistic just given is not asymptotically normal, or even symmetric. Tables of critical values have been tabulated by D. A. Dickey and are reported in, e.g. Fuller (1976). It is instructive to examine these in detail, and they are recorded as Tables 4.1 and 4.2.

The critical values in Fuller's tables pertain to each of three different models: it is important to note at the outset that, as in many other instances, the distributions of test statistics obtained depend not only on the data-generation process, but also on the model with which we investigate it. For the time being, we will consider three possible models:

$$y_t = \rho_a y_{t-1} + u_t, \tag{3a}$$

$$y_t = \mu_b + \rho_b y_{t-1} + u_t, \tag{3b}$$

$$y_t = \mu_c + \gamma_c t + \rho_c y_{t-1} + u_t. \tag{3c}$$

The null hypothesis is that $\rho_i = 1$ for $i = a, b, c$. The applicability of each model depends on what is known about the DGP, since we want to construct similar tests (that is, tests for which the distribution of the test statistic under the null hypothesis is independent of nuisance parameters in the DGP). If a test is not similar, then the appropriate critical values may depend upon unknown nuisance parameters (e.g. a constant), which will invalidate standard inferences. We will return to the similarity of tests below. For the moment, we will follow much of the literature on the topic in assuming that (2) is the DGP, in which case the issue does not arise since (2) contains no nuisance parameters.

Another formulation of the DGP deals with a potential difficulty that arises from (2) concerning the status of the nuisance parameters under the alternative $H_1: \rho < 1$. Reconsider (2) when there is an intercept ϕ:

$$\Delta y_t = \phi + (\rho - 1) y_{t-1} + \varepsilon_t \quad \text{where } \varepsilon_t \sim \mathrm{IID}(0, \sigma_\varepsilon^2) \text{ for } t = 1, \ldots, T.$$

When $H_0: \rho = 1$ is true, y_t is a random walk with drift ϕ, and hence it has a trend for $\phi \neq 0$. When H_0 is false, y_t is stationary (at least asymptotically) around a constant mean of $\phi/(1 - \rho)$, but has no trend. This is a rather asymmetric treatment and, if the data do have a trend, does not do justice to the alternative. Adding a trend to the model compensates, but induces a quadratic trend under the null.

A simple solution was proposed by Bhargava (1986) as follows. Write the DGP as

$$y_t = \phi + u_t \qquad \text{where } u_t = \rho u_{t-1} + \varepsilon_t,$$

which is a common factor model (see Sargan 1980, and Hendry and Mizon 1978). Then

$$\Delta y_t = \phi(1 - \rho) + (\rho - 1)y_{t-1} + \varepsilon_t.$$

Now, for $H_0: \rho = 1$, y_t is a random walk with no drift, whereas when $\rho < 1$ it is stationary around a non-zero mean. Similarly, if γt is added to the process,

$$y_t = \phi + \gamma t + u_t \qquad \text{where } u_t = \rho u_{t-1} + \varepsilon_t,$$

so that

$$\Delta y_t = [\phi(1 - \rho) + \gamma\rho] + \gamma(1 - \rho)t + (\rho - 1)y_{t-1} + \varepsilon_t.$$

When $H_0: \rho = 1$ holds, $\Delta y_t = \gamma + \varepsilon_t$. Thus, a trend at rate $\gamma(1 - \rho)$ is present under the alternative, and drift at rate γ under the null. Bhargava develops several tests based on this formulation. More recently, Schmidt and Phillips (1992) have also investigated the properties and powers of tests of $H_0: \rho = 1$ using this approach and find them preferable, although the power functions cross those of corresponding Dickey–Fuller tests. In practice, unfortunately, the powers of available unit-root tests are low for alternatives different from, but close to, the null of unity.

In interpreting Table 4.1, note that, if the sign of an entry in the table is negative for a given size, say α (where α is the probability of a smaller value), then at least a fraction α of estimates of ρ are less than 1; for models (3*b*) and (3*c*), negative entries persist up to $\alpha = 0.95$ and $\alpha = 0.99$ respectively in large samples. Although it is not explicit in this table, entries even for model (3*a*) are negative at $\alpha = 0.50$. For all of these models, then, most estimates of ρ are less than 1; for the latter two, the overwhelming majority are less than 1. This holds in spite of the fact that the true value is 1: errors are far from symmetric around zero.

Generally, $\hat{\rho}$ is a downwardly biased estimator of ρ; this is true for any of the three models chosen. A test conducted by the method that would typically be used for stationary processes—that is, a test based upon the usual t- or asymptotic normal distribution applied to the t-statistic $(\hat{\rho} - 1)/\mathrm{SE}(\hat{\rho})$, at conventional critical values—therefore seems likely to give misleading results. This can be confirmed by examining Table 4.2, again taken from Fuller (1976) and originally constructed by Monte Carlo simulation.

TABLE 4.1. Empirical cumulative distribution of $T(\hat{\rho} - 1)$
DGP: (2) with $\rho = 1$

Sample size (T)	Probability of a smaller value[a]							
	0.01	0.025	0.05	0.10	0.90	0.95	0.975	0.99
(*a*) Model (3*a*)/(8*a*)								
25	−11.9	−9.3	−7.3	−5.3	1.01	1.40	1.79	2.28
50	−12.9	−9.9	−7.7	−5.5	0.97	1.35	1.70	2.16
100	−13.3	−10.2	−7.9	−5.6	0.95	1.31	1.65	2.09
250	−13.6	−10.3	−8.0	−5.7	0.93	1.28	1.62	2.04
500	−13.7	−10.4	−8.0	−5.7	0.93	1.28	1.61	2.04
∞	−13.8	−10.5	−8.1	−5.7	0.93	1.28	1.60	2.03
(*b*) Model (3*b*)/(8*b*)								
25	−17.2	−14.6	−12.5	−10.2	−0.76	0.01	0.65	1.40
50	−18.9	−15.7	−13.3	−10.7	−0.81	−0.07	0.53	1.22
100	−19.8	−16.3	−13.7	−11.0	−0.83	−0.10	0.47	1.14
250	−20.3	−16.6	−14.0	−11.2	−0.84	−0.12	0.43	1.09
500	−20.5	−16.8	−14.0	−11.2	−0.84	−0.13	0.42	1.06
∞	−20.7	−16.9	−14.1	−11.3	−0.85	−0.13	0.41	1.04
(*c*) Model (3*c*)/(8*c*)								
25	−22.5	−19.9	−17.9	−15.6	−3.66	−2.51	−1.53	−0.43
50	−25.7	−22.4	−19.8	−16.8	−3.71	−2.60	−1.66	−0.65
100	−27.4	−23.6	−20.7	−17.5	−3.74	−2.62	−1.73	−0.75
250	−28.4	−24.4	−21.3	−18.0	−3.75	−2.64	−1.78	−0.82
500	−28.9	−24.8	−21.5	−18.1	−3.76	−2.65	−1.78	−0.84
∞	−29.5	−25.1	−21.8	−18.3	−3.77	−2.66	−1.79	−0.87

[a] e.g., for model (3*a*) with $T = 100$, Pr $[T(\hat{\rho} - 1) < 1.65] = 0.975$. All entries in the left half of the table have standard errors less than 0.15; those in the right half, less than 0.03.

Source: Fuller (1976: 371).

This table gives the cumulative distribution of the t-statistic for H_0: $\rho = 1$ in each of the models (3*a*)–(3*c*). It is especially interesting to compare the results for each of these models with those we would obtain with a stationary process; because the t-statistic would asymptotically be distributed $N(0, 1)$ in that case, the statistics would be distributed as indicated in the last line of the table.

For model (3*a*), we see that the results approximate this outcome reasonably closely if we add (very roughly) 0.3 to each entry in part (*a*) of the table; that is, the entire distribution of the t-statistic is shifted to more negative values, by approximately this amount.

TABLE 4.2. Empirical cumulative distribution of $(\hat{\rho} - 1)/\mathrm{SE}(\hat{\rho})$
DGP: (2) with $\rho = 1$

Sample size (T)	Probability of a smaller value							
	0.01	0.025	0.05	0.10	0.90	0.95	0.975	0.99
(*a*) Model (3*a*)/(8*a*)								
25	−2.66	−2.26	−1.95	−1.60	0.92	1.33	1.70	2.16
50	−2.62	−2.25	−1.95	−1.61	0.91	1.31	1.66	2.08
100	−2.60	−2.24	−1.95	−1.61	0.90	1.29	1.64	2.03
250	−2.58	−2.23	−1.95	−1.62	0.89	1.29	1.63	2.01
500	−2.58	−2.23	−1.95	−1.62	0.89	1.28	1.62	2.00
∞	−2.58	−2.23	−1.95	−1.62	0.89	1.28	1.62	2.00
(*b*) Model (3*b*)/(8*b*)								
25	−3.75	−3.33	−3.00	−2.63	−0.37	0.00	0.34	0.72
50	−3.58	−3.22	−2.93	−2.60	−0.40	−0.03	0.29	0.66
100	−3.51	−3.17	−2.89	−2.58	−0.42	−0.05	0.26	0.63
250	−3.46	−3.14	−2.88	−2.57	−0.42	−0.06	0.24	0.62
500	−3.44	−3.13	−2.87	−2.57	−0.43	−0.07	0.24	0.61
∞	−3.43	−3.12	−2.86	−2.57	−0.44	−0.07	0.23	0.60
(*c*) Model (3*c*)/(8*c*)								
25	−4.38	−3.95	−3.60	−3.24	−1.14	−0.80	−0.50	−0.15
50	−4.15	−3.80	−3.50	−3.18	−1.19	−0.87	−0.58	−0.24
100	−4.04	−3.73	−3.45	−3.15	−1.22	−0.90	−0.62	−0.28
250	−3.99	−3.69	−3.43	−3.13	−1.23	−0.92	−0.64	−0.31
500	−3.98	−3.68	−3.42	−3.13	−1.24	−0.93	−0.65	−0.32
∞	−3.96	−3.66	−3.41	−3.12	−1.25	−0.94	−0.66	−0.33
N(0, 1)								
∞	−2.33	−1.96	−1.65	−1.28	1.28	1.65	1.96	2.33

Source: Fuller (1976: 373).

In models (3*b*) and (3*c*), we see greater deviations from the N(0, 1) pattern above that would hold asymptotically for $|\rho| < 1$. As a constant and then the trend are added to a model, we see more entries that are negative in the tables (parts (*b*) and (*c*)); as in Table 4.1, a greater proportion of estimated $\hat{\rho}$s become negative.

With the information in Table 4.2, however, we can now consider applying a test for $\rho = 1$ using the *t*-statistic from any of the three models. As long as we are aware that the distribution of the statistic is non-standard, and so avoid making the mistake of applying *t*- or normal tables, these significance points tabulated by Dickey and Fuller can be used in their place to provide a valid test. For example, consider model

(3*b*). A t-statistic of $+1.00$ would not lead to rejection of the null against an explosive alternative if we were applying $N(0, 1)$ tables; by Table 4.2*b*, however, the test rejects at the 5 per cent level (or even the 1 per cent level) because the probability of the statistic exceeding even 0.60 is only 0.01. By contrast, a value of -2.50, which would lead to rejection of H_0 using standard normal tables, can no longer be used to infer that H_0 $(\rho = 1)$ is false against a stationary alternative at the 5% level.

This was the first form of 'unit-root test' to have been developed. Its main potential disadvantage lies in the fact that it is based upon the assumption that the data-generation process (2) holds precisely under the null. Many series will be integrated of order 1 but will not have this form; in particular, the DGP may contain nuisance parameters such as a constant or other exogenous variables, or may contain richer dynamics in the variable of interest. As an example of the latter, consider a general AR(p) process in y_t:

$$\alpha(L)y_t = u_t,$$

with $\alpha(L) = (1 - L)\alpha^*(L)$, and where all latent roots of $\alpha^*(L)$ lie within the unit circle. Such a process is I(1), and, depending upon the form of the polynomial, $\alpha^*(L)$ may be well approximated by (2) with $\rho = 1$. To the extent that it is not, however, the critical values in Tables 4.1 and 4.2 may be inaccurate. We will consider several methods of dealing with this in Sections 4.2 and 4.3. First, however, we will consider the possibility of additional exogenous regressors in the DGP, and the problem of constructing similar tests under these conditions.

4.1. Similar Tests and Exogenous Regressors in the DGP

Kiviet and Phillips (1992) consider exact and similar tests for the coefficient on a lagged dependent variable, in a first-order autoregressive model that may include multiple exogenous variables. In order to compute the exact critical values for such tests, these authors use numerical integration based on the Imhof routine. (See Imhof (1961) or Koerts and Abrahamse (1969) for an introduction.) While this procedure can be used to construct exact and similar tests for a DGP with first-order dynamics and also containing arbitrary strictly exogenous processes, the Dickey–Fuller tests already discussed will be similar tests for some DGPs.

Evans and Savin (1981, 1984), Nankervis and Savin (1985, 1987), and Bhargava (1986), as well as Kiviet and Phillips, all consider the properties of Dickey–Fuller tests for various DGPs. Some of the results may be summarized as follows ($\mu \neq 0$; $\gamma \neq 0$).

	DGP	Models yielding similar tests[1]
(i)	$y_t = \rho y_{t-1} + u_t,\ y_0 = 0$	(3*a*), (3*b*), (3*c*)
(ii)	$y_t = \rho y_{t-1} + u_t$, arbitrary y_0	(3*b*), (3*c*)
(iii)	$y_t = \mu + \rho y_{t-1} + u_t$, arbitrary y_0	(3*c*)
(iv)	$y_t = \mu + \gamma t + \rho y_{t-1} + u_t$, arbitrary y_0	Extension of (3*c*) necessary

Thus, for example, in case (i), if the model is given by (3*c*), the appropriate critical values are given by Tables 4.1(*c*) and 4.2(*c*). The same tables can be used to conduct inference in (iii), despite a non-zero value of μ in the DGP, because (3*c*) yields a similar test. Similarity implies that the distributions of $\hat{\rho}$ and its associated *t*-statistic are not affected by the value, under the null, of the nuisance parameter, and the critical values are the same as the ones that would apply for $\mu = 0$, namely, those in Tables 4.1(*c*) and 4.2(*c*).

There are a number of noteworthy additional points. In case (i) there are no nuisance parameters, so that similarity is a trivial property. In general, as this summary suggests, a similar test having a Dickey–Fuller distribution requires that the model used contain *more* parameters than the DGP. In order to have a similar test for (iv), one would then need a model with a term such as t^2, necessitating another block of critical values in each of Tables 4.1 and 4.2. In case (ii), for example, we need at least model (3*b*) (with a constant) to allow for the unknown starting value. In case (iii) we have an unknown constant and need the trend term in model (3*c*) to allow for its effect.

Each of these similar tests is also exact in finite samples, provided appropriate critical values are available. In general, however, it will be necessary to abandon exact tests in order to use variants of the Dickey–Fuller test where there are more unknown parameters. These parameters can typically be estimated, so that asymptotically they can be accounted for and a test provided. Again, Kiviet and Phillips offer general exact and similar tests for DGPs where the dynamics are restricted to first-order, as well as demonstrating the similarity of the tests just mentioned.

In the case of exact parameterizations, such as case (iii) with model (3*b*), we do not have similar tests with the Dickey–Fuller distributions. However, as West (1988) showed, the *t*-statistics in the exactly parameterized case (with exogenous items such as a constant in the DGP) are asymptotically normal, just as are *t*-statistics used for standard problems. In finite samples, however, the Dickey–Fuller distributions may be a better approximation than the normal distribution. We will explore this asymptotic normality further in Chapter 6 below.

[1] Critical values are those corresponding to the model used in Table 4.1 or 4.2.

4.2. General Dynamic Models for the Process of Interest

The first of the methods for allowing richer dynamics in the DGP of the process of interest, $\{y_t\}$, was developed concurrently with the test that we have already described for a unit root in the AR(1) model, and is reported in Fuller (1976). These more general methods yield test statistics that have the same *limiting* distributions as those already discussed, because they are based on consistent estimates of 'nuisance' parameters. Hence we may use the last rows of Tables 4.1(a)–(c) or 4.2(a)–(c) for inference with these statistics in large samples, but in small samples percentage points of their distributions will not in general be the same as for those applicable under the strong assumptions of the simple Dickey–Fuller model.

When y_t follows an AR(p) process,

$$y_t = \sum_{i=1}^{p} \rho_i y_{t-i} + \varepsilon_t, \tag{4}$$

a test can be constructed with the regression model:

$$y_t = \rho y_{t-1} + \sum_{i=1}^{p-1} \gamma_i \, \Delta y_{t-i} + u_t. \tag{5}$$

The coefficient ρ is used to test for a unit root, and $T(\hat{\rho} - 1)$ and $(\hat{\rho} - 1)/\mathrm{SE}(\hat{\rho})$ have the limiting distributions tabulated in Tables 4.1(a) and 4.2(a) for $T \rightarrow \infty$. Moreover, just as in the case of an AR(1) process, we can extend this regression model to allow for the possibility that the data-generation process contains a constant (drift) term or a deterministic time trend. Again, for suitably modified regression models, the asymptotic distributions of the statistics based on $\hat{\rho}$ are those given in Tables 4.1(b)/(c) and 4.2(b)/(c) for $T \rightarrow \infty$. These procedures are called 'augmented' Dickey–Fuller (ADF) tests.

The aim in modifications such as these to the simpler form of the Dickey–Fuller test is to use lagged changes in the dependent variable to capture autocorrelated omitted variables which would otherwise, by default, appear in the (necessarily autocorrelated) error term. With the additional lagged terms it will be possible, if the DGP has the form of (4), to produce a model (5) in which asymptotically the error terms are white noise, because the nuisance parameters are known asymptotically and the terms involving them may be removed from the error term. With white-noise errors, the asymptotic Monte Carlo critical values given in the first two tables may be applied. Moreover, the asymptotic distribution of the coefficient on the y_{t-1} term in (5) is not affected by the inclusion of the additional Δy_{t-i} terms. If y_t is I(1), the differenced terms are all I(0) and appropriate scaling ensures that the variance–covariance matrix is asymptotically block-diagonal. (That is, all cross-product terms of I(0) and I(1) variables in the matrix are asymptotically negligible.) It is this asymptotic *orthogonality* that drives the result, much as, in a standard regression model, one uses the orthogonality of the information matrix to prove the statistical independence of the estimated coefficient vector from the estimate of the standard error. The asymptotic theory and the issue of 'appropriate' scaling are discussed later in this chapter and in Chapter 6.

By allowing the DGP to take the form (4) rather than the much more restrictive AR(1) form (3), we have expanded the class of models to which we can validly apply unit-root tests of this type. Note that, as it will generally be the case that p is unknown even where y_t is strictly an AR(p) process, it is generally safer to take p to be a fairly generous number; if too many lags are present in (5), the regression is free to set them to zero at the cost of some loss in efficiency, whereas too few lags implies some remaining autocorrelation in (5) and hence the inapplicability of even the asymptotic distributions in Tables 4.1 and 4.2. One can, of course, perform tests for autocorrelation on the estimated residuals from (5) in order to check the acceptability of the premise that these residuals are white noise. Alternatively, model selection procedures can be used to choose p, and test for a unit root, jointly (see Hall 1990).

We have, therefore, a class of tests for the unit root which can validly be applied to series that follow AR(p) processes containing no more than one unit root. The next natural step is to attempt to extend further the class of series to which we can apply such tests, ideally in such a way as to allow exogenous variables to enter the process as well. Said and Dickey (1984) provide a test procedure valid for a general ARMA process in the errors; Phillips (1987*a*) and Perron and Phillips (1988) offer a still more general procedure.

While the Said–Dickey approach does represent a generalization of the Dickey–Fuller procedure, it again yields test statistics with the same asymptotic critical values as those tabulated by Dickey and Fuller. The particular advantage of this test is that we can apply it not only to models with MA parts in the errors, but also to models for which (as is typically the case) the orders of the AR and MA polynomials in the error process are unknown. The method involves approximating the true process by an autoregression in which the number of lags increases with sample size.

Begin by assuming that the data-generation process follows:

$$y_t = \rho y_{t-1} + u_t,$$

$$u_t + \sum_{i=1}^{p} \alpha_i u_{t-i} = e_t + \sum_{j=1}^{q} \theta_j e_{t-j}, \qquad e_t \sim \mathrm{IID}(0, \sigma_e^2),$$

so that the error term in the autoregression follows an ARMA(p, q), presumed to be stationary and invertible. The DGP can be rewritten as

$$\Delta y_t = (\rho - 1)y_{t-1} + \sum_{i=1}^{k} \alpha_i \Delta y_{t-i} + v_t, \tag{6}$$

where k is large enough to allow a good approximation to the ARMA(p, q) process $\{u_t\}$, so that $\{v_t\}$ is approximately white noise. The null hypothesis is again that $\rho = 1$. Said and Dickey show that the test is valid in spite of the facts that p and q are unknown and that the ARMA(p, q) is approximated by an AR process, as long as k increases with the sample size T so that there exist numbers c and r, $c > 0$ and $r > 0$, such that $ck > T^{1/r}$ and $T^{-1/3}k \to 0$. Hence $T^{1/3}$ is an upper bound on the rate at which the number of lags, k, should be made to grow with the sample size. Ordinary least-squares estimation of the model (6) is proven to yield a consistent estimator of $(\rho - 1)$; the test can then be based on the t-type statistic, $(\hat{\rho} - 1)/\text{SE}(\hat{\rho})$, using Table 4.2($a$). Clearly, the form of the regression implied by the Said–Dickey test is precisely the same as that of the augmented Dickey–Fuller test.

In this case Table 4.2(a), corresponding to a model containing no drift or trend, is used, but the test can also be adapted to allow for a non-zero drift term μ in the model. The test is modified only in so far as it is then based not on y_t but on $y_t - \bar{y}$, where $\bar{y} \equiv T^{-1}\sum_{t=1}^{T} y_t$. The regression model (6) remains the same except for the first regressor, which becomes $(y_{t-1} - \bar{y})$, and test statistics are calculated in the same way. By analogy to the earlier results for Dickey–Fuller and augmented Dickey–Fuller tests, it is not surprising that we now refer to Table 4.2(b), corresponding to a model containing a drift term, for the significance points of the (asymptotic) distributions of the statistics.

Monte Carlo studies of test power in models with autocorrelated error processes, described by Dickey *et al.* (1986), suggest that the empirical levels of the $T(\hat{\rho} - 1)$ statistics tend to be farther from the nominal test levels than those of the t-type statistics. Dickey *et al.* therefore suggest the use of the t-type statistics in these cases. Deviation of nominal from actual test levels is particularly great in DGPs with MA parts such that the MA lag polynomial contains a factor of $(1 - \theta L)$, with θ near unity. The near-cancellation of such a factor with the factor $(1 - L)$ in the AR lag polynomial (under the null) affects the actual levels of both $T(\hat{\rho} - 1)$ and t-type statistics, but is especially serious for the former.

4.3. Non-parametric Tests for a Unit Root

In extending the original tests above to allow for higher-order autocorrelation, we added extra terms to the regression model to account for the autocorrelation in the residuals that would otherwise be present. By extending the model, it was possible to continue to draw valid inferences from the asymptotic critical values given in Tables 4.1 and 4.2; otherwise it would have been necessary to recompute these critical values for each different DGP, which in turn would require knowledge of the unobservable orders (p) of the processes in these underlying DGPs.

In expanding the set of models to which we can apply these tests, our aim is to avoid increasing the number of tables of critical values that we must find and use while nonetheless allowing for quite general DGPs. Phillips (1987*a*) provides an alternative procedure that largely allows us to do so; our exposition relies on further results reported in Perron (1988) and Phillips and Perron (1988). Rather than taking account of extra elements in the DGP by adding them to the regression model, Phillips suggests accounting for the autocorrelation that will be present (when these terms are omitted) through a non-parametric correction to the standard statistics. That is, while the Dickey–Fuller procedure aims to retain the validity of tests based on white-noise errors in the regression model by ensuring that those errors are indeed white noise, the Phillips procedure acts instead to modify the statistics after estimation in order to take into account the effect that autocorrelated errors will have on the results. Asymptotically, the statistic is corrected by the appropriate amount, and so the same limiting distributions apply. From one perspective, the effect is the same as that of ADF-type tests: we can validly conduct asymptotic inference using Tables 4.1 and 4.2. This procedure does not, however, require the estimation of additional parameters in the regression model.

The data-generation process that is assumed to hold is

$$y_t = \mu + y_{t-1} + u_t \tag{7a}$$

or equivalently

$$y_t = y_0 + \mu t + \sum_{i=1}^{t} u_i. \tag{7b}$$

It is important to note, however, that the error term is not being assumed to follow a white-noise process. The conditions that u_t must satisfy in (7*a*) and (7*b*) are those listed above in Chapter 3 as conditions (3.16*a*)–(3.16*d*) given in Phillips (1987*a*).

As with the Dickey–Fuller tests, tests of the Phillips type are based upon one of three different regression models, differing only in one case from those used earlier, by centring the trend term:

$$y_t = \rho_a y_{t-1} + u_{at} \tag{8a}$$

$$y_t = \mu_b + \rho_b y_{t-1} + u_{bt} \tag{8b}$$

and

$$y_t = \mu_c + \gamma_c(t - T/2) + \rho_c y_{t-1} + u_{ct}. \tag{8c}$$

It is easy to calculate from these regressions the coefficient estimates and the 't-statistics' for each. For tests of the significance of ρ_i, the statistics are then adjusted to reflect autocorrelation in the corresponding u_{it} series. (We will omit subscripts a, b, or c on u_t to simplify notation.) If we define

$$S_t = \sum_{j=1}^{t} u_j, \tag{9}$$

and

$$\sigma^2 = \lim_{T\to\infty} E(T^{-1} S_T^2) \tag{10a}$$

$$\sigma_u^2 = \lim_{T\to\infty} T^{-1} \sum_{t=1}^{T} E(u_t^2), \tag{10b}$$

then the limiting distributions of the test statistics do not depend upon the parameters of the process determining the sequence $\{u_t\}$ if $\sigma^2 = \sigma_u^2$. In the case of tests statistics of the Dickey–Fuller (DF) type that we examined earlier, the model is presumed to capture the relevant features of the process in such a way that the errors are independently and identically distributed; the latter is sufficient to guarantee that $\sigma^2 = \sigma_u^2$. Note that the statistics used in the DF-type parametric tests do emerge as special cases of the non-parametric statistics where the estimates of the parameters σ^2 and σ_u^2 are equal (i.e. where the estimates S_u^2 and $S_{T\ell}^2$, given in (11) and (12) below, are equal).

We will see this more clearly when we examine the non-parametric statistics. In order to do so, we first need consistent estimators of σ^2 and σ_u^2. There are a number of possible choices. If $\mu = 0$ in the DGP (7), then the standard estimator from any of (8a), (8b), (8c) will be consistent for σ_u^2; that is,

$$S_u^2 = T^{-1} \sum_{t=1}^{T} \hat{u}_t^2, \tag{11}$$

where $\hat{u}_t$ represents the residuals from one of (8a), (8b), (8c), above. If $\mu \neq 0$, the estimator is not consistent using the residuals $\{\hat{u}_{at}\}$, but residuals from either of the other two models do yield a consistent estimate.

For the estimator of σ^2, a consistent estimator can be found at the cost of strengthening the assumptions. First, condition (3.16b) is replaced with the condition that $\sup_t E(|u_t|^{2\beta}) < \infty$ for some $\beta > 2$. Next, a condition must be placed on the lag truncation parameter ℓ which will be used in defining the estimator of σ^2. The condition is that $\ell \to \infty$ as $T \to \infty$, such that ℓ is $o(T^{1/4})$. That is, the number of lags used in estimating autocorrelations of the residuals increases with the sample size, but less quickly than its fourth root.

Given these conditions, a consistent estimator of σ^2 is

$$S_{T\ell}^2 = T^{-1}\sum_{t=1}^{T}\hat{u}_t^2 + 2T^{-1}\sum_{j=1}^{\ell}\sum_{t=j+1}^{T}\hat{u}_t\,\hat{u}_{t-j}. \tag{12}$$

The estimator is indexed by the lag truncation parameter ℓ to indicate that different choices of ℓ will lead to different values. It remains only to specify the residuals to be used in (12), and, as in (11) above, we may choose them from any of (8*a*), (8*b*), (8*c*) if $\mu = 0$. Also as in (11), $\mu \neq 0$ requires that we use the residuals from one of the models that does contain a constant term in order to preserve the consistency of this variance estimate. Evidently the safe strategy is to take residual estimates from (8*b*) or (8*c*) in any case where there seems even a small probability that the data-generation process contains a constant (drift) term.

It is important to note that both of the variance estimates S_u^2 and $S_{T\ell}^2$ could be defined using the first differences $y_t - y_{t-1}$ rather than the residuals $\hat{u}_t$. Under the null hypothesis that $\rho = 1$ and that the drift and trend terms are zero, the two will of course be equivalent asymptotically. In finite samples, which of the two methods is used can make a substantial difference, however; we will return to this point below.

While $S_{T\ell}^2$ just defined is consistent for σ^2 given residuals from the appropriate model, it unfortunately does not guarantee a non-negative estimate for finite sample sizes. However, one can guarantee a non-negative estimate with a simple modification of (12) pioneered by Newey and West (1987), which is moreover consistent under precisely the same conditions as is (12). Define

$$\tilde{S}_{T\ell}^2 = T^{-1}\sum_{t=1}^{T}\hat{u}_t^2 + 2T^{-1}\sum_{j=1}^{\ell}\omega_\ell(j)\sum_{t=j+1}^{T}\hat{u}_t\,\hat{u}_{t-j}, \tag{13}$$

where $\omega_\ell(j) = 1 - j(\ell+1)^{-1}$. A few examples of tests using these quantities to transform the test statistics can be presented without further discussion. Thereafter we will present statistics for hypotheses on μ_b, μ_c, and γ_c in (8*b*) and (8*c*), and for hypotheses involving ρ as well as these parameters.

Consider the hypothesis that $\rho_b = 1$ (in (8*b*)).[2] An asymptotically valid test consists of the statistic[3]

$$Z(\hat{\rho}_b) = T(\hat{\rho}_b - 1) - \tfrac{1}{2}(S_{T\ell}^2 - S_u^2)\left[T^{-2}\sum_{t=2}^{T}(y_{t-1} - \bar{y}_{-1})^2\right]^{-1}, \tag{14}$$

[2] We treat the initial observation as fixed at zero; not all statistics here are invariant to the initial value. See Phillips (1987*a*) and Perron (1988).

[3] These statistics are valid for either choice of $S_{T\ell}^2$ given above (i.e. the Phillips or Newey–West forms).

or, alternatively,

$$Z(t(\hat{\rho}_b)) = (S_u/S_{T\ell})t(\hat{\rho}_b) - \tfrac{1}{2}(S_{T\ell}^2 - S_u^2)\left\{S_{T\ell}\left[T^{-2}\sum_{t=2}^{T}(y_{t-1} - \bar{y}_{-1})^2\right]^{1/2}\right\}^{-1}, \quad (15)$$

where $t(\hat{\rho}_b)$ is the t-statistic associated with testing the null hypothesis $\rho_b = 1$. The first of these statistics, $Z(\hat{\rho}_b)$, has under the null hypothesis (H_0: $\rho_b = 1$) the limiting distribution given in Table 4.1(b) ($T \to \infty$); the second has the limiting distribution given in Table 4.2(b) ($T \to \infty$) under the same null. It is especially useful to note again here the fact that the original Dickey–Fuller statistics are special cases of these. Under Dickey and Fuller's assumptions, the $\{u_{bt}\}_{t=1}^{T}$ are independently and identically distributed, implying, as we noted above, that $\sigma_u^2 = \sigma^2$ and therefore that $E(S_{T\ell}^2) = E(S_u^2)$. Hence on average $S_{T\ell}^2 = S_u^2$, and $Z(\hat{\rho}_b)$ reduces to $T(\hat{\rho}_b - 1)$. This is precisely the first of the statistics that Dickey and Fuller examine. Moreover, $Z(t(\hat{\rho}_b))$ reduces to $t(\hat{\rho}_b)$, the ordinary regression t-statistic, and has the distribution given in Table 4.2.

The corresponding statistics for models (8a) and (8c) are also given in Perron (1988), and share this property. For (8a), the test statistics are similar to (14) and (15). They are (with $y_0 \equiv 0$)

$$Z(\hat{\rho}_a) = T(\hat{\rho}_a - 1) - \tfrac{1}{2}(S_{T\ell}^2 - S_u^2)\left(T^{-2}\sum_{t=2}^{T} y_{t-1}^2\right)^{-1} \quad (16)$$

and

$$Z(t(\hat{\rho}_a)) = (S_u/S_{T\ell})t(\hat{\rho}_a) - \tfrac{1}{2}(S_{T\ell}^2 - S_u^2)\left[S_{T\ell}\left(T^{-2}\sum_{t=2}^{T} y_{t-1}^2\right)^{1/2}\right]^{-1}. \quad (17)$$

Analogous to the tests on (8a), (16) has the significance points given in Table 4.1(a) and (17) those in Table 4.2(a). Finally, for model (8c), we have

$$Z(\hat{\rho}_c) = T(\hat{\rho}_c - 1) - (T^6/24)(D_x^{-1})(S_{T\ell}^2 - S_u^2), \quad (18)$$

and

$$Z(t(\hat{\rho}_c)) = (S_u/S_{T\ell})t(\hat{\rho}_c) - [T^3/(4\sqrt{3})](D_x^{-1/2}S_{T\ell}^{-1})(S_{T\ell}^2 - S_u^2), \quad (19)$$

having the limiting distributions tabulated in Tables 4.1(c) and 4.2(c) respectively. The quantity D_x is defined as the determinant of the inner product of the data matrix with itself: for (8c),

$$D_x = [T^2(T^2 - 1)/12]\sum_{t=2}^{T} y_{t-1}^2 - T\left(\sum_{t=2}^{T} ty_{t-1}\right)^2 + T(T+1)\sum_{t=2}^{T} ty_{t-1}\sum_{t=2}^{T} y_{t-1} - [T(T+1)(2T+1)/6]\left(\sum_{t=2}^{T} y_{t-1}\right)^2,$$

where, again, summations are over all available elements of the vectors.

In addition to the extension of the Phillips (1987*a*) results to the case of regression models containing constant and trend, Phillips and Perron (1988) present simulation evidence regarding the power of the Phillips-type procedures *vis-à-vis* that of the Said–Dickey procedure, each being applicable to processes that have general ARMA(p, q) processes in the errors from a regression model that consists of a constant and lagged dependent variable. The data-generation process is taken to be

$$y_t = \rho y_{t-1} + u_t,$$
$$u_t = \varepsilon_t + \theta\varepsilon_{t-1}, \qquad \varepsilon_t \sim \text{IID}(0, \sigma_\varepsilon^2); \qquad y_0 = 0.$$

To characterize the results roughly, the Phillips or Phillips–Perron test generally has higher power, but suffers substantial size distortions for $\theta < 0$, in samples of sizes typically found in economics. The Said–Dickey test also involves size distortions for $\theta < 0$, but much smaller ones: that is, each test rejects a true null of $\rho = 1$ more than the nominal size (5 per cent in these experiments) states, but the problem is much worse for the $Z(\hat{\rho})$ and $Z(t(\hat{\rho}))$ statistics of Phillips and Perron, where rejections of the true null range as high as 99.7 per cent for $\theta = -0.8$. (Size and power also depend upon the number of lags chosen in the Said–Dickey test and on the lag truncation parameter in the Phillips–Perron tests.) For the Said–Dickey test, the largest size distortions (with two lags, a true null is rejected approximately 67.7 per cent of the time at a nominal size of 5 per cent) disappear as the number of lags used increases, falling to only 12 per cent where 12 lags are used.

This simulation study is of course a limited one, dealing as it does with only one ARMA process for the equation errors. It does however suggest that the Phillips-type tests are more likely to reject the null of a unit root, *whether or not* it is false; for errors with strong negative MA components, the difference is quite large. One might suspect as well that the power of the Said–Dickey procedure would be higher for processes involving AR errors, because the test regression captures AR terms precisely.

Phillips and Perron conclude by recommending their own $Z(\hat{\rho})$ test for models with positive MA or IID errors, and the Said–Dickey statistic for models with negative MA errors.

4.4. Tests on More than One Parameter

The tests above have all been directed at testing the level autoregressive parameter alone. In models (8*b*) and (8*c*), however, there are other parameters present, and one may be interested in a formal test of the hypothesis that one of these is zero, or in a joint test. Tests similar to those above can be provided, but a further set of tables must be used to find the significance points of the distributions of the resulting test statistics. Tables 4.4 and 4.5 below are based on those given by Dickey and Fuller (1981), who provide likelihood ratio, t-type, and F-type statistics for tests on the parameters μ_b, μ_c, and γ_c in (8b) and (8c). The tables are again derived from a Monte Carlo simulation.

The statistics that Dickey and Fuller offer are derived under the assumption that u_{bt} and u_{ct} are white-noise processes, but they show that, as was the case with tests above, the same distributions can be applied where the errors follow an autoregressive process and a correctly specified model is used to estimate the parameters of this process. As we noted earlier, however, it is desirable to generalize the tests to be applicable to as broad as possible a class of error processes, of unknown form. This can be done, once again, using a non-parametric correction.

Table 4.3 summarizes the t-type, F-type, and non-parametric test statistics used for several null hypotheses involving the parameters μ and γ. In addition to the quantities defined above, we require

$$S_0^2 = (T-1)^{-1}\sum_{t=2}^{T}(y_t - y_{t-1})^2;$$

$$\bar{y}_0 = (T-1)^{-1}\sum_{t=2}^{T} y_t; \qquad \bar{y}_1 = (T-1)^{-1}\sum_{t=2}^{T} y_{t-1};$$

$$G_x = \left[T^{-6}D_x + (1/12)\left(T^{-3/2}\sum_{t=2}^{T} y_{t-1}\right)^2\right]^{1/2}.$$

The Phillips–Perron corrections to the standard Dickey–Fuller statistics must however be used cautiously. Again, the accumulated evidence of several Monte Carlo simulation studies suggests that the non-parametrically corrected test statistics do not always have the correct sizes even in fairly large samples.

Schwert (1989) makes this point forcefully. His results, amplifying those in the Phillips–Perron simulations reported earlier, show that the critical values of the augmented Dickey–Fuller test statistics, given by the standard Dickey–Fuller tables, are much more robust to the presence of moving average terms in the errors of the random-walk process than are the corresponding non-parametrically adjusted Dickey–Fuller statistics. An example, taken from Schwert, is sufficient to illustrate the point.

The data-generation process is given by[4] $y_t = y_{t-1} + u_t + \theta u_{t-1}$,

[4] For conformity with the notation of Phillips–Perron used earlier, the sign of the coefficient on θ is changed here.

TABLE 4.3(a). Test statistics for simple hypotheses in models with drift and trend[a]

Statistic type	Test Statistic
Model (8b): Null hypothesis: $\mu_b = 0$	
t-type	$\tau_1 = \hat{\mu}_b/\mathrm{SE}(\hat{\mu}_b) = \hat{\mu}_b(c_{11(b)}S_u^2)^{-1/2}$
Non-parametric	$Z(\tau_1) = (S_u/S_{T\ell})\tau_1 + (2S_{T\ell})^{-1}(S_{T\ell}^2 - S_u^2)\left[T^{-2}\sum_{t=2}^{T}(y_{t-1} - \bar{y}_{-1})^2\right]^{-1/2}\left(T^{-2}\sum_{t=2}^{T}y_{t-1}^2\right)^{-1/2}\left(T^{-3/2}\sum_{t=2}^{T}y_{t-1}\right)$
Model (8c): Null hypothesis: $\mu_c = 0$	
t-type	$\tau_2 = \hat{\mu}_c/\mathrm{SE}(\hat{\mu}_c) = \hat{\mu}_c(c_{11(c)}S_u^2)^{-1/2}$
Non-parametric	$Z(\tau_2) = (S_u/S_{T\ell})\tau_2 + T^3(24D_x^{1/2}G_xS_{T\ell})^{-1}(S_{T\ell}^2 - S_u^2)\left(T^{-3/2}\sum_{t=2}^{T}y_{t-1}\right)$
Model (8c): Null hypothesis: $\gamma_c = 0$	
t-type	$\tau_3 = \hat{\gamma}_c/\mathrm{SE}(\hat{\gamma}_c) = \hat{\gamma}_c(c_{22(c)}S_u^2)^{-1/2}$
Non-parametric	$Z(\tau_3) = (S_u/S_{T\ell})\tau_3 - \left\{T^3(2D_x^{1/2}S_{T\ell})^{-1}(S_{T\ell}^2 - S_u^2)\left[T^{-2}\sum_{t=2}^{T}(y_{t-1} - \bar{y}_{-1})^2\right]^{-1/2}\right\}$ $\times\left\{(1/2)[T^{-3/2} + T^{-5/2}]\sum_{t=2}^{T}y_{t-1} - T^{-5/2}\sum_{t=2}^{T}ty_{t-1}\right\}$

[a] Critical values for $Z(\tau_1)$, $Z(\tau_2)$, and $Z(\tau_3)$ are the same as those for τ_1, τ_2, and τ_3 respectively and are tabulated in Table 4.4. Note also that S_u^2 and $S_{T\ell}^2$ are defined with respect to the residuals of a particular model, and so differ across models (8a), (8b), and (8c). $c_{ii}(j)$ is the ith diagonal element of the inverse second-moment matrix of the regressors in model j.

Sources: Dickey and Fuller (1981) and Perron (1988).

TABLE 4.3(b). Test statistics for joint hypotheses[a]

Statistic type	Test statistic
Model (8b): Null hypothesis: $\mu_b = 0$ and $\rho_b = 1$.	
F-type	$\Phi_1 = (2S_u^2)^{-1}[(T-1)S_0^2 - (T-3)S_u^2]$
Non-parametric	$Z(\Phi_1) = (S_u^2/S_{T\ell}^2)\Phi_1 - (2S_{T\ell}^2)^{-1}(S_{T\ell}^2 - S_u^2)\left\{T(\hat{\rho}_b - 1) - (1/4)(S_{T\ell}^2 - S_u^2)\left[T^{-2}\sum_{t=2}^{T}(y_{t-1} - \bar{y}_{-1})^2\right]^{-1}\right\}$
Model (8c): Null hypothesis: $\mu_c = 0,\ \gamma_c = 0,\ \rho_c = 1$.	
F-type	$\Phi_2 = (3S_u^2)^{-1}[(T-1)S_0^2 - (T-4)S_u^2]$
Non-parametric	$Z(\Phi_2) = (S_u^2/S_{T\ell}^2)\Phi_2 - (3S_{T\ell}^2)^{-1}(S_{T\ell}^2 - S_u^2)[T(\hat{\rho}_c - 1) - T^6(48D_x)^{-1}(S_{T\ell}^2 - S_u^2)]$
Model (8c): Null hypothesis: $\gamma_c = 0,\ \rho_c = 1$.	
F-type	$\Phi_3 = (2S_u^2)^{-1}\{(T-1)[S_0^2 - (\bar{y}_0 - \bar{y}_1)^2] - (T-4)S_u^2\}$
Non-parametric	$Z(\Phi_3) = (S_u^2/S_{T\ell}^2)\Phi_3 - (2S_{T\ell}^2)^{-1}(S_{T\ell}^2 - S_u^2)[T(\hat{\rho}_c - 1) - T^6(48D_x)^{-1}(S_{T\ell}^2 - S_u^2)]$

[a] Critical values for $Z(\Phi_1)$, $Z(\Phi_2)$, and $Z(\Phi_3)$ are the same as those for Φ_1, Φ_2, and Φ_3 respectively and are tabulated in Table 4.5. Note also that S_u^2 and $S_{T\ell}^2$ are defined with respect to the residuals of a particular model, and so differ across models (8a), (8b), and (8c).

Sources: Dickey and Fuller (1981) and Perron (1988).

($t = -19, \ldots, T$), where the $\{u_t\}$ process is a normally distributed white-noise process. The first 20 observations are discarded to control for the effect of the initial conditions. Samples of size $T = 25$, 50, 100, 250, 500, and 1000 are used in the experiments and each experiment is replicated 10,000 times. The MA parameter θ is set equal to 0.8, 0.5, 0, -0.5, and -0.8. The model estimated is

$$y_t = \mu_b + \rho_b y_{t-1} + u_t, \qquad t = 1, \ldots, T.$$

Six different test statistics are considered, including the ordinary and augmented Dickey–Fuller statistics and the Phillips–Perron statistics. Both the augmented Dickey–Fuller and the Phillips–Perron statistics are

TABLE 4.4. Empirical cumulative distributions
DGP: (8*a*) with $\rho = 1$

Sample size (T)	Probability of a smaller value[a]			
	0.90	0.95	0.975	0.99
(*a*) Test statistic τ_1; model (8*b*)				
25	2.20	2.61	2.97	3.41
50	2.18	2.56	2.89	3.28
100	2.17	2.54	2.86	3.22
250	2.16	2.53	2.84	3.19
500	2.16	2.52	2.83	3.18
∞	2.16	2.52	2.83	3.18
(*b*) Test statistic τ_2; model (8*c*)				
25	2.77	3.20	3.59	4.05
50	2.75	3.14	3.47	3.87
100	2.73	3.11	3.42	3.78
250	2.73	3.09	3.39	3.74
500	2.72	3.08	3.38	3.72
∞	2.72	3.08	3.38	3.71
(*c*) Test statistic τ_3; model (8*c*)				
25	2.39	2.85	3.25	3.74
50	2.38	2.81	3.18	3.60
100	2.38	2.79	3.14	3.53
250	2.38	2.79	3.12	3.49
500	2.38	2.78	3.11	3.48
∞	2.38	2.78	3.11	3.46

[a] All entries in the table have standard errors of less than 0.01. Distributions are symmetric.

Source: Dickey and Fuller (1981: 1062).

TABLE 4.5. Empirical cumulative distributions

Sample size (T)	Probability of a smaller value[a]							
	0.01	0.025	0.05	0.10	0.90	0.95	0.975	0.99
(a) Test statistic Φ_1; DGP: (8b) with $\rho_b = 1$, $\mu_b = 0$; model (8b)								
25	0.29	0.38	0.49	0.65	4.12	5.18	6.30	7.88
50	0.29	0.39	0.50	0.66	3.94	4.86	5.80	7.06
100	0.29	0.39	0.50	0.67	3.86	4.71	5.57	6.70
250	0.30	0.39	0.51	0.67	3.81	4.63	5.45	6.52
500	0.30	0.39	0.51	0.67	3.79	4.61	5.41	6.47
∞	0.30	0.40	0.51	0.67	3.78	4.59	5.38	6.43
(b) Test statistic Φ_2; DGP: (8c) with $\rho_c = 1$, $\mu_c = 0$, $\gamma_c = 0$; model (8c)								
25	0.61	0.75	0.89	1.10	4.67	5.68	6.75	8.21
50	0.62	0.77	0.91	1.12	4.31	5.13	5.94	7.02
100	0.63	0.77	0.92	1.12	4.16	4.88	5.59	6.50
250	0.63	0.77	0.92	1.13	4.07	4.75	5.40	6.22
500	0.63	0.77	0.92	1.13	4.05	4.71	5.35	6.15
∞	0.63	0.77	0.92	1.13	4.03	4.68	5.31	6.09
(c) Test statistic Φ_3; DGP: (8c) with $\rho_c = 1$, $\gamma_c = 0$; model (8c)								
25	0.74	0.90	1.08	1.33	5.91	7.24	8.65	10.61
50	0.76	0.93	1.11	1.37	5.61	6.73	7.81	9.31
100	0.76	0.94	1.12	1.38	5.47	6.49	7.44	8.73
250	0.76	0.94	1.13	1.39	5.39	6.34	7.25	8.43
500	0.76	0.94	1.13	1.39	5.36	6.30	7.20	8.34
∞	0.77	0.94	1.13	1.39	5.34	6.25	7.16	8.27

[a] All entries in the left half of the table have standard errors of less than 0.005; those in the right half, less than 0.06.

Source: Dickey and Fuller (1981: 1063).

computed for two different lengths of lags. The first lag length is given by $\ell_4 = [4(T/100)^{1/4}]$ and the second by $\ell_{12} = [12(T/100)^{1/4}]$; $[x]$ denotes the largest integer less than or equal to x.

The results of this experiment are presented in Tables 1 and 2 of Schwert (1989: 148–9). They indicate that the distributions of the Phillips–Perron tests are not close to the Dickey–Fuller distribution. The distributions are closest when $\theta = 0.5$ or 0.8 but differ markedly for values of $\theta = -0.5$ and -0.8. The discrepancies persist even with sample sizes as large as $T = 1000$. The ADF statistics, on the other hand, have distributions that are much closer on average to the Dickey–Fuller distribution.

The poor behaviour of the Phillips–Perron tests where negative MA terms are present persists in regressions that incorporate a time trend.

Schwert also reports the distributions of the normalized unit-root estimators (i.e. $T(\hat{\rho}-1)$) in their ADF and non-parametrically corrected DF versions. The conclusions remain unaltered. Finally, Schwert's simulations do suggest that the finite-sample performance under the null of the Phillips–Perron procedures, in the cases where MA terms cause size distortions, is better when S_u^2 and $S_{T\ell}^2$ are calculated using the first differences of y_t than where the regression residuals are used. However, the tests may then fail to be consistent against some stationary alternative hypotheses (Stock and Watson 1988*b*). It seems safest, therefore, to avoid these tests if there is any evidence of the kind of MA component to the errors that causes size distortions.

An alternative procedure is proposed by Hall (1989), who suggests that IV be used in place of OLS in augmented Dickey–Fuller tests. The level instrumental variable used in place of y_{t-1} is $y_{t-(k+1)}$, where the residual autocorrelation function has non-zero elements only up to lag k (see Section 4.6.4 below). Hall's Monte Carlo results suggest that the method performs well, particularly for negative MA error processes.

4.5. Further Extensions

Two more extensions of the testing procedure may be considered. The first concerns testing for multiple unit roots in a process. The second is testing for unit roots at seasonal frequencies. Inventories may be regarded as a good example of a variable that is likely to be I(2) (contains two unit roots), as it is constructed by aggregating a function of flow variables (production and sales) which are individually I(1); a test for multiple unit roots would therefore be important when dealing with stock variables of this kind. Tests for seasonal unit roots are applicable when seasonal data are used. Standard unit-root tests may provide misleading results in the presence of integration at seasonal frequencies.

4.5.1. Multiple Unit Roots

Consider the problem of testing for $d>1$ unit roots in a series. The sequence of testing—which starts with a test for a single unit root in the undifferenced series, then proceeds to a test for a second unit root (that is, tests the first-differenced series) if the first null (of a unit root in levels) is not rejected, and so on—does not constitute a statistically valid testing sequence, since all of the unit-root tests considered in this chapter take the complete absence of unit roots as the alternative hypothesis. Dickey and Pantula (1987) suggest a more natural sequential testing procedure for unit roots which takes the *largest*[5] number of unit roots under consideration as the first maintained hypothesis and then decreases the order of differencing each time the current null hypothesis is rejected. This continues until the first time the null hypothesis is not rejected.

The sequential procedure may be illustrated for the case $d = 2$. Let us consider the AR(2) model,

$$(1 - \rho_1 L)(1 - \rho_2 L)y_t = u_t.$$

This model can be re-parameterized as

$$\Delta^2 y_t = \beta_1 \Delta y_{t-1} + \beta_2 y_{t-1} + u_t,$$

where $\beta_1 \equiv (\rho_1\rho_2 - 1)$ and $\beta_2 \equiv -(1 - \rho_1)(1 - \rho_2)$.

The testing procedure consists of the following steps:

1. Test the null hypothesis of two unit roots against the alternative of a single unit root. Under this null hypothesis $\beta_1 = \beta_2 = 0$ and an F-test may be used to test it. Such a test, however, does not take account of the one-sided nature of the alternative hypothesis. A more powerful procedure follows from noting that, under both the null and the alternative hypotheses, $\beta_2 = 0$. However, $\beta_1 = 0$ under the null hypothesis but is less than zero under the alternative hypothesis. Thus, a more powerful test is given by estimating the regression of $\Delta^2 y_t$ on Δy_{t-1}, computing the t-ratio of $\hat{\beta}_1$, and performing a one-sided lower-tail test using the Dickey–Fuller critical values.

2. If the null hypothesis above is rejected, proceed to test the null of one unit root versus the stationary alternative. Here H_0 and H_1 are given by $\beta_1 < 0$, $\beta_2 = 0$, and $\beta_1 < 0$, $\beta_2 < 0$ respectively. Thus, a one-sided t-test here involves estimating the regression of $\Delta^2 y_t$ on Δy_{t-1} and y_{t-1}, computing the t-ratio of $\hat{\beta}_2$, and comparing it with the Dickey–Fuller values.

This testing procedure may be generalized to testing for three or more unit roots. Dickey and Pantula (1987) contains the results of a simulation study. Their general conclusion is that the sequential procedure, consisting of testing a null hypothesis of k unit roots against an alternative of $k - 1$ unit roots, based on t-tests, is considerably more powerful than an F-test-based procedure.

4.5.2. Seasonal Integration

We have so far focused attention on testing for a unit root at the zero frequency. However, when seasonal data are used, it may be necessary

[5] Note that the first sequence took the *smallest* number (i.e. 1) of unit roots as its first maintained hypothesis.

to allow for seasonal averaging or seasonal differencing to achieve stationarity. For example, the appropriate difference to use to transform to stationarity may not be $x_t - x_{t-1}$, but $x_t - x_{t-4}$ in quarterly data or $x_t - x_{t-12}$ in monthly data. Seasonal integration (and co-integration) and testing for unit roots at seasonal frequencies are discussed by Engle, Granger, and Hallman (1988), Ghysels (1990), Hylleberg, Engle, Granger, and Yoo (1990), Engle, Granger, Hylleberg, and Lee (1993), and Ilmakunnas (1990) among others.

Just as a time series with no seasonal component may be well described by a deterministic process, a stationary stochastic process, or an integrated process, the seasonal component of a time series may be well described by a process from any of these classes, or may combine elements of each. While it is common practice to model a seasonal component as having a deterministic or stationary form, there may be cases where it is appropriate to allow the model of the seasonal component to drift substantially over time. This possibility is implicit in the practice of seasonal differencing (see e.g. Box and Jenkins 1970), whereby a process observed s times per year would be transformed to its s-period difference, $x_t - x_{t-s}$, on the assumption that the process contains an integrated seasonal component.

In order to allow for a unit root at a seasonal frequency, it is useful to factor the lag polynomial of the process. If the lag polynomial contains a factor $(1 - L^s) = \Delta_s$, corresponding to a seasonal unit root, then it can be factorized as

$$(1 - L^s) = (1 - L)(1 + L + L^2 + \ldots + L^{s-1}) = \Delta S(L).$$

That is, the seasonal difference operator can be broken down into the product of the first difference operator and the moving-average seasonal filter $S(L)$ containing further roots of modulus unity.

Engle *et al.* (1988) define a variable x_t to be seasonally integrated of orders d and D (denoted SI(d, D)), if $\Delta^d S(L)^D x_t$ is stationary. Thus, for quarterly data, in the terminology established above, if $\Delta_4 x_t$ is stationary, then x_t is SI(1, 1) with $S(L) = 1 + L + L^2 + L^3$. Further,

$$\begin{aligned}(1 - L^4) &= (1 - L)(1 + L + L^2 + L^3)\\ &= (1 - L)(1 + L)(1 + L^2)\\ &= (1 - L)(1 + L)(1 - iL)(1 + iL).\end{aligned}$$

Hence the quarterly seasonal unit root process has four roots of modulus unity: one at the zero frequency, one at the two-quarter (half-yearly) frequency, and a pair of complex conjugate roots at the four-quarter (annual) frequency. To relate these roots to frequencies in an intuitive way, consider the deterministic process $\alpha(L)x_t = 0$. For

$\alpha(L) = (1 + L)$, then $x_{t+1} = -x_t$ and so $x_{t+2} = x_t$; the process returns to its original value on a cycle with a period of 2. For $\alpha(L) = (1 - iL)$, then $x_{t+1} = ix_t$, $x_{t+2} = i^2x_t = -x_t$, $x_{t+3} = -ix_t$, and $x_{t+4} = -i^2x_t = x_t$, so that the process repeats with a period of 4.

As with a process with a single unit root at the zero frequency (e.g. the random walk $(1 - L)x_t = \varepsilon_t$), a seasonally integrated process such as $(1 - L^4)x_t = \varepsilon_t$ retains the effect of shocks indefinitely, and has a variance which increases linearly with time. However, because the seasonally integrated process contains multiple roots of modulus unity, it does not behave like an I(1) process in all respects. For example, shocks to the system will also alter the seasonal pattern of the series, so that the sequences of observations corresponding to each quarter may evolve in different ways. The first difference of such a seasonally integrated process will not be stationary.

Testing for a unit root at a seasonal frequency has much in common with testing for unit roots at the zero frequency. Tests have been proposed by Hasza and Fuller (1982), Dickey, Hasza, and Fuller (1984), Osborn, Chui, Smith, and Birchenhall (1988), Hylleberg *et al.* (1990), and Engle *et al.* (1993), among others. We will follow Hylleberg *et al.* in describing a testing strategy.

Consider a process observed quarterly and generated by

$$\gamma(L)x_t = \varepsilon_t, \tag{20}$$

where ε_t is IID$(0, \sigma_\varepsilon^2)$ and $\gamma(L)$ is a fourth-order lag polynomial. We wish to test the null hypothesis that the roots of $\gamma(L)$ lie on the unit circle, against the hypothesis that they lie outside. Defining three positive parameters δ_1, δ_2, and δ_3, $\gamma(L)$ can be represented as[6]

$$\gamma(L) = (1 - \delta_1 L)(1 + \delta_2 L)(1 + \delta_3 L^2).$$

For δ_j close to one, this can be further rewritten by using a Taylor series approximation, as

$$\begin{aligned}\gamma(L) = {} & \lambda_1 L(1 + L)(1 + L^2) - \lambda_2 L(1 - L)(1 + L^2) \\ & - \lambda_3 iL(1 - L)(1 + L)(1 - iL) \\ & + \lambda_4 iL(1 - L)(1 + L)(1 + iL) + \gamma^*(L)(1 - L^4),\end{aligned}$$

where the last term is a remainder (see Engle *et al.* (1993) for the approximation theorem). Making the substitutions $\pi_1 = -\lambda_1$, $\pi_2 = -\lambda_2$, $2\lambda_3 = -\pi_3 + i\pi_4$, and $2\lambda_4 = -\pi_3 - i\pi_4$, rewriting the expression for $\gamma(L)$,

[6] The last term appears as $(1 + \delta_3 L^2)$ rather than, as might be expected, as $(1 + \delta_3 L)(1 + \delta_4 L)$ because $\gamma(L)$ is a *real* lag polynomial, and hence at least two of its roots must be complex conjugates of each other.

and grouping terms in π_3 and π_4, we have

$$\gamma(L) = -\pi_1 L(1 + L + L^2 + L^3) + \pi_2 L(1 - L + L^2 - L^3) + (\pi_3 L + \pi_4)L(1 - L^2) + \gamma^*(L)(1 - L^4).$$

Substituting this expression into (20) and rearranging, we have

$$\gamma^*(L)(1 - L^4)x_t = \pi_1 z_{1t-1} + \pi_2 z_{2t-1} + \pi_4 z_{3t-1} + \pi_3 z_{3t-2} + \varepsilon_t, \tag{21}$$

where $z_{1t} = (1 + L + L^2 + L^3)x_t$, $z_{2t} = -(1 - L + L^2 - L^3)x_t$, and $z_{3t} = -(1 - L^2)x_t$.

Equation (21) can be estimated by OLS, possibly with added lags of the dependent variable to capture autocorrelation in the errors. To test the null that there is a unit root at zero frequency, we test $\lambda_1 = 0$, which corresponds to $\pi_1 = 0$; to test for a root of -1 (half-yearly frequency), we test $\lambda_2 = 0$, corresponding to $\pi_2 = 0$; to test for roots of $\pm i$ (annual frequency), we test that λ_3 or $\lambda_4 = 0$, each of which requires a joint test that π_3 and π_4 are equal to zero. Rejection of all of these null hypotheses implies stationarity of the process.

The critical values for these tests are related to the Dickey–Fuller (π_1 and π_2) and Dickey–Hasza–Fuller values, and are tabulated by Hylleberg *et al.*

Various extensions of the basic model are considered by Hasza and Fuller (1982), Dickey *et al.* (1984), and Osborn *et al.* (1988), notably to allow for the presence of a deterministic constant and trend terms in (20) and higher orders of integration.

4.6. Asymptotic Distributions of Test Statistics

We will now consider some examples of the use of a functional central limit theorem to derive the asymptotic distributions of test statistics such as those above, for hypotheses involving integrated variables. Again, recall that results on the sums of powers of trend terms are summarized in Section 1.5.5, and that the relationships among particular sample moments, functionals of Wiener processes, and densities from the normal family are given in Table 3.3.

4.6.1. Example: Dickey–Fuller Tests

The simplest version of this test is based on the null hypothesis that the DGP is $y_t = y_{t-1} + u_t$, $u_t \sim \text{IID}(0, \sigma_u^2)$ and $y_0 = 0$. The model used is

$y_t = \rho y_{t-1} + u_t$. Therefore, estimating the model by OLS,

$$T(\hat{\rho} - 1) = \left(T^{-2} \sum_{t=2}^{T} y_{t-1}^2\right)^{-1} \left(T^{-1} \sum_{t=2}^{T} y_{t-1}u_t\right).$$

By equations (3.22) and (3.23),

$$\left(T^{-2} \sum_{t=2}^{T} y_{t-1}^2\right) \Rightarrow \sigma_u^2 \int_0^1 W(r)^2 \, \mathrm{d}r$$

and

$$\left(T^{-1} \sum_{t=2}^{T} y_{t-1}u_t\right) \Rightarrow (\sigma_u^2/2)[(W(1))^2 - 1].$$

Hence

$$T(\hat{\rho} - 1) \Rightarrow (1/2)[(W(1))^2 - 1] \left(\int_0^1 W(r)^2 \, \mathrm{d}r\right)^{-1}.$$

The percentiles of this distribution are those given in Table 4.1(a).

Further,

$$t(\rho = 1) = \left(T^{-2}\sum_{t=2}^{T} y_{t-1}^2\right)^{1/2} T(\rho - 1)\hat{\sigma}_u$$

$$\Rightarrow \tfrac{1}{2}(W(1)^2 - 1)\left(\int_0^1 W(r)^2 \, \mathrm{d}r\right)^{-1/2}$$

where

$$\hat{\sigma}_u^2 = T^{-1}\left(\sum_{t=2}^{T} (y_t - \hat{\rho} y_{t-1})^2\right).$$

The percentiles of the distribution are given in Table 4.2(a).

Now suppose that y_t is generated by the slightly more elaborate process,

$$y_t = \mu_c + y_{t-1} + u_t, \tag{22}$$

with $u_t \sim \mathrm{IID}(0, \sigma_u^2)$ and $y_0 = 0$. The model is given by

$$y_t = \mu_c + \gamma_c t + \rho_c y_{t-1} + u_t, \tag{23}$$

where $\rho_c = 1$, $\gamma_c = 0$ under the null. The null hypothesis therefore entails that the series is a random walk with possible drift, and the alternative is stationarity around a possibly non-zero deterministic trend.

Consider using the model in (23), with γ_c and μ_c unconstrained, to test null hypotheses of the form H_0^1: $\rho_c = 1$, H_0^2: $\gamma_c = 0$, and H_0^3: $(\rho_c - 1) = \gamma_c = 0$. H_0^1 is the standard Dickey–Fuller null, given as case (iii) in the discussion earlier on similar tests. These tests may all be put within a common framework by using a set of transformations suggested by Sims *et al*. (1990).

Under the null H_0^3, then $y_t = \mu_c t + S_t$, where $S_t = \sum_{i=1}^{t} u_i$. In general, (23) can be rewritten as

$$y_t = (\mu_c + \gamma_c) + \rho_c[y_{t-1} - \mu_c(t-1)] + (\gamma_c + \rho_c\mu_c)(t-1) + u_t,$$

or

$$y_t = \boldsymbol{\theta}'\mathbf{z}_{t-1} + u_t \tag{24}$$

where $\mathbf{z}_t' = (z_{1,t}, z_{2,t}, z_{3,t})$, $\boldsymbol{\theta}' = (\theta_1, \theta_2, \theta_3)$, with $\theta_1 = (\mu_c + \gamma_c)$, $\theta_2 = \rho_c$, $\theta_3 = (\gamma_c + \rho_c\mu_c)$, and $z_{1,t} = 1$, $z_{2,t} = y_t - \mu_c t = S_t$, $z_{3,t} = t$.

The transformed regressors are linear combinations of the original regressors, with the linear combinations chosen to isolate the regressors with different stochastic properties—that is, a constant, an integrated process with no deterministic trend component, and a linear trend, respectively. Given the rates of convergence implied in (3.21)–(3.24), OLS estimators of the coefficients in $\boldsymbol{\theta}$ converge at different rates. Define the scaling matrix $\mathbf{T}_T = \text{diag}(T^{1/2}, T, T^{3/2})$ partitioned conformably with $\mathbf{z}_t$ and $\boldsymbol{\theta}$.

With these definitions, the OLS estimator of $\boldsymbol{\theta}$ is

$$\hat{\boldsymbol{\theta}} = \left(\sum_{t=2}^{T} \mathbf{z}_{t-1}\,\mathbf{z}_{t-1}'\right)^{-1} \sum_{t=2}^{T} \mathbf{z}_{t-1} y_t, \tag{25}$$

so that

$$\mathbf{T}_T(\hat{\boldsymbol{\theta}} - \boldsymbol{\theta}) = \mathbf{V}_T^{-1}\boldsymbol{\phi}_T, \tag{26}$$

where

$$\mathbf{V}_T = \mathbf{T}_T^{-1} \sum_{t=2}^{T} \mathbf{z}_{t-1}\,\mathbf{z}_{t-1}'\,\mathbf{T}_T^{-1} \quad \text{and} \quad \boldsymbol{\phi}_T = \mathbf{T}_T^{-1} \sum_{t=2}^{T} \mathbf{z}_{t-1} u_t.$$

From (3.21)–(3.24) we can derive the limiting distributions of the six elements in the 3×3 symmetric matrix $\mathbf{V}_T$ and the three different elements in $\boldsymbol{\phi}_T$. This is done under the additional assumption that $\mu_c = 0$, without any loss of generality, since, having included the trend in (23), the estimates $\boldsymbol{\theta}$ are invariant to the true value of μ_c given that there is in fact no trend in the DGP.[7] These elements are:

$$V_{T,1,1} = T^{-1} \sum_{t=2}^{T} 1 \to 1;$$

$$V_{T,1,2} = T^{-3/2} \sum_{t=2}^{T} S_{t-1} \Rightarrow \sigma_u \int_0^1 W(r)\,\mathrm{d}r;$$

[7] Refer to the discussion on similar tests earlier in the chapter.

$$V_{T,1,3} = T^{-2} \sum_{t=2}^{T} (t-1) \to 1/2;$$

$$V_{T,2,2} = T^{-2} \sum_{t=2}^{T} S_{t-1}^2 \Rightarrow \sigma_u^2 \int_0^1 (W(r))^2 \, dr;$$

$$V_{T,2,3} = T^{-5/2} \sum_{t=2}^{T} (t-1)S_{t-1} \Rightarrow \sigma_u \int_0^1 rW(r) \, dr;$$

$$V_{T,3,3} = T^{-3} \sum_{t=2}^{T} (t-1)^2 \to 1/3;$$

$$\phi_{T,1} = T^{-1/2} \sum_{t=2}^{T} u_t \Rightarrow \sigma_u W(1);$$

$$\phi_{T,2} = T^{-1} \sum_{t=2}^{T} S_{t-1} u_t \Rightarrow (\sigma_u^2/2)[(W(1))^2 - 1]$$

$$\phi_{T,3} = T^{-3/2} \sum_{t=2}^{T} (t-1)u_t \Rightarrow \sigma_u \int_0^1 r \, dW(r).$$

The analytical densities of $V_{T,1,2}$, $V_{T,2,3}$, $\phi_{T,1}$, $\phi_{T,2}$, and $\phi_{T,3}$ can be found from Table 3.3. In the case of $\phi_{T,2}$ we use the fact that the square of $W(1)$ is distributed as $\chi^2(1)$, recalling that $W(1)$ is standard normal. The closed-form density for the functional to which $V_{T,2,2}$ converges is more difficult to derive, but an asymptotic expansion is given by Abadir (1992).

If, as in this Dickey–Fuller test, we are particularly interested in the estimator of ρ_c and its t-ratio, $t(\hat{\rho}_c)$, choosing the appropriate elements from above gives

$$T(\hat{\rho}_c - 1) \Rightarrow f_1(W) \tag{27}$$

and

$$t(\hat{\rho}_c) = [\hat{\sigma}_u^2 V_T^{22}]^{-1/2} T(\hat{\rho}_c - 1) \Rightarrow f_2(W), \tag{28}$$

where V_T^{22} denotes the second element on the diagonal of $\mathbf{V}_T^{-1}$, and $f_i(W)$, $i = 1, 2$, are combinations of the functionals of Wiener processes derived above. For example, from (24)ff., $\hat{\rho}_c = \hat{\theta}_2$, $\mathbf{T}_{T,22} = T$, and $\theta_2 = 1$ under the null. So from (26),

$$T(\hat{\rho}_c - 1) = (\mathbf{V}_T^{-1} \boldsymbol{\phi}_T)_2,$$

the second element of the 3×1 matrix $\mathbf{V}_T^{-1} \boldsymbol{\phi}_T$. From (27) we note that $(\hat{\rho}_c - 1)$ converges at rate $O_p(T^{-1})$ instead of the conventional $O_p(T^{-1/2})$. Similarly, from (28), the corresponding t-ratio has a non-degenerate distribution differing from the standardized normal distribution which appears in the conventional asymptotic theory appropriate to stationary processes.

There are analogous expressions for general Wald statistics for the tests of joint hypotheses. Suppose that the Wald statistic tests the q hypotheses $\mathbf{R}\boldsymbol{\theta} = \mathbf{r}$ in (24). The test statistic is

$$\zeta_T = (\mathbf{R}\hat{\boldsymbol{\theta}} - \mathbf{r})' \left(\mathbf{R} \sum_{t=2}^{T} \mathbf{z}_{t-1} \mathbf{z}'_{t-1} \mathbf{R}'\right)^{-1} (\mathbf{R}\hat{\boldsymbol{\theta}} - \mathbf{r}) / \hat{\sigma}_u^2. \tag{29}$$

The asymptotic behaviour of this test statistic after suitable scaling by $\mathbf{T}_T$ is then a function of the limiting distributions of $\mathbf{V}_T$ and $\boldsymbol{\phi}_T$.

4.6.2. *Example: Augmented Dickey–Fuller Tests*

In this case we assume that the DGP is similar to (22), but that the error term is an AR($p+1$) process with a unit root. The corresponding model is

$$y_t = \mu_c + \gamma_c t + \rho_c y_{t-1} + \beta(L)\Delta y_{t-1} + u_t, \tag{30}$$

with lag polynomial $\beta(L) = \sum_{i=1}^{p} \beta_i L^i$ where the roots of $[1 - \beta(L)L]$ lie outside the unit circle. Under the null hypothesis H_0: $\{\rho_c = 1, \gamma_c = 0\}$, the DGP is an AR($p$) generalization of (22) so that we can again use the transformed model

$$y_t = \boldsymbol{\theta}'\mathbf{z}_{t-1} + u_t,$$

where now $\mathbf{z}'_t = (\mathbf{z}'_{1,t}, z_{2,t}, z_{3,t}, z_{4,t})$ and $\boldsymbol{\theta}' = (\boldsymbol{\theta}'_1, \theta_2, \theta_3, \theta_4)$. To define the elements of $\mathbf{z}'_t$, let $\bar{\mu}_c = E(\Delta y_t) = (1 - \beta(1))^{-1}\mu_c = b\mu_c$, the unconditional mean of the drift under the null, using $b = (1 - \beta(1))^{-1}$. Next, let

$$\Delta y^*_{t-i} = \Delta y_{t-i} - \bar{\mu}_c$$

$$\mathbf{z}_{1,t} = (\Delta y^*_t, \Delta y^*_{t-1}, \ldots, \Delta y^*_{t-p+1})', \qquad z_{2,t} = 1,$$

$$z_{3,t} = y^*_t = y_t - \bar{\mu}_c t, \qquad \text{and} \qquad z_{4,t} = t.$$

The θ_i are given by $\boldsymbol{\theta}'_1 = (\beta_1, \beta_2, \ldots, \beta_p)$, $\theta_2 = \mu_c + \beta(1)\bar{\mu}_c + \gamma_c$, $\theta_3 = \rho_c$, and $\theta_4 = \gamma_c + \rho_c\bar{\mu}_c$. The scaling matrix $\mathbf{T}_T$ becomes $\operatorname{diag}(T^{1/2}\boldsymbol{\iota}_p, T^{1/2}, T, T^{3/2})$ where $\boldsymbol{\iota}_p$ is the unit vector of dimension p. Finally $\boldsymbol{\Omega}_p = E(\mathbf{z}_{1,t}\mathbf{z}'_{1,t})$, the covariance matrix of $\mathbf{z}_{1,t}$. The elements of the matrices $\mathbf{V}_T$ and $\boldsymbol{\phi}_T$ are similar to those for the simple Dickey–Fuller test. Then, using $\xrightarrow{p}$ to denote convergence in probability

$$\mathbf{V}_{T,1,1} = T^{-1} \sum_{t=2}^{T} \mathbf{z}_{1t-1} \mathbf{z}'_{1t-1} \xrightarrow{p} \boldsymbol{\Omega}_p;$$

$$\mathbf{V}_{T,1,2} \xrightarrow{p} \mathbf{0}; \qquad \mathbf{V}_{T,1,3} \xrightarrow{p} \mathbf{0}; \qquad \mathbf{V}_{T,1,4} \xrightarrow{p} \mathbf{0};$$

$$V_{T,2,2} = T^{-1} \sum_{t=2}^{T} z_{2,t-1}^2 \to 1;$$

$$V_{T,2,3} = T^{-3/2} \sum_{t=2}^{T} y_{t-1}^* \Rightarrow \sigma_u b \int_0^1 W(r)\,\mathrm{d}r;$$

$$V_{T,2,4} = T^{-2} \sum_{t=2}^{T} (t-1) \to 1/2;$$

$$V_{T,3,3} = T^{-2} \sum_{t=2}^{T} z_{3,t-1}^2 \Rightarrow \sigma_u^2 b^2 \int_0^1 (W(r))^2\,\mathrm{d}r;$$

$$V_{T,3,4} = T^{-5/2} \sum_{t=2}^{T} (t-1) y_{t-1}^* \Rightarrow \sigma_u b \int_0^1 rW(r)\,\mathrm{d}r;$$

$$V_{T,4,4} = T^{-3} \sum_{t=2}^{T} (t-1)^2 \to 1/3;$$

$$\boldsymbol{\phi}_{T,1} \Rightarrow \mathrm{N}(\mathbf{0}, \sigma_u^2 \boldsymbol{\Omega}_p);$$

$$\phi_{T,2} \Rightarrow \sigma_u W(1);$$

$$\phi_{T,3} = T^{-1} \sum_{t=2}^{T} z_{3,t-1} u_t \Rightarrow (\sigma_u^2/2) b[(W(1))^2 - 1];$$

$$\phi_{T,4} = T^{-3/2} \sum_{t=2}^{T} (t-1) u_t \Rightarrow \sigma_u \int_0^1 r\,\mathrm{d}W(r).$$

Again, Table 3.3 may be applied to find the densities of the Wiener processes appearing above, with the exception of that appearing in the expression for $V_{T,3,3}$; again, an expansion for this density is given by Abadir (1992).

V is therefore block diagonal, and the estimators of the nuisance parameters $\boldsymbol{\beta}$ are asymptotically normal and do not affect the asymptotic distributions of the Dickey–Fuller statistics, so that the same critical values can be used. The *b*s that appear in some of the expressions cancel appropriately to make this possible. This may be seen in the simplest case where the model does not include either the constant or the trend term but does include the Δy_{t-j} terms. Noting that in this case the terms $\mathbf{V}_{T,1,2}$, $\mathbf{V}_{T,1,4}$, $V_{T,2,3}$, $V_{T,2,4}$, $V_{T,3,4}$, $\phi_{T,2}$, and $\phi_{T,4}$ are not relevant, and that $\mathbf{V}^{-1} = \mathrm{diag}(\omega^{11} \ldots \omega^{pp}, V_{T,3,3}^{-1})$, where ω^{ii} is the *i*th diagonal element of $\boldsymbol{\Omega}_p^{-1}$ the distribution of the *t*-statistic is given by $t = (\sigma_u^2 V_{T,3,3})^{-1/2} \phi_{T,3}$. This has the standard Dickey–Fuller distribution with the critical values given by Tables 4.2(*a*). The results extend to the cases where the constant and (or) trend are (is) included in the model with the critical values given by Tables 4.2(*b*) and 4.2(*c*) respectively.

The inclusion of the I(0) terms Δy_{t-j} leaves unchanged the asymptotic distributions of the parameters of interest.

4.6.3. Example: Non-parametric Test Statistics (Phillips 1987a)

Consider the simple random-walk process $y_t = y_{t-1} + u_t$. The main features of non-parametric corrections may be illustrated by assuming that the only restrictions imposed on the stochastic process $\{u_t\}_{t=1}^{\infty}$ are those given by conditions (3.16*a*)–(3.16*d*); $\{u_t\}_{t=1}^{\infty}$ may therefore be an ARMA(p, q) process in which case the t-statistic for $\hat{\rho}$, in the model $y_t = \rho y_{t-1} + u_t$, does not have the standard Dickey–Fuller distribution.

As discussed earlier in this chapter, a non-parametric correction is one way of accounting for the autocorrelation in the $\{u_t\}_{t=1}^{\infty}$ series. This correction enables us to retain the use of the Dickey–Fuller critical values to conduct inference and therefore expands the range of models to which the Dickey–Fuller tests can be applied.

Using the results in (3.21)–(3.24), the estimator $\hat{\rho}$ and its t-ratio $t(\hat{\rho})$ have the following limiting distributions:

$$T(\hat{\rho} - 1) = T\left(\sum_{t=2}^{T} y_{t-1}^2\right)^{-1}\left(\sum_{t=2}^{T} y_{t-1}u_t\right)$$

$$\Rightarrow \left(\int_0^1 W(r)^2\,\mathrm{d}r\right)^{-1}\left[(1/2)\{W(1)^2 - 1\} + \lambda\sigma^{-2}\right] \tag{31}$$

$$t(\hat{\rho}) = \left(\hat{\sigma}_u^{-2}\,T^{-2}\sum_{t=2}^{T} y_{t-1}^2\right)^{1/2} T(\hat{\rho} - 1)$$

$$\Rightarrow \sigma\sigma_u^{-1}\left[(1/2)\{W(1)^2 - 1\} + \lambda\sigma^{-2}\right]\left[\int_0^1 W(r)^2\,\mathrm{d}r\right]^{-1/2}, \tag{32}$$

where $\lambda = (\sigma^2 - \sigma_u^2)/2$ where σ^2 and σ_u^2 are as defined in (10*a*) and (10*b*). If the u_t are IID$(0, \sigma^2)$, then $\sigma^2 = \sigma_u^2$, and $\lambda = 0$. If so, the distributions of $\hat{\rho}$ and its t-ratio in (31) and (32) above are the usual Dickey–Fuller distributions.

It may then be verified that the limiting distribution of the statistic $Z(\hat{\rho})$, where

$$Z(\hat{\rho}) = T(\hat{\rho} - 1) - \lambda\left(T^{-2}\sum_{t=2}^{T} y_{t-1}^2\right)^{-1}, \tag{33}$$

is the same as the distribution obtained by setting $\lambda = 0$ in (31). This follows from an inspection of (31) and by noting that

$$T^{-2}\sum_{t=2}^{T} y_{t-1}^2 \Rightarrow \sigma^2 \int_0^1 W(r)^2\,dr.$$

Similarly, the limiting distribution of the $Z(t(\hat{\rho}))$, where

$$Z(t(\hat{\rho})) = \sigma_u \sigma^{-1} t(\hat{\rho}) - \lambda\left[\sigma\left(T^{-2}\sum_{t=2}^{T} y_{t-1}^2\right)^{1/2}\right]^{-1}, \qquad (34)$$

is the same as the distribution obtained by setting $\lambda = 0$ in (32).

The limiting distributions of (33) and (34) are unchanged when λ is replaced by $\hat{\lambda}$ in these expressions, where $\hat{\lambda}$ is a consistent estimator of λ. Consistent estimators of σ^2 and σ_u^2 are required in order to obtain a consistent estimator of λ and to implement the non-parametric corrections. A consistent estimator of σ_u^2 is given by either $T^{-1}\sum_2^T(y_t - y_{t-1})^2$ or $T^{-1}\sum_2^T(y_t - \hat{\rho}y_{t-1})^2$. The asymptotic equivalence of the two estimators follows from the property that $\hat{\rho} \rightarrow 1$ in probability.[8] A consistent estimator of σ^2 can be obtained from (12) or (13) as before.

Using arguments similar to those outlined above, the non-parametric corrections for the more elaborate models which include constant or constant and trend, may be derived. In particular, $Z(\hat{\rho}_i)$ and $Z(t(\hat{\rho}_i))$ $(i = b, c)$ may be obtained.

4.6.4. Example: Instrumental Variables Test for Unit Roots (Hall 1989)

The non-parametric statistics described in example 4.6.3 are known not to perform well in finite samples in the presence of negative moving-average errors (see Schwert 1989). Hall (1989) proposed estimation by instrumental variables as an alternative to the use of non-parametric corrections. He showed that in the regression model $y_t = \rho y_{t-1} + u_t$, where u_t is a moving-average process of some specified order and ρ is equal to 1 under H_0, then $\hat{\rho}_{\text{IV}}$ has the standard Dickey–Fuller distribution.

The intuition for this result may be easily described: $\hat{\rho}_{\text{OLS}}$ in the above model does not have the standard Dickey–Fuller distribution because of the bias induced by the correlation between y_{t-1} and u_t (when u_t is an ARMA(p, q) process). It is therefore necessary to use a correction factor to remove this bias. This bias does not appear when, say, y_{t-2} is used as an instrument for y_{t-1} and u_t is an MA(1) process. The

[8] As noted above, the finite-sample behaviour of these two estimators may be quite different (see Schwert 1989).

Dickey–Fuller tables can thus be used directly. We formalize this intuition next by presenting a simple example and by using some of the distributional results derived earlier in the chapter. Throughout, to simplify the algebra, adequate initial observations are assumed to be available, so all sums are taken over $1 \ldots T$.

Let the DGP be given by

$$y_t = y_{t-1} + u_t; \tag{35a}$$

$$u_t = \varepsilon_t + \theta\varepsilon_{t-1}; \tag{35b}$$

$$\varepsilon_t \sim \text{IID}(0, \sigma_\varepsilon^2). \tag{35c}$$

Then $\hat{\rho}_{\text{IV}}$, the instrumental variables estimator of ρ which uses y_{t-2} as an instrument for y_{t-1}, is given by

$$\hat{\rho}_{\text{IV}} = \left(\sum_{t=1}^{T} y_{t-1}y_{t-2}\right)^{-1}\left(\sum_{t=1}^{T} y_t y_{t-2}\right). \tag{36}$$

Next, we want to prove that

$$T(\hat{\rho}_{\text{IV}} - 1) \Rightarrow (1/2)[W(1)^2 - 1]\left(\int_0^1 W(r)^2\,\mathrm{d}r\right)^{-1}, \tag{37}$$

where $W(r)$ is the Wiener process associated with the sequence $\{u_t\}$. The RHS of this expression is the limiting distribution of the simple Dickey–Fuller test for a model like (35) when the u_t are IID (see Section 4.6.1). Thus, we need to show that, for the instrument y_{t-k} $(k \geqslant 2)$,

(i) $T^{-1}\sum_{t=1}^{T} y_{t-k}u_t \Rightarrow (\sigma^2/2)\{W(1)^2 - 1\}$

(ii) $T^{-2}\sum_{t=1}^{T} y_{t-1}y_{t-k} \Rightarrow \sigma^2\left(\int_0^1 W(r)^2\,\mathrm{d}r\right).$

Note that

$$\sigma^2 = \lim_{T\to\infty} T^{-1}E(S_T{}^2) \qquad \text{and} \qquad \sigma_u^2 = \operatorname*{plim}_{T\to\infty} T^{-1}\sum_{t=1}^{T} u_t^2.$$

Proof of (i). From (35*a*),

$$T^{-1}\sum_{t=1}^{T} y_{t-k}u_t = T^{-1}\sum_{t=1}^{T} y_{t-1}u_t - T^{-1}\sum_{t=1}^{T} u_t(u_{t-1} + u_{t-2} + \ldots u_{t-k+1}). \tag{38}$$

This follows from the fact that

$$\begin{aligned} y_{t-k} &= y_{t-1} - (y_{t-1} - y_{t-k}) \\ &= y_{t-1} - [(y_{t-1} - y_{t-2}) + (y_{t-2} - y_{t-3}) + \ldots + (y_{t-k+1} - y_{t-k})]. \end{aligned}$$

Recall now from (3.23) that

$$T^{-1}\sum_{t=1}^{T} y_{t-1}u_t \Rightarrow (\sigma^2/2)\{W(1)^2\} - (\sigma_u^2/2),$$

for the DGP given by (35*a*)–(35*c*). Further, for the error process u_t, $\sigma_u^2 = (1+\theta^2)\sigma_\varepsilon^2$ and $\sigma^2 = (1+\theta)^2\sigma_\varepsilon^2$.

It also follows from (35*b*) that

$$T^{-1}\sum_{t=1}^{T} u_t(u_{t-1} + u_{t-2} + \ldots + u_{t-k+1}) \xrightarrow{\text{p}} \theta\sigma_\varepsilon^2. \tag{39}$$

Using (39), it is now possible to see from (38) that

$$T^{-1}\sum_{t=1}^{T} y_{t-k}u_t \Rightarrow (\sigma^2/2)\{W(1)^2\} - (\sigma_u^2/2) - \theta\sigma_\varepsilon^2. \tag{40}$$

But $\sigma_u^2 = (1+\theta^2)\sigma_\varepsilon^2$. Hence

$$-(\sigma_u^2/2) - \theta\sigma_\varepsilon^2 = [-(1+\theta)^2/2]\sigma_\varepsilon^2 = -(1/2)\sigma^2.$$

The last equality follows from the expression for σ^2 given previously. (i) now follows routinely from (40).

Proof of (ii).

$$\begin{aligned} T^{-2}\sum_{t=1}^{T} y_{t-1}y_{t-k} &= T^{-2}\sum_{t=1}^{T} y_{t-1}[y_{t-1} - (y_{t-1} - y_{t-k})] \\ &= T^{-2}\sum_{t=1}^{T} y_{t-1}^2 \\ &\quad - T^{-2}\sum_{t=1}^{T} y_{t-1}(u_{t-1} + u_{t-2} + \ldots + u_{t-k+1}). \end{aligned}$$

All terms of the form $T^{-2}\sum_{t=1}^{T} y_{t-1}u_{t-j}$, $j = 1, 2, \ldots, (k-1)$, converge in probability to zero. This is because the scaling T^{-1} is appropriate for these sums to have non-degenerate distributions.[9] The scaling T^{-2} induces degeneracy. The distribution of $T^{-2}\sum_{t=1}^{T} y_{t-1}^2$ is given by $\sigma^2(\int_0^1 W(r)^2\,dr)$ for the DGP (35*a*)–(35*c*); (ii) now follows routinely.

Finally, (37) follows from (36), using $k = 2$ in (i) and (ii), since

[9] This follows from arguments similar to those used to prove (3.21)–(3.24).

$$T(\hat{\rho}_{IV} - 1) = \left(T^{-2}\sum_{t=1}^{T} y_{t-1}y_{t-2}\right)^{-1}\left(T^{-1}\sum_{t=1}^{T} y_{t-2}u_t\right).$$

It also follows from (37) that the t-ratio form of the test,

$$t(\hat{\rho}_{IV}) = \left(\sum_{t=1}^{T} y_{t-1}y_{t-2}\right)^{1/2}(\hat{\rho}_{IV} - 1)\hat{\sigma}^{-1},$$

has the Dickey–Fuller t-distribution where $\hat{\sigma}$ is a consistent estimator of σ (possibly equal to $(1 + \hat{\theta})\hat{\sigma}_\varepsilon$, where $\hat{\theta}$ and $\hat{\sigma}_\varepsilon$ are OLS estimators of θ and σ_ε).

Thus, estimation by instrumental variables has the same effect as the non-parametric corrections to $\hat{\rho}$(OLS) proposed by Phillips and Perron.

In a small Monte Carlo study, Hall (1989) shows that the size problems associated with the Phillips–Perron test are partially alleviated by the use of this instrumental variable procedure. However, substantial size distortions remain in the cases where $\theta < 0$ in the null model. No power calculations are reported in Hall's paper.

4.6.5. Example: Bounds Test for Unit Roots (Phillips and Ouliaris 1988)

A limitation of the testing procedures discussed in this chapter is that the distributions of the test statistics are non-standard. Consequently, a number of different sets of critical values have to be used to implement the tests.

This problem is at the heart of a literature which exploits the idea that differencing an I(0) series induces a unit root in the moving-average representation of the process. Use is made of this fact to devise a unit-root test based on the long-run variance, defined in (3.16c), of the first-differenced time series. The critical values are taken from the standard normal table.

In order to illustrate this approach, assume that y_t follows the IMA(1, 1) process,

$$\Delta y_t = (1 - \theta L)\varepsilon_t = u_t, \tag{41}$$

with $\varepsilon_t \sim \text{IID}(0, \sigma_\varepsilon^2)$. The long-run variance of Δy_t is $\sigma^2 = (1 - \theta)^2\sigma_\varepsilon^2$, so $\sigma^2 \neq 0$ if and only if $\theta \neq 1$. In other words, if y_t is I(0), Δy_t will have $\sigma^2 = 0$, while if it is I(1), with $|\theta| < 1$, $\sigma^2 \neq 0$. Phillips and Ouliaris (1988) therefore take as their null hypothesis H_0: $\sigma^2 \neq 0$ or (equivalently, but standardizing to eliminate units of measurement effects) H_0: $\tau^2 = \sigma^2/\sigma_\varepsilon^2 \neq 0$ against the alternative hypothesis H_1: $\tau^2 = 0$. Obtaining an estimate of σ^2 as in (13), they prove that[10]

$$\ell^{1/2}(\hat{\tau}^2 - \tau^2)/\tau^2 \sim \text{N}(0, 1). \tag{42}$$

[10] ℓ is the lag-truncation parameter as defined in (12).

They propose a bounds procedure based upon the confidence interval corresponding to (42) and given by

$$\hat{\tau}^2/[1 + (z_\alpha/\ell^{1/2})] \leqslant \tau^2 \leqslant \hat{\tau}^2/[1 - (z_\alpha/\ell^{1/2})], \tag{43}$$

where z_α is the $(1 - \alpha)$th percentage point of the standard normal distribution. According to the bounds test, H_0 is rejected if the upper limit of τ^2 in (43) is sufficiently small and close to zero. Conversely, H_0 is not rejected if the lower bound is sufficiently large and non-zero; 0.10 is recommended as a thumb-rule value of 'nearness'. Simulation results show that this suggested critical value can lead to very conservative tests in some cases. For example, if the DGP is ARIMA(0, 1, 1) with values of the parameter θ in the interval $(-0.6, 0.6)$, the average upper bound is 0.45 while the average value of the lower bound is close to 0.10.

An implication of this type of test is that, because of asymptotic normality, it can be applied to deal with very general trend-cycle models (for example, linear functions of time or any type of dummy variable). All that is required is to perform the previous test on the differenced *residuals* of the regression of y_t on the deterministic terms.

Phillips and Ouliaris (1988) extend this approach to testing for co-integration among a set of n variables in the vector $\mathbf{x}_t$. If $\mathbf{x}_t$ does not form a co-integrated set of variables, $\boldsymbol{\alpha}'\mathbf{x}_t$ is I(1) for all $\boldsymbol{\alpha}$. Hence, generalizing the analysis given above, $\boldsymbol{\alpha}'\Delta\mathbf{x}_t$ has a positive definite long-run variance matrix $\boldsymbol{\alpha}'\boldsymbol{\Omega}\boldsymbol{\alpha}$, where $\boldsymbol{\Omega}$ is the long-run variance matrix of $\Delta\mathbf{x}_t$. Since $\boldsymbol{\alpha}'\boldsymbol{\Omega}\boldsymbol{\alpha} \neq 0$ implies that $\boldsymbol{\Omega}\boldsymbol{\alpha} \neq \mathbf{0}$, Phillips and Ouliaris (1990) suggest testing for a zero eigenvalue in $\boldsymbol{\Omega}$, using a multivariate estimator of $\boldsymbol{\Omega}$, under the null hypothesis of 'no co-integration'. The test is based on the bounds procedure discussed previously but is applied to the minimum of the estimated eigenvalues of the consistent estimator of $\boldsymbol{\Omega}$.

Taken together, the methods of testing just presented offer a means of discriminating between stationary and non-stationary processes in reasonably general circumstances, without too great a proliferation of tables of critical values. There remains work to be done, however, in improving the power of the tests and in achieving a greater conformity with nominal sizes in finite samples, for particular kinds of error process. Moreover, research is needed into the effects of parameter non-constancy, or even of the possibility that the degree of integration may not be constant, on such tests.

Tests for unit roots are applied for a wide variety of reasons. The tests may, first of all, be directly relevant to economic theory, which offers a number of examples of hypotheses that imply unit roots in observable data series. Moreover, because of the potential problem of spurious regression, investigators working with highly autocorrelated series will often want to test for non-stationarity in these series. If non-stationarity can be rejected, standard regression methods can be applied safely; otherwise, an investigator may choose to transform the series to stationarity, or may investigate co-integrating relationships between the data series which, if present, could again justify regression involving the levels of the variables.

The next chapter takes up the topic of co-integration among different processes and thereby continues the study of regression models of non-stationary data series. Tests for co-integration, which will be considered in Chapter 7, bear a close relationship to tests for unit roots.

5

Co-integration

We define the concept of co-integration of integrated time-series and give several examples. An important theorem due to Granger on alternative representations of a system of co-integrated variables is stated and its proof is sketched. We then discuss the Engle–Granger two-step procedure for estimating the parameters characterizing the co-integrating relationship.

In Chapter 1 we discussed our use of the word 'equilibrium'. The idea that variables hypothesized to be linked by some theoretical economic relationship should not diverge from each other in the long run is a fundamental one.[1] Such variables may drift apart in the short run or because of seasonal effects, but if they were to diverge without bound, an equilibrium relationship among such variables could not be said to exist. The divergence from a stable equilibrium state must be stochastically bounded and, at some point, diminishing over time. 'Co-integration' may be viewed as the statistical expression of the nature of such equilibrium relationships.

The concept of co-integration is a powerful one because it allows us to describe the existence of an equilibrium, or stationary, relationship among two or more time-series, each of which is individually non-stationary.[2] That is, while the component time-series may have moments such as means, variances, and covariances varying with time, some linear combination of these series, which defines the equilibrium relationship, has time-invariant linear properties.

The word 'co-integration' clearly demands a formal definition of 'integration', and this was provided in Chapter 3. Informally, a series is said to be integrated if it accumulates some past effects; such a series is non-stationary because its future path depends upon all such past influences, and is not tied to some mean to which it must eventually

[1] Familiar examples of hypothesized long-run relationships include the quantity theory of money, the Fisher effect, the permanent-income hypothesis of consumption, and purchasing-power parity.

[2] Typically, in economic applications one looks for the existence of co-integrating relationships among variables individually integrated of order one. The deviation from the equilibrium relationship is thus integrated of order zero (i.e. is stationary) when the variables are co-integrated.

return. To transform an integrated series to achieve stationarity, we must difference it at least once. However, a linear combination of series may have a lower order of integration than any one of them has individually. In this case, the variables are said to be co-integrated.[3] Thus, for example, if $\{x_t\}$ and $\{y_t\}$ are integrated of order 1 and are also co-integrated, then $\{\Delta x_t\}$, $\{\Delta y_t\}$, and $\{x_t + \alpha y_t\}$, for some α, are all stationary series.

This chapter provides formal definitions of co-integration and of related concepts. Several theorems are stated, applying in particular to alternative representations of co-integrated processes.

5.1. An example

In order to illustrate the preceding discussion, consider a simple example. Two series $\{x_t\}$ and $\{y_t\}$ are each integrated of order 1 and evolve according to the following data-generation process:[4]

$$x_t + \beta y_t = u_t \tag{1}$$

$$x_t + \alpha y_t = e_t \tag{2}$$

$$u_t = u_{t-1} + \varepsilon_{1t} \tag{3}$$

$$e_t = \rho e_{t-1} + \varepsilon_{2t}, \qquad \text{with } |\rho| < 1; \tag{4}$$

$(\varepsilon_{1t}, \ \varepsilon_{2t})'$ is distributed identically and independently as a bivariate normal with

$$E(\varepsilon_{1t}) = E(\varepsilon_{2t}) = 0 \tag{5}$$

$$\operatorname{var}(\varepsilon_{1t}) = \sigma_{11}; \qquad \operatorname{var}(\varepsilon_{2t}) = \sigma_{22}; \qquad \operatorname{cov}(\varepsilon_{1t}, \varepsilon_{2t}) = \sigma_{12}. \tag{6}$$

Solving for x_t and y_t from the above system with $\alpha \neq \beta$ gives

$$x_t = \alpha(\alpha - \beta)^{-1} u_t - \beta(\alpha - \beta)^{-1} e_t \tag{7}$$

$$y_t = -(\alpha - \beta)^{-1} u_t + (\alpha - \beta)^{-1} e_t. \tag{8}$$

Since $\{u_t\}$ is a random walk and $\{x_t\}$ and $\{y_t\}$ depend linearly on $\{u_t\}$, these may therefore be classified as I(1) variables. Nonetheless, $\{x_t + \alpha y_t\}$ is I(0) because e_t is stationary in (2). In this example the vector $[1 \vdots \alpha]'$ is the co-integrating vector and $x + \alpha y$ is the equilibrium relationship. In the long run, the variables move towards the equilibrium $x + \alpha y = 0$, recognizing that this relationship need not be realized exactly even as $t \to \infty$.

[3] When regarding a co-integrating combination as an 'equilibrium' relationship, it is natural to expect this combination to be integrated of order zero. However, definitionally, any reduction in the order of integration—say, from d to $d - b$ (where $b > 0$)—is sufficient for the variables to be called 'co-integrated'.

[4] The example is taken from Engle and Granger (1987).

Although this is a simple example, much of the method and reasoning can be generalized to more complex cases. What is crucial is that, while $\{x_t\}$ and $\{y_t\}$ are integrated processes, not tied to any fixed means, a linear combination of the two variables makes the resulting series a stationary process and the variables x and y may be said to be linked by the corresponding equilibrium relationship.

It is interesting to note that in the bivariate case we have the added bonus that this equilibrium relationship, if such a relationship exists, is unique. The proof is straightforward and follows by contradiction. Suppose not: that is, suppose that there exist two distinct co-integrating parameters α and γ such that $\{x_t + \alpha y_t\}$ and $\{x_t + \gamma y_t\}$ are both I(0). This implies that $(\alpha - \gamma)y_t$ is also I(0) because *subtracting* one I(d) series from another cannot lead to a series integrated of order $(d + 1)$ (or higher). But since $\{y_t\}$ is I(1), a non-zero constant times $\{y_t\}$ is also I(1). Hence we have a contradiction unless $\alpha = \gamma$.

The analysis is not quite so straightforward in the multivariate case as we must allow for the possibility of several co-integrating vectors. Nevertheless, much of the intuition gained from the analysis of the bivariate case carries through to richer examples.

There are at least three reasons for regarding the concept of co-integration as central to econometric modelling with integrated variables, as well as to the examination of long-run relationships among those variables.

The first is the link that the concept formalizes among variables of higher orders of integration, for which some linear combination is of a lower order of integration. In the most widely used examples, a reduction is made from variables that require first-differencing for stationarity to a composite time-series that is stationary in levels. In addition, this composite stationary variable, constructed by taking a linear combination of the original series, may be said to characterize the equilibrium relationship linking the series. If an equilibrium exists among several variables so that such a stationary linear combination exists, we may count on eventual return of this linear combination to its mean (typically zero).

Second, and following directly from this identification of co-integration with equilibrium, is the complementary idea of meaningful versus spurious regression. Regressions involving levels of time series of non-stationary variables make sense if and only if these variables are co-integrated. A test for co-integration then yields a useful method of distinguishing meaningful regressions from those that Yule (1926) called 'nonsense' and Granger and Newbold (1974, 1977) called 'spurious'.

Finally, another important property characterizes variables that are co-integrated. A set of co-integrated variables is known to have, among other representations, an error-correction representation; that is, the relationship may be expressed so that a term representing the deviation of observed values from the long-run equilibrium enters the model. This is an interesting result by itself, but is even more noteworthy as a contribution to resolving, or synthesizing, the debate between time-series analysts and those favouring econometric methods. It allows a reconciliation, at least in part, of time-series methods of analysing data that traditionally considered only the properties of differenced time-series (which could more legitimately be assumed stationary) and those econometric methods that laid emphasis on the equilibrium relationships between variables and therefore focused on the levels of variables. Both methods as traditionally used could be said to have been flawed, the former by the implied necessity of ignoring information contained in the levels of variables, the latter by its tendency to ignore the spurious regression problem.

Reliance on the use of differenced data, as a potential cure for the spurious regression problem, raises a set of new issues. An example of a potentially controversial recommendation for modelling economic time-series appears in Granger and Newbold (1977 p. 206; emphasis in original): 'In the presence of some autocorrelation of the errors . . . first differencing might be expected to go a long way towards alleviating the problem and is *certainly* preferable to doing nothing at all.'

As an illustration, Granger and Newbold cite the results of Sheppard (1971), who regressed UK consumption on autonomous expenditure and mid-year money stock for both levels and changes, using annual data over the period 1947–62. The results were taken to indicate the existence of a significant relationship in levels which disappeared entirely when first differences were employed. The levels regression, characterized by a high value of R^2 and a low value of the Durbin–Watson statistic, is spurious. However, the first-differenced regression appears to be testing a different hypothesis.[5] The differencing operation, in particular, omits any information about long-run adjustments that the data may contain.

Thus, while the spurious regression problem is a serious one, the practice of differencing integrated series to achieve stationarity, and of treating the resulting series as the proper objects of econometric analysis, is not without costs. Error-correction mechanisms (ECMs) are intended to provide a way of combining the advantages of modelling both levels and differences. In an error-correction model the dynamics of both short-run (changes) and long-run (levels) adjustment processes are modelled simultaneously. This idea of incorporating the dynamic

[5] In the next chapter we discuss the consequences of differencing (and over-differencing) in cases where differencing (any number of times) does not alleviate the problems of non-stationarity and where transforming the series monotonically, prior to differencing, appears to be the appropriate procedure.

adjustment to steady-state targets in the form of error-correction terms, suggested by Sargan (1964) and developed by Hendry and Anderson (1977) and Davidson *et al.* (1978), among others, therefore offers the possibility of revealing information about both short-run and long-run relationships.

The theory of co-integration provides a unified framework for the analysis of ECMs and of time series in which the variables share one or more stochastic trends. We elaborate upon the alternative representations of co-integrated systems in Section 5.3, where we also provide a more formal description of the theory; we first review the theory of polynomial matrices which is necessary for a thorough understanding of several proofs in the next sections and in following chapters.

5.2. Polynomial Matrices

A polynomial matrix $\mathbf{A}(L)$ is a matrix for which the elements $\{a_{ij}(L)\}$ are scalar polynomials in an argument L:

$$a_{ij}(L) = \sum_{r=0}^{k_{ij}} a_{ij,r} L^r, \tag{9}$$

where $k_{ij} < \infty$. Useful references to the algebra of polynomial matrices include Gel'fand (1967) and Gantmacher (1959). The degree, k, of $\mathbf{A}(L)$ is the highest of the orders k_{ij} of the element polynomials:

$$k = \max_{i,j}\{k_{ij}\} < \infty.$$

Thus, $\mathbf{A}(L)$ can be expressed as

$$\mathbf{A}(L) = \sum_{r=0}^{k} \mathbf{A}_r L^r = \mathbf{A}_0 + \mathbf{A}_1 L + \mathbf{A}_2 L^2 + \ldots + \mathbf{A}_{k-1} L^{k-1} + \mathbf{A}_k L^k. \tag{10}$$

The determinant $|\mathbf{A}(L)|$ of a polynomial matrix $\mathbf{A}(L)$ is a scalar polynomial.

A familiar example of a polynomial matrix is $\mathbf{A}(\lambda) = (\mathbf{A}_0 - \lambda\mathbf{I})$, which occurs in the characteristic equation

$$|\mathbf{A}(\lambda)| = |\mathbf{A}_0 - \lambda\mathbf{I}| = 0,$$

which may be solved for eigenvalues of the matrix $\mathbf{A}_0$. Every matrix satisfies its own characteristic equation (the Cayley–Hamilton theorem) in that, if we let $f(\lambda) = |\mathbf{A}(\lambda)|$, then $f(\mathbf{A}) = 0$ (where this is interpreted as a matrix expression). In general, if $\mathbf{A}(L) = \sum_{i=0}^{k} \mathbf{A}_i L^i$, then we will also use the notation $\mathbf{A}(\mathbf{B}) \equiv \sum_{i=0}^{k} \mathbf{A}_i \mathbf{B}^i$, for a matrix argument $\mathbf{B}$.

The *inverse* of a finite polynomial matrix $\mathbf{A}(L)$ of degree k which has all roots of the determinantal equation $|\mathbf{A}(z)| = 0$ strictly outside the unit circle[6] is given, in general, by an infinite-order matrix $\mathbf{C}(L) = \sum_{i=0}^{\infty} \mathbf{C}_i L^i$. This matrix is well defined if and only if $\sum_{i=0}^{k} \mathbf{C}_i L^i$ is a convergent sequence as $k \to \infty$. For $|z| > 1$ (equivalently, $|L| = |z^{-1}| < 1$), a sufficient condition for this to hold is $|\mathbf{C}_i| \leqslant p^i \mathbf{I}$ where $|p| < 1$.[7] The $\mathbf{C}_i$ are defined by an infinite set of matrix identities which may be described in a simple scalar case, where $A(L) = 1 - \rho L = a_0 + a_1 L$, as follows:

$$
\begin{aligned}
C(L) &= (1 - \rho L)^{-1} = 1 + \rho L + \rho^2 L^2 + \ldots \\
&= c_0 + c_1 L + c_2 L^2 + \ldots,
\end{aligned}
$$

such that

$$
\begin{cases}
a_0 c_0 = 1 \\
a_0 c_1 + a_1 c_0 = 0 \\
a_0 c_2 + a_1 c_1 = 0 \\
\qquad \ldots
\end{cases}
\tag{11}
$$

The construction given by (11) is derived by using the property $C(L)A(L) = 1$ and equating powers of L. The algebra generalizes to high-order scalar polynomials $A(L)$ and to matrix polynomials $\mathbf{A}(L)$. In the next section of this chapter and in Chapter 8 we shall need to deal with matrix polynomials that have unit roots ($z = 1$). In these cases, while the matrix $\mathbf{A}(L)$ may not have a well defined inverse because of failure of rank conditions, transforming $\mathbf{A}(L)$ and pre- and post-multiplying it by suitable matrices will lead to an invertible matrix provided certain conditions are satisfied.

Two polynomial matrices $\mathbf{R}(L)$ and $\mathbf{T}(L)$ are said to be *equivalent* if and only if there exist two invertible matrices $\mathbf{U}(L)$ and $\mathbf{V}(L)$ such that

$$\mathbf{R}(L) = \mathbf{U}(L)\mathbf{T}(L)\mathbf{V}(L). \tag{12}$$

Every polynomial matrix $\mathbf{A}(L)$ can be divided on the left by a matrix of the form $(\mathbf{B} - L\mathbf{I})$ for any matrix $\mathbf{B}$ so that, where $\mathbf{A}(L)$ is of degree k,

$$\mathbf{A}(L) = (\mathbf{B} - L\mathbf{I})\mathbf{H}(L) + \mathbf{D}, \tag{13}$$

where $\mathbf{H}(L)$ is of degree $k - 1$ and $\mathbf{D}$ is a constant matrix, the remainder term. To obtain the precise form of $\mathbf{D}$, we will derive this

[6] That is, denoting an arbitrary root of the determinant equation by z, $|z| > 1 + \varepsilon$, for some $\varepsilon > 0$, for all z satisfying this equation.

[7] Note that this exponential decay condition is only sufficient and not necessary to guarantee convergence.

result, which is simply a linear transformation of the original polynomial matrix. We have

$$\begin{aligned}\mathbf{A}(L) &= \mathbf{A}_0 + \mathbf{A}_1 L + \mathbf{A}_2 L^2 + \ldots + \mathbf{A}_{k-1}L^{k-1} + \mathbf{A}_k L^k \\ &= \mathbf{A}_0 + \mathbf{A}_1 L + \mathbf{A}_2 L^2 + \ldots + \mathbf{A}_{k-1}L^{k-1} + L\mathbf{A}_k L^{k-1} \\ &\quad - \mathbf{B}\mathbf{A}_k L^{k-1} + \mathbf{B}\mathbf{A}_k L^{k-1} \\ &= \mathbf{A}_0 + \mathbf{A}_1 L + \mathbf{A}_2 L^2 + \ldots + (\mathbf{A}_{k-1} + \mathbf{B}\mathbf{A}_k)L^{k-1} \\ &\quad - (\mathbf{B} - L\mathbf{I})\mathbf{A}_k L^{k-1} \\ &= \mathbf{A}_0 + \ldots + [\mathbf{A}_{k-2} + \mathbf{B}(\mathbf{A}_{k-1} + \mathbf{B}\mathbf{A}_k)]L^{k-2} \\ &\quad - (\mathbf{B} - L\mathbf{I})(\mathbf{A}_{k-1} + \mathbf{B}\mathbf{A}_k)L^{k-2} - (\mathbf{B} - L\mathbf{I})\mathbf{A}_k L^{k-1}, \qquad (14)\end{aligned}$$

and so on. By induction, we can continue this substitution for any k to get

$$\mathbf{D} = \sum_{i=0}^{k} \mathbf{A}_i \mathbf{B}^i = \mathbf{A}(\mathbf{B}), \qquad \text{and} \qquad \mathbf{H}(L) = -\sum_{i=0}^{k-1}\left(\sum_{j=i+1}^{k} \mathbf{B}^{j-i-1}\mathbf{A}_j\right)L^i.$$

A similar result holds for division on the right. In dealing with integrated series, the case $\mathbf{B} = \mathbf{I}$ is of particular interest; then

$$\mathbf{B} - L\mathbf{I} = (1 - L)\mathbf{I} = \Delta\mathbf{I} \qquad \text{and} \qquad \mathbf{D} = \mathbf{A}(\mathbf{I}) = \mathbf{A}(1), \qquad (15)$$

where $\mathbf{A}(1)$ is equal to $\mathbf{A}(L)$ evaluated at $L = 1$. Note that from (13) and (15), for the case $\mathbf{B} = \mathbf{I}$,

$$\mathbf{A}(L) = (1 - L)\mathbf{I}\mathbf{H}(L) + \mathbf{A}(1) = \mathbf{A}(1) + (1 - L)\mathbf{H}(L)$$

and

$$\mathbf{H}(1) = -\sum_{i=0}^{k-1}\left\{\sum_{j=i+1}^{k} \mathbf{A}_j\right\} = -\sum_{i=1}^{k} i\mathbf{A}_i.$$

Further, $\mathbf{A}(1)$ is called the *total effect*. When $\mathbf{D} = \mathbf{A}(1) = \mathbf{0}$, then $\mathbf{A}(L)$ is divisible on the left by $(1 - L)\mathbf{I}$ without a remainder, and hence can be rewritten in terms of the operator $(1 - L)$ alone.

The next main result to be proved is the isomorphic relationship between polynomial matrices and companion matrices. This will clarify the derivation of *latent roots* of polynomial matrices, which are of great interest in analysing dynamics and co-integration. Consider the system of n deterministic linear equations:

$$\mathbf{A}(L)\mathbf{x}_t = \mathbf{A}_0\mathbf{x}_t + \mathbf{A}_1\mathbf{x}_{t-1} + \mathbf{A}_2\mathbf{x}_{t-2} + \ldots + \mathbf{A}_{k-1}\mathbf{x}_{t-k+1} + \mathbf{A}_k\mathbf{x}_{t-k} = \mathbf{0}. \qquad (16)$$

We set $\mathbf{A}_0 = \mathbf{I}$ as a normalization. The same information can be represented in stacked form (called the *companion form*) by defining the following matrices and vectors:

$$\boldsymbol{\chi}_t = \begin{bmatrix} \mathbf{x}_t \\ \mathbf{x}_{t-1} \\ \vdots \\ \mathbf{x}_{t-k+1} \end{bmatrix} \quad \text{and} \quad \boldsymbol{\Phi} = \begin{bmatrix} \mathbf{A}_1 & \mathbf{A}_2 & \cdots & \mathbf{A}_{k-1} & \mathbf{A}_k \\ -\mathbf{I} & \mathbf{0} & \cdots & \mathbf{0} & \mathbf{0} \\ \mathbf{0} & -\mathbf{I} & \cdots & \mathbf{0} & \mathbf{0} \\ \vdots & \vdots & \cdots & \vdots & \vdots \\ \mathbf{0} & \mathbf{0} & \cdots & -\mathbf{I} & \mathbf{0} \end{bmatrix}, \tag{17}$$

so that

$$\mathbf{A}(L)\mathbf{x}_t = \mathbf{0} \Leftrightarrow \boldsymbol{\chi}_t + \boldsymbol{\Phi}\boldsymbol{\chi}_{t-1} = \mathbf{0}. \tag{18}$$

Direct multiplication of $\boldsymbol{\Phi}$ into $\boldsymbol{\chi}_{t-1}$ and comparison of that outcome with $\boldsymbol{\chi}_t$ reveals that the second expression in (18) merely augments the original system with a set of identities of the form $\mathbf{x}_{t-1} \equiv \mathbf{x}_{t-1}$, etc. The corresponding advantage of companion forms is that, whatever the value of k in (16), the companion form is always of first order, and hence can be analysed using already established tools. This advantage is pronounced when we wish to find the eigenvalues of $\mathbf{A}(L)$, and do so by solving

$$|\boldsymbol{\Phi} - \lambda\mathbf{I}| = 0. \tag{19}$$

It will be convenient to re-express (19) in terms of the negatives of the inverses of the eigenvalues, $\mu = -1/\lambda$, and to solve

$$|\mathbf{I} + \mu\boldsymbol{\Phi}| = 0. \tag{20}$$

Using the definition of $\boldsymbol{\Phi}$ from (17) in (20), we have

$$|\mathbf{I} + \mu\boldsymbol{\Phi}| = \left| \begin{array}{cccc|c} \mathbf{I} + \mu\mathbf{A}_1 & +\mu\mathbf{A}_2 & \cdots & +\mu\mathbf{A}_{k-1} & +\mu\mathbf{A}_k \\ -\mu\mathbf{I} & \mathbf{I} & \cdots & \mathbf{0} & \mathbf{0} \\ \mathbf{0} & -\mu\mathbf{I} & \cdots & \mathbf{0} & \mathbf{0} \\ \vdots & \vdots & \cdots & \vdots & \vdots \\ \hline \mathbf{0} & \mathbf{0} & \cdots & -\mu\mathbf{I} & \mathbf{I} \end{array} \right|. \tag{21}$$

From the partitioned inverse formula, where $|\mathbf{D}| \neq 0$,

$$\begin{vmatrix} \mathbf{E} & \mathbf{F} \\ \mathbf{G} & \mathbf{D} \end{vmatrix} = \begin{vmatrix} \mathbf{I} & -\mathbf{F}\mathbf{D}^{-1} \\ \mathbf{0} & \mathbf{I} \end{vmatrix} \begin{vmatrix} \mathbf{E} & \mathbf{F} \\ \mathbf{G} & \mathbf{D} \end{vmatrix} = \begin{vmatrix} \mathbf{E} - \mathbf{F}\mathbf{D}^{-1}\mathbf{G} & \mathbf{0} \\ \mathbf{G} & \mathbf{D} \end{vmatrix}$$

$$= |\mathbf{E} - \mathbf{F}\mathbf{D}^{-1}\mathbf{G}|\,|\mathbf{D}|. \tag{22}$$

The first equality follows from the fact that the determinant of the first matrix following the equality is one. Repeating these operations in the alternative direction, if $|\mathbf{E}| \neq 0$, establishes that

$$|\mathbf{E} - \mathbf{F}\mathbf{D}^{-1}\mathbf{G}|\ |\mathbf{D}| = |\mathbf{E}|\ |\mathbf{D} - \mathbf{G}\mathbf{E}^{-1}\mathbf{F}|.$$

Both results will be used below. Here, we apply (22) to the determinant in (21), choosing $\mathbf{E}$ as the large $n(k-1) \times n(k-1)$ matrix in the upper-left corner, and $\mathbf{D} = \mathbf{I}$. Then $\mathbf{F}\mathbf{D}^{-1}\mathbf{G}$ is zero except for its top-right block, which is $-\mu^2\mathbf{A}_k$, and $|\mathbf{D}| = 1$. Thus,

$$|\mathbf{I} + \mu\boldsymbol{\Phi}| = \begin{vmatrix} \mathbf{I} + \mu\mathbf{A}_1 & +\mu\mathbf{A}_2 & \cdots & +\mu\mathbf{A}_{k-2} & +(\mu\mathbf{A}_{k-1} + \mu^2\mathbf{A}_k) \\ -\mu\mathbf{I} & \mathbf{I} & \cdots & \mathbf{0} & \mathbf{0} \\ \mathbf{0} & -\mu\mathbf{I} & \cdots & \mathbf{0} & \mathbf{0} \\ \vdots & \vdots & \cdots & \vdots & \vdots \\ \mathbf{0} & \mathbf{0} & \cdots & -\mu\mathbf{I} & \mathbf{I} \end{vmatrix}. \tag{23}$$

Comparing (21) with (23), the analysis can be seen to repeat, leading to $|\mathbf{A}(\mu)|$ after $k-1$ steps. Thus,

$$|\mathbf{I} + \mu\boldsymbol{\Phi}| = |\mathbf{A}(\mu)|;$$

the latent roots can be found by equating either expression to zero and solving. Since $\mathbf{A}(\cdot)$ is $n \times n$, $\boldsymbol{\Phi}$ is $nk \times nk$ and so has nk eigenvalues, as required.

From (13), when $\mathbf{B} = \mathbf{I}$, if $\mathbf{A}(1)$ has rank $r < n$, then $|\mathbf{A}(1)| = 0$ and hence $\mathbf{A}(L)$ has $n - r$ unit roots. Conversely, if $\mathbf{A}(1)$ has rank n, $\mathbf{A}(L)$ has none of its eigenvalues equal to unity.

Next, derivatives of polynomial matrices with respect to their arguments will be needed, and we have

$$\partial\mathbf{A}(L)/\partial L = \sum_{i=1}^{k} i\mathbf{A}_i L^{i-1} \qquad \text{so that} \qquad \partial\mathbf{A}(L)/\partial L\Big|_{L=1} = \sum_{i=1}^{k} i\mathbf{A}_i \equiv \boldsymbol{\Gamma}.$$

This is reminiscent of the mean-lag formula in a scalar distributed lag. From the result that $\mathbf{H}(1) = -\sum_{i=1}^{k} i\mathbf{A}_i$, we now see that $\mathbf{H}(1) = -\boldsymbol{\Gamma}$. Thus, when $\mathbf{A}(1) = \mathbf{0}$, so that $\mathbf{A}(L) = (1-L)\mathbf{H}(L)$, then $|\mathbf{H}(L)| = 0$ delivers the remaining eigenvalues. If $\mathbf{H}(1)$ did not have rank n when $\mathbf{A}(1) = \mathbf{0}$, then $|\mathbf{H}(1)| = 0$, so $\mathbf{H}(L)$ also has unit roots. Using (13) and (15) to write $\mathbf{H}(L) = \mathbf{H}(1) + (1-L)\mathbf{K}(L)$, we note that, in the extreme case that $\boldsymbol{\Gamma} = \mathbf{0}$, $\mathbf{H}(L) \equiv (1-L)\mathbf{K}(L)$, which implies that $\mathbf{A}(L) = (1-L)^2\mathbf{K}(L)$. Consequently, equation (16) would become $(1-L)^2\mathbf{K}(L)\mathbf{x}_t = \mathbf{0}$, yielding a system in second differences. There is a close affinity between the ranks of $\mathbf{A}(1)$, $\mathbf{H}(1)$, etc., and the number of differences that can be extracted from $\mathbf{A}(L)$.

Finally, polynomial matrices are invariant under non-singular linear transformations in that they have many equivalent representations with the same properties. This is clear from (13) above. More generally,

$$\begin{aligned}\mathbf{A}(L) &= \mathbf{A}(1) + (1 - L)\mathbf{H}(L)\\ &= \mathbf{A}(1)L^k + (1 - L)\mathbf{H}^*(L).\end{aligned}$$

In terms of (16),

$$\begin{aligned}\sum_{i=0}^{k}\mathbf{A}_i\mathbf{x}_{t-i} &= \mathbf{A}(1)\mathbf{x}_t + \sum_{i=0}^{k-1}\mathbf{H}_i(1 - L)\mathbf{x}_{t-i}\\ &= \mathbf{A}(1)\mathbf{x}_{t-k} + \sum_{i=0}^{k-1}\mathbf{H}_i^*(1 - L)\mathbf{x}_{t-i}\\ &= \sum_{i=0}^{k}\mathbf{B}_i(1 - L)^i\mathbf{x}_t. \end{aligned} \tag{24}$$

For example, when $k = 1$,

$$\begin{aligned}\mathbf{x}_t + \mathbf{A}_1\mathbf{x}_{t-1} &= (\mathbf{I} + \mathbf{A}_1)\mathbf{x}_t - \mathbf{A}_1(1 - L)\mathbf{x}_t\\ &= (\mathbf{I} + \mathbf{A}_1)\mathbf{x}_{t-1} + (1 - L)\mathbf{x}_t.\end{aligned}$$

Such linear transformations are used regularly in Chapter 8.

5.3. Integration and Co-integration: Formal Definitions and Theorems

Definition 1. (adapted from Engle and Granger 1987). The components of the vector $\mathbf{x}_t$ are said to be co-integrated of order d, b, denoted $\mathbf{x}_t \sim \mathrm{CI}(d, b)$, if (i) $\mathbf{x}_t$ is $\mathrm{I}(d)$ and (ii) there exists a non-zero vector $\boldsymbol{\alpha}$ such that $\boldsymbol{\alpha}'\mathbf{x}_t \sim \mathrm{I}(d - b)$, $d \geqslant b > 0$. The vector $\boldsymbol{\alpha}$ is called the co-integrating vector.

If $\mathbf{x}_t$ has $n > 2$ components, then there may be more than one co-integrating vector $\boldsymbol{\alpha}$; it is possible for several equilibrium relationships to govern the joint evolution of the variables. If there exist exactly r linearly independent co-integrating vectors with $r \leqslant n - 1$, then these can be gathered into an $n \times r$ matrix $\boldsymbol{\alpha}$. The rank of $\boldsymbol{\alpha}$ will be r and is called the *co-integrating rank*.

Definition 2. A vector time-series $\mathbf{x}_t$ has an error-correction representation if it can be expressed as

$$\mathbf{A}(L)(1 - L)\mathbf{x}_t = -\boldsymbol{\gamma}\mathbf{z}_{t-1} + \boldsymbol{\omega}_t,$$

where $\boldsymbol{\omega}_t$ is a stationary multivariate disturbance, with $\mathbf{A}(0) = \mathbf{I}_n$, $\mathbf{A}(1)$ having only finite elements, $\mathbf{z}_t = \boldsymbol{\alpha}'\mathbf{x}_t$, and $\boldsymbol{\gamma}$ a non-zero vector. For the case where $d = b = 1$, and with co-integrating rank r, the Granger Representation Theorem holds (see Section 5.3.1).

Granger's theorem will prove that a co-integrated system of variables can be represented in three main forms: the vector autoregressive (VAR), error-correction, and moving-average forms. These representations are all isomorphic to each other, and the theorem establishes the restrictions that hold between the lag-polynomial matrices in each representation of the process.

We may prove the theorem in at least three (equivalent) ways, depending on the representation from which we choose to start. The theorem is stated in Section 5.3.1. Following this statement, we take the autoregressive representation as our starting-point and derive the main results. This proof is due to Johansen (1991*a*). The sub-section after the proof contains a detailed interpretation of the results. In Chapter 8 we return to the theorem and provide another proof, this time starting from the moving-average representation. Proving the theorem in two ways highlights some interesting symmetries which exist among the equivalent representations of the process.

5.3.1. Granger Representation Theorem (adapted from Engle and Granger 1987 and Johansen 1991a)

Let $\mathbf{x}_t$ be an I(1) vector of n components, each with (possibly) deterministic trend in mean. Suppose that the system can be written as a finite-order vector autoregression:

$$\mathbf{x}_t = \boldsymbol{\mu} + \boldsymbol{\pi}_1\mathbf{x}_{t-1} + \boldsymbol{\pi}_2\mathbf{x}_{t-2} + \dots + \boldsymbol{\pi}_k\mathbf{x}_{t-k} + \boldsymbol{\varepsilon}_t, \qquad t = 1, 2, \dots, T, \tag{25}$$

where the ε_t satisfy assumptions (3.16*a*)–(3.16*d*) and the first k data points $\mathbf{x}_{1-k}, \mathbf{x}_{1-k+1}, \dots, \mathbf{x}_0$ are fixed. The model can then be rewritten in error-correction form as

$$\begin{aligned}\Delta\mathbf{x}_t &= \boldsymbol{\mu} + \boldsymbol{\Gamma}_1\Delta\mathbf{x}_{t-1} + \boldsymbol{\Gamma}_2\Delta\mathbf{x}_{t-2} + \dots + \boldsymbol{\Gamma}_{k-1}\Delta\mathbf{x}_{t-k+1} + \boldsymbol{\pi}\mathbf{x}_{t-k} + \boldsymbol{\varepsilon}_t \\ &= \boldsymbol{\mu} + \sum_{i=1}^{k-1}\boldsymbol{\Gamma}_i(1 - L)L^i\mathbf{x}_t + \boldsymbol{\pi}\mathbf{x}_{t-k} + \boldsymbol{\varepsilon}_t. \end{aligned} \tag{26}$$

Both (25) and (26) can be written as

$$\boldsymbol{\pi}(L)\mathbf{x}_t = \boldsymbol{\mu} + \boldsymbol{\varepsilon}_t, \qquad t = 1, 2, \dots, T,$$

where

$$\boldsymbol{\pi}(L) = (1 - L)\mathbf{I}_n - \sum_{i=1}^{k-1} \boldsymbol{\Gamma}_i(1 - L)L^i - \boldsymbol{\pi} L^k$$

$$\boldsymbol{\Gamma}_i = -\mathbf{I}_n + \boldsymbol{\pi}_1 + \boldsymbol{\pi}_2 + \ldots + \boldsymbol{\pi}_i, \qquad i = 1, 2, \ldots, k$$

$$\boldsymbol{\Gamma}_k = \boldsymbol{\pi} = -\boldsymbol{\pi}(1).$$

Equation (26) may also be written as

$$\boldsymbol{\pi}(L)\mathbf{x}_t = -\boldsymbol{\pi}\mathbf{x}_{t-k} + \boldsymbol{\Psi}(L)\Delta\mathbf{x}_t = \boldsymbol{\mu} + \boldsymbol{\varepsilon}_t, \tag{27}$$

where $\boldsymbol{\Psi}(L) = (1 - L)^{-1}(\boldsymbol{\pi}(L) - \boldsymbol{\pi}(1)L^k) = \mathbf{I}_n - \sum_{i=1}^{k-1}\boldsymbol{\Gamma}_i L^i$. From (13) above, $\boldsymbol{\Psi}(L)$ can always be constructed. Further, the derivative of $\boldsymbol{\pi}(z)$ at $z = 1$ is equal to $-\boldsymbol{\Psi} \equiv -\boldsymbol{\Psi}(1)$.

Define the orthogonal complement $\mathbf{P}_\perp$ of any matrix $\mathbf{P}$ of rank q and dimension $n \times q$ as follows $(0 < q < n)$:

(i) $\mathbf{P}_\perp$ is of dimension $n \times (n - q)$;
(ii) $\mathbf{P}'_\perp\mathbf{P} = \mathbf{0}_{(n-q)\times q}$, $\mathbf{P}'\mathbf{P}_\perp = \mathbf{0}_{q\times(n-q)}$;
(iii) $\mathbf{P}_\perp$ has rank $n - q$, and lies in the null space of $\mathbf{P}$.

Certain key assumptions may now be stated.

Assumption A1. The characteristic polynomial,

$$\boldsymbol{\pi}(z) = (1 - z)\mathbf{I}_n - \sum_{i=1}^{k-1} \boldsymbol{\Gamma}_i(1 - z)z^i - \boldsymbol{\pi} z^k,$$

has roots either equal to or strictly greater than one; that is, $|\boldsymbol{\pi}(z)| = 0$ implies that either $|z| > 1$ or $z = 1$.

Assumption A2. The $n \times n$ matrix $\boldsymbol{\pi}$ has reduced rank $r < n$ and is therefore expressible as the product of two $n \times r$ matrices $\boldsymbol{\gamma}$ and $\boldsymbol{\alpha}$, where $\boldsymbol{\gamma}$ and $\boldsymbol{\alpha}$ have rank r. Thus $\boldsymbol{\pi} = \boldsymbol{\gamma\alpha}'$.

Assumption A3. The $(n - r) \times (n - r)$ matrix $\boldsymbol{\gamma}'_\perp\boldsymbol{\Psi}\boldsymbol{\alpha}_\perp$ has full rank $n - r$.

Assumption A1 guarantees that the non-stationarity of $\mathbf{x}_t$ can be removed by differencing. A2 rules out a stationary $\mathbf{x}_t$ process. If $\boldsymbol{\pi}$ had full rank (that is, if $|\boldsymbol{\pi}(z)|$ had no roots at one), then from (27), $\mathbf{x}_t = \boldsymbol{\pi}^{-1}(L)(\boldsymbol{\mu} + \boldsymbol{\varepsilon}_t)$, which would imply that $\mathbf{x}_t$ was stationary. It is also the statement, in the autoregressive form, that the system has r linearly independent co-integrating vectors. In light of Assumption A2, $\boldsymbol{\gamma\alpha}'$ provides a transformation of the $\boldsymbol{\pi}$ matrix (and hence a linear combination of the x_{it} which is stationary). The significance of A3 will become evident in due course, but essentially, it ensures that $\mathbf{x}_t$ is integrated of order no greater than 1. Under the assumptions stated above, the following results may be proved:

(R1) $\Delta\mathbf{x}_t$ is stationary.

(R2) $\boldsymbol{\alpha}'\mathbf{x}_t$ is stationary.
(R3) $E(\Delta\mathbf{x}_t) = \boldsymbol{\alpha}_\perp(\boldsymbol{\gamma}'_\perp\boldsymbol{\Psi}\boldsymbol{\alpha}_\perp)^{-1}\boldsymbol{\gamma}'_\perp\boldsymbol{\mu}$.
(R4) $E(\boldsymbol{\alpha}'\mathbf{x}_t) = -(\boldsymbol{\gamma}'\boldsymbol{\gamma})^{-1}\boldsymbol{\gamma}'\boldsymbol{\mu} + (\boldsymbol{\gamma}'\boldsymbol{\gamma})^{-1}(\boldsymbol{\gamma}'\boldsymbol{\Psi}\boldsymbol{\alpha}_\perp)(\boldsymbol{\gamma}'_\perp\boldsymbol{\Psi}\boldsymbol{\alpha}_\perp)^{-1}\boldsymbol{\gamma}'_\perp\boldsymbol{\mu}$.
(R5) $\Delta\mathbf{x}_t$ has a moving-average representation given by
$\Delta\mathbf{x}_t = \mathbf{C}(L)(\boldsymbol{\mu} + \boldsymbol{\varepsilon}_t)$.
(R6) $\mathbf{C}(1) = \boldsymbol{\alpha}_\perp(\boldsymbol{\gamma}'_\perp\boldsymbol{\Psi}\boldsymbol{\alpha}_\perp)^{-1}\boldsymbol{\gamma}'_\perp$ has rank $n - r$.
(R7) $\boldsymbol{\alpha}'\mathbf{C}(1) = \mathbf{0}_{r\times n}$
$\mathbf{C}(1)\boldsymbol{\gamma} = \mathbf{0}_{n\times r}$.

(R8) $\mathbf{x}_t = \mathbf{x}_0 + \mathbf{C}(1)\sum_{i=1}^{t}\boldsymbol{\varepsilon}_i + \boldsymbol{\tau}t + \mathbf{S}_t$,

where $\mathbf{C}(L) = \mathbf{C}(1) + (1 - L)\mathbf{C}_1(L)$, $\boldsymbol{\tau} = \mathbf{C}(1)\boldsymbol{\mu}$, $\mathbf{x}_0$ is a constant (vector) of integration, and $\mathbf{S}_t = \mathbf{C}_1(L)\boldsymbol{\varepsilon}_t$.

Proof. Multiply (27) by $\boldsymbol{\gamma}'$ and $\boldsymbol{\gamma}'_\perp$ respectively to obtain the equations

$$-\boldsymbol{\gamma}'\boldsymbol{\gamma}\boldsymbol{\alpha}'\mathbf{x}_t + \boldsymbol{\gamma}'\boldsymbol{\Psi}(L)\Delta\mathbf{x}_t = \boldsymbol{\gamma}'(\boldsymbol{\mu} + \boldsymbol{\varepsilon}_t) \tag{28a}$$

$$\boldsymbol{\gamma}'_\perp\boldsymbol{\Psi}(L)\Delta\mathbf{x}_t = \boldsymbol{\gamma}'_\perp(\boldsymbol{\mu} + \boldsymbol{\varepsilon}_t), \tag{28b}$$

using the decomposition $\boldsymbol{\pi} = \boldsymbol{\gamma}\boldsymbol{\alpha}'$ and the result that $\boldsymbol{\gamma}'_\perp\boldsymbol{\gamma} = \mathbf{0}_{(n-r)\times r}$. The matrix $\boldsymbol{\pi}$ is not invertible, and the system given by (28*a*)–(28*b*) therefore cannot be inverted directly to express the x_{it} in terms of the ε_{it}. To obtain an invertible system, we define two new variables, $\boldsymbol{\omega}_t = (\boldsymbol{\alpha}'\boldsymbol{\alpha})^{-1}\boldsymbol{\alpha}'\mathbf{x}_t$ and $\boldsymbol{v}_t = (\boldsymbol{\alpha}'_\perp\boldsymbol{\alpha}_\perp)^{-1}\boldsymbol{\alpha}'_\perp\Delta\mathbf{x}_t$. Next, define the matrices $\bar{\boldsymbol{\alpha}} = \boldsymbol{\alpha}(\boldsymbol{\alpha}'\boldsymbol{\alpha})^{-1}$ and $\bar{\boldsymbol{\alpha}}_\perp = \boldsymbol{\alpha}_\perp(\boldsymbol{\alpha}'_\perp\boldsymbol{\alpha}_\perp)^{-1}$. Let $\mathbf{R} = (\boldsymbol{\alpha}, \boldsymbol{\alpha}_\perp)$ be an $n \times n$ matrix of rank n. Then $\mathbf{R}(\mathbf{R}'\mathbf{R})^{-1}\mathbf{R}' = \mathbf{I}_n$ and hence $(\boldsymbol{\alpha}\bar{\boldsymbol{\alpha}}' + \boldsymbol{\alpha}_\perp\bar{\boldsymbol{\alpha}}'_\perp) = \mathbf{I}_n$. Thus,

$$\Delta\mathbf{x}_t = (\boldsymbol{\alpha}\bar{\boldsymbol{\alpha}}' + \boldsymbol{\alpha}_\perp\bar{\boldsymbol{\alpha}}'_\perp)\Delta\mathbf{x}_t = \boldsymbol{\alpha}\Delta\boldsymbol{\omega}_t + \boldsymbol{\alpha}_\perp\boldsymbol{v}_t.$$

Substituting in (28*a*)–(28*b*) gives

$$-(\boldsymbol{\gamma}'\boldsymbol{\gamma})(\boldsymbol{\alpha}'\boldsymbol{\alpha})\boldsymbol{\omega}_t + \boldsymbol{\gamma}'\boldsymbol{\Psi}(L)\boldsymbol{\alpha}\Delta\boldsymbol{\omega}_t + \boldsymbol{\gamma}'\boldsymbol{\Psi}(L)\boldsymbol{\alpha}_\perp\boldsymbol{v}_t = \boldsymbol{\gamma}'(\boldsymbol{\mu} + \boldsymbol{\varepsilon}_t), \tag{29a}$$

$$\boldsymbol{\gamma}'_\perp\boldsymbol{\Psi}(L)\boldsymbol{\alpha}\Delta\boldsymbol{\omega}_t + \boldsymbol{\gamma}'_\perp\boldsymbol{\Psi}(L)\boldsymbol{\alpha}_\perp\boldsymbol{v}_t = \boldsymbol{\gamma}'_\perp(\boldsymbol{\mu} + \boldsymbol{\varepsilon}_t), \tag{29b}$$

where in (28*a*) the first term on the left-hand side needs to be written first as $-(\boldsymbol{\gamma}'\boldsymbol{\gamma})(\boldsymbol{\alpha}'\boldsymbol{\alpha})(\boldsymbol{\alpha}'\boldsymbol{\alpha})^{-1}\boldsymbol{\alpha}'\mathbf{x}_t$. The equations for $\boldsymbol{\omega}_t$ and $\boldsymbol{v}_t$ can now be written in autoregressive form as

$$\tilde{\mathbf{A}}(L)(\boldsymbol{\omega}_t{}', \boldsymbol{v}_t{}')' = (\boldsymbol{\gamma}, \boldsymbol{\gamma}_\perp)'(\boldsymbol{\mu} + \boldsymbol{\varepsilon}_t),$$

with

$$\tilde{\mathbf{A}}(z) = \begin{bmatrix} -(\boldsymbol{\gamma}'\boldsymbol{\gamma})(\boldsymbol{\alpha}'\boldsymbol{\alpha}) + \boldsymbol{\gamma}'\boldsymbol{\Psi}(z)\boldsymbol{\alpha}(1 - z) & \boldsymbol{\gamma}'\boldsymbol{\Psi}(z)\boldsymbol{\alpha}_\perp \\ \boldsymbol{\gamma}'_\perp\boldsymbol{\Psi}(z)\boldsymbol{\alpha}(1 - z) & \boldsymbol{\gamma}'_\perp\boldsymbol{\Psi}(z)\boldsymbol{\alpha}_\perp \end{bmatrix}. \tag{30}$$

For $z = 1$, this matrix has determinant

$$|\tilde{\mathbf{A}}(1)| = (-1)^r|\boldsymbol{\gamma}'\boldsymbol{\gamma}|\,|\boldsymbol{\alpha}'\boldsymbol{\alpha}|\,|\boldsymbol{\gamma}'_\perp\boldsymbol{\Psi}\boldsymbol{\alpha}_\perp|,$$

which is non-zero by Assumptions A2 and A3. Hence $z = 1$ is not a root. For $z \neq 1$, straightforward but tedious algebra enables us to express the matrix $\tilde{\mathbf{A}}(z)$ as

$$\tilde{\mathbf{A}}(z) = (\boldsymbol{\gamma}, \boldsymbol{\gamma}_{\perp})'\boldsymbol{\pi}(z)[\boldsymbol{\alpha}, \boldsymbol{\alpha}_{\perp}(1 - z)^{-1}]. \tag{31}$$

To show this, substitute for $\boldsymbol{\Psi}(z)$ in $\tilde{\mathbf{A}}(z)$ in terms of $\boldsymbol{\pi}(z)$ and $\boldsymbol{\pi}(1) \equiv -\boldsymbol{\pi}$ from (27), and use the decomposition $\boldsymbol{\pi} = \boldsymbol{\gamma}\boldsymbol{\alpha}'$ and the orthogonality condition $\boldsymbol{\gamma}'_{\perp}\boldsymbol{\gamma} = \boldsymbol{\alpha}'_{\perp}\boldsymbol{\alpha} = \mathbf{0}_{(n-r)\times r}$. For $z \neq 1$, therefore, from (31),

$$|\tilde{\mathbf{A}}(z)| = |(\boldsymbol{\gamma}, \boldsymbol{\gamma}_{\perp})||\boldsymbol{\pi}(z)||(\boldsymbol{\alpha}, \boldsymbol{\alpha}_{\perp})|(1 - z)^{-(n-r)},$$

where we have used the result that the determinant of a matrix obtained by multiplying $n - r$ columns (or rows) of an $n \times n$ matrix by a constant is the determinant of the original matrix multiplied by the constant raised to the power $n - r$. Thus, for $z \neq 1$, $|\tilde{\mathbf{A}}(z)| = 0$ if and only if $|\boldsymbol{\pi}(z)| = 0$. By Assumption A1, if we exclude $z = 1$, the only remaining roots of this determinant lie outside the unit circle.

This shows that all the roots of $|\tilde{\mathbf{A}}(z)| = 0$ are outside the unit disk. Hence the system defined by (29*a*)–(29*b*) is invertible and $\boldsymbol{\omega}_t$ and $\boldsymbol{v}_t$ can be given initial distributions such that they become stationary. Since $\Delta\mathbf{x}_t = \boldsymbol{\alpha}_{\perp}\boldsymbol{v}_t + \boldsymbol{\alpha}\Delta\boldsymbol{\omega}_t$, stationarity of $\boldsymbol{v}_t$ and $\boldsymbol{\omega}_t$ implies stationarity of $\Delta\mathbf{x}_t$. Further, since $\boldsymbol{\alpha}'\mathbf{x}_t = (\boldsymbol{\alpha}'\boldsymbol{\alpha})\boldsymbol{\omega}_t$, then $\boldsymbol{\alpha}'\mathbf{x}_t$ is also stationary. This completes the proof of (R1) and (R2).

To prove (R3) and (R4), note that

$$(\boldsymbol{\omega}_t{}', \boldsymbol{v}_t{}')' = \tilde{\mathbf{A}}(L)^{-1}(\boldsymbol{\gamma}, \boldsymbol{\gamma}_{\perp})'(\boldsymbol{\mu} + \boldsymbol{\varepsilon}_t). \tag{32}$$

Thus, $E[(\boldsymbol{\omega}'_t, \boldsymbol{v}'_t)'] = \tilde{\mathbf{A}}(1)^{-1}(\boldsymbol{\gamma}, \boldsymbol{\gamma}_{\perp})'\boldsymbol{\mu}$. From (30),

$$\tilde{\mathbf{A}}(1) = \begin{bmatrix} -(\boldsymbol{\gamma}'\boldsymbol{\gamma})(\boldsymbol{\alpha}'\boldsymbol{\alpha}) & \boldsymbol{\gamma}'\boldsymbol{\Psi}(1)\boldsymbol{\alpha}_{\perp} \\ \mathbf{0} & \boldsymbol{\gamma}'_{\perp}\boldsymbol{\Psi}(1)\boldsymbol{\alpha}_{\perp} \end{bmatrix}.$$

Using the formula for inversion of partitioned matrices,

$$\tilde{\mathbf{A}}(1)^{-1} = \begin{bmatrix} -(\boldsymbol{\alpha}'\boldsymbol{\alpha})^{-1}(\boldsymbol{\gamma}'\boldsymbol{\gamma})^{-1} & (\boldsymbol{\alpha}'\boldsymbol{\alpha})^{-1}(\boldsymbol{\gamma}'\boldsymbol{\gamma})^{-1}\boldsymbol{\gamma}'\boldsymbol{\Psi}(1)\boldsymbol{\alpha}_{\perp}(\boldsymbol{\gamma}'_{\perp}\boldsymbol{\Psi}(1)\boldsymbol{\alpha}_{\perp})^{-1} \\ \mathbf{0} & (\boldsymbol{\gamma}'_{\perp}\boldsymbol{\Psi}(1)\boldsymbol{\alpha}_{\perp})^{-1} \end{bmatrix}.$$

Thus,

$$\begin{aligned} E(\boldsymbol{\omega}_t) = & -(\boldsymbol{\alpha}'\boldsymbol{\alpha})^{-1}(\boldsymbol{\gamma}'\boldsymbol{\gamma})^{-1}\boldsymbol{\gamma}'\boldsymbol{\mu} \\ & + (\boldsymbol{\alpha}'\boldsymbol{\alpha})^{-1}(\boldsymbol{\gamma}'\boldsymbol{\gamma})^{-1}\boldsymbol{\gamma}'\boldsymbol{\Psi}(1)\boldsymbol{\alpha}_{\perp}(\boldsymbol{\gamma}'_{\perp}\boldsymbol{\Psi}(1)\boldsymbol{\alpha}_{\perp})^{-1}\boldsymbol{\gamma}'_{\perp}\boldsymbol{\mu}, \end{aligned}$$

and

$$E(\boldsymbol{v}_t) = (\boldsymbol{\gamma}'_{\perp}\boldsymbol{\Psi}(1)\boldsymbol{\alpha}_{\perp})^{-1}\boldsymbol{\gamma}'_{\perp}\boldsymbol{\mu}.$$

From above, $E(\Delta\mathbf{x}_t) = \boldsymbol{\alpha}_{\perp}E(\boldsymbol{v}_t) + \boldsymbol{\alpha}E(\Delta\boldsymbol{\omega}_t)$. Noting that $E(\Delta\boldsymbol{\omega}_t) = \mathbf{0}$, we have that $E(\Delta\mathbf{x}_t) = \boldsymbol{\alpha}_{\perp}(\boldsymbol{\gamma}'_{\perp}\boldsymbol{\Psi}(1)\boldsymbol{\alpha}_{\perp})^{-1}\boldsymbol{\gamma}'_{\perp}\boldsymbol{\mu}$. This proves (R3).

Next,

$$
\begin{aligned}
E(\boldsymbol{\alpha}'\mathbf{x}_t) &= E[(\boldsymbol{\alpha}'\boldsymbol{\alpha})\boldsymbol{\omega}_t] \\
&= (\boldsymbol{\alpha}'\boldsymbol{\alpha})E(\boldsymbol{\omega}_t) \\
&= (-\boldsymbol{\gamma}'\boldsymbol{\gamma})^{-1}\boldsymbol{\gamma}'\boldsymbol{\mu} + (\boldsymbol{\gamma}'\boldsymbol{\gamma})^{-1}\boldsymbol{\gamma}'\boldsymbol{\Psi}(1)\boldsymbol{\alpha}_\perp(\boldsymbol{\gamma}'_\perp\boldsymbol{\Psi}(1)\boldsymbol{\alpha}_\perp)^{-1}\boldsymbol{\gamma}'_\perp\boldsymbol{\mu}.
\end{aligned}
$$

This completes the proof of (R4). From (32),

$$(\boldsymbol{\omega}'_t, \boldsymbol{v}'_t)' = (\widetilde{\mathbf{A}}(L))^{-1}[(\boldsymbol{\gamma}, \boldsymbol{\gamma}_\perp)'(\boldsymbol{\mu} + \boldsymbol{\varepsilon}_t)].$$

But

$$
\begin{aligned}
\Delta\mathbf{x}_t = \boldsymbol{\alpha}\Delta\boldsymbol{\omega}_t + \boldsymbol{\alpha}_\perp\boldsymbol{v}_t &= [\boldsymbol{\alpha}(1 - L), \boldsymbol{\alpha}_\perp](\boldsymbol{\omega}'_t, \boldsymbol{v}'_t)' \\
&= [\boldsymbol{\alpha}(1 - L), \boldsymbol{\alpha}_\perp](\widetilde{\mathbf{A}}(L))^{-1}[(\boldsymbol{\gamma}, \boldsymbol{\gamma}_\perp)'(\boldsymbol{\mu} + \boldsymbol{\varepsilon}_t)] \\
&= \mathbf{C}(L)(\boldsymbol{\mu} + \boldsymbol{\varepsilon}_t),
\end{aligned}
$$

where $\mathbf{C}(L) = [\boldsymbol{\alpha}(1 - L), \boldsymbol{\alpha}_\perp](\widetilde{\mathbf{A}}(L))^{-1}[(\boldsymbol{\gamma}, \boldsymbol{\gamma}_\perp)']$. This completes the proof of (R5).

To prove (R6), note that

$$\mathbf{C}(1) = (\mathbf{0}_{n\times(n-r)}, \boldsymbol{\alpha}_\perp)(\widetilde{\mathbf{A}}(1))^{-1}[(\boldsymbol{\gamma}, \boldsymbol{\gamma}_\perp)'].$$

Substituting for $(\widetilde{\mathbf{A}}(1))^{-1}$ from above gives $\mathbf{C}(1) = \boldsymbol{\alpha}_\perp(\boldsymbol{\gamma}'_\perp\boldsymbol{\Psi}(1)\boldsymbol{\alpha}_\perp)^{-1}\boldsymbol{\gamma}'_\perp$ as required. The matrices $\boldsymbol{\alpha}_\perp$ and $\boldsymbol{\gamma}'_\perp$ and $(\boldsymbol{\gamma}'_\perp\boldsymbol{\Psi}(1)\boldsymbol{\alpha}_\perp)^{-1}$ have rank $(n - r)$ using Assumptions A2, A3, and the definition of the orthogonal complements $\boldsymbol{\alpha}_\perp$ and $\boldsymbol{\gamma}_\perp$. Thus, $\mathbf{C}(1)$ has rank $(n - r)$. This completes the proof of (R6). Note that $E(\Delta\mathbf{x}_t) = \mathbf{C}(1)\boldsymbol{\mu} = \boldsymbol{\tau}$.

(R7) follows immediately from (R6).

Finally, to prove (R8), first write $\mathbf{C}(L) = \mathbf{C}(1) + (1 - L)\mathbf{C}_1(L)$. Thus, from (R5),

$$
\begin{aligned}
\Delta\mathbf{x}_t &= \mathbf{C}(1)\boldsymbol{\mu} + \mathbf{C}(1)\boldsymbol{\varepsilon}_t + (1 - L)\mathbf{C}_1(L)\boldsymbol{\mu} + (1 - L)\mathbf{C}_1(L)\boldsymbol{\varepsilon}_t \\
&= \mathbf{C}(1)\boldsymbol{\mu} + \mathbf{C}(1)\boldsymbol{\varepsilon}_t + (1 - L)\mathbf{C}_1(L)\boldsymbol{\varepsilon}_t.
\end{aligned}
$$

Integrating this expression gives

$$\mathbf{x}_t = \mathbf{x}_0 + \mathbf{C}(1)\sum_{i=1}^{t}\boldsymbol{\varepsilon}_i + \mathbf{C}(1)\boldsymbol{\mu}t + \mathbf{S}_t,$$

as required. This completes the proof of the theorem.

5.3.2. Interpreting the Results of the Granger Representation Theorem

Several features are noteworthy in the theorem proved above. First, it may be seen from (R2) and (R8) respectively that, while $\mathbf{x}_t$ is non-stationary (because it contains the integrated errors $\sum_{i=1}^{t}\boldsymbol{\varepsilon}_i$), $\boldsymbol{\alpha}'\mathbf{x}_t$ is stationary. In fact, $\boldsymbol{\alpha}'\mathbf{x}_t$ provides the set of co-integrated combinations of the x_{it}.

Second, despite the presence of a drift term in the process generating $\mathbf{x}_t$, there is no linear trend in the co-integrated combinations. From (R6) and (R8), the trend in the $\mathbf{x}_t$ process disappears if $\boldsymbol{\gamma}'_\perp \boldsymbol{\mu} = \mathbf{0}_{(n-r)\times 1}$.

Third, (R6) is the condition needed for the process to be integrated of order 1. If this matrix is not of full rank, $|\widetilde{\mathbf{A}}(L)| = 0$ will have a root of 1 and a further unit root can be extracted from the system, leading to a system of I(2) variables.

Fourth, $\mathbf{C}(1)$ is an n-dimensional square matrix but has rank $n - r$. Hence, starting from the assumption of a reduced-rank matrix $\boldsymbol{\pi}$ in the autoregressive representation, we derive a reduced-rank matrix $\mathbf{C}(1)$ in the moving-average representation. As we show in Chapter 8, it is possible to go in the other direction and derive the result that a matrix $\mathbf{C}(1)$ with rank $(n - r)$ implies, for a co-integrated system, a matrix of the form $\boldsymbol{\pi}$ with rank r. Indeed, there is an interesting duality between the singularity of the 'impact' matrix $\boldsymbol{\pi}$ for the autoregressive representation and the singularity of the impact matrix $\mathbf{C}(1)$ for the moving-average representation. The null space for $\mathbf{C}(1)'$ is the range space for $\boldsymbol{\pi}$ and the range space for $\boldsymbol{\pi}'$ is the null space for $\mathbf{C}(1)$. This follows from using (R7) and noting that $\boldsymbol{\pi}(1)\mathbf{C}(1) = \mathbf{C}(1)\boldsymbol{\pi}(1) = \mathbf{0}_n$. This duality will be further in evidence in Chapter 8, when we derive the autoregressive representation of the system from its moving-average representation.

Fifth, if $\boldsymbol{\gamma}'_\perp \boldsymbol{\mu} = \mathbf{0}_{(n-r)\times 1}$, then $\boldsymbol{\mu}$ lies in the orthogonal space of $\boldsymbol{\gamma}_\perp$ and hence in the *space* of $\boldsymbol{\gamma}$. Thus, $\boldsymbol{\mu}$ may be written as $\boldsymbol{\gamma}\boldsymbol{\beta}_0$ where $\boldsymbol{\beta}_0$ is an arbitrary $r \times 1$ vector. From the expression for $E(\boldsymbol{\alpha}'\mathbf{x}_t)$ in (R4), note that $E(\boldsymbol{\alpha}'\mathbf{x}_t) = -\boldsymbol{\beta}_0$, and the constant enters the system only via the error-correction term. This may be seen more clearly by rewriting (26) as

$$\begin{aligned}
\Delta\mathbf{x}_t &= \boldsymbol{\mu} + \sum_{i=1}^{k-1} \boldsymbol{\Gamma}_i(1 - L)L^i\mathbf{x}_t + \boldsymbol{\pi}\mathbf{x}_{t-k} + \boldsymbol{\varepsilon}_t \\
&= \boldsymbol{\gamma}\boldsymbol{\beta}_0 + \sum_{i=1}^{k-1} \boldsymbol{\Gamma}_i(1 - L)L^i\mathbf{x}_t + \boldsymbol{\gamma}\boldsymbol{\alpha}'\mathbf{x}_{t-k} + \boldsymbol{\varepsilon}_t \\
&= \sum_{i=1}^{k-1} \boldsymbol{\Gamma}_i(1 - L)L^i\mathbf{x}_t + \boldsymbol{\gamma}(\boldsymbol{\beta}_0 + \boldsymbol{\alpha}'\mathbf{x}_{t-k}) + \boldsymbol{\varepsilon}_t.
\end{aligned}$$

If this restriction is not satisfied, the intercept enters the system both in the error-correction term and as an autonomous growth component. In Chapter 8, where we present the Johansen maximum-likelihood procedure for estimating the co-integrating relationships, the treatment of the constant is important in determining the estimation procedure and the set of critical values to be used for inference.

Finally, the analysis can be extended to include seasonal components.

The theorem may also be extended (see Hylleberg and Mizon 1989*a*) to incorporate several additional representations of co-integrated systems. Among these are the Bewley and common-trends representations (the latter due to Stock and Watson 1988*b*).

5.3.3. *Granger Representation Theorem (supplement)*

(R9) There exists a Bewley (1979) representation

$$\mathbf{0} = \mathbf{\Omega}_1(L)(1 - L)\mathbf{x}_t + \boldsymbol{\varepsilon}_{1t},$$
$$\boldsymbol{\gamma}^*\boldsymbol{\alpha}'\mathbf{x}_t = \mathbf{\Omega}_2(L)(1 - L)\mathbf{x}_t + \boldsymbol{\varepsilon}_{2t},$$

where $\mathbf{\Omega}_1(L)$ and $\mathbf{\Omega}_2(L)$ are $(n - r) \times n$ and $r \times n$ matrices consisting of stable lag polynomials of order $k - 1$, and where $\mathbf{\Omega}_1(0)$ and $\mathbf{\Omega}_2(0)$ are matrices different from the zero matrix, while $\boldsymbol{\gamma}^*$ is an $r \times r$ matrix of rank r.

(R10) There exists a common-trends representation

$$\mathbf{x}_t = \mathbf{\Phi}\mathbf{\Pi}_t + \boldsymbol{\nu}_t,$$

where $\mathbf{\Phi}$ is an $n \times (n - r)$ matrix of rank $n - r$, $\mathbf{\Pi}_t$ an $(n - r) \times 1$ vector which is a linear transformation of $\sum_{i=1}^{t}\boldsymbol{\varepsilon}_i$, and

$$\boldsymbol{\nu}_t = \mathbf{C}^*(L)\boldsymbol{\varepsilon}_t.$$

The polynomial matrix $\mathbf{C}^*(L)$ is defined as

$$\mathbf{C}^*(L) = (1 - L)^{-1}(\mathbf{C}(L) - \mathbf{C}(1))$$
$$= \sum_{j=0}^{\infty}\left(\sum_{i=0}^{j}\mathbf{C}_i - \mathbf{C}(1)\right)L^j = -\sum_{j=0}^{\infty}\left(\sum_{i=j+1}^{\infty}\mathbf{C}_i\right)L^j \equiv -\sum_{j=0}^{\infty}\mathbf{C}_j^*L^j.$$

The proof of the supplement to the Granger Representation Theorem is given by Hylleberg and Mizon (1989*a*).

Next, we will consider the DGP given by equations (1)–(6) above and derive a few of the above alternative representations. The exercise will then be repeated for another example taken from Engle and Yoo (1987). But first, we need to discuss the importance of each of these alternative representations.[8]

[8] The discussion in Ch. 2, although dealing mainly with I(0) variables, is relevant here. The properties of linear transformations of linear models carry through unchanged, and consequently so do the reasons for estimating particular transformations.

5.4. Significance of Alternative Representations

The moving-average representation is a natural starting-point for analysing variables that are covariance-stationary after first-differencing. However, the error-correction, interim-multiplier, and Bewley representations either offer greater insight into the equilibrium relationships among the co-integrated variables or have operational value in deriving the long-run multipliers or the number of co-integrating vectors.

1. The error-correction representation has the special advantage of separating the long-run and the short-run responses. It is also an important part of what has come to be known as the Engle–Granger two-step procedure, which is discussed later in the chapter. A small modification of the error-correction representation provides the interim-multiplier representation which has been used by Johansen (1988) to develop a maximum-likelihood estimator of the dimension of the co-integration space. Likelihood-ratio tests can be used to determine empirically the value of r, the number of co-integrating vectors.

2. The features of the Bewley representation are described in Chapter 2. In particular, if $n = 2$, one can read directly the estimate of the co-integrating representation. However, as the co-integrating vector is not necessarily unique for $n > 2$,[9] the Bewley transform properly estimated (by IV) will give consistent estimates of the co-integrating *space* although non-unique estimates of the long-run parameters.

3. The common-trends representation decomposes the non-stationary series into a stationary component and a stochastic trend component.

The choice among these equivalent alternative representations is determined primarily by the particular question the investigator wishes to answer.

5.5. Alternative Representations of Co-integrated Variables: Two Examples

5.5.1. *Example 1*

Consider the DGP given by equations (1)–(6). Take $|\rho| < 1$. Then x_t and y_t are co-integrated, and by the Granger Representation Theorem must have vector autoregressive, error-correction, and moving-average representations. We derive each of these in turn.

[9] By this we mean that, if $\mathbf{x}_t$ has $n > 2$ components, then, in general, the dimension of the co-integrating space can be $1 \leqslant r \leqslant n - 1$.

VAR representation

$$\Delta x_t + \beta \Delta y_t = \varepsilon_{1t} \tag{33}$$

$$\Delta x_t + \alpha \Delta y_t = \varepsilon_{2t} - (1-\rho)x_{t-1} - \alpha(1-\rho)y_{t-1} \tag{34}$$

Equations (33) and (34) are derived from (1)–(2) by first-differencing and using $e_t = (x_t + \alpha y_t)$. Thus,

$$\begin{bmatrix} 1 & \beta \\ 1 & \alpha \end{bmatrix} \begin{bmatrix} \Delta x_t \\ \Delta y_t \end{bmatrix} = \begin{bmatrix} \varepsilon_{1t} \\ \varepsilon_{2t} - (1-\rho)x_{t-1} - \alpha(1-\rho)y_{t-1} \end{bmatrix}. \tag{35}$$

Taking the inverse of the matrix multiplying the vector of the first-differenced x_t and y_t, we have

$$\begin{bmatrix} \Delta x_t \\ \Delta y_t \end{bmatrix} = (\alpha-\beta)^{-1} \begin{bmatrix} (\alpha\varepsilon_{1t} - \beta\varepsilon_{2t}) + \beta(1-\rho)x_{t-1} + \beta\alpha(1-\rho)y_{t-1} \\ (\varepsilon_{2t} - \varepsilon_{1t}) - (1-\rho)x_{t-1} - \alpha(1-\rho)y_{t-1} \end{bmatrix} \tag{36}$$

or

$$\begin{bmatrix} \Delta x_t \\ \Delta y_t \end{bmatrix} = (\alpha-\beta)^{-1} \begin{bmatrix} \beta(1-\rho) & \beta\alpha(1-\rho) \\ -(1-\rho) & -\alpha(1-\rho) \end{bmatrix} \begin{bmatrix} x_{t-1} \\ y_{t-1} \end{bmatrix} + \begin{bmatrix} \zeta_{1t} \\ \zeta_{2t} \end{bmatrix}, \tag{36a}$$

which is the VAR representation, where we have relabelled the two linear combinations of ε_{1t} and ε_{2t} as ζ_{1t} and ζ_{2t}.

ECM representation. This follows directly from the VAR representation:

$$\begin{aligned} \Delta x_t &= \beta\delta(x_{t-1} + \alpha y_{t-1}) + \zeta_{1t} \\ &= \beta\delta z_{t-1} + \zeta_{1t} \\ &= \theta_1 z_{t-1} + \zeta_{1t}, \end{aligned} \tag{37}$$

$$\begin{aligned} \Delta y_t &= -\delta(x_{t-1} + \alpha y_{t-1}) + \zeta_{2t} \\ &= -\delta z_{t-1} + \zeta_{2t} \\ &= \theta_2 z_{t-1} + \zeta_{2t} \end{aligned} \tag{38}$$

where we let $\delta = (\alpha-\beta)^{-1}(1-\rho)$ and $z_t = (x_t + \alpha y_t)$.

From the ECM representation, δ is non-zero if and only if ρ is not equal to 1. But $\rho = 1$ is precisely the condition that makes both u_t and v_t random walks and leads to a non-cointegrated system. In other words, if $\rho = 1$, there does not exist an α that makes the linear combination of x and y stationary. From (36*a*), at $\rho = 1$, the levels variables vanish in the VAR, which is then in differences only. Testing for co-integration is considered formally in Chapter 7. Intuitively, however, tests for co-integration in this model may be conducted in two equivalent forms.

1. *Static regression of x_t on y_t.* The test for co-integration is a test of the null hypothesis that $\rho = 1$ in the residuals. This null may be tested by using the Sargan–Bhargava (1983) or Dickey–Fuller statistics and tables.

2. *Regression using the error-correction form of the system, followed by a test of the null hypotheses H_0^1: $\theta_1 = 0$, H_0^2: $\theta_2 = 0$ or of the joint null H_0^J: $\theta_1 = \theta_2 = 0$.* There is a problem here: if α is unknown, it must be estimated from the data. But if the null hypothesis that $\rho = 1$ is valid, α is not identified and the error-correction regression, at least in the form specified by the theorem, is invalid. Only if the series are co-integrated can α be simply estimated by a co-integrating regression, but a test must be based upon the distribution of the statistic assuming that the null is true.

There is however a solution. It consists in specifying the error-correction quite generally, on the lines suggested in Chapter 2, and deducing the values of α, θ_1, and θ_2. That is, in the absence of prior knowledge, one may simply use $x_t - y_t$ in the error-correction term with suitable lags of x and y added to the regression. Recall that in Chapter 2 we showed that the estimates of the short-run adjustment coefficients, given here by θ_1 and θ_2, are invariant to assumptions made about the long-run coefficient. Thus, θ_1 and θ_2 are estimated consistently regardless of whether or not a homogeneous ECM is estimated. Therefore, an equivalent test for the null of no co-integration could be constructed based on the regression coefficients without requiring knowledge of the value of α.

The joint test of H_0^J above is more efficient given that the cross-equation restriction in (37) and (38) implies that the error-correction term z_{t-1} enters both equations. Furthermore, estimating (37) and (38) as a system is likely to lead to estimates more efficient than those derived from estimating (37) and (38) separately. This is because, in general, neither x_t nor y_t is weakly exogenous for the parameters of the other equation, owing to the cross-equation restriction. The issue of single-equation versus systems estimation which this example illustrates is discussed in Chapter 8.

MA representation. From (7)–(8), we have

$$x_t = b_{11}u_t + b_{12}e_t \tag{7'}$$

$$y_t = b_{21}u_t + b_{22}e_t. \tag{8'}$$

The MA representation follows by expressing u_t as $(1 - L)^{-1}\varepsilon_{1t}$ and v_t as $(1 - \rho L)^{-1}\varepsilon_{2t}$. Thus, multiplying both sides of (7′) and (8′) by $(1 - L)$ gives

$$(1 - L)\begin{bmatrix} x_t \\ y_t \end{bmatrix} = \begin{bmatrix} b_{11} & b_{12}(1 - L)(1 - \rho L)^{-1} \\ b_{21} & b_{22}(1 - L)(1 - \rho L)^{-1} \end{bmatrix}\begin{bmatrix} \varepsilon_{1t} \\ \varepsilon_{2t} \end{bmatrix}. \tag{39}$$

5.5.2. Example 2

Assume that, in the MA representation, the DGP is given by

$$(1 - L)\begin{bmatrix} x_t \\ y_t \end{bmatrix} = (1 - 0.4L)^{-1}\begin{bmatrix} 1 - 0.8L & 0.8L \\ 0.1L & 1 - 0.6L \end{bmatrix}\begin{bmatrix} e_{1t} \\ e_{2t} \end{bmatrix}$$

$$= (1 - 0.4L)^{-1}\mathbf{C}(L)\mathbf{e}_t$$

$$= \mathbf{D}(L)\mathbf{e}_t \tag{40}$$

where $\mathbf{e}_t$ is the vector $(e_{1t}, e_{2t})'$.

VAR representation. By direct inversion of the polynomial matrix,

$$\mathbf{C}(L)^{-1} = (1 - L)^{-1}\,(1 - 0.4L)^{-1}\begin{bmatrix} 1 - 0.6L & -0.8L \\ -0.1L & 1 - 0.8L \end{bmatrix}, \tag{41}$$

which implies, upon multiplying both sides of (40) by $\mathbf{C}(L)^{-1}$ and cancelling,

$$\begin{bmatrix} 1 - 0.6L & -0.8L \\ -0.1L & 1 - 0.8L \end{bmatrix}\begin{bmatrix} x_t \\ y_t \end{bmatrix} = \mathbf{e}_t. \tag{42}$$

This is the autoregressive representation.

ECM representation. For the ECM form, we need to express the DGP as

$$(1 - L)(x_t, y_t)' = -(\gamma_1, \gamma_2)'(\alpha_1 x_{t-1} - \alpha_2 y_{t-1}) + \mathbf{e}_t. \tag{43}$$

From the Granger Representation Theorem (R7), $(\alpha_1, \alpha_2)'$ solves

$$(\alpha_1, \alpha_2)\mathbf{D}(1) = (0, 0). \tag{44}$$

From (40),

$$\mathbf{D}(1) = (0.6)^{-1}\begin{bmatrix} 0.2 & 0.8 \\ 0.1 & 0.4 \end{bmatrix},$$

so that $\alpha_1 = 1$ and $\alpha_2 = -2$ solve (44).

Moreover, $(\gamma_1, \gamma_2)'$ solves

$$\mathbf{D}(1)(\gamma_1, \gamma_2)' = (0, 0)'. \tag{45}$$

Equation (45) gives $\gamma_1 = 0.4$ and $\gamma_2 = -0.1$, and so the ECM representation is given by

$$(1 - L)(x_t, y_t)' = -(0.4, -0.1)'(x_{t-1} + 2y_{t-1}) + \mathbf{e}_t.$$

It is easy to see from the ECM representation that the long-run solution is given by

$$x = -2y. \tag{46}$$

5.6. Engle–Granger Two-step Procedure

Engle and Granger (1987) proposed a two-step estimator for models involving co-integrated variables. In the first step, the parameters of the co-integrating vector are estimated by running the static regression in the levels of the variables. In the second step, these are used in the error-correction form. Both steps require only OLS, and the results may be shown to be consistent for all the parameters. In particular, the estimates of the parameters in the first step converge to their probability limits at rate T while the elements of the vector multiplying the error-correction term, in the second step, converge at the usual asymptotic rate of $T^{1/2}$.

This procedure is convenient because the dynamics do not need to be specified until the error-correction structure has been estimated (although it may nevertheless be sensible to do so, as we shall see below). We can illustrate this using a simple argument when there is no intercept.

An important implication of the theory of series x_t integrated of order one is that the variance of Δx_t is asymptotically negligible relative to that of x_t. Assume then that some dynamic relationship links the I(1) series $\{x_t\}$ and $\{y_t\}$, and that these two series are co-integrated. Consider the static regression of y_t on x_t,

$$y_t = \alpha x_t + v_t. \tag{47}$$

Now v_t contains all of the omitted dynamics, but these can be re-parameterized in terms of Δx_{t-j}, Δy_{t-m}, and $(y_{t-r} - \alpha x_{t-r})$, for j, m, $r > 0$, which are all I(0) if co-integrability holds. Thus, α is consistently estimated by the regression despite the complete omission of all dynamics. In fact,

$$\begin{aligned}\hat{\alpha} &= \left(\sum_{t=1}^{T} x_t y_t\right)\left(\sum_{t=1}^{T} x_t^2\right)^{-1} \\ &= \alpha + \left(\sum_{t=1}^{T} x_t v_t\right)\left(\sum_{t=1}^{T} x_t^2\right)^{-1}.\end{aligned} \tag{48}$$

Since $\{v_t\}$ is I(0) under co-integrability but $\{x_t\}$ is I(1),

$$T^{-1}\left(\sum_{t=1}^{T} x_t^2\right) \sim O_p(T), \tag{49}$$

whereas

$$T^{-1}\left(\sum_{t=1}^{T} x_t v_t\right) \sim O_p(1). \tag{50}$$

Thus,

$$T(\hat{\alpha} - \alpha) = \left(T^{-1} \sum_{t=1}^{T} x_t v_t\right)\left(T^{-2} \sum_{t=1}^{T} x_t^2\right)^{-1} \sim O_p(1), \tag{51}$$

which implies that

$$(\hat{\alpha} - \alpha) \sim O_p(T^{-1}). \tag{52}$$

Hence $\hat{\alpha}$ converges to α at a rate of $O_p(T)$ and not at the usual rate of $O_p(T^{1/2})$. Convergence is rapid asymptotically and it is this rapid convergence of the estimates of the coefficients that is used by Engle and Granger as the basis of their two-step estimator.

Since $\hat{\alpha}$ differs from α by terms of $O_p(T^{-1})$, the asymptotic results for estimation of dynamic models with I(1) variables will be the same whether α is estimated or known. Moreover, differencing must reduce the order of integration of an integrated variable by unity, so if Δy_t is related to Δx_t and perhaps lags of both of these, and if $\{x_t\}$ and $\{y_t\}$ are co-integrated, then $y_{t-1} - \alpha x_{t-1}$ is I(0) and can be included in the ECM model as if α were known (that is, the sampling variance of $\hat{\alpha}$ can be ignored). If $\{y_t\}$ and $\{x_t\}$ are not co-integrated, then we have the familiar spurious regression problem; if they are co-integrated, the benefits accruing from a static regression are potentially large.

The so-called 'super-consistency theorem' due to Stock (1987) may be stated formally as follows.

THEOREM (Stock 1987). Suppose that $\mathbf{x}_t$ satisfies $(1 - L)\mathbf{x}_t = \mathbf{C}(L)\mathbf{e}_t$ with $\mathbf{C}(L) = \mathbf{C}(1) + (1 - L)\mathbf{C}^*(L)$, where $\mathbf{C}^*(L)$ has all of its latent roots inside the unit circle. If $\mathbf{C}^*(L)$ is absolutely summable,[10] the disturbances have finite fourth-order absolute moments, and $\mathbf{x}_t$ is CI(1, 1) with r co-integrating vectors (incorporated in a matrix $\boldsymbol{\alpha}$) satisfying, uniquely,

$$\boldsymbol{\alpha}'\mathbf{M} = \mathbf{0}; \qquad \operatorname{vec} \boldsymbol{\alpha} = \mathbf{q} + \mathbf{Q}\boldsymbol{\theta},$$

then[11]

$$T^{1-\delta}(\hat{\boldsymbol{\theta}} - \boldsymbol{\theta}) \xrightarrow{\text{p}} \mathbf{0} \text{ for } \delta > 0.$$

Thus, instead of converging at rate $T^{1/2}$, as in stationary processes,

[10] The infinite sequence $\{c_j\}_1^\infty$ is said to be absolutely summable if $\sum_{j=1}^{\infty}|c_j| < \infty$. For the matrix $\mathbf{C}^*(L)$ to be absolutely summable, the condition is that $\sum_{j=0}^{\infty}\|\mathbf{C}_j^*\| < \infty$.

[11] The elements of $\mathbf{q}$ and $\mathbf{Q}$ will typically be all zeroes and ones, defining one coefficient in each column of $\boldsymbol{\alpha}$ to be unity and defining rotations if $r > 1$. $\mathbf{M} = \operatorname{plim} E(T^{-2} \sum_{i=1}^{T} \mathbf{x}_t \mathbf{x}_t')$.

least-squares estimators converge at a rate of T. This theorem and the error-correction representation of co-integrated systems may be allied to give the following theorem.

> THEOREM (Engle and Granger 1987). The two-step estimator of a single equation of an error-correction system with one co-integrating vector, obtained by taking the estimate $\hat{\boldsymbol{\alpha}}$ of $\boldsymbol{\alpha}$ from the static regression in place of the true value for estimation of the error-correction form at a second stage, will have the same limiting distribution as the maximum-likelihood estimator using the true value of $\boldsymbol{\alpha}$. Least-squares standard errors in the second stage will provide consistent estimates of the true standard errors.

5.6.1. Sketch-proof of Engle–Granger Theorem (Bivariate Case)

The following is a proof of this theorem for the bivariate case. Consider the estimation of β and γ in the two equations given by

$$\Delta y_t = \beta \Delta x_t + \gamma(y_{t-1} - \alpha x_{t-1}) + \varepsilon_t; \tag{53}$$

$$\Delta y_t = \beta \Delta x_t + \gamma(y_{t-1} - \hat{\alpha} x_{t-1}) + \varepsilon_t^*. \tag{54}$$

y_t and x_t are co-integrated I(1) variables with the co-integrating parameter given by α. In the context of the discussion in this chapter, the error-correction mechanism is estimated in (53) using the true value of the co-integrating parameter, while in (54) $\hat{\alpha}$ is substituted for α, where $\hat{\alpha}$ is derived from the static regression of y_t on x_t. Also, $\varepsilon_t^* = \varepsilon_t + \gamma(\hat{\alpha} - \alpha)x_{t-1}$. Let $z_t = y_t - \alpha x_t$.

We need to show that the asymptotic distributions of the estimators $\hat{\beta}$ and $\hat{\gamma}$, of β and γ respectively, are the same regardless of whether one uses α or $\hat{\alpha}$ (that is, whether one estimates (53) or (54)).

In standard fashion, we have from (53) (assuming adequate initial values)

$$T^{1/2}\begin{bmatrix} (\hat{\beta} - \beta) \\ (\hat{\gamma} - \gamma) \end{bmatrix} = \begin{bmatrix} T^{-1}\sum_{t=1}^{T}(\Delta x_t)^2 & T^{-1}\sum_{t=1}^{T}\Delta x_t z_{t-1} \\ T^{-1}\sum_{t=1}^{T}\Delta x_t z_{t-1} & T^{-1}\sum_{t=1}^{T} z_{t-1}^2 \end{bmatrix}^{-1} \begin{bmatrix} T^{-1/2}\sum_{t=1}^{T}\Delta x_t \varepsilon_t \\ T^{-1/2}\sum_{t=1}^{T} z_{t-1}\varepsilon_t \end{bmatrix}. \tag{55}$$

The estimators derived from (54) are also given by (55) but with $\hat{z}_{t-1}$ and ε_t^* replacing z_t and ε_t. From this, it is easy to deduce that the result will be demonstrated if the following conditions are shown to be true:

(i) $\text{plim}\, T^{-1} \sum_{t=1}^{T} \Delta x_t z_{t-1} = \text{plim}\, T^{-1} \sum_{t=1}^{T} \Delta x_t \hat{z}_{t-1}$;

(ii) $\text{plim}\, T^{-1} \sum_{t=1}^{T} z_{t-1}^2 = \text{plim}\, T^{-1} \sum_{t=1}^{T} \hat{z}_{t-1}^2$;

(iii) the asymptotic distributions of $T^{-1/2} \sum_{t=1}^{T} z_{t-1}\varepsilon_t$ and $T^{-1/2} \sum_{t=1}^{T} \hat{z}_{t-1}\varepsilon_t^*$ are the same;

(iv) the asymptotic distributions of $T^{-1/2} \sum_{t=1}^{T} \Delta x_t \varepsilon_t$ and $T^{-1/2} \sum_{t=1}^{T} \Delta x_t \varepsilon_t^*$ are the same.

In (53), we assume that $\{\varepsilon_t\}$ is an innovation process such that $E(\Delta x_t \varepsilon_t) = 0$.

Note first that, by the properties of I(0) and I(1) series, as used and discussed in Chapters 3 and 4, the following expressions are $O_p(1)$ (that is, non-explosive and non-degenerate as $T \to \infty$):

(a) $T^{-2} \sum_{t=1}^{T} x_{t-1}^2$; (56)

(b) $T^{-1} \sum_{t=1}^{T} x_{t-1}\hat{z}_{t-1}$; $T^{-1} \sum_{t=1}^{T} x_{t-1}\Delta x_t$; $T^{-1} \sum_{t=1}^{T} x_{t-1}\varepsilon_t$ (57)

(c) $T(\hat{\alpha} - \alpha)$. (58)

Secondly,

$$z_{t-1} = \hat{z}_{t-1} + (\hat{\alpha} - \alpha)x_{t-1}. \tag{59}$$

Using (59),

$$\begin{aligned} \text{plim}\, T^{-1} \sum_{t=1}^{T} \Delta x_t z_{t-1} &= \text{plim}\, T^{-1} \sum_{t=1}^{T} \Delta x_t \hat{z}_{t-1} + \text{plim}\, T^{-1}(\hat{\alpha} - \alpha) \sum_{t=1}^{T} \Delta x_t x_{t-1} \\ &= \text{plim}\, T^{-1} \sum_{t=1}^{T} \Delta x_t \hat{z}_{t-1} \\ &\quad + \text{plim}\, T^{-1}\{[T(\hat{\alpha} - \alpha)] T^{-1} \sum_{t=1}^{T} \Delta x_t x_{t-1}\}. \end{aligned}$$

Result (i) now follows from (57) and (58). Also,

$$\begin{aligned} \text{plim}\, T^{-1} \sum_{t=1}^{T} z_{t-1}^2 = \text{plim} \Bigg(& T^{-1} \sum_{t=1}^{T} \hat{z}_{t-1}^2 + (\hat{\alpha} - \alpha)^2 T^{-1} \sum_{t=1}^{T} x_{t-1}^2 \\ & + 2(\hat{\alpha} - \alpha) T^{-1} \sum_{t=1}^{T} x_{t-1}\hat{z}_{t-1} \Bigg) \end{aligned}$$

$$= \operatorname{plim} T^{-1}\sum_{t=1}^{T}\hat{z}_{t-1}^{2} + \operatorname{plim} T^{-1}\left\{[T(\hat{\alpha}-\alpha)]^{2}T^{-2}\sum_{t=1}^{T}x_{t-1}^{2}\right\}$$

$$+2\operatorname{plim} T^{-1}\left\{[T(\hat{\alpha}-\alpha)]T^{-1}\sum_{t=1}^{T}x_{t-1}\hat{z}_{t-1}\right\}.$$

Result (ii) now follows from (56), (57), and (58).

Finally,

$$T^{-1/2}\sum_{t=1}^{T}z_{t-1}\varepsilon_t = T^{-1/2}\sum_{t=1}^{T}\hat{z}_{t-1}\varepsilon_t + T^{-1/2}[T(\hat{\alpha}-\alpha)]T^{-1}\sum_{t=1}^{T}x_{t-1}\varepsilon_t$$

$$= T^{-1/2}\sum_{t=1}^{T}\hat{z}_{t-1}\varepsilon_t^{*} - \gamma T^{-1/2}[T(\hat{\alpha}-\alpha)]T^{-1}\sum_{t=1}^{T}\hat{z}_{t-1}x_{t-1}$$

$$+ T^{-1/2}[T(\hat{\alpha}-\alpha)]T^{-1}\sum_{t=1}^{T}x_{t-1}\varepsilon_t.$$

By (57) and (58), the last two expressions on the right-hand side of the above equality are $O_p(T^{-1/2})$. Result (iii) follows, and (iv) is proved analogously from:

$$T^{-1/2}\sum_{t=1}^{T}\Delta x_t\varepsilon_t = T^{-1/2}\sum_{t=1}^{T}\Delta x_t\varepsilon_t^{*} - \gamma T^{-1/2}[T(\hat{\alpha}-\alpha)]T^{-1}\sum_{t=1}^{T}\Delta x_t x_{t-1}.$$

6

Regression with Integrated Variables

We have seen how the presence of integrated variables poses some special problems which do not appear when working with stationary series. These might lead us to believe that a new range of techniques needs to be considered in order to handle such data. However, as we show in this chapter, we can continue to apply standard regressions if we pay attention to orders of integration and use dynamic specifications which take account of any co-integrating relationships among the variables.

The Engle–Granger theorem in Chapter 5, laying emphasis on simple static regressions, implies a good deal about the way in which an investigator ought to proceed with an econometric study of integrated variables. Some of this is related to the evolution of modelling practice among econometricians.

Econometricians of the 1970s began to be suspicious of regressions using data in levels. Their suspicions were reinforced by worries expressed by time-series analysts relating to spurious regressions. The focus of attention began to shift towards the need to have properly specified models with rich dynamic structures. The move, following Mizon (1977), Sims (1977), Hendry and Mizon (1978), and Hendry and Richard (1982), was towards a method of econometric research that preferred models which began with as general a specification as possible, and continued with simplification to a parsimonious econometric model following from imposing constraints consistent with observed data. (See Spanos (1986) for a detailed treatment.) The literature on co-integration reinstated some confidence in static regressions in levels, and good econometric method appeared to have taken a full circle; as long as the I(1) variables were co-integrated, such regressions made sense.

There are nonetheless several reasons for continuing to treat static regressions as being in general sub-optimal. First of all, the estimate $\hat{\alpha}$ is biased for the co-integrating parameter α and, although that bias is $O_p(T^{-1})$, it can be substantial in finite samples. The bias is likely to be a function of some parameter such as the mean lag of the dynamic adjustment process relating $\{y_t\}$ to $\{x_t\}$. In some circumstances, therefore, a return to dynamic modelling would seem to be the appropriate response to the problems of static-regression biases. Already a body of work exists demonstrating the poor performance of static regressions for many types of problem (Banerjee, Dolado, Hendry, and Smith 1986, and Stock 1987). Second, the distributions of coefficient estimates will typically take non-standard forms even where the series are co-integrated. The 'non-standardness', by which we generally mean asymptotic non-normality, comes from the property that the series are integrated of order greater than or equal to 1. The fundamental point is that the distribution theory that applies to non-stationary series is different from the familiar Gaussian asymptotic theory. The estimators have distributions, in general, which are functionals of the Wiener processes discussed in Chapters 1 and 3. However, some of the standard asymptotic theory may be restored in dynamic models.

We will elaborate on the second of these points, leaving a discussion of the first until Chapter 7. It is important to point out at the outset, in order not to mislead readers, that it is not true that single-equation dynamic models are necessarily superior to their static counterparts. The next two sections present examples where single-equation dynamic models do perform satisfactorily. Yet, as the discussion in Chapter 8 shows, it is possible to construct many cases where single-equation dynamic models by themselves are not sufficient for obtaining efficient and unbiased estimates (see Engle *et al.* 1983 and Phillips and Loretan 1991).

There are several interrelated difficulties which are important and which collectively imply that the issue is broader than simply a comparison of dynamic with static models. An informal description of the problems encountered in modelling non-stationary variables in a single-equation framework would identify at least five effects. First, the presence of unit roots induces non-standard distributions of the coefficient estimates. Second, the error process may not be a martingale difference sequence. Third, the explanatory variables may each be generated by processes that display autocorrelation; taken in conjunction with the second effect, this gives rise to 'second-order' biases. Fourth, there may be more than one co-integrating vector. Finally, the explanatory variables in the single equation may not be weakly exogenous for the parameters being estimated. Weak exogeneity can fail if, say, a co-integrating vector enters more than one equation in the system generating the variables.

Static regressions can be affected by all five of the problems listed above, while dynamic models may be able to accommodate the first three effects, as in the examples given in the sections that follow. However, estimates derived from single-equation *dynamic* models are not optimal if weak exogeneity fails to hold. This final observation extends the discussion from the realm of modelling unit-root processes to the all-encompassing realm of general econometric modelling. This discussion is formalized in Chapter 8 and illustrated with several examples.

6.1. Unbalanced Regressions and Orthogonality Tests

Mankiw and Shapiro (1985, 1986) drew attention to a problem that may arise in applying standard distributions to inference where there are non-stationary (or borderline non-stationary) series present, and in particular to the problem of inference concerning orthogonality between series. While the problem is, as with spurious regression, essentially a problem of integrated data, it will appear with near-integrated data in finite samples.[1] With this qualification, the problem may be said to arise in *unbalanced* regressions: that is, regressions in which the regressand is not of the same order of integration as the regressors, or any linear combination of the regressors.[2]

The Mankiw–Shapiro discussion centres on a condition such as

$$E_{t-1}(y_t) = c, \text{ implying } y_t = c + v_t, \qquad E_{t-1}(v_t) = 0, \tag{1}$$

where E_{t-1} is interpreted as the expectation, conditional on information realized at time $t-1$, of the value of some variable which may be dated in the future. That such a condition holds is often tested with a regression such as

$$y_t = c_1 + c_2 x_{t-1} + v_t, \tag{2}$$

where $c_2 = 0$ under the null hypothesis that (1) holds. Examples of such hypotheses and tests arise frequently in models that postulate the full use of all realized information. One such example from macroeconomics is Hall's (1978) formulation of the life-cycle/permanent-income model, which, given a stringent set of assumptions, implies that consumption should follow a random walk. Tests of this hypothesis have typically taken the form of regressions of differenced consumption on a constant and one or more lagged income or consumption terms; under the null hypothesis the coefficients on the lagged terms should not be significantly different from zero.

Mankiw and Shapiro suggest examining the case in which the regressor x_t follows the AR(1) process:

$$x_t = \theta x_{t-1} + \varepsilon_t, \tag{3}$$

[1] While the experiments reported here use borderline stationary data, the results will also apply to integrated series.

[2] These are sometimes called inconsistent regressions. Inconsistency in this sense is unrelated to the concept of an inconsistent estimator of a parameter: see n. 3.

with

$$\text{corr}(\varepsilon_t, v_t) = \rho \quad \text{and} \quad \text{corr}(\varepsilon_{t+j}, v_t) = 0 \; \forall \, j \neq 0.$$

Note that this is not a problem of simultaneity bias: the regressor x_{t-1} is uncorrelated with v_t. A structure such as this is appropriate in many models in which these tests have been used. In the Hall (1978) model, for example, $\rho = 1$ where x_t and y_t represent current income and the change in current consumption respectively. Mankiw and Shapiro use Monte Carlo simulations to tabulate estimates of the actual rejection frequencies and critical values in t-type tests of H_0: $c_2 = 0$, when standard t-values are used. Table 6.1 reproduces a selection of their results for model (2) and also for the model with a linear time trend,

$$y_t = c_1 + c_2 x_{t-1} + c_3 t + v_t. \tag{4}$$

TABLE 6.1. Percentage rejection frequencies of standard t-tests at nominal 5 per cent level[a]

DGP: (1) + (3); Sample size = T; No. of replications = 1000

	Model (2)					Model (4)				
$\theta \setminus \rho$	1.0	0.9	0.8	0.5	0.0	1.0	0.9	0.8	0.5	0.0
(*a*) $T = 50$										
0.999	30	24	20	11	7	60	45	36	16	6
0.99	26	20	15	10	7	54	40	33	15	6
0.98	22	17	15	8	7	50	37	30	14	5
0.95	17	12	10	7	6	38	30	25	12	6
0.90	12	9	8	6	6	28	22	19	10	6
0.00	5	6	6	5	5	6	7	7	5	6
(*b*) $T = 200$										
0.999	29	23	20	10	5	61	48	38	18	5
0.99	18	15	13	8	4	41	32	27	13	5
0.98	13	10	9	7	5	29	24	20	11	6
0.95	9	7	7	6	5	17	14	12	7	6
0.90	7	6	6	6	6	10	9	8	6	7
0.00	5	4	4	5	5	5	5	4	5	5

[a] This table compares two sample sizes. While the test size distortions are generally smaller for the larger sample and will vanish as $T \to \infty$, this feature is specific to the borderline-stationary processes used ($\theta < 1$). For $\theta = 1$, distortions will persist as $T \to \infty$. Each of the entries a_{ij} (expressed as a fraction) has a standard error which can be approximated by $[(a_{ij})(1 - a_{ij})/N]^{1/2}$, where N is the number of replications (equal to 1000 here).

Source: Mankiw and Shapiro (1986).

As with the Dickey–Fuller statistics seen earlier, the size distortions in Table 6.1 spring from bias and skewness in the t-type statistic.

The critical values reported by Mankiw and Shapiro are not reproduced here; Galbraith, Dolado, and Banerjee (1987) show that these are sensitive to unobservable parameters of the underlying DGP, and, in considering a more general DGP, it is possible to relate the problem of size distortions to co-integration among regressors, and so to what has been called the balance or imbalance of the regression model.[3] Generalize (1) and (3) to

$$\begin{bmatrix} y_t \\ x_{1t} \\ x_{2t} \end{bmatrix} = \begin{bmatrix} 0 & 0 & 0 \\ 0 & \theta_{11} & \theta_{12} \\ 0 & 0 & \theta_{22} \end{bmatrix} \begin{bmatrix} y_{t-1} \\ x_{1t-1} \\ x_{2t-1} \end{bmatrix} + \begin{bmatrix} v_t \\ \varepsilon_{1t} \\ \varepsilon_{2t} \end{bmatrix},$$

with $v_t \sim \text{IN}(0, 1)$, $\varepsilon_{it} \sim \text{IN}(0, 1)$, $E(v_t \varepsilon_{1s}) = \delta_{ts}\rho$, $E(\varepsilon_{1t}\varepsilon_{2s}) = 0$, and $\delta_{ts} = 1$ if $t = s$, and 0 otherwise. The fitted model is generalized from (2) to

$$y_t = c_1 + c_2 x_{1,t-1} + c_3 x_{2,t-1} + v_t,$$

incorporating the new regressor. A classification of possible cases is given in Table 6.2. The notation NI(k) (nearly integrated) indicates that the series, although I($k-1$), are close to integrated processes of the given order. Only in case C are the two regressors 'nearly' *co-integrated* series, and in this case the co-integrating slope is $(1-\theta_{11})^{-1}\theta_{12}$.

The size distortions stressed by Mankiw and Shapiro for high values of ρ also appear in the cases B, D, and E (see Galbraith *et al.* 1987), where $\{x_{1t}\}$ is (nearly) I(1) and not co-integrated with $\{x_{2t}\}$. Size distortions begin to appear in case A as θ_{11} rises and case A approaches case E. Where the regressors are co-integrated, however (case C), the

TABLE 6.2. Classification of cases of interest

Case	θ_{11}	θ_{22}	θ_{12}	$\{x_{1t}\}$	$\{x_{2t}\}$
A	$\ll 1.0$	0.999	0.0	I(0)	NI(1)
B	0.999	$\ll 1.0$	0.0	NI(1)	I(0)
C	$\ll 1.0$	0.999	$\neq 0.0$	NI(1)	NI(1)
D	0.999	$\ll 1.0$	$\neq 0.0$	NI(1)	I(0)
E	0.999	0.999	0.0	NI(1)	NI(1)
F	0.999	0.999	$\neq 0.0$	NI(2)	NI(1)

[3] A regression is defined to be balanced if and only if the regressand and the regressors (either individually or collectively, as a co-integrated set) are of the same order of integration. The mere fact that a regression is unbalanced may not be a matter for concern; for example, ADF statistics are computed from models that, in this terminology, are unbalanced. They are nevertheless valid tools for inference as long as the correct critical values are used.

regression is balanced (there exists a linear combination of the regressors that has the same order of integration as the regressand) and size distortions do not appear. Case F resembles C except that θ_{11} is close to 1, indicating that co-integration is broken between the regressors; none the less, size distortions are not detectable as long as θ_{12} remains non-zero. This last finding demonstrates the difficulty of distinguishing, at modest sample sizes, the results of regressions with co-integrated regressors from those with regressors of differing, but both strictly positive, orders.

We see, in summary, that for integrated series (or, in finite samples, for the borderline-stationary series examined in these papers), with $\rho \cong 1$, size distortions may emerge when there is no linear combination of regressors that has the same order of integration as the regressand.[4]

For an intuitive view of these results, let us return to the consumption example and consider the orders of integration of the variables on the two sides of the regression. Consumption and income are both typically variables integrated of order one. Thus, the regression (2) has an I(0) variable (differenced consumption) regressed on an I(1) variable (lagged income in level) and the regression is unbalanced; the investigator is attempting to explain an I(0) variable by a variable integrated of higher order. This strategy will eventually fail, as the two variables must diverge by ever-larger amounts. Therefore, a requirement of estimation with integrated variables must be balance in the orders of integration of the variables on the left-hand and right-hand sides of the regression equation. However, there may be circumstances in which a test will be designed to involve regressand and regressors having different orders of integration—for example, efficiency tests such as those mentioned above. We must bear in mind, of course, that test statistics from such regressions will have non-standard distributions.

The importance of the latter point follows from the observation that, even when the regressand (e.g. y_t) and the regressor (x_t) are both integrated of order 1 and are co-integrated, the t-statistic on the coefficient of x_t still has a non-standard distribution which makes ordinary t and normal tables unusable for purposes of inference. On the other hand, if the order of integration of both sides is zero (which may be ensured by looking for a co-integrated set of regressors and using a sufficiently differenced term as the regressand), the t-statistics can be shown to have asymptotically normal distributions. This implies some advantage to the use of dynamic rather than static regressions, since lagging variables and including them as regressors often has the same effect as providing a co-integrated set of regressor variables. The

[4] Campbell and Dufour (1991) offer, as a way of overcoming the Mankiw–Shapiro problem, an alternative non-parametric test of orthogonality which is independent of some nuisance parameters in the DGP.

essential point is to find some way of re-parameterizing the regression such that in the re-parameterized form, the regressors, either jointly or individually, are integrated of order zero. Correspondingly, the regressand must also be I(0). However, provided no restrictions are imposed, it is irrelevant whether or not the re-parameterization is actually carried out. As we have seen above in Chapter 2, non-singular linear transformations yield numerically equivalent results after transforming back, and so regressions that are linear transformations of each other have identical statistical properties. What is important, therefore, is the *possibility* of transforming in such a way that the regressors are integrated of the same order as the regressand, a possibility that is enhanced in a dynamic model as the probability of a co-integrated set being present is increased, although, as the discussion in the previous section shows, care must be taken if weak exogeneity fails to hold.

6.2. Dynamic Regressions

The remarks above would suggest that a sensible procedure for econometric investigations, even in the presence of integrated variables, is to use a dynamic specification that is as general as the constraints of data and sample allow. The 'general to specific' modelling method is effective here for a straightforward reason: the inclusion of several variables and their lags as regressors increases the chances of obtaining a co-integrated set of regressors. A dependent variable made stationary by differencing can be regressed on this co-integrated set, and standard *t*-, *F*-, and normal tables can be used for inference. The regression would then take the form of a differenced variable as the regressand, and differences and levels of variables as regressors.

A comprehensive account of the asymptotic theory associated with dynamic regressions of this kind appears in Sims *et al.* (1990). In their general formulation, the variables may have drifts and are allowed to be integrated and co-integrated of arbitrary order. The intuition for their results, moreover, is straightforward. They show that estimators of those parameters which can be rewritten as coefficients on mean-zero, non-integrated regressors, will have asymptotically normal joint distributions, converging at a rate $T^{1/2}$ to their probability limits. This rewriting may be accomplished either by differencing the regressors to achieve stationarity or by linearly combining subsets of these regressors as shown in Chapter 4. Stationarity, or more precisely non-integratedness, is achieved in the latter case if and only if subsets of the regressors are co-integrated.

There are three important properties of these transformations. First, starting from the original dynamic regression and transforming linearly in such a way that the regression is rewritten in terms of non-integrated regressors, the original parameters of interest can be identified from the parameters of the transformed regression. Second, because the transformed parameter estimates are asymptotically normally distributed, so are the untransformed estimates. Again, this is because linear transformations do not alter any of the statistical properties of the estimators of the regression coefficients. Finally, as shown by the analysis in Chapter 2, because any information obtained from a transformed regression can be obtained from an untransformed regression as well, the essential point is not that the transformations actually be undertaken, but rather that the scope exists for the appropriate transformations to be made, because appropriate regressors are present.

There is at least one other important case where asymptotic normality of coefficient estimates has been shown to hold. The result is due to West (1988) and occurs when a stochastic trend is present in the regression but is dominated, in the sense of orders of probability, by a non-stochastic trend component. West considers OLS and linear IV models of the form

$$w_t = \mathbf{x}_{1t}'\boldsymbol{\alpha} + \gamma y_t + e_t,$$

where y_t is a scalar I(1) time series the first difference of which has a non-zero unconditional mean, $\mathbf{x}_{1t}$ is a vector of stationary observable variables, and e_t is a stationary disturbance term. The dependent variable w_t is stationary if $\gamma = 0$ but non-stationary otherwise. West shows that the parameter estimates $\hat{\boldsymbol{\alpha}}$ and $\hat{\gamma}$ are asymptotically normal, given that $E(\Delta y_t)$ is non-zero. Note that, where we take $y_t = w_{t-1}$ and let $\mathbf{x}_1$ be a constant term, we have

$$w_t = \mu + \gamma w_{t-1} + e_t;$$

this is the process and model examined by Dickey and Fuller (1979), with the exception that they took $E(\Delta w_t) = 0$. In that case, the asymptotic distribution of the t-statistic for H_0: $\rho = 1$ is given in Table 4.2. Addition of a non-zero constant to the data-generation process, however, makes the asymptotic distribution of this statistic normal.

Asymptotic normality holds only when the non-zero constant (and trend) in the DGP is (are) matched by a constant (and trend) in the model. Including a trend in the model when the DGP does not contain a trend destroys this result. In the latter case, the Dickey–Fuller critical values given in the third block of Table 4.2 are again the appropriate ones to use.[5]

[5] This result follows from the *similarity* properties of the Dickey–Fuller statistics. The third block of Table 4.2 is computed by using a pure random walk (without constant or trend) as the DGP and $y_t = \alpha + \gamma t + \rho y_{t-1} + u_t$ as the model. When the DGP is altered to include a non-zero constant, with the model remaining unchanged, the critical values of the distributions of $\hat{\rho}$ and of the associated t-statistic are not affected: the distributions are invariant to the value of the constant in the DGP which implies similarity. A detailed discussion of this issue appears in Kiviet and Phillips (1992).

Since some non-zero constant seems likely to be present in the first differences of the processes generating many economic time series, we might suspect that the Dickey–Fuller distributions examined in detail in Chapter 4 may be of limited relevance. However, the relevance of the Dickey–Fuller (DF) values is determined by the relative magnitudes of the drift term and the standard deviation of the process.

Hylleberg and Mizon (1989*b*) present some simulation evidence for the AR(1) model. The critical values derived from our simulations, for sample sizes and values of the constant chosen by Hylleberg and Mizon, are given in Table 6.3. Since it is the size of μ relative to $(\text{var}(e_t))^{1/2}$ that is relevant, and $\text{var}(e_t) = 1$ in the experiments reported in Table 6.3, we treat μ as this ratio rather than the value of the constant term in the DGP alone. In general, for $\mu/(\text{var}(e_t))^{1/2} \geqslant 1/2$, the critical values of the normal density are closer to (although less than) the actual critical values than are the DF critical values.

TABLE 6.3. Empirical cumulative distribution of $t(\rho = 1)$
DGP: $x_t = \mu + x_{t-1} + e_t$, $e_t \sim \text{IN}(0, 1)$, $x_0 = 0$;
model: $x_t = \mu + \rho x_{t-1} + e_t$

Sample size (T)	Probability of a smaller value[a]								
	0.01	0.025	0.05	0.10	0.50	0.90	0.95	0.975	0.99
DF[b]	−3.43	−3.12	−2.86	−2.57	−1.56	−0.44	−0.07	0.23	0.60
(*a*) $\mu = 0$									
50	−3.57	−3.22	−2.92	−2.60	−1.55	−0.40	−0.03	0.30	0.66
100	−3.50	−3.17	−2.89	−2.59	−1.56	−0.42	−0.06	0.26	0.62
200	−3.47	−3.15	−2.88	−2.58	−1.56	−0.42	−0.06	0.25	0.62
400	−3.45	−3.13	−2.87	−2.57	−1.56	−0.43	−0.07	0.25	0.62
(*b*) $\mu = 0.001$									
50	−3.57	−3.22	−2.93	−2.60	−1.55	−0.40	−0.03	0.29	0.65
100	−3.49	−3.17	−2.89	−2.58	−1.56	−0.42	−0.06	0.26	0.63
200	−3.47	−3.14	−2.88	−2.57	−1.56	−0.42	−0.06	0.26	0.63
400	−3.46	−3.14	−2.87	−2.57	−1.56	−0.43	−0.07	0.24	0.62
(*c*) $\mu = 0.010$									
50	−3.57	−3.22	−2.93	−2.60	−1.55	−0.40	−0.03	0.29	0.67
100	−3.50	−3.16	−2.90	−2.58	−1.56	−0.41	−0.05	0.27	0.64
200	−3.47	−3.14	−2.88	−2.57	−1.56	−0.41	−0.06	0.26	0.64
400	−3.46	−3.13	−2.87	−2.57	−1.56	−0.42	−0.06	0.26	0.64
(*d*) $\mu = 0.10$									
50	−3.53	−3.17	−2.87	−2.54	−1.46	−0.22	0.16	0.49	0.89
100	−3.41	−3.08	−2.80	−2.48	−1.37	−0.08	0.30	0.61	0.98
200	−3.34	−3.00	−2.71	−2.37	−1.20	0.11	0.48	0.81	1.18
400	−3.17	−2.83	−2.54	−2.19	−0.94	0.34	0.70	1.02	1.39

TABLE 6.3 (*cont.*)

Sample size (T)	Probability of a smaller value[a]								
	0.01	0.025	0.05	0.10	0.50	0.90	0.95	0.975	0.99
(*e*) $\mu = 0.25$									
50	−3.35	−2.95	−2.64	−2.28	−1.02	0.29	0.67	1.00	1.35
100	−3.10	−2.72	−2.41	−2.05	−0.74	0.53	0.90	1.21	1.58
200	−2.86	−2.48	−2.16	−1.80	−0.52	0.74	1.11	1.42	1.77
400	−2.68	−2.31	−2.00	−1.63	−0.36	0.90	1.26	1.58	1.95
(*f*) $\mu = 0.5$									
50	−2.94	−2.53	−2.20	−1.81	−0.51	0.78	1.15	1.47	1.85
100	−2.70	−2.33	−2.01	−1.64	−0.35	0.93	1.29	1.61	1.98
200	−2.60	−2.21	−1.89	−1.53	−0.25	1.02	1.40	1.71	2.06
400	−2.50	−2.14	−1.82	−1.46	−0.18	1.09	1.45	1.79	2.16
(*g*) $\mu = 1$									
50	−2.65	−2.26	−1.93	−1.55	−0.24	1.06	1.44	1.76	2.16
100	−2.52	−2.15	−1.84	−1.47	−0.17	1.12	1.49	1.81	2.19
200	−2.48	−2.10	−1.77	−1.41	−0.12	1.15	1.53	1.84	2.20
400	−2.42	−2.06	−1.74	−1.37	−0.09	1.18	1.54	1.87	2.25
(*h*) $\mu = 10$									
50	−2.44	−2.03	−1.71	−1.32	−0.02	1.28	1.65	1.99	2.39
100	−2.38	−2.00	−1.68	−1.31	−0.02	1.27	1.65	1.97	2.35
200	−2.35	−1.99	−1.67	−1.30	−0.01	1.27	1.65	1.97	2.33
400	−2.35	−1.98	−1.66	−1.30	−0.01	1.27	1.64	1.96	2.33
N(0, 1)	−2.32	−1.96	−1.65	−1.28	0.00	1.28	1.65	1.96	2.32

[a] The entries in this table are based on at least 100,000 replications using GAUSS. For any μ, the samples at the smaller sample sizes are sub-samples of the larger samples, tending to reduce variability across T for any μ. In consequence the results are monotonic in T for given μ.

[b] *Source*: Second block of Table 4.2, in the limiting case $T \to \infty$.

For a data series such as annual GNP, $E(\Delta\log(\text{GNP}_t)) \cong 0.025$, which is roughly the same as the standard deviation of the series. Since the ratio of μ to the standard deviation of the series is close to 1, we refer to the '$\mu = 1$' block, which suggests that for the GNP series the appropriate critical values are quite close to those of the normal distribution.

West's result is in the spirit of the discussion earlier in this section. Asymptotic normality prevails only in the absence of dominating stochastic trends, because in that case conventional[6] central-limit theorems may be used to derive convergence results for the parameter estimates.

[6] By 'conventional' we mean those applying to stationary ergodic processes.

This can be achieved in a regression which can be rewritten in terms of non-stochastically trending components, or where a deterministic trend dominates the stochastic one.

The next section applies the asymptotic theory derived earlier to regressions with integrated variables. The first two examples are derivations, for specific cases, of asymptotic distributions of estimators or test statistics. We then consider the issue of dynamic modelling more generally, by first presenting an example from Stock and West (1988). Five more examples then apply this theory. The final section looks at the issue of co-integration testing when the original data-set has been transformed (for example, by differencing or by taking logarithms).

6.2.1. Asymptotic Normality of Unit-root Tests (West 1988)

Consider a DGP that contains a constant or a constant and a trend. If the same variables appear in the model, the estimator of the coefficient of the lagged dependent variable is *asymptotically* normally distributed and does not have a Dickey–Fuller type distribution.

Assume that y_t is generated by ($\mu_b \neq 0$)

$$y_t = \mu_b + y_{t-1} + u_t; \qquad u_t \sim \text{IID}\,(0, \sigma_u^2); \qquad y_0 = 0. \tag{5}$$

The model is given by

$$y_t = \mu_b + \rho_b y_{t-1} + u_t. \tag{6}$$

Define a scaling matrix $\mathbf{C}_T = \text{diag}\,[T^{1/2}, T^{3/2}]$. Then

$$\mathbf{C}_T \begin{bmatrix} (\hat{\mu}_b - \mu_b) \\ (\hat{\rho}_b - 1) \end{bmatrix} = \begin{bmatrix} 1 & T^{-2}\sum_{t=1}^{T} y_{t-1} \\ T^{-2}\sum_{t=1}^{T} y_{t-1} & T^{-3}\sum_{t=1}^{T} y_{t-1}^2 \end{bmatrix}^{-1} \begin{bmatrix} T^{-1/2}\sum_{t=1}^{T} u_t \\ T^{-3/2}\sum_{t=1}^{T} y_{t-1}u_t \end{bmatrix}. \tag{7}$$

Now, noting that $y_t = \mu_b t + \sum_{s=1}^{t} u_s = \mu_b t + S_t$, it is possible to show that

$$\begin{bmatrix} T^{-1/2}\sum_{t=1}^{T} u_t \\ T^{-3/2}\sum_{t=1}^{T} y_{t-1}u_t \end{bmatrix} \Rightarrow \text{N}\left[\begin{bmatrix} 0 \\ 0 \end{bmatrix}, \sigma_u^2 \begin{bmatrix} 1 & \mu_b/2 \\ \mu_b/2 & \mu_b^2/3 \end{bmatrix}\right]$$

$$= \text{N}(\mathbf{0}, \sigma_u^2 \mathbf{B}). \tag{8}$$

An important feature of this derivation is that, because of the particular scaling matrix chosen, only the deterministic part of y_t plays a role in generating the joint distribution of $T^{-1/2}\sum_{t=1}^{T} u_t$ and $T^{-3/2}\sum_{t=1}^{T} y_{t-1}u_t$. Thus, for example, in deriving the distribution of $T^{-3/2}\sum_{t=1}^{T} y_{t-1}u_t$, we need consider only the distribution of

$$T^{-3/2}\mu_b \sum_{t=1}^{T} (t-1)u_t \xrightarrow{\text{d}} \text{N}(0, \sigma_u^2\mu_b^2/3)$$

(see Table 3.3) because

$$\text{plim}\ T^{-3/2} \sum_{t=1}^{T} S_{t-1}u_t = 0$$

since

$$T^{-1} \sum_{t=1}^{T} S_{t-1}u_t \Rightarrow \int_0^1 W(r)\,\text{d}W(r).$$

The scaling factors are such that any term with the stochastic component of y_t, namely S_t, has a degenerate asymptotic distribution and may be ignored asymptotically.

From (7), we have that

$$\mathbf{C}_T \begin{bmatrix} (\hat{\mu}_b - \mu_b) \\ (\hat{\rho}_b - 1) \end{bmatrix} = \mathbf{B}_T^{-1} \begin{bmatrix} T^{-1/2} \sum_{t=1}^{T} u_t \\ T^{-3/2} \sum_{t=1}^{T} y_{t-1}u_t \end{bmatrix}$$

where

$$\mathbf{B}_T = \begin{bmatrix} 1 & T^{-2} \sum_{t=1}^{T} y_{t-1} \\ T^{-2} \sum_{t=1}^{T} y_{t-1} & T^{-3} \sum_{t=1}^{T} y_{t-1}^2 \end{bmatrix}.$$

Now, $\lim_{T\to\infty} T^{-2}\sum_{t=1}^{T} y_{t-1} = \mu_b/2$ and $\lim_{T\to\infty} T^{-3}\sum_{t=1}^{T} y_{t-1}^2 = \mu_b^2/3$ (where, again, only the deterministic component of y_t is important in determining these limits). Thus $\mathbf{B}_T \xrightarrow{\text{p}} \mathbf{B}$. A simple application of Slutsky's theorem and Cramer's theorem is then needed to prove, using (8), that

$$\mathbf{C}_T \begin{bmatrix} (\hat{\mu}_b - \mu_b) \\ (\hat{\rho}_b - 1) \end{bmatrix} \Rightarrow \text{N}(\mathbf{0}, \sigma_u^2\mathbf{B}^{-1}). \tag{9}$$

From (9) it may then be deduced that $T^{3/2}(\hat{\rho}_b - 1) \Rightarrow N(0, 12\sigma_u^2/\mu_b^2)$. Looking now at the t-ratio,

$$t(\hat{\rho}_b) = s^{-1}(\hat{\rho}_b - 1)\left[\sum_{t=1}^{T} y_{t-1}^2 - T^{-1}\left(\sum_{t=1}^{T} y_{t-1}\right)^2\right]^{1/2}$$

$$= s^{-1}T^{3/2}(\hat{\rho}_b - 1)\left[T^{-3}\sum_{t=1}^{T} y_{t-1}^2 - T^{-4}\left(\sum_{t=1}^{T} y_{t-1}\right)^2\right]^{1/2}. \qquad (10)$$

s^2 is a consistent estimator of σ_u^2, which may be constructed from the residuals of the estimated model, so $\text{plim}\, s = \sigma_u$. Using the results derived earlier,

$$\text{plim}\left[T^{-3}\sum_{t=1}^{T} y_{t-1}^2 - T^{-4}\left(\sum_{t=1}^{T} y_{t-1}\right)^2\right]^{1/2} = 12^{-1/2}|\mu_b|.$$

The result that $t(\hat{\rho}_b)$ is asymptotically distributed as a standard normal variable now follows from an inspection of (10) and by noting that $T^{3/2}(\hat{\rho}_b - 1) \Rightarrow N(0, 12\sigma_u^2/\mu_b^2)$.

This last result is remarkable. The asymptotic distributions of estimators in models where stochastically trending variables are present are typically of the Dickey–Fuller type. In direct contrast, the asymptotic distribution of the estimators in (6) is bivariate normal when $\mu_b \neq 0$.

Similar results apply if both the model and the data-generation process contain a drift term, μ_c, and a trend. In this case $T^{5/2}(\hat{\rho}_c - 1) \Rightarrow N(0, 180\sigma_u^2/\mu_c^2)$, and again $t(\hat{\rho}_c) \Rightarrow N(0, 1)$.

6.2.2. *Co-integrating Regression*

Consider the following bivariate system of co-integrated variables $\{y_t\}_1^\infty$ and $\{x_t\}_1^\infty$:

$$y_t = \beta x_t + u_t \qquad (11)$$

$$\Delta x_t = \varepsilon_t, \qquad (12)$$

$$u_t \sim \text{IN}(0, \sigma_u^2), \qquad \varepsilon_t \sim \text{IN}(0, \sigma_\varepsilon^2), \qquad E(u_t\varepsilon_s) = \delta_{ts}\sigma_{u\varepsilon},$$

where δ_{ts} is the Kronecker delta. The least-squares estimator of β is given by

$$\hat{\beta} = \left(\sum_{t=1}^{T} y_t x_t\right)\left(\sum_{t=1}^{T} x_t^2\right)^{-1}. \qquad (13)$$

Thus,

$$T(\hat{\beta} - \beta) = \left(T^{-1}\sum_{t=1}^{T} x_t u_t\right)\left(T^{-2}\sum_{t=1}^{T} x_t^2\right)^{-1}. \qquad (14)$$

From (3.22),

$$T^{-2}\sum_{1}^{T} x_t^{\,2} \Rightarrow \sigma_\varepsilon^2 \int_0^1 W_\varepsilon(r)^2\,\mathrm{d}r.$$

In order to derive the limiting distribution of $T^{-1}\sum_{t=1}^{T} x_t u_t$, it is convenient to condition u_t on ε_t in the following fashion:

$$u_t = \gamma\varepsilon_t + v_t; \qquad \gamma = \sigma_{u\varepsilon}/\sigma_\varepsilon^2; \qquad \sigma_v^2 = \sigma_u^2 - \sigma_{u\varepsilon}^2/\sigma_\varepsilon^2. \tag{15}$$

By construction, $E(\varepsilon_t v_s) = 0\ \forall\, t \neq s$.

Define $W_\varepsilon(r)$ and $W_v(r)$ as the independent Wiener processes on $C[0,1]$ obtained from the $\{\varepsilon_t\}_1^\infty$ and $\{v_t\}_1^\infty$ series, respectively. Now, using (12) and (15),

$$\begin{aligned} T^{-1}\sum_{t=1}^{T} x_t u_t &= T^{-1}\sum_{t=1}^{T} x_t\,(\gamma\varepsilon_t + v_t) \\ &= \gamma\left(T^{-1}\sum_{t=1}^{T} x_{t-1}\varepsilon_t\right) + \gamma\left(T^{-1}\sum_{t=1}^{T}\varepsilon_t^2\right) + \left(T^{-1}\sum_{t=1}^{T} x_{t-1}v_t\right) \\ &\quad + \left(T^{-1}\sum_{t=1}^{T}\varepsilon_t v_t\right). \end{aligned} \tag{16}$$

Using (3.23) (also see Phillips 1987*a*: 282),

$$T^{-1}\sum_{t=1}^{T} x_{t-1}\varepsilon_t \Rightarrow (\sigma_\varepsilon^2/2)(W_\varepsilon(1)^2 - 1). \tag{17}$$

By the property assumed for the ε_t series,

$$T^{-1}\sum_{t=1}^{T}\varepsilon_t^2 \xrightarrow{\text{p}} \sigma_\varepsilon^2. \tag{18}$$

Finally,

$$T^{-1}\sum_{t=1}^{T} x_{t-1}v_t \Rightarrow \sigma_\varepsilon\sigma_v\int_0^1 W_\varepsilon(r)\,\mathrm{d}W_v(r), \tag{19}$$

$$T^{-1}\sum_{t=1}^{T}\varepsilon_t v_t \xrightarrow{\text{p}} 0. \tag{20}$$

The proof for (19) is similar to those presented in Chapter 3 and is given in Phillips (1986: 327). Equation (20) follows from (i) ε_t and v_t being identically and independently distributed processes with zero means and variances of σ_ε^2 and σ_v^2 respectively, and (ii) the independence of the ε_t and v_t processes (obtained by construction). The limiting distribution of (16) can now be deduced by using (17)–(20) and is

$$(\gamma\sigma_\varepsilon^2/2)(W_\varepsilon(1)^2 + 1) + \sigma_\varepsilon\sigma_v\int_0^1 W_\varepsilon(r)\,\mathrm{d}W_v(r). \tag{21}$$

It can be shown that (see Park and Phillips 1988, and Table 3.3)

$$\int_0^1 W_\varepsilon(r)\,\mathrm{d}W_v(r) \Rightarrow \mathrm{N}\left(0, \int_0^1 W_\varepsilon(r)^2\,\mathrm{d}r\right). \tag{22}$$

Under H_0: $\beta = 0$,

$T\hat{\beta} \Rightarrow$

$$\left[(\gamma\sigma_\varepsilon^2/2)(W_\varepsilon(1)^2 + 1) + \sigma_\varepsilon\sigma_v\int_0^1 W_\varepsilon(r)\,\mathrm{d}W_v(r)\right]\left(\sigma_\varepsilon^2\int_0^1 W_\varepsilon(r)^2\,\mathrm{d}r\right)^{-1}.$$

Further,

$$t_{\beta=0} = \hat{\beta}s^{-1}\left(\sum_{t=1}^{T} x_t^2\right)^{1/2} = T\hat{\beta}s^{-1}\left(T^{-2}\sum_{t=1}^{T} x_t^2\right)^{1/2}. \tag{23}$$

The term s^2 is a consistent estimator of σ_u^2 and may be calculated from the residuals of the estimated regression of y_t on x_t. Thus, using (22),

$$t_{\beta=0} \Rightarrow (\gamma\sigma_\varepsilon\sigma_u^{-1}/2)(W_\varepsilon(1)^2 + 1)\left(\int_0^1 W_\varepsilon(r)^2\,\mathrm{d}r\right)^{-1/2} + \sigma_v\sigma_u^{-1}\mathrm{N}(0, 1). \tag{24}$$

In general, therefore, the t-ratio of $\hat{\beta}$ will not have a standard normal distribution unless $\gamma = 0$ (that is, unless x_t is strongly exogenous for the estimation of β). When $\gamma \neq 0$, the first term in (24) gives rise to 'second-order' or 'endogeneity' bias (see Phillips and Hansen 1990), which, although asymptotically negligible in estimating β due to super consistency, can be important in finite samples.

The Durbin–Watson statistic, computed from the residuals of the estimated regression (11) may be shown to converge in probability limit, to 2. This result follows from our assumption that the u_t are independently and identically distributed. If the u_t are first-order autoregressive with autocorrelation parameter ρ_1, the Durbin–Watson statistic tends to the usual $2(1 - \rho_1)$, familiar from the asymptotic theory for stationary processes. Note that, if $\rho_1 = 1$, $\{y_t\}$ and $\{x_t\}$ are not co-integrated, and the estimated value of the Durbin–Watson statistic should be close to zero. This property is the basis for the Sargan–Bhargava test for co-integration (see Chapter 7).

The existence of nuisance parameters has important effects upon the distribution of $\hat{\beta}$. In the light of Section 6.2.1 this is to be expected. Suppose $\{x_t\}_1^\infty$ is generated by (for $\mu_b \neq 0$)

$$\Delta x_t = \mu_b + \varepsilon_t \text{ which implies } x_t = t\mu_b + \sum_{s=1}^{t} \varepsilon_s.$$

Then

$$T^{-3/2}\sum_{t=1}^{T} x_t u_t = \mu_b T^{-3/2}\sum_{t=1}^{T} t u_t + T^{-3/2}\sum_{t=1}^{T} u_t\left(\sum_{s=1}^{t}\varepsilon_s\right).$$

By results in Stock (1987) and West (1988), and intuitively from the orders of magnitude involved,

$$\operatorname{plim}\left[T^{-3/2}\sum_{t=1}^{T} u_t\left(\sum_{s=1}^{t}\varepsilon_s\right)\right] = 0.$$

Following West (1988) (see also Section 6.2.1 above), it may then be shown that $\mu_b T^{-3/2}\sum_{t=1}^{T} t u_t$, and hence $T^{-3/2}\sum_{t=1}^{T} x_t u_t$, is normally distributed with mean zero and variance $\mu_b^2\sigma_u^2/3$. From Section 6.2.1, $\operatorname{plim} T^{-3}\sum_{t=1}^{T} x_t^{\,2} = \mu_b^2/3$. Hence, by Slutsky's theorem and Cramer's theorem,

$$T^{3/2}(\hat{\beta} - \beta) = \left(T^{-3/2}\sum_{t=1}^{T} x_t u_t\right)\left(T^{-3}\sum_{t=1}^{T} x_t^{\,2}\right)^{-1} \Rightarrow \mathrm{N}(0, 3\sigma_u^2/\mu_b^2).$$

6.2.3. Example (Stock and West 1988)

This example describes how a dynamic regression equation can be transformed to validate the use of asymptotic normal-distribution theory. We next formalize the arguments by presenting a general theoretical framework. All of the examples discussed in this section may be viewed as special cases of this general formulation. This generalization is necessary to illustrate the subtleties inherent in deriving the distribution theory. Four more examples follow the description of the general theory. These elaborate upon and illustrate some special aspects of the theory and yield recommendations for empirical modelling with integrated series.

Stock and West (1988) is one of several papers dealing with tests of the Hall (1978) permanent income hypothesis.[7] Hall's regressions take the following form:

$$c_t = \mu + \beta c_{t-1} + \pi_1 y_{t-1}^d + \ldots + \pi_p y_{t-p}^d + \varepsilon_t, \tag{25}$$

where c_t is consumption in period t and y_t^d is disposable income. The processes generating c_t and y_t^d are assumed to have two important properties. First, c_t and y_t^d have unit roots; that is, they are both integrated of order 1. Second, given that the permanent income hypothesis is correct, y_t^d may be shown to be co-integrated with c_t. Thus,

[7] Other papers include Mankiw and Shapiro (1985, 1986), Banerjee and Dolado (1987), and Galbraith *et al.* (1987).

while c_t and y_t^d are individually non-stationary, $y_t^d - c_t$ is stationary, possibly with a non-zero mean.

The permanent-income hypothesis has two implications: first, $\beta = 1$; and second, $\pi_1 = \pi_2 = \ldots = \pi_p = 0$. In most of the discussion in Stock and West (1988), β is restricted to its hypothesized value of one. Thus, a test of the permanent income hypothesis takes the form of testing the joint exclusion restrictions on the π_i. A joint test of the restrictions on β and the π_i raises several interesting issues, and we will deal with these in the context of a later example. It will become clear that such a joint test will not have the usual F distribution. The F-test on the π_i, with the restriction on β imposed, does however have the standard F distribution asymptotically.

The key feature of the regression given by (25) is that all the coefficients on income can be written as coefficients on mean-zero stationary variables. One possible rearrangement of the variables yields

$$c_t = (\mu + \pi_1 k + \ldots + \pi_p k) + (\beta + \pi_1 + \ldots + \pi_p)c_{t-1} + \pi_1(y_{t-1}^d - c_{t-1} - k) + \ldots + \pi_p(y_{t-p}^d - c_{t-1} - k) + \varepsilon_t \quad (26)$$

or

$$c_t = m + \phi c_{t-1} + \pi_1(y_{t-1}^d - c_{t-1} - k) + \ldots + \pi_p(y_{t-p}^d - c_{t-1} - k) + \varepsilon_t, \quad (27)$$

where k is the intercept of the long-run consumption function,[8] $m = \mu + k\sum_{i=1}^{p}\pi_i$, and $\phi = (\beta + \sum_{i=1}^{p}\pi_i)$.

Theorem 1 in Sims *et al.* (1990) implies that the OLS estimators of $\{\pi_i\}$ are jointly asymptotically normally distributed, converging to the true values at the rate $T^{1/2}$. Theorem 2 of Sims *et al.* implies that the t- or F-tests on any or all subsets of these estimated π_i coefficients have the usual asymptotic distributions. It is worth re-emphasizing that it is only the *existence* of a transformation, to stationary and mean-zero regressors, that is important. There is no unique way to accomplish this transformation, but, because nothing depends on the precise parameterization chosen, uniqueness is not necessary for the results to hold. Tests and coefficient estimates based on any one of the linearly transformed regression models will be equivalent. In particular, then, this will be true of the untransformed regression.

Having established the intuition for the results derived by Sims *et al.*, *inter alia*, it is necessary to proceed to a formalization of the model. This sub-section of the chapter, while relying heavily on Sims, Stock, and Watson (1990) (henceforth SSW), does not present the arguments

[8] Possibly equal to zero.

in all their possible generality. Reference should be made to SSW for a complete description. Their notation is retained for convenience.

6.2.4. General Formulation

Most of the examples usually discussed in this literature may be expressed as special cases of the following linear time-series model:

$$\mathbf{Y}_t = \mathbf{A}\mathbf{Y}_{t-1} + \mathbf{G}\boldsymbol{\Omega}^{1/2}\boldsymbol{\eta}_t, \qquad t = 1, \ldots, T \tag{28}$$

where $\mathbf{Y}_t$ is a k-dimensional vector and $\mathbf{A}$ is a $k \times k$ matrix of coefficients. The $N \times 1$ vector of disturbances $\{\boldsymbol{\eta}_t\}$ is a martingale difference sequence with $E[\boldsymbol{\eta}_t|\boldsymbol{\eta}_1, \ldots, \boldsymbol{\eta}_{t-1}] = \mathbf{0}$ and $E[\boldsymbol{\eta}_t\boldsymbol{\eta}_t'|\boldsymbol{\eta}_1, \ldots, \boldsymbol{\eta}_{t-1}] = \mathbf{I}_N$ for $t = 1, \ldots, T$.[9] The $N \times N$ matrix $\boldsymbol{\Omega}^{1/2}$ is the square root of the covariance matrix $\boldsymbol{\Omega}$ of the errors $(\boldsymbol{\Omega}^{1/2}\boldsymbol{\eta}_t)$. The matrix $\mathbf{G}$ is a selection matrix for the errors. It is of size $k \times N$, is assumed to be known *a priori*, and determines which errors enter which equations. It is also assumed that $\mathbf{A}$ has k_1 eigenvalues with absolute value less than 1, and that the remaining $k - k_1$ eigenvalues are exactly equal to unity.

In general, the components of $\mathbf{Y}_t$ are random terms of various orders of integration, constants, and polynomials in time. Linear combinations of elements of $\mathbf{Y}_t$, with orders of integration lower than those of its component elements, may also be included. As long as the system possesses such *generalized co-integrating vectors*,[10] SSW show that $T^{-p}\sum_{t=1}^{T}\mathbf{Y}_t\mathbf{Y}_t'$ converges to a singular limit, for a suitably chosen p. Thus, the analysis must be undertaken with a transformed set of variables $\mathbf{Z}_t$,

$$\mathbf{Z}_t = \mathbf{D}\mathbf{Y}_t. \tag{29}$$

The variable $\mathbf{Z}_t$ has several important properties. First, the non-singular matrix $\mathbf{D}$ is chosen in such a way that $\mathbf{Z}_t$ is decomposable into its non-stochastic and stochastic components. Second, the moment matrix $\sum_{t=1}^{T}\mathbf{Z}_t\mathbf{Z}_t'$ must be invertible almost surely.

If there are no stochastic trend components in the decomposition of $\mathbf{Z}_t$ into its stochastic and non-stochastic components, or at least no dominating stochastic trend components, then asymptotic normality of

[9] $E[\boldsymbol{\eta}_t|\boldsymbol{\eta}_1, \ldots, \boldsymbol{\eta}_{t-1}] = \mathbf{0}$ is the property that defines a martingale difference sequence; see Ch. 1 (or Hall and Heyde 1980). This martingale difference sequence assumption is not important for the derivation of the results. All convergence theorems in SSW can be proved when the $\boldsymbol{\eta}_t$ are *mixingales* (Hall and Heyde 1980) and follow a process such as the one given in, for example, Phillips (1987*a*).

[10] This is SSW's terminology. They refer to such vectors as generalized co-integrating vectors to allow the possibility that not all of the component elements of the linear combination have the same order of integration.

the regression coefficients holds, both in the transformed and in the untransformed regressions. In this case, we are able to transform the original regressors and express them in terms of variables that do not contain stochastic trends. Normality is then a natural consequence of this transformation for the same reasons as in standard econometrics, where the matrix of sample second moments tends in probability to a non-random positive definite matrix and the usual central-limit theorems apply.

The details of the derivation of the matrix **D** and its existence are contained in SSW. We will proceed by recording the final form of the transformation. Letting $\xi_{1,t} = \sum_{s=1}^{t} \boldsymbol{\eta}_s$, and defining $\xi_{j,t}$ (the j-fold summation of the $\boldsymbol{\eta}_s$) recursively as $\xi_{j,t} = \sum_{s=1}^{t} \xi_{j-1,s}$, $1 \leqslant j \leqslant g$, the transformation **D** is chosen such that

$$\begin{bmatrix} \mathbf{Z}_{1,t} \\ \mathbf{Z}_{2,t} \\ \mathbf{Z}_{3,t} \\ \mathbf{Z}_{4,t} \\ \vdots \\ \mathbf{Z}_{2g,t} \\ \mathbf{Z}_{2g+1,t} \end{bmatrix} = \begin{bmatrix} \mathbf{F}_{11}(L) & \mathbf{0} & \mathbf{0} & \mathbf{0} & \cdots & \mathbf{0} & \mathbf{0} \\ \mathbf{F}_{21}(L) & \mathbf{F}_{22} & \mathbf{0} & \mathbf{0} & \cdots & \mathbf{0} & \mathbf{0} \\ \mathbf{F}_{31}(L) & \mathbf{F}_{32} & \mathbf{F}_{33} & \mathbf{0} & \cdots & \mathbf{0} & \mathbf{0} \\ \mathbf{F}_{41}(L) & \mathbf{F}_{42} & \mathbf{F}_{43} & \mathbf{F}_{44} & \cdots & \mathbf{0} & \mathbf{0} \\ \vdots & \vdots & \vdots & \vdots & & \vdots & \vdots \\ \mathbf{F}_{2g,1}(L) & \mathbf{F}_{2g,2} & \cdots & \cdots & \cdots & \mathbf{F}_{2g,2g} & \mathbf{0} \\ \mathbf{F}_{2g+1,1}(L) & \mathbf{F}_{2g+1,2} & \cdots & \cdots & \cdots & \mathbf{F}_{2g+1,2g} & \mathbf{F}_{2g+1,2g+1} \end{bmatrix} \times \begin{bmatrix} \boldsymbol{\eta}_t \\ 1 \\ \xi_{1,t} \\ t \\ \vdots \\ t^{g-1} \\ \xi_{g,t} \end{bmatrix}$$

or, equivalently

$$\mathbf{Z}_t = \mathbf{F}(L)\boldsymbol{v}_t, \tag{30}$$

where

$$\mathbf{Z}_t = [\mathbf{Z}'_{1,t}, \mathbf{Z}'_{2,t}, \ldots, \mathbf{Z}'_{2g+1,t}]',$$
$$\boldsymbol{v}_t = (\boldsymbol{\eta}'_t, 1, \xi'_{1,t}, t, \xi'_{2,t}, t^2, \xi'_{3,t}, \ldots, t^{g-1}, \xi'_{g,t})'$$

and L is the lag operator. The variates $\boldsymbol{v}_t$ are referred to as the canonical regressors associated with $\mathbf{Y}_t$. The lag polynomial $\mathbf{F}_{11}(L)$ has dimension $k_1 \times N$, and $\sum_{j=0}^{\infty}\mathbf{F}_{11j}\mathbf{F}'_{11j}$ is non-singular. $\mathbf{F}_{jj}$ is assumed to have full row rank k_j (may be equal to zero) for $j = 2, \ldots, 2g+1$, so that $k = \sum_{j=1}^{2g+1} k_j$.

Since we may be interested in estimating only some of the k equations in (28), we next need to define a selection matrix $\mathbf{C}$. If we needed to consider only $n \leqslant k$, we could look at the regression of $\mathbf{CY}_t$ on $\mathbf{Y}_{t-1}$, where $\mathbf{C}$ is an $n \times k$ matrix of constants. The n regression equations to be estimated are then

$$\mathbf{CY}_t = \mathbf{CAY}_{t-1} + \mathbf{CG\Omega}^{1/2}\boldsymbol{\eta}_t. \tag{31}$$

Letting $\mathbf{S}_t = \mathbf{CY}_t$, $\widetilde{\mathbf{A}} = \mathbf{CA}$, and $\boldsymbol{\Sigma}^{1/2} = \mathbf{CG\Omega}^{1/2}$, we have

$$\mathbf{S}_t = \widetilde{\mathbf{A}}\mathbf{Y}_{t-1} + \boldsymbol{\Sigma}^{1/2}\boldsymbol{\eta}_t. \tag{32}$$

The asymptotic analysis in SSW is derived in stacked single-equation form. In order to use this form, we need the symbol $\otimes$ which denotes a Kronecker product defined as follows: consider the $m \times n$ matrix $\mathbf{A} = \{a_{ij}\}$ and the $p \times q$ matrix $\mathbf{B}$; the Kronecker product of $\mathbf{A}$ and $\mathbf{B}$ (in that order) is the $mp \times nq$ matrix,

$$\mathbf{A} \otimes \mathbf{B} = \begin{bmatrix} a_{11}\mathbf{B} & a_{12}\mathbf{B} & \cdots & a_{1n}\mathbf{B} \\ a_{21}\mathbf{B} & a_{22}\mathbf{B} & \cdots & a_{2n}\mathbf{B} \\ \vdots & \vdots & & \vdots \\ a_{m1}\mathbf{B} & a_{m2}\mathbf{B} & \cdots & a_{mn}\mathbf{B} \end{bmatrix}.$$

Vec$(\cdot)$ denotes the column-wise vectoring operator. Thus, writing the matrix $\mathbf{A}$ as $\mathbf{A} = (\mathbf{a}_1, \mathbf{a}_2, \ldots, \mathbf{a}_n)$, where each of the $\mathbf{a}_i$ is an $m \times 1$ vector, vec$(\mathbf{A})$ is given by

$$\begin{bmatrix} \mathbf{a}_1 \\ \mathbf{a}_2 \\ \vdots \\ \mathbf{a}_n \end{bmatrix}.$$

Thus, if $\mathbf{S} = [\mathbf{S}_2, \mathbf{S}_3, \ldots, \mathbf{S}_T]'$, $\boldsymbol{\eta} = [\boldsymbol{\eta}_2, \boldsymbol{\eta}_3, \ldots, \boldsymbol{\eta}_T]'$,

$\mathbf{X} = [\mathbf{Y}_1, \mathbf{Y}_2, \ldots, \mathbf{Y}_{T-1}]'$, $\mathbf{s} = \text{vec}(\mathbf{S})$, $\mathbf{v} = \text{vec}(\boldsymbol{\eta})$, and $\boldsymbol{\beta} = \text{vec}((\widetilde{\mathbf{A}})')$,

then (32) can be written in stacked form as

$$\mathbf{s} = (\mathbf{I}_n \otimes \mathbf{X})\boldsymbol{\beta} + (\boldsymbol{\Sigma}^{1/2} \otimes \mathbf{I}_{T-1})\mathbf{v}. \tag{33}$$

In order to express (33) in terms of the transformed regressors $\mathbf{Z} = [\mathbf{Z}'_1, \mathbf{Z}'_2, \ldots, \mathbf{Z}'_{T-1}]' = \mathbf{XD}'$, note that the coefficient vector corresponding to these is given by $\boldsymbol{\delta} = (\mathbf{I}_n \otimes \mathbf{D}'^{-1})\boldsymbol{\beta}$.[11] Thus, finally,

[11] To show this, substitute for $\mathbf{Z} = \mathbf{XD}'$ and $\boldsymbol{\delta} = (\mathbf{I}_n \otimes \mathbf{D}'^{-1})\boldsymbol{\beta}$ in (34) giving $\mathbf{s} = (\mathbf{I}_n \otimes \mathbf{XD}')(\mathbf{I}_n \otimes \mathbf{D}'^{-1})\boldsymbol{\beta} + (\boldsymbol{\Sigma}^{1/2} \otimes \mathbf{I}_{T-1})\mathbf{v}$. Now $(\mathbf{A}_1 \otimes \mathbf{A}_2)(\mathbf{A}_3 \otimes \mathbf{A}_4) = (\mathbf{A}_1\mathbf{A}_3) \otimes (\mathbf{A}_2\mathbf{A}_4)$, for arbitrary matrices $\mathbf{A}_i$, $i = 1, 2, 3, 4$, provided the matrices are conformable. Using this rule (33) is recovered as required.

$$\mathbf{s} = (\mathbf{I}_n \otimes \mathbf{Z})\boldsymbol{\delta} + (\boldsymbol{\Sigma}^{1/2} \otimes \mathbf{I}_{T-1})\mathbf{v}. \tag{34}$$

The OLS estimator $\hat{\boldsymbol{\delta}}$ of $\boldsymbol{\delta}$ in the stacked transformed regression model (34) is given by

$$\hat{\boldsymbol{\delta}} = (\mathbf{I}_n \otimes \mathbf{Z}'\mathbf{Z})^{-1}(\mathbf{I}_n \otimes \mathbf{Z}')\mathbf{s}. \tag{35}$$

It is possible to see from (30) that the moments involving the different components of $\mathbf{Z}_t$ converge at different rates. For example, $\mathbf{Z}_{1,t}$ and $\mathbf{Z}_{2,t}$ are $O_p(1)$ while $\mathbf{Z}_{3,t}$ is $O_p(t^{1/2})$, $\mathbf{Z}_{4,t}$ is $O_p(t)$, and so on. Hence the sample second moments, which is what we would be interested in when looking at the matrix $\mathbf{Z}'\mathbf{Z}$, converge at a rate of T for the $\mathbf{Z}_{1,t}$ and $\mathbf{Z}_{2,t}$ components, at a rate T^2 for the $\mathbf{Z}_{3,t}$ component, and at a rate T^3 for the $\mathbf{Z}_{4,t}$ component. In order to handle these different orders, SSW use the scaling matrix $\boldsymbol{\Upsilon}_T$, given by

$$\boldsymbol{\Upsilon}_T = \operatorname{diag}(T^{1/2}i_{k_1}, T^{1/2}i_{k_2}, Ti_{k_3}, T^{3/2}i_{k_4}, \ldots, T^{g-1/2}i_{k_{2g}}, T^{g}i_{k_{2g+1}}). \tag{36}$$

All the convergence results use the scaled $\mathbf{Z}'\mathbf{Z}$ matrix $\boldsymbol{\Upsilon}_T^{-1}\mathbf{Z}'\mathbf{Z}\boldsymbol{\Upsilon}_T^{-1}$; let us call this scaled matrix $\mathbf{Q}$.

The first step in the proof is to derive the limiting matrix for $\mathbf{Q}$. SSW show that, under certain regularity conditions, $\mathbf{Q} \Rightarrow \mathbf{V}$ where the elements of $\mathbf{V}$ may be described as follows:

(a) $\mathbf{V}_{11}$ and $\mathbf{V}_{12}$ are non-random matrices given by $\sum_{j=0}^{\infty}\mathbf{F}_{11j}\mathbf{F}'_{11j}$ and $\sum_{j=0}^{\infty}\mathbf{F}_{11j}\mathbf{F}'_{21j}$ respectively. Additionally, $\mathbf{V}_{12} = \mathbf{V}'_{21}$.
(b) $\mathbf{V}_{1p} = \mathbf{V}'_{p1} = \mathbf{0}$, $p = 3, \ldots, 2g + 1$.
(c) $\mathbf{V}_{22}$ is also non-random, given by $\mathbf{F}_{22}\mathbf{F}'_{22} + \sum_{j=0}^{\infty}\mathbf{F}_{21j}\mathbf{F}'_{21j}$.
(d) $\mathbf{V}_{mp}$, where $m, p = 3, 5, 7, \ldots, 2g + 1$, are random matrices involving functionals of multivariate Wiener processes.
(e) $\mathbf{V}_{mp}$, where $m = 2, 4, 6, \ldots, 2g$, $p = 3, 5, 7, \ldots, 2g + 1$, are also random matrices involving functionals of multivariate Wiener processes.
(f) $\mathbf{V}_{mp} = [2/(p + m - 2)]\, \mathbf{F}_{mm}\mathbf{F}'_{pp}$, $p = 4, 6, \ldots, 2g$, $m = 2, 4, 6, \ldots, 2g$.

This is the first time we have used multivariate Wiener processes. The mathematical details involved in going from univariate to multivariate Wiener processes are complex and will not be dealt with here (for a good account, see Phillips and Durlauf 1986). However the generalizations from our analysis in Chapter 3 can be understood intuitively fairly easily and the appendix sketches the bivariate case.

Thus, each element of a standardized $n \times 1$ multivariate Wiener process $\mathbf{W}(r)$ is a univariate Wiener process and the elements of $\mathbf{W}(r)$ are independent. In particular, $\mathbf{W}(1)$ is the multivariate standard normal density, that is, $N(\mathbf{0}, \mathbf{I}_n)$. Further, $\mathbf{W}(r) \in C[0,1]^n$, where $C[0,1]$ is the space of continuous functions defined on $[0,1]$.

Convergence results analogous to (3.17), for a sequence of mean zero random vectors $\{\mathbf{u}_t\}$, can be proved by defining standardized sums such as

$$\mathbf{R}_T(r) = \frac{\boldsymbol{\Omega}^{-1/2}\mathbf{S}_{[Tr]}}{T^{1/2}} = \frac{\boldsymbol{\Omega}^{-1/2}\mathbf{S}_{t-1}}{T^{1/2}},$$

with $(t-1)/T \leqslant r < t/T$ and $t = 1, 2, \ldots, T$, so that $r \in [0,1]$. $\mathbf{S}_t$ is the matrix of the cumulative sum of the $n \times 1$ random vectors $\mathbf{u}_t$, i.e. $\mathbf{S}_t = \sum_{i=1}^{t} \mathbf{u}_i$, and the matrix $\boldsymbol{\Omega}$ is the long-run variance-covariance matrix of $\mathbf{u}_i$ defined by $\boldsymbol{\Omega} = \lim_{T\to\infty} E(T^{-1}\mathbf{S}_T\mathbf{S}_T')$ analogously with (3.16*c*). The $\{\mathbf{u}_t\}$ innovation sequence satisfies conditions equivalent to those given by (3.16*a*)–(3.16*d*) for the univariate case. Provided suitable regularity conditions are satisfied, the following multivariate analogue of (3.18) may be proved:

$$\mathbf{R}_T(r) \Rightarrow \mathbf{W}(r).$$

Finally, multivariate analogues of all the convergence results given earlier for univariate processes may be derived. Thus, for example, referring to Table 3.3, where $\mathbf{y}_t = \mathbf{y}_{t-1} + \mathbf{u}_t$:

$$T^{-1/2}\mathbf{y}_T \Rightarrow \mathbf{W}(1)$$

$$T^{-3/2}\sum_{t=1}^{T}\mathbf{y}_t \Rightarrow \int_0^1 \mathbf{W}(r)\,\mathrm{d}r;$$

$$T^{-1}\sum_{t=1}^{T}(\mathbf{y}_{t-1}\mathbf{u}_t' + \mathbf{u}_t\mathbf{y}_{t-1}') \Rightarrow \mathbf{W}(1)\mathbf{W}(1)' - \mathbf{I}_n.$$

To derive the results above we have assumed, as in Table 3.3, that $\{\mathbf{u}_t\}$ is a white-noise innovation sequence with $\mathbf{I}_n$ as the variance matrix.

The next step of the argument involves rewriting the estimator $\hat{\boldsymbol{\delta}}$ in a form such that its distribution can be derived. This is done by first defining a non-singular matrix $\mathbf{H}$ which, in essence, transposes the stacked version of the matrix $\mathbf{Z}$. Thus,

$$\mathbf{H}(\mathbf{I}_n \otimes \mathbf{Z}') = \begin{bmatrix} \mathbf{I}_n \otimes \mathbf{Z}_1' \\ \mathbf{I}_n \otimes \mathbf{Z}_2' \\ \vdots \\ \mathbf{I}_n \otimes \mathbf{Z}_{2g+1}' \end{bmatrix}. \tag{37}$$

From (35),

$$\begin{aligned} \hat{\boldsymbol{\delta}} &= (\mathbf{I}_n \otimes \mathbf{Z}'\mathbf{Z})^{-1}(\mathbf{I}_n \otimes \mathbf{Z}')\mathbf{s} \\ &= (\mathbf{I}_n \otimes \mathbf{Z}'\mathbf{Z})^{-1}(\mathbf{I}_n \otimes \mathbf{Z}')[(\mathbf{I}_n \otimes \mathbf{Z})\boldsymbol{\delta} + (\boldsymbol{\Sigma}^{1/2} \otimes \mathbf{I}_{T-1})\mathbf{v}], \end{aligned}$$

by substituting for $\mathbf{s}$ from (34). Next, using the result that $(\mathbf{A}_1 \otimes \mathbf{A}_2)(\mathbf{A}_3 \otimes \mathbf{A}_4) = (\mathbf{A}_1\mathbf{A}_3) \otimes (\mathbf{A}_2\mathbf{A}_4)$, we have

$$(\hat{\boldsymbol{\delta}} - \boldsymbol{\delta}) = (\mathbf{I}_n \otimes \mathbf{Z}'\mathbf{Z})^{-1}(\boldsymbol{\Sigma}^{1/2} \otimes \mathbf{Z}')\mathbf{v}.$$

Thus,

$$\begin{aligned}\mathbf{H}(\mathbf{I}_n \otimes \mathbf{T}_T)(\hat{\boldsymbol{\delta}} - \boldsymbol{\delta}) &= \mathbf{H}(\mathbf{I}_n \otimes \mathbf{T}_T)(\mathbf{I}_n \otimes \mathbf{Z}'\mathbf{Z})^{-1}(\mathbf{I}_n \otimes \mathbf{T}_T)\\ &\quad \times [(\mathbf{I}_n \otimes \mathbf{T}_T^{-1})(\boldsymbol{\Sigma}^{1/2} \otimes \mathbf{Z}')\mathbf{v}]\\ &= [\mathbf{H}(\mathbf{I}_n \otimes [\mathbf{T}_T^{-1}(\mathbf{Z}'\mathbf{Z})\mathbf{T}_T^{-1}])\mathbf{H}^{-1}]^{-1}\\ &\quad \times [\mathbf{H}(\boldsymbol{\Sigma}^{1/2} \otimes \mathbf{T}_T^{-1}\mathbf{Z}')\mathbf{v}],\\ &= [\mathbf{H}(\mathbf{I}_n \otimes \mathbf{Q})\mathbf{H}^{-1}]^{-1}\\ &\quad \times [\mathbf{H}(\boldsymbol{\Sigma}^{1/2} \otimes \mathbf{T}_T^{-1}\mathbf{Z}')\mathbf{v}]. \end{aligned} \tag{38}$$

As noted above the matrix $\mathbf{V}$ is the limiting matrix of $\mathbf{Q}$.

The asymptotic distribution of

$$[\mathbf{H}(\boldsymbol{\Sigma}^{1/2} \otimes \mathbf{T}_T^{-1}\mathbf{Z}')\mathbf{v}] \Rightarrow \boldsymbol{\phi}$$

is needed to give us the final result. This limiting vector, denoted by $\boldsymbol{\phi}$, takes the following form:

$$\boldsymbol{\phi} = (\boldsymbol{\phi}_1', \boldsymbol{\phi}_2', \ldots, \boldsymbol{\phi}_{2g+1}')'$$

where

(a) $\boldsymbol{\phi}_m$ for all $m \geqslant 3$ are functionals of multivariate Wiener processes;
(b) $\boldsymbol{\phi}_2 = \boldsymbol{\phi}_{21} + \boldsymbol{\phi}_{22}$, where $\boldsymbol{\phi}_{22} = \text{vec}[\mathbf{F}_{22}\mathbf{W}(1)'\boldsymbol{\Sigma}^{1/2}]$, $\mathbf{W}(1)$ is the multivariate standard normal density function, and

$$\begin{bmatrix}\boldsymbol{\phi}_1\\ \boldsymbol{\phi}_{21}\end{bmatrix} \sim \mathrm{N}(\mathbf{0}, \mathbf{H}\boldsymbol{\Phi}\mathbf{H}').$$

Finally,

$$\boldsymbol{\Phi} = \begin{bmatrix}\boldsymbol{\Sigma} \otimes \mathbf{V}_{11} & \boldsymbol{\Sigma} \otimes \mathbf{V}_{12}\\ \boldsymbol{\Sigma} \otimes \mathbf{V}_{21} & \boldsymbol{\Sigma} \otimes (\mathbf{V}_{22} - \mathbf{F}_{22}\mathbf{F}_{22}')\end{bmatrix},$$

where $(\boldsymbol{\phi}_1, \boldsymbol{\phi}_{21})$ are independent of $(\boldsymbol{\phi}_{22}, \boldsymbol{\phi}_3, \ldots, \boldsymbol{\phi}_{2g+1})$. Consolidating these steps, we have the following theorem.

THEOREM. $\mathbf{H}(\mathbf{I}_n \otimes \mathbf{T}_T)(\hat{\boldsymbol{\delta}} - \boldsymbol{\delta}) \Rightarrow [\mathbf{H}(\mathbf{I}_n \otimes \mathbf{V})\mathbf{H}^{-1}]^{-1}\boldsymbol{\phi}$.

This provides us with several interesting results. First, $\hat{\boldsymbol{\delta}}$, and hence $\hat{\boldsymbol{\beta}}$, is a consistent estimator of $\boldsymbol{\delta}$, respectively $\boldsymbol{\beta}$, in the presence of arbitrarily many unit roots and deterministic time trends. This observation relies on the assumption that the model is correctly specified, in the sense that the errors are martingale difference sequences, and the $\mathbf{T}_T$ may rescale by powers of T greater than $\frac{1}{2}$.

We have already noted that the estimated coefficients on the elements of $\mathbf{Z}_T$ converge to their probability limits at different rates. Hence, if some of the transformed regressors are dominated, in an order of probability sense, by stochastic components, their limiting distributions will be non-normal. On the other hand, if there are no $\mathbf{Z}_t$ regressors dominated by stochastic trends (that is, if $k_3 = k_5 = \ldots = k_{2g+1} = 0$), then $\hat{\boldsymbol{\delta}}$, and hence $\hat{\boldsymbol{\beta}}$, has an asymptotic normal joint distribution. This happens because the terms involving the random integrals are no longer present, as may be seen from (30), where $k_3, k_5, \ldots, k_{2g+1}$ are the ranks of matrices multiplying the stochastic canonical regressors. If these matrices are absent, the transformed regression is considerably simplified as it is expressible solely in terms of stationary variables and deterministic trend terms. In such a case, therefore, $\mathbf{H}(\mathbf{I}_n \otimes \mathbf{T}_T)(\hat{\boldsymbol{\delta}} - \boldsymbol{\delta}) \xrightarrow{d} \mathrm{N}(\mathbf{0}, \mathbf{H}(\boldsymbol{\Sigma} \otimes \mathbf{V}^{-1})\mathbf{H}')$ where $\mathbf{V}$ is now a non-random matrix. Additionally the F-statistic associated with testing an arbitrary set of q linear restrictions $\mathbf{R}\boldsymbol{\beta} = \mathbf{r}$, is asymptotically distributed as χ^2_q in this case.

If a single stochastic trend is dominated by a non-stochastic trend, then, again, asymptotic normality holds. This is the result of West (1988) and may be seen using (30) and keeping track of the rates of convergence of the sample moments of the separate components of $\mathbf{Z}_t$. Consider, for example, the set of canonical regressors given by $(\boldsymbol{\eta}_t, 1, \xi_{1,t}, t)'$ and suppose the transformed regression is expressible in terms of these canonical regressors. Thus, while the sample variability of the stochastic trend term is $O_p(T)$, that of the deterministic trend is $O(T^{3/2})$. As shown by West (1988), and discussed in Section 6.2.1, in deriving the asymptotic distribution for this case, the deterministic trend component dominates the stochastic component and asymptotic normality follows.

The Stock–West (1988) example, discussed earlier, works because we are able to rewrite the regression in terms of canonical regressors which do not have any dominating stochastic component. The issue of domination, in this context, is best addressed by looking at the scaling matrix.

Four more examples will now be given to illustrate these arguments, using the framework developed above. The final example in this set of four contains recommendations for modelling with integrated series.

6.2.5. Example (Sims et al. *1990: 119)*

Let the process $\{x_t\}$ be generated according to the following AR(2) process without drift:

$$x_t = \beta_0 + \beta_1 x_{t-1} + \beta_2 x_{t-2} + \eta_t. \tag{39}$$

Under H_0, $\beta_0 = 0$, $\beta_1 + \beta_2 = 1$ and $|\beta_2| < 1$ so that the autoregressive polynomial in (39) has only one unit root. If a constant is included in the regression of x_t on its two lags, $\mathbf{Y}_t$ (in the notation developed earlier) is given by

$$\mathbf{Y}_t = \begin{bmatrix} x_t \\ x_{t-1} \\ 1 \end{bmatrix} = \begin{bmatrix} \beta_1 & \beta_2 & \beta_0 \\ 1 & 0 & 0 \\ 0 & 0 & 1 \end{bmatrix} \begin{bmatrix} x_{t-1} \\ x_{t-2} \\ 1 \end{bmatrix} + \begin{bmatrix} 1 \\ 0 \\ 0 \end{bmatrix} \eta_t.$$

Transforming to the canonical regressor form,[12] we have

$$x_t = \delta_1 Z_{1,t-1} + \delta_2 Z_{2,t-1} + \delta_3 Z_{3,t-1} + \eta_t, \tag{40}$$

where $\delta_1 = -\beta_2$, $\delta_2 = \beta_0$, and $\delta_3 = \beta_1 + \beta_2$, $Z_{1,t} = \Delta x_t$, $Z_{2,t} = 1$, and $Z_{3,t} = x_t$. It may also be shown that

$$\begin{bmatrix} Z_{1,t} \\ Z_{2,t} \\ Z_{3,t} \end{bmatrix} = \begin{bmatrix} \theta(L) & 0 & 0 \\ 0 & 1 & 0 \\ \theta^*(L) & 0 & \theta(1) \end{bmatrix} \begin{bmatrix} \eta_t \\ 1 \\ \xi_{1,t} \end{bmatrix}, \tag{41}$$

where $\theta(L) = (1 + \beta_2 L)^{-1}$ and $\theta^*(L) = (1 - L)^{-1}[\theta(L) - \theta(1)]$.

Note from (41) that $\mathbf{F}_{21}(L) = 0$. This implies, by referring to the description of the $\mathbf{V}$ matrix above, that $\mathbf{V}$ is block-diagonal. The estimate $\hat{\delta}_1$ of the coefficient on the (differenced) stationary term has an asymptotically normal distribution with mean 0 and variance given by V_{11}^{-1}. The marginal distribution of $\hat{\delta}_2$, however, is not normal; because V_{23} is not equal to zero, $Z_{2,t}$ and $Z_{3,t}$ are asymptotically correlated, and since $Z_{3,t}$ has a Wiener distribution, so does the coefficient on $Z_{2,t}$.

If an intercept is not included in the regression, we have a 2×2 block-diagonal $\mathbf{V}$ matrix. The estimated coefficient $\hat{\delta}_1$ still has an asymptotically normal distribution, with $\hat{\delta}_1$ converging to its probability limit at rate $T^{1/2}$, while $\hat{\delta}_3$ has a Wiener distribution with convergence at rate T. Any joint test involving $\hat{\delta}_1$ and $\hat{\delta}_3$ will also have a non-standard distribution.

The analogy with the Stock–West example is direct. In (27) we had a series of terms integrated of order zero. The coefficient estimates on all these stationary terms were jointly and individually asymptotically normally distributed. The joint distribution of ϕ in (27), with any of the π_i, was of course non-standard. This observation applies equally well here. There is, however, an important difference between the Stock–West

[12] This transformation is not unique, and one could imagine choosing others; however, (39) can be rewritten as $x_t = (\beta_1 + \beta_2)x_{t-1} - \beta_2(x_{t-1} - x_{t-2}) + \eta_t$, because $\beta_0 = 0$ under the null, and this suggests the decomposition given by (40). It has the advantage of making δ_1 $(= -\beta_2)$ the coefficient of a non-integrated random variable, since x_t is an integrated series.

example and the current example. In the former case, because β had already been set equal to 1, our parameters of interest could all be written as coefficients on mean-zero and non-integrated variables. Inference could then be conducted using standard tables. In the latter case, although we can use standard tables to test for the significance of β_2, a test of $\beta_1 + \beta_2 = 1$ still requires us to use non-standard distribution theory (and so tables constructed by simulation). In a sense, our rewriting in terms of stationary variables is not sufficiently successful to enable us to conduct inference solely using standard tables. Example 6.2.6 examines this issue in more detail.

6.2.6. *Example (Sims* et al. *1990: 128)*

Suppose now that x_t is generated as in Section 6.2.5 but β_0 is non-zero under the null. The canonical representation[13] yields

$$x_t = \delta_1 Z_{1,t-1} + \delta_2 Z_{2,t-1} + \delta_4 Z_{4,t-1} + \eta_t, \tag{42}$$

where $Z_{1,t} = \Delta x_t - \mu$, $Z_{2,t} = 1$, $Z_{4,t} = x_t$, $\delta_1 = -\beta_2$, $\delta_2 = \beta_0 - \mu\beta_2$, $\delta_4 = \beta_1 + \beta_2$, and $\mu = \beta_0/(1 + \beta_2)$. Also,

$$\begin{bmatrix} Z_{1,t} \\ Z_{2,t} \\ Z_{4,t} \end{bmatrix} = \begin{bmatrix} \theta(L) & 0 & 0 & 0 \\ 0 & 1 & 0 & 0 \\ \theta^*(L) & 0 & \theta(1) & \mu \end{bmatrix} \begin{bmatrix} \eta_t \\ 1 \\ \xi_{1,t} \\ t \end{bmatrix}, \tag{43}$$

where $\theta(L)$ and $\theta^*(L)$ are defined as in Section 6.2.5 above.

Here, unlike the example in Section 6.2.5, there are no elements of $\mathbf{Z}_t$ *dominated* by a stochastic integrated process. The stochastic-trend term is dominated, in sample variability, by the deterministic-trend term t. A detailed discussion of this case appears in West (1988).

6.2.7. *Example (Banerjee and Dolado 1988)*

This example is a consolidation of most of the principal points discussed in the pages above. It is a variation of the Stock–West example, and all statements concerning the distributions of various parameter estimates may be derived from earlier general principles.

[13] This decomposition again has the advantage of making δ_1 the coefficient of a non-integrated variable. The motivation for choosing this transformation is therefore similar to that given for the example in Sect. 6.2.5.

Consider the following regression:

$$\Delta c_t = \sum_{j=1}^{n-1} \alpha_j \Delta y^d_{t-j} + \sum_{j=1}^{m-1} \gamma_j \Delta c_{t-j} + \beta y^d_{t-n} + \delta c_{t-m} + u_t, \quad (44)$$

where y^d_t denotes the logarithm of disposable income and c_t the logarithm of consumption, and both variables are I(1) in levels. Here, although we have non-stationary variables as regressors, if they are co-integrated with each other, as they must be if any of the permanent-income/life-cycle models of consumption are to make sense, then this co-integration property makes both sides of the regression equation I(0) and the t-tests of the coefficients of all the regressors are asymptotically normal. The long-run multiplier between consumption and income can be deduced much as in any dynamic model.

A variant of (44) is the model

$$\Delta c_t = k + dt + \delta c_{t-1} + \beta y_{t-1} + u_t. \quad (45)$$

Although the individual t-ratios are asymptotically normally distributed, the distribution of the Wald statistic, used for testing the joint null hypothesis $\beta = \delta = 0$, is a functional of a Wiener process and its distribution is non-standard. More interestingly, if (45) were re-parameterized as

$$\Delta c_t = k + dt + \gamma_1 c_{t-1} + \gamma_2 s_{t-1} + u_t, \quad (46)$$

where $s_{t-1} = y_{t-1} - c_{t-1}$, $\gamma_1 = \beta + \delta$, $\gamma_2 = \beta$, and s_{t-1} may be shown to be I(0) under the assumptions of the permanent-income hypothesis, then $t(\gamma_1 = 0)$ would be a functional of a Wiener process whereas $t(\gamma_2 = 0)$ would have an asymptotically normal distribution.

In the general model given by (44), the following results may be proved, using theorems 1 and 2 in SSW (1990):

(*a*) The t-statistic of each coefficient individually is asymptotically normally distributed.

(*b*) The F-statistics of joint significance of any proper subset of the set of stationary regressors have standard asymptotic distributions. Thus, any test of the joint significance of Δy_{t-j} ($j = 1, \ldots, n-1$) and Δc_{t-j} ($j = 1, \ldots, m-1$) will have the correct size if standard tables are used. Further, given that the non-stationary variables are co-integrated, if the regressors in the non-stationary set were combined, say, to give p stationary regressors and q non-stationary regressors,[14] an F-statistic that uses any of the derived p stationary

[14] In (46), for example, $p = q = 1$ and the original number of non-stationary regressors (excluding the trend) is 2.

regressors in combination with any of the original stationary regressors will also have a standard distribution asymptotically.

(*c*) The *F*-statistics of joint significance of any subset of the set of non-stationary regressors have non-standard distributions. Moreover, an *F*-statistic that uses any stationary regressors in combination with any non-stationary regressors will have a non-standard distribution.

Point (*a*) is obtained from the property of the non-stationary regressors forming a co-integrated set; as in Section 6.2.3 above, both δ and β can be written as coefficients on mean–zero stationary variables (with (46) giving one such re-parameterization for β). The next example reconsiders this point in the context of modelling practice. Point (*b*) is not surprising because the *F*-statistics considered use only stationary regressors. The fact that some of these stationary regressors may be re-parameterizations of some or all of the original non-stationary regressors is an interesting feature.

Point (*c*) is surprising in two respects. Consider (44) and (46); the first surprising feature is the non-standard behaviour of the *F*-statistic and the second is that, while the *t*-ratio of the coefficient of c_{t-1} has a standard distribution under parameterization (45), under the linear re-parameterization given by (46) the *t*-ratio has a Wiener distribution. Both results follow from the asymptotic singularity of a particular variance–covariance matrix.[15]

Consider $\hat{\gamma}_1$ in (46), which tends to a non-degenerate distribution at rate T; $T^{1/2}\hat{\gamma}_1$ therefore has a degenerate distribution, and $T^{1/2}\hat{\gamma}_2$ is asymptotically normally distributed. Thus,

$$T^{1/2}\hat{\delta} = T^{1/2}\hat{\gamma}_1 - T^{1/2}\hat{\gamma}_2 = o_p(1) + O_p(1)$$

and so

$$T^{1/2}\hat{\delta} \xrightarrow{\text{p}} -T^{1/2}\hat{\gamma}_2$$

$$T^{1/2}\hat{\beta} \xrightarrow{\text{p}} T^{1/2}\hat{\gamma}_2 \text{ (since } \hat{\beta} \text{ and } \hat{\gamma}_2 \text{ are identical).}$$

This accounts for the asymptotic singularity of the variance–covariance matrix of $[\hat{\delta}, \hat{\beta}]'$ and the corresponding non-standard behaviour of the *F*-statistic in (45). However, the distribution of $T\hat{\gamma}_1$ may be shown to be non-degenerate. $\hat{\gamma}_1$ can be written as a functional of Wiener processes, and the scaling factor (of T) suggests the resulting non-standard distribution.

[15] The asymptotic singularity of the variance–covariance matrix is the problem of multi-collinearity in another guise. On this, also see SSW (1990).

It is instructive to note that the regression given by (44) would not be sensible unless the right-hand variables or regressors were co-integrated. A special example of (44) was discussed in section 6.1, where we spoke of an unbalanced regression. This is a much more general point than that made in the context of spurious regression. A regression involving a right-hand set of variables integrated of an order different from the order of integration of the left-hand side is just as problematic as a regression between two unrelated non-stationary series. In each case, the distributions of the statistics are non-standard.

6.2.8. Example (Stock and Watson 1988a)

Stock and Watson (1988*a*) provide an example of the dangers involved in not properly taking account of the orders of integration of the regressors and the regressand. They set up a simple data-generation process based on the permanent-income hypothesis:

$$y_t = y_t^* + y_t^S \tag{47}$$

$$y_t^* = y_{t-1}^* + u_t \tag{48}$$

$$c_t = y_t^* \tag{49}$$

$$p_t = p_{t-1} + v_t \tag{50}$$

where

- y_t^* = the permanent component of disposable income which is assumed to follow a random walk
- c_t = consumption
- y_t^S = transitory component of disposable income which is a stationary innovation process
- p_t = price level in period t.

The innovation processes u_t and v_t are uncorrelated.

Stock and Watson relate the tale of two econometricians trying to test versions of Friedman's permanent income hypothesis. The misguided econometrician, unaware of or choosing to ignore the orders of integration of the series, estimates the following regressions:

$c_t = \alpha_1 + \beta_1 p_t$ (to check money illusion)

$c_t = \alpha_2 + \beta_2 t$ (to check whether consumption has a trend)

$\Delta c_t = \alpha_3 + \beta_3 \Delta y_t$ (to calculate the marginal propensity to consume)

$\Delta c_t = \alpha_4 + \beta_4 y_{t-1}$ (to test the permanent income hypothesis).

Each of the inferences from these regressions is invalid.

The first regression is a spurious regression of the classical Granger–Newbold kind; c_t and p_t are unrelated random walks, and the econometrician's finding of a large t-statistic for β_1, thereby leading him to conclude in favour of money illusion,[16] is a spurious one.

The second regression is also spurious since it attempts to explain a random walk (or, in other words, a stochastically trending variable) by a deterministic trend. Nelson and Kang (1981) pointed out the dangers of running regressions which attempt to de-trend stochastically trending data in the vain hope of achieving stationarity around a trend. In both cases the problems with the inferences arise because the regressions involve variables that are not co-integrated (see Chapter 3).

The third equation appears to be correctly specified but nevertheless leads to downwardly biased estimates of the coefficient for the marginal propensity to consume because disposable income measures the change in permanent income with error, since it includes the change in transitory income as well. The final regression is what we called an 'unbalanced regression' as it tries to explain a variable integrated of order zero by a variable integrated of order 1. The series of papers noted above (Mankiw and Shapiro 1985, 1986; Banerjee and Dolado 1988; Galbraith *et al.* 1987) consider the extent to which the t-statistics in such cases are biased away from zero, leading to misleading inferences about the significance of coefficients.

Stock and Watson compare the predicament of this econometrician with econometrician B, say, who looks at the results of the following alternative regressions:

$$c_t = \gamma_1 + \delta_1 y_t$$

$$c_t = \gamma_2 + \delta_2 c_{t-1} + \delta_3 c_{t-2}$$

$$c_t = \gamma_3 + \delta_4 c_{t-1} + \delta_5 y_{t-1}.$$

The inferences from each of these regressions will be, by and large, correct. The first regression here is the standard co-integrating regression and this time *is* valid. The estimate of the coefficient δ_1 will have a Wiener distribution but will be super-consistent. The reported standard error will be incorrect owing to untreated autocorrelation.

The second regression can be re-parameterized[17] as

$$c_t = \gamma_2 + (\delta_2 + \delta_3)c_{t-1} - \delta_3(c_{t-1} - c_{t-2}).$$

Thus, δ_3 can be written as a coefficient on a stationary variable (as can δ_2 treated in isolation). The theory, as described above, implies that the

16 Inference of this kind would appear to be faulty, in any case. To consider a rejection of H_0: $\beta_1 = 0$ as a reason for accepting any specific alternative is statistically and logically unjustifiable.

17 Or in a form analogous to that given by (44).

usual t and F distributions[18] will apply. A similar argument applies to the third regression, with the exception that in this case $y_{t-1} - c_{t-1}$ forms the co-integrating relation. Stock and West (1988) and Banerjee and Dolado (1988) discuss regressions of this form in further detail.

The moral of the econometricians' story is the need to keep track of the orders of integration on both sides of the regression equation, which usually means incorporating dynamics; models that have restrictive dynamic structures are relatively likely to give misleading inferences simply for reasons of inconsistency of orders of integration. Specificity was clearly the problem with several of the models proposed by the first econometrician. A general to specific method of econometric modelling would have overcome many of the problems of spurious inferences and non-standard distributions. An initial model, more general than the one postulated by the second econometrician, of the form, say,

$$c_t = \beta_0 + \beta_1 t + \beta_2 p_t + \beta_3 y_t + \beta_4 c_{t-1} + \beta_5 y_{t-1} + \beta_6 p_{t-1},$$

would be more appropriate for inference when weak exogeneity conditions are satisfied.[19] Account must be taken of facts (a)–(c) of Section 6.2.7 when conducting such inference; more generally, the example illustrates ways in which the theory of modelling with integrated variables has contributed to improving our understanding of what constitutes good practice in dynamic modelling.

6.3. Functional Forms and Transformations

We drew attention in Chapter 1 to the fact that many economic time series will come close to conformity with the integrated models only if a logarithmic transformation is applied. The logarithms of many such series may be integrated, but it seems unlikely that the untransformed *levels* of macroeconomic time series such as consumption, national income, and the price level could be made stationary by differencing alone. It is worth examining this transformation more closely, along with the effect that it may be expected to have on an equilibrium relationship. If the levels of two series are co-integrated, do we expect the logarithms to be co-integrated also, and vice versa?

Begin by examining a series with a tendency to grow over time subject to stochastic shocks which tend to grow with the underlying series. For example,

$$Y_t = (1 + \gamma)Y_{t-1}e_t, \tag{51}$$

18 The F-distribution will apply when looking at tests of joint significance of subsets of regressors, each of which is I(0). In this example, because one of the regressors is I(1) and the other is I(0), the F-statistic will have a non-standard distribution.

19 See Ch. 8 and earlier discussion in this chapter.

where e_t has a mean of 1 and is log-normally distributed. A series such as Y_t might describe a number of economic time series, at least in broad outline. Taking the logarithmic transformation of (51) and using lower-case letters to denote the transformed variables with $Y_t > 0$,

$$\log(Y_t) = \log(1 + \gamma) + \log(Y_{t-1}) + \log(e_t) \tag{52}$$

so

$$y_t = \gamma + y_{t-1} + \varepsilon_t, \qquad \varepsilon_t \sim \mathrm{N}(0, \sigma^2),$$

or

$$\Delta y_t = \gamma + \varepsilon_t, \tag{53}$$

where $\log(1 + \gamma) \simeq \gamma$ and $\varepsilon_t = \log(e_t)$.

Equation (53) is indeed commonly used as a simple characterization of the logarithms of economic time series. As a description of such a transformed data series, (52) or (53) seems at least admissible; Δy_t is the growth rate of the level series Y_t, and this growth rate varies around a (typically positive) mean. That this equation could describe the level of the series (so y_t denotes the original data without the logarithmic transformation) seems implausible, however: (53) would then imply that the absolute amount of growth varies around a fixed mean, and therefore that, as the series grows, the average amount of growth falls to zero as a proportion of the series itself. Moreover, $\sigma^2/\mathrm{var}(Y_t)$ would tend to zero, forcing the series to become essentially deterministic in relative terms. This criticism does not apply to (53) since σ is a proportion of Y_t.

Ermini and Hendry (1991) consider the issue of testing 'logarithms versus levels' by formulating a test based on the encompassing principle. The null model M_1 may be said to encompass the rival or alternative model M_2 if M_1 is able to explain the findings of M_2. Alternatively, if the rival model does not adequately characterize the properties of the process generating the series, the null model ought to be able to predict the *form* of mis-specification one would expect to find if the rival model were estimated.

To pursue the last point, suppose a data series $\{Y_t\}$ is well characterized by a random walk in logarithms with a stable drift and homoskedastic errors. Suppose further that this implies that regressing ΔY_t on a constant would yield unstable estimates and heteroskedastic errors. A simple initial test would then be to estimate the random walk in both logarithms and levels and see whether the models displayed the predicted behaviour.[20] If the null model also had predictions to offer about

[20] The processes corresponding to 'random walk in logarithms' and 'random walk in levels' are $\Delta y_t = \mu_1 + \varepsilon_t$ and $\Delta Y_t = \mu_2 + v_t$, respectively.

the form of the instability of the parameters, the test could be sharpened by testing for the presence of particular kinds of misspecification—say, drift or variances of errors increasing exponentially over time. In general, the entire argument should also be run in reverse by taking the rival model as the null; however, linear models do not ensure positive observations, so awkward issues arise.

We illustrate this discussion with the time series analysed in Chapter 1, namely real net national product (Y, in 1929 £million) for the United Kingdom over 1872–1975 (from Friedman and Schwartz 1982). The approach follows that in Ermini and Hendry (1991).

First, we model the level of net national product over the sample 1875–1975 by OLS. Only one lagged difference was needed to remove any residual serial correlation, yielding

$$\Delta Y_t = \underset{(16.6)}{58.2} + \underset{(0.096)}{0.384}\ \Delta Y_{t-1},$$

$$R^2 = 0.138 \qquad \hat{\sigma} = 144.2 \qquad \text{DW} = 1.94 \qquad \text{SC} = 10.01$$

where the standard errors of coefficient estimates are shown in parentheses, $\hat{\sigma}$ is the equation standard error, and SC is the Schwarz criterion. (Smaller values on balance produce preferable models.) Since the mean of Y is 4701.0, the $\hat{\sigma}$ as a percentage of Y is 3.1 per cent. However, the coefficients are not constant over the sample period, as shown in Fig. 6.1 for the intercept, and Fig. 6.2 for the one-step residuals and $\hat{\sigma}$. (See Hendry (1989) for details.)[21] The intercept trends upwards, and $\hat{\sigma}$ increases over time, even ignoring the large shock in 1919–20. On any constancy test, the model is rejected at far beyond the 1 per cent level (e.g. that of Hansen 1992).

Next we model growth in logs. As before, one lagged difference removed residual serial correlation, giving

$$\Delta y_t = \underset{(0.0038)}{0.0138} + \underset{(0.098)}{0.254}\ \Delta y_{t-1}, \tag{54}$$

$$R^2 = 0.064 \qquad \hat{\sigma} = 0.033 \qquad \text{DW} = 1.96 \qquad \text{SC} = -6.73.$$

[21] Recursive estimation involves estimating an equation over successively larger sub-samples, starting from a minimum sub-sample and extending to the full sample. Parameter instability may be tracked by looking at the behaviour of the estimated coefficients, as sample size is increased, to see whether they fluctuate significantly or remain stable. Recursive Chow (1960) tests may be computed in at least two ways. The first involves estimating the equation from, say, $t = 1$ to $t = T_1$, where T_1 is greater than the minimum sample size, and then from $t = 1$ to $t = T_1 + 1$. The one-step-ahead Chow test is based on a comparison of the residual variance of the two estimated equations and is an F-test under the null of parameter constancy. A second test is given by estimating the equation from, say, $t = 1$ to $t = T_1$ and comparing the residual variance of this regression with that of the equation estimated over the full sample. A sequence of these Chow tests is built up by augmenting the sub-sample size by one at each step, e.g. $T_1 + 1$ to $T_1 + 2$, and

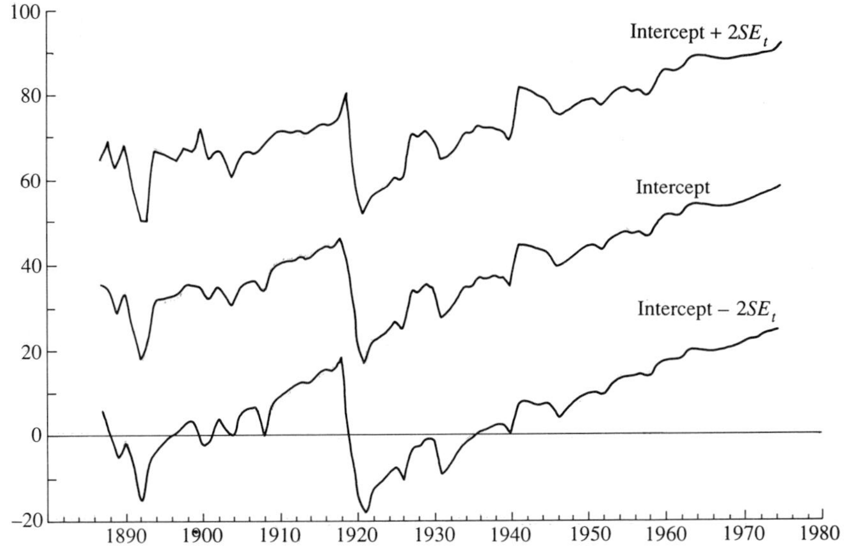

FIG 6.1. Recursive estimates of intercept in levels model

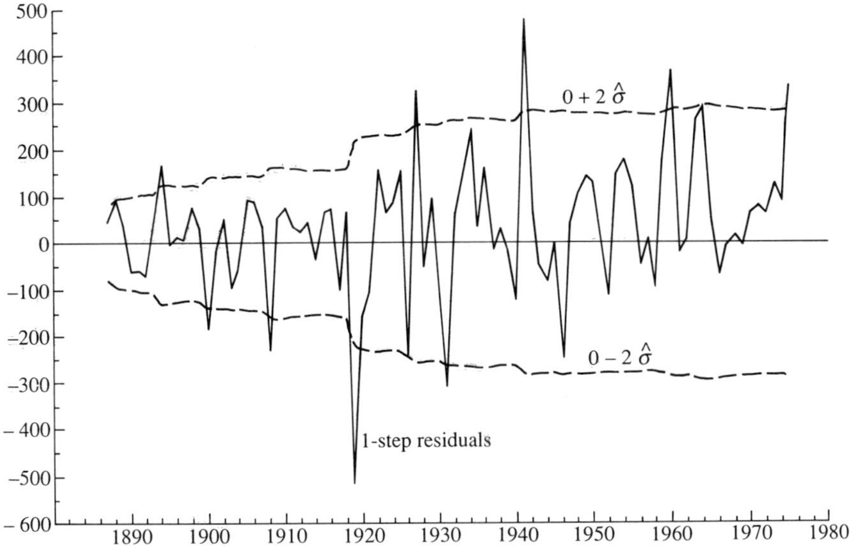

FIG 6.2. One-step residuals in levels model

comparing the residual variance of each of these equations with the full sample residual variance. Alternatively, the sequence of one-step residuals (or forecast errors) can be examined relative to the residual variance at each sample size.

The percentage $\hat{\sigma}$ is 3.3 per cent but now the intercept is constant as shown in Fig. 6.3, and little residual heteroskedasticity remains (see Fig. 6.4). The model fails constancy tests only prior to the large shock in 1919–20.

Ermini and Hendry use results from Ermini and Granger (1991) to describe the particular form of instability and heteroskedasticity one would expect in the model in levels if the data were generated by the logarithmic model. Ermini and Granger show that, if the data are generated by

$$\Delta y_t = \mu + \varepsilon_t, \tag{55}$$

with time-invariant distribution $\Delta y_t \sim \mathrm{IN}(\mu, \sigma^2)$, and if the rival model is

$$\Delta Y_t = \gamma + \eta_t,$$

then $E(\Delta Y_t) = \delta \exp(\lambda t)$; $\mathrm{var}(\Delta Y_t) = \phi \exp[(2\lambda + \sigma^2)t]$, where

$$\lambda = \mu + \sigma^2/2;\ \delta = [1 - \exp(-\lambda)]Y_0;$$

$\phi = \exp(2y_0)\{1 - 2\exp[-(\lambda + \sigma^2)] + \exp[-(2\lambda + \sigma^2)]\}$; and $Y_0 = \exp(y_0)$ is the starting observation postulated for the model in levels.

Thus, if the logarithmic model were true, the model in levels would have both a drift, $\delta \exp(\lambda t)$, and variance, $\phi \exp[(2\lambda + \sigma^2)t]$, exponentially increasing with time. Further, in the regression

$$\Delta Y_t = \gamma + \delta \exp(\hat{\lambda} t) + \eta_t, \tag{56}$$

with $\hat{\lambda} = \hat{\mu} + \hat{\sigma}^2/2$, where $\hat{\mu}$ and $\hat{\sigma}^2$ are obtained from estimating (55),

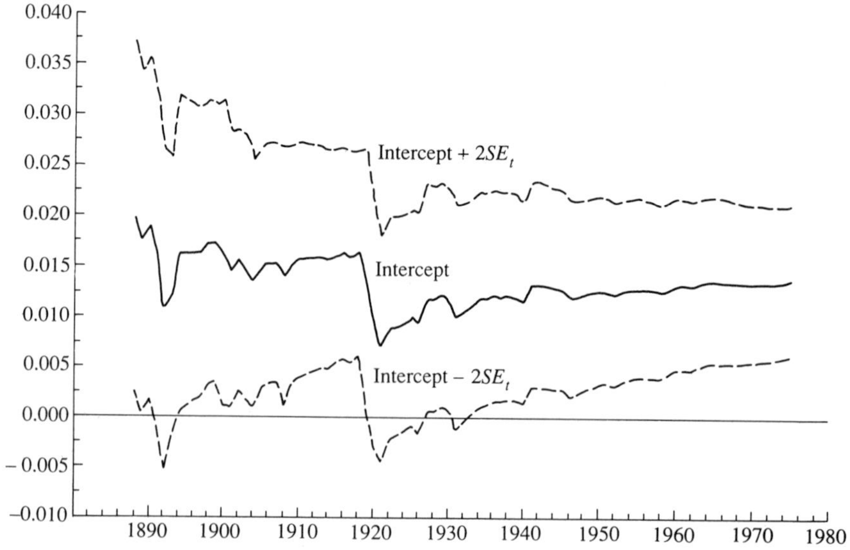

FIG 6.3. Recursive estimates of intercept in log model

M_1 (the logarithmic model) encompasses M_2 (model in levels) only if $\delta \neq 0$ and $\gamma = 0$.

We now apply their test to the linear model of UK national income over the last century. Because of the lagged dependent variable in (54), the long-run solution provides the estimate $\hat{\mu}$ for μ in the Ermini–Hendry test, namely

$$\Delta y = \underset{(0.00445)}{0.01852}.$$

Thus, $\hat{\lambda} t = 0.0191t$; calculate $\exp(\hat{\lambda} t)$ and enter this as an additional regressor in the linear model. The empirical outcome is

$$\Delta Y_t = \underset{(28.8)}{-21.3} + \underset{(0.099)}{0.260}\ \Delta Y_{t-1} + \underset{(8.39)}{27.69}\ \exp(\hat{\lambda} t). \tag{57}$$

$R^2 = 0.224 \quad F(2, 98) = 14.15 \quad \hat{\sigma} = 137.5 \quad \mathrm{DW} = 1.91 \quad \mathrm{SC} = 9.95.$

The coefficient on $\exp(\hat{\lambda} t)$ is significant and makes the intercept insignificant. This result confirms the earlier graphical evidence on the inappropriateness of the linear model against a log-linear form. Finally, dropping the intercept in (57),

$$\Delta Y_t = \underset{(0.099)}{0.264}\ \Delta Y_{t-1} + \underset{(4.60)}{22.50}\ \exp(\hat{\lambda} t). \tag{58}$$

$\hat{\sigma} = 137.2 \quad \mathrm{DW} = 1.91 \quad \mathrm{SC} = 9.91.$

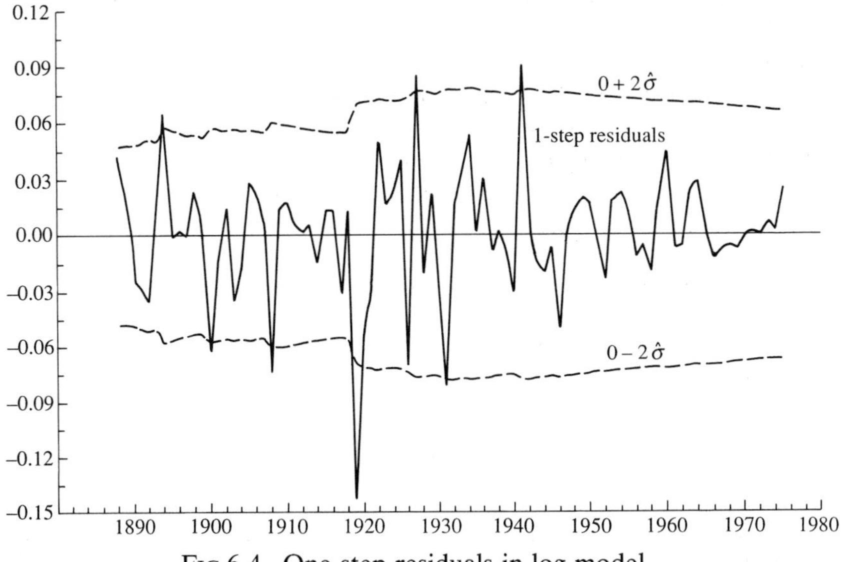

FIG 6.4. One-step residuals in log model

Figure 6.5 shows the recursive estimates of δ from (58) over the sample, and reveals greatly reduced evidence of parameter non-constancy in using the exponential trend relative to an intercept.

These principles may be extended to deciding whether it is the levels or the logarithms of variables that are co-integrated. Thus, consider two I(1) processes $X_t > 0$ and $Z_t > 0$ between which there is a co-integrating relationship in levels:

$$X_t = \beta Z_t + u_t, \qquad u_t \sim \text{ID}(0, \sigma_u^2). \tag{59}$$

Defining the transformed series $x_t = \log(X_t)$ and $z_t = \log(Z_t)$, we have

$$x_t = \log(\beta Z_t + u_t).$$

Using a Taylor series expansion of the logarithmic function, we obtain

$$\log(\beta Z_t + u_t) = \log(\beta Z_t) + \left(\frac{1}{2}\right) u_t(\beta Z_t)^{-1} - \left(\frac{1}{3!}\right)(u_t)^2(\beta Z_t)^{-2} + \ldots$$

so

$$x_t = \log(\beta) + z_t + \sum_{i=0}^{\infty}\left(\frac{(-1)^i}{(i+2)!}\right)\left(\frac{u_t}{\beta Z_t}\right)^{i+1}, \tag{60}$$

from which we can see that the terms in the summation will decline in importance as Z_t grows, since by (59) u_t is of fixed variance, while the variance of Z_t is of $O(t)$. Hence we expect to find an equilibrium relation of some sort among the logarithms of variables that are co-integrated in levels. Asymptotically, this equilibrium relation is of a degenerate kind with the distribution of $x_t - z_t$ collapsing around $\log(\beta)$. This is also a testable prediction of the hypothesis that the random walk model in levels encompasses the logarithmic model,[22] although the test is likely to have low power because the variance in the errors is likely to persist even in fairly large samples.

Conversely, if we begin with a co-integrating relationship between two series which have already been transformed to logarithms,

$$w_t = \alpha v_t + \varepsilon_t, \qquad \varepsilon_t \sim \text{ID}(0, \sigma_\varepsilon^2), \tag{61}$$

then the relationship among the levels of the series is

$$\exp(w_t) = \exp(\alpha v_t + \varepsilon_t),$$

which implies

$$\exp(w_t) = \exp(\alpha v_t)\exp(\varepsilon_t)$$

[22] To see this, simply substitute X_{t-1} for Z_t. The instability of the random walk model in levels made a formal test in the levels → logarithms direction unnecessary in the Ermini–Hendry discussion, although in principle such a test could be carried out.

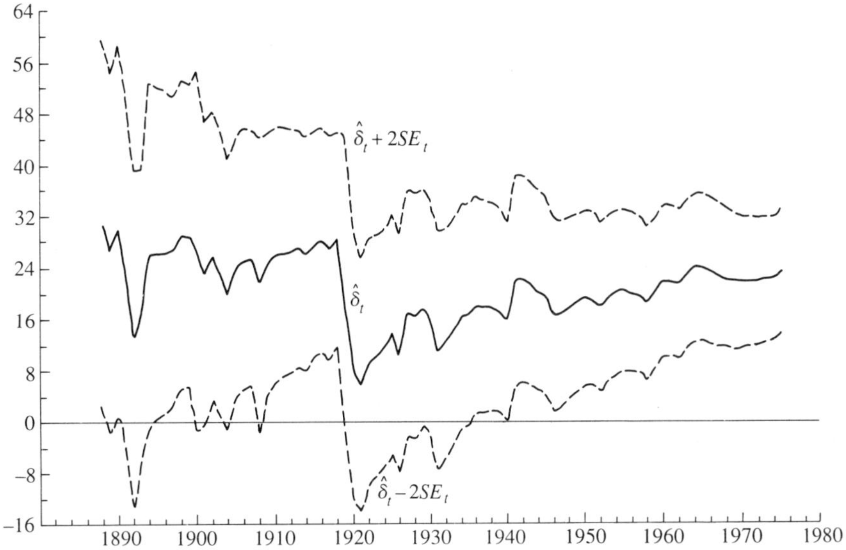

FIG 6.5. Recursive estimates of δ

or

$$W_t = (V_t^{\alpha}) \exp(\varepsilon_t) \equiv V_t^{\alpha} \nu_t.$$

This no longer has the form of a standard co-integrating relationship, since $W_t - kV_t = V_t(V_t^{\alpha-1}\nu_t - k) \equiv \eta_t$; while ν_t may remain a stationary process, the error term η_t in the new relationship depends on the integrated series V_t and is therefore not stationary in general. No co-integrating relationship may therefore appear, and a regression of the form $W_t = kV_t + \eta_t$ is likely to display considerable instability.

At the same time, it should be noted that, in either of the above examples, only one of the logarithm and the level of a variable will be an integrated process (capable of being made stationary by differencing), although stationarity or non-stationarity will be common to both representations. The standard definition of co-integration, which describes equilibrium relations among integrated processes, can be legitimately applied to only one of the two cases at a time.

The fact remains, however, that a co-integrating relationship among the levels of variables suggests the existence of some *linear* equilibrium relationship among the logarithms of those same variables. The converse need not in general be true.

Appendix: Vector Brownian Motion

Consider the bivariate I(1) data generation process given by:

$$\begin{aligned} \Delta y_t &= \eta \Delta z_t + \varepsilon_{1t} \\ \Delta z_t &= \qquad\quad\; + \varepsilon_{2t} \end{aligned} \quad \text{with} \quad \begin{aligned} \varepsilon_{1t} &\sim \mathrm{IN}(0, \sigma_1^2) \\ \varepsilon_{2t} &\sim \mathrm{IN}(0, \sigma_2^2) \end{aligned} \quad \text{where } E[\varepsilon_{1t}\varepsilon_{2s}] = 0 \ \forall t, s. \tag{A1}$$

The DGP in (A1) is a re-parameterization of a general bivariate normal distribution for $(\Delta y_t, \Delta z_t)$ with covariance $\eta\sigma_2^2$, and defines the integrated vector process:

$$\mathbf{x}_t = \mathbf{x}_{t-1} + \mathbf{v}_t \text{ where } \mathbf{v}_t \sim \mathrm{IN}(\mathbf{0}, \boldsymbol{\Sigma}), \tag{A2}$$

when $\mathbf{x}_t = (y_t \colon z_t)'$ and $\mathbf{v}_t = (\varepsilon_{1t} + \eta\varepsilon_{2t}, \varepsilon_{2t})'$. Then $\mathbf{v}_t$ has non-unit error variance matrix $\boldsymbol{\Sigma}$:

$$\boldsymbol{\Sigma} = \begin{bmatrix} \sigma_1^2 + \eta^2\sigma_2^2 & \eta\sigma_2^2 \\ \eta\sigma_2^2 & \sigma_2^2 \end{bmatrix}. \tag{A3}$$

As in Chapter 1, a suitably scaled function of $\mathbf{x}_t$ converges to a vector Brownian motion process, denoted BM($\boldsymbol{\Sigma}$). We first derive the standardized Brownian motion by the transform:

$$\mathbf{m}_t = \mathbf{K}'\mathbf{x}_t \text{ where } \mathbf{K}' = \sigma_1^{-1}\begin{pmatrix} 1 & -\eta \\ 0 & s \end{pmatrix}, \tag{A4}$$

and $s = \sigma_1/\sigma_2$. Then $\mathbf{m}_t$ has a unit error variance matrix since:

$$\mathbf{m}_t = \sigma_1^{-1}\begin{pmatrix} y_t - \eta z_t \\ s z_t \end{pmatrix} = \sum_{j=1}^{t}\begin{pmatrix} \varepsilon_{1j}/\sigma_1 \\ \varepsilon_{2j}/\sigma_2 \end{pmatrix} = \sum_{j=1}^{t}\begin{pmatrix} e_{1t} \\ e_{2t} \end{pmatrix}$$

$$= \sum_{j=1}^{t}\mathbf{e}_j \text{ where } \mathbf{e}_t \sim \mathrm{IN}(\mathbf{0}, \mathbf{I}). \tag{A5}$$

Alternatively, from (A2) and (A4):

$$\mathbf{K}'\mathbf{x}_t = \mathbf{K}'\mathbf{x}_{t-1} + \mathbf{K}'\mathbf{v}_t \text{ where } \mathbf{K}'\mathbf{v}_t = \mathbf{e}_t \sim \mathrm{IN}(\mathbf{0}, \mathbf{K}'\boldsymbol{\Sigma}\mathbf{K}) = \mathrm{IN}(\mathbf{0}, \mathbf{I}). \tag{A6}$$

Next, using a component by component analysis similar to that in Chapter 3, from (A5):

$$T^{-1/2}\sum_{t=1}^{[Tr]}\mathbf{e}_t \Rightarrow \mathbf{B}(r), \tag{A7}$$

where $\mathbf{B}(r) = (B_1(r), B_2(r))'$ (denoted BM($\mathbf{I}$)), and the $B_i(r)$ are the standardized Wiener processes associated with accumulating the $\{e_{it}\}$. Further:

$$T^{-2}\sum_{t=1}^{T}\mathbf{m}_t\mathbf{m}_t' \Rightarrow \int_0^1 \mathbf{B}(r)\mathbf{B}(r)'\,\mathrm{d}r = \begin{bmatrix} \int_0^1 B_1(r)^2\,\mathrm{d}r & \int_0^1 B_1(r)B_2(r)\,\mathrm{d}r \\ \int_0^1 B_1(r)B_2(r)\,\mathrm{d}r & \int_0^1 B_2(r)^2\,\mathrm{d}r \end{bmatrix}, \tag{A8}$$

and:

$$T^{-1}\sum_{t=1}^{T}\mathbf{m}_{t-1}\mathbf{e}_t' \Rightarrow \int_0^1 \mathbf{B}(r)\,\mathrm{d}\mathbf{B}(r)' = \begin{bmatrix} \int_0^1 B_1(r)\,\mathrm{d}B_1(r) & \int_0^1 B_1(r)\,\mathrm{d}B_2(r) \\ \int_0^1 B_2(r)\,\mathrm{d}B_1(r) & \int_0^1 B_2(r)\,\mathrm{d}B_2(r) \end{bmatrix} \tag{A9}$$

These vector formulae are natural generalizations of the scalar Wiener processes in Chapter 3.

Scalar functions of vector I(1) variables can be handled as follows. Consider the distribution of the difference between y_t and z_t, namely $u_t = \mathbf{d}'\mathbf{x}_t$ for $\mathbf{d}' = (1, -1)$. Then from (A4):

$$u_t = \mathbf{d}'\mathbf{K}'^{-1}\mathbf{m}_t = \boldsymbol{\kappa}'\mathbf{m}_t$$

where $\mathbf{d}'\mathbf{K}'^{-1} = \sigma_2(1, -1)\begin{pmatrix} s & \eta \\ 0 & 1 \end{pmatrix} = \sigma_2(s, \eta - 1) = \boldsymbol{\kappa}'$.

Thus, for example:

$$T^{-2}\sum_{t=1}^{T}u_t^2 = T^{-2}\sum_{t=1}^{T}\boldsymbol{\kappa}'\mathbf{m}_t\mathbf{m}_t'\boldsymbol{\kappa} \Rightarrow \boldsymbol{\kappa}'\left[\int_0^1 \mathbf{B}(r)\mathbf{B}(r)'\,\mathrm{d}r\right]\boldsymbol{\kappa},$$

$$= \sigma_2^2(s, \eta - 1)\begin{bmatrix} \int_0^1 B_1(r)^2\,\mathrm{d}r & \int_0^1 B_1(r)B_2(r)\,\mathrm{d}r \\ \int_0^1 B_1(r)B_2(r)\,\mathrm{d}r & \int_0^1 B_2(r)^2\,\mathrm{d}r \end{bmatrix}\begin{bmatrix} s \\ \eta - 1 \end{bmatrix}$$

$$= \sigma_2^2\left[s^2\int_0^1 B_1^2(r)\,\mathrm{d}r + 2s(\eta - 1)\int_0^1 B_1(r)B_2(r)\,\mathrm{d}r + (\eta - 1)^2\int_0^1 B_2^2(r)\,\mathrm{d}r\right]$$

$$= \sigma_1^2 \int_0^1 B_1^2(r)\,dr + 2\sigma_1\sigma_2(\eta - 1)\int_0^1 B_1(r)B_2(r)\,dr$$

$$+ (\eta - 1)^2\sigma_2^2 \int_0^1 B_2^2(r)\,dr. \tag{A10}$$

By direct calculation from (A1) however,
$y_t - z_t = u_t = u_{t-1} + \{\varepsilon_{1t} + (\eta - 1)\varepsilon_{2t}\} = u_{t-1} + w_t$ (say) so:

$$T^{-2}\sum_{t=1}^{T} u_t^2 \Rightarrow \sigma_w^2 \int_0^1 W(r)^2\,dr \text{ where } \sigma_w^2 = \sigma_1^2 + (\eta - 1)^2\sigma_2^2, \tag{A11}$$

and $W(r)$ is the Wiener process associated with $\{w_t/\sigma_w\}$. By definition, $w_t = \varepsilon_{1t} + (\eta - 1)\varepsilon_{2t}$, so that $\sigma_w W(r) = \sigma_1 B_1(r) + (\eta - 1)\sigma_2 B_2(r)$, and hence the expressions in (A10) and (A11) are equal, but provide different insights into the behaviour of the scalar second moment.

Similarly, let $\mathbf{f}' = (1, 0)$ so that $\mathbf{f}'\mathbf{e}_t = \varepsilon_{1t}/\sigma_1$, then we can derive a covariance such as:

$$T^{-1}\sum_{t=1}^{T} u_{t-1}\varepsilon_{1t}$$

$$= \sigma_1 T^{-1}\sum_{t=1}^{T} \boldsymbol{\kappa}'\mathbf{m}_{t-1}\mathbf{e}_t'\mathbf{f}$$

$$\Rightarrow \sigma_1\boldsymbol{\kappa}'\left[\int_0^1 \mathbf{B}(r)\,d\mathbf{B}(r)'\right]\mathbf{f}$$

$$= \sigma_1\sigma_2(s,\ \eta - 1)\begin{bmatrix} \int_0^1 B_1(r)\,dB_1(r) & \int_0^1 B_1(r)\,dB_2(r) \\ \int_0^1 B_2(r)\,dB_1(r) & \int_0^1 B_2(r)\,dB_2(r) \end{bmatrix}\begin{bmatrix} 1 \\ 0 \end{bmatrix}$$

$$= \sigma_1^2 \int_0^1 B_1(r)\,dB_1(r) + \sigma_1\sigma_2(\eta - 1)\int_0^1 B_2(r)\,dB_1(r). \tag{A12}$$

Returning to the standardized vector Brownian motion, let $\mathbf{V}(r) = (V_1(r), V_2(r))'$ (which is $\text{BM}(\boldsymbol{\Sigma})$) be associated with the accumulation of $\{\mathbf{v}_t\}$. Now $V_1(r)$ and $V_2(r)$ are not independent since $E(v_{1t}v_{2t}) \neq 0$. The standardized vector Brownian motion is $\mathbf{B}(r) = \mathbf{K}'\mathbf{V}(r)$ where $\mathbf{K}'$ is defined in (A4). Multiplying out, we have:

$$B_1(r) = \sigma_1^{-1}(V_1(r) - \eta V_2(r)) \quad \text{and} \quad B_2(r) = \sigma_2^{-1}V_2(r). \tag{A13}$$

Indeed, if we condition v_{1t} on v_{2t} (which generates ε_{1t}) and let $V_{1\cdot 2}(r)$ be the associated "conditional" unstandardized Wiener process, then

$V_{1\cdot 2}(r)$ and $V_2(r)$ are independent. Because $\varepsilon_{1t} = v_{1t} - E(v_{1t}|v_{2t}) = v_{1t} - \eta v_{2t}$, we see that $V_{1\cdot 2}(r) = V_1(r) - \eta V_2(r) = \sigma_1 B_1(r)$ from (A13).

Finally, consider an expression of the form:

$$T^{-1}\sum_{t=1}^{T}\mathbf{m}_t\mathbf{e}_t' = T^{-1}\sum_{t=1}^{T}\mathbf{m}_{t-1}\mathbf{e}_t' + T^{-1}\sum_{t=1}^{T}\mathbf{e}_t\mathbf{e}_t' \Rightarrow \int_0^1 \mathbf{B}(r)\,\mathrm{d}\mathbf{B}(r)' + \mathbf{I}. \tag{A14}$$

Then the error covariance matrix is added on if the cross-product under analysis is a contemporaneous rather than a lagged one (see the appendix to Chapter 7 for an extension). Phillips and Durlauf (1986) and Phillips (1988*b*) provide proofs and generalizations.

7

Co-integration in Individual Equations

We first examine methods of testing for co-integration via static regressions, and provide simulation estimates of the upper percentage points of the distributions of statistics used in the tests. Next, we look at the properties of the estimators derived from such static regressions. In particular, we focus on the finite-sample biases in the estimates of co-integrating vectors and the powers of tests to detect co-integration. Finally, we consider modified estimators and dynamic models. In Chapter 8, systems methods of estimating co-integrating relations will be considered.

The previous chapter focused on the properties of co-integrated processes and the implications of modelling with co-integrated variables. We have discussed the 'super-consistency' of the coefficient estimates in the static or co-integrating regression, balanced and unbalanced regressions, and the distributions of the statistics commonly used to test for the significance of regression coefficients.

The two issues of being able to test for the existence of an equilibrium relationship among variables and to accurately estimate such a relationship are complementary. Indeed, as demonstrated in discussing spurious regressions in Chapter 3, static regressions among integrated series are meaningful if and only if they involve co-integrated variables. Thus, it is of interest to discover, first, how well the most frequently used tests of co-integration perform, and second, how accurately the corresponding equilibrium relationship is estimated.

The objective of this chapter is to develop tests applicable to single equations which may be used to detect a long-term relationship of the form discussed and exploited in earlier chapters. We also attempt to formulate some recommendations for efficient estimation of co-integrating parameters and testing for co-integration in finite samples. It will become clear from the discussion that the *asymptotic* properties of static regression estimators are often rather different from their behaviour in empirically relevant sample sizes. Further, lack of weak exogeneity due to co-integrating vectors entering several equations also alters finite sample behaviour. It therefore becomes important, in the face of data limitations, to consider alternative methods which do not rely exclusively on single-equation static regressions. These are the topic of Sections 7–9.

7.1. Estimating a Single Co-integrating Vector

Consider the problem of estimating the single co-integrating vector $\boldsymbol{\alpha}$ using the static model

$$\boldsymbol{\alpha}'\mathbf{x}_t = u_t. \tag{1}$$

We conduct the discussion in this and the following sections in three stages. First, we elaborate upon the theorems presented in Chapter 5 and develop an intuitive discussion of static regressions. Next, we proceed to the issue of testing for co-integration using static regressions. The testing and the parameterization of the equilibrium relationship are seen to be complementary exercises. Finally, we discuss simulation studies which cast light on the behaviour, in finite samples, of the static-regression estimators and the powers of the tests for co-integration.

In order to keep the analysis as tractable as possible, we will restrict ourselves to considering CI(1, 1) systems. Thus, suppose that all the elements in $\mathbf{x}_t$ are I(1). In general, then, any linear combination $\boldsymbol{\delta}'\mathbf{x}_t$ of the elements of $\mathbf{x}_t$ will produce an I(1) series u_t. The only exception, if one exists, is a co-integrating vector $\boldsymbol{\alpha}$ such that $\boldsymbol{\alpha}'\mathbf{x}_t$ is I(0).[1] Ordinary least squares minimizes the residual variance of $\mathbf{x}_t$, and therefore a simple OLS regression of the form (1) should provide an excellent approximation to the true co-integrating vector when one exists, as discussed in Chapter 5.

The simplicity of this method and the elegance of the theoretical argument help explain the popularity of such regressions. All that is needed to parameterize a long-run equilibrium relationship among a set of variables is a static OLS regression. This regression is performed as the first step of the Engle–Granger two-step estimator[2] and serves as a preliminary check on the equilibrium relationships postulated by economic theory to exist among the variables.

[1] Initially we focus on the case where (apart from normalization) the co-integrating vector $\boldsymbol{\alpha}$ is unique and is therefore of dimension $n \times 1$. As the analysis in Ch. 5 showed (especially the discussion of the Granger Representation Theorem), this is clearly a restrictive assumption to make. In general, there will exist r co-integrating vectors, $0 \leqslant r \leqslant n-1$, and when gathered in an array, the matrix $\boldsymbol{\alpha}$ will be of order $n \times r$. The problem of estimating co-integrating vectors in systems is considered in Ch. 8.

[2] The two-step estimator and its asymptotic properties are discussed in Ch. 5. The general case is derived by Engle and Granger (1987: 262, Theorem 2).

However, there are reasons for preferring alternatives to the simple static regression in samples of the size typical in economics. This chapter will consider dynamic regression methods and modified estimators. These techniques help to reduce or eliminate sources of finite-sample biases which arise from static estimation, and which can be very substantial in practice.

7.2. Tests for Co-integration in a Single Equation

The simplest tests for co-integration proposed by Engle and Granger, test for the existence of a unit root in the residuals of the static regression. The methods of Chapter 4 can therefore be followed with minor modifications. We first consider the bivariate case, where $\mathbf{x}_t = (y_t, z_t)'$.

The modifications are necessary because, while the tests for unit roots discussed in Chapter 4 use the original series, say $\{w_t\}$, the co-integration tests are based on the *estimated*, or derived, residual series,

$$\hat{u}_t \equiv y_t - \hat{\beta} z_t. \tag{2}$$

Hence, as the co-integrating regression estimates β *before* the test is performed, the co-integration test is not simply a standard test for a unit root in the series $\hat{u}_t$.

If β were known in the example presented in Chapter 5 (given by equations (5.1)–(5.6)), the null hypothesis of no co-integration, corresponding to ρ equal to 1, could be tested by constructing the series $u_t = y_t - \beta z_t$, treating this series as the one that has the unit root under the null, and using the Dickey–Fuller tables. However, if β is unknown, it must be estimated (e.g.) from the static regression of y_t on z_t. The test is based on the null hypothesis of no co-integration, with the critical values for the test statistics calculated to ensure the appropriate probability of rejection of the null hypothesis.

Some of the most widely used tests of co-integration have been the *co-integrating regression Durbin–Watson* test (CRDW), the Dickey–Fuller test (DF), and the augmented Dickey–Fuller test (ADF).

The CRDW, suggested by Sargan and Bhargava (1983), is computed in exactly the same fashion as the usual DW statistic and is given by

$$\text{CRDW} = \sum_{t=2}^{T} (\hat{u}_t - \hat{u}_{t-1})^2 \Big/ \sum_{t=1}^{T} \hat{u}_t^2, \tag{3}$$

where $\hat{u}_t$ denotes the OLS residual from the co-integrating regression.

The null hypothesis being tested, using the CRDW statistic, is of a single unit root: that is, u_t is a random walk. This is to be contrasted with the conventional use made of this statistic in standard regression analysis where the null of no first-order autocorrelation is tested.

The use of this statistic is problematic in the present setting. First, the test statistic for co-integration depends upon the number of regressors in the co-integrating equation and, more generally, on the data-generation process and hence on the precise data matrix. Only bounds on the critical values are available.[3] Second, the bounds diverge as the number of regressors is increased, and eventually cease to have any practical value for the purposes of inference. Finally, the statistic assumes the null where u_t is a random walk, and the alternative where u_t is a stationary first-order autoregressive process. In such circumstances, Bhargava (1986) demonstrates that it has excellent power properties relative to alternative tests. However, the tabulated bounds are not correct if there is higher-order residual autocorrelation, as will commonly occur. Exact inference is therefore possible if and only if each regression exercise is augmented by the use of algorithms such as that of Imhof (1961) to compute the relevant critical values. In principle, it is possible for simulation methods to be used to compute the critical values. However, in practice this implies a proliferation of tables of different critical values for different data-generation processes and simulation exercises.

As we have argued previously, the only hope for uncomplicated inference lies in generating a robust set of critical values. Robustness is defined by lack of sensitivity of the critical values to a wide range of changes to the data-generation process. Tests that are similar for a wide range of nuisance parameters would ensure this non-sensitivity. In other words, it is important to have a set of tables that could be used regardless of the precise properties of the DGP, as long as the regression model is parameterized to satisfy certain basic properties such as balance. Tests of co-integration based not directly on the residuals but on the regression coefficients themselves, might have higher power. As an alternative method, one could consider using non-parametric corrections of the sort described in Chapter 4 to conduct inference using only a small set of tables, for a range of possible data-generation processes. Examples of both these procedures will be presented in due course.

Similar qualifications apply to the use of the DF statistic and less so to the ADF, if the number of Δu_{t-i} terms appearing in the data-generation process coincides with those used in the implementation of the test. Since the number of such terms appearing in the DGP is unknown, it seems safest to over-specify the ADF regression, and use as many

[3] While the CRDW statistic does not have a limiting distribution with a non-zero variance, $T\,(\text{CRDW}) = T^{-1} \sum_{t=2}^{T}(\hat{u}_t - \hat{u}_{t-1})^2/T^{-2} \sum_{t=1}^{T}\hat{u}_t{}^2$ does.

lagged terms as degrees-of-freedom restrictions will allow. Of course, in practice, the choice of the lag structure in ADF tests may be *ad hoc* and different results can be obtained by changing the length of the autoregression. In particular, the power of the test may be affected adversely.

Table 7.1 provides, for illustration (a more detailed description of applicable critical values will be given below), the 5 per cent critical values of the DW, ADF(1), and ADF(4) tests, for three sample sizes ($T = 50$, 100, 200). The data-generation process is an n-variate random walk with n less than or equal to 5, as in Engle and Yoo (1987).

It is important to emphasize that, in common with the tests for unit roots, tests for co-integration may lack power to discriminate between unit roots and borderline-stationary processes. In a small-scale study of the power properties of this test, Engle and Granger (1987) show that, when the data-generation process of the disturbances of the co-integrating equation is an AR(1) process with the autoregressive parameter equal to 0.9, the powers of the CRDW, DF, and ADF tests at the 5 per cent critical values are 20, 15, and 11 per cent respectively. When the DGP is altered to be a more general AR(1) process with a unit root, the power of the ADF test becomes 60 per cent, dominating strongly both the powers of the CRDW and DF tests at the 5 per cent level.

Engle and Granger (1987) emphasize the robustness to changes in the data-generation process of the ADF critical values. The discussion in Chapter 4 helps to explain this result. Phillips and Ouliaris (1990) show that the limiting distribution of the ADF test statistic is the same as that of the non-parametrically adjusted DF statistic. Because the limiting distribution of the latter statistic is invariant to nuisance parameters in the processes generating the data series, the result follows. Each test manages to correct for various features that may be present in the DGP, in one case by capturing the effects in a regression model, in the other by implicitly adjusting the critical values.

Phillips and Ouliaris (1990) derive the distributions of several tests of co-integration. We close this section by presenting a summary of the theoretical results presented there. They consider the linear co-integrating regressions:

$$y_t = \hat{\boldsymbol{\beta}}'\mathbf{z}_t + \hat{u}_t \tag{4}$$

and

$$y_t = c + \bar{\boldsymbol{\beta}}'\mathbf{z}_t + \bar{u}_t, \tag{5}$$

where y_t and $\mathbf{z}_t$ satisfy (multivariate) unit-root processes. The asymptotic distributions of a number of residual-based tests are discussed, from which we will consider five (this analysis is of course related to the

TABLE 7.1. Five per cent critical values for the co-integration tests

n	T	CRDW	ADF(1)	ADF(4)
2	50	0.72	−3.43	−3.29
	100	0.38	−3.38	−3.17
	200	0.20	−3.37	−3.25
3	50	0.89	−3.82	−3.75
	100	0.48	−3.76	−3.62
	200	0.25	−3.74	−3.78
4	50	1.05	−4.18	−3.98
	100	0.58	−4.12	−4.02
	200	0.30	−4.11	−4.13
5	50	1.19	−4.51	−4.15
	100	0.68	−4.48	−4.36
	200	0.35	−4.42	−4.43

Source: The CRDW critical values (see Sargan and Bhargava 1983) and the ADF(1) critical values were generated by PC-NAIVE using 10,000 replications. The ADF(4) critical values have been taken from Engle and Yoo (1987). The ADF critical values are computed by replicating the regression $\Delta\hat{u}_t = \rho\hat{u}_{t-1} + \sum_{i=1}^{k}\phi_i\Delta\hat{u}_{t-i} + v_t$ for $k = 1, 4$, following estimation of β in (2) augmented by a constant.

analysis of unit-root tests found in Chapter 4):

(i) Dickey–Fuller ρ

$\text{DF}(\rho) = T\hat{\rho}$, where $\hat{\rho}$ is obtained from the regression $\Delta\hat{u}_t = \hat{\rho}\hat{u}_{t-1} + \hat{\eta}_t$;

(ii) Dickey–Fuller t (DF)

$\text{DF}(t) = t_{\rho=0}$ in the regression $\Delta\hat{u}_t = \rho\hat{u}_{t-1} + \hat{\eta}_t$;

(iii) augmented Dickey–Fuller (ADF)

$$\text{ADF} = t_{\rho^*=0} \text{ in the regression } \Delta\hat{u}_t = \rho^*\hat{u}_{t-1} + \sum_{i=1}^{p}\phi_i\Delta\hat{u}_{t-i} + \hat{v}_{tp};$$

(iv) Phillips (1987*a*) Z_α test

$$\hat{Z}_\rho = T\hat{\rho} - (1/2)(S_{T\ell}^2 - S_\eta^2)\left(T^{-1}\sum_{t=2}^{T}\hat{u}_{t-1}^2\right)^{-1}$$

where

$$S_\eta^2 = T^{-1}\sum_{t=1}^{T}\hat{\eta}_t^2, \qquad S_{T\ell}^2 = T^{-1}\sum_{t=1}^{T}\hat{\eta}_t^2 + 2T^{-1}\sum_{j=1}^{\ell}\omega_\ell(j)\sum_{t=j+1}^{T}\hat{\eta}_t\hat{\eta}_{t-j},$$

where $\omega_\ell(j) = 1 - j(\ell + 1)^{-1}$ for some choice of lag window ℓ, and $\hat{\rho}$ and the $\hat{\eta}_t$ are derived from the DF regression given in (i);

(v) $$\hat{Z}_{t(\rho=0)} = \left(\sum_{t=2}^{T} \hat{u}_{t-1}^2\right)^{1/2} \hat{\rho}/S_{T\ell} - (1/2)(S_{T\ell}^2 - S_\eta^2)\left[S_{T\ell}\left(T^{-2}\sum_{t=2}^{T}\hat{u}_{t-1}^2\right)^{1/2}\right]^{-1},$$

with $S_{T\ell}^2$ and S_η^2 as in (iv) and $\hat{\rho}$ and the $\hat{\eta}_t$ are again derived from the DF regression given in (i).

Some properties of these tests may now be enumerated. First, under the maintained hypothesis of no co-integration, the distributions of $\hat{Z}_\rho$ and $\hat{Z}_{t(\rho=0)}$, for any general specification of the error process $\{\eta_t\}$, are the same as those of DF(ρ) and DF(t) respectively, when the distributions are computed under the restrictive assumption of IID errors. The distributions of $\hat{Z}_\rho$ and $\hat{Z}_{t(\rho=0)}$ are independent of nuisance parameters (leading to asymptotically similar tests), although they do depend on the number of regressors in the system; thus, the non-parametric corrections serve the same role in the context of co-integrating regressions as they do in unit-root tests: they eliminate nuisance parameters and enable the use of a standard set of Dickey–Fuller tables. Corrections must still be made for size in the original Dickey–Fuller tables to prevent over-rejection of the null hypothesis. Some of the tables appear in Phillips and Ouliaris (1990).

Second, the ADF test and $\hat{Z}_{t(\rho=0)}$ have the same asymptotic distribution. This is an interesting result because it re-emphasizes the two alternative but equivalent ways of taking account of nuisance parameters. In order to use a standard set of tables, one either augments the Dickey–Fuller regression or adjusts, non-parametrically, the unaugmented Dickey–Fuller statistic.

Third, if the statistics are based on a regression with a fitted intercept or time trend, the interpretation of the tests is not altered although the asymptotic critical values change. This issue is considered in more detail in the next section.

Fourth, if the non-parametrically adjusted statistics were constructed by imposing $\rho = 0$ and therefore using the v_t, where $v_t \equiv \hat{u}_t - \hat{u}_{t-1}$, in the test statistic instead of the $\hat{\eta}_t$, the statistics would have the same asymptotic distribution under the null; however, as shown by Phillips and Ouliaris (1990), these would have inferior power properties.

Finally, an alternative class of tests of co-integration not based on regression residuals has been proposed in the literature. Prominent among the tests are those due to Johansen (1988) and Stock and Watson (1988*b*). These tests also apply to multivariate systems of equations and have their most natural uses when investigating multiple co-integrating vectors. A discussion of the Johansen maximum likelihood procedure appears in the next chapter.

7.3. Response Surfaces for Critical Values

When compared with the corresponding critical values for unit-root tests given in Chapter 4, the critical values in Table 7.1 are illustrative of the changes in test levels implied by the presence of estimated parameters in the relationship yielding the series to be tested for stationarity. In themselves, however, they cover only a limited set of cases. Other tables are provided in Engle and Yoo (1987) and Phillips and Ouliaris (1990). MacKinnon (1991) provides results of a more extensive set of simulations, summarized in *response surfaces*: that is, critical values for particular tests are given as a set of parameters of an equation relating the exact critical value to a constant term and terms involving sample size, from which a critical value for any given sample size can be approximated. We will describe the latter results.

Dickey–Fuller (or augmented Dickey–Fuller) tests for unit roots or co-integration can be considered within a common framework. Consider n time series given by $y_{1t}, y_{2t}, \ldots, y_{nt}$, $n \geqslant 1$, $t = 1, 2, \ldots, T$. If $n = 1$, we are testing for a unit root in a single series, and to establish a uniform notation, we define the time series under test as $\{\hat{u}_t\}_{t=1}^{\infty} \equiv \{y_{1t}\}_{t=1}^{\infty}$. If $n > 1$, we are first interested in obtaining a set of residuals from the estimated relationship among the n variables, and so begin with the (static) co-integrating regression,[4]

$$y_{1t} = \sum_{j=2}^{n} \beta_j y_{jt} + u_t. \tag{6}$$

Let $\mathbf{y}_t \equiv (y_{1t}, y_{2t}, \ldots, y_{nt})$ be the vector of measurements at time t on the n variables. The series to be tested for stationarity then becomes $\hat{u}_t = [1 \vdots -\hat{\boldsymbol{\beta}}']\mathbf{y}_t$, where $\hat{\boldsymbol{\beta}}'$ is the vector of estimated parameters. Subject to the relevance of the normalized variable, the ordering of variables in the co-integrating regression will not affect the asymptotic distribution of the test statistic, although in finite samples the value will depend upon which variable is the regressand. The null hypothesis of no co-integration implies that $\hat{u}_t$ is I(1).

We test this null using the tests considered in Chapter 4. In particular, the augmented Dickey–Fuller test takes the form of one of the following

[4] Below, the parameters δ_0 and δ_1 will denote coefficients on a constant and trend, respectively.

models, with ℓ chosen to eliminate any autocorrelation in the residuals:

$$\Delta\hat{u}_t = \rho\hat{u}_{t-1} + \sum_{i=1}^{\ell}\rho_i\Delta\hat{u}_{t-i} + \varepsilon_t; \tag{7a}$$

$$\Delta\hat{u}_t = \delta_0 + \rho\hat{u}_{t-1} + \sum_{i=1}^{\ell}\rho_i\Delta\hat{u}_{t-i} + \varepsilon_t; \tag{7b}$$

$$\Delta\hat{u}_t = \delta_0 + \delta_1 t + \rho\hat{u}_{t-1} + \sum_{i=1}^{\ell}\rho_i\Delta\hat{u}_{t-i} + \varepsilon_t. \tag{7c}$$

For $n \geqslant 2$, so that a co-integrating regression precedes the use of one of these models,[5] model (6) could also be used with constant and trend, adding δ_0 or $\delta_0 + \delta_1 t$ to the regression. Co-integration tests either include a constant in (6), or include a constant in the regression model (7*b*). If a constant is added to (6) and model (7*a*) is used, the strategy is equivalent to omitting the constant term and using model (7*b*); if constant and trend are added to (6) and model (7*a*) is used, then this is equivalent to using model (7*c*), and so on. The model type referred to in Table 7.2 describes this presence or absence of constant and trend in the models. A test with constant but no trend, for example, implies model (7*b*) with no constant in the co-integrating regression (6), or a constant in (6) used with model (7*a*).

The critical values, or upper quantiles of the distributions, can be calculated from the parameters of Table 7.2 using the relation

$$C(p) = \phi_\infty + \phi_1 T^{-1} + \phi_2 T^{-2}, \tag{8}$$

where $C(p)$ is the p per cent upper-quantile estimate. The parameters were estimated from regression over a set of individual simulation results covering, for most values of n, 40 sets of parameters for each of 15 sample sizes. Model (8) (with an added error term) was found to represent well the various critical values that emerged from the many individual experiments; but other models could in principle have been used to fit a response surface to the results; see MacKinnon (1991) for a description of the experimental technique, including the feasible generalized least squares technique by which estimation of the final response surface model was undertaken, to allow for heteroskedasticity in (8).

As an example, the estimated 1 per cent critical value for 150 observations, $n = 6$ and constant + trend included in the model is given

[5] If $n \geqslant 2$ but the values of the parameters in $\boldsymbol{\beta}$ are known, then the residuals $u_t \equiv [1\colon -\boldsymbol{\beta}']\mathbf{y}_t$ can be constructed without a co-integrating regression, and the test statistic is interpreted as if n were equal to unity. In this case we have one known series of observations to be tested for stationarity, not a series constructed on the basis of estimated parameters. Under the null of no co-integration, however, (6) is a spurious regression so $\hat{\boldsymbol{\beta}}$ has a non-degenerate limiting distribution, which induces different critical values from DF tests.

TABLE 7.2. Response surfaces for critical values of co-integration tests

n	Model	Point (%)	ϕ_∞	SE	ϕ_1	ϕ_2
1	No constant,	1	−2.5658	(0.0023)	−1.960	−10.04
	no trend	5	−1.9393	(0.0008)	−0.398	0.0
		10	−1.6156	(0.0007)	−0.181	0.0
1	Constant,	1	−3.4336	(0.0024)	−5.999	−29.25
	no trend	5	−2.8621	(0.0011)	−2.738	−8.36
		10	−2.5671	(0.0009)	−1.438	−4.48
1	Constant	1	−3.9638	(0.0019)	−8.353	−47.44
	+ trend	5	−3.4126	(0.0012)	−4.039	−17.83
		10	−3.1279	(0.0009)	−2.418	−7.58
2	Constant,	1	−3.9001	(0.0022)	−10.534	−30.03
	no trend	5	−3.3377	(0.0012)	−5.967	−8.98
		10	−3.0462	(0.0009)	−4.069	−5.73
2	Constant	1	−4.3266	(0.0022)	−15.531	−34.03
	+ trend	5	−3.7809	(0.0013)	−9.421	−15.06
		10	−3.4959	(0.0009)	−7.203	−4.01
3	Constant,	1	−4.2981	(0.0023)	−13.790	−46.37
	no trend	5	−3.7429	(0.0012)	−8.352	−13.41
		10	−3.4518	(0.0010)	−6.241	−2.79
3	Constant	1	−4.6676	(0.0022)	−18.492	−49.35
	+ trend	5	−4.1193	(0.0011)	−12.024	−13.13
		10	−3.8344	(0.0009)	−9.188	−4.85
4	Constant,	1	−4.6493	(0.0023)	−17.188	−59.20
	no trend	5	−4.1000	(0.0012)	−10.745	−21.57
		10	−3.8110	(0.0009)	−8.317	−5.19
4	Constant	1	−4.9695	(0.0021)	−22.504	−50.22
	+ trend	5	−4.4294	(0.0012)	−14.501	−19.54
		10	−4.1474	(0.0010)	−11.165	−9.88
5	Constant,	1	−4.9587	(0.0026)	−22.140	−37.29
	no trend	5	−4.4185	(0.0013)	−13.641	−21.16
		10	−4.1327	(0.0009)	−10.638	−5.48
5	Constant	1	−5.2497	(0.0024)	−26.606	−49.56
	+ trend	5	−4.7154	(0.0013)	−17.432	−16.50
		10	−4.4345	(0.0010)	−13.654	−5.77
6	Constant,	1	−5.2400	(0.0029)	−26.278	−41.65
	no trend	5	−4.7048	(0.0018)	−17.120	−11.17
		10	−4.4242	(0.0010)	−13.347	0.0
6	Constant	1	−5.5127	(0.0033)	−30.735	−52.50
	+ trend	5	−4.9767	(0.0017)	−20.883	−9.05
		10	−4.6999	(0.0011)	−16.445	0.0

Source: MacKinnon (1991). We are grateful to James MacKinnon for permission to reproduce this table.

by $-5.5127 - 30.735/150 - 52.50/150^2 \cong -5.7199$. Estimated standard errors for finite-sample critical values such as this are generally less than those reported for ϕ_∞, although MacKinnon argues that these may understate the true standard errors by roughly a factor of 2.

7.4. Finite-sample Biases in OLS Estimates

In the next chapter we will consider systems estimation of co-integrating vectors. Here, we will examine one of the main reasons for using such an estimation strategy: the large finite-sample biases that can arise in static OLS estimates of co-integrating vectors or parameters. While such estimates are super-consistent (T-consistent), Monte Carlo experiments nonetheless suggest that a large number of observations may be necessary before the biases become small (see Banerjee *et al.* 1986).

Some investigators have suggested that we may explain the findings of such Monte Carlo studies by the fact that the particular data-generation processes considered were too specific, or possessed some special properties, which meant that the probability of finding large biases was unusually high. This point is partly valid, in that each DGP can be regarded as specific in some way. Moreover, it is certainly true that, with sufficient patience, the exact expressions for the static biases could be worked out for any data-generation process, as functions of the parameters of the DGP. However, the point is not that some of these data-generation processes are more likely to lead to high biases while others will give lower values, but rather that, in the absence of information on the data-generation process, some method other than static regression may give superior estimates of the co-integrating vector or tests with higher powers. In particular, dynamic regressions may be more robust to a range of data-generation processes. Even where static regressions behave poorly in finite samples, dynamic regressions may provide us with quite good estimates. Since the investigator is in general unaware of the particular properties of the data-generation process (such as whether it will tend to lead to low biases or high biases), it makes sense to allow the regression to be as flexible as possible. Robustness in the sense of adequate performance for a wide range of underlying DGPs is an important property.

Most of the evidence that has been presented in favour of the existence of finite-sample biases has come in the form of Monte Carlo experiments; we present two investigations of the bias properties of OLS estimators. By specifying the data-generation process, Monte Carlo experiments provide complete knowledge and control of the features of interest; in particular, in the present case, we know the co-integrating parameter. Performing regressions on the artificial data, while notionally ignoring the data-generation process, puts us in the position of the empirical investigator; however, we are then able to compare our results with the true parameters, for a set of chosen example cases.

The first experiment considered uses the data-generation process

$$z_t + y_t = v_t \qquad (1 - \rho_1 L)v_t = \varepsilon_{1t} \tag{9}$$

$$y_t + 2z_t = u_t \qquad (1 - \rho_2 L)u_t = \varepsilon_{2t}. \tag{10}$$

The vector $(\varepsilon_{1t}, \varepsilon_{2t})'$ is distributed identically and independently as a bivariate normal with

$$E(\varepsilon_{1t}) = E(\varepsilon_{2t}) = 0 \tag{11}$$

$$\operatorname{var}(\varepsilon_{1t}) = \sigma_1^2; \qquad \operatorname{var}(\varepsilon_{2t}) = \sigma_2^2; \qquad \operatorname{cov}(\varepsilon_{1t}, \varepsilon_{2t}) = 0. \tag{12}$$

The structure of the DGP is the same as that of Engle and Granger (1987). Three cases of interest may be distinguished. In case A, $|\rho_1| < 1$, $|\rho_2| < 1$ so that both z and y are I(0) variables. In case B, $\rho_1 = \rho_2 = 1$ so that both variables are I(1) and are not co-integrated. We will concentrate on case C, where $\rho_1 = 1$, $|\rho_2| < 1$, so that the variables are still I(1) but are now co-integrated. In this last case, the co-integrating coefficient is -2.

For case C, the null hypothesis of a unit root in the error dynamics in (10) is false. Interest therefore lies in investigating the usefulness of the estimate of the co-integrating parameter in the static regression of y_t on z_t and also in checking the ability of unit-root tests to reject the false null of non-stationarity. We use 5000 replications on the parameter space $\mathbf{s} \times \mathbf{T} \times \boldsymbol{\rho}_2$; $\mathbf{s} = \sigma_1/\sigma_2 = (16, 8, 4, 2, 1, \frac{1}{2})$, $\mathbf{T} = (25, 50, 100, 200)$, and $\boldsymbol{\rho}_2 = (0.6, 0.8, 0.9)$ giving rise to 72 experiments. The range of the ratio of standard deviations, the significance of which we will describe below, is very large. Obviously, it would be difficult to distinguish between σ_u^2 and σ_v^2 when σ_1 and T are small and σ_2 and ρ_2 are large; for large values of s, OLS essentially picks up equation (9) instead of equation (10).

The problem of finite-sample biases is illustrated in the figures. Figures 7.1(a)–7.4(a) refer to the simplest form of static model which contains no constant, while Figs. 7.1(b)–7.4(b) pertain to static models which do contain constant terms. The figures show the relationship between bias and sample size for four different values of the ratio of standard deviations. The horizontal scale is implicitly $\log_2(T/25)$ so that the four points shown are equidistant. First of all, it is evident that the bias does not decline at rate T. For example, in Fig. 7.4(a) ($\sigma_1/\sigma_2 = 0.5$), with $\rho_2 = 0.6$, the bias at $T = 25$ is 0.45, at $T = 50$ is 0.32, at $T = 100$ is 0.21, and at $T = 200$ is 0.13. Thus, an eightfold increase in sample size reduces the bias by a factor of approximately

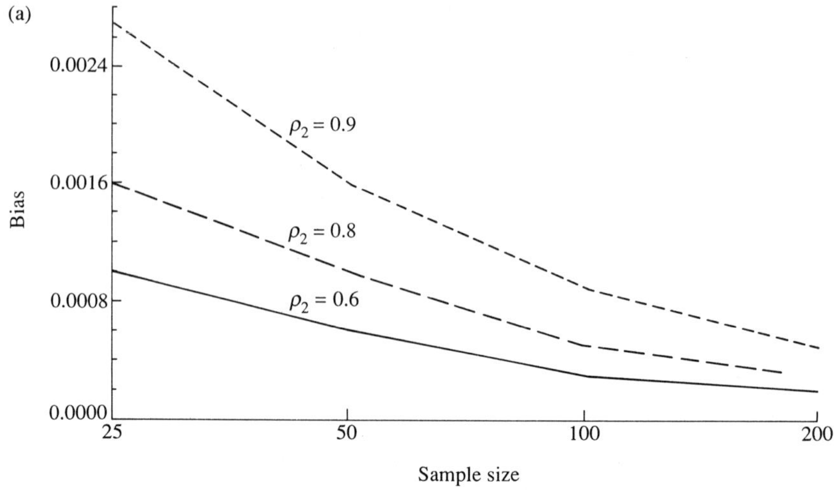

FIG 7.1(*a*). No constant in model, estimated bias *v*. sample size. $s = 16$

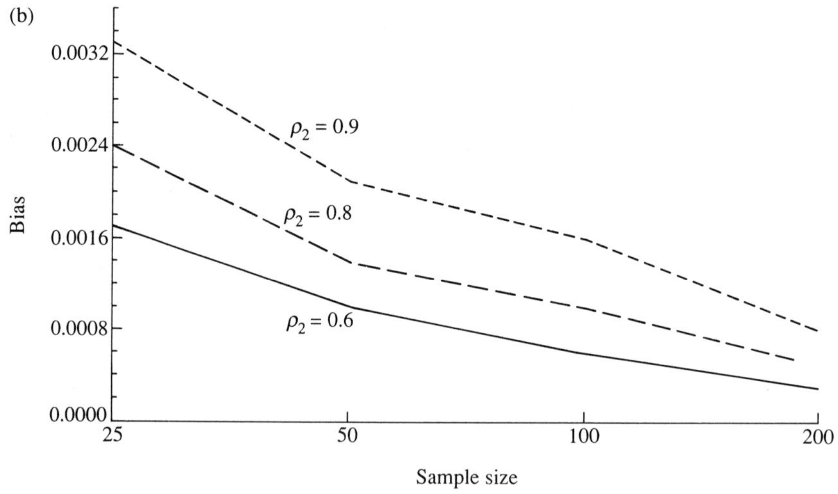

FIG 7.1(*b*). Constant in model, estimated bias *v*. sample size. $s = 16$

3.5. As another example, we see in Fig. 7.2(*a*) ($\sigma_1/\sigma_2 = 4$), with $\rho_2 = 0.6$, the biases at the same set of sample sizes are 0.017, 0.010, 0.005, 0.0026.[6] Here an eightfold increase in sample size reduces the

[6] These numbers are taken from the experimental output rather than read from the figures. The standard error of the smallest of these numbers is roughly 5×10^{-5}.

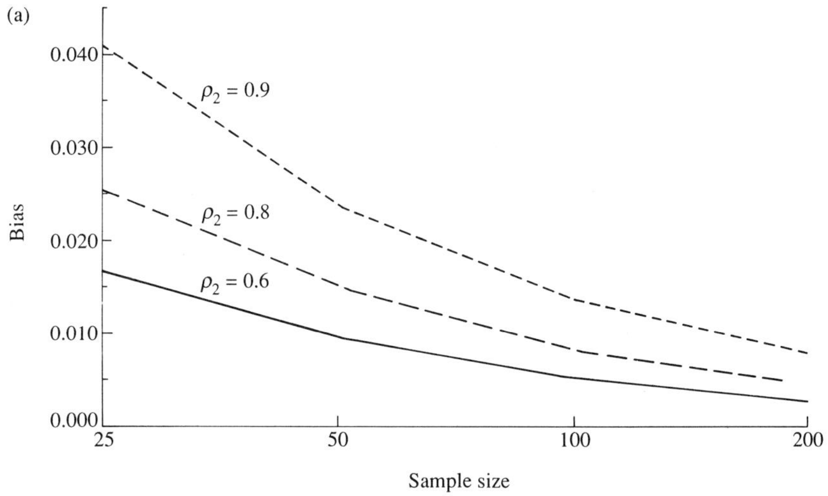

FIG 7.2(*a*). No constant in model, estimated bias *v*. sample size. $s = 4$

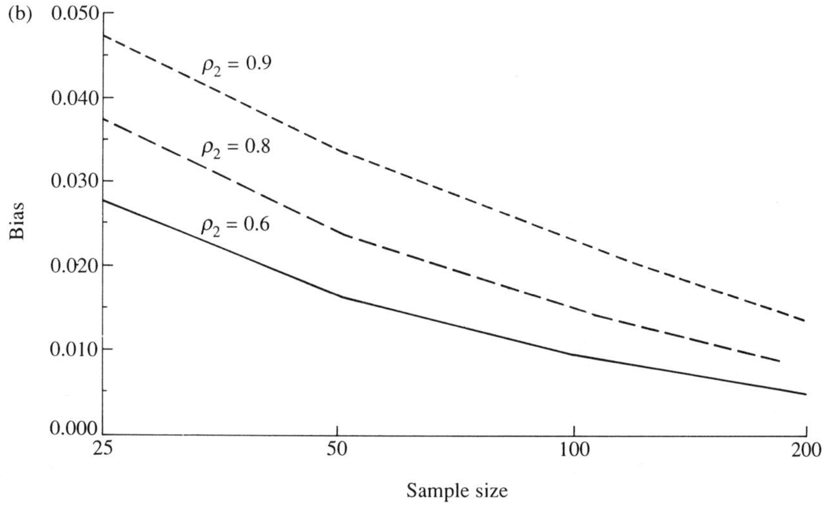

FIG 7.2(*b*). Constant in model, estimated bias *v*. sample size. $s = 4$

bias by a factor of 6.5. Using a standard-deviation ratio of 4 again but a value of $\rho_2 = 0.9$, the biases are 0.04, 0.024, 0.014, and 0.008, a fivefold decrease in bias. The rate of decline of the bias is always faster than $\sqrt{T}$ but not as fast as T for sample sizes up to 200.

Second, the biases increase uniformly in ρ_2 and decrease uniformly in

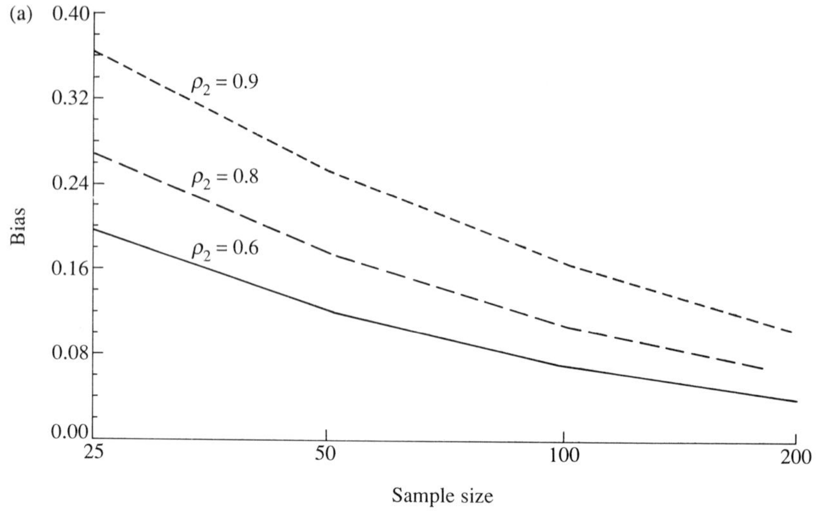

FIG 7.3(*a*). No constant in model, estimated bias *v*. sample size. $s = 1$

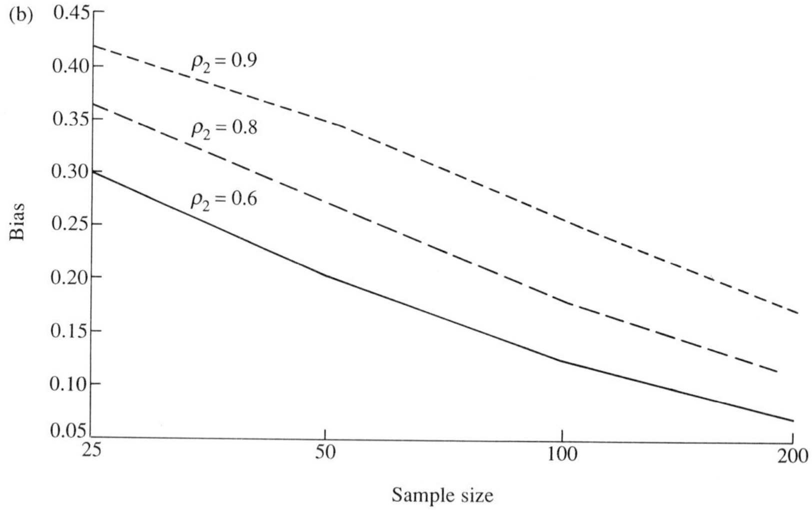

FIG 7.3(*b*). Constant in model, estimated bias *v*. sample size. $s = 1$

σ_1/σ_2. To understand this, we can rewrite (9) and (10) to get

$$z_t = u_t - v_t$$
$$y_t = 2v_t - u_t. \tag{13}$$

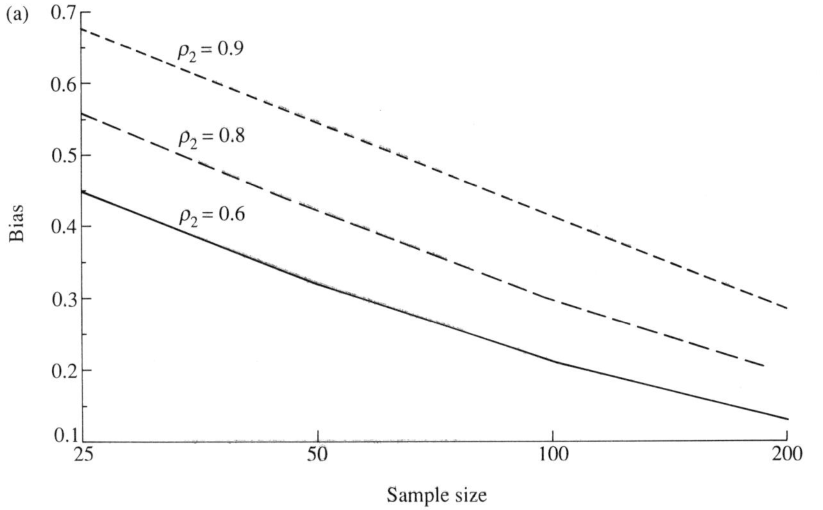

FIG 7.4(a). No constant in model, estimated bias v. sample size. $s = 0.5$

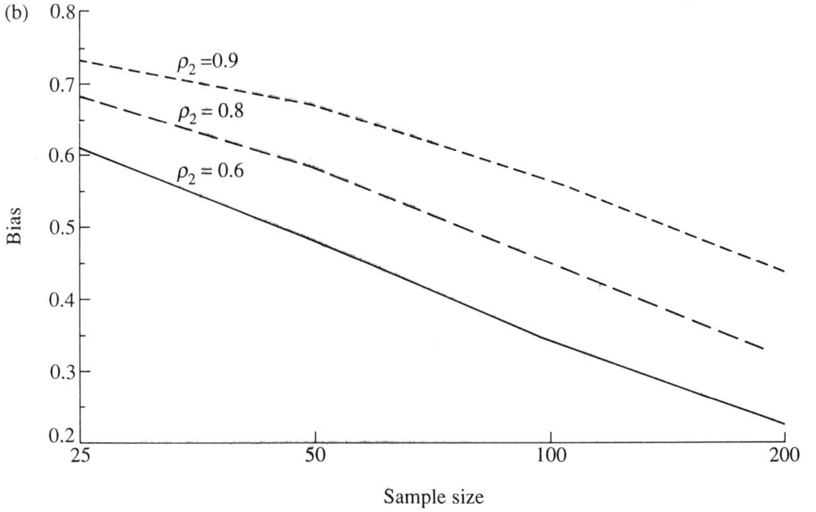

FIG 7.4(b). Constant in model, estimated bias v. sample size. $s = 0.5$

Since $\rho_1 = 1$, $\{v_t\}$ is a random walk and therefore asymptotically dominates $\{u_t\}$. Hence the co-integrating parameter of -2. In finite samples the regression will come closer to revealing this long-run relationship if the variance of u_t is small relative to that of v_t. Recall that by equation (10), u_t is the discrepancy from this long-run relationship. Smaller values of ρ_2 and smaller values of σ_2 (larger values of σ_1/σ_2) make the variance of u_t relatively small, and so we obtain smaller biases as ρ_2 falls or as σ_1/σ_2 rises.

The fact that these biases do disappear less quickly than T, and may remain substantial for sample sizes large relative to many found in economics, suggests that the results from pure static models must be treated with caution. We will later examine ways in which we can improve upon simple static estimation either by including dynamic elements, adjusting the results of the static model, or estimating a system of equations.

Finally, the biases are strongly positively correlated with $(1 - R^2)$, which indicates that co-integrating regressions with values of R^2 well below unity should be viewed with caution.[7] However, in the context of multivariate regressions, a high value of R^2 is not sufficient to guarantee that the biases are small. This is because the R^2 of an equation cannot fall when an additional variable is added to it. Thus, the inference that high values of the R^2 imply low biases, especially where the former may have been achieved by an *ad hoc* addition of regressors, is not valid. Banerjee *et al.* (1986) explore the relationship between bias and $(1 - R^2)$ in more detail.

It is useful to consider an informal explanation for the existence of biases in static regressions. The effect of using static regressions to estimate the co-integrating slope β is to allow the residual $\hat{u}_t$ to capture all the dynamic adjustment terms. According to the super-consistency theorem, this is certainly permissible *asymptotically*. It is important to emphasize that the problem we are discussing here is strictly a finite-sample one; the omission of the dynamics may be justified asymptotically by observing that, as they are of a lower order of magnitude than the non-stationary terms in the regression, they may be ignored in the limit. However, the omitted dynamics, despite being of a lower order of magnitude, can matter considerably in determining biases even in fairly large but finite samples.[8] Hence it seems appropriate to pay attention to modelling the omitted terms.

The dynamic terms can all be parameterized in terms of I(0) series of the form Δy_{t-i}, Δz_{t-j}, and $(y - \gamma z)_{t-k}$ where the values of i, j, and k

[7] We are grateful to Tom Rothenberg for pointing out that R^2 is a random variable in the present context. However, it remains a useful descriptive statistic.

[8] The problem of finite sample biases was also demonstrated by Hendry and Neale (1987). Using recursive procedures for OLS estimation, they estimated a bivariate static regression for sample sizes ranging from 40 to 200, considering the bias of the coefficient estimate for each sample size. The results indicated that, even for sample sizes of 200, the long-run coefficient from the static regression was approximately 0.7 while the true long-run coefficient was 1.0. Convergence to the true value was not nearly as fast in practice as T^{-1} which dominates for sufficiently large T: see (18) below.

will depend upon the nature of the ARIMA process generating $\{y_t\}$ and $\{z_t\}$.[9] Consider a simple model in which $\{z_t\}$ is strongly exogenous for the regression parameters and the true dynamic relationship, apart from deterministic components, is given by

$$y_t = \gamma_1 y_{t-1} + \gamma_2 z_t + \gamma_3 z_{t-1} + \varepsilon_{1t} \tag{14a}$$

$$z_t = z_{t-1} + \varepsilon_{2t}, \tag{14b}$$

where $\{y_t\}$ and $\{z_t\}$ are CI(1, 1).[10] The errors are mean zero, mutually and serially uncorrelated normal variates. The variances of ε_{1t} and ε_{2t} are denoted by σ_1^2 and σ_2^2 respectively. Suppose that economic theory suggests that, in the long run, the homogeneity restriction $\sum_{i=1}^{3}\gamma_i = 1$ holds. Equation (14a) can be rewritten as

$$\Delta y_t = \gamma_2 \Delta z_t + (\gamma_1 - 1)(y - z)_{t-1} + \varepsilon_{1t} \tag{15a}$$

or as

$$y_t = z_t + \gamma_1 (y - z)_{t-1} + (\gamma_2 - 1)\Delta z_t + \varepsilon_{1t}. \tag{15b}$$

Now $(y - z)$ and Δz must both be I(0) using the co-integration assumption, as is ε_{1t}. Hence, by estimating the static regression

$$y_t = \beta z_t + u_t, \tag{16}$$

the dynamics, given by Δz_t and $(y - z)_{t-1}$, are all contained in the residual u_t: when $|\gamma_1| < 1$, $\beta = (\gamma_2 + \gamma_3)/(1 - \gamma_1)$. In general, u_t will be serially correlated. Its long-run variance σ^2, which appears in the expressions for the Wiener distributional limits of the sample moments, is given by

$$\sigma^2 = \sigma_u^2 + 2\lambda \tag{17}$$

where

$$\sigma_u^2 = E(u_i^2) \qquad \text{and} \qquad \lambda = \sum_{j=0, i \neq j}^{\infty} E(u_i u_j).$$

It may then be shown that

$$T(\hat{\beta} - \beta) \Rightarrow \left(\int_0^1 W(r)^2 \, \mathrm{d}r\right)^{-1} \left(\int_0^1 W(r) \, \mathrm{d}W(r) + \lambda\sigma^{-2}\right). \tag{18}$$

Phillips (1986) shows that it is the presence of λ in (18) that causes the biases.

[9] See e.g. the derivation of the ECM representation in Ch. 5 for CI(1, 1) series.

[10] A simple rewriting of equation (10) above, to take account of the structure of the residual autocorrelation, gives us a version of (14a) with the γ_i suitably interpreted. Later in this chapter we consider a generalization of (14) and investigate the consequences of using static and dynamic regressions.

A simple way to reduce the biases is to reparameterize the equation in such a way that λ is set at zero. Both (15a) and (15b) satisfy this property. For comparison, following Banerjee *et al.* (1986), we ran a second set of experiments in order to investigate the effects of such re-parameterizations. Using the DGP given by (14a)–(14b), we estimate equation (15a), with a lagged z included as an extra regressor. The dynamic regression equation estimated is therefore

$$\Delta y_t = b\Delta z_t + c(y_{t-1} - z_{t-1}) + dz_{t-1} + v_t. \tag{19}$$

The extra lagged variable, z_{t-1}, is included to avoid imposing homogeneity (see Chapter 2), as it would be unrealistic to assume that the investigator knows the precise form of the data-generation process. The co-integrating coefficient is estimated by computing the expression $1 - \hat{d}/\hat{c}$: see Sect. 2.4. The static regression given by (16) is also estimated.

The strong exogeneity property required of z_t is guaranteed, in the design of the experiment, by drawing ε_{1t} and ε_{2t} from uncorrelated pseudo-normal distributions. The values of γ_i ($i = 1, \ldots, 3$) are varied as in Table 7.3, while ensuring that long-run homogeneity is preserved. The sample sizes and the ratio of the standard deviations of ε_{1t} and ε_{2t} are also varied, to give a set of 90 experiments. The simulations are all conducted with 5000 replications.

The purpose of the first part of this exercise is to compare the biases in the estimates of the co-integrating parameter obtained from dynamic regression with those obtained from the static regression. (The true value of the co-integrating parameter is 1.) Some of the results for different configurations of the γ_i parameters and standard-deviation ratios are given in Table 7.3. We report the estimated biases, for four different sample sizes, in the static model. The corresponding estimated biases from the dynamic regression (where the co-integrating parameter is calculated as $(1 - \hat{d}/\hat{c})$) are in almost all cases so small as to be within 2 Monte Carlo standard errors of zero and so are not reported. We will return to the comparison of these estimators (static and dynamic) below; for the time being, the noteworthy point is simply that substantial biases remain in static estimates for parameter combinations at which the biases in dynamic estimates are zero, or very close to zero, since the dynamic model has been specified so as to make λ close to zero.

While the dynamic estimates contain negligible biases in these examples, z_t is *strongly* exogenous for the parameter of interest. While it is fairly straightforward to extend this specification to include weakly exogenous z_t, the usefulness of estimates from dynamic single equations is reduced substantially if the regressors are not weakly exogenous. It also becomes difficult to make unambiguous comparisons between

TABLE 7.3. Biases in static models[a]
DGP: (14*a*) + (14*b*); 5000 replications

	Sample size (T)				
	25	50	100	200	400
$\gamma_1 = 0.9$, $\gamma_2 = 0.5$, $s = 3$	−0.39	−0.25	−0.15	−0.07	−0.04
$\gamma_1 = 0.9$, $\gamma_2 = 0.5$, $s = 1$	−0.32	−0.22	−0.14	−0.08	−0.04
$\gamma_1 = 0.5$, $\gamma_2 = 0.1$, $s = 3$	−0.23	−0.13	−0.07	−0.03	−0.02
$\gamma_1 = 0.5$, $\gamma_2 = 0.1$, $s = 1$	−0.21	−0.12	−0.06	−0.03	−0.02

[a] Standard errors of these estimates vary widely, but the estimated biases are in almost all cases significantly different from zero, for sample sizes of 50 or greater. Note that again the biases appear to decline less quickly than T^{-1}, but more quickly than $T^{-1/2}$. Calculations were undertaken using GAUSS.

dynamic and static single-equation estimates. We discuss this issue below.

Recalling the discussion in Chapter 5, a test of the null hypothesis $H_0: c = 0$, based on the t-statistic $t_{c=0}$, is a valid test for co-integration.[11] This statistic, under the null of no co-integration, is not asymptotically normally distributed. Therefore a second part of the exercise was used to compute the critical values of the distribution of $t_{c=0}$ and to use these critical values to derive the power of this statistic, for a range of cases, to detect co-integration. This is an example of a test of co-integration based not directly on the residuals, but on a regression coefficient. A power comparison, between a residual-based test and the t-test, is given in Table 7.7; but first we use a more general DGP to consider further the issue of finite sample biases.

7.4.1. General Data-generation Processes

Consider now the comparison of static and dynamic estimates of the long-run multiplier when the time series are derived from a more

[11] When y and z are not co-integrated, $(y - z)_{t-1}$ is I(1), in which case (19) can only be balanced if $c = 0$. This observation forms the logical basis for a test of co-integration based on $t_{c=0}$. The strong exogeneity of z_t (for the parameters in (14*a*)) ensures that a test based on estimates from a single equation such as (19) is fully efficient.

general DGP. The experiments described above are special cases of this more general DGP. The 'static' estimate of the co-integrating coefficient β is called $\hat{\beta}_s$, while the dynamic estimate is denoted $\hat{\beta}_d$.

The exogenous variable is generated as

$$z_t = \phi z_{t-1} + v_t, \qquad v_t \sim \mathrm{IN}(0, 1), \tag{20}$$

so that z_t can be made either I(0) or I(1) by choice of ϕ. The process generating $\{y_t\}$ is an autoregressive-distributed lag model with three lags on both endogenous and exogenous variables:

$$y_t = \sum_{i=1}^{3} \rho_i y_{t-i} + \sum_{i=0}^{3} \rho_{i+4} z_{t-i} + \varepsilon_t, \qquad \varepsilon_t \sim \mathrm{IN}(0, 1). \tag{21}$$

Finally, the dynamic regression model[12] is

$$y_t = \sum_{i=1}^{2} \lambda_i y_{t-i} + \sum_{i=0}^{2} \psi_i z_{t-i} + v_t. \tag{22}$$

In comparing the data-generation process with the model, three interesting cases can be identified. These are the cases in which the model is over-parameterized, under-parameterized, and exactly parameterized.

For each of these cases, several sub-cases, which derive from the integration properties of the $\{z_t\}$ and the $\{y_t\}$ series, are of interest. In particular, we might be interested in determining whether the relative performances of the static and dynamic regressions depend upon the proximity of the largest latent root of either of the processes to unity—whether, for example, performance when the $\{z_t\}$ series is I(0) and the $\{y_t\}$ series is very nearly I(1) differs from that which holds when the $\{z_t\}$ series is I(1) and the $\{y_t\}$ series is nearly I(2), or whether in general the results are affected by specifying the $\{z_t\}$ series to be non-stationary ($\phi = 1.0$) rather than clearly stationary ($\phi = 0.5$).

In order to facilitate interpretation, a typology of the particularly interesting cases is presented in Table 7.4. The simulation results appear in Table 7.5 and were computed using GAUSS.

It is important to note that the series $\{y_t\}$ has the same order of integration as $\{z_t\}$ in each of the cases treated below; it is simply *close to* deviating from the order of integration of $\{z_t\}$ if the sum of the parameters $\rho_1 + \rho_2 + \rho_3$ is close to 1. In finite samples, it will be difficult to distinguish this proximity ('borderline' stationarity, in case B) from an actual difference in orders of integration.

[12] This produces an estimate of the co-integrating parameter equal to that produced by linear transformations such as the error-correction form.

TABLE 7.4. Examples of properties of $\{z_t\}$ and $\{y_t\}$ for various parameter values[a]

	$\rho_1 + \rho_2 + \rho_3$[b]	ϕ[b]	Property of $\{z_t\}$	Property of $\{y_t\}$[c]
A	$\ll 1$	$\ll 1$	I(0)	I(0)
B	$\cong 1$	$\ll 1$	I(0)	nearly I(1)
C	$\cong 1$	1.0	I(1)	nearly I(2)
D	$\ll 1$	1.0	I(1)	I(1)

[a] Parameters are those appearing in equations (20) and (21).

[b] In Table 7.5 below we treat values of 0.99 as '$\cong 1$' and values of 0.95 or lower (in absolute value) as '$\ll 1$'. Note that we cannot have $\rho_1 + \rho_2 + \rho_3 = 1$ exactly, since the term $(1 - \rho_1 - \rho_2 - \rho_3)^{-1}$ appears in the equation for the long-run equilibrium solution.

[c] By 'nearly', we mean that the series in question is on the borderline between two orders of integration: in finite samples the difference between, for example, an AR(1) with parameter 1.0 and an AR(1) with parameter 0.99 is a difference of degree rather than of kind. We say that $z_t = 0.99z_{t-1} + e_t$ is *nearly* I(1): see Ch. 3.

The Monte Carlo results are organized as follows. Table 7.5 contains three sections, applying to models that are exactly parameterized, over-, and under-parameterized. For each case we report percentage biases in the estimation of a scalar co-integration parameter and the standard errors of the experimental estimates of those biases, for a range of parameter values representative of each of the cases A, B, C, D above. Entries are marked as being examples of either case A, B, C, or D.

Our intent in examining the results is not simply to draw conclusions about the relative merits of the static and dynamic regressions, bearing in mind that in practice the investigator does not know the form of the DGP, and so cannot in general produce a model that contains precisely the correct number of lags of relevant variables. We are also interested in discovering the cases in which one or both of the methods (static and dynamic regression) yield especially large finite-sample biases. All results pertain to a sample size of 120 observations.

The following conclusions emerge from examination of Table 7.5 and the examples of each of the four cases A–D.

First, the dynamic regression tends to produce lower biases in estimates of the co-integration parameter. This result does not depend upon a close correspondence between the dynamic model and the data-generation process: for example, even in the case where the DGP is a simple one, so that the model used here is substantially over-parameterized, estimates from a dynamic model tend to be at least as good as from the static model.

TABLE 7.5. Some Monte Carlo estimates of percentage biases in static and dynamic estimates of long-run multipliers[a]
DGP: (20) + (21); 5000 replications; 120 observations

(*a*) Dynamic model correctly parameterized[b] ($\rho_3 = \rho_7 = 0$, $\rho_4 = 1$)

ϕ	ρ_1	ρ_2	ρ_5	ρ_6	β	$100(\beta - \hat{\beta}_s)/\beta$	(SE)	$100(\beta - \hat{\beta}_d)/\beta$	(SE)	
0.0	0.9	0.0	0.5	0.5	20	−96	(0.026)	0.4	(0.319)	A
0.0	0.9	0.09	0.5	0.5	200	−100	(0.004)	52	(42.6)	B
0.8	0.9	0.0	0.5	0.5	20	−77	(0.119)	−0.2	(0.084)	A
0.8	0.9	0.09	0.5	0.5	200	−99	(0.022)	128	(128.0)	B
1.0	0.9	0.0	0.5	0.5	20	−30	(0.252)	−0.01	(0.020)	D
1.0	0.9	0.09	0.5	0.5	200	−82	(0.209)	0.5	(0.103)	C
0.0	0.9	0.0	0.5	−0.5	10	−91	(0.036)	0.8	(0.507)	A
0.0	0.9	0.09	0.5	−0.5	100	−99	(0.005)	−636	(567.0)	B
0.8	0.9	0.0	0.5	−0.5	10	−69	(0.113)	−0.3	(0.161)	A
0.8	0.9	0.09	0.5	−0.5	100	−98	(0.023)	−6	(27.30)	B
1.0	0.9	0.0	0.5	−0.5	10	−26	(0.223)	−0.07	(0.039)	D
1.0	0.9	0.09	0.5	−0.5	100	−82	(0.207)	1.3	(0.389)	C
0.0	0.9	−0.4	0.5	0.5	4	−76	(0.080)	−0.2	(0.142)	A
0.8	0.9	−0.4	0.5	0.5	4	−25	(0.100)	−0.05	(0.050)	A
1.0	0.9	−0.4	0.5	0.5	4	−4	(0.055)	−0.01	(0.014)	D

(*b*) Dynamic model over-parameterized[c] ($\rho_2 = \rho_6 = \rho_3 = \rho_7 = 0,\ \rho_4 = 1$)

ϕ	ρ_1	ρ_5	β	$100(\beta - \hat{\beta}_s)/\beta$	(SE)	$100(\beta - \hat{\beta}_d)/\beta$	(SE)	
0.0	0.0	0.0	1	−3	(0.132)	−1	(0.232)	A*
0.0	0.5	0.0	2	−52	(0.084)	−0.8	(0.255)	A
0.0	0.9	0.0	10	−91	(0.034)	−2	(2.80)	A
0.0	0.99	0.0	100	−99	(0.006)	−24	(44.0)	B
0.8	0.0	0.0	1	−2	(0.089)	−0.2	(0.091)	A*
0.8	0.5	0.0	2	−21	(0.097)	−0.3	(0.097)	A
0.8	0.9	0.0	10	−71	(0.114)	−0.1	(0.164)	A
0.8	0.99	0.0	100	−98	(0.025)	44	(33.6)	B
1.0	0.0	0.0	1	−0.03	(0.038)	−0.02	(0.028)	D*
1.0	0.5	0.0	2	−4	(0.059)	−0.04	(0.029)	D
1.0	0.9	0.0	10	−28	(0.023)	−0.02	(0.038)	D
1.0	0.99	0.0	100	−81	(0.217)	1	(0.309)	C
0.0	0.0	0.5	1.5	−35	(0.099)	−0.7	(0.159)	A
0.0	0.5	0.5	3	−68	(0.070)	−0.6	(0.189)	A
0.0	0.9	0.5	15	−94	(0.028)	0.7	(0.405)	A
0.0	0.99	0.5	150	−100	(0.004)	2	(30.5)	B
0.8	0.0	0.5	1.5	−9	(0.069)	−0.2	(0.061)	A
0.8	0.5	0.5	3	−27	(0.095)	−0.2	(0.068)	A
0.8	0.9	0.5	15	−74	(0.115)	−0.09	(0.112)	A
0.8	0.99	0.5	150	−99	(0.024)	25	(17.6)	B
1.0	0.0	0.5	1.5	−2	(0.031)	−0.02	(0.019)	D
1.0	0.5	0.5	3	−5	(0.066)	−0.02	(0.019)	D
1.0	0.9	0.5	15	−29	(0.242)	−0.01	(0.026)	D
1.0	0.99	0.5	150	−81	(0.218)	1	(0.732)	C

TABLE 7.5 (*cont.*)

(*c*) Dynamic model under-parameterized ($\rho_4 = 1$, $\rho_5 = \rho_6 = \rho_7 = 0.5$)

ϕ	ρ_1	ρ_2	ρ_3	β	$100(\beta - \hat{\beta}_s)/\beta$	(SE)	$100(\beta - \hat{\beta}_d)/\beta$	(SE)	
0.0	0.5	0.15	−0.15	5	−85	(31.0)	−1	(16.0)	A
0.0	0.9	0.15	−0.15	25	−137	(3.76)	−69	(6.06)	A
0.0	0.99	0.15	−0.15	250	−101	(0.433)	−21	(5.71)	B
0.8	0.5	0.15	−0.15	5	−281	(9.67)	50	(2.12)	A
0.8	0.9	0.15	−0.15	25	−80	(1.53)	11	(0.498)	A
0.8	0.99	0.15	−0.15	250	−99	(0.101)	145	(77.1)	B
1.0	0.5	0.15	−0.15	5	−10	(5.51)	1	(0.436)	D
1.0	0.9	0.15	−0.15	25	−24	(0.977)	5	(0.098)	D
1.0	0.99	0.15	−0.15	250	−79	(0.253)	406	(380.0)	C
0.0	0.5	0.00	0.49	250	−99	(0.850)	102	(21.8)	B
0.0	0.5	0.00	0.45	50	−99	(1.90)	−41	(7.78)	A
0.0	0.5	0.00	0.30	12.5	−89	(3.10)	−39	(4.22)	A
0.8	0.5	0.00	0.49	250	−100	(0.085)	−5	(6.38)	B
0.8	0.5	0.00	0.45	50	−95	(0.690)	−51	(0.750)	A
0.8	0.5	0.00	0.30	12.5	−79	(1.33)	−25	(0.500)	A
1.0	0.5	0.00	0.49	250	−90	(0.144)	−15	(0.373)	C
1.0	0.5	0.00	0.45	50	−59	(2.86)	−36	(0.865)	D
1.0	0.5	0.00	0.30	12.5	432	(13.4)	−25	(0.468)	D

[a] Rounding: to nearest integer for raw figures ⩾1 in absolute value; to nearest 0.1 for figures between 0.1 and 1; to nearest 0.01 otherwise. Negative biases indicate biases towards zero, since all co-integrating parameters are positive.

[b] The dynamic model is in fact slightly over-parameterized in the cases where $\rho_2 = 0$.

[c] The symbol * indicates a case for which the *static* model is correctly parameterized: that is, the DGP is a static equation.

Second, an especially troublesome case arises where the roots of the lag polynomial in the series $\{y_t\}$ are such that $\{y_t\}$ is close to being an I(1) series in spite of the stationarity of $\{z_t\}$. This case leads to the largest biases of those examined here. As it is already known that regression of I(0) series on I(1) series produces troublesome results, especially in the form of non-standard distributions of test statistics, this result in the opposite case is unsurprising. It suggests that the investigation of the properties of t- and F-statistics that would be generated in the co-integrating regressions examined here may be of independent interest.

A feature of these *nearly* unbalanced regressions is that the biases in the estimates of the long-run multiplier in the static regressions tend to be associated with much lower standard errors than those in the corresponding dynamic regressions. This is attributable to the result that the variance of $\hat{\beta}_s$ is of order T^{-2} while in the dynamic regression, because of the asymptotic normality of the coefficient estimates, the variance of $\hat{\beta}_d$ is of order T^{-1}.[13] Expressed differently, when $\hat{c}$ is small, $\hat{\beta}_d$ can take extremely large values, and in finite samples may not have any analytical moments (see Sargan 1980 and Hendry 1991*a*).

Finally, the under-parameterized dynamic regressions, for a wide range of parameter values, perform notably worse than their correctly and over-parameterized counterparts. In the absence of *a priori* information about lag structures this would appear to support the inclusion of a fairly rich dynamic structure in the regression. Note also that in parts (*a*) and (*c*) of Table 7.5 there is at least one case in which the static regression appears to be superior to the dynamic. Hence a preference for the dynamic form seems reasonable based on the overall results, but the results should not be interpreted to mean that the dynamic regression is *invariably* superior even with strong exogeneity.

The classification recorded in Table 7.4 helps us to interpret further the results appearing in Table 7.5. Cases labelled A and D are examples of balanced regressions. However while case A represents regressions of an I(0) variable on other I(0) variables, case D represents regressions of an I(1) variable on other I(1) variables. Thus in case A experiments, the omitted dynamics are important and the dynamic model should perform noticeably better than the corresponding static model. An examination of parts (*a*) and (*b*) of Table 7.5 shows that this is indeed true.

The more interesting case, from the point of view of the study of co-integration, is case D, in which we have two I(1) processes that are co-integrated. It may be seen that, for this case too, in a substantial majority of experiments the dynamic regression estimates of the long-run coefficient are more accurate than the static estimates. This recalls,

[13] The rates of convergence are determined by using the SSW theorems, discussed in Ch. 6.

in the context of this more general data-generation process, the character of the results in Banerjee *et al.* (1986).

Cases B and C denote nearly unbalanced regressions, and the results here should be interpreted with caution. In a sense, one might argue that the regressions are spurious because variables of different orders of integration cannot be linked by an equilibrium relationship. Hence, following from the work of Phillips (1986), these regressions are likely to be characterized by asymptotically divergent coefficient estimates and t-statistics. We would also expect both the static and dynamic regressions to behave rather badly, with the behaviour worsening the further the regression moves away from balance. For example, in case B, the greater the absolute discrepancy between ϕ and $\rho_1 + \rho_2 + \rho_3$, the larger the biases in the estimates. As ϕ approaches 1 (for $\rho_1 + \rho_2 + \rho_3$ close to the unit circle), case B approaches case C, and the biases are generally lower. Case C represents unbalanced regressions of a rather special kind—namely, regressions of a near-I(2) variable on I(1) and near-I(2) variables—and the properties of such regressions appear to be better than might have been expected (see Chapter 3).

Where the exogenous variable is I(1), the regression estimates are super-consistent and the bias for the properly specified model is close to zero. Where each of the series is I(0) larger biases can appear; the largest arise where one series deviates from another by a quantity that is close to being non-stationary.

In sum, substantial biases in static OLS estimators exist, and specifying dynamic regressions can help alleviate the problem. The desirability of using dynamic regressions is reinforced by a consideration of their ability to detect co-integration, so we can compare the power properties of a test based on dynamic models with one based on the residuals from static regressions. Section 7.6 illustrates the two methods empirically. In Section 7.7, we consider methods of correcting static estimators of co-integrating vectors and discuss their properties.

7.5. Powers of Single-equation Co-integration Tests

A range of alternative tests for co-integration has been discussed in earlier sections, and here we comment on a number of features that influence test power, following the analysis in Kremers, Ericsson, and Dolado (1992).

Reconsider the DGP in (9)–(12) above, in case C:

$$\Delta z_t + \Delta y_t = \varepsilon_{1t} \tag{9'}$$

$$\Delta y_t + 2\Delta z_t = (\rho_2 - 1)(y_{t-1} + 2z_{t-1}) + \varepsilon_{2t}. \tag{10'}$$

The static regression involves estimating an equation of the form

$$y_t = \beta z_t + v_t, \tag{23}$$

and the DF test is conducted on

$$\Delta \hat{v}_t = \phi \hat{v}_{t-1} + \omega_t, \tag{24}$$

where $\hat{v}_t = y_t - \hat{\beta} z_t$. The DGP is optimal for the DF test here because (10′) has a valid common factor when $E(\varepsilon_{1t}\varepsilon_{2t}) = 0$ (see Hendry and Mizon 1978, and Sargan 1980). Since $\beta = -2$, $v_t = y_t + 2z_t$, so that (10′) corresponds to $\Delta v_t = (\rho_2 - 1)v_{t-1} + \varepsilon_{2t}$ and hence ω_t coincides with ε_{2t} except for terms involving $(\hat{\beta} - \beta)z_t$, etc. For this reason, the DGP selected by Engle and Granger (1987) is relatively favourable to the DF test.

By contrast, consider the DGP in (14) with the static regression in (16) and the same form of DF test as in (24):

$$\Delta \hat{u}_t = \phi \hat{u}_{t-1} + w_t. \tag{25}$$

In this case, $u_t = y_t - \beta z_t$ so that in (25), evaluated at $\hat{\beta} = \beta$,

$$\Delta(y_t - \beta z_t) = \phi(y_{t-1} - \beta z_{t-1}) + w_t;$$

hence

$$\Delta y_t = \beta \Delta z_t + \phi(y_{t-1} - \beta z_{t-1}) + w_t. \tag{26}$$

In (26), a common-factor restriction is imposed on the dynamics, but this time it is not necessarily a valid representation of (14*a*). Indeed, since $\beta = 1$ by homogeneity, (14*a*) can be written as

$$\Delta y_t = \Delta z_t + (\gamma_1 - 1)(y_{t-1} - z_{t-1}) + [\varepsilon_{1t} + (\gamma_2 - 1)\Delta z_t]. \tag{27}$$

Comparison with (26) reveals that the new error $[\varepsilon_{1t} + (\gamma_2 - 1)\Delta z_t]$ is white noise, but has a larger variance than that of the error in (14*a*). Kremers *et al.* (1992) show that t_ϕ in (24) retains the Dickey–Fuller distribution under the null, $\phi = 0$, whereas for a fixed β (such as unity) $t(\gamma_1 - 1)$ in (14*a*) can be approximated by N(0, 1) when $(\gamma_2 - 1)^2\sigma_2^2/\sigma_1^2$ is sufficiently large. However, when β is estimated under the null of no co-integration, the second test ceases to have a normal distribution.

Under the alternative of co-integration, $t(\gamma_1 - 1) \cong (\sigma_w/\sigma_1)t_\phi$ and hence has higher power, a result verified by power approximations based on near-integrated processes. To illustrate this form of power analysis, consider testing the null $H_0: \rho = 1$ in $y_t = \rho y_{t-1} + v_t$ against the local alternative $H_T: \rho = \exp(\varepsilon/T)$, $\varepsilon < 0$, using the Dickey–Fuller t-test. When the v_t are IID, then under H_0

$$t(\rho = 1) = \left(\hat{\sigma}^{-1}\sum_{t=2}^{T} y_{t-1}^2\right)^{1/2}(\hat{\rho} - 1) = T^{-1}\left(\sum_{t=2}^{T} y_{t-1}\varepsilon_t\right)\left(\hat{\sigma}^{-1}T^{-2}\sum_{t=2}^{T} y_{t-1}^2\right)^{-1/2}$$

$$\Rightarrow \left(\int_0^1 W(r)\,\mathrm{d}W(r)\right)\left(\int_0^1 W(r)^2\,\mathrm{d}r\right)^{-1/2}, \tag{28}$$

using results demonstrated in Chapter 3.

Under H_T, however, using results on near-integrated processes in (3.40)–(3.42),

$$t(\rho = 1) \Rightarrow (\varepsilon + \eta)\left(\int_0^1 K_\varepsilon(r)^2\,\mathrm{d}r\right)^{1/2} \tag{29}$$

where $\eta = (\int_0^1 K_\varepsilon(r)\,\mathrm{d}W(r))\,(\int_0^1 K_\varepsilon(r)^2\,\mathrm{d}r)^{-1}$. When $\varepsilon = 0$, we reproduce the distribution under H_0. Otherwise, for $\varepsilon < 0$, the distribution is shifted to the left by $\varepsilon(\int_0^1 K_\varepsilon(r)^2\,\mathrm{d}r)^{1/2}$. When $T = 100$, $\varepsilon = -1$ implies that $\rho = 0.99$, and $\varepsilon = -5$ implies that $\rho = 0.95$; as $\varepsilon \to -\infty$, the power tends to 1.

Kremers *et al.* (1992) argue that similar considerations show that the non-centrality parameter of the ECM-based test for co-integration is larger than that of the non-parametric statistics discussed in Chapter 4. Their Monte Carlo results support these asymptotic results.

Return now to the Monte Carlo experiment given by equations (14*a*)–(14*b*). One appealing test for co-integration that we have mentioned consists in using the model (15*a*), where, under the null of no co-integration, $\gamma_1 = 1$ so that the second coefficient is equal to zero. A t-test for this condition is therefore a test for co-integration. While we would expect the distribution of this test statistic to be non-standard, it is a straightforward test and would therefore be especially useful if its power were high. In particular, for strongly exogenous regressors it is similar (see Kiviet and Phillips 1992).

We examine the test with a small Monte Carlo experiment, comparing its power with that of the ADF test based on a static model to estimate the co-integrating parameter, in the DGP given by (14*a*)–(14*b*). The first test is the ADF test with one lag, computed from the residuals of the static regression (16). The second test is based on the t-statistic for $\hat{c}$ in (19). As noted earlier, if the null of no co-integration is true, $c = 0$.

Under the null (i.e. $\gamma_1 = 1$, $\gamma_2 = \gamma_3 = 0$, $\sigma_1 = \sigma_2 = 1$ in (14*a*)–(14*b*)), $t_{c=0}$ has a Wiener distribution. The critical values of this distribution and the ADF were computed by simulating the null model for 5000 replications using PC-NAIVE (Hendry, Neale, and Ericsson 1990). These critical values were then used for computing the test power, and are shown in Table 7.6 for regressions like (19) with an intercept. (The population constant is zero.) The same critical values result for $\gamma_2 + \gamma_3 = 0$ when these parameters are individually non-zero, so the test

TABLE 7.6. Fractiles of t-statistic for H_0: $c = 0$ in (19)

Fractiles of $t_{c=0}$ in (19)				Fractiles of ADF(1)		
T	0.10	0.05	0.01	0.10	0.05	0.01
25	−2.99	−3.42	−4.22	−3.15	−3.51	−4.30
50	−2.95	−3.33	−4.06	−3.10	−3.41	−4.08
100	−2.93	−3.28	−3.95	−3.09	−3.39	−4.00

is similar for the impact of Δz_t: this finding is based on replicating the null experiment at different parameter values using the same random numbers. The ADF(1) critical values are also the same for all the values of the null model's parameters since the ADF test is known to be similar. (The same Monte Carlo trick was used to check that feature: see Banerjee and Hendry 1992.)

The $t_{c=0}$ fractiles are slightly closer to zero than the corresponding fractiles of the augmented Dickey–Fuller distribution. Under the alternative hypothesis of co-integration, $t_{c=0}$ is asymptotically normally distributed.

Each entry in Table 7.7 shows the proportional frequency of rejection of the *false* null hypothesis of no co-integration.[14] The power of each test for each set of parameter values of the DGP and sample size is shown separately. At small values of $\gamma_1 - 1$, the power P_a of the ADF(1) test is very close to that of the $t_{c=0}$ test (P_c), but the latter dominates as $\gamma_1 - 1$ increases. Increasing the signal–noise ratio σ_2/σ_1 or $(1 - \gamma_2)$ also favours P_c. The powers converge to unity as the sample size T increases, but slowly when $(1 - \gamma_1) = 0.1$.

Thus, the power of $t_{c=0}$ relative to the ADF increases with $(1 - \gamma_1)$, $(1 - \gamma_2)\sigma_2/\sigma_1$, and T, matching the results in Kremers *et al.* noted above. The first three experiments have dynamics that are close to satisfying a common factor restriction: the ADF equation has a residual standard error that is only about 4 per cent larger in (a) than the DGP. On these experiments the ADF test does relatively well, although both tests do poorly in absolute terms. When a common factor approximation is poor as in (f), the ADF test suffers about an 85 per cent increase in the residual standard error by imposing the common factor and does relatively badly, in some cases dramatically so (e.g. $T = 50$ at the 1% significance level). Owing to the large value of $(1 - \gamma_1)$, both tests do well absolutely for sample sizes of 100.

The test powers respond in a nonlinear way to changes in the design parameter values, but some understanding of the rejection frequencies

[14] As in Table 7.6, all the results are based on 5000 replications.

TABLE 7.7. Test rejection frequencies in ECMs
DGP: (14*a*) + (14*b*); 5000 replications

	Estimated power at given fractile		
	0.10	0.05	0.01
	$t_{c=0}$/ADF	$t_{c=0}$/ADF	$t_{c=0}$/ADF
(*a*) $\gamma_1 = 0.9,\ \gamma_2 = 0.5,\ s = 3$[a]			
$T =$ 25	0.13/0.13	0.06/0.06	0.01/0.01
50	0.21/0.17	0.10/0.10	0.02/0.02
100	0.44/0.31	0.26/0.20	0.07/0.05
(*b*) $\gamma_1 = 0.9,\ \gamma_2 = 0.5,\ s = 1$			
$T =$ 25	0.14/0.11	0.06/0.05	0.01/0.01
50	0.21/0.15	0.10/0.09	0.02/0.02
100	0.49/0.30	0.30/0.19	0.08/0.04
(*c*) $\gamma_1 = 0.9,\ \gamma_2 = 0.5,\ s = 1/3$			
$T =$ 25	0.13/0.10	0.07/0.05	0.02/0.01
50	0.24/0.13	0.12/0.07	0.03/0.01
100	0.59/0.24	0.40/0.14	0.13/0.03
(*d*) $\gamma_1 = 0.5,\ \gamma_2 = 0.1,\ s = 3$			
$T =$ 25	0.66/0.35	0.45/0.20	0.16/0.05
50	0.99/0.84	0.97/0.72	0.78/0.34
100	1.00/1.00	1.00/1.00	1.00/0.97
(*e*) $\gamma_1 = 0.5,\ \gamma_2 = 0.1,\ s = 1$			
$T =$ 25	0.79/0.31	0.66/0.18	0.29/0.04
50	1.00/0.80	1.00/0.67	0.94/0.28
100	1.00/1.00	1.00/1.00	1.00/0.96
(*f*) $\gamma_1 = 0.5,\ \gamma_2 = 0.1,\ s = 1/3$			
$T =$ 25	0.94/0.23	0.87/0.12	0.64/0.03
50	1.00/0.75	1.00/0.60	1.00/0.22
100	1.00/1.00	1.00/1.00	1.00/0.94

[a] $s = \sigma_1/\sigma_2$.

in Table 7.7 can be obtained from the following analysis. Neglecting the intercept, the ADF test essentially involves testing $\gamma_1 = 1$ in

$$\Delta(y_t - \beta z_t) = (\gamma_1 - 1)(y_{t-1} - \beta z_{t-1}) + \delta\Delta(y_{t-1} - \beta z_{t-1}) + v_t,$$

where the first step regression of y_t on z_t estimates β, which here has a population value of unity. Under the alternative, $y_{t-1} - \beta z_{t-1}$ is stationary, and for $\beta = 1$ the non-centrality of the ADF pseudo t-test will be given approximately by

$$NC_{adf} \approx \sqrt{T}(\gamma_1 - 1)/\text{ASE} \approx \sqrt{T}(\gamma_1 - 1)/(1 - \gamma_1^2)^{1/2},$$

(see Mizon and Hendry 1980), where ASE denotes the coefficient asymptotic standard error calibrated to a sample size of T. For given design parameter values, the ASE is easily calculated using PC-NAIVE, and some outcomes are shown below.

Similarly, the $t_{c=0}$ test is actually based on testing $\gamma_1 = 1$ in

$$\Delta y_t = \gamma_2 \Delta z_t + (\gamma_1 - 1)(y_{t-1} - z_{t-1}) + (\gamma_3 + \gamma_2 + \gamma_1 - 1)z_{t-1} + \varepsilon_t.$$

Since the regressor $y_{t-1} - z_{t-1}$ is stationary under the alternative, if $\gamma_3 + \gamma_2 + \gamma_1 = 1$ is imposed and hence z_{t-1} omitted, the asymptotic non-centrality of the t-test of $\gamma_1 = 1$ (again in PC-NAIVE), yields the following illustrative values for $T = 25$:

Case	(*a*)	(*b*)	(*c*)	(*d*)	(*e*)	(*f*)
NC_{adf}	−1.15	−1.15	−1.15	−2.89	−2.89	−2.89
NC_{ecm}	−1.19	−1.28	−1.52	−3.25	−3.88	−5.32

In practice, these approximate non-centralities were close to the mean values of the corresponding test statistics in the Monte Carlo, except for (*a*)–(*c*) for the ADF, which had a mean of about −2.15 (see (4.28)). Their values help explain both the increasing powers of both tests across the experiments and the relatively better performance of $t_{c=0}$. Compared with the critical values in Table 7.6, and given the sampling standard deviations of the tests of about 0.8 for ADF and 1.0 for $t_{c=0}$, the non-centralities also account for the absolute powers of the tests: when the mean outcome is below the critical value, a power of less than 0.5 usually results; when the mean is more than one standard deviation below the critical value, the resulting power is under 0.2; two standard deviations lower induces a very low power; and so on. Similar arguments apply for deviations of the mean above the critical value.

Overall, there would seem to be some advantage in modelling dynamics less restrictively than by common factors when the latter is a poor approximation. Note that the absence of any contemporaneous effect from Δz_t always induces a violation of common factors. Finally, since the long-run parameter is not assumed known in these experiments, the $t_{c=0}$ test procedure is an operational one, and has the same number of parameters here as the ADF test.

The main drawback to such an approach is its dependence on strong exogeneity. Boswijk (1991) proposes a Wald test for co-integration in individual equations when the regressors are not even weakly exogenous. This jointly tests the null for the coefficients of all the lagged levels in a Bårdsen formulation. The resulting test is asymptotically similar and in effect tests for a common factor of unity (see Hendry and Mizon 1978). Boswijk and Franses (1992) investigate the power of this test.

7.6. An Empirical Illustration

To illustrate several tests for co-integration in single equations, we return to consider the UK seasonally adjusted quarterly data on money demand. The raw data series were shown in Chapter 1, and we concentrate here on the DW, DF, and ADF tests based on a static regression, and on their comparison with a dynamic regression, which is heavily over-parameterized. In all cases, we assume that there is only one co-integrating vector and that it enters the money-demand model. See Kremers *et al.* (1992) and Ericsson, Campos, and Tran (1990) for related analyses.

The long-run determinants of the demand for transactions money M, as measured by M1, are the price level P, real income as measured by constant 1985-price total final expenditure X_{85}, and the opportunity cost of holding money measured by R_n. (See Hendry and Ericsson (1991*b*) for details of its calculation.) We assumed a log-linear equation, consonant with price and income homogeneity, given by

$$m = a_0 + a_1 p - a_2 R_n + a_3 x_{85},$$

where lower-case letters denote logs, $a_1 = 1$ is anticipated, and $a_i > 0, i = 1, 2, 3$. Least-squares estimation of the static regression over the sample 1963(I)–to 1989(II) yielded

$$\underset{}{\hat{m}} = \underset{(0.038)}{0.749\, p} - \underset{(0.245)}{3.440\, R_n} + \underset{(0.144)}{1.305\, x_{85}} - \underset{(1.686)}{3.958} + \hat{u}, \qquad (30)$$

$$R^2 = 0.987 \qquad \sigma = 0.0919 \qquad DW = 0.250$$

$$SC = -4.637.$$

The residuals were then tested for a unit root using the DF and ADF tests, the latter commencing with four lags and testing down. The following results were obtained:

$$\Delta\hat{u} = -\underset{(0.063)}{0.118\, \hat{u}_1} + \underset{(0.109)}{0.085\, \Delta\hat{u}_1} + \underset{(0.106)}{0.022\, \Delta\hat{u}_2} - \underset{(0.105)}{0.072\, \Delta\hat{u}_3} + \underset{(0.105)}{0.037\, \Delta\hat{u}_4},$$

$$R^2 = 0.056 \qquad \sigma = 0.046.$$

No lagged values of $\Delta\hat{u}$ proved significant, leading to the DF test:

$$\Delta\hat{u} = -\underset{(0.051)}{0.108\, \hat{u}_1},$$

$$R^2 = 0.043 \qquad \sigma = 0.045.$$

In no case does any test reject the null of no co-integration, as the t-values on the estimated coefficient of $\hat{u}_1$ are in the neighbourhood of 2 in both the DF and the ADF regressions. That outcome continues to hold if a trend is added to the basic static-regression model (30), or if price homogeneity is imposed and Δp added as a regressor, corresponding to allowing m and p to be I(2), with $(m - p)$ and Δp being I(1). In that last case, R^2 for real money is equal to only 0.68.

We assume now that Δp, x_{85}, and R_n are weakly exogenous for the parameters in the conditional money demand model. The outcome of estimating a dynamic equation in the levels of the variables with five lags on each of $m - p$, Δp, x_{85}, and R_n (plus a constant) by least squares is shown in Table 7.8.

TABLE 7.8. Empirical results

Variable	Lag 0	1	2	3	4	5	Sum of lags
$m - p$	−1.000	0.549	0.240	0.251	0.152	0.164	−0.147
SE	0.	0.118	0.132	0.135	0.131	0.109	0.028
x_{85}	−0.041	0.293	−0.067	−0.240	0.130	0.087	0.162
SE	0.115	0.135	0.139	0.139	0.139	0.119	0.026
R_n	−0.411	−0.361	−0.122	−0.046	−0.084	−0.045	−1.070
SE	0.117	0.178	0.185	0.176	0.175	0.130	0.187
Δp	−0.757	0.020	0.307	−0.412	−0.329	0.069	−1.102
SE	0.210	0.255	0.253	0.246	0.246	0.203	0.222
CONSTANT	−0.124	—	—	—	—	—	−0.124
SE	0.169						0.169

$R^2 = 0.9966$ $\sigma = 0.0130$ $F(23, 76) = 975.38$ $DW = 1.976$
SC = −7.853 Mean = 10.896131 SD = 0.196173
Normality $\chi^2(2) = 4.29$
AR 1–5 $F[5, 71] = 0.20$ ARCH 4 $F[4, 68] = 0.22$
X_i^2 $F[37, 38] = 0.66$ RESET $F[1, 75] = 0.98$
COMFAC $F[15, 76] = 3.14$

Tests on the significance of each variable

Variable	F[num., denom.]	Value	Probability	Unit-root t-test
$m - p$	$F[5, 76]$	340.201	0.000	−5.168
x_{85}	$F[6, 76]$	7.801	0.000	6.171
R_n	$F[6, 76]$	12.127	0.000	−5.719
Δp	$F[6, 76]$	6.846	0.000	−4.963
CONSTANT	$F[1, 76]$	0.536	0.466	−0.732

Solved static long-run equation

$$m - p = \underset{(0.112)}{1.102 x_{85}} - \underset{(0.528)}{7.278 R_n} - \underset{(1.482)}{7.493 \Delta p} - \underset{(1.230)}{0.842}$$

These dynamic estimates are well behaved: the unit-root t-tests are all in the neighbourhood of 5 or larger in absolute value and every regressor matters as a set (i.e. testing all five lags); the solved long run is well defined and compares favourably with (30) since the three economic variables have highly significant coefficients with sensible signs and magnitudes; the goodness of fit is reasonable; and the diagnostic tests of the dynamic specification are all acceptable. Note that the sum of all the lags of the dependent variable, as shown in the final column of Table 7.8, is similar to that found in the DF regression, but has a much smaller standard error.

Only the first lag is strongly significant, as is shown in Table 7.9. Tests of common factors in the lag polynomials using the procedure in Sargan (1980) yield the results in Table 7.10.

Thus, the hypothesis of five common factors can be rejected at any reasonable level of significance. Recalling the discussion in Section 7.5 above, this outcome helps explain why the DF and ADF tests did not reject the null of no co-integration, whereas the dynamic model has done so decisively. Given that the common factor restrictions are rejected, the DF and ADF tests are not well suited to detecting co-integration. The ECM version of this equation, reported in Hendry and Ericsson (1991*b*), has a t-value greater than 10 in absolute value for the ECM coefficient, in a model which parsimoniously encompasses the unrestricted equation fitted above. Thus, the evidence favours rejecting no co-integration, and the results in the next chapter support that claim.

TABLE 7.9. Tests on the significance of each lag

Lag	F[num., denom.]	= Value	Probability
5	$F[4, 76]$	0.691	0.600
4	$F[4, 76]$	1.615	0.179
3	$F[4, 76]$	1.654	0.170
2	$F[4, 76]$	1.416	0.237
1	$F[4, 76]$	12.967	0.000

TABLE 7.10. COMFAC Wald test statistic summary table

Order	χ^2 d.f.	Value	Incremental χ^2 d.f.	Value
1	3	0.086	3	0.086
2	6	0.196	3	0.110
3	9	4.176	3	3.980
4	12	8.101	3	3.925
5	15	47.128	3	39.028

7.7. Fully Modified Estimation

This section considers methods for correcting the finite-sample biases in static regressions. Park and Phillips (1988), Phillips and Durlauf (1986), Phillips and Hansen (1990), and Phillips (1988*a*, 1991) have argued that the performance of estimators of co-integrating vectors based on static regressions is adversely affected by the existence of *second-order* biases. As shown in the examples below, these biases have no effect on the consistency of the estimators, but result in the asymptotic distributions of scaled estimators, such as $T(\hat{\beta} - \beta)$ in (31) below, having non-zero means.

Such biases play a potentially important role in finite samples. For example, let the variables y_{1t} and y_{2t} be generated by

$$y_{1t} = \beta y_{2t} + u_{1t} \tag{31}$$

$$y_{2t} = y_{2t-1} + u_{2t}. \tag{32}$$

When the $\{u_{it}\}$ are autocorrelated and intercorrelated, a static regression of y_{1t} on y_{2t}, by not using any information about the process generating y_{2t}, provides an estimate of β which can be quite severely biased even in fairly large samples. Phillips *et al.* therefore recommend full-system maximum likelihood estimation of co-integrated systems. As an alternative to estimation of the full system, they propose correcting the single-equation estimates non-parametrically in order to obtain median-unbiased and asymptotically normal estimates. These recommended corrections, for simultaneity bias and residual autocorrelation, use expressions derived from the asymptotic distributions of the estimators although the corrections are made to estimators from finite samples. Phillips and Hansen (1990) show that these corrections work effectively in sample sizes as small as 50.[15] Their example is presented in Section 7.10.4 below.

The estimates obtained from fully modified and full-information methods are asymptotically equivalent. This equivalence is of interest because it links the discussion with a third possible method of reducing finite-sample biases, namely, estimating single-equation *dynamic* regressions. The aim of the analysis in this section is to compare the non-parametrically corrected estimates (which are also asymptotically efficient and median-unbiased) with estimates obtained from dynamic regressions in either their ADL or ECM forms. The form of the autocorrelation in the error process in (31) and (32) is crucial to this comparison. For some specifications of the error process, a dynamic

[15] While it is possible to derive exact expressions for the biases in finite samples to any desired level of accuracy, using Edgeworth-type expansions, this is a complicated procedure.

regression equation implicitly performs the same corrections as those achieved by the non-parametric correction terms. The long-run estimates obtained from this properly specified dynamic equation are then equivalent, asymptotically, to the non-parametrically corrected estimates.[16] In such cases, therefore, two ways of incorporating information about the marginal process (that is, the process generating y_{2t}) present themselves: non-parametric correction, or dynamic specification. However, for other specifications of the autocorrelation process a single-equation dynamic regression may fail to achieve efficiency, or eliminate the effects of second-order bias, regardless of the richness of the parameterization, owing to a failure of the conditioning variables to be weakly exogenous for the parameters of the dynamic equation.

Our theoretical discussion is based on Phillips (1988*a*). Although it is fairly straightforward to describe and categorize the circumstances under which dynamic single-equation estimates will perform well, the detailed theoretical background for this description is lengthy and complex. Readers interested in implementing the non-parametric corrections are referred to the papers by Phillips and his co-authors cited previously. We shall focus on presenting the arguments intuitively and will illustrate the theoretical analysis with two simulation exercises, the first taken from Phillips and Hansen (1990), and the second from Gonzalo (1990).

7.8. A Fully Modified Least-squares Estimator

Consider the data-generation process given by (31) and (32) and disregard, for the moment, the precise autocorrelation structure of $\mathbf{u}_t = [u_{1t}, u_{2t}]'$. Assume only that $\mathbf{u}_t$ is weakly stationary with its mean vector and long-run covariance matrix given by $[0, 0]'$ and $\mathbf{\Omega}$ respectively, where $\mathbf{\Omega} = \{\omega_{ij}\}_{i,j=1,2}$.[17] The following decomposition of the $\mathbf{\Omega}$ matrix is useful in understanding its structure: $\mathbf{\Omega} = \mathbf{V} + \mathbf{\Gamma} + \mathbf{\Gamma}'$, where $\mathbf{V} = E[\mathbf{u}_0\mathbf{u}_0']$ and $\mathbf{\Gamma} = \sum_{k=1}^{\infty} E[\mathbf{u}_0\mathbf{u}_k']$. Thus, if the $\mathbf{u}$ process is serially uncorrelated and stationary, the $\mathbf{\Omega}$ matrix is the usual covariance matrix. In the presence of serial correlation, additional terms in the form of $\mathbf{\Gamma}$ need to be incorporated. The appendix explains the derivation of $\mathbf{\Omega}$.

[16] In Ch. 3 we compared the performance of the ADF test with the performance of the non-parametrically corrected DF test. The two tests were equivalent asymptotically, in their ability to mop up the effects of residual autocorrelation in the DF regression, but they could behave quite differently in finite samples. The same comparisons apply here. Even when a particular dynamic specification estimator is asymptotically equivalent to a non-parametric correction, it is still of interest to compare the performances of the estimates obtained from each method.

[17] The long-run covariance matrix is given by $2\pi\mathbf{f}_{uu}(0)$, where $\mathbf{f}_{uu}(0)$ is the spectral density matrix of $\mathbf{u}_t$ evaluated at zero. The corrections discussed below are termed 'non-parametric' because consistent estimates of this covariance matrix, and of related matrices, must be obtained non-parametrically.

The fully modified least-squares estimator of β takes the form

$$\beta^{+} = \left(\sum_{t=1}^{T} y_{2t}^{2}\right)^{-1}\left[\left(\sum_{t=1}^{T} y_{1t}^{+} y_{2t}\right) - T\hat{\delta}^{+}\right], \tag{33}$$

where

$$y_{1t}^{+} = y_{1t} - \hat{\omega}_{12}\hat{\omega}_{22}^{-1}\Delta y_{2t} \tag{34}$$

$$\hat{\delta}^{+} = \hat{\mathbf{\Lambda}}\begin{bmatrix} 1 \\ -\hat{\omega}_{22}^{-1}\hat{\omega}_{21} \end{bmatrix} \tag{35}$$

$$\mathbf{\Lambda} = \sum_{k=0}^{\infty} E(u_{20}\mathbf{u}_k'). \tag{36}$$

In (33)–(36), $\hat{\delta}^{+}$ is a bias correction term, $\hat{\omega}_{21}$ and $\hat{\omega}_{22}$ are consistent estimates of the corresponding elements in the long-run covariance matrix, and $\hat{\mathbf{\Lambda}}$ is a consistent estimate of $\mathbf{\Lambda}$. Under quite general conditions,

$$T(\beta^{+} - \beta) \Rightarrow \left(\int_0^1 B_2(r)^2\,\mathrm{d}r\right)^{-1}\left(\int_0^1 B_2(r)\,\mathrm{d}B_{1.2}(r)\right), \tag{37}$$

where

$$\begin{bmatrix} B_{1.2}(r) \\ B_2(r) \end{bmatrix} = \mathrm{BM}(\mathbf{\Omega}_{11.2}), \qquad \mathbf{\Omega}_{11.2} = \begin{bmatrix} \omega_{11.2} & 0 \\ 0 & \omega_{22} \end{bmatrix},$$

$$\text{and } \omega_{11.2} = \omega_{11} - \omega_{21}^{2}\omega_{22}^{-1}.$$

The notation $\mathrm{BM}(\mathbf{\Omega}_{11.2})$ is used to denote a bivariate Brownian motion process with covariance matrix $\mathbf{\Omega}_{11.2}$ and is a matrix generalization of scalar Wiener processes, as discussed in Chapter 6. The limiting distribution (37) is a covariance matrix mixture of normals (see Table 3.3).

The 'full modification' in (33) achieves two notable aims. First, by taking account of any serial correlation in the residuals, the bias correction term $\hat{\delta}^{+}$ mitigates the effects of second-order bias. Second, the corrections for long-run simultaneity in the system made by using y_{1t}^{+} (in place of y_{1t}) permit the use of conventional (asymptotic) procedures for inference. Thus, defining the fully modified standard error by s^{+} where,

$$(s^{+})^2 = \hat{\omega}_{11.2}\left(\sum_{t=1}^{T} y_{2t}^{2}\right)^{-1},$$

where $\hat{\omega}_{11.2}$ is a consistent estimator of $\omega_{11.2}$, we have the following result:

$$t^{+} = (\beta^{+} - \beta)/s^{+} \Rightarrow \mathrm{N}(0, 1). \tag{38}$$

Phillips and Hansen (1990) show that this approach is asymptotically equivalent to systems procedures such as full maximum likelihood estimation discussed in Chapter 8. Both (38), which simplifies the process of inference, and the reduction in the second-order bias in β^+ help estimation and testing of single equations in co-integrated systems. Our use of a simple data-generation process is solely for the purposes of exposition; the literature to which we have referred is capable of treating co-integrated systems at a high level of generality.

7.9. Dynamic Specification

Is it possible, by suitable dynamic specification alone, to make the same corrections as those made by the technique described above? In order to answer this question, Phillips (1988*a*) considers a dynamic version of equation (31):

$$y_{1t} = \beta y_{2t} + \boldsymbol{\gamma}'\mathbf{x}_t + \eta_t, \tag{39}$$

where $\mathbf{x}_t$ is a vector with jointly stationary elements. Thus, $\mathbf{x}_t$ contains lagged values of Δy_{1t} and current and lagged values of Δy_{2t}. While far from being a general dynamic model, (39) is a linear-in-parameters ADL model.

The process of constructing a regression equation such as (39) has been extensively discussed in the literature (see, in particular, Engle *et al.* 1983). Thus, focusing on the DGP given by (31) and (32) and imposing no restrictions upon the autocorrelation structure of the u_{it},

$$\begin{aligned}\eta_t &= y_{1t} - E(y_{1t}|y_{2t}, \mathcal{F}_{t-1})\\ &= u_{1t} - E(u_{1t}|y_{2t}, \mathcal{F}_{t-1})\\ &= u_{1t} - E(u_{1t}|u_{1t-1}, u_{1t-2}, \ldots; u_{2t}, u_{2t-1}, \ldots),\end{aligned} \tag{40}$$

where $\mathcal{F}_{t-1}$ is the information set containing information on past realizations of y_{1t}, y_{2t} and hence of u_{it-j}, $i = 1, 2$; $j \geqslant 1$. By construction, $\{\eta_t\}$ in (40) is a martingale difference sequence.

If the process generating $\mathbf{u}_t$ is now specialized to the case where it is a linear process, so that

$$\mathbf{u}_t = \sum_{j=0}^{\infty} \mathbf{A}_j \boldsymbol{\varepsilon}_{t-j}, \tag{41}$$

where $\boldsymbol{\varepsilon}_t = (\varepsilon_{1t}, \varepsilon_{2t})' \sim \mathrm{IN}(\mathbf{0}, \boldsymbol{\Sigma})$, $\mathbf{A}_0 = \mathbf{I}_2$, and $\sum_{j=0}^{\infty}\|\mathbf{A}_j\| < \infty$, then[18]

$$\eta_t = \varepsilon_{1t} - E(\varepsilon_{1t}|\varepsilon_{2t}) = \varepsilon_{1t} - \sigma_{21}\sigma_{22}^{-1}\varepsilon_{2t}.$$

The variance of η_t is given by $\sigma_{11.2} = \sigma_{11} - \sigma_{21}^2\sigma_{22}^{-1}$, and η_t is orthogonal to ε_{2t} as well as to the entire history of $\boldsymbol{\varepsilon}_t$ given by $(\boldsymbol{\varepsilon}_{t-1}, \boldsymbol{\varepsilon}_{t-2}, \ldots)$.

[18] Note that $\boldsymbol{\Sigma} = \{\sigma_{ij}\}_{i,j=1,2}$ and $\mathbf{I}_2$ is the (2×2) identity matrix.

Estimating the regression (39) is asymptotically equivalent to maximizing the conditional likelihood function of $(\varepsilon_{11}, \varepsilon_{12}, \ldots, \varepsilon_{1T})$, given $(\varepsilon_{2t}, t = 1, 2, \ldots, T)$. Assuming invertibility of $\mathbf{A}(L)$ in (41), we have

$$\mathbf{B}(L)\mathbf{u}_t = \boldsymbol{\varepsilon}_t, \qquad \mathbf{B}(L) = \sum_{j=0}^{\infty} \mathbf{B}_j L^j, \qquad \mathbf{B}_0 = \mathbf{I}_2. \tag{42}$$

Equation (42) implies

$$\varepsilon_{1t} = b_{11}(L)u_{1t} + b_{12}(L)u_{2t}$$

and

$$\varepsilon_{2t} = b_{21}(L)u_{1t} + b_{22}(L)u_{2t}.$$

Thus, to maximize the conditional likelihood requires

$$\max\left[-(T/2)\log\sigma_{11.2} - (1/2)\sigma_{11.2}^{-1}\sum_{t=1}^{T}(\varepsilon_{1t} - \sigma_{21}\sigma_{22}^{-1}\varepsilon_{2t})^2\right],$$

which involves

$$\min\left\{\sum_{t=1}^{T}[(b_{11}(L), b_{12}(L))\mathbf{u}_t - \sigma_{21}\sigma_{22}^{-1}(b_{21}(L), b_{22}(L))\mathbf{u}_t]^2\right\}. \tag{43}$$

Solving (43) is equivalent to least-squares estimation of the regression model

$$y_{1t} = \beta y_{2t} + d_1(L)(y_{1t} - \beta y_{2t}) + d_2(L)\Delta y_{2t} + v_t; \tag{44}$$

where $d_1(L) = \sum_{j=1}^{\infty} d_{1j}L^j$, $d_2(L) = \sum_{j=0}^{\infty} d_{2j}L^j$, and $v_t \sim \mathrm{IN}(0, \sigma_{11.2})$ which is independent of the regressors.

It is then possible to show that

$$T(\hat{\beta} - \beta) \Rightarrow \left(\int_0^1 B_2(r)^2\,\mathrm{d}r\right)^{-1}\left(\int_0^1 B_2(r)\,\mathrm{d}B_v(r)\right), \tag{45}$$

where $\hat{\beta}$ is the estimate of the coefficient of y_{2t} in (44). $B_v(r)$ and $B_2(r)$ comprise a bivariate Brownian motion process with a well-defined variance–covariance matrix.

The question posed at the beginning of this sub-section can now be answered. Comparing (37) and (45), the fully modified estimator β^+ and the dynamic single-equation least-squares estimator are equivalent if and only if $B_v(r) = B_{1.2}(r)$. These two Brownian motion processes are not necessarily equal to each other. This is because $B_v(r)$ can be correlated with $B_2(r)$, despite its construction in (40). The generating mechanism for u_{2t} may therefore be informative, and optimal inference then requires joint estimation with the error-correction model. Phillips (1988) describes this as a failure of weak exogeneity or valid conditioning. If, on the other hand, $B_v(r)$ and $B_2(r)$ are uncorrelated at all frequencies, the conditional process is completely informative for the purposes of estimation of β and the marginal process generating u_{2t} may be ignored. In such a case, $B_v(r) = B_{1.2}(r)$.

The examples following this sub-section will elaborate upon these conditions, but we will close this section with an interpretation. The non-equivalence of the dynamic regression estimator and the fully modified estimator arises from possible correlation between the residuals η_t of the conditional process and the residuals u_{2t} of the marginal process. This correlation arises because, although η_t is orthogonal to u_{2t} and the past history of u_{2t} (η_t is orthogonal to its own past by construction), u_{2t} is not necessarily orthogonal to the past of u_{1t} and hence $(\eta_t, u_{2t})'$ jointly is not a martingale difference sequence (MDS).

Three examples are presented below. They are adapted from Phillips (1988*a*) and are special cases of the examples appearing in that paper. Three different specifications of the autocorrelation structure of the $\mathbf{u}_t$ process are considered while the data-generation process continues to be (31) and (32).

The examples help to integrate and interpret the discussions on weak exogeneity, dynamic modelling, and fully modified estimation. Exogeneity plays an important role in dealing with non-stationary variables. Dynamic regression equations in which the conditioning is on weakly or strongly exogenous variables (for the parameters of interest) provide asymptotically unbiased estimates. Further, inference may be conducted with standard tables. In cases where such conditioning is not possible, improperly conditioned equations lead to inefficient and biased estimates. The full system must therefore be estimated or the non-parametrically modified estimates used. It is seen that fully modified estimation is another way of addressing the issue of the completeness of conditional models for purposes of estimation and inference.

7.10. Examples

7.10.1. Example (Phillips 1988a: 352)

$$\begin{bmatrix} u_{1t} \\ u_{2t} \end{bmatrix} \sim \mathrm{IN}\left[\begin{bmatrix} 0 \\ 0 \end{bmatrix}, \begin{bmatrix} \phi_{11} & \phi_{21} \\ \phi_{21} & \phi_{22} \end{bmatrix}\right].$$

In reduced form, the DGP (31) and (32) is given by

$$\begin{aligned} y_{1t} &= \beta y_{2t-1} + u_{1t} + \beta u_{2t} = \beta y_{2t-1} + v_{1t} \\ y_{2t} &= y_{2t-1} + u_{2t}. \end{aligned} \tag{46}$$

Hence

$$\begin{aligned} \begin{bmatrix} v_{1t} \\ u_{2t} \end{bmatrix} &\sim \mathrm{IN}\left[\begin{bmatrix} 0 \\ 0 \end{bmatrix}, \begin{bmatrix} \phi_{11} + \beta^2\phi_{22} + 2\beta\phi_{21} & \beta\phi_{22} + \phi_{21} \\ \beta\phi_{22} + \phi_{21} & \phi_{22} \end{bmatrix}\right] \\ &\sim \mathrm{IN}\left[\begin{bmatrix} 0 \\ 0 \end{bmatrix}, \begin{bmatrix} \zeta_{11} & \zeta_{21} \\ \zeta_{21} & \phi_{22} \end{bmatrix}\right]. \end{aligned} \tag{47}$$

Thus, using the formula for the conditional expectation of bivariate normal random variables, we have

$$E(y_{1t}|y_{2t}, \mathscr{F}_{t-1}) = \beta y_{2t-1} + \zeta_{21}\phi_{22}^{-1}(y_{2t} - y_{2t-1}). \tag{48}$$

Defining

$$\eta_t = y_{1t} - E(y_{1t}|y_{2t}, \mathscr{F}_{t-1})$$

and using (48), we obtain

$$y_{1t} = \beta y_{2t-1} + \zeta_{21}\phi_{22}^{-1}(y_{2t} - y_{2t-1}) + \eta_t \tag{49}$$

or, alternatively,

$$\Delta y_{1t} = \boldsymbol{\alpha}'\mathbf{y}_{t-1} + \zeta_{21}\phi_{22}^{-1}\Delta y_{2t} + \eta_t, \tag{50}$$

where $\boldsymbol{\alpha} = (-1, \beta)'$ and $\mathbf{y}_t = (y_{1t}, y_{2t})'$.

Finally, substituting for $\zeta_{21} = \beta\phi_{22} + \phi_{21}$ in (49), from (46):

$$\eta_t = u_{1t} - \phi_{21}\phi_{22}^{-1}u_{2t}.$$

Several features are now evident. By construction, η_t is an MDS. Second, again by construction, η_t is uncorrelated with u_{2t}.[19] From (47), we have that the u_{2t} process is serially uncorrelated both with past u_{2t} and with past u_{1t}. It follows that η_t and u_{2t} are incoherent (that is, uncorrelated at all lags or frequencies), that the long-run covariance matrix of $[\eta_t, u_{2t}]'$ is diagonal, and that the estimation of a single dynamic equation should provide a fully efficient and unbiased estimate of the vector $\boldsymbol{\alpha}$.

Looking at the conditional and marginal processes given by (50) and the second equation in (46) respectively, and at the properties identified in the previous paragraph, single-equation least squares on (50) is equivalent to full-information maximum likelihood for estimating β. The orthogonality of the η_t and u_{2t} processes ensures that the joint likelihood function for the system factorizes into the likelihood functions for the marginal and conditional models given by the second equation in (46) and (50) respectively. There are no cross-equation restrictions; the parameter of interest β can be estimated and identified from (50) alone; and, recalling the discussion of weak exogeneity in Chapter 1, the marginal process generating u_{2t} need not be modelled when estimating β.

7.10.2. Example (Phillips 1988a: 355)

$$u_{1t} = \varepsilon_{1t} \tag{51}$$

$$u_{2t} = \lambda u_{2t-1} + \varepsilon_{2t} \tag{52}$$

where,

$$\begin{bmatrix}\varepsilon_{1t}\\ \varepsilon_{2t}\end{bmatrix} \sim \text{IN}\left[\begin{bmatrix}0\\0\end{bmatrix}, \begin{bmatrix}\sigma_{11} & \sigma_{21}\\ \sigma_{21} & \sigma_{22}\end{bmatrix}\right].$$

[19] From above, $E(\eta_t u_{2t}) = E(u_{1t}u_{2t}) - \phi_{21}\phi_{22}^{-1}E(u_{2t}^2)$. Thus, $\text{cov}(\eta_t, u_{2t}) = E(\eta_t u_{2t}) = \phi_{21} - \phi_{21}\phi_{22}^{-1}\phi_{22} = 0$.

Then

$$\begin{aligned}\eta_t &= u_{1t} - E(u_{1t}|u_{2t}, \mathscr{F}_{t-1}) \\ &= u_{1t} - \sigma_{21}\sigma_{22}^{-1}(u_{2t} - \lambda u_{2t-1}) \\ &= \varepsilon_{1t} - \sigma_{21}\sigma_{22}^{-1}\varepsilon_{2t}. \end{aligned} \tag{53}$$

The long-run covariance matrix of $(\eta_t, u_{2t})'$ is given by

$$\mathbf{\Omega}_{11.2} = \begin{bmatrix} \sigma_{11.2} & 0 \\ 0 & (1-\lambda)^{-2}\sigma_{22} \end{bmatrix}$$

where $\sigma_{11.2} = \sigma_{11} - \sigma_{12}^2\sigma_{22}^{-1}$. The expression for $\mathbf{\Omega}_{11.2}$ follows from application of the conditional-expectations formula and from inspection of (53). η_t and u_{2t} are again incoherent, and the limit Brownian motions are

$$\begin{bmatrix} B_\eta(r) \\ B_2(r) \end{bmatrix} = \mathrm{BM}(\mathbf{\Omega}_{11.2}),$$

where B_η and B_2 are independent and $B_\eta = B_{1.2}$. Thus, estimating a dynamic single-equation model (the conditional model) provides estimates identical, asymptotically, to those provided by the Phillips–Hansen procedure. Here the conditional model is given by

$$y_{1t} = \beta y_{2t} + \sigma_{21}\sigma_{22}^{-1}\Delta y_{2t} - \lambda\sigma_{21}\sigma_{22}^{-1}\Delta y_{2t-1} + \eta_t. \tag{54}$$

In error-correction format, we may rewrite (54) as

$$\Delta y_{1t} = -(y_{1t-1} - \beta y_{2t-1}) + (\sigma_{21}\sigma_{22}^{-1} + \beta)\Delta y_{2t} - \lambda\sigma_{21}\sigma_{22}^{-1}\Delta y_{2t-1} + \eta_t. \tag{55}$$

Equation (54) is the one that must be estimated in order to obtain an asymptotically unbiased estimator of β. The static regression is augmented in (54) by the terms Δy_{2t} and Δy_{2t-1}. These additional terms are incorporated to reduce or eliminate, in finite samples, the effects of second-order bias, without estimating the full system.

Phillips (1988*a*) notes that the bias correction term δ^+ for this example is equal to zero since $\mathbf{\Lambda} = (\omega_{12}, \omega_{22})'$. However, to obtain fully modified estimates, from (34) y_{1t} needs to be corrected for long-run endogeneity as follows:

$$y_{1t}^+ = y_{1t} - \sigma_{21}\sigma_{22}^{-1}(1-\lambda)\Delta y_{2t}.$$

The same correction is achieved in the dynamic regression by the two Δy_{2t-i} terms in (55). The static regression produces biases by ignoring these corrections.

7.10.3. Example (Phillips 1988a: 356)

$$u_{1t} = \varepsilon_{1t} + \theta_{11}\varepsilon_{1t-1} + \theta_{12}\varepsilon_{2t-1} \tag{56}$$

$$u_{2t} = \varepsilon_{2t} + \theta_{21}\varepsilon_{1t-1} + \theta_{22}\varepsilon_{2t-1}. \tag{57}$$

We take the process $(\varepsilon_{1t}, \varepsilon_{2t})'$ to be distributed as in Section 7.10.2. Then it may be shown that

$$\eta_t = u_{1t} - E(u_{1t}|u_{2t}, \mathscr{F}_{t-1}) = \varepsilon_{1t} - \sigma_{21}\sigma_{22}^{-1}\varepsilon_{2t}.$$

The long-run covariance matrix is given by

$$\mathbf{\Omega}_{11.2} = \begin{bmatrix} \sigma_{11.2} & \theta_{21}\sigma_{11.2} \\ \theta_{21}\sigma_{11.2} & H \end{bmatrix},$$

where $\sigma_{11.2}$ is as defined in Section 7.10.2, and

$$H = \theta_{21}^2\sigma_{11} + 2(1 + \theta_{22})\sigma_{21}\theta_{21} + (1 + \theta_{22})^2\sigma_{22}.$$

The Brownian motions B_η and B_2 are correlated and the single-equation dynamic estimator and the fully modified estimator are no longer equivalent, unless $\theta_{21} = 0$. For the structure of the correlation between B_η and B_2 (see Phillips 1988*a*):

$$B_\eta(r) = \sigma_{11.2}\theta_{21}H^{-1}B_2(r) + B_{\eta.2}(r), \tag{58}$$

where $B_{\eta.2}(r)$ is a univariate Brownian motion process with variance given by $\sigma_{11.2} - \sigma_{11.2}^2\theta_{21}^2H^{-1}$ and is independent of $B_2(r)$. Further,

$$T(\hat{\beta} - \beta) \Rightarrow \left(\int_0^1 B_2(r)^2\,\mathrm{d}r\right)^{-1}\left(\theta_{21}\sigma_{11.2}H^{-1}\int_0^1 B_2(r)\,\mathrm{d}B_2(r) + \int_0^1 B_2(r)\,\mathrm{d}B_{\eta.2}(r)\right). \tag{59}$$

From (58) setting θ_{21} equal to zero makes the $B_\eta(r)$ and $B_{\eta.2}(r)$ equivalent to each other. Further, $B_{\eta.2}(r)$ has a variance of $\sigma_{11.2}$ and is in all respects equivalent to the $B_{1.2}(r)$ process given in (37) above. Thus, the $B_\eta(r)$ and $B_{1.2}(r)$ processes are equivalent, and, in accordance with the previous discussion, this equivalence leads to the equivalence of the single-equation dynamic estimator and the fully modified estimator.

It should be noted that $\theta_{21} \neq 0$ also implies that the $\mathbf{\Gamma}$-type terms (see Section 7.8) are important in the long-run variance matrix for the $(\eta_t, u_{2t})'$ process. This is just another way of saying that the past of the process is important (and so, in the $(\eta_t, u_{2t})'$ construction we have not achieved a martingale difference sequence). Thus, the equivalence of dynamic single-equation estimators and fully modified estimators may also be assessed by looking for the presence of $\mathbf{\Gamma}$-type terms in the long-run variance matrix. These are the terms (for example, the first term in (59)) that give rise to biases in the single-equation dynamic estimates of the co-integrating vector.

The necessary and sufficient condition for non-equivalence has a natural interpretation in the language of an earlier literature on dynamic modelling. It is evident that the condition $\theta_{21} \neq 0$ violates weak exogeneity[20] as may be verified from (57); and once again, it may be seen that the issues of a fully modified estimation and dynamic specification are closely related. This example forms the basis for the simulation exercise discussed in the final sub-section.

7.10.4. *Simulation Example (Phillips and Hansen 1990: 116)*

The data-generation process for their simulation study is given by

$$\begin{aligned} y_{1t} &= \beta y_{2t} + u_{1t} \\ y_{2t} &= y_{2t-1} + u_{2t}, \qquad t = 1, 2, \ldots, 50 \\ u_{1t} &= \varepsilon_{1t} + 0.3\varepsilon_{1t-1} - 0.4\varepsilon_{2t-1} \\ u_{2t} &= \varepsilon_{2t} + \theta_{21}\varepsilon_{1t-1} + 0.6\varepsilon_{2t-1} \end{aligned}$$

$$\begin{bmatrix} \varepsilon_{1t} \\ \varepsilon_{2t} \end{bmatrix} \sim \mathrm{IN}\left[\begin{bmatrix} 0 \\ 0 \end{bmatrix}, \begin{bmatrix} 1 & \sigma_{21} \\ \sigma_{21} & 1 \end{bmatrix}\right].$$

The design of the experiment consisted in allowing σ_{21} and θ_{21} to vary. Thus, four values of σ_{21} and three values of θ_{21} were used. The values of σ_{21} considered were -0.8, -0.4, 0.4, and 0.8, and the three values of the moving-average parameter θ_{21} were 0.8, 0.4, and 0.0.[21] β was set equal to 2 for all twelve combinations of the values of σ_{21} and θ_{21}. The aim was to calculate and compare the distributions of estimators and t-statistics for the co-integrating parameter obtained by OLS, single-equation dynamic, and fully modified methods.

For the fully modified method, Phillips and Hansen used a Bartlett triangular window of lag length 5 and the OLS residuals $\hat{u}_{1t}$ to calculate non-parametric estimates of $\mathbf{\Lambda}$, $\mathbf{\Omega}$ and hence of δ^+. We shall denote these estimates by $\hat{\mathbf{\Lambda}}$, $\hat{\mathbf{\Omega}}$, and $\hat{\delta}^+$. The OLS t-statistic was estimated by using $\hat{\omega}_{11}$ (the (1, 1) element from the non-parametrically estimated long-run variance matrix) as an estimate of the standard error. The dynamic equation regressed y_{1t} on $(y_{2t}, \Delta y_{2t}, \Delta y_{2t-1}, \Delta y_{2t-2}, \Delta y_{1t-1}, \Delta y_{1t-2})$, using 30,000 replications for each simulation (that is, for each pair of values of $(\theta_{21}, \sigma_{21})$). Given the nature of the DGP, the dynamic

[20] The correlation between u_{2t} and ε_{1t-1}, introduced by a non-zero value of θ_{21}, implies that the marginal process contains information relevant for the η_t process. Thus, the construction of η_t in this example does not lead to a complete purging of information relating to the marginal process, and efficient estimation therefore requires that the u_{2t} also be modelled. This is of course just a restatement of the weak-exogeneity condition.

[21] In light of the simulation findings presented by Schwert (1989), this experiment design is open to one criticism. No negative values of the moving-average parameter were considered. Negative MA values were the ones that were most troublesome, for the Phillips–Perron non-parametric corrections, in the study by Schwert.

equation is only an approximation. The results are presented in Tables 7.11 and 7.12.

Table 7.11 presents the Monte Carlo means and standard deviations of $(\hat{\beta} - \beta)$ for the OLS, dynamic (D), and fully modified (FM) estimators. It is clear from this table that, in general, OLS gives the most heavily biased estimator. However, there seems to be little to choose between the fully modified estimator (FM) and the dynamic estimator (D). No consistent pattern of superiority (measured in terms of lower *absolute* values of biases and standard errors) appears to be present.

Consider first the cases where $\theta_{21} \neq 0$. For a value of $\sigma_{21} = -0.8$, D is more biased than FM when $\theta_{21} = 0.8$ but is less biased when $\theta_{21} = 0.4$. When $\sigma_{21} = 0.8$, the opposite is true. For the two intermediate values of σ_{21} considered, the bias in FM is less than or equal to the bias in D. Thus, although FM provides lower biases in a larger number of cases than D, the evidence is mixed. For the cases where $\theta_{21} = 0$, and the single-equation and fully modified estimator have distributions that are asymptotically equivalent, D out-performs FM on three out of four occasions. In the only case where FM provides a lower bias ($\sigma_{21} = 0.4$), the D and FM biases are 0.009 and 0.004 (in absolute value) respectively. This comparison is therefore made in the context of both D and FM performing well in providing low biases.

TABLE 7.11. Mean (standard deviation) of $(\hat{\beta} - \beta)$

	$\theta_{21} = 0.8$	$\theta_{21} = 0.4$	$\theta_{21} = 0.0$
$\sigma_{21} = -0.8$			
OLS	−0.137 (0.125)	−0.090 (0.089)	−0.055 (0.061)
D	−0.062 (0.106)	−0.021 (0.066)	−0.003 (0.041)
FM	−0.025 (0.127)	−0.028 (0.079)	−0.025 (0.052)
$\sigma_{21} = -0.4$			
OLS	−0.067 (0.081)	−0.057 (0.079)	−0.040 (0.061)
D	−0.051 (0.086)	−0.030 (0.077)	−0.007 (0.060)
FM	−0.042 (0.094)	−0.027 (0.081)	−0.015 (0.063)
$\sigma_{21} = 0.4$			
OLS	−0.024 (0.040)	−0.020 (0.046)	−0.011 (0.050)
D	−0.023 (0.046)	−0.019 (0.053)	−0.009 (0.060)
FM	−0.023 (0.048)	−0.012 (0.052)	0.004 (0.060)
$\sigma_{21} = 0.8$			
OLS	−0.015 (0.025)	−0.010 (0.028)	−0.004 (0.036)
D	−0.009 (0.024)	−0.008 (0.030)	−0.005 (0.039)
FM	−0.016 (0.028)	−0.005 (0.030)	0.015 (0.043)

Reproduced from Phillips and Hansen (1990).

Phillips and Hansen also estimate the probability density functions for the D and FM estimators. When $\theta_{21} = 0.8$, the density function of FM is better centred (at zero) than D, while the opposite is true when $\theta_{21} = 0$.[22]

Based then on a consideration of biases alone, there do not appear to be strong grounds for preferring the FM over the D estimator. This observation must be qualified by two cautionary remarks. First, the experiment considered here is very limited, and a more extensive simulation exercise might reveal the superiority of FM over D. Second, both FM (in finite samples) and D could be out-performed by full-information maximum likelihood estimation of the two-equation system. Such a comparison is undertaken in the next chapter.

The argument in favour of using fully modified methods is stronger when one considers the evidence presented in Table 7.12, wherein the means and standard deviations of the distributions of the t-statistics are tabulated. Here the conclusions are more nearly unambiguous. When $\theta_{21} \neq 0$, the t-statistics from D are more heavily biased than those obtained from FM (in all but one case) and have higher standard errors. The FM t-statistic comes much closer to achieving a distribution that is roughly normal than does the t-statistic from D. As noted by Phillips and Hansen, the relatively inferior behaviour of the dynamic t-statistic may have been caused by the inclusion of an insufficient number of lag terms in the D regression. When $\theta_{21} = 0$, the dynamic t-statistic is substantially less biased (in all but one case) than the FM t-statistic, but its variance is much higher.

Since the use of the normal distribution is a considerable simplification and the bias comparisons are at best ambiguous for the dynamic estimates (when $\theta_{21} \neq 0$), there may be reasons to prefer the FM estimator over the D estimator when only long-run parameters are of interest. This recommendation must be qualified by noting that a more richly parameterized dynamic model may have provided lower biases and a distribution of the t-statistic closer to the normal distribution. Performance with a negative MA parameter is also important; some early studies have suggested that the FM estimator performs less well in such cases. Both these qualifications point to the need for more extensive simulation studies.

What is clear from all the studies considered so far is the poor performance of unmodified estimates derived from static regressions. Some form of incorporation of the dynamic structure of the data-generation process, either by means of a non-parametric correction of the static regression estimates or by running dynamic regressions, is

[22] Phillips and Hansen rationalize this behaviour by stating that 'when this condition [$\theta_{21} = 0$] does hold, the parametric nature of the [dynamic] method gives it a natural advantage over our semi-parametric approach' (1990: 119).

TABLE 7.12. Mean (standard deviation) of $t_{(\hat{\beta}-\beta)}$

	$\theta_{21} = 0.8$	$\theta_{21} = 0.4$	$\theta_{21} = 0.0$
$\sigma_{21} = -0.8$			
OLS	−1.616 (1.268)	−1.240 (1.105)	−0.930 (1.00)
D	−1.259 (2.040)	−0.563 (1.701)	−0.003 (1.40)
FM	−0.388 (1.432)	−0.449 (1.092)	−0.025 (0.896)
$\sigma_{21} = -0.4$			
OLS	−1.156 (1.32)	−0.986 (1.25)	−0.754 (1.149)
D	−1.058 (1.69)	−0.636 (1.57)	−0.163 (1.388)
FM	−0.729 (1.49)	−0.516 (1.35)	−0.335 (1.193)
$\sigma_{21} = 0.4$			
OLS	−0.711 (1.19)	−0.520 (1.21)	−0.267 (1.24)
D	−0.664 (1.29)	−0.478 (1.34)	−0.213 (1.37)
FM	−0.606 (1.26)	−0.267 (1.30)	0.096 (1.36)
$\sigma_{21} = 0.8$			
OLS	−0.575 (0.955)	−0.302 (0.979)	−0.098 (1.04)
D	−0.445 (1.15)	−0.339 (1.25)	−0.184 (1.36)
FM	−0.519 (0.922)	−0.102 (0.962)	0.418 (1.12)

Reproduced from Phillips and Hansen (1990).

necessary for inference. While super-consistency theorems show that I(0) terms may be ignored asymptotically in regressions with I(1) variables, these asymptotic results have little bearing on sample sizes common in econometrics, where I(0) terms are important and need to be accommodated.

The other important issue raised by these examples is the weak exogeneity of the conditioning variables for the parameters of interest. Reconsider the DGP in (31) and (32) where $\mathbf{u}_t$ is a first-order autoregressive process, so that a finite lag length dynamic model is valid:

$$y_{1t} - \beta y_{2t} = u_{1t}$$

$$\Delta y_{2t} = u_{2t}$$

where

$$\begin{bmatrix} u_{1t} \\ u_{2t} \end{bmatrix} = \begin{bmatrix} c_{11} & c_{12} \\ c_{21} & c_{22} \end{bmatrix} \begin{bmatrix} u_{1t-1} \\ u_{2t-1} \end{bmatrix} + \begin{bmatrix} \varepsilon_{1t} \\ \varepsilon_{2t} \end{bmatrix}. \tag{60}$$

Then

$$y_{1t} = \beta y_{2t} + c_{11}(y_{1t-1} - \beta y_{2t-1}) + c_{12}\Delta y_{2t-1} + \varepsilon_{1t},$$

or

$$\Delta y_{1t} = \beta \Delta y_{2t} + (c_{11} - 1)(y_{1t-1} - \beta y_{2t-1}) + c_{12}\Delta y_{2t-1} + \varepsilon_{1t},$$

in terms of I(0) variables. Let $E[\varepsilon_{1t}|\varepsilon_{2t}] = \sigma_{12}\sigma_{22}^{-1}\varepsilon_{2t} = \gamma\varepsilon_{2t}$ so $\varepsilon_{1t} = v_t + \gamma\varepsilon_{2t}$; then

$$\begin{aligned}\Delta y_{1t} &= \beta\Delta y_{2t} + (c_{11} - 1)(y_{1t-1} - \beta y_{2t-1}) + c_{12}\Delta y_{2t-1} + v_t + \gamma\varepsilon_{2t} \\ &= (\beta + \gamma)\Delta y_{2t} + (c_{11} - 1 - \gamma c_{21})(y_{1t-1} - \beta y_{2t-1}) \\ &\quad + (c_{12} - \gamma c_{22})\Delta y_{2t-1} + v_t \\ &= \beta^*\Delta y_{2t} + \alpha(y_{1t-1} - \beta y_{2t-1}) + \delta\Delta y_{2t-1} + v_t \\ &= E[\Delta y_{1t}|\Delta y_{2t}, y_{1t-1}, y_{2t-1}, \Delta y_{2t-1}] + v_t. \end{aligned} \tag{61}$$

Further, assume that $\boldsymbol{\theta} = (\beta^* : \alpha : \beta : \delta)'$ denotes the parameters of interest, and indeed that $\boldsymbol{\theta}$ is both constant and invariant to regime shifts affecting Δy_{2t}. Nevertheless, although (61) appears to define a valid conditional model for all values of $\boldsymbol{\theta}$, if $c_{21} \neq 0$ then Δy_{2t} is not weakly exogenous for $\boldsymbol{\theta}$. Because of the resulting non-diagonality of the long-run covariance matrix, this loss of weak exogeneity can have a detrimental impact on the bias and efficiency of the least-squares estimator of $\boldsymbol{\theta}$ in finite samples.

In fact, $c_{21} \neq 0$ jointly violates the weak and strong exogeneity of y_{2t} for $\boldsymbol{\theta}$. To sort out which aspect is dominant, three cases merit comment: the following implications are based on Monte Carlo studies of (61). First, even if $\gamma = 0$, so that there is no simultaneity and $\beta^* = \beta$, the previous conclusion holds. Second, if $\gamma \neq 0$ whereas $c_{21} = 0$, y_{2t} is strongly exogenous for $\boldsymbol{\theta}$ and no problems result. Finally, if strong exogeneity alone is violated, but weak exogeneity holds, as would happen if Δy_{1t-1} directly affected Δy_{2t} when $c_{21} = 0$, there are again no serious bias effects. Thus, the presence of the co-integrating vector in another equation appears to be the primary determinant of the finite-sample bias. Consequently, co-integration forces a renewed emphasis on systems methods if potentially misleading inferences are to be avoided. That is the focus of Chapter 8.

Appendix: Covariance Matrices

Consider the DGP in (A1) where $\mathbf{y}_t$ is the stationary first-order vector autoregressive process:

$$\mathbf{y}_t = \mathbf{A}\mathbf{y}_{t-1} + \boldsymbol{\varepsilon}_t \text{ where } \boldsymbol{\varepsilon}_t \sim \mathsf{IN}(\mathbf{0}, \boldsymbol{\Sigma}), \tag{A1}$$

and all the latent roots of $\mathbf{A}$ lie inside the unit circle. There are three distinct covariance matrices relevant to the analysis, as follows, noting that $E(\mathbf{y}_t) = \mathbf{0}$.

(a) *The conditional (or contemporaneous) covariance matrix*

$$E[(\mathbf{y}_t - E[\mathbf{y}_t|\mathbf{y}_{t-1}])(\mathbf{y}_t - E[\mathbf{y}_t|\mathbf{y}_{t-1}])'|\mathbf{y}_{t-1}] = E(\boldsymbol{\varepsilon}_t\boldsymbol{\varepsilon}_t') = \boldsymbol{\Sigma}. \tag{A2}$$

(b) *The unconditional covariance matrix*

$$E(\mathbf{y}_t\mathbf{y}_t') = \mathbf{G} = E[(\mathbf{A}\mathbf{y}_{t-1} + \boldsymbol{\varepsilon}_t)(\mathbf{y}_{t-1}'\mathbf{A}' + \boldsymbol{\varepsilon}_t')]$$
$$= \mathbf{A}E[\mathbf{y}_{t-1}\mathbf{y}_{t-1}']\mathbf{A}' + E(\boldsymbol{\varepsilon}_t\boldsymbol{\varepsilon}_t')$$
$$= \mathbf{AGA}' + \boldsymbol{\Sigma}, \tag{A3}$$

obtained as shown by substituting (A1) for $\mathbf{y}_t$, multiplying out, and using stationarity. The elements of $\mathbf{G}$ can be obtained by vectoring (A3) and solving.

(c) *The long-run covariance matrix*

Consider the finite sample expression, analogous to $E[T^{-1}S_T^2]$ in the scalar case:

$$E\left[T^{-1}\left(\sum_{t=1}^{T}\mathbf{y}_t\right)\left(\sum_{s=1}^{T}\mathbf{y}_s'\right)\right] = E\left[T^{-1}\sum_{t=1}^{T}\sum_{s=1}^{T}\mathbf{y}_t\mathbf{y}_s'\right]$$
$$= E\left[T^{-1}\sum_{t=1}^{T}\mathbf{y}_t\mathbf{y}_t'\right] + E\left[T^{-1}\sum_{t=1}^{T}\sum_{s=t+1}^{T}\mathbf{y}_t\mathbf{y}_s'\right]$$
$$+ E\left[T^{-1}\sum_{t=1}^{T}\sum_{s=t+1}^{T}\mathbf{y}_s\mathbf{y}_t'\right]$$
$$= \mathbf{G} + \sum_{s=1}^{T-1}E[\mathbf{y}_t\mathbf{y}_{t-s}'] + \sum_{s=1}^{T-1}E[\mathbf{y}_{t-s}\mathbf{y}_t']$$
$$= \mathbf{G} + \mathbf{A}(\mathbf{I} + \mathbf{A} + \mathbf{A}^2 + \mathbf{A}^3 + \ldots + \mathbf{A}^{T-2})\mathbf{G}$$
$$+ \mathbf{G}(\mathbf{I} + \mathbf{A} + \mathbf{A}^2 + \mathbf{A}^3 + \ldots + \mathbf{A}^{T-2})'\mathbf{A}'$$
$$\rightarrow \mathbf{G} + \mathbf{A}(\mathbf{I} - \mathbf{A})^{-1}\mathbf{G} + \mathbf{G}(\mathbf{I} - \mathbf{A}')^{-1}\mathbf{A}'$$
$$= \mathbf{G} + \boldsymbol{\Lambda} + \boldsymbol{\Lambda}' = \boldsymbol{\Omega}. \tag{A4}$$

Rewriting $\boldsymbol{\Omega}$ as $(\mathbf{I} - \mathbf{A})(\mathbf{I} - \mathbf{A})^{-1}\mathbf{G} + \boldsymbol{\Lambda} + \boldsymbol{\Lambda}' + \mathbf{G}(\mathbf{I} - \mathbf{A}')^{-1}(\mathbf{I} - \mathbf{A}') - \mathbf{G}$, on simplifying we have that:

$$\boldsymbol{\Omega} = (\mathbf{I} - \mathbf{A})^{-1}\mathbf{G} + \mathbf{G}(\mathbf{I} - \mathbf{A}')^{-1} - \mathbf{G}.$$

However, a more convenient form of $\boldsymbol{\Omega}$, directly related to the spectral density at the origin, results from (A3):

$$\boldsymbol{\Sigma} = \mathbf{G} - \mathbf{AGA}' = (\mathbf{I} - \mathbf{A})\mathbf{G} + \mathbf{G}(\mathbf{I} - \mathbf{A}') - (\mathbf{I} - \mathbf{A})\mathbf{G}(\mathbf{I} - \mathbf{A}'), \tag{A5}$$

so that on pre-multiplying $\boldsymbol{\Sigma}$ by $(\mathbf{I} - \mathbf{A})^{-1}$ and post-multiplying by $(\mathbf{I} - \mathbf{A}')^{-1}$ and using (A4):

$$\boldsymbol{\Omega} = (\mathbf{I} - \mathbf{A})^{-1}\boldsymbol{\Sigma}(\mathbf{I} - \mathbf{A}')^{-1}. \tag{A6}$$

Similar principles apply to deriving these three matrices in more general weakly stationary processes. As a second example, if (A1) is altered to the first-order moving average:

$$\mathbf{y}_t = \boldsymbol{\varepsilon}_t + \mathbf{B}\boldsymbol{\varepsilon}_{t-1}, \tag{A7}$$

then, using $\mathcal{I}_{t-1}$ to denote available information:

$$E[(\mathbf{y}_t - E[\mathbf{y}_t|\mathcal{I}_{t-1}])(\mathbf{y}_t - E[\mathbf{y}_t|\mathcal{I}_{t-1}])'|\mathcal{I}_{t-1}] = E(\boldsymbol{\varepsilon}_t\boldsymbol{\varepsilon}_t') = \boldsymbol{\Sigma}; \tag{A8}$$

$$E(\mathbf{y}_t\mathbf{y}_t') = \mathbf{H} = E[(\boldsymbol{\varepsilon}_t + \mathbf{B}\boldsymbol{\varepsilon}_{t-1})(\boldsymbol{\varepsilon}_t' + \boldsymbol{\varepsilon}_{t-1}'\mathbf{B}')] = \mathbf{B}\boldsymbol{\Sigma}\mathbf{B}' + \boldsymbol{\Sigma}; \tag{A9}$$

and:

$$\boldsymbol{\Omega} = \mathbf{H} + \mathbf{B}\boldsymbol{\Sigma} + \boldsymbol{\Sigma}\mathbf{B}' = \mathbf{B}\boldsymbol{\Sigma}\mathbf{B}' + \boldsymbol{\Sigma} + \mathbf{B}\boldsymbol{\Sigma} + \boldsymbol{\Sigma}\mathbf{B}' = (\mathbf{I} + \mathbf{B})\boldsymbol{\Sigma}(\mathbf{I} + \mathbf{B}'). \tag{A10}$$

Following Phillips and Durlauf (1986), consider a general I(1) vector process:

$$\mathbf{x}_t = \mathbf{x}_{t-1} + \boldsymbol{v}_t \text{ where } \mathbf{x}_0 = \mathbf{0}, \tag{A11}$$

and $\boldsymbol{v}_t$ is a weakly stationary stochastic process with unconditional covariance $E(\boldsymbol{v}_t\boldsymbol{v}_t') = \mathbf{G}$ and long-run covariance $\boldsymbol{\Omega} = \mathbf{G} + \boldsymbol{\Lambda} + \boldsymbol{\Lambda}'$. From (A4), $\boldsymbol{\Lambda}$ can be written as:

$$\boldsymbol{\Lambda} = \sum_{j=1}^{\infty} E(\boldsymbol{v}_0\boldsymbol{v}_j'). \tag{A12}$$

Extending the analysis in Chapter 3 to allow for vector processes, and in the appendix to Chapter 6 to allow for non-IID errors, $\mathbf{x}_T/\sqrt{T}$ converges to the vector Brownian motion BM($\boldsymbol{\Omega}$):

$$T^{-1/2}\sum_{t=1}^{[Tr]} \boldsymbol{v}_t \Rightarrow \mathbf{B}(r). \tag{A13}$$

Then:

$$T^{-1}\sum_{t=1}^{T} \mathbf{x}_{t-1}\boldsymbol{v}_t' \Rightarrow \int_0^1 \mathbf{B}(r)\,\mathrm{d}\mathbf{B}(r)' + \boldsymbol{\Lambda}; \tag{A14}$$

$$T^{-1}\sum_{t=1}^{T} \mathbf{x}_t\boldsymbol{v}_t' \Rightarrow \int_0^1 \mathbf{B}(r)\,\mathrm{d}\mathbf{B}(r)' + \mathbf{G} + \boldsymbol{\Lambda}. \tag{A15}$$

These vector formulae could be standardized using $\mathbf{V}(r) = \mathbf{K}'\mathbf{B}(r)$ where $\boldsymbol{\Omega}^{-1} = \mathbf{KK}'$.

8

Co-integration in Systems of Equations

We have so far considered only single-equation estimation and testing. While the estimation of single equations is convenient and often efficient, for some purposes only estimation of a system provides sufficient information. This is true, for example, when we consider the estimation of multiple co-integrating vectors, and inference about the number of such vectors. Traditionally, systems have been estimated when there is a failure of weak exogeneity in a single equation, and these considerations also apply here. This chapter examines methods of finding the co-integrating rank, considers circumstances when dynamic single-equation methods will be asymptotically equivalent to systems methods, and provides examples to illustrate these issues. Asymptotic distributions are also derived.

In earlier chapters, we investigated data series containing unit roots in their scalar autoregressive representations (i.e. their marginal distributions), and denoted such series as I(1). In this chapter we will consider a vector time series of dimension n, $\mathbf{x}_t = (x_{1t}, x_{2t}, \ldots, x_{nt})'$ (generalizing the analysis to any number of variables), where $\mathbf{x}_t$ is I(1) so that $\Delta\mathbf{x}_t$ is I(0). Generally, any arbitrary linear combination of the elements of $\mathbf{x}_t$, say $\mathbf{w}_t = \boldsymbol{\alpha}'\mathbf{x}_t$, will also be I(1), and such linear combinations imply or give rise to *spurious regressions*. However, there may exist vectors $\boldsymbol{\alpha}_i$ such that

$$\mathbf{w}_t = \boldsymbol{\alpha}_i'\mathbf{x}_t \sim \mathrm{I}(0), \qquad i = 1, 2, \ldots, r,$$

in which case the relevant components of $\mathbf{x}_t$ are co-integrated.

In the simplest bivariate case, as we have seen, we may take $\mathbf{x}_t = (y_t, z_t)'$, where y_t and z_t are individually I(1). The arbitrary linear combination $(y_t - \kappa z_t)$ will also be I(1), but if there exists a value κ_1 of κ such that $(y_t - \kappa_1 z_t) \sim \mathrm{I}(0)$, then y_t and z_t are co-integrated. Letting $\boldsymbol{\alpha}_1' = (1, -\kappa_1)$ be the co-integrating vector in this case, $\boldsymbol{\alpha}_1$ must be unique, since for any other value κ^*, then $y_t - \kappa^* z_t = y_t - \kappa_1 z_t + (\kappa_1 - \kappa^*)z_t = w_t + (\kappa_1 - \kappa^*)z_t$, which is the sum of an I(0) process and an I(1) process, and therefore I(1) unless $\kappa_1 = \kappa^*$.

For n elements in $\mathbf{x}_t \sim I(1)$, there can be, at most, $n-1$ co-integrating combinations.[1] Hence $0 \leqslant r \leqslant n-1$ and the r vectors may be gathered in an $n \times r$ matrix $\boldsymbol{\alpha} = [\boldsymbol{\alpha}_1, \boldsymbol{\alpha}_2, \ldots, \boldsymbol{\alpha}_r]$. Outside the bivariate model, $n > 2$ and the co-integrating matrix is no longer unique in the absence of prior information. We noted in Chapter 2 the related issue for stationary equilibria, only some of which need correspond to substantive economic hypotheses.

A simple case of non-uniqueness occurs when subsets of the x_{it} are co-integrated. In fact, for any non-singular $r \times r$ matrix $\mathbf{F}$, $\mathbf{w}_t^* = \mathbf{F}\boldsymbol{\alpha}'\mathbf{x}_t = \boldsymbol{\alpha}^{*\prime}\mathbf{x}_t$ is also I(0). This last result shows that linear combinations of the co-integrating vectors themselves form co-integrating combinations. Since $\boldsymbol{\alpha}_j'\mathbf{x}_t$ and $\boldsymbol{\alpha}_i'\mathbf{x}_t$ are I(0), so is any linear combination thereof. In the terminology of linear algebra, the dimension of the co-integrating space (given by the rank of the matrix $\boldsymbol{\alpha}$) is r and the columns of $\boldsymbol{\alpha}$ form the *basis* vectors of this space. Pre-multiplying $\boldsymbol{\alpha}'$ by an $r \times r$ non-singular matrix $\mathbf{F}$ does not alter either the co-integrating space or its dimensions. Therefore, strictly speaking, estimating the co-integrating matrix $\boldsymbol{\alpha}$ essentially involves deriving the basis vectors. The matrix $\boldsymbol{\alpha}$ is non-unique in the absence of prior information.

A brief justification may be offered for focusing on the open interval $(0, n)$ of $\mathbb{N}$, as the domain of values for r. When $r = n$, $\mathbf{x}_t$ must be I(0), as shown in Section 8.1 below. We therefore exclude this case when we know that $\mathbf{x}_t$ is I(1) and only consider stochastic processes where variables are marginally I(1). Thus, $n - r > 0$, and we can re-express the process $\{\mathbf{x}_t\}$ in terms of I(0) processes, using the r co-integrating relationships and $n - r$ first differences of the process. The case of $r = 0$ is a trivial one as it implies the absence of even a single co-integrating vector and suggests respecification of the system in differences.

As we saw in Chapter 5, Engle and Granger (1987) established an isomorphism between co-integration and error-correction models. In order to examine co-integration in systems of equations, we will derive that result, formulating the system in ECM form, in some detail below, starting this time from the moving-average representation of the process. From that system, a maximum likelihood estimator (MLE) of r, the number of co-integrating relationships, will be obtained based on a method proposed by Johansen (1988). This will in turn enable us to test hypotheses concerning the dimension of the co-integration space, and establish a 'central value' of $\boldsymbol{\alpha}$.

[1] A proof of this result is given in Sect. 8.1.

8.1. Co-integration and Error Correction

We now return to the representation of a co-integrated system in autoregressive or (equivalently) in error-correction form. When $\{\Delta\mathbf{x}_t\}$ is a stationary process (possibly) with drift, we can express it as a multivariate moving average using the Wold (1954) decomposition theorem:

$$\Delta\mathbf{x}_t = \mathbf{C}(L)(\mathbf{m} + \mathbf{e}_t), \tag{1}$$

where $\mathbf{e}_t \sim \text{IID}(\mathbf{0}, \boldsymbol{\Omega})$; L is again the lag operator, and $\mathbf{C}(L)$ is a polynomial matrix in L given by

$$\mathbf{C}(L) = \sum_{i=0}^{\infty} \mathbf{C}_i L^i, \qquad \mathbf{C}_0 = \mathbf{I}_n.$$

The cumulative or total effect from $\mathbf{C}(L)$ is given by

$$\mathbf{C}(1) = \left(\mathbf{I}_n + \sum_{i=1}^{\infty} \mathbf{C}_i\right) < \infty,$$

where the $\mathbf{C}_i$ again obey an exponential decay condition of the form discussed in Chapter 5. Using $\mathbf{C}(1)$, we can rewrite $\mathbf{C}(L)$ as

$$\mathbf{C}(L) = \mathbf{C}(1) + (1 - L)\mathbf{C}^*(L) \tag{2}$$

where $\mathbf{C}^*(L) = \sum_{i=0}^{\infty} \mathbf{C}_i^* L^i$ and $\mathbf{C}_i^* = -\sum_{j=i+1}^{\infty} \mathbf{C}_j$ so that $\mathbf{C}_0^* = \mathbf{I}_n - \mathbf{C}(1)$. Note that the existence of these matrices is again guaranteed by the exponential decay condition. Thus, from (1),

$$\Delta\mathbf{x}_t = \mathbf{C}(1)\mathbf{m} + \mathbf{C}(1)\mathbf{e}_t + \mathbf{C}^*(L)\Delta\mathbf{e}_t,$$

or

$$(\Delta\mathbf{x}_t - \boldsymbol{\mu}) = \mathbf{C}(1)\mathbf{e}_t + \mathbf{C}^*(L)\Delta\mathbf{e}_t, \tag{3}$$

where $\boldsymbol{\mu} = \mathbf{C}(1)\mathbf{m}$.

The key assumptions needed to derive the autoregressive representation of the process are given below. As in Chapter 5, the proof follows Johansen (1991*a*).

Assumption B1. The characteristic polynomial,

$$\mathbf{C}(z) = \sum_{i=1}^{\infty} \mathbf{C}_i z^i,$$

has roots either equal to or strictly greater than 1; that is, $|\mathbf{C}(z)| = 0$ implies that either $|z| > 1$ or $z = 1$.

Assumption B2. The matrix $\mathbf{C}(1)$ has reduced rank $n - r$ and is therefore expressible as the product of two $n \times (n - r)$ matrices $\boldsymbol{\phi}$ and $\boldsymbol{\eta}$, where $\boldsymbol{\phi}$ and $\boldsymbol{\eta}$ have rank $n - r$. Thus, $\mathbf{C}(1) = \boldsymbol{\phi}\boldsymbol{\eta}'$.

Assumption B3. The $r \times r$ matrix $\boldsymbol{\phi}'_{\perp}\mathbf{C}^*(1)\boldsymbol{\eta}_{\perp}$ has full rank r.[2]

Assumptions B1–B3 are analogous to Assumptions A1–A3 in Chapter 5. Given our results on $\mathbf{C}(1)$ in Chapter 5, it is natural to require that $\mathbf{C}(1)$ be of reduced rank and have rank $n - r$. Also, $r = n$ implies that $\mathbf{C}(1)$ is identically the null matrix. Thus, from (3), $(\Delta\mathbf{x}_t - \boldsymbol{\mu}) = \mathbf{C}^*(L)\Delta\mathbf{e}_t$, which implies, after integration, that $\mathbf{x}_t$ is integrated (at most) of order 0. Assumption B3 then rules out the possibility that $\mathbf{C}^*(L)$ has a root on the unit circle, so $\mathbf{x}_t$ cannot be integrated of order -1. In either case, we have a contradiction of the assumption that the components of $\mathbf{x}_t$ are I(1).

To derive the autoregressive representation, multiply (3) by $\boldsymbol{\phi}'$ and $\boldsymbol{\phi}'_{\perp}$ respectively to obtain the equations

$$\boldsymbol{\phi}'\boldsymbol{\phi}\boldsymbol{\eta}'\mathbf{e}_t + \boldsymbol{\phi}'\mathbf{C}^*(L)\Delta\mathbf{e}_t = \boldsymbol{\phi}'(\Delta\mathbf{x}_t - \boldsymbol{\mu}) \tag{4a}$$

$$\boldsymbol{\phi}'_{\perp}\mathbf{C}^*(L)\Delta\mathbf{e}_t = \boldsymbol{\phi}'_{\perp}(\Delta\mathbf{x}_t - \boldsymbol{\mu}), \tag{4b}$$

using the decomposition $\mathbf{C}(1) = \boldsymbol{\phi}\boldsymbol{\eta}'$ and the result that $\boldsymbol{\phi}'_{\perp}\boldsymbol{\phi} = \mathbf{0}_{r\times(n-r)}$. The matrix $\mathbf{C}(1)$ is not invertible and the system given by (4a) and (4b) therefore cannot be inverted directly to express the x_{it} in terms of the e_{it}. An invertible system is obtained by defining, as in Chapter 5, two new variables, $\mathbf{w}_t = (\boldsymbol{\eta}'\boldsymbol{\eta})^{-1}\boldsymbol{\eta}'\mathbf{e}_t$ and $\mathbf{y}_t = (\boldsymbol{\eta}'_{\perp}\boldsymbol{\eta}_{\perp})^{-1}\boldsymbol{\eta}'_{\perp}\Delta\mathbf{e}_t$. Repeating the steps used in Chapter 5, the matrices $\bar{\boldsymbol{\eta}}$ and $\bar{\boldsymbol{\eta}}_{\perp}$ are defined as $\boldsymbol{\eta}(\boldsymbol{\eta}'\boldsymbol{\eta})^{-1}$ and $\boldsymbol{\eta}_{\perp}(\boldsymbol{\eta}'_{\perp}\boldsymbol{\eta}_{\perp})^{-1}$ respectively. Next, again as in Chapter 5,

$$\Delta\mathbf{e}_t = (\boldsymbol{\eta}\bar{\boldsymbol{\eta}}' + \boldsymbol{\eta}_{\perp}\bar{\boldsymbol{\eta}}'_{\perp})\Delta\mathbf{e}_t = \boldsymbol{\eta}_{\perp}\mathbf{y}_t + \boldsymbol{\eta}\Delta\mathbf{w}_t.$$

Substituting into (4a) and (4b) gives

$$(\boldsymbol{\phi}'\boldsymbol{\phi})(\boldsymbol{\eta}'\boldsymbol{\eta})\mathbf{w}_t + \boldsymbol{\phi}'\mathbf{C}^*(L)\boldsymbol{\eta}\Delta\mathbf{w}_t + \boldsymbol{\phi}'\mathbf{C}^*(L)\boldsymbol{\eta}_{\perp}\mathbf{y}_t = \boldsymbol{\phi}'(\Delta\mathbf{x}_t - \boldsymbol{\mu}) \tag{5a}$$

$$\boldsymbol{\phi}'_{\perp}\mathbf{C}^*(L)\boldsymbol{\eta}\Delta\mathbf{w}_t + \boldsymbol{\phi}'_{\perp}\mathbf{C}^*(L)\boldsymbol{\eta}_{\perp}\mathbf{y}_t = \boldsymbol{\phi}'_{\perp}(\Delta\mathbf{x}_t - \boldsymbol{\mu}). \tag{5b}$$

We therefore have

$$\widetilde{\mathbf{B}}(L)(\mathbf{w}'_t, \mathbf{y}'_t)' = (\boldsymbol{\phi}, \boldsymbol{\phi}_{\perp})'(\Delta\mathbf{x}_t - \boldsymbol{\mu})$$

with

$$\widetilde{\mathbf{B}}(z) = \begin{bmatrix} (\boldsymbol{\phi}'\boldsymbol{\phi})(\boldsymbol{\eta}'\boldsymbol{\eta}) + \boldsymbol{\phi}'\mathbf{C}^*(z)\boldsymbol{\eta}(1 - z) & \boldsymbol{\phi}'\mathbf{C}^*(z)\boldsymbol{\eta}_{\perp} \\ \boldsymbol{\phi}'_{\perp}\mathbf{C}^*(z)\boldsymbol{\eta}(1 - z) & \boldsymbol{\phi}'_{\perp}\mathbf{C}^*(z)\boldsymbol{\eta}_{\perp} \end{bmatrix}. \tag{6}$$

For $z = 1$, this matrix has determinant

$$|\widetilde{\mathbf{B}}(1)| = |\boldsymbol{\phi}'\boldsymbol{\phi}||\boldsymbol{\eta}'\boldsymbol{\eta}||\boldsymbol{\phi}'_{\perp}\mathbf{C}^*(1)\boldsymbol{\eta}_{\perp}|,$$

[2] The orthogonal complement of a matrix is defined in Sect. 5.3.1. Using this definition, $\boldsymbol{\phi}_{\perp}$ and $\boldsymbol{\eta}_{\perp}$ are $n \times r$ dimensional matrices with rank r.

which is non-zero, using Assumptions B2 and B3. Thus, $\widetilde{\mathbf{B}}(z)$ does not have a root at 1. For $|z| > 1$,

$$\widetilde{\mathbf{B}}(z) = (\boldsymbol{\phi}, \boldsymbol{\phi}_\perp)'\mathbf{C}(z)[\boldsymbol{\eta}, \boldsymbol{\eta}_\perp(1 - z)^{-1}], \tag{7}$$

where (7) may be shown by substituting for $\mathbf{C}^*(z)$ in $\widetilde{\mathbf{B}}(z)$ in terms of $\mathbf{C}(z)$ and $\mathbf{C}(1) = \boldsymbol{\phi\eta}'$, and using the orthogonality condition $\boldsymbol{\phi}'_\perp\boldsymbol{\phi} = \boldsymbol{\eta}'_\perp\boldsymbol{\eta} = \mathbf{0}_{r\times(n-r)}$. For $z > 1$, from (7),

$$|\widetilde{\mathbf{B}}(z)| = |(\boldsymbol{\phi}, \boldsymbol{\phi}_\perp)||\mathbf{C}(z)||(\boldsymbol{\eta}, \boldsymbol{\eta}_\perp)|(1 - z)^{-r}.$$

Thus for $z > 1$, $|\widetilde{\mathbf{B}}(z)| = 0$ if and only if $|\mathbf{C}(z)| = 0$. Excluding $z = 1$, by Assumption B1 the only remaining roots of this determinant lie outside the unit circle.

All the roots of $|\widetilde{\mathbf{B}}(z)| = 0$ are therefore outside the unit disk, and the system defined by (5*a*) and (5*b*) is invertible. Thus, from (6),

$$(\mathbf{w}'_t, \mathbf{y}'_t)' = \widetilde{\mathbf{B}}(L)^{-1}(\boldsymbol{\phi}, \boldsymbol{\phi}_\perp)'(\Delta\mathbf{x}_t - \boldsymbol{\mu}).$$

Also from (6), note that

$$\widetilde{\mathbf{B}}(1) = \begin{bmatrix} (\boldsymbol{\phi}'\boldsymbol{\phi})(\boldsymbol{\eta}'\boldsymbol{\eta}) & \boldsymbol{\phi}'\mathbf{C}^*(1)\boldsymbol{\eta}_\perp \\ \mathbf{0} & \boldsymbol{\phi}'_\perp\mathbf{C}^*(1)\boldsymbol{\eta}_\perp \end{bmatrix},$$

and, using the formula for inversion of partitioned matrices,

$$\widetilde{\mathbf{B}}(1)^{-1} = \begin{bmatrix} (\boldsymbol{\eta}'\boldsymbol{\eta})^{-1}(\boldsymbol{\phi}'\boldsymbol{\phi})^{-1} & -(\boldsymbol{\eta}'\boldsymbol{\eta})^{-1}(\boldsymbol{\phi}'\boldsymbol{\phi})^{-1}\boldsymbol{\phi}'\mathbf{C}^*(1)\boldsymbol{\eta}_\perp(\boldsymbol{\phi}'_\perp\mathbf{C}^*(1)\boldsymbol{\eta}_\perp)^{-1} \\ \mathbf{0} & (\boldsymbol{\phi}'_\perp\mathbf{C}^*(1)\boldsymbol{\eta}_\perp)^{-1} \end{bmatrix}. \tag{8}$$

From the definition of $\Delta\mathbf{e}_t$,

$$\begin{aligned} \Delta\mathbf{e}_t = \boldsymbol{\eta}\Delta\mathbf{w}_t + \boldsymbol{\eta}_\perp\mathbf{y}_t &= [\boldsymbol{\eta}(1 - L), \boldsymbol{\eta}_\perp](\mathbf{w}'_t, \mathbf{y}'_t)' \\ &= [\boldsymbol{\eta}(1 - L), \boldsymbol{\eta}_\perp](\widetilde{\mathbf{B}}(L))^{-1}[(\boldsymbol{\phi}, \boldsymbol{\phi}_\perp)'(\Delta\mathbf{x}_t - \boldsymbol{\mu})] \\ &= \mathbf{F}(L)(\Delta\mathbf{x}_t - \boldsymbol{\mu}), \end{aligned} \tag{9}$$

where $\mathbf{F}(L) = [\boldsymbol{\eta}(1 - L), \boldsymbol{\eta}_\perp](\widetilde{\mathbf{B}}(L))^{-1}[(\boldsymbol{\phi}, \boldsymbol{\phi}_\perp)']$.

Integrating (9) gives

$$\mathbf{F}(L)\mathbf{x}_t = \mathbf{F}(1)t\boldsymbol{\mu} + \mathbf{e}_t + \mathbf{x}_0,$$

where $\mathbf{x}_0$ is the constant of integration. To derive the value of $\mathbf{F}(1)$, note that

$$\mathbf{F}(1) = (\mathbf{0}_{n\times(n-r)}, \boldsymbol{\eta}_\perp)(\widetilde{\mathbf{B}}(1))^{-1}[(\boldsymbol{\phi}, \boldsymbol{\phi}_\perp)'].$$

Substituting for $(\widetilde{\mathbf{B}}(1))^{-1}$ from (8) gives $\mathbf{F}(1) = \boldsymbol{\eta}_\perp(\boldsymbol{\phi}'_\perp\mathbf{C}^*(1)\boldsymbol{\eta}_\perp)^{-1}\boldsymbol{\phi}'_\perp$. Thus, recalling that $\boldsymbol{\mu} = \mathbf{C}(1)\mathbf{m} = (\boldsymbol{\phi\eta}')\mathbf{m}$, $\mathbf{F}(1)\boldsymbol{\mu} = \mathbf{0}_{n\times 1}$. The autoregressive representation, in its final form, is therefore given by

$$\mathbf{F}(L)\mathbf{x}_t = \mathbf{x}_0 + \mathbf{e}_t.$$

Several features of the derivations above are noteworthy, particularly with respect to the $\mathbf{F}(1)$ matrix. First, $\mathbf{F}(1)\mathbf{C}(1) = \mathbf{C}(1)\mathbf{F}(1) = \mathbf{0}_n$. This result follows from substituting $\boldsymbol{\eta}_\perp(\boldsymbol{\phi}'_\perp\mathbf{C}^*(1)\boldsymbol{\eta}_\perp)^{-1}\boldsymbol{\phi}'_\perp$ for $\mathbf{F}(1)$ and $\boldsymbol{\phi\eta}'$ for $\mathbf{C}(1)$ and using the orthogonality conditions. This re-emphasizes the duality, first mentioned in Chapter 5, between the impact matrix in the MA representation, given by $\mathbf{C}(1)$, and the impact matrix in the AR representation, given here by $\mathbf{F}(1)$. The null space of the former is the range space of the latter and vice versa.

Second, the isomorphism of $\mathbf{F}(1)$ with the $\boldsymbol{\gamma\alpha}'$ matrix in Chapter 5 can be demonstrated easily. Note that

(i) $\mathbf{C}(1)\boldsymbol{\eta}_\perp(\boldsymbol{\phi}'_\perp\mathbf{C}^*(1)\boldsymbol{\eta}_\perp)^{-1} = \mathbf{0}_{n\times r}$;

(ii) $\boldsymbol{\phi}'_\perp\mathbf{C}(1) = \mathbf{0}_{r\times n}$.

Both $\boldsymbol{\eta}_\perp(\boldsymbol{\phi}'_\perp\mathbf{C}^*(1)\boldsymbol{\eta}_\perp)^{-1}$ and $\boldsymbol{\phi}_\perp$ are matrices of rank r and dimension $n \times r$. Thus, redefining $\boldsymbol{\phi}'_\perp$ as $\boldsymbol{\alpha}'$ and $\boldsymbol{\eta}_\perp(\boldsymbol{\phi}'_\perp\mathbf{C}^*(1)\boldsymbol{\eta}_\perp)^{-1}$ as $\boldsymbol{\gamma}$, we have $\mathbf{F}(1) = \boldsymbol{\gamma\alpha}'$, which is an $n \times n$ matrix with rank r and is isomorphic to $\boldsymbol{\pi}$. It is natural to define $\boldsymbol{\phi}'_\perp\mathbf{x}_t$ ($\boldsymbol{\alpha}'\mathbf{x}_t$ in Chapter 5) as the co-integrated combinations of the x_{it}. Integrating (4*b*) shows that $\boldsymbol{\phi}'_\perp\mathbf{x}_t$ does not contain an integrated component of the form $\sum_{i=1}^t \mathbf{e}_i$. Further, by the orthogonality of $\boldsymbol{\mu}$ with $\boldsymbol{\phi}_\perp$, the co-integrating combinations do not contain a trend. Both these results match exactly the corresponding results on $\boldsymbol{\alpha}'\mathbf{x}_t$ in Chapter 5.

Third, if $\widetilde{\mathbf{B}}(L)$ were not of full rank, it would be possible to extract another unit root in the representation given by (6), and the system would be I(0) instead of I(1), as assumed originally. The importance of Assumption B3 is now clear. Finally, using the result that the rank of $\mathbf{F}(1)$ is r, it is possible to rewrite the model in error-correction form as

$$\Delta\mathbf{x}_t = \mathbf{D}(L)\Delta\mathbf{x}_{t-1} + \mathbf{x}_0 + \mathbf{F}(1)\mathbf{x}_{t-k} + \mathbf{e}_t, \tag{10}$$

where $\mathbf{F}(1)$, like $\boldsymbol{\pi}$ in Chapter 5, is a matrix of rank r and can therefore be decomposed into two $n \times r$ matrices, each of rank r. The steps involved in going from the final autoregressive form of the system to the ECM form are given in (5.25)–(5.27), with $\boldsymbol{\pi}$ playing the role of $\mathbf{F}(1)$.

Sections 5.3 and 8.1 have demonstrated the isomorphism of the moving-average, error-correction, and autoregressive representations of co-integrated processes. The next section returns to the autoregressive representation and relates this to the method used by Johansen (1988) which tests the rank of $\boldsymbol{\pi} = \boldsymbol{\gamma\alpha}'$, since, if there are r co-integrating vectors and $\boldsymbol{\gamma\alpha}' = \boldsymbol{\pi}$, then rank $(\boldsymbol{\pi}) = r$. The non-uniqueness of these vectors (in the absence of *a priori* information) is easily seen:

$$\boldsymbol{\pi} = \boldsymbol{\gamma\alpha}' = \boldsymbol{\gamma}\mathbf{P}\mathbf{P}^{-1}\boldsymbol{\alpha}' = \boldsymbol{\gamma}^*\boldsymbol{\alpha}^{*\prime},$$

for all $r \times r$ non-singular matrices $\mathbf{P}$. However, since rank $(\boldsymbol{\alpha}) = r$, we can normalize $\boldsymbol{\alpha}^*$ (perhaps after suitable rearrangement of the variables) such that $\boldsymbol{\alpha}^{*\prime} = (\mathbf{I}_r : \boldsymbol{\beta}')$, and so $\boldsymbol{\alpha}^{*\prime}\mathbf{x}_t = \mathbf{x}_{at} + \boldsymbol{\beta}'\mathbf{x}_{bt}$ where $\mathbf{x}'_t = (\mathbf{x}'_{at} : \mathbf{x}'_{bt})$.

An important point for inference, given (10), is that the ECM terms $\boldsymbol{\alpha}'\mathbf{x}_{t-k}$ will generally enter more than one equation. This will violate weak exogeneity when $\boldsymbol{\alpha}$ is a parameter of interest, since the ECMs will be present in some of the other marginal distributions, and will therefore necessitate joint estimation for efficiency as discussed in Chapter 7 (see e.g. Phillips 1991, and Phillips and Hansen 1990). Hence a necessary condition for the use of single-equation methods to be appropriate in the analysis of co-integrated systems is that the relevant ECM terms enter *only* the equation under study; this is clearly not a sufficient condition, since it is possible that there can be links between other parameters.

As an illustration of (10), consider the case where $n = 2$ and $r = 1$. Let $\boldsymbol{\alpha}' = (1, -\kappa)$ and $\mathbf{x}_0 = \mathbf{0}$, so that the respective systems become

$$x_{1t} - \kappa x_{2t} = u_{1t},$$
$$\Delta x_{2t} = u_{2t}, \tag{11}$$

and

$$\left.\begin{aligned} \Delta x_{1t} &= d_{12}(L)\Delta x_{2t} + d_{11}(L)\Delta x_{1t-1} + \gamma_1(x_{1t-k} - \kappa x_{2t-k}) + e_{1t} \\ \Delta x_{2t} &= d_{21}(L)\Delta x_{1t} + d_{22}(L)\Delta x_{2t-1} + \gamma_2(x_{1t-k} - \kappa x_{2t-k}) + e_{2t} \end{aligned}\right\}. \tag{11'}$$

The form in (11) is the 'canonical' representation in I(0) space, and Phillips (1991) focuses on estimation of this system. When $E(u_{1t}u_{2t}) \neq 0$, a 'simultaneity problem' is present, but this can be dealt with by the inclusion of Δx_{2t} as a regressor in the first equation of (11). The functional central-limit theorems for Wiener processes noted in earlier chapters apply despite the serial dependence in $\mathbf{u}_t = [u_{1t}, u_{2t}]'$, and direct estimation of κ in the first equation of (11) can be seen as the method originally proposed by Engle and Granger (1987). Inference must, however, allow for the serial dependence in $\mathbf{u}_t$.

The latter system, (11′), highlights the 'structural' form. At least one of γ_1 or γ_2 must be non-zero, since otherwise the system can be expressed in terms of differenced variables alone. Weak exogeneity is violated by (among other possibilities) $\gamma_1\gamma_2 \neq 0$. Since we are unlikely to know *a priori* which other equations are influenced by any given ECM, we turn now to a method of estimating the co-integrating rank r of a system, which will also allow tests of this aspect of weak exogeneity.

8.2. Estimating Co-integrating Vectors in Systems

Consider the linear system in (10) rewritten as

$$\Delta\mathbf{x}_t = \sum_{i=1}^{k-1} \mathbf{D}_i \Delta\mathbf{x}_{t-i} + \boldsymbol{\pi}\mathbf{x}_{t-k} + \mathbf{e}_t, \qquad t = 1, \ldots, T, \tag{12}$$

where, for simplicity, we have excluded deterministic terms such as trends or constants. We shall return to a consideration of these in Section 8.5. In general, the number of co-integrating vectors will be unknown in empirical modelling, and must first be determined from the data. This step is important, because both under- and over-estimation of r have potentially serious consequences for estimation and inference.

Under-estimation implies the omission of empirically relevant error-correction terms, with these omitted terms being relegated to $\mathbf{e}_t$. Over-estimation implies that the distributions of statistics will be non-standard. This may be demonstrated by inspection of (12). If $\boldsymbol{\pi}$ is correctly specified, all the variables in (12) are I(0) and standard distributional results apply. However $\boldsymbol{\pi}\mathbf{x}_{t-k}$ will not be I(0) if the matrix $\boldsymbol{\alpha}$ contains vectors $\boldsymbol{\alpha}_\ell$, say, such that $\boldsymbol{\alpha}'_\ell \mathbf{x}_{t-k}$ is not a co-integrating combination and is therefore I(1). The vector $\boldsymbol{\pi}\mathbf{x}_{t-k}$ will have a mixture of I(0) and I(1) terms corresponding to the correct and incorrect (or over-estimated) co-integrating vectors respectively. Incorrect inferences will result from the use of conventional critical values in tests. We will see later that this may also have an adverse effect on forecasting accuracy.

Once r is known, we can proceed to estimate $\boldsymbol{\alpha}$ and $\boldsymbol{\gamma}$, noting that non-singular linear combinations of these matrices provide equivalent representations. Indeed, $(\boldsymbol{\alpha} : \boldsymbol{\gamma})$ is an over-parameterization of $\boldsymbol{\pi}$, so only the dimension of the co-integrating space can be established directly.

A test for the null hypothesis that there are r co-integrating vectors can be based on the maximum likelihood approach proposed by Johansen (1988). The test is equivalent to testing whether $\boldsymbol{\pi} = \boldsymbol{\gamma}\boldsymbol{\alpha}'$, where $\boldsymbol{\alpha}$ and $\boldsymbol{\gamma}$ are $n \times r$; hence it is a test of the hypothesis that $\boldsymbol{\pi}$ has less than full rank.

We emphasize that, of the three distinct cases, (i) $r = n$, (ii) $r = 0$, and (iii) $0 < r < n$, only case (iii) will be considered formally. We have already shown that case (i) implies that all the variables in $\mathbf{x}_t$ are I(0) and would only be of interest if our initial assumption, that $\mathbf{x}_t$ is I(1), were incorrect. In case (ii), $\boldsymbol{\pi} = \mathbf{0}$ and the system ought to be respecified in differences to achieve stationarity. We can potentially cover this case as an extreme of case (iii).

For $0 < r < n$, under the assumptions that (12) is the DGP, that all coefficient matrices are constant, that $\mathbf{x}_{1-k} \ldots \mathbf{x}_0$ are given and that[3]

$$\mathbf{e}_t \sim \mathrm{IN}(\mathbf{0}, \boldsymbol{\Omega}),$$

[3] Phillips and Durlauf (1986) derive the limiting distribution of the least-squares estimator of (the equivalent of) $\boldsymbol{\pi}$, allowing for more general error processes.

the log-likelihood function is derived from the multivariate normal distribution:[4]

$$L(\mathbf{D}_1, \ldots, \mathbf{D}_{k-1}, \boldsymbol{\pi}, \boldsymbol{\Omega}|(\mathbf{x}_1, \ldots, \mathbf{x}_T)) = \frac{Tn}{2}\log(2\Pi) - \frac{T}{2}\log|\boldsymbol{\Omega}| - \frac{1}{2}\sum_{t=1}^{T}\mathbf{e}_t'\boldsymbol{\Omega}^{-1}\mathbf{e}_t. \tag{13}$$

The first step is to concentrate $L(\cdot)$ with respect to $\boldsymbol{\Omega}$, which involves no new considerations, and yields the conventional result that $\hat{\boldsymbol{\Omega}} = T^{-1}\sum_{t=1}^{T}\mathbf{e}_t\mathbf{e}_t'$. Next, we remove the known I(0) variables from (12) to focus on the matrix of interest $\boldsymbol{\pi}$, which requires concentrating $L(\cdot)$ with respect to $(\mathbf{D}_1, \ldots, \mathbf{D}_{k-1})$. To do so, since the $\{\mathbf{D}_i\}$ are unrestricted, we can partial out the effects of $(\Delta\mathbf{x}_{t-1}, \ldots, \Delta\mathbf{x}_{t-k+1})$ from both $\Delta\mathbf{x}_t$ and $\mathbf{x}_{t-k}$ by regression, to obtain residuals $\mathbf{R}_{0t}$ and $\mathbf{R}_{kt}$ respectively. Let $\mathbf{q}_t = (\Delta\mathbf{x}_{t-1}', \ldots, \Delta\mathbf{x}_{t-k+1}')'$; then

$$\mathbf{R}_{0t} = \Delta\mathbf{x}_t - \sum_{i=1}^{k-1}\hat{\mathbf{D}}_i\Delta\mathbf{x}_{t-i}, \tag{14}$$

where

$$(\hat{\mathbf{D}}_1, \ldots, \hat{\mathbf{D}}_{k-1}) = \left(\sum_{t=1}^{T}\Delta\mathbf{x}_t\mathbf{q}_t'\right)\left(\sum_{t=1}^{T}\mathbf{q}_t\mathbf{q}_t'\right)^{-1} \tag{15}$$

and

$$\mathbf{R}_{kt} = \mathbf{x}_{t-k} - \sum_{i=1}^{k-1}\tilde{\mathbf{D}}_i\Delta\mathbf{x}_{t-i}, \tag{16}$$

$$(\tilde{\mathbf{D}}_1, \ldots, \tilde{\mathbf{D}}_{k-1}) = \left(\sum_{t=1}^{T}\mathbf{x}_{t-k}\mathbf{q}_t'\right)\left(\sum_{t=1}^{T}\mathbf{q}_t\mathbf{q}_t'\right)^{-1}. \tag{17}$$

The concentrated likelihood function $L^*(\boldsymbol{\pi})$ now depends only on $\{\mathbf{R}_{0t}, \mathbf{R}_{kt}\}$ and takes the form

$$L^*(\boldsymbol{\pi}) = K - \frac{T}{2}\log\left|\sum_{t=1}^{T}(\mathbf{R}_{0t} - \boldsymbol{\pi}\mathbf{R}_{kt})(\mathbf{R}_{0t} - \boldsymbol{\pi}\mathbf{R}_{kt})'\right|. \tag{18}$$

Next, we compute the second-moment matrices of all of these residuals and their cross-products, $\mathbf{S}_{00}, \mathbf{S}_{0k}, \mathbf{S}_{k0}, \mathbf{S}_{kk}$, where

$$\mathbf{S}_{ij} = T^{-1}\sum_{t=1}^{T}\mathbf{R}_{it}\mathbf{R}_{jt}', \qquad i, j = 0, k. \tag{19}$$

[4] Note that we use the upper-case Π for the ratio of the circumference of a circle to its diameter, as opposed to the lower-case $\boldsymbol{\pi}$ defined earlier as the matrix product $\boldsymbol{\gamma\alpha}'$.

Consequently, from (18),

$$L^*(\boldsymbol{\pi}) = K_0 - \frac{T}{2}\log|\mathbf{S}_{00} - \boldsymbol{\pi}\mathbf{S}_{k0} - \mathbf{S}_{0k}\boldsymbol{\pi}' + \boldsymbol{\pi}\mathbf{S}_{kk}\boldsymbol{\pi}'|. \qquad (20)$$

If $\boldsymbol{\pi}$ were unrestricted, a conventional regression estimator would result. However, we are interested in the class of solutions that result from the imposition of the restriction that

$$\boldsymbol{\pi} = \boldsymbol{\gamma}\boldsymbol{\alpha}'.$$

Hence, from (20),

$$L^*(\boldsymbol{\gamma}, \boldsymbol{\alpha}) = K_0 - \frac{T}{2}\log|\mathbf{S}_{00} - \boldsymbol{\gamma}\boldsymbol{\alpha}'\mathbf{S}_{k0} - \mathbf{S}_{0k}\boldsymbol{\alpha}\boldsymbol{\gamma}' + \boldsymbol{\gamma}\boldsymbol{\alpha}'\mathbf{S}_{kk}\boldsymbol{\alpha}\boldsymbol{\gamma}'|. \qquad (21)$$

Next, concentrate $L^*(\boldsymbol{\gamma}, \boldsymbol{\alpha})$ with respect to $\boldsymbol{\gamma}$, which will deliver an expression for the MLE of $\boldsymbol{\gamma}$ as a function of $\boldsymbol{\alpha}$, and yields a further concentrated likelihood function which depends only on $\boldsymbol{\alpha}$. Once the MLE of $\boldsymbol{\alpha}$ is obtained, we can solve backwards for estimates of all the other unknown parameters as functions of the MLE of $\boldsymbol{\alpha}$. Thus, from (21),

$$\frac{\partial L^*(\boldsymbol{\gamma}, \boldsymbol{\alpha})}{\partial \boldsymbol{\gamma}} = \mathbf{0} \text{ which implies } \hat{\boldsymbol{\gamma}} = \mathbf{S}_{0k}\boldsymbol{\alpha}(\boldsymbol{\alpha}'\mathbf{S}_{kk}\boldsymbol{\alpha})^{-1}. \qquad (22)$$

Substituting $\hat{\boldsymbol{\gamma}}$ into (21) yields $L^{**}(\boldsymbol{\alpha})$:

$$L^{**}(\boldsymbol{\alpha}) = K_1 - \frac{T}{2}\log|\mathbf{S}_{00} - \mathbf{S}_{0k}\boldsymbol{\alpha}(\boldsymbol{\alpha}'\mathbf{S}_{kk}\boldsymbol{\alpha})^{-1}\boldsymbol{\alpha}'\mathbf{S}_{k0}|. \qquad (23)$$

At first sight, differentiating $L^{**}(\boldsymbol{\alpha})$ with respect to $\boldsymbol{\alpha}$ looks formidable, but in fact the algebra involved is close to that underlying the well-known LIML estimator for a single equation from a simultaneous system; both depend on reduced-rank restrictions being imposed. In order to solve the problem, we apply partitioned inversion results to (23) and obtain

$$\begin{aligned}|\mathbf{S}_{00} - \mathbf{S}_{0k}\boldsymbol{\alpha}(\boldsymbol{\alpha}'\mathbf{S}_{kk}\boldsymbol{\alpha})^{-1}\boldsymbol{\alpha}'\mathbf{S}_{k0}| &= |\boldsymbol{\alpha}'\mathbf{S}_{kk}\boldsymbol{\alpha}|^{-1}|\mathbf{S}_{00}||\boldsymbol{\alpha}'\mathbf{S}_{kk}\boldsymbol{\alpha} - \boldsymbol{\alpha}'\mathbf{S}_{k0}\mathbf{S}_{00}^{-1}\mathbf{S}_{0k}\boldsymbol{\alpha}| \\ &= |\boldsymbol{\alpha}'\mathbf{S}_{kk}\boldsymbol{\alpha}|^{-1}|\mathbf{S}_{00}||\boldsymbol{\alpha}'(\mathbf{S}_{kk} - \mathbf{S}_{k0}\mathbf{S}_{00}^{-1}\mathbf{S}_{0k})\boldsymbol{\alpha}|.\end{aligned} \qquad (24)$$

Then maximizing $L^{**}(\boldsymbol{\alpha})$ with respect to $\boldsymbol{\alpha}$ corresponds to minimizing the generalized variance ratio,

$$|\boldsymbol{\alpha}'(\mathbf{S}_{kk} - \mathbf{S}_{k0}\mathbf{S}_{00}^{-1}\mathbf{S}_{0k})\boldsymbol{\alpha}| / |\boldsymbol{\alpha}'\mathbf{S}_{kk}\boldsymbol{\alpha}|, \qquad (25)$$

noting that $|\mathbf{S}_{00}|$ is a constant. To locate that minimum, we proceed as with LIML and impose the normalization that $\boldsymbol{\alpha}'\mathbf{S}_{kk}\boldsymbol{\alpha} = \mathbf{I}$. The MLE now requires that we minimize, with respect to $\boldsymbol{\alpha}$,

$$|\boldsymbol{\alpha}'(\mathbf{S}_{kk} - \mathbf{S}_{k0}\mathbf{S}_{00}^{-1}\mathbf{S}_{0k})\boldsymbol{\alpha}| \qquad \text{subject to } \boldsymbol{\alpha}'\mathbf{S}_{kk}\boldsymbol{\alpha} = \mathbf{I}. \tag{26}$$

This involves finding the saddle-point of the Lagrangian,

$$|\boldsymbol{\alpha}'(\mathbf{S}_{kk} - \mathbf{S}_{k0}\mathbf{S}_{00}^{-1}\mathbf{S}_{0k})\boldsymbol{\alpha}| - \phi[\text{trace}(\boldsymbol{\alpha}'\mathbf{S}_{kk}\boldsymbol{\alpha} - \mathbf{I})],$$

where ϕ is the Lagrangian associated with the constraint. The minimization has now been translated into a generalized eigenvalue problem, where we need to solve a set of equations of the form[5]

$$(\lambda\mathbf{S}_{kk} - \mathbf{S}_{k0}\mathbf{S}_{00}^{-1}\mathbf{S}_{0k})\boldsymbol{\alpha} = \mathbf{0},$$

where λ is given by solving

$$|\lambda\mathbf{S}_{kk} - \mathbf{S}_{k0}\mathbf{S}_{00}^{-1}\mathbf{S}_{0k}| = 0 \tag{27}$$

for the r largest eigenvalues $\lambda_1 \geqslant \lambda_2 \geqslant \ldots \geqslant \lambda_r \ldots \geqslant \lambda_n \geqslant 0$. The columns of $\boldsymbol{\alpha}$ are the corresponding eigenvectors

$$\boldsymbol{\alpha} = (\mathbf{v}_1, \mathbf{v}_2, \ldots, \mathbf{v}_r). \tag{28}$$

The complete set of eigenvectors is given by solving

$$(\lambda_i\mathbf{S}_{kk} - \mathbf{S}_{k0}\mathbf{S}_{00}^{-1}\mathbf{S}_{0k})\mathbf{v}_i = \mathbf{0}, \qquad i = 1, 2, \ldots, n, \tag{29}$$

subject to the normalization

$$\mathbf{V}'\mathbf{S}_{kk}\mathbf{V} = \mathbf{I}.$$

Thus $\boldsymbol{\alpha}$ simultaneously diagonalizes $\mathbf{S}_{kk}$ (to a unit matrix) and $\mathbf{S}_{k0}\mathbf{S}_{00}^{-1}\mathbf{S}_{0k}$ (to $\boldsymbol{\Lambda}$, the matrix of eigenvalues). These two diagonalizations impose r^2 restrictions in total on the system.

Defining a selection matrix $\mathbf{P}' = (\mathbf{I}_r, \mathbf{0}')$, we may deduce from (28) that (a) $\hat{\boldsymbol{\alpha}} = \mathbf{VP}$ and (b) $\hat{\boldsymbol{\alpha}}'\mathbf{S}_{kk}\hat{\boldsymbol{\alpha}} = \mathbf{I}$. Further, we can set $\mathbf{V} = (\hat{\boldsymbol{\alpha}}, \hat{\boldsymbol{\delta}})$, for instance, where the columns of $\hat{\boldsymbol{\delta}}$ are the estimates of the $n - r$ eigenvectors corresponding to the $n - r$ smallest eigenvalues. Once $\hat{\boldsymbol{\alpha}}$ has been calculated, all the other intermediate MLEs can be obtained. For example, from (22),[6] $\hat{\boldsymbol{\gamma}} = \mathbf{S}_{0k}\hat{\boldsymbol{\alpha}}$ and thus, $\hat{\boldsymbol{\pi}} = \hat{\boldsymbol{\gamma}}\hat{\boldsymbol{\alpha}}' = \mathbf{S}_{0k}\hat{\boldsymbol{\alpha}}\hat{\boldsymbol{\alpha}}'$. Also, from (13) and (23),[7] $T\hat{\boldsymbol{\Omega}} = \mathbf{S}_{00} - \mathbf{S}_{0k}\hat{\boldsymbol{\alpha}}\hat{\boldsymbol{\alpha}}'\mathbf{S}_{k0} = \mathbf{S}_{00} - \hat{\boldsymbol{\pi}}\mathbf{S}_{k0}$.

Johansen (1988) proves that $\hat{\boldsymbol{\Omega}}$ and $\hat{\boldsymbol{\pi}}$ are consistent for $\boldsymbol{\Omega}$ and $\boldsymbol{\pi}$ respectively. The expression for $\hat{\boldsymbol{\Omega}}$ given above is a natural one, in the sense that an unrestricted estimator of $\boldsymbol{\Omega}$ would be similar in form but would use an unrestricted estimator $\tilde{\boldsymbol{\pi}}$ of $\boldsymbol{\pi}$. Thus, denoting the unrestricted estimator of $\boldsymbol{\Omega}$ by $\tilde{\boldsymbol{\Omega}}$, then $\tilde{\boldsymbol{\Omega}} = \mathbf{S}_{00} - \tilde{\boldsymbol{\pi}}\mathbf{S}_{k0}$ and $\tilde{\boldsymbol{\pi}} = \mathbf{S}_{0k}\mathbf{S}_{kk}^{-1}$.

Conventional methods may be used to solve (27). Since $\mathbf{S}_{kk}$ is a

[5] By a standard result from the theory of canonical correlations, an expression of the form $|\zeta'(\mathbf{M}_1 - \mathbf{M}_2)\zeta||\zeta'\mathbf{M}_1\zeta|^{-1}$ can be minimized by solving the equation $|\lambda\mathbf{M}_1 - \mathbf{M}_2| = 0$. This is the result used above. Details are contained in Anderson (1958).

[6] Note that we have used the restriction that $\hat{\boldsymbol{\alpha}}'\mathbf{S}_{kk}\hat{\boldsymbol{\alpha}} = \mathbf{I}$.

[7] From (13) and (20), $\hat{\boldsymbol{\Omega}} = T^{-1}\sum_{t=1}^{T}\hat{\mathbf{e}}_t\hat{\mathbf{e}}_t' = T^{-1}(\mathbf{S}_{00} - \hat{\boldsymbol{\pi}}\mathbf{S}_{k0} - \mathbf{S}_{0k}\hat{\boldsymbol{\pi}}' + \hat{\boldsymbol{\pi}}\mathbf{S}_{kk}\hat{\boldsymbol{\pi}}')$. Substituting for $\hat{\boldsymbol{\pi}} = \mathbf{S}_{0k}\hat{\boldsymbol{\alpha}}\hat{\boldsymbol{\alpha}}'$ and simplifying gives the desired result.

symmetric, positive-definite matrix for finite T, its inverse can be factorized as

$$\mathbf{S}_{kk}^{-1} = \mathbf{GG}',$$

where $\mathbf{G}$ is non-singular. Substituting this expression into (27) produces a conventional eigenvalue problem:

$$|\lambda\mathbf{I} - \mathbf{G}'\mathbf{S}_{k0}\mathbf{S}_{00}^{-1}\mathbf{S}_{0k}\mathbf{G}| = 0. \tag{30}$$

In deriving (30), we have made use of the fact that $\mathbf{G}'\mathbf{S}_{kk}\mathbf{G} = \mathbf{I}$. Thus, only conventional estimation tools are needed.

Further, from (29),

$$\mathbf{S}_{k0}\mathbf{S}_{00}^{-1}\mathbf{S}_{0k}\mathbf{V} = \mathbf{S}_{kk}\mathbf{V}\mathbf{\Lambda}, \tag{31}$$

where $\mathbf{\Lambda}$ is the diagonal matrix of eigenvalues. Hence, as $\mathbf{V}'\mathbf{S}_{kk}\mathbf{V} = \mathbf{I}$,

$$\mathbf{V}'\mathbf{S}_{k0}\mathbf{S}_{00}^{-1}\mathbf{S}_{0k}\mathbf{V} = \mathbf{V}'\mathbf{S}_{kk}\mathbf{V}\mathbf{\Lambda} = \mathbf{\Lambda}, \tag{32}$$

so that $\mathbf{S}_{k0}\mathbf{S}_{00}^{-1}\mathbf{S}_{0k}$ is diagonalized to $\mathbf{\Lambda}$ by the $\mathbf{V}$, $\mathbf{V}'$ transformation. Moreover, $\mathbf{\Lambda}$ is ordered such that the first r elements (denoted $\mathbf{\Lambda}_r$) are the largest eigenvalues, and the remaining $(n - r)$ (denoted $\mathbf{\Lambda}_{n-r}$) are the smallest. These eigenvalues will play a primary role in inference about the dimension r of the co-integrating space. We focus on this issue in the next section where the asymptotic distribution of the estimators of the eigenvalues is also discussed. Finally, from (32),

$$\mathbf{\Lambda}_r = \hat{\boldsymbol{\alpha}}'\mathbf{S}_{k0}\mathbf{S}_{00}^{-1}\mathbf{S}_{0k}\hat{\boldsymbol{\alpha}} = \hat{\boldsymbol{\gamma}}'\mathbf{S}_{00}^{-1}\hat{\boldsymbol{\gamma}} \quad \text{and} \quad \mathbf{\Lambda}_{n-r} = \hat{\boldsymbol{\delta}}'\mathbf{S}_{k0}\mathbf{S}_{00}^{-1}\mathbf{S}_{0k}\hat{\boldsymbol{\delta}} = \hat{\boldsymbol{\rho}}'\mathbf{S}_{00}^{-1}\hat{\boldsymbol{\rho}},$$

where $\hat{\boldsymbol{\rho}}$ is the $(n - r) \times n$ matrix, analogous to $\hat{\boldsymbol{\gamma}}$, and corresponds to the omitted eigenvectors.

8.3. Inference about the Co-integration Space

From (24) and (32), the maximized value of the likelihood function (23) is given by

$$\begin{aligned} L^{**}(\hat{\boldsymbol{\alpha}}) &= K_2 - (T/2)\log|\hat{\boldsymbol{\alpha}}'(\mathbf{S}_{kk} - \mathbf{S}_{k0}\mathbf{S}_{00}^{-1}\mathbf{S}_{0k})\hat{\boldsymbol{\alpha}}| \\ &= K_2 - (T/2)\log|\mathbf{I} - \mathbf{\Lambda}_r| \\ &= K_2 - (T/2)\sum_{i=1}^{r}\log(1 - \lambda_i), \end{aligned} \tag{33}$$

since $\mathbf{\Lambda}_r$ is the sub-matrix of $\mathbf{\Lambda}$ corresponding to the r largest eigenvalues.

Denote by H_r the hypothesis that there are r co-integrating vectors in the system (i.e. there are $n - r$ unit roots). When $\boldsymbol{\pi}$ is unrestricted, all n eigenvalues are retained and the unrestricted maximum of the likelihood function is given by

$$L^{**}(\mathbf{V}) = K_3 - (T/2)\sum_{i=1}^{n} \log(1 - \lambda_i). \tag{34}$$

Since the r largest eigenvalues deliver the co-integration vectors, and since $\lambda_{r+1}, \lambda_{r+2}, \ldots, \lambda_n$ should be zero for the non-co-integrating combinations, tests of the hypothesis that there are at most r co-integrating vectors $0 \leqslant r < n$, and thus $n - r$ unit roots, can be based on twice the difference between the log-likelihood in (33) and that in (34); that is,

$$\eta_r = -T \sum_{i=r+1}^{n} \log(1 - \lambda_i), \qquad r = 0, 1, 2, \ldots, n-2, n-1. \tag{35}$$

The distribution of the η_r or *trace* statistic is derived under the hypothesis that there are r co-integrating vectors and tests H_r within H_n. The test strategy is, therefore, the multivariate analogue of the DF test: the potentially stationary variant is estimated, the coefficient (matrix) of the levels is tested for significance, and unit roots are imposed where the null cannot be rejected. The testing therefore proceeds in sequence from $\eta_0, \eta_1, \ldots, \eta_{n-1}$. The number of co-integrating vectors selected is $r + 1$ where the last significant statistic is η_r, which thereby rejects the hypothesis of $n - r$ unit roots. H_0 is not rejected if η_0 is insignificant; H_0 is rejected in favour of H_1 if η_1 is significant; etc. Since $\eta_r = -T \log|\mathbf{I} - \boldsymbol{\Lambda}_r|$, from (32) η_r measures the 'importance' of the adjustment coefficients on the eigenvectors to be potentially omitted. The distribution of η_r will be discussed shortly; however, it will not be the conventional χ^2 distribution because $\mathbf{x}_t$ is a (multivariate) I(1) process. Thus, while η_r still measures the cost in likelihood terms of omitting $n - r$ linear combinations of the levels of $\mathbf{x}_{t-k}$, the metric for judging a significant loss of likelihood is different from that in the I(0) case.

Alternatively, tests of significance of the largest λ_r could be based on

$$\zeta_r = -T \log(1 - \lambda_{r+1}), \qquad r = 0, 1, 2, \ldots, n-2, n-1. \tag{36}$$

From (36), ζ_r tests H_r within H_{r+1}. The ζ_r statistic is often called the *maximal-eigenvalue* or *λ-max* statistic.

Both η_r and ζ_r have non-standard distributions which are functionals of multivariate Wiener processes. For η_r, this process is of dimension $n - r$. These distributions are generalizations of the scalar (Dickey–Fuller) Wiener processes considered in earlier chapters. The crucial feature that makes these methods operational is that the distributions only depend on the dimension n of the process under analysis. Thus, although there are no analytical forms for the distributions, critical values under their respective nulls can be obtained by Monte Carlo simulation. For example, critical values for the above tests have been tabulated by Johansen (1988) and Osterwald-Lenum (1992), *inter alia*, for a range of values of n. The upper percentiles of the Osterwald-Lenum tables are given in Table 8.1.[8] Even though the distributions are non-standard, Johansen (1988) suggests a χ^2-based approximation to the distribution of η_r of the form

$$\eta_r \approx h\chi^2(2m^2),$$

where $h = 0.85 - 0.58/(2m^2)$ for $m = n - r$.

Once the degree of co-integration has been established, the co-integrating combinations are given by

$$\hat{\mathbf{w}}_t = \hat{\boldsymbol{\alpha}}'\mathbf{x}_t,$$

and these linear combinations of the data are the estimated ECMs. As before, linear transformations are also valid co-integrating vectors, and a choice among these could be made either on the basis of prior information or by following tests for hypothesized vectors as considered in Section 8.52.

Moreover, once the ECMs have been defined, $\hat{\gamma}$ reveals the importance of each co-integrating combination in each equation, and is related to the speeds of adjustment of each dependent variable to the associated disequilibria. If a given ECM enters more than one equation, the co-integration parameters are inherently cross-linked between such equations, and hence their dependent variables cannot be weakly exogenous in the related equations. This implies that joint estimation is required to compute fully efficient estimators. By way of contrast, if a given column of γ is zero except for a single entry, and there is only one co-integrating vector, single-equation estimation of that relation will not lead to any loss of information on co-integration.

8.4. An Empirical Illustration

To illustrate the calculation involved in the MLE, we consider the relationship between the (logs of) the prices of new and second-hand

[8] The tables in Osterwald-Lenum (1992) give critical values for values of n running from 1 to 11 and are therefore more extensive than those in Johansen (1988). We are grateful to Michael Osterwald-Lenum for permission to reproduce this table.

TABLE 8.1. Quantiles of the asymptotic distribution of the co-integration rank test statistics η_r and ζ_r

DGP and model: $\Delta \mathbf{x}_t = \sum_{i=1}^{k-1} \mathbf{D}_i \Delta \mathbf{x}_{t-i} + \boldsymbol{\pi} \mathbf{x}_{t-k} + \mathbf{e}_t$; $\mathbf{e}_t \sim \mathrm{IN}(\mathbf{0}, \boldsymbol{\Omega})$

$n - r$	90%	95%	97.5%	99%
		ζ_r (λ–max)		
1	2.86	3.84	4.93	6.51
2	9.52	11.44	13.27	15.69
3	15.59	17.89	20.02	22.99
4	21.58	23.80	26.14	28.82
5	27.62	30.04	32.51	35.17
6	33.62	36.36	38.59	41.00
7	38.98	41.51	44.28	47.15
8	44.99	47.99	50.78	53.90
9	50.65	53.69	56.55	59.78
10	56.09	59.06	61.57	65.21
11	61.96	65.30	68.35	72.36
		η_r (trace)		
1	2.86	3.84	4.93	6.51
2	10.47	12.53	14.43	16.31
3	21.63	24.31	26.64	29.75
4	36.58	39.89	42.30	45.58
5	55.44	59.46	62.91	66.52
6	78.36	82.49	86.09	90.45
7	104.77	109.99	114.22	119.80
8	135.24	141.20	146.78	152.32
9	169.45	175.77	181.44	187.31
10	206.05	212.67	219.88	226.40
11	248.45	255.27	261.71	269.81

Source: Osterwald-Lenum (1992: Table 0).

houses in the U.K., denoted $p_{n,t}$ and $p_{h,t}$ respectively, over the quarterly (seasonally unadjusted) sample 1957(III)–1981(II). A lag length of two periods is selected to capture the main short-run dynamics in a parsimonious way, and the system to be estimated takes the form (see Ericsson and Hendry 1985)

$$\Delta p_{n,t} = \sum_{i=1}^{4} \mu_{1i} q_{it} + d_{11} \Delta p_{n,t-1} + d_{12} \Delta p_{h,t-1} + \pi_{11} p_{n,t-2} + \pi_{12} p_{h,t-2} + e_{1t}$$

$$\Delta p_{h,t} = \sum_{i=1}^{4} \mu_{2i} q_{it} + d_{21} \Delta p_{n,t-1} + d_{22} \Delta p_{h,t-1} + \pi_{21} p_{n,t-2} + \pi_{22} p_{h,t-2} + e_{2t}.$$

The constant and the three seasonal dummy variables (denoted q_{it}) included unrestrictedly in both equations were first concentrated out of the likelihood by regressing the remaining variables on them and taking the residuals as the 'new' data set. Next, the lagged differenced variables were removed in a similar way (see equations (14)–(17)) to leave the $\mathbf{R}_{0t}$ and $\mathbf{R}_{2t}$ terms used in calculating the second moments $\mathbf{S}_{ij}$ in (19). Given these moments, (27) can be solved for the eigenvalues λ_j, which yielded

$$\lambda_1 = 0.154 \qquad \text{and} \qquad \lambda_2 = 0.0042.$$

The test-statistics η_r and ζ_r based on these, together with their 5 per cent critical values from Table 1 of Osterwald-Lenum (1992) (denoted by $\eta_r(0.05)$ etc.) are given in Table 8.2. The hypothesis that there are two unit roots can be rejected in favour of one unit root (and hence one co-integrating vector) at the 5 per cent level using both statistics, but the hypothesis that there is one unit root cannot be rejected against the maintained hypothesis of no unit roots. We therefore select $r = 1$ in this case.

The corresponding estimated eigenvectors (normalized by their diagonal elements) are given in Table 8.3. The rows are the rows of $\boldsymbol{\alpha}'$, and both are approximately $(1, -1)$ and $(-1, 1)$, which corresponds to the relative price $(p_n - p_h)$ being the co-integrating relation, as might be expected for an ECM.

The estimates of γ are given in Table 8.4. The first column corresponds to the first column of γ and reveals one reasonably large feedback coefficient of -0.06 from $(p_{n,t-2} - p_{h,t-2})$ on to $\Delta p_{n,t}$; most of the remaining coefficients are relatively close to being negligible, given the meaning and units of the ECM here. Thus, it would not be possible to reject the hypothesis that $p_{h,t}$ was weakly exogenous in the $p_{n,t}$ equation on the basis of this evidence alone. The small values of the coefficients in the second column are consistent with the very small values of η_1 and ζ_1, so little loss of likelihood would result from respecifying the system in terms of the I(0) variables $\Delta p_{n,t}$, $\Delta p_{h,t}$, and $(p_{n,t-1} - p_{h,t-1})$.

TABLE 8.2. Tests and Critical values

	ζ_r	ζ_r (0.05)	η_r	η_r (0.05)
$n - 2 = r = 0$	16.1	14.1	16.5	15.4
$n - 1 = r = 1$	0.41	3.76	0.41	3.76

Source: Osterwald-Lenum (1992), Table 1.

TABLE 8.3. Normalized eigenvectors $\boldsymbol{\alpha}'$

Variable	p_n	p_h
p_n	1.000	−1.077
p_h	−1.063	1.000

TABLE 8.4. Adjustment coefficients $\boldsymbol{\gamma}$

Variable	p_n	p_h
p_n	−0.063	−0.007
p_h	0.022	−0.019

8.5. Extensions

The preceding results hold for a simple model. Several possible extensions and other considerations arise in this model and we shall briefly consider eight of these:
1. dummy variables (such as constants and trends);
2. linear restrictions on co-integrating vectors;
3. powers of tests;
4. forecasting in co-integrated processes;
5. finite-sample properties;
6. selecting lag length;
7. I(2) variables;
8. weak exogeneity and conditional models.

8.5.1. Dummy Variables

The first issue of practical importance is the potential presence of intercepts in the equations. The inclusion of intercepts in the estimated system alters the critical values of the tests from those that obtain when no intercepts are present (as a comparison of Table 8.1 (no constant) with Table 8.5 below shows). Under the null of no co-integrating vectors, non-zero intercepts would generate trends. However, even in equations with ECMs, two possibilities arise: that the intercept enters only in the ECM, or that it also enters as an autonomous growth factor in the equation. Both cases are considered by Osterwald-Lenum (1992) and Johansen and Juselius (1990). In terms of (12), the model becomes

$$\Delta \mathbf{x}_t = \sum_{i=1}^{k-1} \mathbf{D}_i \Delta \mathbf{x}_{t-i} + \boldsymbol{\pi} \mathbf{x}_{t-k} + \boldsymbol{\mu} + \mathbf{e}_t, \tag{37}$$

where $\boldsymbol{\mu}$ is an $n \times 1$ vector of intercepts. When $\boldsymbol{\mu}$ is unrestricted, it can be concentrated out of the likelihood function, and merely makes all variables deviations about their sample means. After estimation of $\boldsymbol{\gamma}$ and $\boldsymbol{\alpha}$, the MLE of $\boldsymbol{\mu}$ can be derived in the same way as the other parameters, concentrated out of the likelihood function, were estimated in Section 8.2.

If any given equation contains an ECM, then the estimated (unrestricted) intercept could be included in that term, perhaps at the cost of having ECMs with non-zero means. However, this could lead to the system having different means for the same ECM in different equations.

An interesting alternative possibility is that $\boldsymbol{\mu}$ is restricted to entering only the ECMs, namely,

$$\boldsymbol{\mu} = \boldsymbol{\gamma}\boldsymbol{\alpha}_0,$$

where $\boldsymbol{\alpha}_0$ is $r \times 1$. In that case, (37) becomes

$$\Delta \mathbf{x}_t = \sum_{i=1}^{k-1} \mathbf{D}_i \Delta \mathbf{x}_{t-i} + \boldsymbol{\gamma}(\boldsymbol{\alpha}' \mathbf{x}_{t-k} + \boldsymbol{\alpha}_0) + \mathbf{e}_t.$$

Equations without ECMs clearly are random walks without drift (but may have lagged differences), while equations with ECMs have a common mean given by $\boldsymbol{\gamma}\boldsymbol{\alpha}_0$, and hence also have no drift. Models of the term structure of interest rates might be expected to have such a property. Hall, Anderson, and Granger (1992), Johansen and Juselius (1990), and Osterwald-Lenum (1992) discuss testing for this possibility.

More specifically, consider a system written in first-order autoregressive form (either set $k = 1$ or regard the system as being stacked as in Chapter 5):

$$\mathbf{x}_t = (\mathbf{I} + \boldsymbol{\pi})\mathbf{x}_{t-1} + \boldsymbol{\mu} + \mathbf{e}_t = \boldsymbol{\pi}^* \mathbf{x}_{t-1} + \boldsymbol{\mu} + \mathbf{e}_t, \tag{38}$$

where $\boldsymbol{\pi} = \boldsymbol{\gamma}\boldsymbol{\alpha}'$ and $\boldsymbol{\pi}^* = \mathbf{I} + \boldsymbol{\gamma}\boldsymbol{\alpha}'$. Reformulate (38) in I(0) space by partitioning $\mathbf{x}_t$ into $(\mathbf{x}'_{at}:\mathbf{x}'_{bt})'$ where $\boldsymbol{\alpha}'\mathbf{x}_t$ and $\Delta \mathbf{x}_{bt}$ are I(0) by construction. From (38),

$$\Delta \mathbf{x}_t = \boldsymbol{\gamma}\boldsymbol{\alpha}' \mathbf{x}_{t-1} + \boldsymbol{\mu} + \mathbf{e}_t = \boldsymbol{\gamma} \mathbf{w}_{at-1} + \boldsymbol{\mu} + \mathbf{e}_t,$$

where $\mathbf{w}_t = (\mathbf{x}'_t \boldsymbol{\alpha} : \Delta \mathbf{x}'_{bt})' = (\mathbf{w}'_{at}:\mathbf{w}'_{bt})'$ and $\boldsymbol{\gamma}' = (\boldsymbol{\gamma}'_a:\boldsymbol{\gamma}'_b)$ which is $(r \times r{:}r \times (n-r))$, so that normalizing by $\boldsymbol{\alpha}'(\mathbf{I}_r : \boldsymbol{\alpha}^{*\prime})$ then

$$\mathbf{w}_t = \mathbf{C}\mathbf{w}_{t-1} + \mathbf{P}\boldsymbol{\mu} + \boldsymbol{\varepsilon}_t,$$

where $\boldsymbol{\varepsilon}_t \sim \mathrm{IN}(\mathbf{0}, \boldsymbol{\Sigma})$. Letting $\mathbf{J}' = (\mathbf{0}{:}\mathbf{I})$, it is seen that

$$\mathbf{P} = \begin{bmatrix} \boldsymbol{\alpha}' \\ \mathbf{J}' \end{bmatrix}, \quad \mathbf{C} = \begin{bmatrix} (\mathbf{I} + \boldsymbol{\alpha}'\boldsymbol{\gamma}) & \mathbf{0} \\ \boldsymbol{\gamma}_b & \mathbf{0} \end{bmatrix} = \begin{bmatrix} \boldsymbol{\psi} & \mathbf{0} \\ \boldsymbol{\gamma}_b & \mathbf{0} \end{bmatrix},$$

and
$$\mathbf{\Sigma} = \begin{bmatrix} \boldsymbol{\alpha}'\mathbf{\Omega}\boldsymbol{\alpha} & \boldsymbol{\alpha}'\mathbf{\Omega}\mathbf{J} \\ \mathbf{J}'\mathbf{\Omega}\boldsymbol{\alpha} & \mathbf{J}'\mathbf{\Omega}\mathbf{J} \end{bmatrix}.$$

This I(0) form allows us to determine the unconditional means and variances of the variables and hence to establish the impact of $\boldsymbol{\mu}$ on the growth of the variables. When $\boldsymbol{\alpha}'\boldsymbol{\gamma}$ is non-singular, the long-run solution for the system is defined by

$$E[\mathbf{w}_t] = (\mathbf{I} - \mathbf{C})^{-1}\mathbf{P}\boldsymbol{\mu} = \begin{bmatrix} -(\boldsymbol{\alpha}'\boldsymbol{\gamma})^{-1}\boldsymbol{\alpha}'\boldsymbol{\mu} \\ \boldsymbol{\gamma}_b(\boldsymbol{\alpha}'\boldsymbol{\gamma})^{-1}\boldsymbol{\alpha}'\boldsymbol{\mu} + \boldsymbol{\mu}_b \end{bmatrix},$$

so that

$$E[\Delta\mathbf{x}_t] = \boldsymbol{\gamma}E[\mathbf{w}_{at-1}] + \boldsymbol{\mu} = [\mathbf{I} - \boldsymbol{\gamma}(\boldsymbol{\alpha}'\boldsymbol{\gamma})^{-1}\boldsymbol{\alpha}']\boldsymbol{\mu} = \mathbf{K}\boldsymbol{\mu} = \mathbf{g}_x,$$

which determines the growth in the system. Since $\boldsymbol{\pi}^*\boldsymbol{\gamma} = (\mathbf{I} + \boldsymbol{\gamma}\boldsymbol{\alpha}')\boldsymbol{\gamma} = \boldsymbol{\gamma}(\mathbf{I} + \boldsymbol{\alpha}'\boldsymbol{\gamma}) = \boldsymbol{\gamma}\boldsymbol{\psi}$ where, matching the structure of $\mathbf{C}$, $\boldsymbol{\psi} = (\mathbf{I} + \boldsymbol{\alpha}'\boldsymbol{\gamma})$, it follows that $\boldsymbol{\pi}^{*s}\boldsymbol{\gamma} = \boldsymbol{\gamma}\boldsymbol{\psi}^s$. But since $\mathbf{C}$ defines the I(0) representation, $\boldsymbol{\psi}^s \to \mathbf{0}$ as $s \to \infty$, so that $\boldsymbol{\pi}^*$ has some roots equal to unity and a convergent component $\boldsymbol{\psi}$. In a bivariate case, $\boldsymbol{\psi}$ would be the stationary root of $\boldsymbol{\pi}^*$.

The matrix $\mathbf{K}$ is non-symmetric and idempotent with $\boldsymbol{\alpha}'\mathbf{K} = \mathbf{0}'$ and $\mathbf{K}\boldsymbol{\gamma} = \mathbf{0}$ so that $\boldsymbol{\pi}^*\mathbf{K} = \mathbf{K}$. Also, when $\boldsymbol{\gamma} = \mathbf{0}$ then $\mathbf{K} = \mathbf{I}$. Since the condition that $\boldsymbol{\mu}$ falls in the co-integrating space is $\boldsymbol{\mu} = \boldsymbol{\gamma}\boldsymbol{\alpha}_0$ where $\boldsymbol{\alpha}_0$ is $r \times 1$, then

$$E[\Delta\mathbf{x}_t | \boldsymbol{\mu} = \boldsymbol{\gamma}\boldsymbol{\alpha}_0] = \mathbf{K}\boldsymbol{\gamma}\boldsymbol{\alpha}_0 = \mathbf{0},$$

confirming the absence of any linear trend in $\mathbf{x}_t$ when $\boldsymbol{\mu} = \boldsymbol{\gamma}\boldsymbol{\alpha}_0$.

Further, the unconditional variance matrix of $\mathbf{w}_t$, $\text{var}[\mathbf{w}_t] = \mathbf{G}$, is $\mathbf{G} = \mathbf{CGC}' + \mathbf{\Sigma}$, or

$$\begin{bmatrix} \mathbf{G}_{aa} & \mathbf{G}_{ab} \\ \mathbf{G}_{ba} & \mathbf{G}_{bb} \end{bmatrix} = \begin{bmatrix} \boldsymbol{\psi}\mathbf{G}_{aa}\boldsymbol{\psi}' & \boldsymbol{\psi}\mathbf{G}_{aa}\boldsymbol{\gamma}_b' \\ \boldsymbol{\gamma}_b\mathbf{G}_{aa}\boldsymbol{\psi}' & \boldsymbol{\gamma}_b\mathbf{G}_{aa}\boldsymbol{\gamma}_b' \end{bmatrix} + \begin{bmatrix} \mathbf{\Sigma}_{aa} & \mathbf{\Sigma}_{ab} \\ \mathbf{\Sigma}_{ba} & \mathbf{\Sigma}_{bb} \end{bmatrix}.$$

This long-run variance matrix can be solved by vectorizing, and reveals the dependence of $\mathbf{G}$ on $\boldsymbol{\pi}$ only through $\boldsymbol{\gamma}_b$ and $\boldsymbol{\psi}$. The diagonality or otherwise of $\mathbf{G}$ is important for determining the quality of single-equation least-squares estimation of co-integrating relations (see Chapter 7).

Tables 8.5–8.7 provide critical values, again taken from Osterwald-Lenum, for the trace and λ-max statistics for both treatments of intercepts. The two possibilities may be dealt with more explicitly by rewriting (37) as

$$\Delta\mathbf{x}_t = \sum_{i=1}^{k-1} \mathbf{D}_i\Delta\mathbf{x}_{t-i} + \boldsymbol{\pi}\mathbf{x}_{t-k} + \boldsymbol{\gamma}\boldsymbol{\alpha}_0 + \boldsymbol{\gamma}_\perp\boldsymbol{\beta}_0 + \mathbf{e}_t,$$

where $\boldsymbol{\gamma}_\perp$ is an $n \times (n - r)$ matrix orthogonal to $\boldsymbol{\gamma}$ and $\boldsymbol{\mu} = \boldsymbol{\gamma}\boldsymbol{\alpha}_0 + \boldsymbol{\gamma}_\perp\boldsymbol{\beta}_0$

without loss of generality. Thus, $\boldsymbol{\beta}_0 = \mathbf{0}$ corresponds to the case where the intercept enters only via the ECM terms. Equivalently, the constant $\boldsymbol{\mu}$ lies in the space spanned by $\boldsymbol{\gamma}$ and hence $\boldsymbol{\gamma}'_\perp\boldsymbol{\mu} = \boldsymbol{\gamma}'_\perp\boldsymbol{\gamma}\boldsymbol{\alpha}_0 + \boldsymbol{\gamma}'_\perp\boldsymbol{\gamma}_\perp\boldsymbol{\beta}_0 = \boldsymbol{\gamma}'_\perp\boldsymbol{\gamma}_\perp\boldsymbol{\beta}_0 = \mathbf{0}$ when $\boldsymbol{\beta}_0 = \mathbf{0}$. The case $\boldsymbol{\beta}_0 \neq \mathbf{0}$ allows the intercepts to enter autonomously as growth factors. The critical values in the tables apply to three interesting DGP–model combinations.

Table 8.5 provides critical values when $\boldsymbol{\alpha}_0 \neq \mathbf{0}$, $\boldsymbol{\beta}_0 \neq \mathbf{0}$ in both the DGP and the model (i.e. the intercept enters separately). Critical values for $\boldsymbol{\alpha}_0 \neq \mathbf{0}$, $\boldsymbol{\beta}_0 = \mathbf{0}$ in the DGP and $\boldsymbol{\alpha}_0 \neq \mathbf{0}$, $\boldsymbol{\beta}_0 \neq \mathbf{0}$ in the model are given in Table 8.6 (intercept enters only ECM but model is over-parameterized). Table 8.7 considers the DGP–model combination given by $\boldsymbol{\alpha}_0 \neq \mathbf{0}$,

TABLE 8.5. Quantiles of the asymptotic distribution of the co-integration rank test statistics η_r and ζ_r

DGP and model: $\Delta\mathbf{x}_t = \sum_{i=1}^{k-1}\mathbf{D}_i\Delta\mathbf{x}_{t-i} + \boldsymbol{\pi}\mathbf{x}_{t-k} + \boldsymbol{\gamma}\boldsymbol{\alpha}_0 + \boldsymbol{\gamma}_\perp\boldsymbol{\beta}_0 + \mathbf{e}_t$;
$\boldsymbol{\alpha}_0 \neq \mathbf{0}, \boldsymbol{\beta}_0 \neq \mathbf{0}$; $\mathbf{e}_t \sim \mathrm{IN}(\mathbf{0}, \boldsymbol{\Omega})$

$n - r$	90%	95%	97.5%	99%
		ζ_r (λ–max)		
1	2.69	3.76	4.95	6.65
2	12.07	14.07	16.05	18.63
3	18.60	20.97	23.09	25.52
4	24.73	27.07	28.98	32.24
5	30.90	33.46	35.71	38.77
6	36.76	39.37	41.86	45.10
7	42.32	45.28	47.96	51.57
8	48.33	51.42	54.29	57.69
9	53.98	57.12	59.33	62.80
10	59.62	62.81	65.44	69.09
11	65.38	68.83	72.11	75.95
		η_r (trace)		
1	2.69	3.76	4.95	6.65
2	13.33	15.41	17.52	20.04
3	26.79	29.68	32.56	35.65
4	43.95	47.21	50.35	54.46
5	64.84	68.52	71.80	76.07
6	89.48	94.15	98.33	103.18
7	118.50	124.24	128.45	133.57
8	150.53	156.00	161.32	168.36
9	186.39	192.89	198.82	204.95
10	225.85	233.13	239.46	247.18
11	269.96	277.71	284.87	293.44

Source: Osterwald-Lenum (1992: Table 1).

TABLE 8.6. Quantiles of the asymptotic distribution of the co-integration rank test statistics η_r and ζ_r

DGP: $\Delta \mathbf{x}_t = \sum_{i=1}^{k-1} \mathbf{D}_i \Delta \mathbf{x}_{t-i} + \boldsymbol{\pi} \mathbf{x}_{t-k} + \boldsymbol{\gamma} \boldsymbol{\alpha}_0 + \mathbf{e}_t$, $\boldsymbol{\alpha}_0 \neq \mathbf{0}$ $\quad \mathbf{e}_t \sim \mathrm{IN}(\mathbf{0}, \boldsymbol{\Omega})$;

Model:[a] $\Delta \mathbf{x}_t = \sum_{i=1}^{k-1} \mathbf{D}_i \Delta \mathbf{x}_{t-i} + \boldsymbol{\pi} \mathbf{x}_{t-k} + \boldsymbol{\mu} + \mathbf{e}_t$

$n - r$	90%	95%	97.5%	99%
		ζ_r (λ–max)		
1	6.50	8.18	9.72	11.65
2	12.91	14.90	17.07	19.19
3	18.90	21.07	22.89	25.75
4	24.78	27.14	29.16	32.14
5	30.84	33.32	35.80	38.78
6	36.35	39.43	41.86	44.59
7	42.06	44.91	47.59	51.30
8	48.43	51.07	53.85	57.07
9	54.01	57.00	59.80	63.37
10	59.19	62.42	64.98	68.61
11	65.07	68.27	70.69	74.36
		η_r (trace)		
1	6.50	8.18	9.72	11.65
2	15.66	17.95	20.08	23.52
3	28.71	31.52	34.48	37.22
4	45.23	48.28	51.54	55.43
5	66.49	70.60	74.04	78.87
6	90.39	95.18	99.32	104.20
7	118.99	124.25	129.75	136.06
8	151.38	157.11	162.75	168.92
9	186.54	192.84	198.06	204.79
10	226.34	232.49	238.26	246.27
11	269.53	277.39	283.84	292.65

[a] In the model, $\boldsymbol{\mu} = \boldsymbol{\gamma}\boldsymbol{\alpha}_0 + \boldsymbol{\gamma}_{\perp}\boldsymbol{\beta}_0$ enters unrestrictedly; that is, $\boldsymbol{\alpha}_0 \neq 0$, $\boldsymbol{\beta}_0 \neq 0$.

Source: Osterwald-Lenum (1992: Table 1.1*).

$\boldsymbol{\beta}_0 = \mathbf{0}$ in both the DGP and the model (intercept enters only ECM and model is correctly parameterized). Note that the critical values for the DGP–model combination given by $\boldsymbol{\alpha}_0 = \mathbf{0}$, $\boldsymbol{\beta}_0 = \mathbf{0}$ in both the DGP and the model appear in Table 8.1.

Other possible dummy variables include a trend, which would allow the possibility that some variables were trend stationary, and seasonal dummy variables in quarterly data (or equivalent dummies in data of other frequencies). Critical values for some of these additional cases are given by Osterwald-Lenum, although the necessary critical values to

TABLE 8.7. Quantiles of the asymptotic distribution of the co-integration rank test statistics η_r and ζ_r
DGP and model: $\Delta \mathbf{x}_t = \sum_{i=1}^{k-1} \mathbf{D}_i \Delta \mathbf{x}_{t-i} + \boldsymbol{\pi} \mathbf{x}_{t-k} + \boldsymbol{\gamma} \boldsymbol{\alpha}_0 + \mathbf{e}_t$;
$\boldsymbol{\alpha}_0 \neq \mathbf{0} \quad \mathbf{e}_t \sim \mathsf{IN}(\mathbf{0}, \boldsymbol{\Omega})$

$n - r$	90%	95%	97.5%	99%
		ζ_r (λ–max)		
1	7.52	9.24	10.80	12.97
2	13.75	15.67	17.63	20.20
3	19.77	22.00	24.07	26.81
4	25.56	28.14	30.32	33.24
5	31.66	34.40	36.90	39.79
6	37.45	40.30	43.22	46.82
7	43.25	46.45	48.99	51.91
8	48.91	52.00	54.71	57.95
9	54.35	57.42	60.50	63.71
10	60.25	63.57	66.24	69.94
11	66.02	69.74	72.64	76.63
		η_r (trace)		
1	7.52	9.24	10.80	12.97
2	17.85	19.96	22.05	24.60
3	32.00	34.91	37.61	41.07
4	49.65	53.12	56.06	60.16
5	71.86	76.07	80.06	84.45
6	97.18	102.14	106.74	111.01
7	126.58	131.70	136.49	143.09
8	159.48	165.58	171.28	177.20
9	196.37	202.92	208.81	215.74
10	236.54	244.15	251.30	257.68
11	282.45	291.40	298.31	307.64

Source: Osterwald-Lenum (1992: Table 1*).

implement tests for all r and for all possible DGP–model combinations are not available.

8.5.2. Linear Restrictions on Co-integrating Vectors

A different set of generalizations concerns testing linear restrictions on $\boldsymbol{\alpha}$ and $\boldsymbol{\gamma}$. These would correspond to investigating *a priori* theories about the co-integrating vectors, and about their roles in different equations. Conditional on r being the number of co-integrating relationships, and the model being transformed to I(0) space, the relevant hypotheses generally involve standard χ^2 distributions. (Again, see Johansen 1988, and Johansen and Juselius 1990.)

As an example, consider testing linear restrictions on $\boldsymbol{\alpha}$ of the form

$$H_J\text{: } \boldsymbol{\alpha} = \mathbf{J}\boldsymbol{\Psi},$$

where $\mathbf{J}$ is a known $n \times s$ matrix and $\boldsymbol{\Psi}$ is an $s \times r$ matrix of unknown parameters and $r \leqslant s < n$. Maximization of the likelihood function is unaltered until equation (26), which becomes

$$\min_{\boldsymbol{\Psi}} |\boldsymbol{\Psi}'\mathbf{J}'(\mathbf{S}_{kk} - \mathbf{S}_{k0}\mathbf{S}_{00}^{-1}\mathbf{S}_{0k})\mathbf{J}\boldsymbol{\Psi}|. \tag{39}$$

In place of (27), we must solve for the eigenvalues $\lambda_1^* \geqslant \lambda_2^* \geqslant \ldots \geqslant \lambda_s^*$ from the equation

$$|\lambda^*\mathbf{J}'\mathbf{S}_{kk}\mathbf{J} - \mathbf{J}'\mathbf{S}_{k0}\mathbf{S}_{00}^{-1}\mathbf{S}_{0k}\mathbf{J}| = 0, \tag{40}$$

using the principles applied above. A likelihood-ratio test against the unrestricted value of $\boldsymbol{\alpha}$ can be calculated and amounts to testing H_J within H_r, and is therefore based on

$$\xi_r = T\sum_{i=1}^{r} \log[(1 - \lambda_i^*)/(1 - \lambda_i)].$$

The ξ_r test results in an asymptotic $\chi^2[r(n-s)]$ distribution. It is important to note that the analysis is now in I(0) space, conditional on having selected r earlier. Similar results obtain for testing the hypothesis that a subset of $\boldsymbol{\alpha}$ equals a known matrix.

8.5.3. Test Power

Johansen (1989) has investigated the power function of the η_r test using the theory of 'near-integrated' processes as developed in Phillips (1991) and discussed in Chapter 3. In place of $\boldsymbol{\pi} = \boldsymbol{\gamma}\boldsymbol{\alpha}'$, Johansen considers

$$\boldsymbol{\pi} = \boldsymbol{\gamma}\boldsymbol{\alpha}' + \boldsymbol{\psi}\boldsymbol{\tau}'/T,$$

where $\boldsymbol{\psi}$ and $\boldsymbol{\tau}$ are $n \times 1$ fixed vectors. For a given standardized importance of the co-integrating vector effect, the power falls as $n - r$ rises (since a larger space has to be searched to find the co-integrating vector), and depends both on the magnitude of the ECM impact and on the position of the 'local' co-integrating vectors in the space. In the simple case where $r = 1$, two scalar measures of the impact of the 'local' co-integrating vector are given by

$$\boldsymbol{\psi}'\boldsymbol{\tau} \quad \text{and} \quad [(\boldsymbol{\psi}'\boldsymbol{\psi})(\boldsymbol{\tau}'\boldsymbol{\tau}) - (\boldsymbol{\psi}'\boldsymbol{\tau})^2].$$

When either is zero, power rises with the other, but their effects also interact. Otherwise, not much is known as yet about the power properties of this systems approach.

An implication of this lack of knowledge is that more than usual care should be taken in deciding upon the relevant value of r. To reject the null of $r + 1$ co-integrating vectors, a critical value from an $(n - r - 1)$-dimensional Brownian motion is consulted. This is a much larger value than that associated with the usual χ^2-distribution, so a larger absolute value of the likelihood ratio seems acceptable if only r co-integrating vectors are retained. However, if the end result of a modelling exercise is an overall test of the validity of all the over-identifying restrictions imposed, an investigator who regarded the $(r + 1)$th co-integrating vector as I(0) would obtain a large value of the test statistic for omitting this component. Since tests of over-identification tend to have high numbers of degrees of freedom, that additional likelihood loss could be highly significant. Thus, it may not be wise simply to omit co-integrating vectors which are close to some conventional significance value. Alternatively, all over-identification tests should be conducted in I(0) space, and the reduction from the original levels system for $\mathbf{x}_t$ tested first as $I(1) \rightarrow I(0)$ and then for further restrictions conditional on the first test (see Hendry and Mizon 1992).

8.5.4. Forecasting with Co-integrated Systems

Engle and Yoo (1987) investigated the possible gains from utilizing co-integration information when making h-step-ahead forecasts from dynamic systems for large h. They consider a dynamic bivariate system and contrasted an ECM formulation based on the Engle and Granger (1987) two-step approach with an unrestricted VAR. From the common trends formulation of the system (Stock and Watson 1988*b*) discussed in Chapter 5,

$$\mathbf{x}_{t+h} = \mathbf{C}(1) \sum_{j=0}^{t+h-1} \mathbf{e}_{t+h-j} + \mathbf{C}^*(L)\mathbf{e}_{t+h}, \tag{41}$$

where the first term on the right-hand side is a stochastic trend of rank $n - r$. If the $\mathbf{C}^*(L)$ weights decline rapidly as functions of powers of L, then for large h, the h-step-ahead forecast conditional on information available at time t is approximately

$$\mathbf{x}_{t+h|t} \cong \mathbf{C}(1) \sum_{j=0}^{t-1} \mathbf{e}_{t-j}. \tag{42}$$

Forecast errors are given by

$$\mathbf{f}_{t+h|t} = \mathbf{x}_{t+h} - \mathbf{x}_{t+h|t} \cong \mathbf{C}(1) \sum_{j=0}^{h-1} \mathbf{e}_{t+h-j} + \mathbf{C}^*(L)\mathbf{e}_{t+h}. \tag{43}$$

Such forecast errors have variances of $O(h)$ for individual series, but remain $O(1)$ for combinations of the form $\boldsymbol{\alpha}'\mathbf{f}_{t+h|t}$ since $\boldsymbol{\alpha}'\mathbf{C}(1) = \mathbf{0}$. Thus, the n time series share only $n - r$ trends, so forecasts of the series move together in linear combinations even though forecasts of individual series diverge from outcomes. Hence

$$E[\boldsymbol{\alpha}'\mathbf{f}_{t+h|t}] = \mathbf{0} \qquad \text{and} \qquad \operatorname{var}(\boldsymbol{\alpha}'\mathbf{f}_{t+h|t}) < \infty$$

to the order of approximation in (42). An ECM imposes this condition whereas a VAR does not; hence the former may be expected to forecast better for long horizons. Engle and Yoo present a Monte Carlo example with this property. However, they find that the VAR does slightly better on short horizons; we comment on this below.

When the process has a non-zero mean $\boldsymbol{\mu}$, a term of the form $\boldsymbol{\mu}(t + h)$ should be included in the above analysis, which otherwise is unchanged: see Section 8.5.1 for the case where $\boldsymbol{\mu}$ lies in the co-integration space.

The fact that variances of forecast errors for co-integrated combinations remain bounded does not resolve the problem of long-run forecasting with integrated variables. A simple scalar example illustrates the difficulty. Consider the process

$$x_t = \pi_0 + \pi x_{t-1} + \varepsilon_t,$$

where $|\pi| < 1$. Then, by repeated substitution, the h-step-ahead forecast at time t, denoted $\hat{x}_{t+h|t}$, is given by

$$\hat{x}_{t+h|t} = \pi_0(1 - \pi)^{-1}(1 - \pi^h) + \pi^h x_t.$$

As $h \to \infty$, $\hat{x}_{t+h|t} \to \pi_0(1 - \pi)^{-1}$, which is the unconditional mean of the process.[9] This argument, when applied to stationary variables such as $\boldsymbol{\alpha}'\mathbf{x}_t$ or Δx_{it} (where $\mathbf{x}_t = (x_{1t}, x_{2t}, \ldots, x_{nt})'$), implies that the system of equations, if rewritten entirely in terms of I(0) variables, loses the ability to forecast future values based on its past. As the forecast horizon increases, the best predictor turns out to be the unconditional mean. Working in the levels of I(1) variables is equally problematic—now the past is apparently informative, but forecast errors have variances increasing with h.

An example from Hendry (1991*b*) demonstrates the important features of the problem. Consider a system of three variables, 'consumption', 'income', and 'saving', denoted by C, Y, and S respectively. The data-set is artificial but matches important properties of actual UK series, such as the growth rate of income, when the variables are viewed as logarithms of the original data (so S_t is the log of the savings ratio). Using PC-NAIVE, data are generated by

[9] The algebra generalizes to the case where $\mathbf{x}_t$ is an n-dimensional vector and $\boldsymbol{\pi}$ is a matrix. The necessary and sufficient conditions for stationarity of a vector process are given in Ch. 1.

$$\Delta C_t = 0.05 + 0.5\Delta Y_t + 0.2S_{t-1} + \varepsilon_{1t}$$

$$\Delta Y_t = 0.05 + 0.5\Delta Y_{t-1} + \varepsilon_{2t}$$

$$S_t \equiv Y_t - C_t,$$

where $\varepsilon_{it} \sim \mathrm{IN}(0, \sigma_{ii})$ with $E(\varepsilon_{1t}\varepsilon_{2s}) = 0 \quad \forall\, t, s,$ $\sigma_{11} = 0.02,$ and $\sigma_{22} = 0.05$. The system can be written in levels as

$$C_t = 0.075 + 0.45Y_{t-1} - 0.25Y_{t-2} + 0.8C_{t-1} + \varepsilon_{1t} + 0.5\varepsilon_{2t}$$

$$Y_t = 0.05 + 1.5Y_{t-1} - 0.5Y_{t-2} + \varepsilon_{2t}$$

$$S_t = -\ 0.025 + 0.25\Delta Y_{t-1} + 0.8S_{t-1} - \varepsilon_{1t} + 0.5\varepsilon_{2t}.$$

Note now that consumption and income are both I(1) variables, consumption and income are co-integrated, and saving is a stationary variable. The equations

$$\Delta Y_t = 0.05 + 0.5\Delta Y_{t-1} + \varepsilon_{2t}$$

$$S_t = -\ 0.025 + 0.25\Delta Y_{t-1} + 0.8S_{t-1} - \varepsilon_{1t} + 0.5\varepsilon_{2t},$$

define the system in I(0) space. The discussion above provided two implications, both of which may now be confirmed.

A: The system in I(0) space loses predictive power but variances of forecast errors remain bounded.

The confirmation of this prediction is twofold. First, defining the vector $\mathbf{w}_t = (S_t, \Delta Y_t)'$ and the matrix $\mathbf{\Lambda}$ as

$$\begin{bmatrix} 0.8 & 0.25 \\ 0.0 & 0.50 \end{bmatrix},$$

we have $\mathbf{w}_t = \mathbf{k} + \mathbf{\Lambda}\mathbf{w}_{t-1} + \mathbf{v}_t$, where $\mathbf{k} = (-0.025,\ 0.050)'$ and $\mathbf{v}_t = (0.5\varepsilon_{2t} - \varepsilon_{1t}, \varepsilon_{2t})'$. The various powers of $\mathbf{\Lambda}$ are as follows:

$$\mathbf{\Lambda}^2 = \begin{bmatrix} 0.64 & 0.33 \\ 0.0 & 0.25 \end{bmatrix}; \quad \mathbf{\Lambda}^3 = \begin{bmatrix} 0.51 & 0.32 \\ 0.0 & 0.13 \end{bmatrix};$$

$$\mathbf{\Lambda}^4 = \begin{bmatrix} 0.41 & 0.29 \\ 0.0 & 0.06 \end{bmatrix}; \quad \mathbf{\Lambda}^5 = \begin{bmatrix} 0.33 & 0.25 \\ 0.0 & 0.03 \end{bmatrix}.$$

Thus, noting that $\mathbf{w}_{t+h|t} = (\mathbf{I}_2 - \mathbf{\Lambda})^{-1}(\mathbf{I}_2 - \mathbf{\Lambda}^h)\mathbf{k} + \mathbf{\Lambda}^h\mathbf{w}_t$, the ability to predict ΔY_t vanishes rapidly and little remains five periods ahead. This is also true for S_t, although the rate of decay is slower.

Forecasting from the system using the artificially generated data provides additional confirmation of implication A. Figure 8.1 shows the forecast behaviour for the change in consumption. The forecast variances rapidly converge to a constant size, spanning about one unit, which matches the range of the observed changes in consumption in the sample used to estimate the system. The forecast reveals a return of the

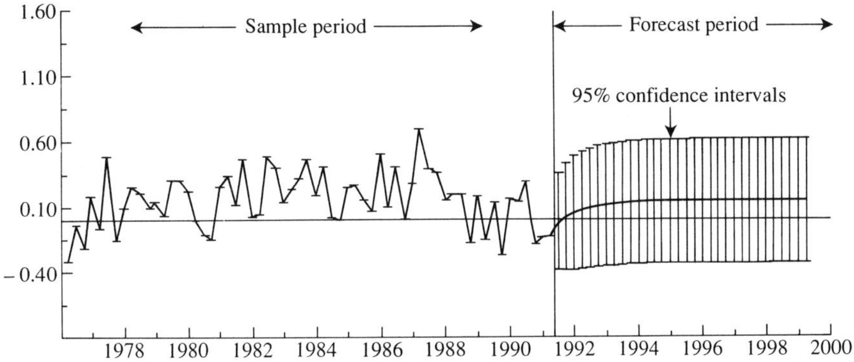

FIG 8.1. Eight-year-ahead forecast of ΔC

growth rate to its unconditional mean of 0.1 after about five periods, where it then settles.

Figure 8.2 shows the corresponding forecast behaviour for saving. The outcome is similar to that depicted in Fig. 8.1. The forecast variances stabilize rapidly, there is some information up to about eight periods ahead, but thereafter conditional forecasts are no better than the unconditional mean of −0.125.

B: The system in I(1) space has variances of forecast errors increasing linearly with h.

Figure 8.3 reports the dynamic forecasts for the level of consumption together with the forecast error bars. The huge increase in the forecast

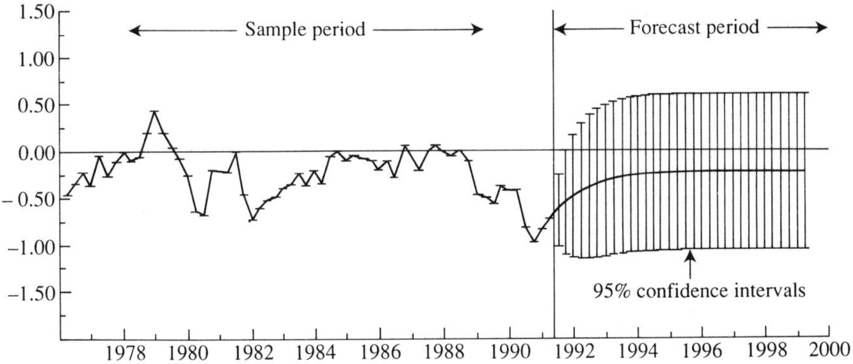

FIG 8.2. Eight-year-ahead forecast of S

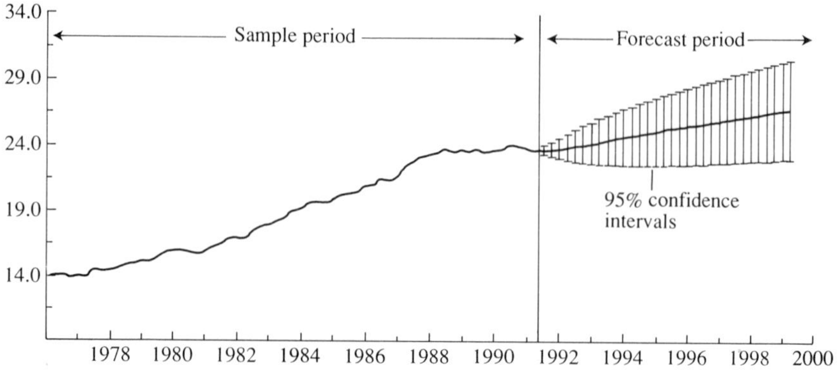

FIG 8.3. Eight-year-ahead forecast for C

standard errors as the horizon increases is obvious. They trend upwards, and at 32 periods ahead, corresponding to eight years of quarterly data, span a range almost as large as that of the previous 60 data observations. That range is about 7.5 units, whereas saving never varies outside ± 1. The mean forecast quickly becomes a trend since the series is I(1) and the forecasts are uninformative after 10 periods because of the large variances. Either a large recession or a major boom would be compatible with the confidence intervals calculated. Figure 8.4 reports a recession scenario for consumption that induces a fall of over 10 per cent in final-period consumption relative to the central forecast, but nevertheless lies entirely within the 95 per cent confidence bands of the latter.

The discussion so far has abstracted from the problems arising from parameter uncertainty. The analysis has been conducted in what might be regarded as a utopian world for an economic forecaster. The model coincides with the mechanism that generated the data, an assumption that seriously underestimates the uncertainty likely to be present in any realistic setting. Allowing for, say, parameter uncertainty makes forecasts even more uncertain.

Sampson (1991) describes the effects of parameter uncertainty on the variances of conditional forecast errors. The conditional forecast variance grows with the *square* of the forecast horizon, both for unit-root (difference-stationary) and trend-stationary models. Chong and Hendry (1986) discuss the same issue for a stationary example. Brandner and Kunst (1990) show that a marked deterioration in forecast accuracy occurs if I(1) combinations are retained, so some of the supposed ECMs are spurious.

Clements and Hendry (1991) also find that poor estimates of $\boldsymbol{\alpha}$ induce a similar effect, which helps account for the Engle–Yoo Monte Carlo results. However, they also show that mean-square forecast errors

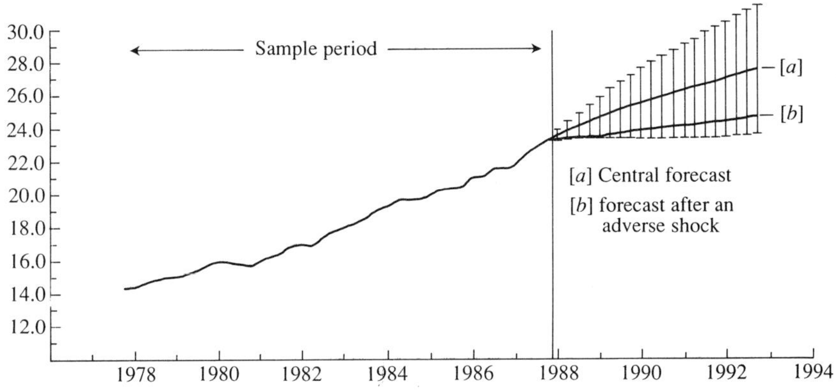

FIG 8.4. Alternative future trajectories for C

(MSFEs) constitute an inadequate basis for selecting forecasting models or methods because of a lack of invariance of MSFEs to non-singular, scale-preserving linear transforms. As a result, for multi-step forecasts in systems of equations, minimum MSFE for one linear function of predicted variables does not imply minimum MSFE on another. One method can dominate all others for comparisons in the levels of variables, yet lose to one of the others for differences, to a second for co-integrating vectors, and to a third for combinations of variables. Thus, the outcome of a forecast comparison can depend on which representation is selected.

By re-examining the Monte Carlo study of Engle and Yoo (1987), Clements and Hendry (1991) find that different rankings of VAR and Engle–Granger (EG) estimators do indeed result from the I(0) and I(1) representations of the process. For MSFE calculations using co-integrating combinations rather than levels, the VAR dominates EG for all forecast horizons even though the differences of the variables are predicted with approximately the same accuracy. They propose an alternative invariant criterion which ensures a unique ranking across models or methods and shows that there is little to choose between the VAR and EG estimators in a bivariate process. However, both are dominated, for most of the parameter values considered, by the Johansen maximum likelihood estimator (MLE).

The asymptotic formulae for the h-step-ahead forecast variances in co-integrated autoregressive systems are derived by Clements and Hendry (1992). The h-step-ahead realizations for known parameters in terms of (38) for $\mathbf{x}_t$ over the forecast period $T+1$ to $T+h$ are

$$\mathbf{x}_{T+h} = \boldsymbol{\pi}^{*h}\mathbf{x}_T + \left(\sum_{s=0}^{h-1} \boldsymbol{\pi}^{*s}\right)\boldsymbol{\mu} + \sum_{s=0}^{h-1} \boldsymbol{\pi}^{*s}\mathbf{e}_{T+h-s}, \qquad (44)$$

where

$$\boldsymbol{\pi}^* = \mathbf{I} + \boldsymbol{\pi}.$$

The conditional expectation $E[\mathbf{x}_{T+h}|\mathbf{x}_T]$ at T is

$$\hat{\mathbf{x}}_{T+h} = \left(\sum_{s=0}^{h-1} \boldsymbol{\pi}^{*s}\right)\boldsymbol{\mu} + \boldsymbol{\pi}^{*h}\mathbf{x}_T,$$

with forecast error

$$\mathbf{v}_{x,T+h} = \mathbf{x}_{T+h} - \hat{\mathbf{x}}_{T+h} = \sum_{s=0}^{h-1} \boldsymbol{\pi}^{*s}\mathbf{e}_{T+h-s}.$$

Thus, the forecast error variance matrix is

$$\mathrm{var}\,[\mathbf{v}_{x,T+h}|\mathbf{x}_T] = \sum_{s=0}^{h-1} \boldsymbol{\pi}^{*s}\boldsymbol{\Omega}\boldsymbol{\pi}^{*s\,\prime}. \tag{45}$$

For $\mathbf{C}$ and $\boldsymbol{\Sigma}$ in the model defined in Section 8.5.1, using $\mathbf{w}_t$,

$$\mathrm{var}\,[\mathbf{v}_{w,T+h}|\mathbf{x}_T] = \sum_{s=0}^{h-1} \mathbf{C}^s\boldsymbol{\Sigma}\mathbf{C}^{s\,\prime}. \tag{46}$$

Hence, the MSFE for $\mathbf{x}_t$ in (45) is $O(h)$, while the MSFE for $\mathbf{w}_t$ in (46) is $O(1)$ in h since $\mathbf{C}^s \to \mathbf{0}$ as $s \to \infty$. These results reflect the fact that $\mathbf{x}_t$ is I(1) but $\mathbf{w}_t \sim$ I(0). The covariance between forecast errors at h and l, denoted by cov $[\cdot]$, is

$$\mathrm{cov}\,[\mathbf{v}_{x,T+h}, \mathbf{v}_{x,T+l}] = \sum_{s=1}^{m} \boldsymbol{\pi}^{*h-s}\boldsymbol{\Omega}\boldsymbol{\pi}^{*l-s\,\prime} \tag{47}$$

when $m = \min(l, h)$.

When the system is expressed in differences to forecast $\Delta\mathbf{x}_{T+h}$, outcomes are given by

$$\Delta\mathbf{x}_{T+h} = \boldsymbol{\pi}^{*h-1}(\boldsymbol{\gamma}\boldsymbol{\alpha}'\mathbf{x}_T + \boldsymbol{\mu}) + \mathbf{e}_{T+h} + \sum_{s=0}^{h-2} \boldsymbol{\pi}^{*s}\boldsymbol{\gamma}\boldsymbol{\alpha}'\mathbf{e}_{T+h-s-1}. \tag{48}$$

Letting $\widehat{\Delta\mathbf{x}}_{T+h}$ denote the conditional expectation $E[\Delta\mathbf{x}_{T+h}|\mathbf{x}_T]$,

$$\widehat{\Delta\mathbf{x}}_{T+h} = \boldsymbol{\pi}^{*h-1}(\boldsymbol{\gamma}\boldsymbol{\alpha}'\mathbf{x}_T + \boldsymbol{\mu}). \tag{49}$$

Then, subtracting (49) from (48),

$$\mathbf{v}_{\Delta x,T+h} = \Delta\mathbf{x}_{T+h} - \widehat{\Delta\mathbf{x}}_{T+h} = \mathbf{e}_{T+h} + \sum_{s=0}^{h-2} \boldsymbol{\pi}^{*s}\boldsymbol{\gamma}\boldsymbol{\alpha}'\mathbf{e}_{T+h-s-1},$$

and so for known parameters, the variance formula is $\boldsymbol{\Omega}$ for $h = 1$ and

$$\mathrm{var}\,[\mathbf{v}_{\Delta x,T+h}|\mathbf{x}_T] = \boldsymbol{\Omega} + \sum_{s=0}^{h-2} \boldsymbol{\gamma}\boldsymbol{\psi}^s\boldsymbol{\alpha}'\boldsymbol{\Omega}\boldsymbol{\alpha}\boldsymbol{\psi}^{s\,\prime}\boldsymbol{\gamma}' \qquad \text{for } h > 1. \tag{50}$$

Thus, the MSFE in (50) is again $O(1)$. In all cases, when parameters need to be estimated, more complicated formulae with additional terms result.

These asymptotic forecast error variance formulae reveal a great deal about the behaviour of forecast errors as horizons increase. Clements and Hendry (1992) report a Monte Carlo study for a bivariate system which shows that the formulae above reflect the main finite sample effects when $T = 100$. Their evidence also suggests that there is little benefit from imposing reduced rank co-integration restrictions in a bivariate VAR unless the forecast horizon is short or the sample size is small. However, there are losses from omitting relevant co-integrating vectors. Their conclusions are based on experiments where the number of co-integrating combinations is known. When the number of co-integrating vectors has to be determined from the data, the performance of the MLE will reflect both under- and over-specification of the degree of co-integration. Also, the MLE might be expected to dominate the unrestricted vector autoregression in larger systems when co-integrating relations impose many more restrictions.

8.5.5. Finite Sample Properties

Gonzalo (1990) has undertaken a Monte Carlo study of the small-sample behaviour of the Johansen procedure in a bivariate model, and has compared its performance with the Engle and Granger (1987) two-step approach, as well as several other procedures based on canonical correlations and principal components. Even though the parameter estimates in I(1) processes converge at a rate of T, rather than $T^{1/2}$, quite large differences in estimates emerge from the various methods considered. The findings are reasonably encouraging for the maximum-likelihood method. Specifically, Gonzalo finds that the MLE frequently has the smallest mean-squared error across a range of parameter values of interest to empirical research. He also delineates several features of the DGP which influence the relative performances of the various estimators significantly. For example, when there is one co-integrating vector and a common factor error representation (COMFAC) is valid (see Hendry and Mizon 1978, and Sargan 1980), then the Engle–Granger two-step method is asymptotically equivalent to MLE. Generally, MLE does better at larger sample sizes and when COMFAC does not hold. The effects of non-normal errors seem minimal. However, given the similarities of the MLE to LIML, particularly the normalizations in $\boldsymbol{\alpha}$, the MLE may have no finite sample moments (see Anderson 1976).

Gonzalo's paper also provides useful derivations of the asymptotic distributions of all the estimators he considers in the Monte Carlo, and relates the simulation findings to these limiting distributions. We return to this below.

Reimers (1991) compares the powers of various tests for co-integration for bivariate and trivariate processes. He finds that the Johansen procedure over-rejects when the null is true, in small samples, and suggests correcting this using $(T-p)\log(1-\lambda_i)$ instead of $T\log(1-\lambda_i)$ for the test statistics where $p = nk$ takes account of the number of estimated parameters. While nk/T is asymptotically negligible, it can be large in small samples. The power of the tests is dependent on the specification of the DGP, but Reimers does not relate his simulation findings to the type of analysis in Section 8.5.3.

8.5.6. Selecting Lag Length

Both Gonzalo's (1990) and Reimers's (1991) studies consider the effects on the MLE of using incorrect lag lengths for the short-run dynamics. Gonzalo finds that the loss of efficiency from choosing too long a lag is small, and that the MLE performs best even if a lag of four periods is used for the short-run dynamics instead of the correct value of 0. However, if too short a lag length is used (for example, zero lags instead of one) then the MLE is no longer the best method. More practical experience is required before a final judgement can be reached on the relative costs of under-specifying versus over-specifying the lag-length, but Gonzalo's simulation evidence seems intuitively reasonable since under-specification will induce residual autocorrelation. Reimers finds that the Schwarz criterion does well in a data-based lag-length selection exercise. However, since the role of the $\Delta\mathbf{x}_{t-i}$ is to whiten the error, it is not clear that the use of the Schwarz criterion, which penalizes the addition of lags strongly, will prove optimal in this context.

8.5.7. The Analysis of I(2) Variables

Reconsider the basic autoregressive system with lag length k, written as

$$\mathbf{A(L)x}_t = \mathbf{A}_0\mathbf{x}_t - \sum_{s=1}^{k} \mathbf{A}_s\mathbf{x}_{t-s} = \boldsymbol{\mu} + \mathbf{e}_t \tag{51}$$

where $\mathbf{A}_0 = \mathbf{I}$, so that

$$\mathbf{x}_t = \boldsymbol{\mu} + \mathbf{x}_{t-1} + (\mathbf{A}_1 - \mathbf{I})\mathbf{x}_{t-1} - (\mathbf{A}_1 - \mathbf{I})x_{t-2} + (\mathbf{A}_2 + \mathbf{A}_1 - \mathbf{I})\mathbf{x}_{t-2}$$
$$+ \ldots + \left(\sum_{s=1}^{k} \mathbf{A}_s - \mathbf{I}\right)\mathbf{x}_{t-k} + \mathbf{e}_t.$$

Writing this system in the usual form,

$$\Delta \mathbf{x}_t = \sum_{s=1}^{k-1} \mathbf{D}_s \Delta \mathbf{x}_{t-s} + \boldsymbol{\pi} \mathbf{x}_{t-k} + \boldsymbol{\mu} + \mathbf{e}_t, \tag{52}$$

we see that

$$\boldsymbol{\pi} = \left(\sum_{s=1}^{k} \mathbf{A}_s - \mathbf{I} \right) = -\mathbf{A}(1).$$

The mean-lag matrix is given by

$$\boldsymbol{\Phi} = \left. \frac{\partial \mathbf{A}(z)}{\partial z} \right|_{z=1} = -\sum_{s=1}^{k} s\mathbf{A}_s. \tag{53}$$

To preclude $\mathbf{x}_t$ being integrated of order 2, $\boldsymbol{\gamma}'_\perp \boldsymbol{\Phi} \boldsymbol{\alpha}_\perp$ must be a full-rank matrix, where $\boldsymbol{\gamma}_\perp$ and $\boldsymbol{\alpha}_\perp$ are full-column-rank $n \times (n-r)$ matrices such that $\boldsymbol{\gamma}' \boldsymbol{\gamma}_\perp = \boldsymbol{\alpha}' \boldsymbol{\alpha}_\perp = \mathbf{0}$ (see Section 5.2). A natural issue is whether or not rank $(\boldsymbol{\gamma}'_\perp \boldsymbol{\Phi} \boldsymbol{\alpha}_\perp) = (n-r)$ can be tested and, if so, what can be done if a rank failure is found. This problem is analysed in Johansen (1991*b*).

First, note that the I(2) model is a sub-model of the I(1) model. This can be seen most easily in the univariate case:

$$x_t = a_1 x_{t-1} + a_2 x_{t-2} + e_t.$$

If the process is not explosive, then the coefficients (a_1, a_2) of the polynomial $(1 - a_1 z - a_2 z^2)$ must lie on or inside a triangular region bounded by the points (0, 1), (2, −1) and (−2, −1). The line connecting the first two of these points describes a single unit root (the sum of the coefficients is unity), and only its right end-point determines two unit roots.

Second, we can repeat the trick used earlier for characterizing reduced-rank matrices and express $\boldsymbol{\gamma}'_\perp \boldsymbol{\Phi} \boldsymbol{\alpha}_\perp$ as $\boldsymbol{\phi} \boldsymbol{\eta}'$ where $\boldsymbol{\phi}$ and $\boldsymbol{\eta}$ are $(n-r) \times p$ matrices of rank $p \leq (n-r)$. When $p < (n-r)$, an additional condition is needed to prevent I(3) variables, similar in form to the earlier mean-lag condition. We assume that $\mathbf{x}_t$ is I(2) so $\Delta \mathbf{x}_t$ is I(1), and $\Delta^2 \mathbf{x}_t$ is I(0). However, the original series $\boldsymbol{\alpha}' \mathbf{x}_t$ will usually be I(1), and combinations of the form $\boldsymbol{\alpha}^{*\prime} \Delta \mathbf{x}_t$ and $\boldsymbol{\alpha}' \mathbf{x}_t + \boldsymbol{\delta}' \Delta \mathbf{x}_t$ will be I(0). This result helps explain why investigators often need variables such as inflation in long-run money demand equations. When nominal money and prices are I(2) but co-integrate to I(1) as real money, and real income is I(1), velocity may still be I(1) and require inflation to co-integrate to I(0). Further, the concepts of multi-co-integration (see Granger and Lee 1990) or polynomial co-integration (see Engle and Yoo 1991) can be linked by such results to the analysis of I(2) processes. Thus, earlier models of, for example, consumers' expenditure involving the wealth–income ratio as an integral correction mechanism can be appropriately re-interpreted (see Hendry and Ungern-Sternberg 1981).

Johansen (1991*b*) provides a statistical procedure based on an extension of the I(1) MLE, which essentially consists in repeating the I(1) method twice. The first stage proceeds as usual for the reduced-rank analysis of the levels of the variables, correcting for the lagged first differences and any dummy variables, to determine r, $\boldsymbol{\gamma}$, and $\boldsymbol{\alpha}$. Next, one transforms the variables to I(1) combinations as just described by creating $\boldsymbol{\alpha}'_{\perp}\Delta\mathbf{x}_{t-1}$ and $\boldsymbol{\alpha}'\mathbf{x}_{t-1}$, $\boldsymbol{\gamma}'_{\perp}\Delta^2\mathbf{x}_t$ and regresses on those two plus lagged $\Delta^2\mathbf{x}_{t-i}$ up to lag length $k-2$ to establish $\boldsymbol{\phi}$, $\boldsymbol{\eta}$, and p. Johansen shows that, asymptotically, this procedure determines the correct parameters. He also obtains the relevant limiting distributions of the estimators.

8.5.8. Weak Exogeneity and Conditional Models

Most large-scale econometric systems and many other empirical models are open in the sense that they treat a subset of the variables as 'exogenous'. In this sub-section, we will focus on the potential weak exogeneity of contemporaneous conditioning variables for the parameters of interest in I(1) co-integrated systems (see Engle *et al.* 1983). As discussed in Chapter 1, weak exogeneity requires that there is no loss of information about the parameters of interest in reducing the analysis from the joint distribution to a conditional model. The concept was developed initially in the context of stationary processes, but as the results in Chapter 7 suggested, it plays an important role in I(1) systems as well.

In particular, when the vector of observables $\mathbf{x}_t$ is I(1) there can be cross-equation links between parameters, which are induced by the occurrence in several equations of common co-integrating combinations $\boldsymbol{\alpha}'\mathbf{x}_t$. If $\boldsymbol{\alpha}'\mathbf{x}_t$ enters both the ith and jth equations, then x_{jt} cannot be weakly exogenous for the parameters of the ith equation since the parameters of the two equations share common components of $\boldsymbol{\alpha}'\mathbf{x}_t$ and so cannot be variation free. Failure to account for such parameter dependencies can adversely affect the validity of inference in finite samples (see Chapter 7, Phillips 1991, Phillips and Loretan 1991, and Hendry and Mizon 1992).

To develop notation for an I(1) open system, two partitions of $\mathbf{x}_t$ are needed. To exposit the basic idea, it is convenient to return to the first-order system in (38) above, written as

$$\Delta\mathbf{x}_t = \boldsymbol{\pi}\mathbf{x}_{t-1} + \boldsymbol{\mu} + \mathbf{e}_t = \boldsymbol{\gamma}\boldsymbol{\alpha}'\mathbf{x}_{t-1} + \boldsymbol{\mu} + \mathbf{e}_t, \tag{54}$$

where $\mathbf{e}_t \sim \mathrm{IN}(\mathbf{0}, \boldsymbol{\Sigma})$ and $\boldsymbol{\alpha}'$ is $r \times n$ of rank r. First, we have the usual transformed partition of $\mathbf{x}_t$ into $\mathbf{w}_t = (\mathbf{x}_t'\boldsymbol{\alpha}:\Delta\mathbf{x}_{bt}')'$, capturing the locations of the unit roots and the co-integrating vectors, where there are r elements in $\mathbf{x}_t'\boldsymbol{\alpha}$ and $(n-r)$ in $\Delta\mathbf{x}_{bt}'$. The history of the process up to time $t-1$ is denoted in I(0) space by $\mathbf{W}_{t-1}^1 = (\mathbf{w}_1, \ldots, \mathbf{w}_{t-1})$. Second, we partition $\Delta\mathbf{x}_t$ into $(\Delta\mathbf{x}_{1t}':\Delta\mathbf{x}_{2t}')'$, where $\Delta\mathbf{x}_{2t}$ is $m \times 1$ and is to be treated as weakly exogenous for the vector parameter of interest $\boldsymbol{\phi} \in \boldsymbol{\Phi}$, which includes those elements of $\boldsymbol{\alpha}$ and $\boldsymbol{\gamma}$ relevant to $\Delta\mathbf{x}_{1t}$. For later use, we explicitly write out $\boldsymbol{\pi}\mathbf{x}_{t-1}$ in terms of $(\mathbf{x}_{1t-1}':\mathbf{x}_{2t-1}')'$, when there are $r_1 + r_2 = r$ co-integrating relations in the two blocks, namely

$$\boldsymbol{\gamma}\boldsymbol{\alpha}'\mathbf{x}_{t-1} = \begin{bmatrix} \boldsymbol{\gamma}_{11} & \boldsymbol{\gamma}_{12} \\ \boldsymbol{\gamma}_{21} & \boldsymbol{\gamma}_{22} \end{bmatrix} \begin{bmatrix} \boldsymbol{\alpha}_{11}' & \boldsymbol{\alpha}_{12}' \\ \boldsymbol{\alpha}_{21}' & \boldsymbol{\alpha}_{22}' \end{bmatrix} \begin{bmatrix} \mathbf{x}_{1t-1} \\ \mathbf{x}_{2t-1} \end{bmatrix}$$
$$= \begin{bmatrix} \boldsymbol{\gamma}_{11} & \boldsymbol{\gamma}_{12} \\ \boldsymbol{\gamma}_{21} & \boldsymbol{\gamma}_{22} \end{bmatrix} \begin{bmatrix} \boldsymbol{\alpha}_{11}'\mathbf{x}_{1t-1} + \boldsymbol{\alpha}_{12}'\mathbf{x}_{2t-1} \\ \boldsymbol{\alpha}_{21}'\mathbf{x}_{1t-1} + \boldsymbol{\alpha}_{22}'\mathbf{x}_{2t-1} \end{bmatrix}. \tag{55}$$

The dimensions of $\boldsymbol{\gamma}_{11}$, $\boldsymbol{\gamma}_{12}$, $\boldsymbol{\gamma}_{21}$, and $\boldsymbol{\gamma}_{22}$ are $(n-m) \times r_1$, $(n-m) \times r_2$, $m \times r_1$, and $m \times r_2$ respectively; and, correspondingly, $\boldsymbol{\alpha}_{11}'$, $\boldsymbol{\alpha}_{12}'$, $\boldsymbol{\alpha}_{21}'$, and $\boldsymbol{\alpha}_{22}'$ are $r_1 \times (n-m)$, $r_1 \times m$, $r_2 \times (n-m)$, and $r_2 \times m$. If $r_2 = 0$, then the relevant elements are set to zero. Since the analysis in terms of $\mathbf{w}_t$ is in I(0) space, the approach in Engle *et al.* applies.

The complete set of parameters of the joint distribution is $\boldsymbol{\theta} \in \boldsymbol{\Theta}$, and these are mapped one-for-one to $\mathbf{f}(\boldsymbol{\theta}) = \boldsymbol{\lambda} \in \boldsymbol{\Lambda}$, and partitioned into $\boldsymbol{\lambda} = (\boldsymbol{\lambda}_1':\boldsymbol{\lambda}_2')'$ where $\boldsymbol{\lambda}_1 \in \boldsymbol{\Lambda}_1$ and $\boldsymbol{\lambda}_2 \in \boldsymbol{\Lambda}_2$. Factorize the joint sequential density $D_X(\Delta\mathbf{x}_t|\mathbf{W}_{t-1}^1, \boldsymbol{\theta})$ of $\Delta\mathbf{x}_t$ into its conditional and marginal components:

$$D_X(\Delta\mathbf{x}_t|\mathbf{W}_{t-1}^1, \boldsymbol{\theta}) = D_{X_1|X_2}(\Delta\mathbf{x}_{1t}|\Delta\mathbf{x}_{2t}, \mathbf{W}_{t-1}^1, \boldsymbol{\lambda}_1)D_{X_2}(\Delta\mathbf{x}_{2t}|\mathbf{W}_{t-1}^1, \boldsymbol{\lambda}_2). \tag{56}$$

Since $\mathbf{w}_{t-1} = (\mathbf{x}_{t-1}'\boldsymbol{\alpha}:\Delta\mathbf{x}_{bt-1}')'$, all the information on the co-integrating vectors is retained in $\mathbf{W}_{t-1}^1$. Consequently, $\Delta\mathbf{x}_{2t}$ is weakly exogenous for $\boldsymbol{\phi}$ if $\boldsymbol{\phi}$ depends on $\boldsymbol{\lambda}_1$ alone, and $\boldsymbol{\lambda}_1$ and $\boldsymbol{\lambda}_2$ are variation free, so that $\boldsymbol{\Lambda} = \boldsymbol{\Lambda}_1 \times \boldsymbol{\Lambda}_2$. Weak exogeneity of $\Delta\mathbf{x}_{2t}$ for $\boldsymbol{\phi}$ cannot occur when $\boldsymbol{\lambda}_1$ and $\boldsymbol{\lambda}_2$ both depend on common components of $\boldsymbol{\alpha}$.

As a consequence of the normality assumption, and using the expression in (55) for $\boldsymbol{\gamma}\boldsymbol{\alpha}'\mathbf{x}_{t-1}$, conditioning $\Delta\mathbf{x}_{1t}$ on $\Delta\mathbf{x}_{2t}$ leads to the mean of the conditional density:

$$\begin{aligned} E[\Delta\mathbf{x}_{1t}|\Delta\mathbf{x}_{2t}, \mathbf{W}_{t-1}^1] = {} & \boldsymbol{\Psi}\Delta\mathbf{x}_{2t} + \{\boldsymbol{\gamma}_{11} - \boldsymbol{\Psi}\boldsymbol{\gamma}_{21}\}(\boldsymbol{\alpha}_{11}'\mathbf{x}_{1t-1} + \boldsymbol{\alpha}_{12}'\mathbf{x}_{2t-1}) \\ & + (\boldsymbol{\mu}_1 - \boldsymbol{\Psi}\boldsymbol{\mu}_2) \\ & + \{\boldsymbol{\gamma}_{12} - \boldsymbol{\Psi}\boldsymbol{\gamma}_{22}\}(\boldsymbol{\alpha}_{21}'\mathbf{x}_{1t-1} + \boldsymbol{\alpha}_{22}'\mathbf{x}_{2t-1}), \end{aligned} \tag{57}$$

where $\mathbf{\Psi} = \mathbf{\Sigma}_{12}\mathbf{\Sigma}_{22}^{-1}$. Thus, a necessary condition for the weak exogeneity of $\Delta \mathbf{x}_{2t}$ for $(\gamma_{11}:\boldsymbol{\alpha}_{11}:\boldsymbol{\alpha}_{12})$ is that either $\{\gamma_{12} - \mathbf{\Psi}\gamma_{22}\} = \mathbf{0}$ or $\gamma_{22} = \mathbf{0}$; i.e. $(\boldsymbol{\alpha}_{21}'\mathbf{x}_{1t-1} + \boldsymbol{\alpha}_{22}'\mathbf{x}_{2t-1})$ appears in only one of $D_{X_1|X_2}(\cdot)$ or $D_{X_2}(\cdot)$, but not both. Further, unless $\gamma_{21} = \mathbf{0}$, then $(\boldsymbol{\alpha}_{11}'\mathbf{x}_{1t-1} + \boldsymbol{\alpha}_{12}'\mathbf{x}_{2t-1})$ will appear in the marginal distribution of $\Delta \mathbf{x}_{2t}$, so $\gamma_{21} = \mathbf{0}$ is also necessary. There are sufficient conditions for these necessary conditions to hold, including $\gamma_{21} = \mathbf{0}$, $\gamma_{22} = \mathbf{0}$ and $\gamma_{12} = \mathbf{0}$ where the latter two arise because $r_2 = 0$. Such conditions can be tested using the approach in Johansen (1992*b*) and Johansen and Juselius (1990).

Short-run parameters may depend on some of the elements in $\boldsymbol{\alpha}$ without jeopardizing efficient inferences about long-run parameters of interest. However, if all the elements of $\boldsymbol{\lambda}_1$ are of interest, then again variation-free parameters are required, and any cross-restrictions violate weak exogeneity.

To illustrate this analysis, reconsider the example in equations (31) and (32) and (60) of Chapter 7. There is one co-integrating vector with parameter β, $r_1 = r = 1$, $r_2 = 0$, $m = 1$, and $n = 2$:

$$\begin{bmatrix} x_{1t} - \beta x_{2t} \\ \Delta x_{2t} \end{bmatrix} = \begin{bmatrix} u_{1t} \\ u_{2t} \end{bmatrix} = \begin{bmatrix} c_{11} & c_{12} \\ c_{21} & c_{22} \end{bmatrix} \begin{bmatrix} u_{1t-1} \\ u_{2t-1} \end{bmatrix} + \begin{bmatrix} \varepsilon_{1t} \\ \varepsilon_{2t} \end{bmatrix} \tag{58}$$

where

$$\begin{bmatrix} \varepsilon_{1t} \\ \varepsilon_{2t} \end{bmatrix} \sim \mathrm{IN}\left[\begin{bmatrix} 0 \\ 0 \end{bmatrix}, \begin{bmatrix} \sigma_{11} & \sigma_{12} \\ \sigma_{21} & \sigma_{22} \end{bmatrix}\right].$$

This representation is in terms of $\mathbf{w}_t$ (see (38) above) but is written as a triangular system error correction as in Phillips (1991), imposing a specific first-order autoregressive parametric form for the error process $\mathbf{u}_t$ (compared with the general processes allowed by Phillips):

$$\mathbf{w}_t = \mathbf{u}_t \qquad \text{where } \mathbf{u}_t = \mathbf{C}\mathbf{u}_{t-1} + \boldsymbol{\varepsilon}_t \text{ and } \boldsymbol{\varepsilon}_t \sim \mathrm{IN}(\mathbf{0}, \mathbf{\Sigma}).$$

The unconditional covariance matrix of $\mathbf{u}_t$ is $\operatorname{plim} T^{-1}\sum \mathbf{u}_t\mathbf{u}_t' = \mathbf{G}$, derived in Section 8.5.1. Let $c_{12} = c_{22} = 0$ since these parameters only determine the presence of the lagged difference of x_{2t}, and do not affect co-integration vectors. Then the long-run covariance matrix is (see Ch. 7 appendix):

$$\mathbf{\Omega} = (\mathbf{I} - \mathbf{C})^{-1}\mathbf{\Sigma}(\mathbf{I} - \mathbf{C}')^{-1} = \begin{bmatrix} \omega_{11} & c_{21}\omega_{11} + \psi_{12} \\ c_{21}\omega_{11} + \psi_{12} & c_{21}^2\omega_{11} + \sigma_{22} + 2c_{21}\psi_{12} \end{bmatrix} \tag{59}$$

where $\omega_{11} = \sigma_{11}/(1 - c_{11})^2$ and $\psi_{12} = \sigma_{12}/(1 - c_{11})$. The non-diagonality of $\mathbf{\Omega}$ implies that there is information about the parameters of each equation in the other. However, by conditioning $\Delta \mathbf{x}_{1t}$ on $\Delta \mathbf{x}_{2t}$ in the first equation, the σ_{12} effect is removed. Then even if the first equation is dynamic, so $c_{11} \neq 0$, the diagonality of $\mathbf{\Omega}$ only depends on $c_{21} = 0$. When $c_{21} \neq 0$, the long-run covariance matrix is non-diagonal and there is a loss of weak exogeneity, which can have a detrimental impact on the bias and efficiency of the least-squares estimator of β in finite samples. Note that $c_{12} \neq 0$ can be corrected within the first equation treated in isolation by adding lagged Δx_{2t}, but that $c_{21} \neq 0$ requires modelling the system (although corrections based on adding leads of Δx_{2t} have been proposed to exploit the obverse Granger causality of x_1 on x_2: see Stock and Watson 1991).

We now derive the conditional and marginal factorizations. In terms of observables, the original system from Chapter 7 can be written as $\mathbf{w}_t = \mathbf{C}\mathbf{w}_{t-1} + \boldsymbol{\varepsilon}_t$, or

$$\begin{bmatrix} x_{1t} - \beta x_{2t} \\ \Delta x_{2t} \end{bmatrix} = \begin{bmatrix} c_{11} & c_{12} \\ c_{21} & c_{22} \end{bmatrix} \begin{bmatrix} x_{1t-1} - \beta x_{2t-1} \\ \Delta x_{2t-1} \end{bmatrix} + \begin{bmatrix} \varepsilon_{1t} \\ \varepsilon_{2t} \end{bmatrix}. \quad (60)$$

Rewritten as a VAR in I(0) variables as in (37), we have

$$\begin{bmatrix} \Delta x_{1t} \\ \Delta x_{2t} \end{bmatrix} = \begin{bmatrix} 0 & d_{12} \\ 0 & d_{22} \end{bmatrix} \begin{bmatrix} \Delta x_{1t-1} \\ \Delta x_{2t-1} \end{bmatrix} + \begin{bmatrix} \gamma_{11} \\ \gamma_{21} \end{bmatrix} (1{:}-\beta) \begin{bmatrix} x_{1t-1} \\ x_{2t-1} \end{bmatrix} + \begin{bmatrix} \varepsilon_{1t} + \beta\varepsilon_{2t} \\ \varepsilon_{2t} \end{bmatrix}, \quad (61)$$

where $d_{12} = c_{12} + \beta c_{22}$, $\gamma_{11} = (c_{11} - 1 + \beta c_{21})$, $d_{22} = c_{22}$, and $\gamma_{21} = c_{21}$. The restricted first column of $\mathbf{D}$ is an incidental effect from assuming a first-order autoregressive error initially.

Finally, solving for the conditional and marginal representations, we have

$$\Delta x_{1t} = \lambda_{11}\Delta x_{2t} + \lambda_{12}(x_{1t-1} - \beta x_{2t-1}) + \lambda_{13}\Delta x_{2t-1} + v_t \quad (62a)$$

$$\Delta x_{2t} = \lambda_{21}(x_{1t-1} - \beta x_{2t-1}) + \lambda_{22}\Delta x_{2t-1} + \varepsilon_{2t}, \quad (62b)$$

where $\Psi = \sigma_{12}\sigma_{22}^{-1}$, $\lambda_{11} = (\beta + \Psi)$, $\lambda_{12} = (c_{11} - 1 - \Psi c_{21})$, $\lambda_{13} = (c_{12} - \Psi c_{22})$, $\lambda_{21} = c_{21}$, $\lambda_{22} = c_{22}$, and $E[v_t \varepsilon_{2t}] = 0$. Assume that $\boldsymbol{\phi} = (\lambda_{11}{:}\lambda_{12}{:}\lambda_{13}{:}\beta)'$ is the vector parameter of interest. When $\lambda_{21} = 0$, least-squares estimation of $\boldsymbol{\phi}$ from the first equation involves no loss of information. In fact, x_{2t} is strongly exogenous for $\boldsymbol{\phi}$ in such a system. However, when $\lambda_{21} \neq 0$, Δx_{2t} is not weakly exogenous for $\boldsymbol{\phi}$ and the analysis is not fully efficient. Monte Carlo studies (e.g. Phillips and Loretan 1991) confirm the impact of this loss of efficiency in finite samples (see Chapter 7).

Irrespective of the value of λ_{21}, the first equation in (62) is the conditional expectation from (58), namely

$$E[\Delta x_{1t} | \Delta x_{2t}, \mathbf{W}_{t-1}^1].$$

Thus, once data are I(1) but co-integrated, the fact that an equation coincides with the conditional expectation is not sufficient to justify single-equation least-squares modelling. Rather surprisingly, weak exogeneity is at least as important in I(1) processes as in I(0) processes.

8.6. A Second Example of the Johansen Maximum Likelihood Approach

We reconsider the UK seasonally adjusted quarterly data from Sect. 7.6 on money, prices, output, and interest rates, this time treated as a system, represented by a VAR with two lags on each of $m - p$, Δp, x_{85}, and R_n, plus a constant and a trend. The lag length was selected by commencing at five lags on every variable, and sequentially testing from the highest order. The sample was 1964(3)–1989(2). The residual standard deviations of the four equations were 0.0161, 0.0069, 0.0126, and 0.0127 respectively, and on recursive F-tests all four equations had acceptably constant coefficients using one-off I(0) critical values. The residuals also yielded insignificant outcomes on χ^2 tests for autocorrelation but not for normality.

In almost every instance, two co-integrating combinations were significant (i.e. two unit roots were rejected); the second of these was virtually the same in all lag specifications, but the first was often a linear combination of the first two rows reported in Table 8.9. Such a finding matches that in Hendry and Mizon (1992) and Ericsson *et al.* (1991). Beginning with the largest statistics, two of the tests in each column are significant (see Osterwald-Lenum 1992: Table 2).

The corresponding eigenvectors are shown in Table 8.9, in rows, augmented by the two non-co-integrating combinations in the last two

TABLE 8.8. Eigenvalues, test statistics, and 5 per cent critical values

Eigenvalues	0.013817	0.060350	0.249694	0.517240
Statistics	$-T\log(1-\mu_i)$	$\zeta_r(0.05)$	$-T\log(1-\mu_i)$	$\eta_{n-r}(0.05)$
$n-4=r=0$	72.82	30.33	109.17	54.64
$n-3=r=1$	28.73	23.78	36.34	34.55
$n-2=r=2$	6.22	16.87	7.62	18.17
$n-1=r=3$	1.39	3.74	1.39	3.74

TABLE 8.9. Normalized eigenvectors $\boldsymbol{\alpha}'$

Variable	$m-p$	Δp	x_{85}	R_n
$\boldsymbol{\alpha}_1'$	1.0000	6.3966	−0.8938	7.6838
$\boldsymbol{\alpha}_2'$	0.0311	1.0000	−0.3334	−0.1377
$\boldsymbol{\upsilon}_1'$	−0.2633	0.9435	1.0000	−1.2117
$\boldsymbol{\upsilon}_2'$	0.9838	4.5659	−0.7701	1.0000

rows. The first row suggests the following long-run solution for the money equation:

$$m - p = 0.89x_{85} - 7.68R_n - 6.40\Delta p.$$

This is close to that found from the single-equation dynamic analysis in Chapter 7. No trend is required. The γ matrix is given in Table 8.10. Only the first entry in the first column is at all large, so that the first co-integrating vector only affects the first equation consistent with the weak exogeneity of x_{85}, R_n, and Δp for the parameters of the money-demand equation. This again matches the finding over a shorter sample in Hendry and Mizon (1992).

The second row of Table 8.9 delivers the approximate long-run solution

$$\Delta p \approx 0.333(x_{85} - \delta t) + 0.138R_n.$$

This corresponds to the impact of excess demand, as measured by the deviation from its linear trend, on inflation with a small and possibly insignificant effect from interest rates. No additional trend is then required. The second column of γ shows a large effect of this ECM on all four equations, violating any possibility of treating any of the four variables as weakly exogenous in a model of inflation or excess demand when the parameters of interest include the long-run multipliers.

When the ordering of variables is $(m - p, \Delta p, x_{85}, R_n)$ the long-run π matrix is

$$\begin{bmatrix} -0.082 & -0.245 & -0.081 & -0.761 \\ -0.009 & -0.474 & 0.164 & 0.112 \\ 0.007 & 0.146 & -0.108 & -0.147 \\ -0.021 & -0.119 & 0.149 & -0.059 \end{bmatrix}.$$

8.7. Asymptotic Distributions of Estimators of Co-integrating vectors in I(1) systems

Gonzalo (1990) reviews and compares the various alternatives to OLS for the estimation of co-integrating vectors, including those proposed by

TABLE 8.10. Adjustment coefficients γ

Variable	γ_1	γ_2	γ_1^*	γ_2^*
$m - p$	−0.0952	0.4268	−0.0300	−0.0076
Δp	0.0048	−0.5147	−0.0013	0.0024
x_{85}	−0.0210	0.2578	−0.0318	0.0116
R_n	−0.0001	−0.2253	0.0796	0.0069

Stock (1987), Stock and Watson (1988*b*), Johansen (1988), Phillips (1988*a*), and Phillips and Hansen (1990). While all of the suggested methods share the super-consistency property, we have seen that there can be substantial differences in their performance on moderately sized samples.

Gonzalo makes the comparison on a simple data generation process in which co-integration holds between the I(1) series z_t and y_t:

$$y_t = \beta z_t + v_t, \qquad v_t = \rho v_{t-1} + \varepsilon_{1t}, \qquad z_t = z_{t-1} + \varepsilon_{2t}, \tag{63a}$$

and

$$\begin{bmatrix} \varepsilon_{1t} \\ \varepsilon_{2t} \end{bmatrix} \sim \mathrm{IN}\left[\begin{bmatrix} 0 \\ 0 \end{bmatrix}, \begin{bmatrix} \sigma_1^2 & \theta\sigma_1\sigma_2 \\ \theta\sigma_1\sigma_2 & \sigma_2^2 \end{bmatrix}\right]. \tag{63b}$$

This system is a special case of (58) and can therefore be represented in the error-correction form

$$\begin{bmatrix} \Delta y_t \\ \Delta z_t \end{bmatrix} = \begin{bmatrix} \rho - 1 & \beta(1-\rho) \\ 0 & 0 \end{bmatrix} \begin{bmatrix} y_{t-1} \\ z_{t-1} \end{bmatrix} + \begin{bmatrix} u_{1t} \\ u_{2t} \end{bmatrix}, \tag{64}$$

where $u_{1t} = \beta\varepsilon_{2t} + \varepsilon_{1t}$, $u_{2t} = \varepsilon_{2t}$, and $E(\mathbf{uu}') = \mathbf{\Lambda}$, with

$$\mathbf{\Lambda} = \begin{bmatrix} \beta^2\sigma_2^2 + \sigma_1^2 + 2\beta\theta\sigma_1\sigma_2 & \beta\sigma_2^2 + \theta\sigma_1\sigma_2 \\ \beta\sigma_2^2 + \theta\sigma_1\sigma_2 & \sigma_2^2 \end{bmatrix}. \tag{65}$$

The logarithm of the likelihood function for the ECM is therefore

$$L(\boldsymbol{\alpha}, \boldsymbol{\gamma}, \mathbf{\Lambda}) = K - (T/2)\ln|\mathbf{\Lambda}| - \frac{1}{2}\sum_{t=1}^{T} (\Delta\mathbf{x}_t - \boldsymbol{\gamma\alpha}'\mathbf{x}_{t-1})'\mathbf{\Lambda}^{-1}(\Delta\mathbf{x}_t - \boldsymbol{\gamma\alpha}'\mathbf{x}_{t-1}), \tag{66}$$

where $\mathbf{x}_t = (y_t, z_t)'$, $\boldsymbol{\gamma} = (\rho - 1, 0)'$, $\boldsymbol{\alpha}' = (1, -\beta)$, and $\boldsymbol{\gamma\alpha}'$ is the 2×2 matrix of rank 1 given in (64).

The systems (63) and (64) have the property that z_t is weakly exogenous for β. Since the u_{it} are normally distributed (from (63)), take conditional expectations in (64)

$$E(\Delta y_t|\Delta z_t, \mathbf{Z}_{t-1}, \mathbf{Y}_{t-1}) = (\rho - 1)y_{t-1} + \beta(1-\rho)z_{t-1} + \frac{\operatorname{cov}(u_{1t}, u_{2t})}{\operatorname{var}(u_{2t})}[\Delta z_t - E(\Delta z_t|\mathbf{Z}_{t-1}, \mathbf{Y}_{t-1})].$$

Taking the covariances of the u_i from (65), we have

$$E(\Delta y_t|\Delta z_t, \mathbf{Z}_{t-1}, \mathbf{Y}_{t-1}) = (\rho - 1)y_{t-1} + \beta(1-\rho)z_{t-1} + \left(\frac{\beta\sigma_2^2 + \theta\sigma_1\sigma_2}{\sigma_2^2}\right)\Delta z_t$$
$$= (\beta + \phi)\Delta z_t + (\rho - 1)(y_{t-1} - \beta z_{t-1}), \tag{67}$$

where $\phi = \theta\sigma_1/\sigma_2$.

The parameter β is recoverable from (67). Moreover, β does not enter the marginal distribution.

Weak exogeneity of z_t for β implies that inference concerning β can be carried out with no loss of information by using the density of y_t conditional on z_t and ignoring the marginal density of z_t (that is, the DGP of z_t). It is then not surprising that, when the log-likelihood is formally split into a conditional and a marginal likelihood, the marginal density contains no information about β. That is, (66) can be rewritten as

$$L(\boldsymbol{\alpha}, \gamma, \boldsymbol{\Lambda}) = K - \frac{T}{2}\ln|\Lambda_0| - \frac{1}{2}\sum_{t=1}^{T} \zeta_t \Lambda_0^{-1} \zeta_t$$
$$- \left(\frac{T}{2}\ln|\Lambda_{22}| - \frac{1}{2}\sum_{t=1}^{T} \Delta z_t \Lambda_{22}^{-1} \Delta z_t\right), \qquad (68)$$

with $\Lambda_0 = \Lambda_{11} - \Lambda_{12}\Lambda_{22}^{-1}\Lambda_{21}$, $\zeta_t = \Delta y_t - (\rho - 1)(y_{t-1} - \beta z_{t-1}) - \psi \Delta z_t$, and, finally, $\psi = \Lambda_{12}\Lambda_{22}^{-1} = (\beta + \theta\sigma_1/\sigma_2)$; ψ can be interpreted as a short-run multiplier, being the coefficient on Δz_t in (67), while the long-run multiplier is β, from (63). The term in parentheses in (68) is the marginal likelihood of z_t (or Δz_t) and does not involve β; estimation of β can be carried out by maximizing the conditional likelihood alone. The estimate is that which would be obtained from OLS in the regression corresponding to (67).

In order to discuss the asymptotic properties of different estimation methods, we use the multivariate functional central-limit theorem and transformation to the unit interval described in Chapter 6. For the vector $\mathbf{e}_t = (v_t, \varepsilon_{2t})'$, let $\mathbf{p}_t = \mathbf{p}_{t-1} + \mathbf{e}_t$. Then

$$T^{-1/2}\mathbf{P}_{[\mathrm{Tr}]} = T^{-1/2}\sum_{t=1}^{[\mathrm{Tr}]} \mathbf{e}_t \Rightarrow \mathbf{B}(r), \qquad r \in [0, 1],\ T \to \infty,$$

with $\mathbf{B}(r) = (B_1(r),\ B_2(r))'$. The long-run covariance matrix of this bivariate Brownian motion process can be calculated as in the appendix to Chapter 7:

$$\lim_{T\to\infty} T^{-1} E\left(\left(\sum_{t=1}^{T} \mathbf{e}_t\right)\left(\sum_{t=1}^{T} \mathbf{e}_t\right)'\right) \equiv \boldsymbol{\Omega} = \begin{pmatrix} \sigma_1^2/(1-\rho)^2 & \theta\sigma_1\sigma_2/(1-\rho) \\ \theta\sigma_1\sigma_2/(1-\rho) & \sigma_2^2 \end{pmatrix}$$

Further,

$$T^{-1}\sum_{t=1}^{T} \mathbf{p}_t \mathbf{e}_t \Rightarrow \int_0^1 \mathbf{B}(r)\,\mathrm{d}\mathbf{B}(r)' + \mathbf{G} + \boldsymbol{\Gamma}$$

where

$$\mathbf{G} = \begin{pmatrix} \sigma_1^2/(1-\rho^2) & \theta\sigma_1\sigma_2 \\ \theta\sigma_1\sigma_2 & \sigma_2^2 \end{pmatrix} \text{ and } \boldsymbol{\Gamma}' = \frac{\rho}{1-\rho}\begin{pmatrix} \sigma_1^2/(1-\rho^2) & \theta\sigma_1\sigma_2 \\ 0 & 0 \end{pmatrix}.$$

Hence

$$T^{-1}\sum_{t=1}^{T} z_t v_t = (0:1)\left[\int_0^1 \mathbf{B}(r)\,\mathrm{d}\mathbf{B}(r)' + \mathbf{G} + \mathbf{\Gamma}\right]\binom{1}{0}$$
$$= \int_0^1 B_2(r)\,\mathrm{d}B_1(r) + \theta\sigma_1\sigma_2/(1-\rho).$$

Results on the asymptotic distributions of the different estimators of co-integrating parameters will be stated without proof, but can be found in Gonzalo (1990).

(i) Static regression estimated by OLS. For $\mathbf{x}_t$ generated by (63), the OLS estimator of β in a static regression has the asymptotic distribution

$$T(\hat{\beta}_{\text{OLS}} - \beta) = \left[T^{-2}\sum_{t=1}^{T} z_t^2\right]^{-1} T^{-1}\sum_{t=1}^{T} z_t v_t$$
$$\Rightarrow \left[\int_0^1 B_2^2(s)\,\mathrm{d}s\right]^{-1}(A_1 + A_2 + A_3); \tag{69}$$
$$A_1 = [\sigma_1/(1-\rho)](1-\theta^2)^{1/2}\int_0^1 B_2(s)\,\mathrm{d}W(s) \tag{70a}$$
$$A_2 = [1/(1-\rho)](\psi - \beta)\int_0^1 B_2(s)\,\mathrm{d}B_2(s) \tag{70b}$$
$$A_3 = [1/(1-\rho)]\theta\sigma_1\sigma_2, \tag{70c}$$

using the decomposition $B_1(s) = \omega_{12}\omega_{22}^{-1}B_2(s) + (\omega_{11} - \omega_{12}^2\omega_{22}^{-1})^{1/2}W(s)$ where ω_{ij} is the (i, j)th element of $\mathbf{\Omega}$ and $W(s)$ is a Brownian motion process independent of B_2 since $\omega_{12}\omega_{22}^{-1} = \theta\sigma_1/\sigma_2(1-\rho)$ and $(\omega_{11} - \omega_{12}^2\omega_{22}^{-1}) = \sigma_1^2(1-\theta^2)/(1-\rho)^2$.

The important properties of static estimation of β are apparent from (69) and (70). The estimator is super-consistent, but contains second-order biases reflected in (70*b*) and (70*c*); these terms also make standard distributions inappropriate for hypothesis testing. Estimation will be improved to the extent that (70*b*) and (70*c*) can be reduced or eliminated, and they will vanish if the short-run and long-run multipliers are equal, since $\psi = \beta$ implies $\theta = 0$, and so $A_2 = A_3 = 0$. While the limiting distribution above is specific to the DGP (63), $\psi = \beta$ will typically only arise because of an absence of lagged values of z_t and y_t from the DGP; if for example $y_t = \psi z_t + \gamma_1 y_{t-1} + \gamma_2 z_{t-1} +$ error, then the long-run multiplier is $\beta = (\psi + \gamma_2)/(1-\gamma_1)$, in which case $\gamma_1 = \gamma_2 = 0$ is sufficient for $\beta = \psi$. A common factor ($\gamma_2 = -\psi\gamma_1$) is necessary and sufficient.

The terms A_2 and A_3 above can be eliminated when $\psi \neq \beta$ by the use of other estimation methods, as will be seen below.

(ii) Non-linear least squares (Stock 1987). This method, which eliminates the bias contained in (70*c*), consists in minimizing the sum of squared residuals defined as

$$\sum_{t=2}^{T} \{[\Delta y_t - \gamma_1(y_{t-1} - \beta z_{t-1})]\}^2,$$

which is non-linear in that the coefficient on z_{t-1} in the corresponding regression model is $\gamma_1\beta$. The coefficient β can however be recovered from the ordinary linear regression

$$\Delta y_t = \pi_1 y_{t-1} + \pi_2 z_{t-1} + \boldsymbol{\theta}(L)'\Delta \mathbf{x}_{t-1} + u_t,$$

with $\hat{\beta} = \hat{\pi}_2/\hat{\pi}_1$.

The asymptotic distribution of this NLS estimator is similar to that in (69), but with the term (70*c*) omitted and (70*b*) modified to

$$A_2' = [\psi/(1-\rho)] \int_0^1 B_2(s)\,\mathrm{d}B_2(s). \tag{70b'}$$

Comparing (70*b*) and (70*b*′), we see that (70*b*′) contains a factor of ψ rather than $(\psi - \beta)$. As (70*b*) is one of the terms responsible for second-order bias, it seems likely that OLS will perform relatively well when $\psi - \beta \cong 0$, reducing the bias in (70*b*), and that NLS will perform relatively well when $\psi \cong 0$, reducing the bias in (70*b*′). In the Monte Carlo study of Stock (1987), the DGP chosen implies that $\psi = 0$, leading to the superiority of the NLS technique; where $\psi \cong \beta$, however, OLS may do better. Recall from the definition of ψ that $\psi = \beta$ if θ, a scaling factor for the correlation between the underlying white-noise disturbances in y_t and z_t, is equal to zero.

(iii) Full-information maximum likelihood (FIML). The FIML procedure of Johansen (1988) for estimating the matrix $\boldsymbol{\alpha}$ of co-integrating vectors in a system is described above. Gonzalo shows that, for the DGP (63), the FIML estimator of β has the asymptotic distribution

$$T(\hat{\beta}_{\text{FIML}} - \beta) \Rightarrow \left[\int_0^1 B_2^2(s)\,\mathrm{d}s\right]^{-1} A_1, \tag{71}$$

where A_1 is as given in (70*a*). Therefore (71) is equivalent to (69) with terms A_2 and A_3 eliminated. FIML estimation eliminates two sources of bias: the non-symmetry caused by $\psi \neq \beta$ which leads to a bias in median (term (70*b*)), and the simultaneous-equations bias, which is a bias in mean (term (70*c*)), which results when the long-run covariance between z_t and v_t in (63) is not accounted for. The FIML estimator is asymptotically symmetrically distributed.

Moreover, the asymptotic distribution given in (71) is a mixture of normals. (Recall that in (70a) $B_2(s)$ and $W(s)$ are independent Brownian motion processes.) As a result, standard asymptotic chi-squared hypothesis tests are valid.

(iv) Other estimators. Stock and Watson (1988b) and Bossaerts (1988) propose additional methods of estimation based on principal components and canonical correlations respectively.

The principal-component method finds the linear combination of y_t and z_t with minimum variance, which amounts to finding the co-integrating vector. Given the covariance matrix of (y_t, z_t), the principal-component estimate of the co-integrating vector is the eigenvector corresponding to the smallest eigenvalue of this covariance matrix. For the DGP (63), its asymptotic distribution is like that of OLS as given in (69), with the addition of a fourth term grouped with A_1, A_2 and A_3. Calling this term A_4,

$$A_4 = [\beta/(1 + \beta^2)][\sigma_1^2/(1 - \rho^2)].$$

The additional term affects the bias in mean, which may be larger or smaller than that of OLS as this term may be positive or negative. Like FIML, the principal-component method lends itself naturally to the estimation of more than one co-integrating vector.

The method of canonical correlation is based on a search for the linear combination of (y_t, z_t) and (y_{t-1}, z_{t-1}) which has the maximal correlation subject to normalization and identification constraints.

Gonzalo compares the methods in a Monte Carlo simulation that uses a DGP similar to (63), but with (63a) modified to

$$y_t = x_t + v_t, \qquad v_t = \rho v_{t-1} + \varepsilon_{1t},$$

$$a_1 y_t = 0.5 x_t + \omega_t, \qquad \omega_t = \omega_{t-1} + \varepsilon_{2t},$$

where $a_1 = 0$ or 1 and with $\sigma_1^2 = 1$. The results are consistent with the analysis of biases given above, and in particular support the contention that the Johansen-type FIML estimator will tend to be superior. Which of OLS and NLS is superior depends, as anticipated, on the parameters ψ and $\psi - \beta$. Moreover, as we have seen above, it appears that the efficiency cost of over-parameterization of the FIML or NLS estimators is modest, while the consequences of under-parameterization may be more serious.

9

Conclusion

We briefly summarize the main themes of the book, and then consider the invariance of the matrix of co-integrating vectors in a linear system under both linear transformations and seasonal adjustment. Next, co-integration is related to structured time-series models, which offer an alternative approach to modelling integrated data. Recent research on integration and co-integration is described, and the book concludes by re-interpreting some old econometric problems in the light of co-integration theory.

9.1. Summary

Many economic time series appear to be non-stationary and to drift over time. Efficient inference in time-series econometrics requires taking account of this phenomenon. This book described the modelling of economic variables as integrated processes, allowing for the possibility that variables may be linked in the long run, implying that linear combinations of them are co-integrated.

We first presented the background to the theory of integrated series, building on concepts from time-series analysis and the theory of stochastic processes. The resulting distributions of estimators and tests applied to integrated data were functionals of Wiener processes, which when combined with a functional central-limit theorem led to a powerful and general method for deriving their limiting distributions. These were different from the limiting distributions conventionally applied to stationary processes, both because the normalization factor was the sample size rather than its square root, and because the form of the asymptotic distribution was non-normal. An important implication was that the critical values of test statistics differed between I(0) and I(1) data. Although the asymptotic distribution theory involved new types of derivations, it was feasible to master the logic of Wiener processes without excessive effort; the pay-off was that the approach simplified other derivations (such as constancy tests, as in Hansen 1992), and, in addition, was very general.

The Wiener process tools then allowed us to analyse such diverse problems as spurious (or nonsense) regressions, spurious detrending, parametric and non-parametrically adjusted univariate tests for unit roots, regressions on I(1) data, and tests for co-integration. We showed that even with I(1) data many tests had conventional distributions, but some did not, so care was required in conducting inference. For example, tests such as the Johansen statistic $T \log(1-\lambda)$ for co-integration had distributions which were functionals of Wiener processes, although tests on co-integrating vectors were asymptotically normal. In particular, over-identification tests needed to be formulated *after* mapping to the space of I(0) variables to ensure that their distributions were not a mixture of these two types of distributions (see Hendry and Mizon 1992). Conditioning tests on the I(1) decision for the number of co-integrating relations allowed the tests to be treated as having conventional distributions.

Co-integration provided a conceptual framework for mapping to I(0) space and therefore we examined it as a data-reduction tool and investigated some of its wide-ranging implications. Tests for co-integration based on residuals from static regressions and on systems were derived. The Granger Representation Theorem linked co-integration to a variety of other representations, including error-correction mechanisms (ECMs) which have been widely used since the late 1970s.

This link in turn entails a new view of dynamics: lagged feedbacks and ECMs do not necessarily violate rationality in an I(1) world. Further, as in Davidson *et al.* (1978), the role of differencing is as a transform, which preserves co-integration, and not as a filter, which eliminates levels variables and hence loses co-integration. Conversely, omitting an ECM generally induces a negative moving-average error, a point elaborated upon below.

9.2 The Invariance of Co-integrating Vectors

Linear systems, perhaps formulated after suitable data transformations (such as logarithms) intended to make linearity a reasonable approximation, play a leading role in co-integration analysis. A linear system is invariant under non-singular linear transforms, but usually its parameters are altered by such transforms. Chapter 2 discussed the properties of linear autoregressive distributed lag (ADL) models for stationary data, relating transformations of ADLs to ECMs to demonstrate the equivalence of estimators of long-run multipliers from any of the transforms even though the parameters of the equation were altered. In I(1) processes, the corresponding result is that co-integration defines an invariant of a linear system, as we now show.

Consider an identified $n \times r$ co-integration matrix $\boldsymbol{\alpha}$ in the I(1) system:

$$\Delta \mathbf{x}_t = \boldsymbol{\mu} + \boldsymbol{\Gamma}\Delta \mathbf{x}_{t-1} + \boldsymbol{\gamma\alpha}'\mathbf{x}_{t-1} + \boldsymbol{\varepsilon}_t \tag{1}$$

where $\boldsymbol{\varepsilon}_t \sim \mathrm{IN}(\mathbf{0}, \boldsymbol{\Sigma})$. The system in (1) has parameters $(\boldsymbol{\Gamma}, \boldsymbol{\gamma}, \boldsymbol{\alpha}, \boldsymbol{\mu}, \boldsymbol{\Sigma})$. Then, $\mathbf{x}_t$ is I(1) if and only if *rank* $(\boldsymbol{\gamma}_\perp'\boldsymbol{\Psi}\boldsymbol{\alpha}_\perp) = n - r$ where $\boldsymbol{\Psi}$ is the mean lag matrix defined in Chapter 8. Here $(\boldsymbol{\gamma} : \boldsymbol{\gamma}_\perp)$ has rank n, with $\boldsymbol{\gamma}_\perp$ being $n \times (n - r)$ such that $\boldsymbol{\gamma}_\perp'\boldsymbol{\gamma} = \mathbf{0}$ and $(\boldsymbol{\alpha} : \boldsymbol{\alpha}_\perp)$ has rank n with $\boldsymbol{\alpha}_\perp'\boldsymbol{\alpha} = \mathbf{0}$ for $\boldsymbol{\alpha}_\perp$ of size $n \times (n - r)$. Pre-multiplying (1) by a known $n \times n$ non-singular matrix $\mathbf{B}$ (so $|\mathbf{B}| \neq 0$),

$$\begin{aligned}\mathbf{B}\Delta \mathbf{x}_t &= \mathbf{B}\boldsymbol{\mu} + \mathbf{B}\boldsymbol{\Gamma}\Delta \mathbf{x}_{t-1} + \mathbf{B}\boldsymbol{\gamma\alpha}'\mathbf{x}_{t-1} + \mathbf{B}\boldsymbol{\varepsilon}_t \\ &= \boldsymbol{\mu}^* + \boldsymbol{\Gamma}^*\Delta \mathbf{x}_{t-1} + \boldsymbol{\gamma}^*\boldsymbol{\alpha}'\mathbf{x}_{t-1} + \boldsymbol{\varepsilon}_t^*. \end{aligned} \tag{2}$$

The system in (2) has the same likelihood as (1), but with parameters $(\boldsymbol{\Gamma}^*, \boldsymbol{\gamma}^*, \boldsymbol{\alpha}, \boldsymbol{\mu}^*, \boldsymbol{\Sigma}^*)$ where $\boldsymbol{\Sigma}^* = \mathbf{B}\boldsymbol{\Sigma}\mathbf{B}'$; an example of an admissible transform is any just-identified reformulation of (1). Only $\boldsymbol{\alpha}$ is unaffected by the linear transform, and $\boldsymbol{\alpha}'\mathbf{x}_{t-1}$ remains the co-integrating combination, so $\boldsymbol{\alpha}$ is an invariant parameter of the system.

The I(1) property of the system is also preserved as follows. The mean-lag matrix becomes $\boldsymbol{\Psi}^* = \mathbf{B}\boldsymbol{\Psi}$ and, letting $(\boldsymbol{\gamma}^* : \boldsymbol{\gamma}_\perp^*) = (\mathbf{B}\boldsymbol{\gamma} : \mathbf{B}^{-1\prime}\boldsymbol{\gamma}_\perp)$ so that $\boldsymbol{\gamma}^{*\prime}\boldsymbol{\gamma}_\perp^* = \mathbf{0}$, then

$$\boldsymbol{\gamma}_\perp^{*\prime}\boldsymbol{\Psi}^*\boldsymbol{\alpha}_\perp = \boldsymbol{\gamma}_\perp'\mathbf{B}^{-1}\mathbf{B}\boldsymbol{\Psi}\boldsymbol{\alpha}_\perp = \boldsymbol{\gamma}_\perp'\boldsymbol{\Psi}\boldsymbol{\alpha}_\perp,$$

and hence the two matrices have the same rank. The invariance of $\boldsymbol{\alpha}$ is a natural property of reduced-rank systems and extends to I(2) processes and to conditional systems. Thus, for a given vector $\mathbf{x}_t$, reduced forms, marginal models, conditional models, and structural forms all can be modelled with the same set of co-integration vectors.

9.3. Invariance of Co-integration Under Seasonal Adjustment

The co-integrating vector $\boldsymbol{\alpha}$ is invariant to seasonal adjustment by a diagonal seasonal filter $\mathbf{S}(L)$ which satisfies the scale-preserving property $\mathbf{S}(1) = \mathbf{I}$, as does a procedure like X-11. The results in this section are drawn from Ericsson, Hendry, and Tran (1992). It is assumed that $\mathbf{S}(L)$ annihilates any deterministic seasonal dummies. The invariance result holds because $\mathbf{S}(L)$ can be written as (see Chapter 5):

$$\mathbf{S}(L) = \mathbf{S}(1) + \mathbf{S}^*(L)\Delta = \mathbf{I} + \mathbf{S}^*(L)\Delta. \tag{3}$$

We first show the co-integration relation between adjusted and unadjusted data and then establish the invariance of the co-integration matrix $\boldsymbol{\alpha}$ of $\mathbf{x}_t$. Let $\mathbf{x}_t^a = \mathbf{S}(L)\mathbf{x}_t$ denote the seasonally adjusted vector variable. Then

$$\mathbf{x}_t^a = [\mathbf{S}(1) + \mathbf{S}^*(L)\Delta]\mathbf{x}_t = \mathbf{x}_t + \mathbf{S}^*(L)\Delta\mathbf{x}_t, \tag{4}$$

so that $\mathbf{x}_t^a - \mathbf{x}_t = \mathbf{S}^*(L)\Delta\mathbf{x}_t$. Hence $\mathbf{x}_t^a$ and $\mathbf{x}_t$ co-integrate with a unit coefficient to I(0) when $\mathbf{x}_t$ is I(1). Most seasonal adjustment filters are two-sided and symmetric for most of the available sample, so that in fact $\mathbf{S}^*(1) = \mathbf{0}$ and $\mathbf{S}(L) = \mathbf{I} + \mathbf{S}^{**}(L)\Delta^2$. Then $\mathbf{x}_t^a - \mathbf{x}_t = \mathbf{S}^{**}(L)\Delta^2\mathbf{x}_t$ so that co-integration to I(0) occurs between adjusted and unadjusted data even when $\mathbf{x}_t$ is I(2). Alternatively, if $\Delta\mathbf{x}_t$ is I(0) with a non-zero mean (as in GNP), then $\mathbf{x}_t^a - \mathbf{x}_t$ has a zero mean, as seems sensible for the seasonal residual. Generally, if $\mathbf{S}(L) = \mathbf{I} + \mathbf{S}^\dagger(L)\Delta^d$, then $\mathbf{x}_t^a$ and $\mathbf{x}_t$ co-integrate with a unit coefficient to I(0) when $\mathbf{x}_t$ is I(d), and also have a zero mean difference when $\mathbf{x}_t$ is I($d-1$). When $\mathbf{x}_t^a - \mathbf{x}_t$ is at most I(0), any co-integrating vector $\boldsymbol{\alpha}'$ of either $\mathbf{x}_t^a$ or $\mathbf{x}_t$ is a co-integrating vector of the other, so co-integration parameters are unaffected by $\mathbf{S}(L)$. Since $\mathbf{x}_t^a = \mathbf{x}_t + \mathbf{S}^{**}(L)\Delta^2\mathbf{x}_t$, we have that

$$\boldsymbol{\alpha}'\mathbf{x}_t^a - \boldsymbol{\alpha}'\mathbf{x}_t = \boldsymbol{\alpha}'\mathbf{S}^{**}(L)\Delta^2\mathbf{x}_t$$

and hence the difference is at least two orders of integration lower than that of $\mathbf{x}_t$.

However, the adjustment parameter $\boldsymbol{\gamma}$ is altered as follows. Multiply (1) by $\mathbf{S}(L)$ to give

$$\begin{aligned}\Delta\mathbf{x}_t^a &= \mathbf{S}(L)\boldsymbol{\mu} + \mathbf{S}(L)\boldsymbol{\Gamma}\Delta\mathbf{x}_{t-1} + \mathbf{S}(L)\boldsymbol{\gamma}\boldsymbol{\alpha}'\mathbf{x}_{t-1} + \mathbf{S}(L)\boldsymbol{\varepsilon}_t \\ &= \boldsymbol{\mu} + \boldsymbol{\Gamma}\Delta\mathbf{x}_{t-1} + \mathbf{S}^\dagger(L)\boldsymbol{\Gamma}\Delta^{d+1}\mathbf{x}_{t-1} + \boldsymbol{\gamma}\boldsymbol{\alpha}'\mathbf{x}_{t-1} + \mathbf{S}^\dagger(L)\boldsymbol{\gamma}\boldsymbol{\alpha}'\Delta^d\mathbf{x}_{t-1} \\ &\quad + \boldsymbol{\varepsilon}_t^a. \end{aligned} \tag{5}$$

By suitable addition and subtraction of lags and differences of $\mathbf{x}_t^a$ on the right-hand side,

$$\begin{aligned}\Delta\mathbf{x}_t^a &= \boldsymbol{\mu} + \boldsymbol{\Gamma}\Delta\mathbf{x}_{t-1}^a + \boldsymbol{\Gamma}(\Delta\mathbf{x}_{t-1} - \Delta\mathbf{x}_{t-1}^a) + \boldsymbol{\gamma}\boldsymbol{\alpha}'\mathbf{x}_{t-1}^a + \boldsymbol{\gamma}\boldsymbol{\alpha}'(\mathbf{x}_{t-1} - \mathbf{x}_{t-1}^a) \\ &\quad + \mathbf{S}^\dagger(L)\Delta^d(\boldsymbol{\Gamma}\Delta + \boldsymbol{\gamma}\boldsymbol{\alpha}')\mathbf{x}_{t-1} + \boldsymbol{\varepsilon}_t^a \\ &= \boldsymbol{\mu} + \boldsymbol{\Gamma}\Delta\mathbf{x}_{t-1}^a + \boldsymbol{\gamma}\boldsymbol{\alpha}'\mathbf{x}_{t-1}^a - [(\boldsymbol{\Gamma}\Delta + \boldsymbol{\gamma}\boldsymbol{\alpha}')\mathbf{S}^\dagger(L) \\ &\quad - \mathbf{S}^\dagger(L)(\boldsymbol{\Gamma}\Delta + \boldsymbol{\gamma}\boldsymbol{\alpha}')]\Delta^d\mathbf{x}_{t-1} + \boldsymbol{\varepsilon}_t^a \\ &= \boldsymbol{\mu} + \boldsymbol{\Gamma}\Delta\mathbf{x}_{t-1}^a + \boldsymbol{\gamma}\boldsymbol{\alpha}'\mathbf{x}_{t-1}^a + \boldsymbol{v}_t^a. \end{aligned} \tag{6}$$

When $\mathbf{S}^\dagger(L)$ is a scalar times the unit matrix (the same filter for all x_{it}), $\boldsymbol{v}_t^a = \boldsymbol{\varepsilon}_t^a$. In (6), it looks as if $\boldsymbol{\gamma}$ is also an invariant, but as $\boldsymbol{v}_t^a$ involves lagged, current, and future differences of $\mathbf{x}_t$ of dth or higher order, as well as $\boldsymbol{\varepsilon}_t^a$, then one of $\boldsymbol{v}_t^a$ or $\boldsymbol{\varepsilon}_t$ is likely to be autocorrelated. Since $\boldsymbol{\alpha}'\mathbf{x}_{t-1}^a$ is an I(0) variable, conventional serial correlation biases apply to it, and hence $\boldsymbol{\gamma}$ will usually be affected by whether or not the data are seasonally adjusted. The short-run dynamics will be changed when $\boldsymbol{\varepsilon}_t$ is an innovation, because $\boldsymbol{v}_t^a$ is correlated with $\Delta\mathbf{x}_{t-1}^a$, and additional lags are needed to remove its autocorrelation.

9.4. Structured Time-series Models and Co-integration

An alternative approach to modelling integrated processes is offered by structured time-series models (see Harvey 1989).[1] In this section, we briefly explain their form and relate their data description properties to a co-integrated system. A simple univariate example is given by

$$y_t = \mu_t + \varepsilon_t \qquad \text{where } \varepsilon_t \sim \text{IN}(0, \sigma_\varepsilon^2); \tag{7}$$

$$\mu_t = \mu_{t-1} + v_t \qquad \text{with } v_t \sim \text{IN}(0, \sigma_v^2); \tag{8}$$

and $E[\varepsilon_t v_s] = 0 \ \forall t,s$. Their form generally leads to the presence of negative moving-average errors, since (7) and (8) imply that

$$\Delta y_t = \Delta\mu_t + \Delta\varepsilon_t = \varepsilon_t - \varepsilon_{t-1} + v_t. \tag{9}$$

The process $\{\varepsilon_t - \varepsilon_{t-1} + v_t\}$ can be re-expressed as a first-order moving average $\{e_t - \theta e_{t-1}\}$, where the moments of the derived process are identical to those of the original process and determine θ. The variance of the former is $2\sigma_\varepsilon^2 + \sigma_v^2$, and that of the latter, $\{e_t - \theta e_{t-1}\}$, is $(1 + \theta^2)\sigma_e^2$, and these must be equal to each other; their first-order auto-covariances are $-\sigma_\varepsilon^2$ and $-\theta\sigma_e^2$, and again these must be equal. All longer lag covariances vanish. Equating the first-order serial correlation coefficients of the two representations yields

$$-1/(2 + q) = -\theta/(1 + \theta^2) \tag{10}$$

where $q = \sigma_v^2/\sigma_\varepsilon^2$. Equation (10) is a quadratic in θ that, given q, can be solved for a value of θ between 0 and 1. Finally, equating first-order covariances $\sigma_e^2 = \sigma_\varepsilon^2/\theta$. Thus, Δy_t is I(0) and has a negative moving-average error with parameter θ: $\Delta y_t = e_t - \theta e_{t-1}$.

There are close links between negative moving-average errors and error-correction mechanisms as remarked earlier (see e.g. Gregoir and Laroque 1991). Consider a simple co-integrated system,

$$\Delta y_t = -\lambda(y_{t-1} - \beta z_{t-1}) + u_t, \qquad \text{where } u_t \sim \text{IN}(0, \sigma_u^2); \tag{11}$$

$$\Delta z_t = v_t, \qquad \text{with } v_t \sim \text{IN}(0, \sigma_v^2). \tag{12}$$

To marginalize with respect to z at all lags in (11), first rewrite it as

$$y_t = (1 - \lambda)y_{t-1} + \lambda\beta z_{t-1} + u_t, \tag{13}$$

so that, in terms of differences,

$$\Delta y_t = (1 - \lambda)\Delta y_{t-1} + \lambda\beta v_{t-1} + \Delta u_t = (1 - \lambda)\Delta y_{t-1} + w_t. \tag{14}$$

In (14), $w_t = \lambda\beta v_{t-1} + \Delta u_t$ and as with (9), when $\{v_t\}$ and $\{u_s\}$ are mutually independent, we can rewrite w_t as $\xi_t - \tau\xi_{t-1}$, where equating

[1] Harvey calls such models 'structural', but as that word is heavily over-used in econometrics, we have substituted 'structured'.

moments yields $-\tau/(1+\tau^2) = -1/(2+s)$ for $s = \lambda^2\beta^2\sigma_v^2/\sigma_u^2$. Thus, a negative moving-average error also results from the marginalization providing $\lambda \neq 0$ (the unit root in (14) cancels when $\lambda = 0$ since then $s = 0$ and so $\tau = 1$). If (7) and (8) allowed for a short-run dynamic element, the observed outcome would be similar to that entailed by (14).

A structured time-series model that generalizes (8) by including a time-varying slope generates an I(2) series,

$$\mu_t = \mu_{t-1} + \zeta_t + v_t, \qquad \text{where } v_t \sim \mathrm{IN}(0, \sigma_v^2); \tag{15}$$

$$\zeta_t = \zeta_{t-1} + \eta_t, \qquad \text{when } \eta_t \sim \mathrm{IN}(0, \sigma_\eta^2). \tag{16}$$

Thus, as long as $\sigma_\eta^2 \neq 0$,

$$\Delta\mu_t = \Delta\mu_{t-1} + \eta_t + \Delta v_t. \tag{17}$$

Hence from (7),

$$\Delta^2 y_t = \Delta^2\mu_t + \Delta^2\varepsilon_t = \eta_t + \Delta v_t + \Delta^2\varepsilon_t. \tag{18}$$

When $\sigma_\eta^2 = 0$, we have $\zeta_t = \zeta_{t-1} = \zeta_0$, say, so that

$$\Delta y_t = \zeta_0 + \Delta\varepsilon_t + v_t, \tag{19}$$

and ζ_0 is the mean growth rate $E[\Delta y_t] = g_y = \zeta_0$. When $\sigma_\eta^2 \neq 0$, (18) entails changes in $E[\Delta y_t] = g_y(t)$ over time and generates y_t as I(2).

The alternative possibility to evolving growth rates is that of changes in means over time, so that $g_y(t)$ takes different values in different epochs. Such behaviour could be approximated by a model in which the distribution $D_\eta(\eta_t)$ was non-normal, with a large mass at zero and small probabilities of large values. Then ζ_t would usually be constant, but would occasionally jump to a new level. Thus, it is unsurprising that discrimination between integrated and regime-change models is difficult (see Perron 1989). Conversely, there are close affinities between structured time-series and econometric models for integrated data. Indeed, several researchers have suggested switching from a unit-root null to one of I(0) or co-integration. For example, one might seek to test $\sigma_v^2 = 0$ when $\sigma_\eta^2 = 0$ (so $\zeta_t = \zeta \,\forall t$) as a test for a unit root (see e.g. Kwiatkowski, Phillips, and Schmidt (1991) and Leybourne and McCabe (1992)).

9.5. Recent Research on Integration and Co-integration

During the last decade there has been an explosion of research on integrated and co-integrated processes. Dozens of papers appeared while we were writing the book, and many will appear between completion of writing and its appearance in print. With such a rapidly moving target, we focused on central research topics to explain what seem likely to remain the major concepts, tools, techniques, models, methods, and tests.

Consequently, some research areas received scant treatment, including other estimation methods for co-integration vectors, as well as studies of their properties: see *inter alia* Ahn and Reinsel (1988), Bewley, Orden, and Fisher (1991), Boswijk (1991), Box and Tiao (1977), Engle and Yoo (1991), Phillips (1991), Saikkonen (1991). Some comparative Monte Carlo studies of finite sample behaviour and related econometric theory have been noted, but others appear apace and we can expect many more over the next few years clarifying the choice of method, and the likely problems confronting each proposal. Researchers will also study the problems of joint selection of, e.g. lag length and the number of co-integration vectors. Another research topic is the order in which hypothesis tests should be conducted. Intuition suggests that it should be constancy, lag length, co-integration, congruence of the system, weak exogeneity, structural restrictions, encompassing, intercepts (and whether they lie in the co-integration space), etc. However, the distributions of tests of the first hypothesis are affected by the presence of co-integration, and it may well be difficult to implement a good order, although if the data are indeed I(1), tests for lag length based on lagged first differences will be in I(0) space. One recommendation concerning choices of methods and estimators that emerged as we proceeded was for a systems approach in preference to single-equation modelling until weak exogeneity has been ascertained.

Further developments have occurred in testing for unit roots in univariate processes such as instrumental variables tests and Durbin–Hausman tests (see e.g. Hall 1991, Choi 1992, Schmidt and Phillips 1992, Kremers *et al.* 1992; and Banerjee and Hendry 1992 for a summary). However, the previous recommendation of modelling the system rather than using univariate representations brings into question the point of conducting unit-root tests in marginal processes. One purpose might be to reject the null of integration against trend stationarity. Here, the available tests are known to have relatively low power. In particular, investigators often use $t(\rho = 1)$ rather than $T(\hat{\rho} - 1)$ (see Sect. 4.6) although Monte Carlo evidence shows the latter to have higher power. In any case, failure to reject the null does not entail accepting it as 'true'. For example, univariate unit-root tests can reflect other non-modelled forms of non-stationarity such as regime shifts, and inherent non-stationarity in mean and variance functions. Further, variables inherit unit roots from marginalizing with respect to other unit-root processes on which they depend. Thus, failure to reject a null of a unit root tells us little about the persistence of shocks to the variable being considered in isolation or in a small, highly marginalized system as discussed in Campbell and Perron (1991).

A second purpose might be to check that variables in a system are not I(2) (see e.g. Pantula 1991), so the null would be a unit root in the differences of the original variables. However, if the intention is to model the system, then it seems better to proceed from the general to the specific here as well and test the necessary rank conditions on the mean lag matrix of the system (see following (1) above). Nevertheless, sequential tests in this context raise some new problems. For example, the outcome of a pretest for a unit root (i.e. reject or not reject) affects the critical values used to test economic hypotheses, so the possibility of Type-I errors at the first stage may lead to size or power distortions at the second stage when conventional initial values are used.

Finally, a unit root may be of interest in order to validate a specific estimator (e.g. Engle–Granger) by appealing to super-consistency. Here a unit root test may be of descriptive value as it depends on the ratio of the covariance of the first difference with the level to the variance of the level, and so should be close to zero when there is a unit root, although we showed in Section 3.6 that similar distributions will result for integrated and near-integrated processes. The ratio of the variance of the first difference to that of the level is another index of the rapidity of accrual of information (either from trends or from drift).

Other likely research interests concern tests of structural, long-run, exogeneity, causality, and encompassing hypotheses (see e.g. Boswijk 1991, Hendry and Mizon 1992, and Banerjee and Hendry 1992). Modelling I(2) systems is in its infancy (see Johansen 1991*b*), but has close links to multi-co-integration and the analysis of stock-flow relations (see Granger and Lee 1990). This last development provides an additional explanation for such phenomena as the role of inflation in real money demand equations: if nominal money and the price level are I(2), and real money and inflation are I(1), then the last may be needed to create an I(0) co-integration vector. Extensive developments also seem likely to occur in estimation and dynamic modelling, since for many objectives in econometrics, including forecasting and policy, the focus of interest must be all parameters of the system and not just the long-run parameters.

In co-integrated processes, weak exogeneity of the conditioning variables for the parameters of interest remains as vital as it did in stationary processes—even for the long-run parameters. Thus, it is important to test for the presence of co-integrating vectors in other equations as discussed in Chapter 8. Doing so, however, implies system modelling even for an LM test (see Boswijk 1991). Further, Urbain (1992) shows that tests for orthogonality between regressors and errors lack power to detect such a weak exogeneity failure.

9.6. Reinterpreting Econometrics Time-series Problems

Integration and co-integration also lead to the re-interpretation of many extant econometrics time-series problems. We consider a few of these, commencing with multi-collinearity.

9.6.1. Multi-collinearity

When $\mathbf{x}_t \sim \mathrm{I}(1)$ and $\boldsymbol{\alpha}'\mathbf{x}_t \sim \mathrm{I}(0)$, then including all the elements of $\mathbf{x}_t$ or $\mathbf{x}_{t-1}$ as regressors in a single equation will induce an apparently serious collinearity problem. The second moment matrix $(\mathbf{X}'\mathbf{X})$ will be $O(T^2)$, whereas the linear combination $(\boldsymbol{\alpha}'\mathbf{X}'\mathbf{X}\boldsymbol{\alpha})$ will be $O(T)$. Consequently, $(T^{-2}\mathbf{X}'\mathbf{X})$ will converge on a singular matrix. Generally, it is inadvisable to 'solve' this problem by deleting variables; for I(1) data, doing so jeopardizes the possibility of co-integration. If the dependent variable is I(0), then the solution is to find the co-integrating combination $\boldsymbol{\alpha}'\mathbf{x}_t$ or $\boldsymbol{\alpha}'\mathbf{x}_{t-1}$ and use that as an explanatory variable. This strategy corresponds to the usual recommendation of transforming to near-orthogonal and interpretable variables. In other cases, where the dependent variable is I(1) but is co-integrated with a subset of $\mathbf{x}_t$, say, elimination may be sensible, but Wiener-based critical values should be used for variables that cannot be written implicitly as an I(0) function (see Chapter 7). These ideas are related to the earlier technique of confluence analysis in Hendry and Morgan (1989).

9.6.2. Measurement Errors

Measurement errors are a second problem where treatment recommendations can differ in the light of data being integrated. When $\mathbf{x}_t \sim \mathrm{I}(1)$, then $\Delta\mathbf{x}_t \sim \mathrm{I}(0)$, and if the data are in logarithms, then the changes are growth rates. If observed growth rates are to be at all sensible, then the error with which they are measured must not be I(1) or higher. Letting $\mathbf{x}_t^0$ denote the observed series, one possible model is $\Delta\mathbf{x}_t^0 = \Delta\mathbf{x}_t + \mathbf{u}_t$, where $\mathbf{u}_t$ is I(0), so that

$$\mathbf{x}_t^0 - \mathbf{x}_t = \mathbf{x}_{t-1}^0 - \mathbf{x}_{t-1} + \mathbf{u}_t. \tag{20}$$

If the measurement error in levels is denoted $\mathbf{w}_t = \mathbf{x}_t^0 - \mathbf{x}_t$, then $\mathbf{w}_t$ is apparently I(1). This consideration therefore only rather weakly bounds the scale of measurement error. Indeed, if the DGP is of the form that $\Delta\mathbf{x}_t = \boldsymbol{\varepsilon}_t$, then $\mathbf{u}_t$ and $\boldsymbol{\varepsilon}_t$ are essentially indistinguishable in models of $\mathbf{x}_t^0$.

However, when $\boldsymbol{\alpha}'\mathbf{x}_t$ is an I(0) co-integrating combination, then, on pre-multiplying (20) by $\boldsymbol{\alpha}'$,

$$\boldsymbol{\alpha}'\mathbf{x}_t^0 - \boldsymbol{\alpha}'\mathbf{x}_t = \boldsymbol{\alpha}'\mathbf{x}_{t-1}^0 - \boldsymbol{\alpha}'\mathbf{x}_{t-1} + \boldsymbol{\alpha}'\mathbf{u}_t. \tag{21}$$

Since $\Delta\boldsymbol{\alpha}'\mathbf{x}_t$ is I(-1) and

$$\Delta\boldsymbol{\alpha}'\mathbf{x}_t^0 = \Delta\boldsymbol{\alpha}'\mathbf{x}_t + \boldsymbol{\alpha}'\mathbf{u}_t,$$

$\boldsymbol{\alpha}'\mathbf{x}_t^0$ will be I(0) only if $\boldsymbol{\alpha}'\mathbf{u}_t$ is I(-1). Thus, I(0) measurement errors on growth rates must co-integrate to I(-1) with co-integration matrix $\boldsymbol{\alpha}$ if the observed series are to co-integrate in the same way as the latent variables when the measurement errors are I(0) on growth rates. Nowak (1990) calls a failure to observe $\boldsymbol{\alpha}'\mathbf{x}_t^0$ being I(0) when $\boldsymbol{\alpha}'\mathbf{x}_t$ is I(0) a problem of 'hidden co-integration'. However, many co-integration relationships, such as consumption and income, are likely to have connected measurement errors. Governmental statistical bureaux may even correct the data on such series in a related way to avoid divergence, which suggests an I(0) measurement error for, say, the ratio between them.

An alternative model of measurement error for logarithms is one with a constant-percentage standard deviation, so that the size of the absolute error grows with the variable. This leads to $\mathbf{x}_t^0 = \mathbf{x}_t + \mathbf{v}_t$ where var$[\mathbf{v}_t]$ is constant. Such a measurement error would not impede co-integration analyses, in that inconsistency would not result as in an I(0) setting, but would have the usual impact in I(0) representations since $\boldsymbol{\alpha}'\mathbf{v}_t$ could be I(0). An important instance is when $\mathbf{v}_t$ is an expectations error, in which case the distributions of the long-run parameter estimates are unaffected but short-run parameter estimates may be biased (see Engle and Granger 1987, and Hendry and Neale 1988).

9.6.3. *Incorrectly Omitted and Included Variables*

When a relevant I(1) variable is omitted from a relationship, I(0) co-integration is impossible and serious biases can result. In particular, for an I(0) dependent variable, all the remaining I(1) regressors may cease to be significant given the appropriate critical values, leading the model to collapse to one in differences. Including an irrelevant I(1) variable or vector will probably lower the efficiency of estimates of the co-integrating vectors but should be detectable in large enough samples, with the usual possibility of Type-I errors.

If one incorrectly includes an I(0) variable in a co-integration vector in a static regression, its coefficient will be biased when that variable is correlated with omitted I(0) variables. The consequences in the maximum likelihood procedure seem less serious as it is possible to test for a unit vector (i.e. one of the form (0 . . . 0 1 0 . . . 0)) lying in the co-integration space (see Sect. 8.5.2.). However, conditioning on the estimated coefficients of I(0) variables is inappropriate, and spuriously small confidence intervals for the remaining I(0) effects will usually result. Finally, excluding an I(0) variable from a model will not affect the long-run parameter estimates in large samples, but will usually bias the short-run parameters as in conventional econometric derivations.

9.6.4. Parameter Change in Integrated Processes

The most serious problem arising from possible parameter change in econometrics is the predictive failure of models that fail to incorporate the necessary effects. Unfortunately, it is difficult even to diagnose the problem since it is easy to confuse an I(1) process with an I(0) subject to shifts (see e.g. Perron 1989, Rappoport and Reichlin 1989, and Hendry and Neale 1991). Indeed, as noted in Section 9.4 above, structured time-series models implement the latter and produce the former. Whether it is more useful to view economic data as integrated (in the sense of having a unit root in the autoregressive representation subject to regular small shocks) or as subject to large and persistent regime shifts (the abolition of fixed exchange rates following Bretton Woods, or their reinstatement in the ERM; the formation of OPEC; the denationalization of large sectors of an economy; new forms of monetary control or their removal; financial and technological innovation; etc.) remains to be seen. However, both types are bound to play important roles, and although we have focused on the former in this book, understanding economic behaviour will necessitate modelling both integrated data and breaks appropriately. *Ex ante*, structural breaks can lead to bad predictions, which I(1) data alone do not seem to cause. *Ex post*, testing for parameter change in I(1) data must allow for a wide range of possible choices for break points. Useful developments are occurring in deriving appropriate tests based on Wiener distributions, and decision taking in this area should improve rapidly (see Nyblom 1989, Chu and White 1991, 1992, Andrews and Ploberger 1991, Hansen 1991, and Lin and Teräsvirta 1991).

9.6.5. Conditional Models of Co-integrated Processes

Chapter 8 emphasized the maximum-likelihood approach to testing for and estimating co-integrating vectors in the context of a VAR. This imposed the minimum conditioning assumptions and allowed a clear focus on the properties of co-integration estimation. However, many papers have begun to develop approaches in the context of systems that treat a subset of variables as weakly exogenous for all the parameters of interest: see Johansen (1992*a*, 1992*b*), Johansen and Juselius (1990), and Boswijk (1991), *inter alia*. Related work includes that on testing for Granger causality in co-integrated systems (see Toda and Phillips 1991, Mosconi and Giannini 1992, and Hunter 1992).

For a long time, econometricians have 'talked' co-integration without realizing it: for example, Klein (1953) discusses various great ratios of economics, namely consumption–income, capital–output, wage share in total income, and so on, implicitly assuming a stationary, or I(0), world. From our perspective, given that the components of these relations are I(1), Klein's ratios are early examples of co-integration hypotheses. In a log-linear multivariate analysis, these postulate particular forms for the rows of the co-integration matrix, highlighting the potential confirmatory role of the methods discussed in Chapter 8. Econometricians need no longer simply assume long-run equilibrium relations since it is feasible to test for their existence. Once that is established the analysis is reduced from I(1) to I(0) space, allowing the application of well established tools.

Thus, the recent focus on conditional or open models takes us back to the 1970s in an important sense with the links between economic theory or long-run equilibrium reasoning and data modelling having been placed on a sounder footing.

As we have shown in this book, there still remain many difficult theoretical and empirical problems to be overcome. However, the literature on co-integration, error correction and the econometric analysis of non-stationary data has enabled us to gain many important insights into modelling relationships among integrated variables. This has enhanced rather than replaced existing methods of dynamic econometric modelling of economic time series.

References

ABADIR, K. M. (1992), 'The Limiting Distribution of the Autocorrelation Coefficient Under a Unit Root', *Annals of Statistics*, forthcoming.

AHN, S. K., and REINSEL, G. C. (1988), 'Nested Reduced-Rank Autoregressive Models for Multiple Time Series', *Journal of the American Statistical Association*, 83: 849–56.

ANDERSON, T. W. (1958), *An Introduction to Multivariate Statistical Analysis*, John Wiley, New York.

—— (1976), 'Estimation of Linear Functional Relationships: Approximate Distributions and Connections with Simultaneous Equations in Econometrics (with discussion)', *Journal of the Royal Statistical Society* B, 38: 1–36.

ANDREWS, D. W. K., and PLOBERGER, W. (1991), 'Optimal Tests of Parameter Constancy', mimeo., Yale University Press.

BANERJEE, A., and DOLADO, J. (1987), 'Do We Reject Rational Expectations Models Too Often? Interpreting Evidence using Nagar Expansions', *Economics Letters*, 24: 27–32.

—— —— (1988), 'Tests of the Life Cycle–Permanent Income Hypothesis in the Presence of Random Walks: Asymptotic Theory and Small Sample Interpretations', *Oxford Economic Papers*, 40: 610–33.

—— —— and GALBRAITH, J. W. (1990*a*), 'Orthogonality Tests with De-trended Data: Interpreting Monte Carlo Results using Nagar Expansions', *Economics Letters*, 32: 19–24.

—— —— HENDRY, D. F., and SMITH, G. W. (1986), 'Exploring Equilibrium Relationships in Econometrics through Static Models: Some Monte Carlo Evidence', *Oxford Bulletin of Economics and Statistics*, 48: 253–77.

—— GALBRAITH, J. W., and DOLADO, J. (1990*b*), 'Dynamic Specification with the General Error-Correction Form', *Oxford Bulletin of Economics and Statistics*, 52: 95–104.

—— and HENDRY, D. F. (eds.) (1992), *Testing Integration and Cointegration*, special issue of the *Oxford Bulletin of Economics and Statistics*, 54, 225–55.

BÅRDSEN, G. (1989), 'The Estimation of Long-Run Coefficients from Error-Correction Models', *Oxford Bulletin of Economics and Statistics*, 51: 345–50.

BEWLEY, R. A. (1979), 'The Direct Estimation of the Equilibrium Response in a Linear Model', *Economics Letters*, 3: 357–61.

BEWLEY, R. A., ORDEN, D., and FISHER, L. (1991), 'Box-Tiao and Johansen Canonical Estimators of Cointegrating Vectors', University of New South Wales, Economics Discussion Paper, 91/5.

BHARGAVA, A. (1986), 'On the Theory of Testing for Unit Roots in Observed Time Series', *Review of Economic Studies*, 53: 369–84.

BILLINGSLEY, P. (1968), *Convergence of Probability Measures*, John Wiley, New York.

BOSSAERTS, P. (1988), 'Common Non-Stationary Components of Asset Prices', *Journal of Economic Dynamics and Control*, 12: 347–64.

Boswijk, H. P. (1991), 'Testing for Cointegration in Structural Models', University of Amsterdam, Econometrics Discussion Paper AE7/91.

—— (1992), 'Efficient Inference on Cointegration Parameters in Structural Error Correction Models', University of Amsterdam, Econometrics Discussion Paper.

—— and Franses, P. H. (1992), 'Dynamic Specification and Cointegration', *Oxford Bulletin of Economics and Statistics*, 54: 369–81.

Box, G. E. P., and Jenkins, G. M. (1970), *Time Series Analysis Forecasting and Control*, Holden-Day, San Francisco.

—— and Tiao, G. C. (1977), 'A Canonical Analysis of Multiple Time Series', *Biometrika*, 64: 355–65.

Brandner, P., and Kunst, R. (1990), 'Forecasting Vector Autoregressions: The Influence of Cointegration', Memorandum 265, IAS, Vienna.

Campbell, B., and Dufour, J.-M. (1991), 'Over-Rejections in Rational Expectations Models: A Non-Parametric Approach to the Mankiw–Shapiro Problem', *Economics Letters*, 35: 285–90.

Campbell, J. Y., and Perron, P. (1991), 'Pitfalls and Opportunities: What Macroeconomists Should Know About Unit Roots', in Blanchard, O. J. and Fischer, S. (eds), *NBER Economics Annual 1991*, MIT Press.

—— and Shiller, R. J. (1991), 'Cointegration and Tests of Present Value Models', *Journal of Political Economy*, 95: 1062–88.

Chambers, M. J. (1991), 'A Note on Forecasting in Co-Integrated Systems', Department of Economics, University of Essex.

Chan, N. H., and Wei, C. Z. (1988), 'Limiting Distributions of Least-Squares Estimates of Unstable Autoregressive Processes', *Annals of Statistics*, 16: 367–401.

Choi, I. (1992), 'Durbin–Hausman Tests for Unit Roots', *Oxford Bulletin of Economics and Statistics*, 54: 289–304.

Chong, Y. Y., and Hendry, D. F. (1986), 'Econometric Evaluation of Linear Macroeconomic Models', *Review of Economic Studies*, 53: 671–90.

Chow, G. C. (1960), 'Tests of Equality Between Sets of Coefficients in Two Linear Regressions', *Econometrica*, 52: 211–22.

Chu, C.-S. J., and White, H. (1991), 'Testing for Structural Change in some Simple Time Series Models', Discussion Paper 91–6, University of California, San Diego, Dept. of Economics.

—— (1992) 'A Direct Test for Changing Trend', *Journal of Business and Economic Statistics*, 10: 289–99.

Clements, M. P., and Hendry, D. F. (1991), 'On the Limitations of Mean Square Error Forecast Comparisons', Discussion paper 138, Oxford Institute of Economics and Statistics. Forthcoming, *Journal of Forecasting*.

—— —— (1992), 'Forecasting in Cointegrated Systems', Discussion paper 139, Oxford Institute of Economics and Statistics.

Davidson, J. E. H., Hendry, D. F., Srba, F., and Yeo, S. (1978), 'Econometric Modelling of the Aggregate Time-Series Relationship Between Consumers' Expenditure and Income in the United Kingdom', *Economic Journal*, 88: 661–92.

Davidson, R., and MacKinnon, J. G. (1992), *Estimation and Inference in Econometrics*, Oxford University Press.

Deaton, A. S., and Muellbauer, J. N. J. (1980), *Economics and Consumer*

Behavior, Cambridge University Press.

Dickey, D. A. (1976), 'Estimation and Hypothesis Testing for Nonstationary Time Series', Ph.D. dissertation, Iowa State University.

—— and Fuller, W. A. (1979), 'Distribution of the Estimators for Autoregressive Time Series with a Unit Root', *Journal of the American Statistical Association*, 74: 427–31.

—— —— (1981), 'Likelihood Ratio Statistics for Autoregressive Time Series with a Unit Root', *Econometrica*, 49: 1057–72.

—— and Pantula, S. G. (1987), 'Determining the Order of Differencing in Autoregressive Processes', *Journal of Business and Economic Statistics*, 15: 455–61.

—— and Said, S. E. (1981), 'Testing ARIMA$(p, 1, q)$ against ARMA $(p+1, q)$', *Proceedings of the Business and Economic Statistics Section, American Statistical Association*, 28: 318–22.

—— Bell, W. R., and Miller, R. B. (1986), 'Unit Roots in Time Series Models: Tests and Implications', *American Statistician*, 40: 12–26.

—— Hasza, D. P., and Fuller, W. A. (1984), 'Testing for a Unit Root in Seasonal Time Series', *Journal of the American Statistical Association*, 79: 355–67.

Durlauf, S. N., and Phillips, P. C. B. (1988), 'Trends versus Random Walks in Time Series Analysis', *Econometrica*, 56: 1333–54.

Engle, R. F., and Granger, C. W. J. (1987), 'Co-integration and Error Correction: Representation, Estimation and Testing', *Econometrica*, 55: 251–76.

—— and Yoo, B. S. (1987), 'Forecasting and Testing in Co-integrated Systems', *Journal of Econometrics*, 35: 143–59.

—— —— (1991), 'Cointegrated Economic Time Series: An Overview with New Results', in R. F. Engle and C. W. J. Granger (eds.), *Long-Run Economic Relationships*, Oxford University Press, 237–66.

—— Granger, C. W. J., and Hallman, J. (1988), 'Merging Short- and Long-run Forecasts: An Application of Seasonal Co-integration to Monthly Electricity Sales Forecasting', *Journal of Econometrics*, 40: 45–62.

—— —— Hylleburg, S., and Lee, H. S. (1993), 'Seasonal Co-Integration: The Japanese Consumption Function', *Journal of Econometrics*, 55: 275–98.

—— Hendry, D. F., and Richard, J.-F. (1983), 'Exogeneity', *Econometrica*, 51: 277–304.

Ericsson, N. R. (1992), *Cointegration, Exogeneity and Policy Analysis*, Special Issue, *Journal of Policy Modeling*, 14, 3 and 4.

—— Campos, J., and Tran, H.-A. (1990), 'PC-GIVE and David Hendry's Econometric Methodology', *Revista de Econometrica,* X, 7–117.

—— and Hendry, D. F. (1985), 'Conditional Econometric Modelling: An Application to New House Prices in the United Kingdom', in Atkinson, A. C. and Fienberg, S. E. (eds), *A Celebration of Statistics*, Springer-Verlag, 251–85.

—— Hendry, D. F. and Tran, H.-A. (1992) 'Cointegration, Seasonality, Encompassing and the Demand for Money in the United Kingdom', Discussion Paper, Board of Governors of the Federal Reserve System, Washington, DC.

Ermini, L., and Granger, C. W. J. (1991), 'Some Generalizations on the

Algebra of $I(1)$ Processes', Working Paper, Department of Economics, University of Hawaii at Manoa.
ERMINI, L., and HENDRY, D. F. (1991), 'Log Income vs. Linear Income: An Application of the Encompassing Principle', Working Paper no. 91-11, Department of Economics, University of Hawaii at Manoa.
EVANS, G. B. A., and SAVIN, N. E. (1981), 'Testing for Unit Roots: 1', *Econometrica*, 49: 753–79.
—— —— (1984), 'Testing for Unit Roots: 2' *Econometrica*, 52: 1241–69.
FRIEDMAN, M., and SCHWARTZ, A. J. (1982), *Monetary Trends in the United States and the United Kingdom: Their Relation to Income, Prices, and Interest Rates, 1867–1975,* University of Chicago Press.
FULLER, W. A. (1976), *Introduction to Statistical Time Series*, John Wiley, New York.
GALBRAITH, J. W., DOLADO, J., and BANERJEE, A. (1987), 'Rejections of Orthogonality in Rational Expectations Models: Further Monte Carlo Results for an Extended Set of Regressors', *Economics Letters*, 25: 243–7.
GANTMACHER, F. R. (1959), *Applications of the Theory of Matrices*, Interscience, New York.
GEL'FAND, J. M. (1967), *Lectures on Linear Algebra*, Interscience, New York.
GEWEKE, J. (1986), 'The Super-Neutrality of Money in the United States: An Interpretation of the Evidence', *Econometrica*, 54: 1–21.
GHYSELS, E. (1990), 'On the Economics and Econometrics of Seasonality', paper presented to the Sixth World Congress of the Econometric Society.
GONZALO, J. (1990), 'Comparison of Five Alternative Methods of Estimating Long-Run Equilibrium Relationships', Discussion Paper, University of California at San Diego.
GRANGER, C. W. J. (1981), 'Some Properties of Time Series Data and their Use in Econometric Model Specification', *Journal of Econometrics*, 16: 121–30.
—— (1983), 'Forecasting White Noise', in A. Zellner (ed.), *Applied Time Series Analysis of Economic Data*, Bureau of the Census, Washington, DC, 308–14.
—— (1986), 'Developments in the Study of Co-integrated Economic Variables', *Oxford Bulletin of Economics and Statistics*, 48: 213–28.
—— and HALLMAN, J. (1991), 'The Algebra of I(1) Processes', *Journal of Time Series Analysis*, 12: 207–24.
—— and LEE, T.-H. (1990), 'Multicointegration', in G. F. Rhodes Jr. and T. B. Fomby (eds.), *Advances in Econometrics*, JAI Press, Greenwich Conn., 71–84.
—— and NEWBOLD, P. (1974), 'Spurious Regressions in Econometrics', *Journal of Econometrics*, 2: 111–20.
—— —— (1977), 'The Time Series Approach to Econometric Model Building', in C. A. Sims (ed.), *New Methods in Business Cycle Research*, Federal Reserve Bank of Minneapolis.
—— —— (1978), *Forecasting Economic Time Series,* Academic Press, New York.
—— and WEISS, A. A. (1983), 'Time-Series Analysis of Error-Correction Models', in S. Karlin, T. Amemiya, and L. A. Goodman (eds.), *Studies in Econometrics, Time Series and Multivariate Statistics*, Academic Press, New York.

GREGOIR, S., and LAROQUE, G. (1991) 'Multivariate Integrated Time Series: A General Error Correction Representation with Associated Estimation and Test Procedures', Discussion paper 53/G305, INSEE, Paris.

GRIMMET, G. R., and STIRZAKER, D. R. (1982), *Probability and Random Processes*, Oxford University Press.

HALDRUP, N., and HYLLEBERG, S. (1991), 'Integration, Near-Integration and Deterministic Trends', Discussion Paper no. 1991-15, Aarhus University, Denmark.

HALL, A. (1989), 'Testing for a Unit Root in the Presence of Moving Average Errors', *Biometrika*, 79: 49–56.

——(1990), 'Testing for a Unit Root in Time Series using Instrumental Variables Estimators with Pre-test Data-Based Model Selection', Discussion Paper, North Carolina State University.

——(1991), 'Model Selection and Unit Root Tests based on Instrumental Variables Estimators', Discussion paper, North Carolina State University.

HALL, A. D., ANDERSON, H. M., and GRANGER, C. W. J. (1992), 'A Cointegration Analysis of Treasury Bill Yields', *Review of Economics and Statistics*, 74: 116–25.

HALL, P., and HEYDE, C. C. (1980), *Martingale Limit Theory and Applications*, Academic Press, New York.

HALL, R. E. (1978), 'Stochastic Implications of the Life-Cycle Permanent Income Hypothesis', *Journal of Political Economy*, 86: 971–87.

HAMMERSLEY, J. M., and HANDSCOMB, D. C. (1964), *Monte Carlo Methods*, Methuen, London.

HANSEN, B. E. (1991), 'Tests for Parameter Instability in Regressions with I(1) Processes', Discussion paper. University of Rochester.

——(1992), 'Testing for Parameter Instability in Linear Models', *Journal of Policy Modeling*, 14: 517–33.

HARVEY, A. C. (1989), *Forecasting, Structural Time Series Models and the Kalman Filter*, Cambridge University Press.

HASZA, D. P., and FULLER, W. A. (1982), 'Testing for Nonstationary Parameter Specifications in Seasonal Time-Series Models', *Annals of Statistics*, 10: 1209–16.

HENDRY, D. F. (1984), 'Monte Carlo Experimentation in Econometrics', ch. 16 in Z. Griliches and M. D. Intrilligator (eds.), *Handbook of Econometrics*, ii, North-Holland, Amsterdam, 937–76.

——(1989), *PC-GIVE: An Interactive Econometric Modelling System*, Institute of Economics and Statistics, Oxford University, Oxford.

——(1991*a*), 'Using PC-NAIVE in Teaching Econometrics', *Oxford Bulletin of Economics and Statistics*, 53, 199–223.

——(1991*b*), 'Economic Forecasting', Report to the Treasury and Civil Service Committee, UK.

——and ANDERSON, G. J. (1977), 'Testing Dynamic Specification in Small Simultaneous Models: An Application to a Model of Building Society Behavior in the United Kingdom', ch. 8*c* in M. D. Intrilligator (ed.), *Frontiers of Quantitative Economics*, iii(*a*), North-Holland, Amsterdam, 361–83.

——and CLEMENTS, M. P. (1992), 'Towards a Theory of Economic Forecasting', unpublished paper, Institute of Economics and Statistics, Oxford University.

HENDRY, D. F., and ERICSSON, N. R. (1991*a*), 'An Econometric Appraisal of U.K. Money Demand in *Monetary Trends in the United States and the United Kingdom* by Milton Friedman and Anna J. Schwartz', *American Economic Review*, 81: 8–38.

—— and ERICSSON, N. R. (1991*b*), 'Modelling the Demand for Narrow Money in the United Kingdom and the United States', *European Economic Review*, 35: 833–81.

—— and MIZON, G. E. (1978), 'Serial Correlation as a Convenient Simplification, not a Nuisance: A Comment on a Study of the Demand for Money by the Bank of England', *Economic Journal*, 88: 549–63.

—— —— (1992), 'Evaluating Dynamic Models by Encompassing the VAR', in P. C. B. Phillips (ed.), *Models, Methods, and Applications of Econometrics*, Basil Blackwell, Oxford.

—— and MORGAN, M. S. (1989), 'A Re-analysis of Confluence Analysis', *Oxford Economic Papers*, 41: 35–52: reprinted in N. de Marchi and C. L. Gilbert (eds.), *History and Methodology of Econometrics*, Clarendon Press, Oxford, 1990.

—— MUELLBAUER, J. N. J., and MURPHY, A. (1990), 'The Econometrics of DHSY', in J. D. Hey and D. Winch (eds.), *A Century of Economics*, Basil Blackwell, Oxford, 298–334.

—— and NEALE, A. J. (1987), 'Monte Carlo Experimentation using PC-NAIVE', in T. Fomby and G. Rhodes (eds.), *Advances in Econometrics*, vi, JAI Press, Greenwich, Conn., 91–125.

—— —— (1988), 'Interpreting Long-Run Equilibrium Solutions in Conventional Macro Models: A Comment', *Economic Journal*, 98: 808–17.

—— —— (1991), 'A Monte Carlo Study of the Effects of Structural Breaks on Unit Root Tests', in P. Hackl and A. H. Westlund (eds.), *Economic Structural Change: Analysis and Forecasting*, Springer-Verlag, Vienna, 95–119.

—— —— and ERICSSON, N. R. (1990), *PC-NAIVE: An Interactive Program for Monte Carlo Experimentation in Econometrics*, Institute of Economics and Statistics, Oxford University, Oxford.

—— PAGAN, A. R., and SARGAN, J. D. (1984), 'Dynamic Specification', ch. 18 in Z. Griliches and M. D. Intrilligator (eds.), *Handbook of Econometrics*, ii, North-Holland, Amsterdam, 1023–100.

—— and RICHARD, J.-F. (1982), 'On the Formulation of Empirical Models in Dynamic Econometrics', *Journal of Econometrics*, 20: 3–33.

—— and UNGERN-STERNBERG, T. VON (1981), 'Liquidity and Inflation Effects on Consumers' Behaviour', ch. 9 in A. S. Deaton (ed.) *Essays in the Theory and Measurement of Consumers' Behaviour*, Cambridge University Press, 237–60.

HUNTER, J. (1992), 'Tests of Cointegrating Exogeneity for PPP and Uncovered Interest Rate Parity in the UK', *Journal of Policy Modeling*, 14: 453–64.

HYLLEBERG, S. (1991), *Modelling Seasonality*, Oxford University Press.

—— and MIZON, G. E. (1989*a*), 'Cointegration and Error Correction Mechanisms', *Economic Journal* (Supplement), 99: 113–25.

—— —— (1989*b*), 'A Note on the Distribution of the Least Squares Estimator of a Random Walk with Drift', *Economics Letters*, 29: 225–30.

—— ENGLE, R. F., GRANGER, C. W. J., and YOO, B. S. (1990), 'Seasonal Integration and Co-Integration', *Journal of Econometrics*, 44: 215–28.

ILMAKUNNAS, P. (1990), 'Testing the Order of Differencing in Quarterly Data: An Illustration of the Testing Sequence', *Oxford Bulletin of Economics and Statistics*, 52: 79–88.

IMHOF, P. (1961), 'Computing the Distribution of Quadratic Forms in Normal Variates', *Biometrika*, 48: 419–26.

JARQUE, C. M., and BERA, A. K. (1980), 'Efficient Tests for Normality, Homoskedasticity and Serial Independence of Regression Residuals', *Economics Letters*, 6: 255–9.

JAZWINSKI, A. H. (1970), *Stochastic Processes and Filtering Theory*, Academic Press, New York.

JOHANSEN, S. (1988), 'Statistical Analysis of Cointegration Vectors', *Journal of Economic Dynamics and Control*, 12: 231–54.

—— (1989), 'The Power of the Likelihood Ratio Test for Cointegration', mimeo, Institute of Mathematical Statistics, University of Copenhagen.

—— (1991*a*), 'Estimation and Hypothesis Testing of Cointegration Vectors in Gaussian Vector Autoregressive Models', *Econometrica*, 59: 1551–80.

—— (1991*b*), 'A Statistical Analysis of Cointegration for I(2) variables', Institute of Mathematical Statistics, University of Copenhagen.

—— (1992*a*), 'Cointegration in Partial Systems and the Efficiency of Single Equation Analysis', *Journal of Econometrics*, 52: 389–402.

—— (1992*b*), 'Teşting Weak Exogeneity and the Order of Cointegration in UK Money Demand', *Journal of Policy Modeling*, 14: 313–34.

—— and JUSELIUS, K. (1990), 'Maximum Likelihood Estimation and Inference on Cointegration—with Applications to the Demand for Money', *Oxford Bulletin of Economics and Statistics*, 52: 169–210.

KELLY, C. M. (1985), 'A Cautionary Note on the Interpretation of Long-Run Equilibrium Solutions in Conventional Macro Models', *Economic Journal*, 95: 1078–86.

KIVIET, J., and PHILLIPS, G. D. A. (1992), 'Exact Similar Tests for Unit Roots and Cointegration, *Oxford Bulletin of Economics and Statistics*, 54: 349–67.

KLEIN, L. R. (1953), *A Textbook of Econometrics*, Row, Peterson and Company, Evanston, Ill.

KOERTS, J., and ABRAHAMSE, A. P. J. (1969), *On the Theory and Application of the General Linear Model*, Rotterdam University Press.

KREMERS, J. J. M., ERICSSON, N. R., and DOLADO, J. (1992), 'The Power of Co-integration Tests', *Oxford Bulletin of Economics and Statistics*, 54: 325–48.

KWIATKOWSKI, D., PHILLIPS, P. C. B., and SCHMIDT, P. (1991), 'Testing the Null Hypothesis of Stationarity against the Alternative of a Unit Root: How Sure Are We that Economic Time Series Have a Unit Root', Cowles Foundation Discussion Paper No. 979.

LEYBOURNE, S. J., and MCCABE, B. P. M. (1992), 'A Simple Test for Cointegration', typescript Nottingham University.

LIN, C.-F., and TERÄSVIRTA, T. (1991), 'Testing the Constancy of Regression Parameters against Continuous Structural Change', Discussion paper, University of California at San Diego.

MCCALLUM, B. T. (1984), 'On Low-Frequency Estimates of Long-Run Relationships in Macroeconomics', *Journal of Monetary Economics*, 14: 3–14.

MACKINNON, J. G. (1991), 'Critical Values for Co-Integration Tests', in R. F.

Engle and C. W. J. Granger (eds.), *Long-Run Economic Relationships*, Oxford University Press, 267–76.

Mankiw, N. G., and Shapiro, M. D. (1985), 'Trends, Random Walks and Tests of the Permanent Income Hypothesis', *Journal of Monetary Economics*, 16: 165–74.

—— —— (1986), 'Do We Reject Too Often? Small Sample Properties of Tests of Rational Expectations Models', *Economics Letters*, 20: 139–45.

Mann, H. B., and Wald, A. (1943), 'On Stochastic Limit and Order Relationships', *Annals of Mathematical Statistics*, 14: 217–77.

Mizon, G. E. (1977), 'Model Selection Procedures', in M. J. Artis and A. R. Nobay (eds.), *Studies in Modern Economic Analysis*, Basil Blackwell, Oxford.

—— and Hendry, D. F. (1980), 'An Empirical Application and Monte Carlo Analysis of Tests of Dynamic Specification', *Review of Economic Studies*, 47: 21–45.

Morgan, M. S. (1990), *The History of Econometric Ideas*, Cambridge University Press.

Mosconi, R., and Giannini, C. (1992), 'Non-Causality in Cointegrated Systems: Representation, Estimation and Testing', *Oxford Bulletin of Economics and Statistics*, 54: 399–417.

Nankervis, J. C., and Savin, N. E. (1985), 'Testing the Autoregressive Parameter with the *t*-statistic', *Journal of Econometrics*, 27: 143–61.

—— —— (1987), 'Finite Sample Distributions of t and F Statistics in an AR(1) model with an Exogenous Variable', *Econometric Theory*, 3: 387–408.

Nelson, C. R., and Kang, H. (1981), 'Spurious Periodicity in Inappropriately Detrended Time Series', *Journal of Monetary Economics*, 10: 139–62.

Newey, W. K., and West, K. D. (1987), 'A Simple Positive Semi-Definite Heteroskedasticity and Autocorrelation-Consistent Covariance Matrix', *Econometrica*, 55: 703–8.

Nowak, E. (1990), 'Hidden Cointegration', Discussion paper, University of California at San Diego.

Nyblom, J. (1989), 'Testing for the Constancy of Parameters over Time', *Journal of the American Statistical Association*, 84: 223–30.

Osborn, D. R., Chiu, A. P. L., Smith, J. P., and Birchenhall, C. R. (1988), 'Seasonality and the Order of Integration for Consumption', *Oxford Bulletin of Economics and Statistics*, 50: 361–78.

Osterwald-Lenum, M. (1992), 'A Note with Fractiles of the Asymptotic Distribution of the Maximum Likelihood Cointegration Rank Test Statistics: Four Cases', *Oxford Bulletin of Economics and Statistics*, 54: 461–72.

Pantula, S. G. (1991), 'Testing for Unit Roots in Time Series Data', *Econometric Theory*, 5: 265–71.

Park, J. Y., and Phillips, P. C. B. (1988), 'Statistical Inference in Regressions with Integrated Processes: Part I', *Econometric Theory*, 4: 468–97.

Perron, P. (1988), 'Trends and Random Walks in Macroeconomic Time Series: Further Evidence from a New Approach', *Journal of Economic Dynamics and Control*, 12: 297–332.

—— (1989), 'The Great Crash, the Oil Shock and the Unit Root Hypothesis', *Econometrica*, 57: 1361–402.

Phillips, P. C. B. (1986), 'Understanding Spurious Regressions in Economet-

rics', *Journal of Econometrics*, 33: 311–40.
—— (1987*a*), 'Time Series Regression with a Unit Root', *Econometrica*, 55: 277–301.
—— (1987*b*), 'Towards a Unified Asymptotic Theory of Autoregression', *Biometrika*, 74: 535–48.
—— (1988*a*), 'Reflections on Econometric Methodology', *Economic Record*, 64: 344–59.
—— (1988*b*), 'Multiple Regression with Integrated Time Series', *Contemporary Mathematics*, 80: 79–105.
—— (1991), 'Optimal Inference in Co-integrated Systems', *Econometrica*, 59: 282–306.
—— and Durlauf, S. N. (1986), 'Multiple Time Series Regression with Integrated Processes', *Review of Economic Studies*, 53: 473–95.
—— and Hansen, B. E. (1990), 'Statistical Inference in Instrumental Variables Regression with I(1) Processes', *Review of Economic Studies*, 57: 99–125.
—— and Loretan, M. (1991), 'Estimating Long-Run Economic Equilibria', *Review of Economic Studies*, 58: 407–36.
—— and Ouliaris, S. (1988), 'Testing for Co-integration using Principal Components Methods', *Journal of Economic Dynamics and Control*, 12: 205–30.
—— —— (1990), 'Asymptotic Properties of Residual Based Tests for Cointegration', *Econometrica*, 58: 165–93.
—— and Park, J. Y. (1988), 'Asymptotic Equivalence of Ordinary Least Squares and Generalized Least Squares in Regressions with Integrated Variables', *Journal of the American Statistical Association*, 83: 111–15.
—— and Perron, P. (1988), 'Testing for a Unit Root in Time Series Regression', *Biometrika*, 75: 335–46.
Priestley, M. B. (1989), *Nonlinear and Nonstationary Time Series Analysis*, Academic Press, New York.
Quandt, R. E. (1978), 'Tests of Equilibrium vs. Disequilibrium Hypotheses', *International Economic Review*, 19: 435–52.
—— (1982), 'Econometric Disequilibrium Models', *Econometric Reviews*, 1: 1–63.
Rappoport, P., and Reichlin, L. (1989), 'Segmented Trends and Non-Stationary Time Series', *Economic Journal*, 99: 168–77.
Reimers, H. E. (1991), 'Comparisons of Tests for Multivariate Co-integration', Discussion Paper no. 58, Christian-Albrechts University, Kiel.
Ripley, B. D. (1987), *Stochastic Simulation*, John Wiley, New York.
Said, S. E., and Dickey, D. A. (1984), 'Testing for Unit Roots in Autoregressive-Moving Average Models of Unknown Order', *Biometrika*, 71: 599–607.
Saikkonen, P. (1991), 'Asymptotically Efficient Estimation of Cointegrating Regressions', *Econometric Theory*, 7: 1–21.
Sampson, M. (1991), 'The Effect of Parameter Uncertainty on Forecast Variances and Confidence Intervals for Unit Root and Trend Stationary Time-Series Models', *Journal of Applied Econometrics*, 6: 67–76.
Sargan, J. D. (1964), 'Wages and Prices in the United Kingdom: A Study in Econometric Methodology', in P. E. Hart, G. Mills, and J. K. Whitaker (eds.), *Econometric Analysis for National Economic Planning*, Butterworth,

London; reprinted in D. F. Hendry and K. F. Wallis (eds.), *Econometrics and Quantitative Economics*, Basil Blackwell, Oxford, 1984.

SARGAN, J. D. (1980), 'Some Tests of Dynamic Specification for a Single Equation', *Econometrica*, 48: 879–97.

—— and BHARGAVA, A. (1983), 'Testing Residuals from Least Squares Regression for Being Generated by the Gaussian Random Walk', *Econometrica*, 51: 153–74.

SCHMIDT, P., and PHILLIPS, P. C. B. (1992), 'LM test for a Unit Root in the Presence of Deterministic Trends', *Oxford Bulletin of Economics and Statistics*, 54: 257–87.

SCHWERT, G. W. (1989), 'Tests for Unit Roots: A Monte Carlo Investigation', *Journal of Business and Economic Statistics*, 7: 147–59.

SHEPPARD, D. K. (1971), *The Growth and Role of UK Financial Institutions 1890–1962*, Methuen, London.

SIMS, C. A. (ed.) (1977), *New Methods in Business Cycle Research*, Federal Reserve Bank of Minneapolis.

—— STOCK, J. H., and WATSON, M. W. (1990), 'Inference in Linear Time Series with Some Unit Roots', *Econometrica*, 58: 113–44.

SPANOS, A. (1986), *Statistical Foundations of Econometric Modelling*, Cambridge University Press.

STOCK, J. H. (1987), 'Asymptotic Properties of Least-Squares Estimators of Co-integrating Vectors', *Econometrica*, 55: 1035–56.

—— and WATSON, M. W. (1988*a*), 'Variable Trends in Economic Time Series', *Journal of Economic Perspectives*, 2: 147–74.

—— —— (1988*b*), 'Testing for Common Trends', *Journal of the American Statistical Association*, 83: 1097–107.

—— —— (1991) 'A Simple MLE of Cointegrating Vectors in General Integrated Systems', Typescript, Northwestern University.

—— and WEST, K. D. (1988), 'Integrated Regressors and Tests of the Permanent Income Hypothesis', *Journal of Monetary Economics*, 21: 85–96.

TODA, H., and PHILLIPS, P. C. B. (1991), 'Vector Autoregressions and Causality', Cowles Foundation Discussion Paper, 997.

URBAIN, J.-P. (1992), 'On Weak Exogeneity in Error Correction Models', *Oxford Bulletin of Economics and Statistics*, 54: 187–207.

WEST, K. D. (1988), 'Asymptotic Normality, when Regressors have a Unit Root', *Econometrica*, 56: 1397–418.

WHITE, H. (1980), 'A Heteroskedasticity-Consistent Covariance Matrix Estimator and a Direct Test for Heteroskedasticity', *Econometrica*, 48: 817–38.

—— (1984), *Asymptotic Theory for Econometricians*, Academic Press, New York.

WICKENS, M. R., and BREUSCH, T. S. (1988), 'Dynamic Specification, the Long Run and the Estimation of Transformed Regression Models', *Economic Journal*, 98 (Conference 1988): 189–205.

WOLD, H. (1954), *A Study in the Analysis of Stationary Time Series*, Almqvist and Wiksell, Stockholm.

YULE, G. U. (1926), 'Why Do We Sometimes Get Nonsense Correlations Between Time Series? A Study in Sampling and the Nature of Time Series', *Journal of the Royal Statistical Society*, 89: 1–64.

Acknowledgements for Quoted Extracts

The authors are grateful to the following for permission to reproduce extracts:

Elsevier Science Publishers, for material from N. G. Mankiw and M. D. Shapiro (1986), 'Do we reject too often: Small-sample properties of rational expectations models', *Economics Letters*, 20: 142–3.

The *Review of Economic Studies*, for material from P. C. B. Phillips and B. E. Hansen (1990), 'Statistical Inference in Instrumental Variables Regression with I(1) Processes', *Review of Economic Studies*, 57: 116–17.

The Econometric Society for material from D. A. Dickey and W. A. Fuller (1981), 'Likelihood Ratio Statistics for Autoregressive Time Series with a Unit Root', *Econometrica*, 49: 1062–3.

David A. Dickey, Professor of Statistics, North Carolina State University.

John Wiley & Sons, Inc., for material from Wayne A. Fuller (1976), *Introduction to Statistical Time Series*, 371–3.

Author Index

Subject Index